I0110258

GERMAN ETHNOGRAPHY
IN AUSTRALIA

GERMAN ETHNOGRAPHY
IN AUSTRALIA

EDITED BY NICOLAS PETERSON
AND ANNA KENNY

MONOGRAPHS IN
ANTHROPOLOGY SERIES

Australian
National
University

PRESS

ANU PRESS

Published by ANU Press
The Australian National University
Acton ACT 2601, Australia
Email: anupress@anu.edu.au
This title is also available online at press.anu.edu.au

National Library of Australia Cataloguing-in-Publication entry

Title: German ethnography in Australia / editors: Nicolas
           Peterson, Anna Kenny.

ISBN: 9781760461317 (paperback) 9781760461324 (ebook)

Series: Monographs in Anthropology.

Subjects: Ethnology--Australia.
           Germans--Australia--History.
           Ethnology--Germany.
           Australia--Ethnic relations.

Other Creators/Contributors:
           Peterson, Nicolas, 1941- editor.
           Kenny, Anna, editor.

All rights reserved. No part of this publication may be reproduced, stored in a retrieval system or transmitted in any form or by any means, electronic, mechanical, photocopying or otherwise, without the prior permission of the publisher.

Cover design and layout by ANU Press. Cover image: Aranda Lutherans and a group of visiting Luritja people at Hermannsburg Mission, 1910s. Source: Strehlow Research Centre, Alice Springs, SRC 06192.

This edition © 2017 ANU Press

Contents

Introduction

Part I: First encounters

Part II: Impact of the Aranda

Part III: Widening the interest

Part IV: Academic anthropology

Abbreviations

AADFAS	Association of Australian Decorative and Fine Arts Societies
AAPA	Aboriginal Affairs Planning Authority
AIAS	Australian Institute of Aboriginal Studies
AIATSIS	Australian Institute of Aboriginal and Torres Strait Islander Studies
AILC	Australian Indigenous Languages Collection
ARC	Australian Research Council
AVC	active verbal concept
CHB	Catherine Berndt
DFG	German Research Foundation
LSE	London School of Economics
MP	Member of Parliament
PVC	passive verbal concept
RMB	Ronald Berndt
SAC	Society of the Catholic Apostolate
SWR	*Südwestrundfunk*
WAC	Work Area Clearance

Figures and tables

Maps

Plates

Preface and acknowledgements

This volume has its origins in a conference held at The Australian National University on 18 and 19 June 2015 titled 'The German Anthropological Tradition in Australia', in connection with an Australian Research Council (ARC) Linkage grant (LP110200803), 'Rescuing Carl Strehlow's Indigenous cultural heritage legacy: The neglected German tradition of Arandic ethnography'. This grant was a collaborative project between the Central Land Council and the Strehlow Research Centre, both in Alice Springs, the University of Western Australia and The Australian National University. The project had several aims. First, to make better known the seven-volume ethnography on the Aranda by Carl Strehlow that has not been published in English. This has been achieved by the publication of *The Aranda's Pepa: An introduction to Carl Strehlow's masterpiece Die Aranda- und Loritja-Stämme in Zentral-Australien (1907–1920)*, by Dr Anna Kenny, the postdoctoral fellow on the project, which discusses the distinctive and interesting findings. Second, to translate the 7,600-word Aranda and Luritja dictionary compiled by Carl Strehlow between 1905 and 1909. This has been achieved, with publication of the dictionary and accompanying essays by Dr Kenny, Dr John Henderson of the University of Western Australia and David Moore scheduled for early 2018. Third, to bring together scholars to explore the significance of German-language ethnography in Australia, particularly, but not only, in relation to native title claims. This volume is the result of the third aim. We could not have realised these outcomes without the unfailing support of both the Central Land Council and the Strehlow Research Centre.

It would not have been possible to realise the conference had we not received a A$10,000 grant from The Australian National University's College of Arts and Social Sciences Internal Grants Scheme. This grant made it possible to bring Professor André Gingrich and Professor Erich Kolig to the conference, for which we are most grateful.

In holding the conference and preparing this volume for publication, we have received valuable help from the following people, whom we would like to thank: Adam Macfie and Shaun Angelis at the Strehlow Research Centre and Lea Gardam at the South Australian Museum for assisting with sourcing and providing images, Karina Pelling for the cartography, Jan Borrie for the copyediting and Lyn North for organising our conference food and dinner. Finally, we are greatly indebted to Emily Hazlewood and the team at ANU Press for the enormous care and attention to detail they provided in guiding the book through the publication process.

Orthography

In this book, many of the original spellings used by early ethnographers such as Schürmann, Reuther, the Strehlows, Spencer and Gillen, Howitt, Róheim and Berndt have been retained. The early writings include well-known spellings of group or language names and of complex terms such as *altjira* or *tjurunga*. Some authors in this volume have adopted modern phonemic spelling systems developed by linguists, while others have opted to stick with the original spellings of the authors they are discussing. For example, in the common Institute of Aboriginal Development orthography, the language name 'Aranda' is spelt 'Arrernte', and elsewhere the name Dieri is now rendered 'Diyari'. However, in some instances, the Aboriginal groups involved have clear and strong preferences for the spelling of their language name. Thus, the people belonging to the Arandic areas on the Upper Finke River in Central Australia prefer to spell their language name 'Aranda' and the native title holders east of Lake Eyre prefer their language name to be spelt 'Dieri'. Otherwise, the spelling of Aboriginal words—including names of individuals, subsections, sites, countries (estates) and dreamings—that are in use today follow modern phonemic spelling systems unless they are established placenames or personal names of people who have long passed away or no longer in use.

Contributors

Diane Austin-Broos is Professor Emerita of Anthropology at the University of Sydney, a Fellow of the Academy of Social Sciences in Australia and a doctoral graduate from the University of Chicago. Her two main research areas have been in the Caribbean, with a focus on Jamaica, and in Central Australia, among Western Arrernte people at Ntaria/Hermannsburg. Her principle research themes have been social and economic marginalisation and cultural change. She has published eight books, including *Jamaica Genesis* (1997), *Creating Culture* (1987), *Arrernte Present, Arrernte Past* (2009) and *A Different Inequality* (2011). Her current research concerns the politics of moral order in market societies.

Corinna Erckenbrecht is a German cultural anthropologist who has worked since the 1980s on issues relating to Indigenous Australia. She worked mainly at museums of ethnology (primarily in Cologne) with collections of cultural artefacts from Australia and the Pacific. From 2013 to 2015, she conducted a research project at the Moravian Church Archive and the Museum of Ethnology in Herrnhut, Germany, focusing on the Moravian mission stations in western Cape York Peninsula. This research was based on the Moravian archival documents, historical photographs and ethnographic artefacts, and was financed by the German Research Foundation. She currently works in the Junior Research Group 'The Transcultural Heritage of Northwestern Australia: Dynamics and resistencies'.

Deane Fergie is a social anthropologist whose academic training was undertaken in Papua New Guinea and Australia. She is a Senior Lecturer in Anthropology at the University of Adelaide. She is also manager and principal consultant of a small interdisciplinary team—the Locus of Social Analysis and Research (LocuSAR)—at the University of Adelaide. Since 1989, she has undertaken research and assessment processes under state or Commonwealth heritage legislation, working with people who identify as Antakirinja, Arabunna, Diyari, Eastern Maar, Kaurna, Kokatha, Kuyani, Barngarla, Gawler Ranges, Ngarrindjeri, Nukunu, Wangkanguru and Yankunytjatjara. Since 2002, she has researched 'connection reports' for successful consent determinations in four native title claims, including Eastern Maar (Victoria), and co-authoring (with Rod Lucas) expert reports for the Arabunna, Diyari and Gawler Ranges peoples in South Australia.

Regina Ganter (Fellow of the Academy of Humanities in Australia (FAHA)) is Professor of History at Griffith University, currently researching German-speaking missionaries in Australia as an Australian Research Council (ARC) Future Fellow. She is a multi–award-winning author and has taught Australian history at Griffith University since 1992.

Jason Gibson is Curator within the Humanities Department at the Melbourne Museum. For more than 15 years, he has worked extensively on Central Australia's intercultural history and has a particular interest in the Arrernte and Anmatyerr regions. His previous appointments include teaching and research positions at Swinburne University and the University of Technology Sydney, research coordinator of The Australian National University's 'Reconstructing Spencer and Gillen' ARC Linkage project, coordinator of the Northern Territory Libraries 'Libraries and Knowledge Centres' initiative and various research consultancies with the Strehlow Research Centre. He is currently working on the completion of his PhD thesis on T. G. H. Strehlow's Anmatyerr ethnography.

André Gingrich received his doctoral degree from the University of Vienna. He is Director of the Institute for Social Anthropology at the Austrian Academy of Sciences and Professor of Social Anthropology at the University of Vienna. He has researched and published on the history of German-speaking anthropology, including his chapters in the book co-authored with Fredrik Barth, Robert Parkin and Sydel Silvermann *One Discipline, Four Ways: British, German, French, and American anthropology* (2005), and in the volume edited by Deborah James, Evelyn Plaice and Christina Toren, *Culture Wars: Context, Models, and Anthropologists' Accounts* (2010).

Luise Hercus was a fellow of St Anne's College Oxford and university lecturer (1948–54), and began work on Aboriginal languages in Victoria in 1962. From 1967 to 1969, she was a part-time research fellow at the University of Adelaide (T. G. H. Strehlow's department). From 1969 to

1991, she was a lecturer and then reader in Sanskrit at The Australian National University. During this time, her main research has been in far western New South Wales, north-eastern South Australia and adjacent parts of Queensland. Since retiring in 1991, she has continued this work, especially the study of Arabana-Wangkangurru song cycles and traditions.

David Kaus is a Senior Curator at the National Museum of Australia in Canberra, and has worked with the Indigenous collections there since 1979. Until recently, he managed the museum's repatriation program and now has a more traditional curatorial role working on collections and exhibitions. His chief research interests are in the history of collections of Indigenous artefacts, their documentation and material culture. He has had a long-term interest in Herbert Basedow's collections and has spent considerable time improving the documentation of his collections. He is the author of two books: *Ernabella Batiks in the Hilliard Collection* of the National Museum of Australia (2004) and *A Different Time* (2008), on the photographs of Herbert Basedow.

Anna Kenny is an ARC Postdoctoral Fellow in the School of Archaeology and Anthropology at The Australian National University and a consultant anthropologist based in Alice Springs. She has conducted field research with Aboriginal people in the Northern Territory since 1991, as well as in Queensland and Western Australia. She has written 12 Connection Reports for native title claims and a book based on her PhD thesis called *The Aranda's Pepa: An introduction to Carl Strehlow's masterpiece Die Aranda- und Loritja-Stämme in Zentral-Australien (1907–1920)*. Currently, she is finalising the translation of Carl Strehlow's unpublished Aranda–German–Loritja–Diyari dictionary (c. 1900) with Aranda and Luritja people and working on a book about T. G. H. Strehlow called *Shadows of A Father* and a number of native title claims.

Erich Kolig is an Honorary Fellow in Religion at Otago University, New Zealand. He was a senior lecturer (reader) in social anthropology at Otago and visiting professor of cultural anthropology at Vienna University. He was also a research fellow at the University of Western Australia and a government anthropologist in Western Australia. Erich has done fieldwork in Afghanistan, Australia, Austria, Indonesia, New Zealand and Vanuatu. He has published several books (authored and edited) and many articles on Australian Aboriginal culture and religion, but also on indigenous politics in New Zealand, Vanuatu and Australia;

on historical exploration in New Zealand; on Muslims and Islam in Afghanistan, Indonesia and New Zealand; and on freedom of speech, Muslim integration and several other topics.

Rod Lucas is a social anthropologist with a PhD in anthropology and psychiatry from the University of Adelaide, where he has lectured since 1999. He has worked in the field of Aboriginal cultural heritage since 1989, co-researched three native title claims to successful consent determination and peer-reviewed several others. In these contexts, he has worked with Aboriginal people who identify as Diyari, Arabana, Kokatha, Antakirinja, Yankunytjatjara, Wangkangurru/Yarluyandi, Barngarla, Gawler Ranges, Kaurna and Ngarrindjeri. He has worked in the north-east of South Australia for nearly three decades, in which context he has become familiar with Reuther's work. He and Deane Fergie are currently working on a large-scale photographic project with the Dieri Aboriginal Corporation.

Kim McCaul is a consulting anthropologist and linguist who works in urban and remote contexts on native title and heritage processes. When he began his work in Aboriginal Australia in 2000, one of his first tasks was to review the correspondence between the Killalpaninna-based Lutheran missionary Otto Siebert and A. W. Howitt. More recently, he had to consider the ethnographic record left by another Lutheran missionary, Clamor Schürmann, who worked among the Aboriginal peoples of both the Adelaide region and the Eyre Peninsula.

William B. McGregor (FAHA, Member of the Academia Europaea (MAE)) is Professor of Linguistics in the School of Communication and Culture, Aarhus University. He is primarily a descriptive linguist, with special focus on the languages of the Kimberley, Western Australia. Since 2010, he has been working on Shua, a Khoe ('Khoisan') language of Botswana. He has published widely on these languages, including descriptive grammars and articles on grammatical topics. Other interests include linguistic typology, theoretical linguistics, social cognition in grammar and the history of linguistics, on which he has published a number of articles and edited a book, *Encountering Aboriginal Languages* (2008), and a special issue of the journal *Language and History*, entitled '19th and 20th century studies of Pacific languages' (Vol. 54, No. 2, 2011).

Francesca Merlan is Professor of Anthropology in the School of Archaeology and Anthropology at The Australian National University. Her interest in the German tradition in Australia, as one aspect of her research concerning relations between Indigenous and other Australians, has been especially focused on several key events and people: first, the Twenty-Second Frobenius Expedition (1938–39) and especially the work of its leader, Helmut Petri (*Sterbende Welt in nordwest Australien*, 1954); second, on that of Andreas Lommel (*Fortschritt ins Nichts: Die Modernisierung der Primitiven Australiens: Beschreibung und Definition eines psychischen Verfalls*, Zürich, 1969); third, she returns often to the main work of Erhard Eylmann (*Die Eingeborenen der Kolonie Suedaustralien*, Berlin, 1908), the subject of her contribution to this volume. It has been useful to consult his account of the upper-central parts of the Northern Territory where she has done research. Francesca was the Jensen Lecturer at the Frobenius Institut in Frankfurt-am-Main in 2010, on the topic of early contact between settlers and Aborigines in Australia.

John Morton is a research associate in anthropology in the School of Humanities and Social Sciences at La Trobe University, Melbourne, where he previously lectured for more than 20 years. His principal research interests lie in the fields of Australian Aboriginal religion, land tenure and social organisation, with which he has been involved for several decades. He has worked variously as lecturer, curator and consultant and has published widely, mainly in relation to the Arrernte (Aranda, Arunta) people of Central Australia. His publications include two earlier papers (1995, 2004) about the life and work of T. G. H. Strehlow.

Nicolas Peterson is Professor of Anthropology in the School of Archaeology and Anthropology at The Australian National University. He has a longstanding interest in Australian Aboriginal anthropology, land and sea tenure, economic anthropology, Fourth World people and the state and history of the discipline in Australia. He is Director of the Centre for Native Title Anthropology. His most recent books are *The Makers and Making of Indigenous Australian Museum Collections* (2008, co-edited with L. Allen and L. Hamby) and *Experiments in Self-Determination: Histories of the outstation movement* (2016, co-edited with Fred Myers).

Anthony Redmond has worked in the northern Kimberley region of Australia since 1994 with Ngarinyin people and their neighbours, in Central Australia since 2002 and in Cape York Peninsula since 2005. During this time, he has conducted ethnographic research (into transformations in local economies, Indigenous relationships with pastoralists, traditional cosmology, sung traditions and bodily experiences of time and country) and also conducted applied native title and land rights research. His most recent work has been focused on death and grieving, the comic in everyday Ngarinyin life, the social and ritual importance of body fat and a phenomenology of travelling in community trucks. Anthony is currently a Visiting Professor at Ca Foscari University, Venice, and, until this year, a visiting research fellow at the Centre for Aboriginal Economic Policy Research at The Australian National University, where he was an ARC partner working on a pan-Australian project on Aboriginal involvement in frontier and intercultural economies.

Nick Thieberger helped establish the Pacific and Regional Archive for Digital Sources in Endangered Cultures (paradisec.org.au), a digital archive of mainly audio language and music records, and is now its director. He is developing methods for the creation of reusable datasets from fieldwork on previously unrecorded languages. He is the editor of the journal *Language Documentation & Conservation* and edited *The Oxford Handbook of Linguistic Fieldwork* (2012). He taught in the Department of Linguistics at the University of Hawai'i at Mānoa and is an ARC Future Fellow at the University of Melbourne, where he is a chief investigator in the Centre of Excellence for the Dynamics of Language.

Introduction

1

The German-language tradition of ethnography in Australia

Nicolas Peterson and Anna Kenny[1]

Native title and statutory land claims under the *Aboriginal Land Rights (Northern Territory) Act 1976* (Cth) and the *Native Title Act 1993* (Cth) have been central to creating a renewed interest in early ethnographic accounts of Aboriginal life at a time when most current academic research into Aboriginal issues is focused on contemporary social problems, health matters and development. This is because to prove the existence of native title, Aboriginal claimants have to define the rights and interests in land that existed at sovereignty, identify the group that held these rights at that time, demonstrate a continued connection between these original rights holders, the contemporary claimants and their land and show how the rights and interests in the land are being exercised today. This has led anthropologists preparing claims to turn to the earliest ethnographic sources across the continent to establish what the original situation was likely to have been in a region and to demonstrate continuity of connection.

The Francophone emphasis in Australian and British education that lasted well into the middle of the twentieth century has meant that even other European languages such as Spanish and German are not widely known.

---

1   We would like to acknowledge the very useful comments from one of the anonymous referees on a draft of this chapter.

Thus, without translations, there has been very limited incorporation of ethnography in German into Australian anthropological scholarship until recently, when translations have started to become available. Yet even so, this body of ethnography is not well known.

The purpose of this volume is to draw attention to this ethnographic corpus and to highlight interesting aspects of it to attract people to look into it further. While this volume provides a guide to the history of German-language approaches to ethnography and theorising, it is not an academic history of this field nor is there unanimity of views about that history. The approaches to the work of the various people discussed are eclectic, ranging from straight historical to others who choose to locate their account in terms of the relevance of old material to the present context. Further, most of the ethnographers in the earlier part of Australia's contact history whose work is discussed here were not professional anthropologists but often missionaries or interested people of means.

A specifically German anthropological orientation emerged in late Enlightenment and early Romanticist thought, which André Gingrich (Chapter 2, this volume) suggests embodied a tension in understanding other human lives between a universalism derived from Immanuel Kant and the Johann and Georg Forster father and son collaboration, on the one hand, and a relativism derived from Johann Gottfried Herder and the von Humboldt brothers, Alexander and Wilhelm, on the other. The relativistic approach emphasised the significance of language for understanding other people's particularity, because language was seen as the embodiment of a people's *Geist*. As early as 1828, Goethe observed that a number of Herderian ideas had become absorbed into the mainstream of philosophical and, ultimately, anthropological thought (Marchand 1982: 20). In his memoirs, *Dichtung und Wahrheit*, Goethe (1998: 430) commented that one of the most significant occurrences in his life was his acquaintance with Herder, whom he had met by chance in the Gasthof zum Geist. A key focus of this German tradition was '*Ethnologie*', which was a concern with the relationship between cultural groups in historical and geographical perspective but was broader than the later American usage of ethnology because it included a concern with material culture, as well as mythology, ritual and language.

The emphasis on cultural multiplicity reflected in language was taken up by Adolf Bastian and his anthropological circle in Germany—in particular, by Franz Boas, who exported it to North America—and became their main methodological tool for empirical investigations. The meticulous and diligent study and collection of language data, especially through original texts of myths and songs, were central particularly because language was seen as the marker of humanity. It is not surprising, therefore, that linguists working in Australia are the ones who have made the most use of the material in German. As far as native title goes, the early work of the Lutheran missionaries in South and Central Australia (e.g. see McCaul, Chapter 3; Lucas and Fergie, Chapter 4, both this volume) has been most important, but later work has also been significant in demonstrating continuity of practices (see Redmond, Chapter 16, this volume). This German ethnography has also become of interest in contemporary Australia in the context of intellectual repatriation of cultural materials to Aboriginal communities concerned with cultural revitalisation of languages, traditional art forms and social practices.

However, it would be wrong to assume that just because missionaries paid attention to language, they automatically paid attention to culture. In most cases, the recording of mythical narratives and Aboriginal customs was a by-product of their linguistic work, which was focused on Bible translations. The major ethnographies by missionaries such as J. G. Reuther (1861–1914) and Carl Strehlow (1871–1922) were mainly the result of the guidance of mentors from the scientific world in urban centres in Germany (Völker 2001) and Australia. It is very unlikely, for example, that Carl Strehlow would have made his ethnographic investigations without the constant probing and support of his armchair anthropologist friend and mentor, Baron Moritz von Leonhardi (1856–1910) (Kenny 2013), who also corresponded with Reuther and Otto Siebert (1871–1957). Reuther and Siebert were correspondents as well of Alfred Howitt (1830–1908) in Melbourne.

Beyond native title, interest in German-language ethnography has come from outside social and cultural anthropology, with the growth of research into the rock art of the Kimberley region and material culture studies. Although the existence of this art has been known since the mid-1830s and there had been some documentation of it beginning with Ian Crawford (see 1968), it was the systematic work by Grahame Walsh, a self-funded researcher (Morwood 2002: 52), that has resulted in the documentation of nearly 1,000 sites on the Kimberley Plateau and has been principally responsible for the growth of interest. Because members of the 1938–39 Frobenius Institute Expedition had published major untranslated ethnographies on the Kimberley, Walsh was keen to gain access to them. His work stimulated the interest of local pastoralist Susan Bradley in the art, and influenced the Myer family of Melbourne to purchase two pastoral leases in the area to support his research. With Bradley's help, Walsh organised the translation and publication in 1997 of Andreas Lommel's *Die Unambal*, originally published in 1952, and in 2011 of Helmut Petri's *Sterbende Welt in Nordwest Australien*, originally published in 1954. The Association of Australian Decorative and Fine Arts Societies (AADFAS) funded both translations.[2] More recently, this translation of German ethnography has received another boost under the influence of Kim Akerman, an anthropologist with a strong interest in Kimberley material culture, who has been instrumental in having Petri's 'Der Australische Medizinmann' (1952) translated and published by Hesperian Press in 2014, and, in 2015, a collection of translations of articles by German ethnographers on northern Western Australia (Akerman 2015).

Australian ethnography produced by German speakers can be divided into three broad phases. The initial work was almost entirely by German-speaking missionaries of Lutheran and Moravian background, who gathered their material from the 1830s until the early twentieth century. A second phase overlapping with this first period runs from the beginning of the twentieth century until the 1930s, during which time a very small number of researchers, who may be broadly characterised as 'men of science', were active. A third phase runs from the late 1930s to the present and is characterised by the work of professionally trained anthropologists writing mainly in German, but more recently in English. Taken together, this work has three principal regional focuses: north-eastern South Australia among the Diyari (Dieri)[3] and their neighbours; Central Australia among the Aranda; and the Kimberley region of Western Australia. There is important work from elsewhere such as Cape York and southern South Australia, too, as emerges clearly from the chapters in this book by Corinna Erckenbrecht (Chapter 6) and Kim McCaul.

---

2   Neither the publications that have been translated with AADFA support nor the various websites provide any detailed information as to which of the many Australian branches supported the translation.

3   Diyari is a modern rendering of the people's name. The common spelling in the past was Dieri, which is still used by the people themselves today.

First encounters: Missionary anthropology

The prejudice of anthropologists towards missionaries and their missionising is well known but that has not extended to their ethnographic work in anything like the same degree. It is safe to generalise that most missionaries arrived in remote regions well before anthropologists and, until anthropology became a fieldwork-based discipline, the founding fathers of anthropology worldwide relied heavily on the reports of missionaries in particular, and, to a lesser extent, on travellers and explorers for their information.

Kenelm Burridge, in his neglected book *Encountering Aborigines* (1973: 5), makes a persuasive case that anthropology has a European signature. Indeed, he asks whether there would have been ethnographic studies of Aboriginal social and cultural life if Australia had been colonised from outside Europe. Colonisation, he argues, is only one aspect of that European signature. Another is anthropology's Christian inflexion that combines objective accounts of things as they are with engagement. While Christianity keeps these in a dialectical engagement, anthropology placed them in a 'taut and unsynthesised opposition' (Burridge 1973: 23). Both also share, in their different ways, a concern with how things might be. Thus, Burridge argues that a Christian ambience has contributed to an awareness of otherness and a desire to incorporate it. He also points out that missionary activity and anthropological monographs were:

> continually infusing the European homeland with experiences of otherness … It has been the collective and accumulated experience of the missionary tradition, in short, which has prepared the European mind to accept rather than reject the strange or new experiences, and then come to terms with it. (Burridge 1973: 17)

Missionaries, particularly German missionaries, were substantial contributors to early accounts of 'otherness' here in Australia. One clear reason for this was their accomplishment as linguists and the emphasis their training placed on learning local languages. It was surely Clamor Schürmann's (1815–93) command of the Barngarla language of the Eyre Peninsula in South Australia that led to him being the first person to report matrimoieties in 1846, and it was only command of local languages that could have resulted in the detail in the work of A. H. Kempe (1844–1928), L. G. Schulze (1851–1924), Reuther, Siebert and Carl Strehlow. The concern to learn local languages is testament to their education, especially those educated at the Neuendettelsau seminary, as is the marvellous photograph of Reuther in his study in remotest north-eastern South Australia in the 1890s (see Plate 4.3). Acquisition of the local languages required intensive work with Aboriginal people and led to further intensive work on the translation of hymns and sections of the Bible. While the Protestant theologian Gustav Warneck urged ethnography as a precondition of successful proselytisation, for some missionaries it seems the initial work on the language led to an interest in Aboriginal culture itself, way beyond what was required for their practical purposes. This is most clearly the case in respect of Otto Siebert at Killalpaninna (Bethesda Mission) and Carl Strehlow at Hermannsburg Mission—both of whom were criticised for spending too much time on ethnographic inquiry.

Their ethnographic zeal was also combined with a very active involvement in the collection of material culture for sale to support the mission. On the other hand, J. G. Reuther, who was also at Killalpaninna, initially claimed in 1892 that his only purpose in acquiring knowledge of the Diyari language and life was to 'find the points of contact with the Christian faith, and thereby to destroy their pagan concepts' (quoted in Scherer 1979: 14). Nevertheless, his ethnographic corpus of material eventually filled 13 volumes, with considerable attention paid to placenames and their associated mythology, and seems to clearly indicate a change of heart. Rod Lucas and Deane Fergie explore in fascinating detail Reuther's realisation of the importance of place to the Diyari and how he engaged his co-worker, Harry Hillier, to prepare a map to show some of the 2,449 placenames he recorded. He also commissioned an extensive collection of *toas*, the somewhat mysterious so-called direction signs—objects that have been the focus of considerable research and debate (e.g. see Morphy 1977; Jones and Sutton 1986). Indeed, Reuther's interest in material culture— so dramatically displayed in the photograph of the central corridor of his house, with its more than 1,000 artefacts (see Plate 4.4)—when added to the reports of Siebert and Hillier organising the sale of artefacts from the community at Killalpaninna to museums, clearly underlines the intensity of the artefact industry, especially in light of the fact that there were only 200 adults at Killalpaninna and most, if not all, of the wooden items would have been made by the 50 or so adult men. This focus on artefacts was driven not just by the need to generate income for the mission, but also, more generally, by the place of museums and material culture in German anthropology of the time (see Gingrich, Chapter 2, this volume).

Plate 1.1 A Dieri family at a camp just outside of Killalpaninna Mission.
Source: SRC 06182, Strehlow Research Centre, Alice Springs.

Luise Hercus (Chapter 5) explores linguistic aspects of Reuther's 4,000-word Diyari dictionary, his comparative wordlists of seven other languages of the Lake Eyre region with 1,744 single gloss entries for Arabana, Yawarrawarrka, Wangkangurru, Kuyani, Ngamini, Thirrari and Yandruwandha and the related volume with the 2,449 placenames to reflect on his methodology and the enormous amount of detailed information his work contains. She shows the richness of his ethno-linguistic oeuvre and what can be learnt from it, but also demonstrates the problems these types of raw data pose. She uses particular words as examples to show how these problems might be overcome with the help of comparative linguistic materials and comparison with later ethnographic records, some of which she collected in the 1960s and 1970s from Aboriginal people from the Lake Eyre Basin.

In his consideration of the intellectual influences on these Lutheran missionaries, André Gingrich warns against drawing too strong a contrast between the social evolutionism of Baldwin Spencer and the British school, and the romantic humanism of the German researchers. Although Herder's views were important, they included a moderate evolutionism, reflecting his acceptance of universalism. The essential point was the acceptance that people such as the Aborigines had souls, even if they were seen as inferior, and, as a result, it was important to learn their language as a key to accessing their belief system and mythology. This emphasis on language learning, mythology and beliefs makes these early German missionary recorders' work invaluable in terms not only of general ethnography, but also linguistically, and marks it out from much of the work of the Anglophone ethnographers of the time.[4]

Although the Moravian missionaries first arrived in Australia in 1849, with their main efforts in Victoria, they extended their work to western Cape York in 1891, first by establishing Mapoon, then Weipa in 1898 and Aurukun in 1904. The training provided to these missionaries was quite different from that given to those with Lutheran backgrounds and was a great deal more practical, including not only gardening and farming, but also, interestingly, photography. Corinna Erckenbrecht has found an enormously rich archive in Herrnhut, Saxony, documenting the early years of these missions, which includes a fascinating visual record along with the many letters, journals and reports sent back to the mission headquarters. One particularly intriguing reference is to the early establishment of an orphanage at Mapoon in 1892, initially with three orphans brought by John Douglas from Thursday Island. The Cape York missionaries seem to have encountered greater difficulty in learning the languages of the region than the Lutherans in Central Australia, especially because of their number. Like the Lutherans, they, too, made collections of artefacts for sale to German museums.[5]

Impact of the Aranda ethnography

Although the ethnographic work by missionaries to the Aranda falls within this first phase, the key figure, Carl Strehlow, deserves separate treatment because of the role that Aranda ethnography has played in Australian anthropology, the size of his corpus, his engagement with Moritz von Leonhardi in Germany and his influence on his son, T. G. H. Strehlow (1908–78).

---

4   Of course, Malinowski emphasised the importance of fieldworkers learning the local language and Radcliffe-Brown, then foundation professor of anthropology at the University of Sydney, arranged funding for an American linguist of German background, Gehard Laves, to work in Australia towards a doctorate, which he never finished. Nonetheless, Laves's fieldnotes in the Australian Institute of Aboriginal and Torres Strait Islander Studies (AIATSIS) in Canberra have proved valuable to linguists and in native title claims.
5   An important secular collector was Amalie Dietrich, active in Queensland between 1863 and 1972, and working for a private museum in Hamburg (see Sumner 1993).

If there is one thing that has long been known about German ethnography in Australia, it is the conflict between this Lutheran missionary to the Aranda at Hermannsburg, west of Alice Springs in Central Australia, and Sir Baldwin Spencer, professor of biology at the University of Melbourne and co-author with Frank Gillen of *The Native Tribes of Central Australia* (1899). The details of this conflict have been examined at length by a number of authors (e.g. see Strehlow 1947; Veit 2004; Strehlow 2004; Kenny 2013). The central issue was whether there was a concept of 'high god(s)' (see Hiatt 1996) among the Aranda and more generally in Australia and the full significance of the term *altjira*, which the Lutherans used as the translation for 'God'. Spencer aligned himself with Edward Tylor and Sir James Frazer and a strong evolutionary perspective that saw Aranda ceremonies as magical and the precursor to religion. Carl Strehlow's report of high gods among the Aranda was at complete odds with this view, as was treating Aboriginal beliefs and practices as religious. In Spencer's view, Strehlow failed to realise that his report of high gods as Indigenous was quite wrong and that such beliefs were the result of Christian missionary activity. In this conflict, which was a key factor in marginalising Strehlow's work, the Australian anthropological fraternity clearly sided with Spencer until recently, as Walter Veit (2004: 108–9) notes, mainly because of their view that missionaries were 'prejudiced interlopers'. However, a number of scholars in the United Kingdom referred very favourably to Carl Strehlow's work. In 1933, A. M. Hocart (1933), for instance, pointed out that Strehlow's works were much stronger in their textual evidence than Spencer's and Gillen's. Hocart, however, belonged to a very different anthropological tradition than either Frazer or Alfred Radcliffe-Brown. Northcote Thomas (1905) also corresponded in German with Strehlow, raising questions over Spencer and Gillen's published accounts.[6]

Schulze and Kempe, the original missionaries who helped establish Hermannsburg Mission in 1877, 125 km west of Alice Springs, were not trained at the Neuendettelsau seminary in southern Germany, but were graduates of the Hermannsburg seminary in northern Germany, which was less academically oriented. Nevertheless, it was Kempe's work on the Aranda language that laid the foundation for Carl Strehlow's rapid competency in the local language when he arrived in 1894. As early as 1880, they had produced a school primer and a book of Bible stories as

---

6   We are grateful to one of the anonymous reviewers for pointing out this evidence about the reception of Strehlow's work in the United Kingdom.

well as hymns in Aranda. From Schulze's brief ethnographic output, it is clear that he was a sensitive observer recognising the ceremonies for what they were: religious celebrations.

Carl Strehlow was said to be preaching in Aranda within six months of his arrival at Hermannsburg and to be collecting material on linguistics and mythology at that time as well. However, he started writing his ethnographic work only in response to the inquiries from Leonhardi after the turn of the twentieth century, completing it in a five-year period (1905–10). The known manuscripts of Carl Strehlow's published work were destroyed in World War II during the bombing of the Ethnological Museum of Frankfurt. However, these were only duplicates provided to his editor. The original handwritten manuscripts survived because Strehlow had copied them and sent them in segments to Germany for comment and publication (Kenny 2013: 37). These manuscripts consist of three volumes, titled *Sagen* ('myths'/'legends'), *Cultus* ('cults') and *Leben* ('life'), and are now held at the Strehlow Research Centre in Alice Springs in Central Arrernte territory. *Sagen* contains the collection of myths, *Cultus* contains the songs that were sung during ceremonies and describes the choreography and paraphernalia of these rites and ceremonies and *Leben* describes aspects of social life. They were published in seven instalments as *Die Aranda- und Loritja-Stämme in Zentral-Australien* between 1907 and 1920 and are the richest and densest ethnographic writing on Western Aranda and Loritja cultures of Central Australia at the beginning of the twentieth century. His meticulous ethno-linguistic work also included a comparative dictionary of more than 7,600 Aranda and Loritja terms glossed in German, along with 1,200 Dieri (Diyari) words that remained unpublished at the time due to the death of his editor, and a comparative grammar of Aranda and Loritja. The comparative dictionary and grammar had the purpose 'to ascertain by comparison that Loritja and Aranda were two distinct languages, in structure and vocabulary'[7] and to illustrate some theoretical points of the emerging *Kulturkreislehre* ('culture circle theory'; see below) school.

---

7   Letter from Moritz von Leonhardi to Carl Strehlow, 3 April 1909, held at the Strehlow Research Centre, Alice Springs.

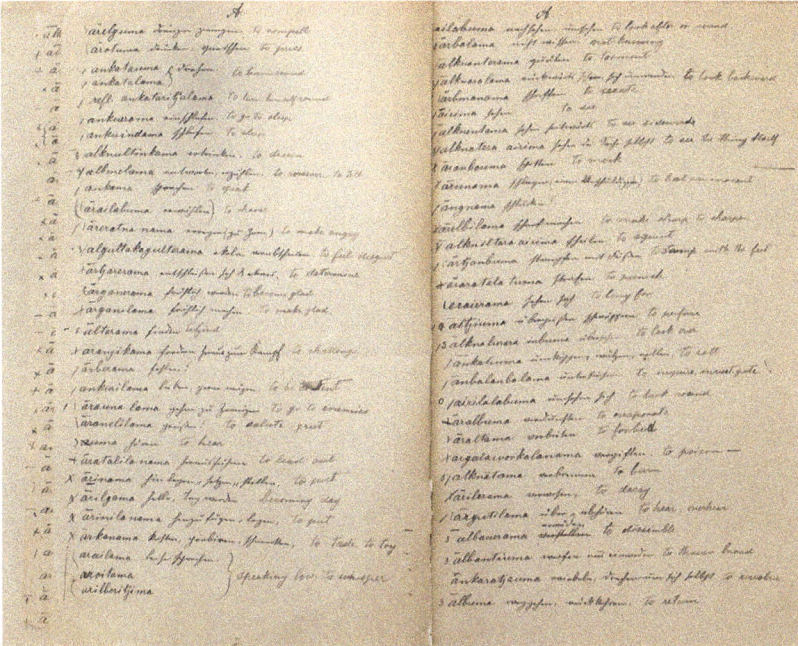

Plate 1.2 Kempe's Aranda to German wordlist with English translation by T. G. H. Strehlow, 1877–91.
Source: Image courtesy of Strehlow Research Centre, Alice Springs.

In her contribution, Anna Kenny (Chapter 7) concentrates on three key ethnographic topics discussed in the works of Kempe, Schulze and Strehlow senior that have direct relevance today: the *altjira* concept mentioned above, the subsection system and the links to the mother's country (place). It is a tribute to Schulze that he discovered the eight-class system, even if he struggled to get on top of it, leaving it to Carl Strehlow to do so. The significance of the mother's country is a major theme of most native title claims today and is central to ceremonial life. Although the concern with the eight-class system and links to the mother's country relate to social organisation, as well as genealogy to some degree, more detailed investigation of kinship and marriage were clearly avoided, as Gingrich emphasises—an avoidance that lasted until the 1970s among missionaries to the Aranda.[8]

---

8   Despite the continuing tradition of the Lutheran missionaries mastering Aranda, they had no grasp of the social and territorial organisation of the people at Hermannsburg until two of them took a course in anthropology at the University of Queensland in the mid-1970s, in which they learnt about the significance of patrilineal descent groups and ideology.

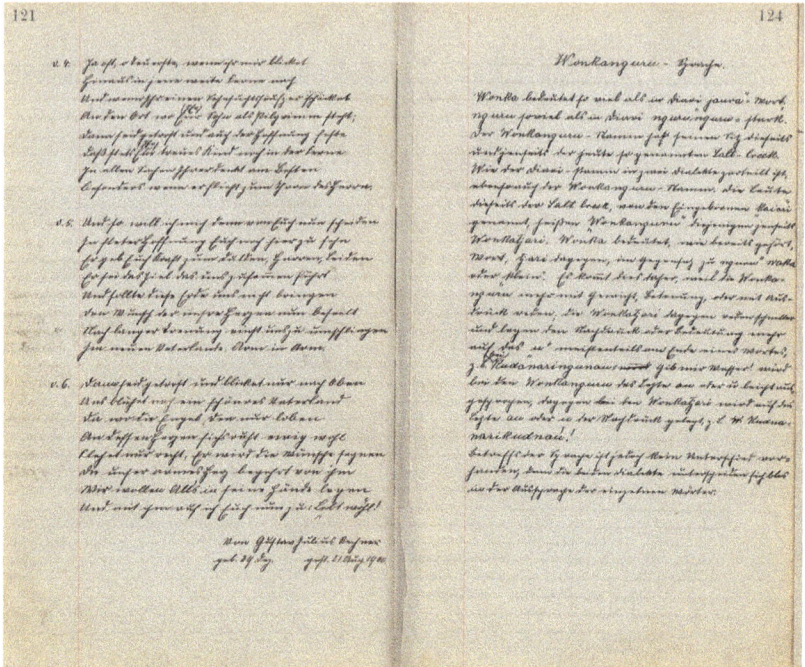

Plate 1.3 Pages of Reuther's manuscript of volume 5 containing data about eight languages of the Lake Eyre Basin, date range 1891–1904.
Source: South Australian Museum, Adelaide, AA-9-5, pp. 121, 124.

Because there is no published translation of Carl Strehlow's work, there is little awareness of its significance in the Anglophone world, although Kenny's (2013) book on Carl Strehlow describes his key findings to make them accessible to people outside a small cadre of regional specialists.[9] At the time of the work's original publication, both Andrew Lang and N. W. Thomas in the Anglophone world recognised its importance, and Strehlow's work had considerable impact in Europe, where Marcel Mauss, Arnold van Gennep and others made good use of it (Kenny 2013: 101). However, besides the language problem, and Spencer's denigration of Strehlow's work, the outbreak of the war and the rise of Nazism resulted in any further interest in his ethnography dropping off.

Carl Strehlow's work was, however, a major influence on his son's anthropological research starting in the 1930s, and indeed provided the blueprint for his son's oeuvre. But, as John Morton (Chapter 8) argues,

---

9   The work has not been published in English as Aranda men are concerned about the amount of restricted information included in the seven volumes.

there is clear evidence of a strongly oedipal relationship across successive generations in the Strehlow line, and, even though, as he says, T. G. H. Strehlow's 'anthropological journey is inseparable from his father's', T. G. H. never acknowledged his enormous debt to Carl. This despite drawing on every aspect of his father's work, from his extensive Aranda and Luritja dictionary to his extended genealogies and his translations of myths and songs. Indeed, T. G. H. was poor at acknowledging the works of others more generally and there are, according to Jason Gibson (Chapter 10), no references to either German or American anthropologists in his work or notes. It was only late in his career that he started looking towards North America, where his work might have found greater acceptance, and that he began to incorporate more theoretical thoughts on language into his papers as well as references (Kenny and Mitchell 2005).

Although T. G. H. Strehlow's work is well known because it is all in English, neither he nor his work was ever fully embraced by British social anthropology. Despite two years at the London School of Economics (LSE) that he had hoped would bring the recognition of a PhD, on the basis of his published work, neither Raymond Firth, the head of anthropology there, nor A. P. Elkin in Sydney was really impressed with his anthropology (see Austin-Broos, Chapter 9, this volume). Both Diane Austin-Broos and Jason Gibson suggest that the reason for this was because T. G. H. Strehlow's interests were too particularistic and highly empirical, which, together with the focus on ritual, did not fit the prevailing social anthropological interests in kinship and social organisation. Nevertheless, Austin-Broos argues that, with access to his father's rich genealogical work, to which he made very substantial additions by linking kinship and marriage with totemic affiliations so assiduously marked for most people, T. G. H. has in fact mapped out the wider regional social system. This regional emphasis is shown as a ritual network and the fact that the genealogies have no ego reference point, but are named in relation to one or more apical ancestors, underlines this.

There was another, quite different aspect to Strehlow junior's regionalism that has been ignored, as Gibson documents. He worked much more widely in Central Australia than just with the Western, Eastern and Southern Aranda, spending considerable time with people to the north speaking Anmatyerr. Gibson emphasises just how keenly T. G. H. took up film and wire recording in the documenting of ceremonies. Interestingly, many of these recordings were made at religious festivals—very much in the tradition of Baldwin Spencer and Frank Gillen in 1896. This work on ceremonial life is yet another reason T. G. H. Strehlow's work, like that of his father, is not well known, since it is restricted mainly because of the secret-sacred content.

In his chapter, Morton examines the currents that link T. G. H. Strehlow's work with that of Freud, mediated by Géza Róheim (1891–1953). Although Hungarian, Róheim wrote in both German and English and conducted fieldwork for nine months with the Aranda and Pitjantjatjara in 1929. Morton outlines the influence of Róheim and his psychoanalytic approach on T. G. H., who commented that he felt 'the Freudian school has some excellent suggestions to offer in regard to the elucidation of aboriginal sacred myths and songs' (1971: xvi–xvii). But T. G. H.'s concern for 'absolute accuracy' in whatever he documented meant that he found Róheim's 'generally reckless and uneconomical approach to writing', as Morton puts it, problematic. Regardless of this, given the lack of credibility that psychoanalysis had among social anthropologists, it became yet another reason to add to the concern with ritual and his difficult personality for T. G. H.'s work not entering the mainstream of Australian anthropological scholarship in his lifetime. His time at the LSE had little impact on his orientation, and it is clear from both his writing and the fact that the Froebenius Institute approached him to join their 1938–39 expedition to Australia that his anthropological approach was still seen as being in tune with German orientations to anthropology.

Widening the interest

In terms of the chronology of work by German ethnographers in Australia, we need to go back to 1896 when the first of the published non-missionary investigators arrived, making them more or less contemporary with Baldwin Spencer. This was Erhard Eylmann (1860–1926), a man of private means with a medical and natural science background. His book *Die Eingeborenen der Kolonie Südaustralien* (*The Natives of the Colony of South Australia*; 1908) has not been translated into English and for this reason alone is not well known. In her examination of Eylmann's book, Francesca Merlan (Chapter 11) draws attention to the rather unusual nature of his writing, which combines a scientific reporting style with personal writing that gives a feeling for the subjective experience of fieldwork, and a touch of a modern sensibility to his writing.

At much the same time (1904–07), Hermann Klaatsch (1863–1916) was in Australia. He, too, had a medical background, with a particular interest in physical anthropology and the theory of his friend Otto Schoetensack that the human race had originated in Australia—an idea he soon realised was unlikely. Gingrich comments that there was a growth of interest in physical anthropology at this period. Klaatsch's life and work have been given extended treatment by Corinna Erckenbrecht (2010). Although he was interested in and made a large collection of material culture and wrote about aspects of social life, being critical of Spencer's ideas on totemism (see Erckenbrecht 2010: 194), Klaatsch's only book-length work in English was an analysis of the W. E. Roth collection of skulls in the Australian Museum (see Klaatsch 1907) and he died before publishing a major work on Australia.

The first scholar with a German background to publish an encyclopedic text on Aboriginal ethnography was Herbert Basedow (1881–1933), author of *The Australian Aboriginal*, published in English in 1925. Apart from three years of primary education in Germany, Basedow was educated in Adelaide, going on to do science at the University of Adelaide. When he was 26, he travelled to Germany for postgraduate work, studying science and medicine under Hermann Klaatsch. For one of his two PhDs, Basedow wrote on Aboriginal crania in relation to the ideas that Aboriginal people were 'black Caucasians'. In Basedow's complex career following his return to Australia, David Kaus (Chapter 12) shows that his anthropological work was always secondary to his prospecting or medical employment. There was considerable scepticism about his medical training, because of the rapidity with which it was acquired, and this scepticism seems to have spilt over to his ethnographic work, which was not held in high regard by his contemporaries, all the more so because his book does not reference other people's work even where he has drawn on it.

The first person to work with an explicitly *Kulturkreislehre* or diffusionist approach in Australia was Father Ernest Worms (1891–1963) of the Pallottine mission, who arrived in the Kimberley in 1930. Although a missionary, his concern with anthropological research in Aboriginal languages and religion was of a professional standard, as William McGregor (Chapter 13) shows, so he can be seen as a 'man of science'. Almost immediately after arrival, he began research on the Indigenous languages of the region, and was joined by his former teacher Hermann Nekes (1875–1948) in 1935. Together, while effectively 'interned' in Melbourne during the war, they prepared a magnum opus on Australian languages, which was distributed on microfilm in 1953 but not published until 2006. Worms was also interested in Aboriginal religion but had little involvement in either sociolinguistics or social anthropology. He was concerned with the historical sequence of influences from the desert on Kimberley religion, which was eventually published as *Australische Eingeborenen-Religionen* in 1968, but not translated until 1986. Following Virchow, Worms saw the role of missionaries as being to collect information, leaving the theorising to the metropole. Regina Ganter (Chapter 14) reports that his strongly anti-evolutionist position led him to dismiss the work of Frazer, Tylor, Spencer and Morgan as 'pre-modern ethnology', preferring the new ethnology of Ratzel, Graebner, Frobenius and Schmidt because it 'harmonised with Catholic thought'. Indeed, it was through Worms's work that Schmidt's work on Australian languages and their sequencing was most influential. Ganter reports that 'in the early 1950s, one of Elkin's students ... produced a scathing critique of Catholic mission policy', so that, from then on, Worms no longer published in *Oceania* (which was edited by Elkin), but only in *Anthropos*.

Despite the rift with Elkin, W. E. H. Stanner (1905–81) invited Worms to present at the inaugural conference for the Australian Institute of Aboriginal and Torres Strait Islander Studies (AIATSIS) in 1961.

Indirectly, these *Kulturkreislehre* ideas influenced Norman Tindale (1976) and D. S. Davidson (1928), both of whom were interested in the spatial distribution of material culture and patterns of diffusion in Australia.

Academic researchers

The beginning of this phase is clearly marked by the Frobenius Institute Expedition to north-west Australia in 1938–39, with its two male anthropologists, Andreas Lommel (1912–2005) and Helmut Petri (1907–86), both of whom published book-length accounts of their work. Because Lommel's and Petri's books were not translated into English until 1997 and 2011, respectively, the impact of their work in Australia has been limited and is known largely through a few chapters in edited volumes and journal articles that were of interest mainly to regional specialists. However, Erich Kolig (Chapter 15) was very much an exception to this ignorance as a native German speaker from Austria who received his anthropological education at the University of Vienna. He was not only familiar with these works but also knew Helmut Petri and his wife,

Gisela Petri-Odermann. Kolig reflects on his anthropological education to ask about the nature of this German anthropological tradition and the diverse influences on his approach. Although this includes Durkheim and Weber, the majority of people who have influenced his work are quite different from those influencing people in the social anthropological tradition until the recent phenomenological turn, and the nature of his own publications could never be mistaken for those of an Anglophone social anthropologist. Kolig came to the Kimberley region of Western Australia in 1970 as a postdoctoral researcher with full knowledge of Lommel's and Petri's works from the time of the Frobenius Expedition in 1938. Each wrote a book that was framed by a pessimistic historical perspective on the future, a framing influenced by Frobenius's ideas on cultural morphology and the analogy of cultures having 'life cycles'. Their historical orientation, even if negative, contrasted strongly in Kolig's eyes with the backward-looking and reconstructive bias of much of the work of Australian anthropologists going on when he arrived. Kolig's own work relates directly to Petri's concern with travelling cults and brought a strong interest in cultural change, which he saw in much more positive terms of resilience and cultural revivalism. Petri, too, became more positive, Kolig believes, as a result of his postwar research in Australia.

Silke Beinssen-Hess (1991) provides a comprehensive account of the background to Frobenius's interest in Australia and the organisation of the expedition, comprising originally Helmut Petri and Gisela Petri-Odermann and then joined by Lommel as the third anthropologist. There were also two women painters for the recording of rock art, and later they were joined by Patrick Pentony, who worked on dreams and ended up as professor of psychology at The Australian National University. Beinssen-Hess provides a comparative account of the work of Petri and Lommel. While there is no doubt that Petri was the better scholar, Lommel was more widely known in Europe because of writings on Aboriginal art in German and extensively in English (e.g. see Lommel and Lommel 1959, and its translation), which have been strongly criticised by at least one Australian scholar (Beinssen-Hess 1991: 148). Beinssen-Hess also briefly mentions another member of the Frobenius research group on Australia, F. J. Micha, who had several publications in English (see 1959, 1970) and one major one in German (1958).

Lommel's work on the *jurnba* song cycle was the jumping off point for Anthony Redmond (Chapter 16) when he began his PhD research in the Kimberley in 1994. Redmond worked with some of Lommel's informants and collected further song texts from them and others, but also gained insights into how the Europeans of the Frobenius Expedition in 1938 were perceived and received by the Aboriginal people of Munja. He shows how they, as well as events occurring in the war years, left records of their social impact in their various song cycles.

Of the researchers working in an academic mode, the most problematic is Carl von Brandenstein (1909–2005), who started academic life as a Hurrinan-language expert at the Berlin Ethnological Museum. After internment in Australia during the war, he became involved with the Australian Institute of Aboriginal Studies early on, carrying out language surveys in Western Australia. His linguistic career can be divided into two phases: the earlier period in which he carried out extensive fieldwork recording and the latter period when his work became increasingly speculative. This speculation included his dubious views on Portuguese influence on the language of the Kimberley region, fitting with diffusionist thinking, but more significantly on the attempts at linking the classification of human temperaments and somatic types with the section and subsection systems. This work is highly controversial and made all the more problematic by his book *Names and Substance of the Australian Subsection System*, which was published by Chicago University Press in 1982. As Patrick McConvell points out, '[m]uch of his linguistic evidence is coincidence, dressed up as historical connection' (quoted in Thieberger, Chapter 17, this volume). No doubt, as Nick Thieberger suggests, von Brandenstein's lasting contribution will be the extensive field recordings he made of languages, many of which are no longer in daily use.

It is no accident that both Kolig and von Brandenstein received support and encouragement from Ronald Berndt (1916–90), the foundation professor of anthropology in Western Australia. Ronald Berndt was born in Adelaide to German-speaking parents but received his anthropological education at the University of Sydney and the LSE, and so was firmly in the social anthropological tradition. He wrote only in English. However, his own interests and sensibilities seem to be at odds with his training and his focus was on ritual, religion, mythology, art and collecting extensive texts with interlinear translations. Nicolas Peterson (Chapter 18) argues that this gives a Germanic inflexion to his work—the exact sources of which are a little unclear, but which he believes are related to Berndt's pride in his German background and the experiences of working in the South Australian Museum early in his life, in the context of a general empiricism that pervaded anthropology in Adelaide, influenced as it was by the natural and medical scientists who were the supporters of the discipline. In his concern for ethnography over anthropology, Berndt also had a soulmate in T. G. H. Strehlow, with whom he was good friends and who was one of his few supporters right up to Strehlow's death.

If Ronald Berndt marked the end of one era, educational and political currents in Europe have opened a new one, bringing a new wave of anthropologists with German backgrounds to Australia since the late 1980s. This has been in the form of a steady stream of German postgraduate students coming to work with Aboriginal people, some registered in German-speaking countries and others in Australia (e.g. see Musharbash 2008; Eickelkamp 2001; Heil 2003; Kenny 2013; Duelke 1998; Stotz 1993; Widlok 1992; Weichart 1997). Their interests in psychoanalysis, phenomenology and material culture are now partly tinged with the form of British social anthropological practice found in Australia today, which itself is more correctly seen as a mid-Atlantic mix.

Conclusion

There are several important ethnographers whose work has been left out of consideration here. Two people who worked in South Australia, Christian Gottlieb Teichelmann (1841) and Heinrich Meyer (1846) from the Dresden Mission Society have some profile as their work was written in English and reprinted early, in 1879 (see Woods 1879), but there are others whose work was quite unknown until recently. Foremost among these is William Blandowski (1822–78), who has now received considerable attention, thanks to the work of Harry Allen (see 2010; Darragh 2009). Although working in the 1850s and 1860s, Blandowski was certainly a man of science, becoming the first director of what is now Museum Victoria. Allen has quite clearly understood Blandowski's intention to publish the first visual ethnography of Aboriginal life based on the assumption that it was similar across the continent. This assumption allowed him to draw, unacknowledged, on other people's imagery where he had gaps in what he was unable to document while on his expedition to the lower River Murray in 1859. What is so powerful in the images is, as Allen puts it, their 'highly engaging sense of Aboriginal sociality' (Allen 2010: 12); even if this was an artistic artifice, it captures so nicely the dense sociality of Aboriginal life, and, in that respect, many of the images could only have been drawn from the experience of being with Aboriginal people. The publication of the images he assembled for his book included the documentation of aspects of Aboriginal culture in the south of the continent that are elsewhere recorded only in words.

Another scholar whose work is not dealt with here because much of it is in English is Wolfgang Laade (1925–2013), professor of ethnomusicology at the University of Zurich from 1971 to 1990, who carried out field research in the Torres Strait. In 1971, he published the first of five to seven planned volumes devoted to the ethno-history and ethnography of Torres Strait oral traditions. He also made a very extensive collection of musical recordings (e.g. see Laade 1971, 1974).

Taking all the scholars who have been mentioned here together, it would clearly be an error to manufacture a coherent and self-conscious German tradition where it did not exist. However, it is also clear that whether the ethnographers were missionaries, scientists or academics, the interest in mythology, song and religion more generally, grounded in enormous respect for local languages, plus the skills and motivations to learn them, permeates the work of all the people reported here. It has, as a result, created a body of work that is quite distinctive and that has greatly enriched the ethnographic corpus on Australian Aboriginal life.

References

Akerman, K. (ed.). 2015. *Cologne to the Kimberley: Studies of Aboriginal life in northwest Australia by five German scholars in the first half of the 20th century*. Perth: Hesperian Press.

Allen, H. (ed.). 2010. *William Blandowski's Illustrated Encyclopaedia of Aboriginal Life*. Canberra: Aboriginal Studies Press.

Baessler, A. 1983 [1895]. *A Picnic with Australian Aborigines at Wallaga Lake (NSW)*. Translated by D. Fraser. Canberra: Department of the Parliamentary Library.

Basedow, H. 1925. *The Australian Aboriginal*. Adelaide: F.W. Preece and Sons.

Beinssen-Hesse, S. 1991. The study of Australian Aboriginal culture by German anthropologists of the Frobenius Institute. In *From Berlin to the Burdekin: The German contribution to the development of Australian science, exploration and the arts*, (eds) D. Walker and J. Tanpke, pp. 135–50. Sydney: UNSW Press.

Burridge, K. 1973. *Encountering Aborigines: Anthropology and the Australian Aborigines*. New York: Pergamon.

Campbell, I. (trans.). 1997. *The Unambal: A tribe in northwest Australia by A. Lommel*. Carnarvon Gorge, Qld: Takarakka Nowan Kas Publications.

Campbell, I. (trans.). 2011. *The Dying World in Northwest Australia*. Perth: Hesperian Press.

Crawford, I. 1968. *The Art of the Wandjina: Aboriginal cave painting in Kimberley, Western Australia*. Melbourne: Oxford University Press.

Crawford, I. (trans.). 2014. *The Australian Medicine Man*. Perth: Hesperian Press.

Darragh, T. 2009. William Blandowski: A frustrated life. *Proceedings of the Royal Society of Victoria* 121(1): 11–60.

Davidson, D. S. 1928. *The Chronological Aspects of Certain Australian Social Institutions as Inferred from Geographical Distribution*. Philadelphia: University of Philadelphia.

Duelke, B. 1998. *Same but Different: Vom Umgang mit Vergangenheit. Traition und Geschichte im Alltak einer nordaustralilischen Aborigines-Kommune*. Cologne: R. Koppe.

Eickelkamp, U. 2001. Pitjantjatjara women's art at Ernabella: Genesis and transformations. Unpublished PhD thesis. Heidelberg University, Heidelberg.

Erckenbrecht, C. 2010. Auf der Suche nach den Ursprungen: Die Australienreise des Anthropologen und Sammlers Hermann Klaatsch 1904–1907. *Ethnologica NF Band 27*.

Eylmann, E. 1908. *Die Eingeborenen der Kolonie Südaustralien*. Berlin: Dietrich Reimer (Ernst Vohsen).

Goethe, J. 1998. *Dichtung und Wahrheit.* Stuttgart: Reclam.

Heil, D. 2003. Well-being and bodies in trouble: Situating health practices within Australian Aboriginal socialities. Unpublished PhD thesis. University of Sydney, Sydney.

Hiatt, L. 1996. *Arguments about Aborigines: Australia and the evolution of social anthropology.* Cambridge: Cambridge University Press.

Hocart, A. M. 1933. Arunta language: Strehlow v. Spencer and Gillen. *Man* 33(May): 92.

Jones, P. and Sutton, S. 1986. *Aboriginal Sculptures of the Lake Eyre Region.* Adelaide: South Australian Museum and Wakefield Press.

Kenny, A. 2013. *The Aranda's Pepa: An introduction to Carl Strehlow's masterpiece Die Aranda- und Loritja-Stämme in Zentral-Australien (1907–1920).* Canberra: ANU E Press.

Kenny, A. and Mitchell, S. (eds). 2005. *Collaboration and language.* Occasional Paper No. 4. Strehlow Research Centre, Alice Springs, NT.

Klaatsch, H. 1907. The skull of the Australian Aboriginal New South Wales. *Pathological Laboratory Reports* 1(3): 44–167. Lunacy Department, Sydney.

Laade, W. 1971. *Oral Traditions and Written Documents on the History and Ethnography of the Northern Torres Strait Islands, Saibai-Dauan-Boigu. Volume 1: Aeh—Myths, legends, fairy tales.* Wiesbaden, Germany: Franz Steiner.

Laade, W. 1974. *Das Geisterkanu: Südseemythen und-märchen aus der Torres-Strasse.* Kassel, Germany: Eric Roth.

Lally, J. 2008. The Australian Aboriginal collection and the Berlin Ethnological Museum. In *The Makers and Making of Indigenous Australian Museum Collections,* (eds) N. Peterson, L. Allen and L. Hamby, pp. 190–205. Melbourne: Melbourne University Press.

Langham, I. 1981. *The Building of British Social Anthropology.* Dordrecht: D. Reidel Publishing Company. doi.org/10.1007/978-94-009-8464-6.

Lommel, A. 1952. *Die Unambal: Ein Stamm in Nordwest Australien.* Hamburg. [English version 1997. *The Unambal.* Translated by I. Campbell. Carnarvon Gorge, Qld: Takarakka Nowan Kas Publications.]

Lommel, A. 1969. *Fortschritt ins Nichts: die Modernisierung der Primitiven Australiens—Beschreibung und Definition eines psychischen Verfalls.* Zurich: Atlantis.

Lommel, A. and Lommel, K. 1959. *Die Kunst des fünften Erdteils Australien.* Munich: Staatliches Museum fur Volkerkunde.

Marchand, J. W. 1982. Herder: Precursor of Humboldt, Whorf, and modern language philosophy. In *Johann Gottfried Herder: Innovator through the ages,* (ed.) W. Koepke with S. B. Knoll, pp. 20–34. Bonn: Bouvier Verlag Herbert Grundmann.

Meyer, H. A. 1846. *Manners and Customs of the Aborigines of the Encounter Bay Tribe.* Adelaide: G. Dehane. [Reprinted in Woods, J. 1879. *The Native Tribes of South Australia.* Adelaide: E. S. Wigg & Son.]

Micha, F. J. 1958. Der Handel der zentralaustralischen Eingeborenen. *Annali Lateranensi* [Vatican City] 22: 41–228.

Micha, F. J. 1959. Die Tauschmittel an den Märkten der zentralaustralischen Eingeborenen. *Anthropos* 54(S): 377–400.

Micha, F. J. 1970. Trade and change in Aboriginal Australian cultures: Australian Aboriginal trade as an expression of close culture contact and as a mediator of cultural change. In *Diprotodon to Detribalization,* (eds) A. Pilling and R. Waterman, pp. 285–313. East Lansing: Michigan State University Press.

Morphy, H. 1977. Schematisation, meaning and communication in *toa*s. In *Form in Indigenous Art: Schematisation in the art of Aboriginal Australia and prehistory Europe,* (ed.) P. Ucko, pp. 77–89. London: Duckworth Humanities Press.

Morwood, M. 2002. *Visions from the Past: The archaeology of Australian Aboriginal art.* Washington, DC: Smithsonian Press.

Musharbash, Y. 2008. *Yuendumu Everyday: Contemporary life in remote Aboriginal Australia.* Canberra: Aboriginal Studies Press.

Nekes, H. and Worms, E. 2006. *Australian Languages*. Edited by W. McGregor. Berlin: Mouton de Gruyter.

Petri, H. 1952. Der Australische Medizinmann. *Annali Lateranensi* 16: 159–317. [English version 2014. *The Australian Medicine Man*. Translated by I. Campbell. Perth: Hesperian Press.]

Petri, H. 1954. *Sterbende Welt in Nordwest Australien*. Brunswick, Germany: Albert Limbach Publishers. [English version 2011. *The Dying World in Northwest Australia*. Translated by I. Campbell. Perth: Hesperian Press.]

Reim, H. 1962. *Die Insektennahrung der Australischen Ureinwohner: Eine Studie zur Frühgeschichte Menschlicher Wirtschaft und Ernährung*. Berlin: Akademie-Verlag.

Scherer, P. A. 1979. Donor of Aboriginal heritage. *The Lutheran* 13(12): 12–15.

Semon, R. 1899. *In the Australian Bush and on the Coast of the Coral Sea*. London: Macmillan.

Spencer, W. B. and Gillen, F. J. 1899. *The Native Tribes of Central Australia*. London: Macmillan & Co.

Stotz, G. 1993. Kurdungurlu got to drive Toyota: Differential colonizing process among the Warlpiri. Unpublished PhD thesis. Deakin University, Melbourne.

Strehlow, C. 1907–1920. *Die Aranda- und Loritja-Stämme in Zentral-Australien*. 7 vols. Frankfurt am Main: Joseph Baer & Co.

Strehlow, J. 2004. *Reappraising Carl Strehlow: Through the Spencer–Strehlow debate*. In Occasional Paper No. 3, (ed.) W. Veit, pp. 59–91. Strehlow Research Centre, Alice Springs, NT.

Strehlow, T. G. H. 1947. *Aranda Traditions*. Melbourne: Melbourne University Publishing.

Strehlow, T. G. H. 1971. *Songs of Central Australia*. Sydney: Angus & Robertson.

Sumner, R. 1993. Amalie Dietrich and the Aborigines: Her contribution to Australian anthropology and ethnography. *Australian Aboriginal Studies* 2: 2–19.

Teichelmann, C. 1841. *Aborigines of South Australia: Illustrative and explanatory notes of the manners, customs, habits, and superstitions of the natives of South Australia*. Adelaide.

Thomas, N. 1905. The religious ideas of the Arunta. *Folklore* 16(4): 428–33. doi.org/10.1080/0015587X.1905.9719976.

Tindale, N. 1976. Some ecological bases for Australian tribal boundaries. In *Tribes and Boundaries in Australia*, (ed.) N. Peterson, pp. 12–29. Canberra: Australian Institute of Aboriginal Studies.

Veit, W. 2004. *The struggle for souls and science: Constructing the fifth continent, German missionaries and scientists in Australia*. Occasional Paper No. 3, Strehlow Research Centre, Alice Springs, NT.

Völker, H. 2001. Missionare als Ethnologen. Moritz Freiherr von Leonhardi, australische Mission und europäische Wissenschaft. In *Sammeln, Vernetzen, Auswerten. Missionare und ihr Beitrag zum Wandel europäischer Weltsicht*, (ed.) R. Wendt, pp. 173–218. Tübingen, Germany: Gunter Narr Verlag.

von Brandenstein, C. G. 1982. *Names and Substance of the Australian Subsection System*. Chicago: Chicago University Press.

Walsh, G. 2000. *Bradshaw Art of the Kimberley*. Brisbane: Takarakka Nowan Kas Publications.

Weichart, G. 1997. Art in the centre: An overview of the production of art in Central Australia and its role in contemporary society. Unpublished thesis. University of Vienna, Austria.

Widlok, T. 1992. Practice, politics and ideology of the travelling business in Aboriginal religion. *Oceania* 63(2): 114–36. doi.org/10.1002/j.1834-4461.1992.tb02408.x.

Woods, J. (ed.). 1879. *The Native Tribes of South Australia*. Adealide: G. S. Wigg & Sons.

Worms, E. and Petri, H. 1968. Australische Eingeborenen-Religionen. In *Eingeborenen-Religionen der Sudsee und Australiens*, pp. 125–329. Stuttgart: W. Kohlhammer. [English version 1986. *Australian Aboriginal Religions*. Sydney and Melbourne: Spectrum Publications.]

2

German-language anthropology traditions around 1900: Their methodological relevance for ethnographers in Australia and beyond

André Gingrich

This overview will outline the main chapters of anthropology's development in German before 1900 and thereafter, while paying special attention to the connections to and interactions with respective ethnographic research in Australia.[1] The general rationale of this examination is therefore to explore which intellectual and methodological inspirations emerged inside the history of anthropology in German throughout the nineteenth and early twentieth centuries in such a way that they directly or indirectly inspired ethnographically relevant research that was carried out in Australia while being written up in German.

1   The author wishes to acknowledge with gratitude the substantial academic discussions that have helped to improve this chapter: first, by Nic Peterson and Anna Kenny (both in Canberra), as this volume's editors as well as academic hosts to the conference that preceded it; second, by Gabriele Weichart and Peter Schweitzer (both in Vienna); third, by the publishing house's anonymous reviewers. My special thanks go to Eva-Maria Knoll (Vienna) for elaborating Figures 2.1, 2.2, 2.3 and 2.4, which accompany this text.

There are general and particular dimensions to this task. One of the more general challenges lies in presenting, in a humble and modest manner, elements of an overview on the main phases and connections of anthropology in German before and after 1900 while experts continue to investigate that history. If such a provisional overview on anthropology in German is the more general side of my topic, my special attention will attempt to focus on how that 'general' dimension intersected with the 'particular' challenges of ethnography and anthropology in Australia while it was in the making during those decades, with specific attention to those sources that were written in German. I shall strive to address this specific interplay between the general 'anthropology in German' topic and the particular challenges of the 'ethnographic Australian sources in German' side through three short sections followed by a conclusion.

The first section will focus on legacies before 1850 that continued to profoundly shape anthropology in German by the mid-nineteenth century—that is, when German-speaking explorers had entered the scene and while missionaries began to come to Australia in somewhat larger numbers and stayed on for longer periods. I will start with a short review of those legacies from the Enlightenment and Romanticist periods that continued to have an impact in the 1850s and beyond. I will then move on to discuss the early phases of German-speaking anthropology's institutionalisation between the 1850s and the last decades of that century. This will help us to identify a fairly coherent conceptual frame of reference that became quite relevant for most ethnographically active people in Australia with a German-speaking background. That conceptual frame of reference was informed by elements of those earlier Romanticist legacies, but also by the more recent requirements of institutional museum life. Section three then follows up by discussing my core topic, the 'main conceptual trajectories before and after 1900', by demonstrating how that conceptual frame of reference differentiated into the main so-called schools of German-speaking anthropology in their dimensions of some relevance for Australia. Finally, my conclusions will address continuities and discontinuities in this regard after World War I through the theme of 'transitions'.

My approach is oriented according to historical phases and sequences, as I think is befitting for historians of anthropology and, also, for historical anthropologists. Beyond that, I will pay somewhat closer attention to the histories of ideas and methods, rather than to those of institutions or individual biographies, and I shall follow a general observance of transnational and postcolonial interests into the field's historical trajectories. It is to be mentioned merely in passing that a German nation-state was founded as late as 1871. Regina Ganter has made this point abundantly clear on her websites and in her other published texts. I shall follow her example and carefully avoid any late-nationalist terminology, so the term 'German-speaking' and corresponding equivalents will provide my general frame of reference in this regard.

Earlier legacies by 1850

Most scholars of the history of anthropology in German agree about especially long intellectual trajectories of relevance that preceded those subsequent phases of increasing institutionalisation that were setting in after 1850.[2] Regarding the content of those long precursor trajectories, most experts also seem to agree, by and large, on two additional basic points. Those earlier intellectual trajectories had received decisive impulses and orientations at the turn of the nineteenth century—that is, first, from the late and unfinished philosophical Enlightenment era in German; and second, from early Romanticist academic interests in philology, languages, literature and art traditions. In short, it has come to be an accepted insight today about a global understanding of the history of anthropology that one of its main roots can be identified in German-speaking Enlightenment and early Romanticism (Figure 2.1).

Johann Forster and his son, Georg (especially after accompanying James Cook on his second voyage), Johann Gottfried Herder in his critical interaction with Immanuel Kant and the von Humboldt brothers, Alexander and Wilhelm, represented the key authors and influences in this enduring intellectual scenario—with Adelbert von Chamisso and many others as less influential but contributing players who should not be ignored.

---

2   For some of the central studies in English of the history of German-language anthropology during the main periods under scrutiny here, see Brandewie (1990); Gingrich (2005); Johler et al. (2010); Penny and Bunzl (2003); Vermeulen (2015); Zammito (2002).

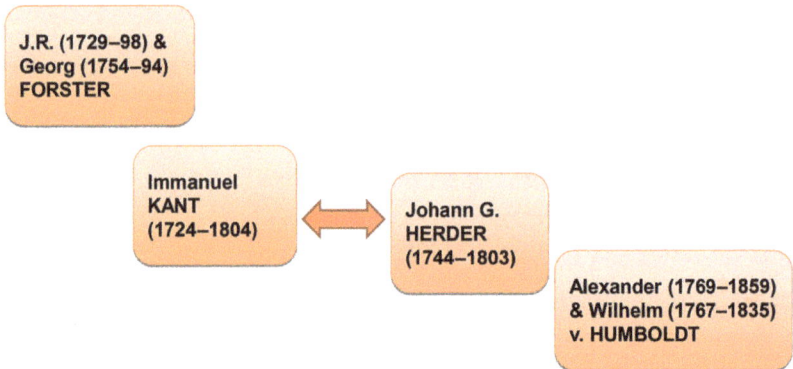

J.R. (1729–98) &
Georg (1754–94)
FORSTER

Immanuel
KANT
(1724–1804)

Johann G.
HERDER
(1744–1803)

Alexander (1769–1859)
& Wilhelm (1767–1835)
v. HUMBOLDT

Figure 2.1 Key influences in late Enlightenment and early Romantic movement thought.

Source: A. Gingrich and E. M. Knoll.

In my view, that scenario may be best understood through the lasting intellectual and methodological impact it exerted on the humanities in German. That impact may be addressed in a balanced way as the productive and unstable tension between universalism and relativism as modalities of investigating human lives and human relations. Kant and the Forsters were more explicitly on the universalist side of that tension, which is one among several reasons they upheld some expectations concerning the relevance of biological factors that included their occasional but systematic reference to notions of race. Parallel with that, Johann F. Blumenbach elaborated on biological paradigms of the first universalist classification of hierarchical human races that represented those of dark skin colour as the lowest level. It seems that some early German travellers with training in biology or medicine already were at least partially influenced by that universalist and natural sciences part of the spectrum, as indicated in Hermann Koeler's reports on South Australia from 1837 to 1838.

By contrast, Herder and the von Humboldt brothers put a much stronger emphasis on the notion of 'unity through diversity' and saw little need for integrating ideas about race into that. So Herder and the Humboldt brothers did pursue some early versions of a 'relativist' or 'weak' universalism that indeed has remained relevant for the main subsequent trends in German-speaking, but also North American, anthropology, as we know through the biographies of Franz Boas, Robert Lowie and Alfred Kroeber.

In spite of significant epistemological differences between late Enlightenment and early Romanticist thinkers in German, it would be quite one-sided if we emphasised beyond proportion only the differences between them. This is why a friendly caveat is in place here. As a Protestant theologian, Herder believed not only in humanity's unity by creation, but also in its mission towards improvement. It therefore would be inappropriate to characterise him as an 'anti-evolutionist' before the term. In fact, some of Herder's writing can be easily read as if he was sympathising with a tree or a bush model of multiple evolution rather than with a staircase model of unilinear progress upward. Having emphasised this point of general agreement among most Herder experts, I would like to add that neither the Humboldts' nor Herder's work should be idealised. Although they refrained from constructing any racial hierarchies, their universalist relativism was not an egalitarian one. The hierarchies they attributed to relations among large groups of humans were not of a racial but of a cultural kind.

The most significant early connection between the Herder–Humboldt strand of reasoning in the German-language zone and research in Australia is featured in the work of Friedrich W. L. Leichhardt (1813–48), who famously disappeared (presumed perished) with his team in Central Australia during the third of his expeditions. Although hardly appreciated in Europe, Leichhardt's biography and legacy are well known in Australia, and his scholarly diaries have been made available recently in a fine translation (Darragh and Fensham 2013). They demonstrate quite clearly that this geographer and biologist also had a keen interest in Aboriginal matters, and how the Humboldts indeed served as intellectual role models for the pursuit of his expeditions.

Another important connection between scientific reasoning in German during the mid-nineteenth century and research in Australia was established by the Imperial Austrian *Novara* frigate's expedition during the 1850s (in fact, preparations for this first circumnavigation of the world by a German-speaking crew and captain had begun during the 1840s). That expedition also included sojourns by expedition members in New South Wales and Victoria in 1858–59. While the expedition's medical members carried out some case examples of physical measurements among Aboriginal groups and also collected human remains, Carl von Scherzer was responsible for a fairly broad and systematic linguistic and ethnographic survey. The results of these investigations were published during the 1860s as part of the expedition's results in

20 volumes, with Friedrich Müller as responsible author for the volumes on ethnography and linguistics (1867, 1868). The expedition's general orientation was positioned within the wide and contradictory tension between the legacies of late Enlightenment and colonial Romanticism and racism. Müller, who never would visit Australia himself, was able to integrate von Scherzer's linguistic material into his first attempt towards a systematic overview of linguistic diversity in Australia[3] and elsewhere, which he would then try to correlate with a specific version of racial classification. In this manner, Müller represented a good example of those in the German-speaking humanities who tried to combine Humboldtian relativism with the emerging racism in the biological and medical fields. Müller eventually became an influential founding figure for linguistic ethnography in Vienna and beyond, by further elaborating this often overlooked collection of Aboriginal linguistic material as an element in his treatise (Müller 2004) on linguistic diversity and racial hierarchies.

The Humboldts had been fairly close to an early form of linguistic relativism (as elaborated much later by Sapir and Whorf), but the basic differences they had seen between various groups of languages also included what they understood as different levels of potential linguistic (and mental) sophistication. For Herder, by contrast, the main cultural differentiation beyond the particular originated with the absence or presence of writing, and of the state. This led to his influential and fateful distinction between 'natural' and 'cultural' peoples—and it is easy to envision where this particularly popular, nineteenth-century classification in German would situate Australian Aborigines. It is true that distinguishing '*Naturvölker*' from '*Kulturvölker*' became fetishised by later followers of Herder in ways that were alien to him, yet the distinction per se did already feature quite prominently in his own work—together with his valuable emphasis on songs, proverbs and myths as the collective 'soul' of a people to be explored and expressed through language.

All of this may be fairly well known, but, in a volume on the German-language tradition's influence on Australian anthropology for which Herder and the Humboldts were in fact quite important, the integration of a balanced perspective on these authors and their influence is indispensable. With all due appreciation for their productive legacies, it would be misleading to morally classify them as more 'positive' in

---

3   I am indebted to Stefan Sienell (Archives of the Austrian Academy of Sciences) and to Clara Stockigt (Department of Linguistics, University of Adelaide) for helping me to establish these points.

contrast with others—for example, those working in the British traditions. Those lines of tradition were more dominant and more continuous, and this more marginalised and more frequently interrupted sequence in German certainly had alternative merits in its own right, but it also featured a number of substantial biases and specific shortcomings.

This also concerns an open debate rather than the more established insights as addressed so far. The notions of humanity and humanism have caused some discussions with regard to the history of anthropology in German and, as I see it, some confusion. I consider one of these two terms as being quite clear—namely, humanity in its German-language meaning since the early nineteenth century, that is *Menschheit*. In fact, Australia played some role in this notion; after all, since the 1810s and 1820s, it had dawned on German-speaking thinkers that, in an empirical sense, it could be taken for granted that all the continents inhabited by humans were now known. So, in a positive and affirmative way, knowledge of Australia sealed and completed the acknowledgement of a globally existing humanity. Humanism, by contrast, is a contested term in its German version (*Humanismus*) without any clear philosophical qualities. I remain fairly sceptical of the validity and usefulness of this term for understanding the history of research in nineteenth-century German-speaking academia in general. For anthropology, in particular, we might not even need that term at all. It designates two very different movements that had very little to do with each other. First, an early humanism of the fifteenth and sixteenth centuries—basically, the philosophical side of the Renaissance, emanating from Italy and culminating with Erasmus of Rotterdam's work, but having limited impact in the German lands. Second, about 300 years later, neo-humanism emerged in its German version—namely, as an educational ideal to be instrumentalised for the aspiration of nation-building processes towards a unified German state. Neo-humanism implied a certain obsession with antiquity as one of two alleged roots of German nationhood (Nordic culture was seen as the second of these two roots). In short, I suspect that the so-called humanist tradition is an artificial and fictional invention by liberal German nationalism seeking to invent a 'longue durée' where there never was any, by combining neo-humanism of the nineteenth century with Renaissance thought of the fifteenth and sixteenth centuries. I thus do not really see how neo-humanism, with its preoccupation for Mediterranean antiquity, could have been important to anthropology in German, as some authors have claimed. It is quite sufficient to understand that, by the 1850s, German-speaking explorers, most missionaries and early ethnographers agreed that indigenous peoples in remote areas such as Australia were basically part of humanity, although they usually regarded it as an inferior part, and thus these humans had souls—therefore it was important to learn their languages and to come to know their myths and songs.

Early institutional phase: 1850s to 1900

The two crucial conceptual elements of language and of culture were thus already firmly in place by the 1850s in German-language anthropology. This field gradually emerged inside and outside academia, in book publications and articles, in civil associations and in private collections, as well as inside more general university teaching programs. During the 1840s, the time had come to further advance and popularise the collectors' side among these various activities. Upon initiatives by members of the urban elite in one of the most affluent commercial and industrial city communes anywhere in the German-speaking lands, the first anthropology museum was inaugurated in Basel in 1849. Somewhat later, Leipzig and Hamburg followed up through similar initiatives, until, by the 1870s and 1880s, the three capital cities of Bern, Vienna and Berlin completed the vast landscapes of anthropology museums or museum departments that would remain so characteristic for the German-speaking parts of our field until this day. After its foundation, the Berlin Museum gradually emerged to become one of the world's largest (and most chaotically organised) anthropology museums, as described by Glenn Penny (e.g. 2002) and others. It continued to hold that position until its destruction during World War II.

These institutional developments between the 1840s and the 1870s in turn promoted organisational and conceptual consequences that are important for our contexts. Throughout the next 50 to 70 years, most professional anthropologists in the German-speaking lands would be museum experts. As a result, they had to be especially interested in material objects that could be put on display for visitors. Since many—albeit not all—of these museum experts were armchair anthropologists, the analysis of what came to be known as 'material culture' gradually attained the status of these museum anthropologists' true intellectual and academic mission. In turn, that type of intellectual specialisation through overviews on the material sides of life enhanced methodological priorities for the dissemination of fields of cultural elements in their spatial ranges of distribution. A self-understood by-product of these professional and methodological constellations between the 1850s and the 1920s was that the majority of German-speaking armchair anthropologists at their home museums sought to establish and maintain well-functioning, smooth interactions with their networks of correspondents out in the field. Of course, missionaries were among the most preferred correspondents whenever they stayed on for longer periods than others, and if they spoke local languages better than other potential correspondents.

By the 1860s, a fairly stable and coherent conceptual and organisational frame of reference was operating. In that frame of reference, out of museum practices the two notions of 'material culture' and of 'space' had been added to the conceptual priorities for 'language' and 'culture', as inherited from Herder and the Humboldts. The conceptual result, as outlined in Figure 2.2, would identify any particular culture first of all as the interplay (by means of language) between 'material culture' and 'mental culture'. That local examination of particular ethnographic examples, however, always should go hand in hand with a wider regional examination of the spatial distribution of similarities and differences among this and all other cases under scrutiny. In consequence, such spatial analyses of diversities and parallels would allow insights into those cases that might be directly related to each other, and those with less affinity. Once these relationships in space were established, it was expected to be possible to move on towards elaborating relative chronologies across (pre-)historical times. A very similar conceptual frame would also become part of the young Franz Boas's training at the Berlin Museum a few decades later. Yet it had existed before as a largely unquestioned set of priorities of interest, as Han Vermeulen (2015) has shown in his recent volume *Before Boas*. The conceptual frame served as a roadmap for fieldwork that the museum expert and armchair anthropologist would communicate in implicit or explicit ways to their correspondents out in the field. Whether or not those correspondents were missionaries and whether or not they had already acquired some ethnographic instructions or training units, they were expected to focus on these four or five topical fields; as was befitting for an epistemological orientation of particularism, a primary emphasis was put on exploring cultural and linguistic specificities within and among one smaller or larger group or subgroup in its particular dimensions. If time and opportunity allowed, exploring similarities and differences between this and neighbouring groups or subgroups in space came next. In addition to representing a rather clear-cut and straightforward set of ethnographic priorities, this frame of reference communicated a number of additional advantages to the missionaries in the field.

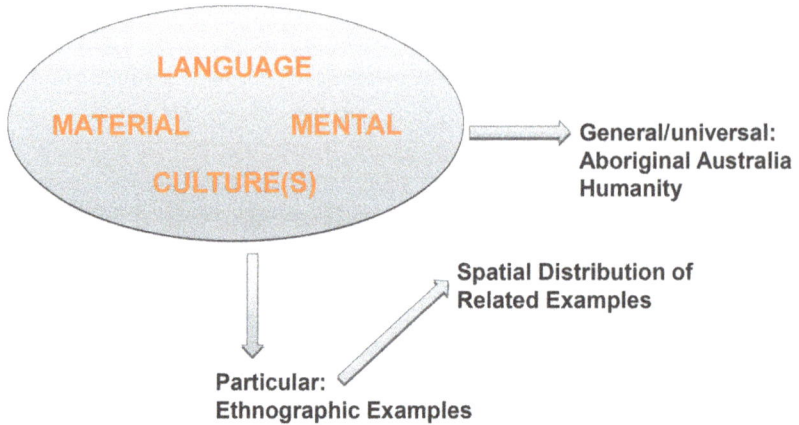

Figure 2.2 The conceptual framework that had emerged by the 1860s.
Source: A. Gingrich and E. M. Knoll.

First, it upgraded and supported some of the activities the missionaries were committed to pursue anyhow, such as learning and practising the local language and exploring its relation to the local conceptual, mental and spiritual world, including its myths and rituals. Second, the same frame of reference conspicuously avoided such themes as gender, sex, marriage and kinship. That, again, was compatible with the missionaries' own priorities—since, to an extent, they were merely interested in these more sensitive matters to change them as rapidly as possible into other practices, which, as they saw it, were closer to those eternal values in which they believed. It also should be said that most armchair anthropologists in the German-language zones supported views that were not too far away from that—namely, views on the nuclear family's basic eternal existence, especially so after a certain Heinrich Schurtz at the Hamburg Museum had published his volume on *Altersklassen und Männerbünde* (*Age Classes and Male Associations*) in 1902.[4] That was a very popular booklet in many ways but anti-evolutionist in this particular regard, emphasising women's alleged timeless immobility in privacy in contrast to men's eternal socialising mobility in public. So the armchair anthropologists at home also were not really systematically interested in exploring social variations of gender relations or in understanding the diversities of sexual life and marriage or kinship ties, but, instead, they subsumed most

---

4   The book was subsequently used in conservative and even Nazi political propaganda as 'evidence' of women's allegedly timeless mission to primarily take care of the household and children. It is perhaps for this very reason that it is freely available online. See: archive.org/details/altersklassenun00schugoog.

of that under the heading of terminology and language. Third, that loose yet fairly straightforward frame of reference (Figure 2.2), with its basic underlying idea that Aborigines were humans with souls, did envision Aboriginal Australia as part of 'general' (or universal) humanity, albeit with 'particular' features and characteristics to be determined.

By and large, the museum expert at home and the missionary out in the field were thus both interested in intersecting and related topics, which could be organised as guiding priorities by that conceptual frame of reference for further implementation and exploration on the ground. In many ways, that frame was indeed curiosity driven, and, simultaneously, it was inspired by basic convictions about Aboriginal people being humans with souls and dignity.

My example to illustrate this general point comes from several years later—namely, from 1912. It concerns the Hermannsburg Lutheran missionary Oskar Liebler, to be seen next to his wife, who is sitting on a camel (see Plate 2.1). Liebler was a contemporary of Carl Strehlow, and was responsible for acquiring significant ethnographic elements that are in part stored or displayed in the South Australian Museum collection. In 1912, he had compiled a fairly large set of Aboriginal objects in Central Australia. The other part of the collection was transported to Berlin, and dedicated as a personal gift for Emperor Wilhelm II. The Kaiser ordered that this gift should be passed on to the Hamburg Museum, where it continues to represent a core portion of that museum's Australian collection—in fact, one of the largest of its kind in Germany to this day. Now, if we try to find out more about Liebler's ethnographically relevant papers it turns out that many of them are of course in Australia, but quite a significant amount are in German archives. Some of them are part of the Hamburg Museum collection, meticulously putting each single object into wider contexts. Others, however, are part of the archives of Liebler's Lutheran mission, which today has its central offices in Bavaria. There the relevant 'Findbuch'—that is, the archival orientation guide—informs us (see Plate 2.1) about his reports and letters back home. They contain highly interesting ethnographic materials, which some experts on Central Australia have analysed to a limited extent. There is still work to be carried out in this regard. As for methodology and ethnography, Liebler's expert contact was usually the Hamburg Museum director Georg Thilenius, born in 1868 and a lifelong armchair anthropologist and colonial strategist. Thilenius maintained a close and continuous correspondence with his old colleague Franz Boas until they broke in 1933 because of Thilenius's support for Hitler (Fischer 1990; Geisenhainer 2002: 46–50; Mischek 2002: 29, notes 6 and 8, cf. also pp. 30–6). Yet the point here is that, as a leading figure in German anthropology before and after the Great War, Thilenius was a fairly typical empirical diffusionist in his time, with close ties to Boas—and, as we shall see, empirical or secular diffusionism was one of the trajectories that came out of the stable frame of reference that has been discussed here. Beyond illustrating several of the above points, Liebler's example also demonstrates that, from the perspective of a historical anthropology of Australia, some of the more ethnographically interesting letters and reports by these missionaries-cum-ethnographers still wait to be examined and assessed by German-speaking PhD students and other research projects that could be supported by Australian and German, Austrian or Swiss institutions.

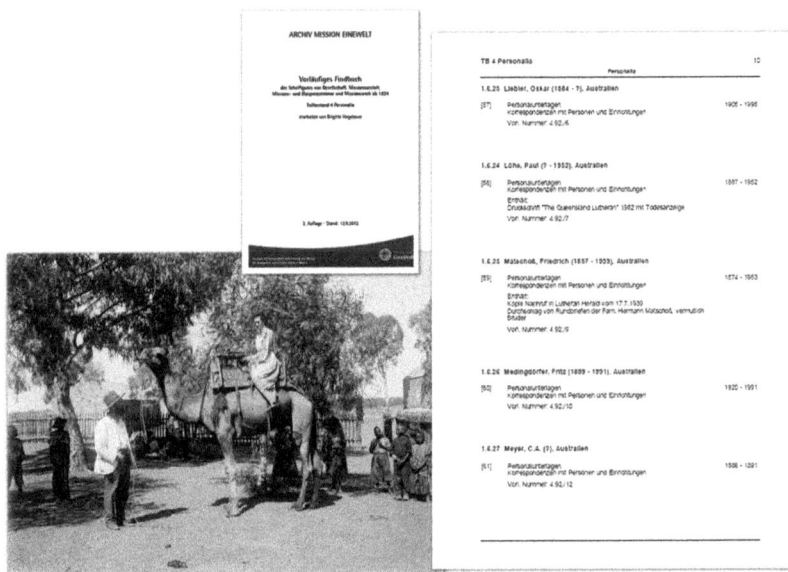

Plate 2.1 Oskar Liebler of Hermannsburg Mission and his *Findbuch*.
Source: National Library of Australia, nla.pic-vn6157043-v.

Main trajectories before and after 1900

The Prussian-led German unification process was completed in 1871; the Austro-Hungarian monarchy was formally installed in 1867; Swiss neutrality simultaneously consolidated for Europe's only republic at the time. As the nineteenth century's last quarter set in, the German-speaking lands had attained those political forms that would last until at least 1918. Germany, as a newly incoming colonial competitor, was also quick to establish its colonial presence in Africa, Oceania and elsewhere. Academic anthropology continued to be concentrated largely in those many major and minor museums of the German-language zone, but now they became linked to neighbouring universities and to their teaching and training programs. Together with that, imperial state interests, in contrast to civil commercial interests prevailing since the 1840s, attained increasing influence in the field.

The German Melanesian expedition is a case in point. For the purpose of these expeditions and beyond them, biological anthropologists claimed their own field's increasing relevance. In fact, the small Berlin–Vienna Melanesian expedition of 1904–06 under Rudolf Pöch also had a brief sojourn (in 1905) and investigation series of less than four months in the Sydney area of New South Wales, in addition to their main sojourn in New Guinea's Kaiser Wilhelm's territory. For Pöch (1915, 1916), the ensuing publications, including his analysis of a Tasmanian skull in Vienna, were promoting his career as Vienna's leading physical anthropologist at the time and as a contributor to proliferating racist theorising on the features and qualities of what he classified as primitive races.[5]

For some time, ethnography and physical anthropology had understood themselves and each other as closely cooperating fields, such as during the Virchow and Bastian era at the Berlin Museum since its foundation. Many ethnographers trained by Virchow and Bastian received their first degrees in the natural sciences, such as Franz Boas, but also Erhard Eylmann (see Merlan, Chapter 11, this volume). In fact, Eylmann, as one of the very first trained German freelance ethnographers in Australia, may be seen as a close associate of the Berlin Museum's rather liberal Bastian period. Yet as influential as Bastian was in his own time, his approach to identifying 'elementary ideas' had few German-speaking followers in the next generation. On the contrary, those cultural anthropologists who came immediately after Bastian felt they had to reassert their own field against growing claims by physical anthropologists. They did so by leaving

---

5   Major elements of those collections of Aboriginal human remains that had been acquired during the 1850s by members of the Novara expedition, by Pöch in 1905 and by Lebzelter in 1935, continued to be in the possession of Vienna museums until most of them were officially returned to representatives of Australia in 2009 and 2011 (Krejci-Weiss 2013). On Amalie Dietrich's skeleton collections from Queensland, see Scheps (2013).

Bastian's structural reasoning[6] behind and by embracing a historicising '*Völkerkunde*' more explicitly than before. Against the rising tide of fairly aggressive claims by biological anthropologists, especially after the deaths of Bastian (in 1905) and Virchow (in 1902), sociocultural anthropologists—or *Völkerkundler*, as they came to be called—thus had to increasingly mark their own relevance by competition.

The first theoretical and methodological schools of thought emerged in these contexts around the turn of the century in German-speaking anthropology. In many ways, these 'schools' were organic continuations of the earlier frame of reference. An exception to that was Richard Thurnwald's German variety of functionalism and economic anthropology that would emerge primarily during the 1920s. Yet all the other main schools of thought at the time were markedly anti-sociological and also anti-evolutionist in their efforts to compete not only with the biological anthropologists at home, and not only with sociocultural anthropology in the United Kingdom and France, but also with the materialist evolutionism as advocated by the labour movement, which in the Habsburg and Prussian empires was stronger than almost everywhere else.

By and large, these first trends and schools of German-speaking *Völkerkunde* followed various forms of historical diffusionism. Their focus continued to be on material and mental elements of culture through language, as examined in their respective spatial distribution. From here, historical conclusions would be possible through specific ways of approaching relative chronologies. In one way or another, diffusionism would remain influential in *Völkerkunde* until the 1950s and 1960s. I will now examine somewhat more closely these schools through their manifest forms around 1900 (see Figure 2.3).

---

6   Still firmly rooted in the traditions of German Enlightenment and Humboldtian relativism, which also shaped his junior museum collaborator Franz Boas, Bastian had embraced the 'psychic unity of mankind' as his key paradigm. From this point of departure, he developed his main research strategy towards identifying fairly stable 'elementary ideas' that humans had developed, according to Bastian, in line with their respective experience and linguistic skills across sociocultural and biological diversity. In his view, these elementary ideas could be identified by means of (museum) objects and their related terminology through analytical abstraction and condensation (see Koepping 1984). In view of his approaches, Bastian thus may be seen as a precursor to early structural reasoning, as elaborated shortly thereafter by Durkheim and Mauss in France.

Cultural Morphology	Secular Diffusionism	Culture Circle Theory
(Frankfurt)	(Cologne, Hamburg, Berlin)	(Vienna)
Frobenius, Jensen	Graebner, Thilenius, Ankermann	Schmidt, Koppers

Figure 2.3 The principal schools of thought around 1900.
Source: A. Gingrich and E. M. Knoll.

In 1904 and 1905, Fritz Graebner and Bernhard Ankermann gave two famous lectures at the Berlin Museum, where, based on anthropogeographer Friedrich Ratzel's earlier reasoning, they proposed a more historically oriented *Völkerkunde* approach, which they called *Kulturkreislehre* ('culture circle' theory). Leo Frobenius had already coined that particular term, theory and methodology somewhat earlier, but distanced himself from it soon thereafter. Graebner (1911) further elaborated his own take on the historicity and relative chronology of cultural circles (or areas) by publishing his best-known book, *Methode der Ethnologie*. Parallel with, yet partly before, that the Westphalian-born Catholic priest Wilhelm Schmidt from the Steyl missionary order (Societas Verbi Divini: the Society of the Divine Word or SVD) had, since the 1890s, begun to establish near Vienna his own anthropological and missionary orientations. This also included his substantial and, in its time, relevant contributions to the issue of Austronesian languages (e.g. Schmidt 1899). In short, since the very first years of the twentieth century, the core elements of three diffusionist orientations existed in German-speaking anthropology that would gain some limited relevance also for the anthropology of Australia: Leo Frobenius would after the war establish his 'cultural morphology' in Frankfurt; Wilhelm Schmidt's 'Vienna school' of culture circle theory began to proliferate near Vienna (Brandewie 1990); and, as the most widespread tendency, a more secular and more empirically oriented version of diffusionism tried to remain most faithful to Graebner, who eventually (after being interned in Australia) moved to Cologne. Best known among the Graebnerians during those years were Ankermann and von Luschan in Berlin and Thilenius in Hamburg.

Some of the values and key theoretical interests pursued by these schools differed widely from each other, as briefly characterised below. The subsequent positioning of these directions and their representatives vis-à-vis fascism and Nazism is quite another story, largely but not entirely a political one. In fact, one does not even have to particularly sympathise with any of these directions at all, but still a minimum of critical respect would be in place since most of them in fact were serious and committed anthropologists. If only in partial and fragmentary ways, some of their insights retain some value for understanding specific problems for the historical ethnography of Australia—mostly, I would add, from my personal perspective, in empirical contexts rather than in theoretical fields.

Among these three directions, Schmidt embarked on a lifelong preoccupation with 'high gods', by picking up on a contemporary debate in British anthropology evoked by Tylor's student Andrew Lang, as will be recalled from Lang's (1898, 1899) arguments on Australian 'gods', as well as from Les Hiatt's careful discussion of the issue in *Arguments about Aborigines* (1996). In that ideological and theological focus on high gods, the Vienna school of anthropologists certainly was biased and misguided; but it has to be said to their credit that they at least helped to put the study of hunter-gatherer societies, including large portions of anthropology in Australia, into some early, empirically grounded comparative perspectives. In addition, they promoted substantial fieldwork among many foraging societies in Asia and Africa to that purpose. Schmidt also elaborated the Heidelberg economic anthropologist Ernst Grosse's distinction between more mobile 'simple' and quasi-sedentary 'complex' hunters and gatherers, and he productively pursued Eduard Hahn's early ideas about female contributions to subsistence in foraging societies half a century before feminist anthropologists would reactivate that important topic, as shown by Peter Schweitzer (2004). Among ethnographic and linguistic works grounded in Australia, the impact of Schmidt's version of anthropology is specifically present in the writings and collections of Ernst A. Worms (Society of the Catholic Apostolate, SAC) after his arrival in Australia in 1930 (see McGregor, Chapter 13, and Ganter, Chapter 14, this volume). That clear and explicit interaction between Worms and Schmidt also included a typically diffusionist theory about earlier and more recent waves of migration into Australia, by which Tasmania was seen as representing the retreat area of earlier migrations while northern Australian Aboriginal populations were viewed as representing the more recent waves of migration near the main 'entrance' of those waves.

Frobenius, on the other hand, focused in a deeply romanticising neo-Herderian manner on a culture's inner being or '*Paideuma*', and researched the expressions of that primarily in art, from sculpture to rock art. Frobenius still inspired and managed preparations for the German–Australian expedition of 1938, the year in which he passed away. That expedition is thus a well-known outcome of his orientation, which mostly used an anthropomorphic chronology of emergence, maturity and decay to make its main points about the cycles of cultural life. Art and its phenomenological analysis were understood as key avenues towards identifying a culture's innermost essence and its articulation in world views or cosmo-visions. The Frankfurt school is often referred to as cultural morphology[7] and, in addition to Frobenius and Jensen, also included Helmut Petri and Andreas Lommel, some of whose works have been made available in English (Petri 2011; Lommel 1997). Similar to Worms and the Schmidt school, one need not accept the cultural morphologists' theoretical paradigms to respect their ethnographic results, yet to make appropriate use of their ethnographic results, it is necessary to critically understand their theoretical and methodological priorities.

The secular diffusionists such as Thilenius in Hamburg pursued Graebner's methodological program somewhat more rigidly than the other two schools, and in a manner that was more empirically grounded. In that sense one could situate them between the two other schools (also in view of the fact that the Frankfurtians were quite close to Protestant theology). Yet basically, the Graebner program (see references in Gaillard 2004: 43–4; and a useful early discussion in Lowie 1937) was also shared by the two other directions to an extent. I have already said that it was striving to document and assess the dissemination of mental and material cultures in space, to arrive at relative chronologies about what had come

---

7   Between 1904 and 1935, Frobenius carried out a number of famous research expeditions to various parts of sub-Saharan and North Africa that provided the ethnographic material for his most influential publications on African myth, lore, art and cosmo-vision. For Frobenius, Saharan rock art represented an especially important source for reconstructing African cultural history. Based on these empirical features and on assumptions about their migration and diffusion, he developed the methodology and theory of what he came to call 'cultural morphology'—that is, a quasi-phenomenological approach towards cultures that were seen as organisms with life cycles and a cultural 'soul' ('*Paideuma*', which was also the name of the journal he founded in 1938) to be accessed through key cultural features such as art, lore or myths. Frobenius had already attained some celebrity status when the Nazis came to power; they courted him during the Nazi 'peace period' until he passed away in 1938. Adolf E. Jensen, as his main disciple and successor at the Frankfurt Institute, however, soon had to face Nazi reprisals, which had partly to do with Jensen's refusal to divorce his Jewish wife (which saved her life). After 1945, Jensen therefore was seen with some justification as one of the few leading anthropologists who had remained in Germany during the war and had nevertheless maintained a fairly clean political record. That reputation also facilitated the publication of some of Jensen's work after the war in English, as part of a modestly successful attempt to gain some new respect for anthropologists in West Germany (Kohl and Platte 2006).

earlier and what more recently. By so doing, the program distinguished more recent elements near hypothetical points of entry to the continent and older elements in remote zones of retreat, by applying non-functional criteria of form and quality as well as of quantity. If combined with modern methods of triangulation for determining age and historical background, one should not hesitate to acknowledge that some of these procedures may continue to be useful as auxiliary methodological tools for specified problems.

Before 1914, therefore, thinking about Australia was certainly developing and proliferating in productive ways inside German-speaking anthropology. The outbreak of World War I introduced a profound rupture to these tendencies.

Conclusions: Transitions after 1918

In the end, a few lines of transition may be identified that seem to have characterised the German-speaking legacies in the anthropology of Australia after the end of World War I. We know that the Great War represented an unavoidable interruption in this regard. At its outbreak, some German-speaking missionaries and anthropologists left Australia immediately, such as Felix von Luschan, while others were interned until 1918, such as Fritz Graebner. Some had to register as enemy aliens but could continue their ethnographic work if their loyalties moved in the right direction, as in Malinowski's case (in 1914, he was still a citizen of the Austro-Hungarian Empire). Still others had to register as enemy aliens—like Malinowski—even though they had Australian papers, such as Carl Strehlow, who had some of his children educated in Germany (as we know from Kenny 2013). Even more importantly, the lines of communication with offices and institutions in Germany and Austria had to be cut for years.

The relaunch of anthropological activities after 1918 was slow in Central Europe, and especially so with regard to a region such as Australia, which had been on the winners' side in the war. The three locally and regionally hegemonic schools that were outlined in the previous section took some time to re-establish themselves in new ways, which in turn allowed some room for anti-hegemonic orientations to gain ground, in contrast to their beginnings before the war. In fact, there were two especially anti-hegemonic approaches in German with some keen interest in the anthropology of Australia whose representatives continued with their earlier interests. On the one hand, Sigmund Freud in Vienna, in part through his and his daughter Anna's personal acquaintance with the Malinowski family, had developed a growing interest, together with Freud's disciple Géza Róheim, in understanding Aboriginal lives, rituals and, of course, 'dreaming' through psychoanalysis (see Morton, Chapter 8, this volume). On the other hand, across all major cities of the German-language zone, a second and third generation of left-leaning intellectuals inspired by the work of Marx and Engels developed an immense theoretical interest in the non-state and non-scriptural sides of Australian Aboriginal societies. This was addressed by Rosa Luxemburg in her texts written before and during the Great War (Luxemburg 1975: 624–34), by Friedrich Engels's previous associate Heinrich Cunow at the Berlin Museum during the 1920s and early 1930s (Ulrich 1987), by the young Karl August Wittfogel (1970: 488–92) in his early text sections on Australia and by Paul Kirchhoff (Gray 2006), who studied with Cunow. From that spectrum, there was indeed a multilayered Marx-inspired anthropological interest inside and around the German labour movement that would in some ways resurface after 1945 in those East German contexts that were to host Fredrick Rose (Monteath and Munt 2015), from the 1950s onwards in East Berlin.[8]

The 15 pre-Nazi years after 1918 and the subsequent six Nazi prewar years feature a few significant changes with regard to the anthropology of Australia, if compared with what has been discussed for the time before 1914. Some of these changes are indicated by the three main elements of illustration (Figure 2.4). First, some of the missionaries-cum-ethnographers with a background in German continued. Although this occurred on a smaller scale, it also included new arrivals such as Ernst A. Worms (SAC) in 1930. These missionaries were somewhat less welcome inside Australia after the experience of the Great War, while they also received far less support from those weakened parts of German-speaking Europe that had lost that war.

---

8   Let it be noted at least in passing that those East German contexts included some interesting archival studies in Australian historical ethnography, among them most notably Helmut Reim's (1962) analysis of Australian insect food.

AFTER 1918:
Some continuation by German-speaking missionaries with ethnographic interests (e.g. Worms)

BY LATE 1920s:
New interests by trained German ethnographers from mainstream academia (e.g. Petri, Lommel)

AFTER 1933:
Asylum-seeking German anthropologists
Rejected: e.g. Kirchhoff
Accepted: e.g. Adam

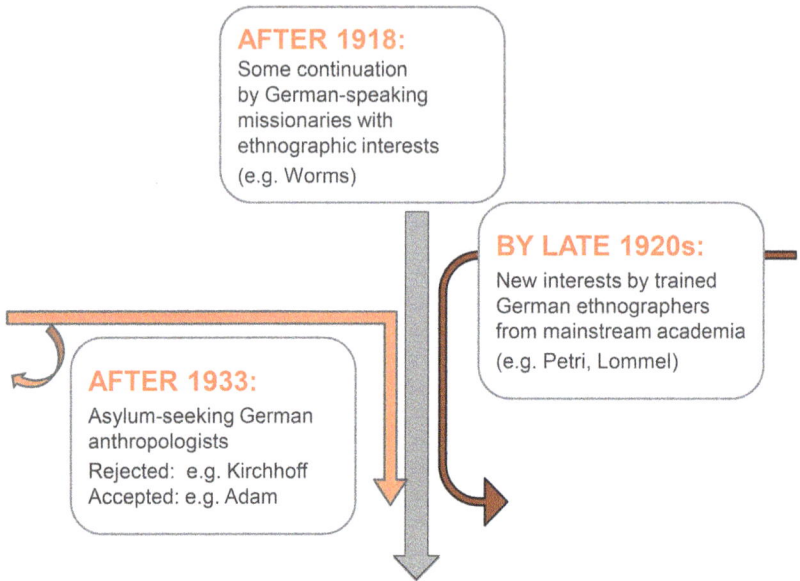

Figure 2.4 The three main schools post-1918.
Source: A. Gingrich and E. M. Knoll.

Second, from the late 1920s until the Frobenius Expedition of 1938, a new, small but relevant sequence of interventions set in from trained mainstream ethnographers from German-speaking academia—some of whom had no political interests in mind while others were at least partially involved with the rising forces of Nazism. That element is perhaps best known through the publication and translation of some of the relevant books—that is, by Lommel and Petri.[9]

Third, after the early 1930s, some of those German-speaking anthropologists who were fleeing from Nazism were seeking asylum in Australia. Several were rejected, such as Paul Kirchhoff, who eventually made it to Mexico. Quite a few were accepted, however, such as legal anthropologist Leonhard Adam (1944, 1954; Sloggett 2015), whose papers at his new Melbourne home institution might still deserve a fair assessment today.

---

9   In addition, a number of doctoral theses were submitted during the Nazi years, discussing various aspects of Australian Aboriginal ethnographic materials from local museums and archival sources in German. Two examples from the University of Vienna's Völkerkunde (Ethnology) Institute from 1940 were Frank's (1940) study of material means of communication among Aboriginal societies and Fischer-Colbrie's (1940) thesis on various types of traditional Australian weapons.

To sum up, these transitions after 1918 already indicated that the end of an era was gradually approaching. It would come about with World War II and its aftermath. Erich Kolig (Chapter 15) and Nicolas Peterson (Chapter 18) discuss other aspects of that final phase in this volume. We may therefore conclude with the hypothesis that the three or four decades after 1918 represented the discontinuous and contradictory transition phase that put an end to the entire period and to those sets of influences under scrutiny here.

In such a perspective, the century from the 1850s to the 1950s included many diverse interactions between German-speaking and Australian anthropology. What was to an extent hegemonic on the continental European side of this twisted and broken interrelation often was deviant or marginal on the Australian side, including significant counterexamples. Some of these interactions were more of a methodological orientation while others are worth remembering or even retrieving today, if primarily for their historical and ethnographic value. At any rate, these sources, narratives and records need not be glorified or idealised, but they also can no longer be flatly ignored. Critical and sober assessment of them in context is quite sufficient and, in fact, is long overdue for making use of the ethnographic harvest of evidence and the interpretations included, with all their limits, but also in view of their richness and potential. A lot of work remains to be carried out to that purpose.

References

Adam, L. 1944. Has Australian Aboriginal art a future? *Angry Penguins* [*Australian Journal of Literature and Art*, Adelaide University Arts Association]: 42–50.

Adam, L. 1954 [1940]. Primitive Art. 3rd edn, rev. & enlarged. Baltimore: Penguin.

Brandewie, E. 1990. *When Giants Walked the Earth: The life and times of Wilhelm Schmidt, SVD. Volume 44.* Fribourg, Switzerland: Studia Instituti Anthropos.

Darragh, T. A. and Fensham, R. J. (eds). 2013. *The Leichhardt Diaries: Early travels in Australia during 1842–1844.* Brisbane: Queensland Museum.

Fischer, H. 1990. *Völkerkunde im Nationalsozialismus: Aspekte der Anpassung, Affinität und Behauptung einer wissenschaftlichen Disziplin.* Berlin and Hamburg: Dietrich Reimer.

Fischer-Colbrie, M. 1940. Speere, Speerschleudern und Keulen der Parnkala (Süd-Australien). Doctoral thesis. Institut für Völkerkunde, University of Vienna, Vienna.

Frank, A. 1940. Botenstäbe und Wegzeichen in Australien. Doctoral thesis. Institut für Völkerkunde, University of Vienna, Vienna.

Gaillard, G. 2004 [1997]. *The Routledge Dictionary of Anthropologists.* London and New York: Routledge.

Geisenhainer, K. 2002. 'Rasse ist Schicksal': Otto Reche (1879–1966)— ein Leben als Anthropologe und Völkerkundler. Leipzig: Evangelische Verlagsanstalt.

Gingrich, A. 2005. Ruptures, schools and nontraditions: Re-assessing the history of sociocultural anthropology in German. In *One Discipline, Four Ways: British, German, French, and American anthropology*, (eds) F. Barth, A. Gingrich, R. Parkin and S. Silverman, pp. 61–153. Chicago: University of Chicago Press.

Graebner, F. 1911. *Methode der Ethnologie.* Heidelberg: Winter.

Gray, G. 2006. The 'ANRC has withdrawn its offer': Paul Kirchhoff, academic freedom and the Australian academic establishment. *Australian Journal of Politics and History* 52(3): 362–77. doi.org/10.1111/j.1467-8497.2006.00424.x.

Hiatt, L. R. 1996. *Arguments about Aborigines: Australia and the evolution of social anthropology.* Cambridge: Cambridge University Press.

Johler, R., Marchetti, C. and Scheer, M. (eds). 2010. Doing anthropology in wartime and war zones: World War I and the cultural sciences in Europe. Transcript. Bielefeld, Germany.

Kenny, A. 2013. *The Aranda's Pepa: An introduction to Carl Strehlow's masterpiece Die Aranda- und Loritja-Stämme in Zentral-Australien (1907–1920).* Canberra: ANU E Press.

Koepping, K.-P. 1984. *Adolf Bastian and the Psychic Unity of Mankind: The foundations of anthropology in nineteenth-century Germany.* Brisbane: University of Queensland Press.

Kohl, K.-H. and Platte, E. (eds). 2006. *Gestalter und Gestalten: 100 Jahre Ethnologie in Frankfurt am Main.* Frankfurt and Basel: Stroemfeld.

Krejci-Weiss, E. 2013. Abschied aus dem Knochenkabinett: Repatriierung als Instrument kultureller und nationaler Identitätspolitik am Beispiel österreichischer Restitutionen. In *Sammeln, Erforschen, Zurückgeben? Menschliche Gebeine aus der Kolonialzeit in akademischen und musealen Sammlungen,* (eds) H. Stoecker, T. Schnalke and A. Winkelmann, pp. 447–76. Berlin: Ch. Links Verlag.

Lang, A. 1898. *The Making of Religion.* London: Longmans, Green & Co.

Lang, A. 1899. Australian gods: A reply. *Folk-Lore* 10: 1–46. doi.org/10.1080/0015587X.1899.9720479.

Lommel, A. 1997. *The Unambal.* Canarvon Gorge, Qld: Takarakka Nowan Kas Publications.

Lowie, R. H. 1937. *The History of Ethnological Theory.* New York: Farrar & Rinehart.

Luxemburg, R. 1975 [1925]. Einführung in die Nationalökonomie. In *Gesammelte Werke. Volume 5,* pp. 524–778. Berlin: Dietz Verlag.

Mischek, U. 2002. *Leben und Werk Günter Wagners (1908–1952).* Veröffentlichungen des Instituts für Ethnologie der Universität Leipzig, Reihe Fachgeschichte, Band 2. Gehren, Germany: Escher.

Monteath, P. and Munt, V. (eds). 2015. *Red Professor: The Cold War life of Fred Rose.* Adelaide: Wakefield Press.

Müller, F. 1867. *Reise der Oesterreichischen Fregatte Novara um die Erde, Linguistischer Theil* [The journey of the Austrian Novara around the World, Linguistic Part]. Wien: Kaiserliche Akademie der Wissenschaften.

Müller, F. 1868. *Reise der Oesterreichischen Fregatte Novara um die Erde, Anthropologischer Theil, 3. Abtheilung; Ethnographie (auf Grund des von Dr. Karl v. Scherzer gesammelten Materials)* [The journey of the Austrian Novara around the World, Anthropological Part/Volume/Section]. Wien: Kaiserliche Akademie der Wissenschaften.

Müller, F. 2004 [1882]. *Grundriß der Sprachwissenschaft. Volume 2: Die Sprachen der schlichthaarigen Rassen.* 4 vols. Hildesheim, Germany: Olms [Vienna: Hölder].

Penny, G. H. 2002. *Objects of Culture: Ethnology and ethnographic museums in imperial Germany.* Chapel Hill, NC: University of North Carolina Press.

Penny, G. H. and Bunzl, M. (eds). 2003. *Worldly Provincialism: German anthropology in the age of empire.* Ann Arbor: University of Michigan Press.

Petri, H. 2011. *The Dying World in Northwest Australia.* Perth: Hesperian Press.

Pöch, R. 1915. Studien an Eingeborenen von Neu-Südwales und an australischen Schädeln. *Mitteilungen der Anthropologischen Gesellschaft in Wien* 45: 12–94.

Pöch, R. 1916. Ein Tasmanierschädel im kk. Naturhistorischen Hofmuseum: Die anthropologische und ethnographische Stellung der Tasmanier. *Mitteilungen der Anthropologischen Gesellschaft in Wien* 46: 37–91.

Reim, H. 1962. *Die Insektennahrung der australischen Ureinwohner.* Berlin: Akademie-Verlag.

Scheps, B. 2013. Skelette aus Queensland: Die Sammlerin Amalie Dietrich. In *Sammeln, Erforschen, Zurückgeben? Menschliche Gebeine aus der Kolonialzeit in akademischen und musealen Sammlungen,* (eds) H. Stoecker, T. Schnalke and A. Winkelmann, pp. 130–45. Berlin: Ch. Links Verlag.

Schmidt, W. 1899. Die sprachlichen Verhältnisse Oceaniens (Melanesiens, Polynesiens, Mikronesiens und Indonesiens) in ihrer Bedeutung für die Ethnologie. *Mitteilungen der Anthropologischen Gesellschaft in Wien* 29: 245–58.

Schurtz, H. 1902. *Altersklassen und Männerbünde: Eine Darstellung der Grundformen der Gesellschaft*. Berlin: Reimer.

Schweitzer, P. 2004. No escape from being theoretically important: Hunter-gatherers in German-language debates of the late nineteenth and early twentieth centuries. In *History, Archaeology, and Anthropology*, (ed.) A. Barnard, pp. 69–76. Oxford: Berg.

Sloggett, R. 2015. 'Has Aboriginal art a future?' Leonhard Adam's 1944 essay and the development of the Australian Aboriginal art market. *International Journal of Cultural Studies* 18(2): 167–83. doi.org/10.1177/1367877913515871.

Ulrich, M. 1987. Heinrich Cunow (1862–1936): Sein ethnologisches Werk vor dem Hintergrund der Persönlichkeit, der Zeitgeschichte und der wissenschaftlichen Traditionen. Doctoral dissertation. University of Vienna, Vienna.

Vermeulen, H. 2015. *Before Boas: The genesis of ethnography and ethnology in the German Enlightenment*. Critical Studies in the History of Anthropology. Lincoln: University of Nebraska Press.

Wittfogel, K. A. 1970 [1932]. *Die natürlichen Ursachen der Wirtschaftsgeschichte. Archiv für Sozialwissenschaft und Sozialpolitik 67*. Vols 4, 5 and 6. Frankfurt: Junius.

Zammito, J. H. 2002. *Kant, Herder, and the Birth of Anthropology*. Chicago: University of Chicago Press.

Part I: First encounters

3

Clamor Schürmann's contribution to the ethnographic record for Eyre Peninsula, South Australia

Kim McCaul

The Barngarla native title claim,[1] which received a largely positive determination from the Federal Court in 2014, covered an area that essentially corresponds to the eastern part of Eyre Peninsula in South Australia, from just north of Port Augusta to Sleaford Bay, south of Port Lincoln (see Map 3.1). The determination followed a contested trial that carried with it the usual forensic analysis of both contemporary Aboriginal evidence and the ethno-historical record.

Because native title law requires a comparison of the present system of 'laws and customs' with that maintained by the claimants' ancestors at the time of sovereignty, the early ethnographic record is especially sought after in such matters. It is rare, however, for this record to include material that is both as close to first contact and as detailed as that produced by the Lutheran missionary Clamor Schürmann.

This chapter will briefly contextualise Schürmann's ethnographic activities and provide an overview of some of the key elements of his record, which consists of significant linguistic, anthropological and historical data.

---

1   *Croft on behalf of the Barngarla Native Title Claim Group v State of South Australia* [2015] FCA 9.

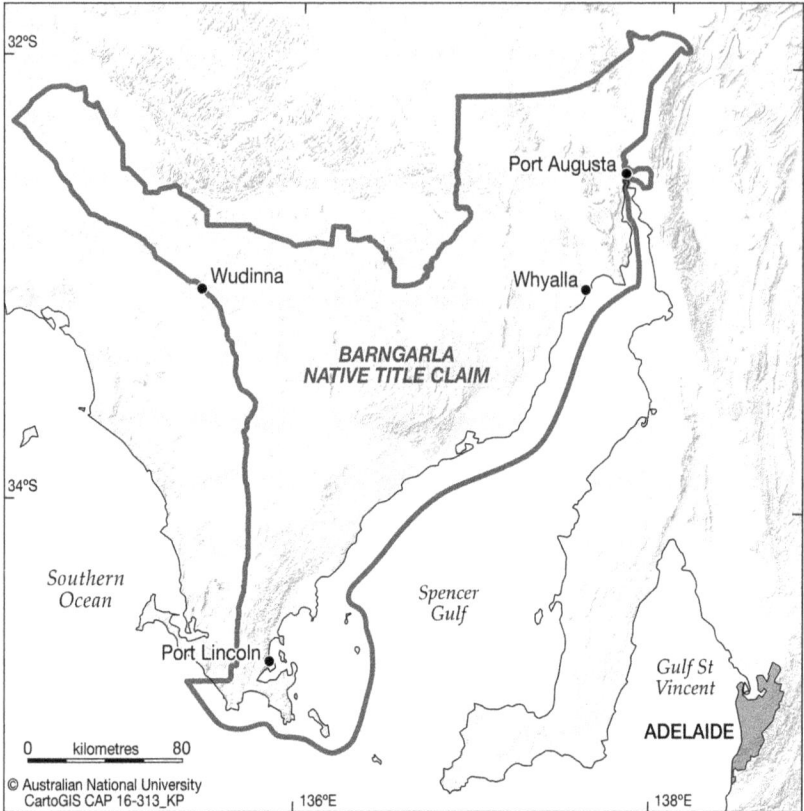

Map 3.1 Barngarla native title claim area.
Source: CartoGIS, The Australian National University.

Clamor Schürmann and the Lutheran ethnographic tradition

Clamor Schürmann was born in June 1815 in Schledehausen near Osnabrück, in what is today the state of Lower Saxony. He entered a missionary seminary in Berlin in July 1832. In 1836, he entered the seminary of the Evangelical Lutheran Mission Society of Dresden together with Gottlieb Teichelmann, his future collaborator in Australia. Two years later, Schürmann and Teichelmann left for South Australia, where they arrived on 12 October and immediately began work in Adelaide (Lockwood 2011). While their brief missionary work was fraught with setbacks and by all measures unsuccessful, their work on the language of the Adelaide Plains (Teichelmann and Schürmann 1840) eventually became a crucial source for language reclamation (Amery 2000). It also marked the beginnings of the remarkable contribution Lutheran missionaries made to the ethnographic record of South Australia.

In addition to Teichelmann and Schürmann's work on Kaurna and Schürmann's solo work on Barngarla, which I will discuss here, their colleague Heinrich Meyer produced linguistic and ethnographic material about the language and culture of the Ramindjeri and other Ngarrindjeri peoples of the Encounter Bay area, where he attempted missionary work in the 1840s (Meyer 1843, 1846).

Starting in the 1870s, a new wave of Lutherans began work in Central Australia: first, at Killalpaninna Mission on Cooper Creek among the Diyari people, and, later, at the famous Hermannsburg Mission among the Arrernte. Otto Siebert, Johann Georg Reuther and Carl Strehlow produced the most significant ethnographic contributions from this era. Siebert and Reuther both conducted extensive ethnographic work with the peoples at Killalpaninna, the former in close communication with A. W. Howitt, which resulted in a number of publications (Howitt and Siebert 1904; Howitt 1996, in which Siebert is acknowledged as a major informant; Siebert 1910).

Siebert's colleague and rival Reuther was unable to publish his own ethnographic work in his lifetime, but he produced an incredible multivolume oeuvre that provides unique insights into traditional life among the Diyari and neighbouring peoples (Reuther 1976) and has been the source of much analysis by subsequent researchers (e.g. Hercus and Potezny 1991; Jones 2002; Jones and Sutton 1986). Finally, while only published in German and still not fully translated into English, the work of Carl Strehlow on Arrernte culture and language is widely known among anthropologists, because of his rivalry with Baldwin Spencer and indirectly due to the subsequent work of his son, T. G. H. Strehlow (1907–20, see also 1971; Kenny 2013).

This Lutheran ethnographic legacy is no coincidence. At a time when anthropology had not yet developed as a formal discipline (Meyer, Schürmann, Teichelmann) or was essentially in its infancy (Reuther, Siebert, Strehlow), the motivation of these young Germans to enter the cultural world of Aboriginal people arose directly from a missionary philosophy that required spreading the word of God in the language of the people whose conversion was sought. And this meant not only using the words of that language, but also being sufficiently fluent in the local cultural lexicon so as to be able to adapt one's teaching to the existing world view and judge what to combat as anti-Christian and what to accept as anodyne (Völker 1999: 9). Due to their own priorities, this inspired the missionaries to learn about Aboriginal marriage laws, ceremonial life and religious beliefs—all essential areas of anthropological inquiry.

In Schürmann's case at least, one other factor that helped him establish a rapport with Aboriginal people seems to have been that he genuinely saw them as equal human beings at a time when for so many other Europeans they were something lesser. This is reflected not only in the compassion with which he reports some of the deaths he witnessed and in the friendships he seems to have developed, but also in the large number of personal Aboriginal names found in his correspondence. While so many early European commentators would only identify Aboriginal people by imposed and at times demeaning European names, or even in formal correspondence refer to grown men as 'boys' and women as 'gins', Schürmann consistently identifies the people he is talking about by their own names, reflecting a respect and familiarity that explain the detail available in his ethnographic text.

Schürmann's complex social positioning

The Lutheran approach to the missionary enterprise was extremely frugal. Essentially, missionaries were expected to be financially self-sufficient or obtain donations from local Lutherans (Lockwood 2011: 25). There was no institutional fund as such. As a result, the missionaries were heavily reliant on assistance from the colonial government. Yet the relationship with the government was complex. On the one hand, the missionaries felt they were providing a service to the government by assisting in the education of the Aboriginal population, but, on the other, they strongly and at times vocally disagreed with English colonial policy (Lockwood 2011: 22). And, from the perspective of the English authorities, the position of German Lutheran missionaries always seems to have been ambiguous. Schürmann and Teichelmann had befriended South Australian governor George Gawler on their voyage to Australia and originally received some support in setting up the 'Native Location' in Adelaide for the purposes of providing a European education to Aboriginal children, but this support was soon withdrawn in favour of an English boarding school. This pattern was to be repeated on Eyre Peninsula, where, after years of service on a meagre wage, Schürmann saw his position usurped by a generously funded Anglican mission (Lockwood 2011).

When Schürmann moved to Port Lincoln in 1840, his support from the governor was contingent on him assisting the authorities as interpreter and liaison with the Barngarla and Nawu[2] people of the peninsula. Eyre Peninsula had been colonised only in the previous year and Schürmann witnessed significant early frontier conflict between the colonisers and the original inhabitants. His first encounter with Aboriginal people, as recorded in his correspondence, was with a group of nine men who came to camp at Port Lincoln. With an ethnographer's eye already trained from his work with diverse Aboriginal peoples around Adelaide, his description of this meeting noted that the men were circumcised and had long beards plaited together and wrapped with grey fur.[3] He also noted that even though some words seemed similar to the 'Adelaide language', he could not really make himself understood. According to Schürmann's subsequent letter to Gawler, the men were beaten and arrested by police in supposed connection with the recent murder of a shepherd, even though it was clear that they had nothing to do with that incident (Schurmann 1987: 117–18).

This harsh introduction set the tone for the next five years of Schürmann's work around Port Lincoln. Aboriginal violence against settlers—often committed by inland peoples who withdrew after the attacks—was met with indiscriminate retaliation by the English authorities. And Schürmann was caught in the middle, expected on the one hand to liaise with the Aboriginal people, only to have his subsequent advice about guilt and innocence ignored by the authorities in favour of summary executions. This in turn undermined the trust he was trying so hard to build with the Barngarla and Nawu people. On one occasion when Schürmann accompanied a group of soldiers in pursuit of the murderers of a colonist, the troopers shot an innocent man whom Schürmann had befriended. Schürmann left the party in disgust, 'feeling it inconsistent with my missionary character and good faith with the natives to witness such actions' (Schurmann 1987: 151–2).

---

2   The name of this group is often spelt Nauo in the literature, but I spell it Nawu in accordance with the contemporary orthography of the languages in this area.
3   He would have noted their circumcision as significant, because not all the peoples he met around Adelaide practised that custom.

While beyond the scope of this chapter, there are numerous passages like the following in Schürmann's correspondence that would offer rich material for a history of the frontier conflict on Eyre Peninsula:

> This morning I went to see the natives released from captivity to find out about them for myself. Wornama told me that the following natives had been shot: Ngulga, Munta, Tubu, and two children named Tyilye and Tallerilla, aged ten and 12 years. Munta and Tubu accompanied us to Mallei (in the search party which left on April 2), and the former was in my house when the news arrived of Biddle's murder. So heinous are the Whites! Mr Driver said the butchery will continue until they hand over the guilty ones. But it hasn't even been proved that the guilty ones are among them. It is possible, as they insist, that the real murderers are somewhere in the north. (Schurmann 1987: 152)

Not only do his data provide an insight into an often-ignored violent aspect of South Australia's colonial history, they also show the complex dynamics of the broader Aboriginal polity, which was not in agreement on whether or not to resist colonial invasion by force, and was trying to maintain its regular social and economic life patterns in the face of dramatic and rapid social changes. This chapter, however, is not the place for this analysis.

One thing is certain: for most contemporary anthropologists, it is hard to imagine the working conditions Schürmann had to contend with, which makes his ethnographic productions even more remarkable.

Schürmann's ethnographic contributions

Schürmann's record consists of two major publications, both published in English. A grammar and vocabulary (Schürmann 1844) and an ethnographic account covering such varied details as material culture, initiation ceremonies and mythological stories (Schürmann 1879). In addition, Schürmann wrote a significant number of letters containing interesting historical and cultural information. Much of this correspondence was translated and compiled by a descendant (Schurmann 1987), although some important pieces of information remain unpublished in the Lutheran Archives in Adelaide (Schürmann 1840–45).

Linguistics

I will not comment in detail here on Schürmann's linguistic work. It is discussed by Hercus and Simpson (2001), who make the following comments:

> Schürmann's dictionary contains over 3,000 head words … He notes about seventy-six synonyms or paraphrases (distinct from variant forms), but there are many more. The surprisingly high number indicates a conflation of dialects, perhaps of the coastal and the scrub-gum people dialects of Barngarla, but perhaps also of Nauo. This is suggested by pairs such as kuma, kubmanna 'one' and kuttara, kalbelli 'two' in which one member of the pair is definitely Nauo, but also by pairs such as kappa, kulbarri 'three', kapi, kauo 'water', and mialla, mena 'eye' in which one member is shared with Wirangu. (Hercus and Simpson 2001: 283)

Hercus and Simpson engaged with his work primarily for the purpose of re-creating the Nawu language, but, more recently, Schürmann's record has provided the foundation for contemporary Barngarla language revival, initiated by the community in 2012.

Social data

In his paper on the social organisation of South Australian tribes, R. H. Matthews acknowledged Schürmann's 1846 account of the two intermarrying matrimoieties found among the Barngarla as:

> the first accurate record of the divisions of aboriginal tribes, not only in the colony mentioned, but in any part of the Australian continent. Owing to this priority and convenience of reference I have adopted the name of the Parnkalla tribe for the whole nation. (Matthews 1900: 79)

Matthews's 'nation' encompassed essentially the entire north-east of South Australia—the area that was subsequently termed the 'Lakes cultural bloc' by Elkin in the 1930s (Elkin 1931). The Barngarla are located at the south-western–most extent of his cultural bloc and Schürmann's was the first account to identify numerous key cultural features defining this region, including a particular set of initiatory ceremonies known as *wilyaru*, which he describes in unparalleled detail (Schürmann 1879: 231–4).

Many years after Matthews, one of Australia's most eminent anthropologists was less flattering of Schürmann's work. Despite relying heavily on Schürmann for his chapter on the Aboriginal culture of Eyre Peninsula, Ronald Berndt (1985: 127) described his work as 'not based on systematic anthropological enquiry' and 'often misleading'.

The basis for Berndt's casual dismissal of Schürmann's work is not apparent from Berndt's article. He does not elaborate on where he thinks Schürmann's information is misleading and, for the most part, simply reproduces material from Schürmann's 1846 publication.

One area where Berndt's article explores questions not contemplated by Schürmann is a discussion of hypothetical historical migrations across Eyre Peninsula. In Berndt's view, Barngarla people migrated down Eyre Peninsula following European colonisation, gradually pushing southward the original Nawu population. As this view is of direct relevance to the native title inquiry into the ongoing connection between people and land, it was naturally canvassed before the court. Schürmann's material was fundamental in refuting Berndt's thesis. But before discussing this issue in more detail, I will give a brief outline of some other details in Schürmann's data.

While much of what Schürmann points out about Aboriginal society— for example, its acephalous social structure—has since become a given in our understanding of these societies, his work pre-dated any detailed observations published to that point and as such was groundbreaking.

Schürmann referred to the lack of clear leadership structures, with some ethnocentric judgement:

> It is a curious fact, as well as a strong proof of the degraded social condition of the aboriginal inhabitants of this country, that they have no chief, or any persons of acknowledged superior authority among them. All grown up men are perfectly equal, and this is so well understood that none ever attempt to assume any command over their fellows; but whatever wishes they may entertain with regard to the conduct and actions of others, they must be expressed in the shape of entreaty or persuasion. Considerable deference, however, is shown to the old men by the younger generation, proceeding, perhaps, partly from the respect which superior age and experience inspire, but greatly increased and kept up by the superstitious awe of certain mysterious rites, known only to the grown up men, and to the knowledge of which the young are only very gradually admitted. (Schürmann 1879: 226)

3. CLAMOR SCHÜRMANN'S CONTRIBUTION TO THE ETHNOGRAPHIC RECORD

Schürmann's negative views of the lack of hierarchy among the Aboriginal people may simply reflect his Germanic background, but from his correspondence with the mission authorities it appears that his feelings may also have been tainted, because the absence of social stratification posed added challenges to his missionary work. Thus, in a letter to his mission society on 3 July 1843, Schürmann complained about the difficulty of converting Aboriginal people, caused by the way they roamed about and the fact they could not be controlled in any way, saying:

> If they had chiefs or just recognized some kind of authority through which one could effect uniformity in their movements and actions, much or even all could be achieved. But as long as each one is unfettered master of himself, I see this desirable goal as remaining unobtainable. (Schürmann 1840–45: 170; my translation)

Elsewhere, Schürmann provides a brief synopsis of daily camp life that captures the practical impacts of this lack of social leadership and at the same time could have served nicely as an exemplar for Sahlins's 'original affluent society' (Sahlins 1972):

> They seem never in a hurry to start in the morning, and it usually requires a great deal of talking and urging, on the part of the more eager, before a movement is made. When arrived at the camp, which is always some time before sunset, the first thing to be done is to make a fire and roast the small animals that they may have killed (kangaroo and other large game, being roasted on the spot where it is killed, and what is not eaten then, carried piece-meal to the camp.) After the meat is consumed, the women produce the roots or fruit picked up by them during the day; and this dessert also over, the rest of the evening is spent in talking, singing or dancing. (Schürmann 1879: 221)

Such detailed firsthand insights into the everyday life of an Aboriginal population so close to pre-contact are rare indeed.

Name avoidance of the deceased and beliefs in spiritual punishments are two well-known features of classic Aboriginal society that Schürmann illustrates with a level of insight well beyond what is commonly found in material that pre-dates formal anthropological inquiries. Regarding the former, which early commentators would often deride as deriving from superstitions, he offers an emic logic focused instead on human emotions, richly illustrated with practical implications:

> Never, upon any account, is the name of the deceased mentioned again for many years after, not from any superstition, but for the professed reason that their mournful feelings may not be excited, or, to use their own expression, 'that it may not make them cry too much.' If they have occasion to allude to dead persons, it is done by circumlocution, such as these: I am a widower, fatherless child, childless, or brotherless, as the case may be, instead of saying: my wife is dead, my father, child or brother is dead. If a death occurs among them in the bush, it is with great difficulty that the name of the deceased can be ascertained. In such a case, the natives will remind you of incidents that may have happened in his lifetime, that he did such a thing, was present on such an occasion, &c., but no persuasion on earth will induce them to pronounce his name. (Schürmann 1879: 247–8)

The belief that bad things will happen to people who misbehave is a common feature of contemporary Aboriginal culture, where illness and accidents are often attributed to some kind of socially unacceptable conduct. Schürmann documents the ancient origins of this belief with an example that shows that it was not culturally limited to Aboriginal people but considered a universal principle:

> [T]hey seem to think that the fate of man in this world is in some degree dependent on his good or bad conduct. The following anecdote will best illustrate their views on the subject: It was reported by a native that at or near Streaky Bay a black man had been shot by a whaling party for spearing a dog belonging to them, and which had been furiously attacking the native; some time after, the crew of a whaler wrecked in that neighbourhood came overland to Port Lincoln, and when it was hinted that perhaps one of them had shot the black man, the natives at once assigned that act of cruelty as the cause of the shipwreck. (Schürmann 1879: 235)

From an applied anthropological perspective, it is significant that both these cultural insights are easily referenced in contemporary culture. Even if name avoidance may have become less absolute, it is still readily observed; in my experience of interviewing Aboriginal people about their family history, the names of deceased people are regularly avoided unless directly prompted for.

Such examples of continuity are important in legislative frameworks of not only native title, but also heritage laws that include requirements of 'traditionality' and cultural continuity. In other words, Aboriginal people are regularly required to demonstrate their cultural authenticity when seeking recognition of some form of rights under the Anglo-Australian legal system. As such, being able to identify traditional practices that have clear contemporary counterparts is very valuable.

The ability to demonstrate continuity is especially important in practices relating to land, which in Aboriginal society essentially amount to religious practices, an area of logical interest to Schürmann. He recorded initiatory practices in remarkable detail and was able to personally witness a third-stage initiation practice that is known as *wilyaru* across much of eastern South Australia (Schürmann 1879: 231; Elkin 1931: 53).

More relevant to the question of continuity in relationship to land, however, is a passing observation Schürmann makes regarding the importance of areas associated with an earlier stage of initiation. On Eyre Peninsula, as across much of settled Australia, actual initiation ceremonies have been in abeyance for a couple of generations (although men are still sometimes initiated elsewhere). However, it is common for people to know areas that were traditionally associated with initiation ceremonies and consider them to be culturally restricted. In contemporary contexts, the underlying approach to Aboriginal people by non-Aboriginal laypeople (in the context of land access issues, these are most commonly mining company or government representatives) is often tainted by preconceptions regarding cultural loss. Against this backdrop, when Aboriginal people emphasise the importance of initiation sites, despite the fact that initiations are no longer practised, this can be interpreted as an attempt to re-create cultural significance in the face of fundamental loss. However, in one brief passage, Schürmann's record establishes that the significance of such places has a deeply traditional origin:

> To illustrate how early and systematically the native children are trained to view these ceremonies [referring to Warrara or circumcision ceremonies] with feelings of awe, it may be mentioned, that they are never allowed to approach the spot where a warrara has been made; if such a place should happen to fall in the line that the men are traveling, the little boys are directed to take a round, in order to avoid the sacred spot. (Schürmann 1879: 228)

Any contemporary restrictions on accessing such historical initiation sites clearly have traditional foundations.

Creation narratives

When it comes to the actual creation narratives that we now know fundamentally underpin the Aboriginal relationship to land, Schürmann's work was unfortunately hampered by his cultural preconceptions. Schürmann bookended the handful of abbreviated creation narratives that he published with the following comments, first at the introduction: 'The Aborigines have a great number of fabulous traditions handed down to them by their forefathers, all of which are characterized by a high degree of improbability and monstrosity' (Schürmann 1879: 238).

And he follows his accounts with this conclusion: 'The natives have many more similar tales among them; the above … will be sufficient to show their monstrous and in every respect ridiculous character' (Schürmann 1879: 241).

It is almost as if Schürmann feared that his audience might think he in some way endorsed or accepted the accounts if he did not deride and belittle them. He adopts the same tone in a letter to his mission society:

> The original concepts of the Aborigines regarding religious matters are very childish and often so meaningless that one spends a lot of time doubting that one has properly understood them. About the origin of visible nature they do not seem to have any concept, or at least they always respond to questions about this as though everything had come into being by itself, while the creation of some particular things is tied to some very ridiculous fairytales. For example, they attribute the creation or separation of the ocean from the land to two women, who some time ago came from the far north and caused the separation of land and water by throwing their sticks (such as are still today used to dig up roots). (Schürmann 1840–45: 178; my translation)

This prejudice against Aboriginal creation narratives would persist among Lutheran clergy and dominate some of the correspondence between missionaries and their society in the 1880s and 1890s (e.g. Hercus and McCaul 2004: 36).

While it is tempting to lament the lost opportunity of establishing a comprehensive record of creation narratives for Eyre Peninsula caused by this prejudice, it is more productive to focus on what was recorded. In his published record, Schürmann documented four stories (1879: 238–41; also reproduced in Berndt 1985: 132). They are already in the record, but I will mention two here because during the Barngarla native title hearing claimants gave evidence about these stories that was clearly not derived from Schürmann's work, thereby establishing important continuities.

The first one concerns the actions of an ancestral man now linked to thunder and lightning on the southern part of Eyre Peninsula:

> Pulyállana was in days of yore a great man, who conferred on succeeding generations the benefit of having given names to many localities in the southern and western parts of this district, which they retain to this day.
>
> He had, however, the misfortune to lose both his wives, who absconded from him—an event that by no means contributed to keep him in good humour. After a great deal of fruitless search he at last hit upon their track, and, following it; overtook them somewhere about Cape Catastrophe, where they were both killed by him. They were then converted into stone, together with their children, and all may be seen there at the present day in the shape of rocks and islands; and their breathing and groaning be heard in a cave, into which the roaring sea rushes a long way underground. Pulyallana himself was subsequently raised in the sky, at or near Puyundu (the native name for Cape Sir Isaac) where he is sometimes seized with violent fits of rage. On such occasions he raves and storms about among the clouds, and keeps shouting most lustily ... thus producing what is commonly called thunder ... The lightening is also his production, being caused by the sudden jerking or opening of his legs in his furious gestures. (Schürmann 1879: 238–9)

The second story concerns *marnpi* ('pigeon') and *tata* ('bat'):

> Between Coffin's and Sleaford Bays there is a line of bare, white sandhills, erroneously laid down in Flinders' map as white cliffs. These masses of drifting sand have most probably been piled up by the westerly gales, which often now alter their shape and position; but, according to a tradition of the natives, they were raised by Marnpi and Tatta, two of their ancestors. A great fire, coming from the ocean, spread far and wide on the sea-coast, and seemed likely to envelop the whole country in its flames. Deliberating how to prevent such a calamity, it occurred to the abovementioned personages, that the best method of quenching the fire would be to bury it; they accordingly betook themselves to the task, and, in executing it, threw up those sandhills which testify to this day the vastness of the undertaking. (Schürmann 1879: 240–1)

In 2014, claimants gave evidence of both of these stories in terms suggesting convincingly that they had learned them from the previous generations. As such, Schürmann's record played the important role of evidencing the antiquity of the narratives, which clearly pre-date the arrival of Europeans in Australia.

I will now turn to the issue of population movement, about which Berndt expressed such definitive views in his account of traditional Aboriginal life on Eyre Peninsula.

Berndt's migration hypothesis

In his desktop study of Eyre Peninsula Aboriginal people, Berndt argued that there had been substantial population movement across the peninsula from the very beginning of European colonisation. In the native title claim, this argument was essentially expressed as representing a Barngarla population shift into much of their claim area, potentially post-sovereignty. Because native title rights and interests claimed today must arise from rights and interests enjoyed by the claimants' ancestors at the time of sovereignty, this argument could have been fatal to the native title claim. Berndt summarised his views as follows:

> According to the available information, then, while the Gugada traditionally came as far south as the north-western end of the Gawler Ranges and to at least part of Lake Gairdner, they were also spreading from the north-west into Eyre Peninsula prior to 1850. The evidence dealt with in this paper suggests that culturally, if not socially, they virtually overwhelmed, especially the Wirangu, and were certainly making inroads into both Banggala and Nauo territories. On the northeastern side of the Peninsula, the Banggala were being forced southward to take over Nauo land. The Wirangu, essentially not a Western Desert population, had been forced southward by expanding Desert groups. While the Nauo were obviously influenced by (if not culturally akin to) the Banggala, it is tempting to speculate that the Wirangu and Nauo were protohistorically the original inhabitants of a large part of the Peninsula. The Banggala belonged culturally to the lakes Eyre and Torrens groups … They traditionally occupied the northeastern sector of the Peninsula … Nevertheless, on the face of the evidence available to us today, we must conclude that at the time of early European settlement on the Eyre Peninsula the two dominant Aboriginal socio-cultural systems were Banggala and Gugada. (Berndt 1985: 128)

A map that graphically illustrates Berndt's migration theory accompanies his article (Map 3.2).

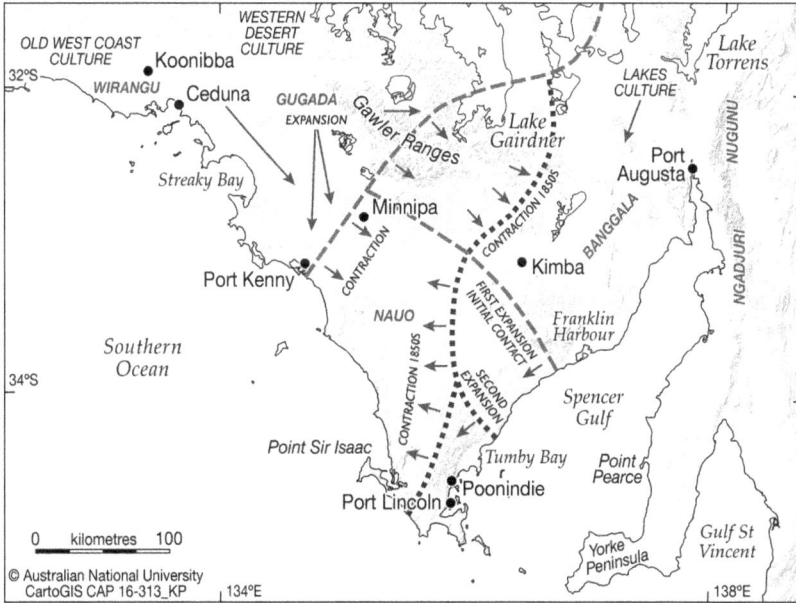

Map 3.2 Berndt's map showing the expansion and contraction of Aboriginal groups on Eyre Peninsula at the time of early European settlement.
Source: CartoGIS, The Australian National University, after Berndt (1985: 129).

Unfortunately, Berndt does not actually identify the information and evidence alluded to in the above quote that supports such major social movements. As his theory closely mirrors accounts found in Tindale (1974), one has to assume that Berndt was influenced by those. Tindale makes relevant comments in his catalogue entries for both Nawu and Barngarla. Under Barngarla, Tindale claims:

> Prehistoric and protohistoric pressure from the Kokata was modifying their northern boundary, causing a shift of their southern limits also between Port Augusta and the Gawler Ranges down towards Franklin Harbour. In their last years they ventured as far south as Tumby Bay to obtain whipstick mallee wood for spears (Hossfeld). After white settlement they lived around Port Lincoln where both Schürmann and Wilhelmi studied them. (Tindale 1974: 216)

Correspondingly, under Nawu, he asserts the following:

> Pressure from Pangkala was causing contraction to southwest at time of early white settlement; their protohistoric boundary ran from about the Gawler Ranges to Port Augusta; extinct, all my data from Wirangu and Pangkala informants. (Tindale 1974: 214)

Schürmann arrived on Eyre Peninsula as part of the first wave of permanent colonisation, one year after Port Lincoln was established. If the sudden presence of Europeans had caused major population shifts, Schürmann did not perceive it. His published work testifies to a seemingly stable situation on Eyre Peninsula, and does not support Berndt's suggestion that Barngarla and Kukata were the dominant Aboriginal sociocultural systems at the time of early European settlement:

> The Aborigines inhabiting the Peninsula of Port Lincoln are divided into several tribes, with two of whom the European settlers are in daily contact, namely, the Nauo and Parnkalla tribes. Besides these, three other tribes are mentioned by the natives as known to them: the Nukunnus in the north-east, the Kukatas in the north-west, and the Ngannityiddis in the north, between the last two mentioned of whom a few have now and then visited the settlement. All these tribes seem in general to be on tolerably good terms with each other, at least it does not appear that there are any hereditary feuds between them, such as exist in other parts of the colony. It is true that the Kukatas are universally feared and abominated, but apparently more on account of their reputed skill in witchcraft and various other dangerous tricks than for their warlike qualities. (Schürmann 1879: 248–9)

In his unpublished writings, Schürmann provided additional details that allow further appreciation of the traditional demographics of Eyre Peninsula. In a letter of 18 May 1842 to the Protector of Aborigines, Matthew Moorhouse, Schürmann provides the following account of the distribution of tribes around Port Lincoln:

> The natives of Port Lincoln are divided into two principal tribes called in their own languages the one Nauo + the other Parnkallas. The former of these frequent the coast to the south and west of the settlement + live chiefly upon fish; they are generally speaking a strong race of people + often meet in comparatively large bodies, not unlike the natives of Encounter Bay. They differ considerably in dialect + custom from the other tribe + the males have the distinguishing mark of a small ring or circle engraved on each shoulder. The Parnkalla tribe are spread over a far greater extent of country from Port Lincoln to the northward beyond

Franklin Harbour and over the greater part of the interior country. They divide themselves again into two smaller tribes, viz. Wambirri yurarri, i.e. coast people and Battara yurarri, i.e. gum tree people, so called from their living in the interior country where the gum is plentiful. It is to be understood however, that these tribes are not so entirely separated as not to mix occasionally, on the contrary they often visit each other in small numbers. (Schürmann 1840–45: 143–5)

Schürmann touches on the relationship between Nawu and Barngarla people in numerous other letters (e.g. Schürmann 1840–45: 167, 195), and it is consistently implicit in his correspondence that Nawu people and country are primarily to the immediate south and west of Port Lincoln, and Barngarla people are at Port Lincoln and north from there.

It is possible, as was suggested by some during the Barngarla trial, that Barngarla people had only recently moved as far south as Port Lincoln in response to the novelty of the emerging white township.

Against this suggestion, in my view, is the fact that there is no mention in any of Schürmann's writings of disputes among Aboriginal people about ownership or authority in Port Lincoln. The overall image conveyed is one of generally peaceful coexistence between Nawu and Barngarla, or at least no more tension between those two groups than there appears to have been between coastal and inland Barngarla—that is, the Batara yurari and Wambirri yurari. For the most part, these tensions seem to have been fuelled by conflicts with Europeans. For example, it seems to have frequently been the Batara yurari who would attack homesteads or shepherds and the Wambirri yurari who would suffer the consequences of white retaliation, which in turn led to the latter being angry with the former.

The lack of perceivable conflict about traditional matters or, as Schürmann said, 'hereditary feuds' (something he had become alerted to during his time in Adelaide) suggests that whatever population movements may have happened in this area, the intra-Aboriginal situation was relatively stable by the time Schürmann lived at Port Lincoln, which was essentially at effective sovereignty.[4]

---

4   In the native title context, 'sovereignty' is the time in which the British Crown legally annexed land, which, for Eyre Peninsula and most of South Australia, was 1788. 'Effective sovereignty' refers to the time physical colonisation actually took place, and courts will usually use that as the relevant point from which to assess cultural change.

In 1853, Schürmann left South Australia for Victoria, where he became the minister to a German congregation in Portland and eventually president of the Victorian district of the Evangelical Lutheran Synod of Australia. He died on 3 March 1893 while attending synod at Bethany, South Australia (Kneebone 2005).

Conclusion

Schürmann's ethnographic observations clearly have their limitations. His cultural biases inhibited his recording of religious narratives and quite possibly other cultural features, and, of course, he had not been trained as an ethnographic observer. Ultimately, creating an ethnographic record was not his main concern, but rather a means to an end. And yet his record contains a unique level of detail from a period of colonisation for which ethnographic information is largely absent. His intimate and personal relationships with Barngarla and Nawu people allowed Schürmann to convey insights not usually found outside dedicated anthropological fieldwork, which he pre-dated by more than half a century. His information on the traditional population patterns on Eyre Peninsula on the one hand cancelled out the migration argument against the Barngarla claim. On the other hand, it meant that areas south of Port Lincoln were not determined on behalf of Barngarla, because they were found to have been traditional Nawu country. As such, he joins an ever-increasing list of posthumous 'experts' in the native title process (Burke 2011). Ultimately, Schürmann has left a record that continues to offer valuable data to linguists, anthropologists and historians, and be of ongoing relevance to the descendants of the people with whom he worked.

References

Amery, R. 2000. *Warrabarna Kaurna! Reclaiming an Australian language.* Lisse, Netherlands: Swets & Zeitlinger.

Berndt, R. 1985. Traditional Aborigines. In *Natural History of Eyre Peninsula*, Occasional Publications for the Royal Society of South Australia No. 4, (eds) C. R. Twidale, M. J. Tyler and M. Davies, pp. 127–38. Adelaide: Royal Society of South Australia.

Burke, P. 2011. *Law's Anthropology: From ethnography to expert testimony in native title*. Canberra: ANU E Press.

Elkin, A. P. 1931. The social organization of South Australian tribes. *Oceania* 2: 44–73. doi.org/10.1002/j.1834-4461.1931.tb00022.x.

Hercus, L. and McCaul, K. 2004. *Otto Siebert: The missionary ethnographer*. Occasional Paper No. 3, (ed.) Walter Veit, pp. 36–50. Strehlow Research Centre, Alice Springs, NT.

Hercus, L. and Potezny, V. 1991. Locating Aboriginal sites: A note on JG Reuther and the Hillier map of 1904. *Records of the South Australian Museum* 24(2).

Hercus, L. and Simpson, J. 2001. The tragedy of Nauo. *In Forty Years On: Ken Hale and Australian languages*, (eds) J. Simpson, D. Nash, M. Laughren, P. Austin and B. Alpher, pp. 263–90. Canberra: Pacific Linguistics.

Howitt, A. W. 1996 [1904]. *The Native Tribes of South-East Australia*. Canberra: Aboriginal Studies Press.

Howitt, A. W. and Siebert, O. 1904. Legends of the Dieri and kindred tribes of Central Australia. *Journal of the Anthropological Institute of Great Britain* (34): 100–29.

Jones, P. 2002. Naming the dead heart: Hillier's map and Reuther's gazetteer of 2,468 place names in north-eastern South Australia. In *The Land is a Map: Placenames of Indigenous origins in Australia*, (eds) L. Hercus, F. Hodges and J. Simpson, pp. 187–200. Canberra: Pandanus Books.

Jones, P. and Sutton, P. 1986. *Art and Land: Aboriginal sculptures of the Lake Eyre Basin*. Adelaide: Wakefield Press.

Kenny, A. 2013. *The Aranda's Pepa: An introduction to Carl Strehlow's masterpiece Die Aranda- und Loritja-Stämme in Zentral-Australien (1907–1920)*. Canberra: ANU E Press.

Kneebone, H. 2005. Teichelmann, Christian Gottlieb (1807–1888). In *Australian Dictionary of Biography*. Canberra: National Centre of Biography, The Australian National University. Available from: adb.anu.edu.au/biography/teichelmann-christian-gottlieb-13213/text23925. Published first in hardcopy 2005. Accessed online 19 January 2016.

Lockwood, C. 2011. A vision frustrated: Lutheran missionaries to the Aborigines of South Australia 1838–1853. In *Germans: Travelers, settlers and their descendants in South Australia*, (ed.) P. Monteath, pp. 17–40. Adelaide: Wakefield Press.

Matthews, R. M. 1900. Divisions of the South Australia Aborigines. *Proceedings of the American Philosophical Society* 39: 78–93.

Meyer, H. A. E. 1843. *Vocabulary of the Language Spoken by the Aborigines of the Southern and Eastern Portions of the Settled Districts of South Australia*. Adelaide: James Allen.

Meyer, H. A. E. 1846. *Manners and Customs of the Aborigines of the Encounter Bay Tribe: South Australia*. Adelaide: State Library of South Australia.

Reuther, J. G. 1976. The Diari. Translated by Rev. P. A. Scherer. Unpublished ms, AA226, South Australian Museum, Adelaide.

Sahlins, M. 1972. *Stone Age Economics*. London: Tavistock Publications.

Schürmann, C. 1840–45. Correspondence of missionary Clamor Schürmann from Port Lincoln. Unpublished ms, Lutheran Archives, Adelaide.

Schürmann, C. 1844. *Vocabulary of the Parnkalla Language: Spoken by the natives inhabiting the western shores of Spencer's Gulf.* Adelaide: Dehane.

Schürmann, C. 1879 [1846]. The Aboriginal tribes of Port Lincoln in South Australia: Their mode and life, manners, customs etc. In *The Native Tribes of South Australia*, (ed.) J. Woods, pp. 209–51. Adelaide: E. S. Wigg & Son.

Schurmann, E. 1987. *I'd Rather Dig Potatoes: Clamor Schurmann and the Aborigines of South Australia 1838–1853*. Adelaide: Lutheran Publishing House.

Siebert, O. 1910. Sagen und Sitten der Dieri und Nachbarstämme in Zentral-Australien. *Globus* 97(3): 44–50; 97(4): 53–9.

Strehlow, C. 1907–1920. *Die Aranda- und Loritja-Stämme in Zentral-Australien.* 7 vols. Frankfurt am Main: Joseph Baer & Co.

Strehlow, T. G. H. 1971. *Songs of Central Australia.* Sydney: Angus & Robertson.

Teichelmann, C. G. and Schürmann, C. 1840. Outlines of a grammar, vocabulary, and phraseology, of the Aboriginal language of South Australia, spoken by the natives in and for some distance around Adelaide. Adelaide.

Tindale, N. 1974. *Aboriginal Tribes of Australia.* Canberra: Australian National University Press.

Völker, H. 1999. Projektion des Fremden: Beiträge deutscher lutherischer Missionare zur Darstellung der australischen Urbevölkerung um 1900—Johann Georg Reuther, Carl Strehlow, Otto Siebert. PhD thesis. Albert Ludwig University of Freiburg, Freiburg im Breisgau, Germany.

4

Pulcaracuranie: Losing and finding a cosmic centre with the help of J. G. Reuther and others

Rod Lucas and Deane Fergie[1]

J. G. Reuther's collecting—of language, myth, material objects, natural history specimens, biographies and *Volksgut* in general—among the Dieri[2] and other Aboriginal groups of South Australia's north-east is

1   We are especially grateful to Helen Gordon, Reuther's granddaughter, for providing generous access to her personal archive of documents, genealogical records, letters, translations of Reuther's résumé and diary, family photographs and objects (including Pauline's treasured wedding ring). We are equally indebted to the generous support and encouragement of Colin Jericho, grandson of the staunch *Kolonist* Hermann Vogelsang, whose tenure at Killalpaninna and Kopperamanna exceeded that of Reuther himself. Colin provided us access to his personal archive and outstanding knowledge of all things Lutheran in South Australia. We are hugely appreciative of Anna Kenny for her work on the Reuther manuscript in the South Australian Museum. We would also like to thank the wonderful staff of the Lutheran Archive.
2   There has been a range of renderings of the name for both language and group across time. One of the earliest uses of the form 'Dieri' is the first instructional primer, called *Nujanujarajinkiniexa: Dieri Jaura jelaribala* (1870), probably written by Koch and Homann, who were members of the second Lutheran missionary expedition that sought to settle at Killalpaninna in early 1868 (Austin 1986: 190; 2015: 4). Missionary Karl Schoknecht compiled *Wörterbuch*: Deutsch–Dieri & Dieri–Deutsch at Cooranina (Cooryanna), in January 1873, together with a *Grammatik* (Schoknecht and Schoknecht 1997). Missionary Johannes Flierl revised the orthography and wrote a detailed grammar during his time at the mission from 1878 to 1884. His Christianieli Ngujangujara-Pepa Dieri Jaurani (1880) is a translation of the Lutheran catechism, epistles and gospels in the new orthography. This orthography remained the standard for all mission writings (published and unpublished) until the mission closed in 1915. Reuther and Strehlow employed the same orthography in their translation of the New Testament, as did Reuther, including in his four-volume dictionary (Austin 1986: 176). The mission (and Reuther) adopted the spelling 'Diari', although Siebert—the 'bush' missionary and

comparable with Carl Strehlow's pioneering work among the Western Arrernte. Reuther's unpublished handwritten 13-volume 'The Diari' (1899–1908)[3] in many ways reflects Strehlow's published seven-volume *Die Aranda- und Loritja-Stämme in Zentral-Australien* (1907–20). Both contain an unprecedented (and unrepeatable) compendium of materials that continue to inform contemporary ethnography, as well as Aboriginal responses to their own country. The two Germans worked together at Killalpaninna on Coopers Creek (now known as Cooper Creek) from 1892 to 1894, resulting in the first publication of the New Testament in an Aboriginal language (in 1897). They had both been seminarians at Neuendettelsau.[4]

Lutheran missiology since the seventeenth century had emphasised the need to study local languages to preach the Gospel—since the Reverend John Campanius prepared the first known vocabulary of the Amerindian tribes on the Delaware (where Sweden had established its New World colony in 1638), founded the first known Lutheran school on North American soil and produced the first translation of Luther's *Catechism* in a 'heathen' tongue (Peters n.d.). In his commentary on Psalm 117, Luther had placed language at the heart of his mission:

---

counter ethnographer—used 'Dieri' in the title for 'Sagen und Sitten der Dieri und Nachbarstämme in Zentral-Australien', published in *Globus* in 1910. 'Diyari' is the rendering developed from Peter Austin's fieldwork carried out in 1974–77 while a postgraduate student at The Australian National University, in the resulting PhD thesis and in the published *A Grammar of Diyari* (Austin 1981). Pedagogical materials for the maintenance and propagation of cultural and linguistic heritage produced since 2008 use a practical orthography based on the phonological analyses of Austin (1981) and later works. Contemporary people have chosen to adopt the name and spelling 'Dieri'. In what originated as two competing native claims, the groups Ngayana Dieri Karna ('We the Dieri people') and the Dieri Mitha ('Dieri ground/country') both adopted 'Dieri' as their identity, despite other differences. Later the two groups joined in a combined 'Dieri' native title claim (SCD2012/001, *Lander v. State of South Australia*) in which Dieri native title was determined by consent in 2012. With that and a subsequent determination, 'Dieri' now has an existence in Australian case law.

3   J. G. Reuther's 13 handwritten volumes are held at the South Australian Museum (SAM) in Adelaide. Their call numbers are SAM AA266/09/1 to SAM AA266/09/13. These volumes are numbered with Arabic numerals (i.e. 1–13), while P. A. Scherer's English translation of Reuther's work of the 1970s uses Roman numerals (i.e. I–XIII). Scherer's translation was made available on microfiche in 1981. See Appendix 4.1 for the titles of the original 13 volumes.

4   Carl Strehlow was admitted to the Neuendettelsau seminary on 1 August 1888. He graduated on 31 August 1891. Having been assigned as a pastor to the Lutheran Church in North America, Strehlow responded to a call from Australia for missionary work at Bethesda. He was ordained at Light Pass in South Australia on 3 July 1892 and immediately appointed an assistant to J. G. Reuther at Killalpaninna, where he arrived on 11 July.

If all heathen are to praise God, this assumes that he has become their God. If he is to be their God, then they must know him, believe in him, and give up all idolatry. One cannot praise God with an idolatrous mouth or an unbelieving heart. And if they are to believe, they must first hear his word and thereby receive the Holy Spirit, who through faith purifies and enlightens their hearts. One cannot come to faith or lay hold on the Holy Spirit without hearing the word first, as St. Paul has said (Rom. 10: 14): 'How are they to believe in him of whom they have never heard?' and (Gal. 3: 2): 'You have received the Spirit through the proclamation of faith.' If they are to hear his word, then preachers must be sent to proclaim God's word to them; for not all the heathen can come to Jerusalem. (L. W. 14: 9, 10, cited in Valleskey 1993: 2)

It is for this reason that Reuther collected (Dieri) words. Vernacular language was a path to a peoples' soul and mimicked the directness of Luther's aim of bypassing theological hierarchy. In line with Neuendettelsau teachings, Reuther, like Strehlow, pursued understanding of Dieri culture, language and belief as a vehicle for introducing his own. He, like Strehlow, was a great philologist. But there are materials in his four-volume 'Dictionary' (encompassing Dieri, Wangkangurru and Yandruwandha) that disclose more than words; there are ethnographic riches that reveal the preoccupations, passions, values and perceptions of a world that few others have recorded from north-east South Australia.[5]

In this chapter, we present Reuther as the ultimate collector with religious intent: he collected objects to find their names and all the words associated with them. He collected language on the basis of a fundamental Lutheran principle that the word of God must be received in the vernacular so that people knowingly and freely (and according to the patterns of their own thought) choose their acceptance of Christian faith.

Although the time and location of his training were suffused with ideas and theories of culture, historical particularism and *Volksgeist*, there is no evidence that these intellectual currents particularly informed Reuther's practice. In his own words, his secondary education was 'inadequate' and he found seminary training 'difficult'. He was not, we contend, an anthropological theorist or an ethnographer in a post-Malinowskian sense. His was a practical theology of conversion through language, to ensure belief and thus the possibility of resurrection after death. This religious perspective is, we suggest, a critical key for understanding Reuther and his work.

---

5   Reuther, J. G. 1904–06, Wörterbuch, Vols 1–4, SAM AA266/09/1-4, SAM.

What he left to us is a remarkable cache of words, facts and objects that, a century later, become especially valuable to contemporary Dieri people under legislative conditions that Reuther could never have anticipated. For him, the Dieri, after all, were a vanishing people.

Where Reuther documented language as a precursor to conversion and salvation, Australian regimens of heritage and native title demand 'collecting' evidence of connection. In those contexts, prior documentation in a written record is highly valued, indeed privileged (Lucas 1996). Where Reuther attended to language, the state, courts and anthropologists working for them are required to address the record and the material trace of a previously oral tradition. Reuther's 'data' become key elements in a new knowledge practice documenting endurance, persistence and reproduction (of Dieri knowledge, social norms and connection to country). By this means, his material is used by contemporary Dieri people to reinscribe meaning in the landscape, rehabilitate connection, repatriate the past and build identity. Of this process, we provide a brief case study. We explore the ways in which a pivotal place can be elucidated using the work of Reuther and others. We reconstruct—through triangulating the records of missionaries, explorers and anthropologists—how a place has been relocated and reinvested with meaning by contemporary Dieri people, drawing on and seeing with the aid of Reuther's earlier records. Pulcaracuranie enfolds philological collecting, the recording of myth, *toa*-making, the salvage ethnography of a modernist discipline and the hopes and aspirations of a people reconnecting with their land.

J. G. Reuther

Origins

Johann Georg Reuther was born on 3 September 1861. He was the eldest of seven siblings who survived childhood, the children of Martin and Anna Barbara (née Riffelmacher) Reuter. All were born in Rosstal, Middle Franconia, near Neuendettelsau, and all were baptised in the Laurentius-Kirche in Rosstal. Church records have all Reuther siblings sharing the surname 'Reuter'; the family today does not know when or why the 'h' began appearing in the spelling of the surname, but presumably some time in J. G. Reuther's generation.[6]

---

6   Helen Gordon, personal communication.

Reuther's education was undertaken in Rosstal, but he complains in his résumé of an elderly teacher he had in the upper classes, from whom he did not learn much. School was supplemented by his religious education: 'what was left undone at school was made up for spiritually in the preparatory and confirmation instructions that I received in Rosstal'.[7] He was confirmed and received into the church at Pentecost in 1875.

Vocationally, Reuther trained as a weaver (his father's trade) until age 22, during which time he also helped manage the family household (which he says became difficult when a younger sister became deaf and mute at age four). On the basis of this domestic difficulty, he was able to defer military training for two years, but was eventually taken into the reserve for military service, which he served at Neuburg on the Danube.

Reuther had known of the mission school (Neuendettelsau) from the age of 15 and long wished to enter it, but was thwarted in this ambition for a number of years. After military service, he returned to Rosstal and worked as a postman, then as a postal assistant in Nürnberg.

An epiphany or 'awakening' (Veit n.d.) came on Christmas Eve 1885:

> It was Christmas 1885 when on Christmas Eve I was at the railway station waiting for the arrival of mail trains. Suddenly in the night at 12 o'clock all the bells of Nürnberg were ringing in the holy festival. This affected me so deeply that I thought, if only all people knew about the holy Christ child. I had to weep because of the great joy which has been granted us Christians, but I was also sad because of the sorry plight of the heathens.[8]

With this new vision and determination, Reuther applied to the Mission Institute and was admitted on 2 April 1886.

On strict Lutheran grounds there is no earthly purpose post baptism other than propagation and proselytising of the Christian Gospel. In a sermon on 1 Peter 1, Luther stated that a Christian really had only one reason for continuing to live on this earth after he had been brought to faith in Jesus:

> We have no other reason for living on earth than to be of help to others. If this were not the case, it would be best for God to kill us and let us die as soon as we are baptized and have begun to believe. But he permits us to live here in order that we may bring others to faith, just as he brought

---

7   Reuther, résumé, Neuendettelsau, 24 July 1888.
8   ibid.

us … The greatest work that comes from faith is this, that I confess Christ with my mouth and, if it has to be, bear testimony with my blood and risk my life … in order that others, too, may be brought to faith. (L. W. 30: 30, 31, cited in Valleskey 1993: 2)

This was Reuther's mission, and it filled the whole of his life, except that for several decades the Aboriginal worlds and languages of Cooper Creek were its vehicle—capturing the hearts and mouths that Luther required.

Of his time at Neuendettelsau, Reuther wrote (in the *Zusammenfassung* that all graduates had to submit before leaving, on the assumption that they may never return):

> My stay in the mission school of Dettelsau was partly a difficult one, partly full of blessing for me. Difficult insomuch as I had received unsatisfactory [inadequate] schooling and had to endeavour to make up for what my education lacked; full of blessing insomuch as I with the help of God and that of my tireless teachers, had reached the point where I was to be a servant of the Lord in His kingdom amongst the heathens in Bethesda. For this purpose I sat for my exams beginning on 16th July, 1888, and, God willing, will be inducted and commissioned on 12th August and on 17th September will embark in Genoa.[9]

Two things stand out from the passage: Reuther's prior education was, in his own eyes, academically inadequate, but he worked hard to overcome any deficiency; and he already knew on graduating that he was being sent to Bethesda at Killalpaninna in northern South Australia.

To the north of South Australia

Disembarking in South Australia, Reuther began a whirlwind tour of Lutheran communities, preached in a number of churches and prepared for ordination. In this brief period he met his future wife, Pauline Stolz née Rechner, the daughter of a pivotal South Australian Lutheran family.[10] Pauline's first husband, Johannes Martin Stolz, had died three years earlier.

9   ibid.
10   Pauline Stolz née Rechner was the daughter of Gustav Julius Rechner (1830–1900), schoolteacher, cantor, clerk to George Fife Angas (founding chair of the South Australian Company, which was populating the colony with free settlers), pastor, president of the Evangelical Lutheran Immanuel Synod of South Australia and chairman of the Mission Committee, and thus J. G. Reuther's 'boss' (Proeve 1976). Pauline's eldest son, J. J. Stolz, became the general president of the United Evangelical Lutheran Church of Australia, serving from 1925 to 1953.

Plate 4.1 Reuther's graduation portrait.
Source: C. Schmidt, jnr, Nürnberg, 1888. Lutheran Archives, M00313.

Plate 4.2 Reverend J. G. Reuther and the widow Pauline Stolz around the time of their engagement, 1888.

Source: Lutheran Archives, M00277.

Pauline and Georg were engaged after an eight-day acquaintance in Point Pass (Reuther 1970: 2), where Pauline Stolz and her three children were living in the church vestry. The engagement was celebrated at Light Pass, where Reuther had gone to be ordained, during a pastors' conference on 23 November 1888, which was also the anniversary of Pauline's husband's death (Reuther 1970: 2). At this strange conjunction, Pauline's father, G. J. Rechner:

> mentioned that this day was the day the whole family was in deepest sorrow when my bride [fiancée] was deprived of her husband through death. Today he would also bring joy to the bride … After this he blessed our union [engagement]. (Reuther 1970: 2)

Five days later (on 28 November 1888), Reuther left Adelaide with Johann Flierl, but without Pauline, on his first trip to the mission station on Lake Killalpaninna, then called Bethesda, arriving on 2 December (Scherer 1966a: 304). He was joined three months later by Pauline, whose first Reuther child was born on the couple's first wedding anniversary; she was to bear a child each year for the next eight years, all at Killalpaninna on Cooper Creek.

Plate 4.3 Pauline and J. G. Reuther in the missionary's study, Killalpaninna.
Source: Lutheran Archives, P027/41/05316.

Although principally taken up with the practical and moral duties of Lutheran *Mutterschaft*, Pauline was also a helpmate and facilitator of Reuther's work, as epitomised in the frequently used portrait of them together in Reuther's study (see Plate 4.3). This is the room in which

Reuther worked on the 'Dictionary', the Dieri manuscript volumes and (with Strehlow) the New Testament translation. In his diary, Reuther recorded the 'dedication' of the newly built study on 6 May 1891. He added:

> Give Your blessing, O Lord, to the work I will be doing in this room. Especially send Thy Holy Spirit Who evermore give me the wisdom to study Thy Word, so that it may become a power for me and for the others, the heathen, to save all who believe it. (Reuther 1970)

With the aid of Strehlow, Reuther commenced translation of the New Testament on 10 April 1893 (Scherer 1966a: 305; 1979: 13). Strehlow was transferred to Hermannsburg 18 months later. Reuther's diary records that Strehlow and Reuther left Killalpaninna for Finke on 27 September 1894, arriving at Hermannsburg on 11 October; Reuther stayed five weeks then left on 16 November 1894. During this absence, Reuther's child Georg Edwin died, aged three months. Reuther continued with the translation alone until, on 29 October 1895, he noted on a calendar: 'Thanks to God, today I finished the New Testament in Diari [Dieri]' (Reuther 1970). On 18 November, he added a short preface and continued revising the text and preparing the manuscript until August 1896 (Scherer 1966b: 314). According to Scherer (1979: 13), Reuther 'transcribed the New Testament into Diari three times before he was satisfied with the textual result'. On the debate as to who contributed most to the linguistic work, Scherer (1966b: 314) points out that Strehlow had been at the mission only nine months by the time of commencing the translation, but Reuther had already spent four-and-a-half years learning the language; Strehlow spent less than 18 months assisting Reuther in the task, but the latter spent at least five-and-a-half years on the translation.

G. J. Rechner (Reuther's father-in-law) supervised publication of the *Dieri New Testament* by G. Auricht of Tanunda, South Australia. This took two years as:

> every proof sheet had to be forwarded to Mr. Reuther in the Far North for correction and revision ... The book is likely to remain a monument of piety and industry long after the tribe for which it has been specifically produced is extinct.[11]

---

11   A new 'New Testament', *The Advertiser*, [Adelaide], 22 September 1898: 4.

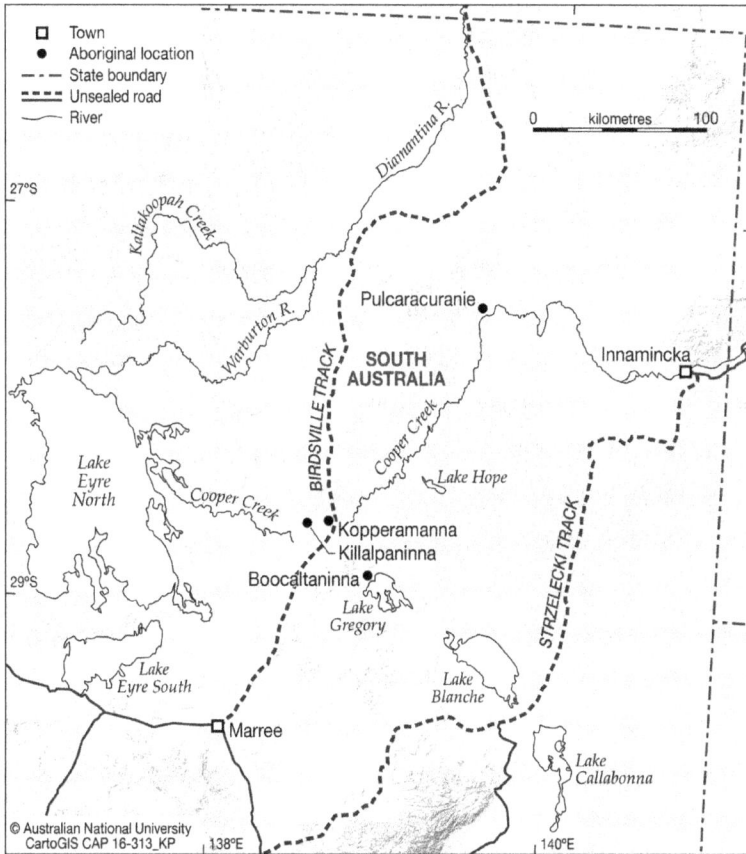

Map 4.1 The location of Lutheran missions in the vicinity of Cooper Creek, northern South Australia.
Source: CartoGIS, The Australian National University.

Collections

A contemporary account of Reuther's collection around the time of his leaving Killalpaninna is as follows:

> The interior of Mr. Reuther's dwelling is a veritable museum. The passage contains over 1,000 pieces of native weapons, ornaments and apparel, including 100 boomerangs, suspended from the ceiling. Four hundred symbols [*toas*], composed of almost every kind of material available, form an interesting collection. These symbols correspond to European finger posts, and through their agency the blacks indicate to each other the place to which they have gone.[12]

---

12 A missionary among Aborigines, *Register*, [Adelaide], 7 February 1906: 4.

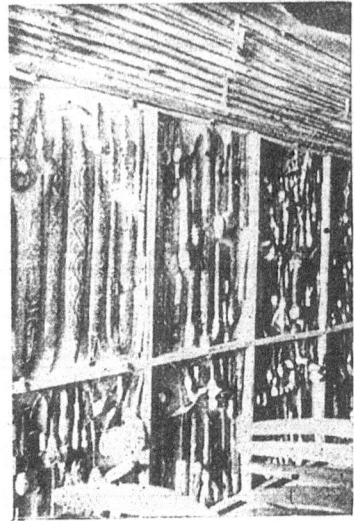

NATIVE WEAPONS AND SYMBOLS.

Plate 4.4 The central corridor of Reuther's Killalpaninna house.
Source: *Kapunda Herald*, 10 May 1907.

Plate 4.5 Reuther's artefact collection, including *toas*, in his Killalpaninna house.
Source: *Observer*, [Adelaide], 10 February 1906.

This collecting subserved Reuther's desire to collect everything that would facilitate access to the Aboriginal mind and thereby act as a medium for its transformation. Reuther collected things to find the words attached to them, along with all their associations. This can be seen in the multilayered entries in the 'Dictionary', which is replete with contextualised renderings, uses, conjunctions and examples.

A. C. H. Zietz, a curator at the South Australian Museum, visited Reuther at his Gumvale property in 1907 'to inspect an extensive ethnological collection made by him at Cooper Creek'.[13] It was described at the time as follows:

> The comprehensive collection represents the results of 20 years' work by an enthusiastic ethnological expert, and includes a vast variety of boomerangs, spears, mats, charms and sacred articles, concerning which little had been hitherto known. There is also over a score of bottles of seeds and roots, which formed a considerable part of the food of the aborigines

---

13   Museum report, *The Advertiser*, [Adelaide], 5 November 1908: 12.

… Apparently Mr. Reuther was always on the alert for new discoveries, and he assured Mr. A. H. C. Zietz … that once anything was brought under his notice for the first time he never rested until he had gained all the information available in regard to it.[14]

The material culture collection was bought by the museum in October 1907 for £400 (Scherer 1979: 15).

Seven years later, following Reuther's death, the museum board purchased a set of manuscript ledgers and three maps for £75 (Scherer 1979). The 'Manuscript' (as it has come to be known) included the four-volume *Wörterbuch* ('Dictionary') that Reuther had worked on from 1903 to 1906, a '*Diari Gramatik*' he had completed in 1899, together with Wangkangurru and Yandruwantha grammars in 1901 (see Jones and Sutton 1986: 53; Stevens 1994: 211) and wordlists of eight Aboriginal languages, with each having approximately 1,744 single glosses in volume 5, notes on subjects such as *Farben* ('colours') and *Verbote für alle* ('general prohibitions') in volume 6,[15] a collection of 2,468 placenames (volume 7), explanations of 303 personal names (volumes 8 and 9), a collection of myths and legends (volume 10), a volume (11) called '*Von der Götter- und Geisterwelt der Eingeborenen Australiens*' ('About the world of the gods and spirits of Aboriginal Australians') and two volumes (12 and 13) describing his material culture collection (see Kenny 2017).

A focus on language

The role of language in the conversion of the Dieri was articulated by Goessling, who was among the first missionaries to settle (unsuccessfully) in Dieri country.[16] Mission was a 'battlefield' and language was the 'weapon carrier' (*Waffenträger*) that was to aid the fight:

> *Die Reise mit Allem, was damit zusammenhängt, liegt jetzt hinter uns. Der Marsch nach dem Kampfplatz ist nun vollendet. Und weil das eigentliche Kriegsleben erst mit dem Ausbruche des Krieges seinen Anfang nimmt, so geht auch für uns der eigentliche Krieg jetzt erst an. Wir sind nun auf dem Platze, den der Herr uns gezeigt hat, und unter dem Volke, welchem unsere*

---

14 A splendid ethnological collection, *Register*, [Adelaide], 29 October 1907.

15 The notes in this small notebook are sparse and mainly crossreference entries in the other volumes.

16 Missionary Johann F. Goessling was in the very first party that departed Langmeil for Lake Killalpaninna to found the Bethesda Mission in October 1866, confusingly, originally called Hermannburg. Others included missionary Ernst Homann and *Kolonists* ('lay assistants') Hermann Vogelsang and Ernst Jacob (Proeve and Proeve 1952).

Sendung gilt. Jetzt gilt es nun sich zu beweisen als treue Streiter Jesu Christi, denn es wird Niemand gekrönt, er kämpfe denn recht. Und das möchten wir auch gerne, recht kämpfen und keine Luftstreiche thun; denn Luftstreiche ermüden nur, richten aber nichts aus, als daß sie den Kämpfer dem Feind zum Spott machen. Nun kennen wir ja unsere Waffen und wissen auch, wie sie geführt werden müssen, wenn wir nur erst den Waffenträger der Sprache in unsere Gewalt hätten. Und es hält oft sehr schwer das richtige Wort für einen Gegenstand, Begriff oder Bewegung zu bekommen. Man kann oft Stunden lang an einem Worte klauben und kriegt es mitunter doch nicht heraus. Zuerst bekamen wer eine Anzahl Worte von Herrn Gassen (?) in Lake Hope, und nachher haben wir uns, so viel wir eben konnten, dazu gesammelt und suchen so bei Kleinem immer weiter zu kommen. Man muß sich zuerst in ihren Gedankenkreis hineinfinden.[17]

[The journey and everything associated with it is now behind us. The march to the battlefield is completed. And because actual war life starts only with the outbreak of war, so for us the actual war begins only now. We are now at the place that the Lord has shown us and among the people whom our is aimed at. Now it is necessary to prove ourselves as Jesus Christ's loyal fighters, as nobody will be crowned unless he fights well. And that is what we would like, fight well and not beat the air, as beating the air tires only, but achieves nothing other than that it holds the fighter up to ridicule in front of the enemy. Now we surely know our weapons and also know how we must use them, if only we had the weapon carrier of the language under our control. And it is often very difficult to get the right word for an object, a term or a movement. One can often spend hours pondering over//gathering a word and does not find it in the end. At first we received a number of words from Mr Gassen (?) [Police Trooper Samuel Gason] in Lake Hope and later we have collected as much as we could, and seek, little by little, to always progress. One must first acquaint oneself with their body of thought// world of thoughts//way of thinking.]

Language learning was a way of unlocking the 'heathen' mind so that Christ's message could find fertile ground. The study of Aboriginal religion—and Indigenous thought in general—was to service conversion.

The great Lutheran theorist Warneck, in *Missionsmotiv und Missionsaufgabe nach der modernen religionsgeschichtlichen Schule* (*The Missionary Motive and Missionary Commission According to the Modern School of the History of Religion*; 1907, cited in Veit n.d.), provided instructions for a theoretical

---

17   Schreiben des Missionar Gößling an das Missions-Comité, 15 April 1867, Kirchen und Missionsblatt, p. 49.

comparison of religions, together with a practical apology of Christianity. He proposed that both were required of Lutheran missionaries and both should be taught as part of training. He wrote:

> It is not sufficient that the missionary knows Christianity, he also needs to know deeply the Heathen religions which he has been sent to overcome. Before he can confront that religion in discussion, sermon, teaching and literary work, he must have earlier fought the internal context [of the relativity of religions] in his own mind. That demands study. Objects of these studies must be 1) the sacred documents including the most important religious literature which the respective religions possess; 2) the religious traditions where religious sources do not exist; and 3) the religious life and activities as they come presently before our eyes: the religious practices as they can be known from the forms of cults, customs, organisations, sacrifices, prayers, sorceries and, particularly, from their morals. (Warneck 1907, quoted in Veit n.d.: 11–12)

Although written at the end of Reuther's tenure and long after his seminary training, this seems an apt summation of his interests and passions—including the collection of what we perceive today as ethnographic details—for the purpose of overcoming heathen belief. Both the knowing and the overcoming—the documenting and the dismissal—were integral to Reuther's vision of an essentially religious, not anthropological, task:

> Feeling my way into the mental world of these people I searched through their legends and the god-and-spirit world of heathendom in an attempt to discover points of contact with the Christian faith, and thereby to destroy their pagan concepts. Indeed, it cost me much time and labour to become a Dieri to my Dieri people, for in my opinion a missionary without a thorough knowledge of the language and customs of his people is, in the best instance, like a clock that works but has no hands. (Reuther, quoted in Scherer 1979: 14)

Warneck, in *Evangelische Missionslehre: Ein missiontheorestischer Versuch* (*Evangelical Doctrine: From the perspective of theory*; 1897), emphasised the learning of local languages as the means of spreading the word of God (hence the—tautological—need to make the Gospel available in Indigenous languages):

> He maintained that since there were no peoples in the world who were speechless, there could also be no people who were without religion. This was evident in the fact that the gospel could be preached in all languages and all languages were capable of Bible translation. (Kenny 2009: 101–2)

Kenny (2009: 102) says that it is *not* clear that Strehlow was explicitly taught Warneck's principles on language and religion, but follows Veit by suggesting that it is 'reasonable to assume' a familiarity with these ideas, pointing to the presence of Warneck's pamphlets in the seminary's library (p. 103). This would apply equally to Strehlow's fellow seminarian, Reuther. We do not deny that these ideas were 'in the air', most especially at Neuendettelsau in the late nineteenth century. We do not doubt that they infiltrated Reuther's thought and led to his profound attention to language. But we have found little evidence that this was a theoretical interest per se. While it may represent a missiological 'anthropology' in the broadest sense, it is not an anthropology in the twentieth-century disciplinary sense (of a secular, descriptive or analytic science à la Radcliffe-Brown or Malinowski).

Reuther's was not ethnography in the style of a later age. In his diary entry for 11 March 1891, he wrote:

> I was field-preacher in the camp near the station. Thou crucified One open their hearts, that Your anxiety and pain not be in vain for them. O Lord of the harvest see that many are not lost. Open Thou their hearts that they may take heed of Thy word. (Reuther 1970)

The following day (12 March), he recorded: 'I was in the camp again this evening with the heathen to put the word of God close to their heart' (Reuther 1970).

Two days later (on 14 March), he witnessed preparations for an 'Emu' ceremony (probably *Mindiri*) at Lake Allalana:

> On Saturday afternoon I went to Ngalangalani on foot with Joseph [Ngantjalina] to preach the word of God to the natives camping there … On Sunday morning I first had a devotion with those [natives] who had been on the station before and then I visited the shearers who were just ready to make [the ceremony/*wima* of] Warukati [Emu]. I gathered them and then gave an address on the love of Christ who seeks us and also them. During my talk there was one continually knocking, so that the Emu-making does not stop. Soon three men were sent away, dressed up, so that they could return as Emus. O poor people. God give me the strength of the Holy Spirit to follow these people in all humility and faithfulness. May he also bring the Holy Spirit's reign in His time into the hearts of these poor heathen. (Reuther 1970)

Throughout Reuther's diary and other records, there is little evidence of his engagement with the everyday life of Dieri people and he seems rarely to have left the station itself. The above are among the few comments he makes about such excursions. It seems that he left such contact to the Dieri evangelist Joseph Ngantjalina, and (after 1894) specifically to Otto Siebert as 'bush missionary'. It seems from these entries that, in the face of an actual ceremony, Reuther proselytises to the participants and then prayed for his own strength and faith to survive the strain and weariness of his task of overcoming heathenism.

Later years

Reuther laboured at Killalpaninna for 18 years. The early years of a new century had been fraught with financial difficulties and a declining Aboriginal population. Stevens (1994: 158 ff.) sets out in detail the disappointments and outright conflicts of Reuther's final year.

When Reuther left Killalpaninna in 1906 he acquired a lease of land from the South Australian Government. About 160 hectares was excised from the Dutton family property, Anlaby, to the west of Eudunda. The Reuther family called their farm 'Gumvale'. It was close to the Lutheran Church at Julia (Rechner 2008: 259, see also p. 235). From here, Reuther served the Point Pass congregation as secretary, treasurer and organist (Scherer 1979: 15). The homestead was a former boundary rider's hut.[18] Reuther still had to make a living (which he did from wheat and sheep) and support his sons' education back at Neuendettelsau. He spent his entire life enveloped by Lutheranism and its close-knit community. For all his insight into a Dieri view of the land, its cosmogony and its sung manifestation, Reuther never abandoned the faith and pity that had been rung in by the Christmas bells of Nürnberg.

---

18 *Kapunda Herald*, 14 December 1906: 2.

Plate 4.6 J. G. and Pauline Reuther with two Stolz sons, five Reuther sons and only daughter, Alma. Laura Reuther is sitting in the foreground.

Source: Rechner (2008: 235).

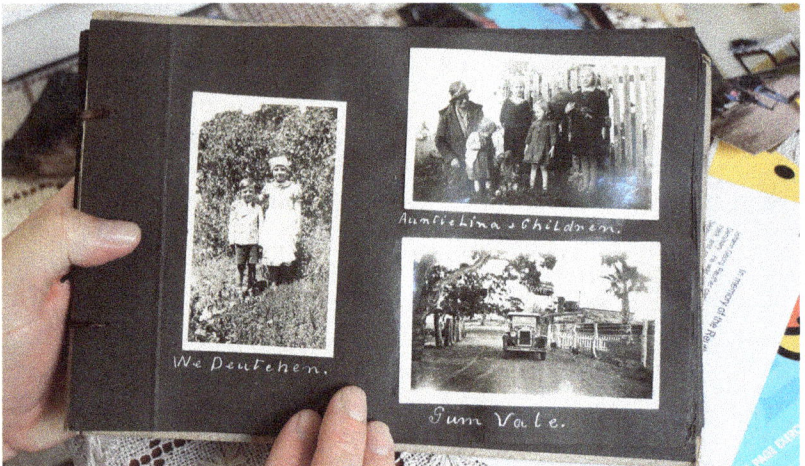

Plate 4.7 Reuther family album from Gumvale, in the possession of Alma's only daughter, Helen Gordon.

Source: Deane Fergie, May 2015.

Death by drowning

Reuther's death was as extraordinary as his working life. With a passenger, Reuther was riding in a trap to Hampden Siding to meet his son Martin, who was coming home from Queensland for his parents' silver wedding anniversary. At the Freshwater Ford, the passenger—a Mr Richards with whom Reuther was sharecropping—got out to test the strength of the stream and, as it was fine, they rode on. At the next crossing of Julia Creek, Mr Richards found the water to be up to his chest. He returned to Reuther in the trap and they proceeded. Witnesses suggested that either the horse was taken from its feet or they entered the Julia not quite at the ford. A flash flood had come downstream and the water in the middle was over the hooded trap. The horse fell and the trap was overthrown. It appears Reuther was kicked in the head by the flailing horse. His body was found 16 kilometres downstream.[19] The planned anniversary celebration turned into a wake.

Following J. G. Reuther's death in 1914:

> the home and wheat farm was managed by mother Pauline with help from … Oscar, and assistance from Alma and a part Aboriginal girl, Laura, who was always considered part of the family. (Rechner 2008: 267)

Laura Reuther was the daughter of Reuther's Aboriginal housekeeper, Frieda, over whom so much gossip, innuendo and inquiry had taken place in Reuther's final year at Killalpaninna (Stevens 1994: 160). It was rumoured that she was Reuther's child, a point dismissed by Reuther at the time and his descendants today (some of whom knew and lived with Laura well into the twentieth century). Even if she was not his child, Reuther had been chastised by Kaibel, chair of the Mission Committee, for spending too much time in his study and neglecting the moral shepherding of even his own staff: 'you are not leaving your own cell and don't know what is going on at the station. You cannot condone such depravity'.[20]

And, again, in early 1906:

> This has gone too far … In your extensive work that you wish to bring to print … you have not been driven to further God's word, but to a large extent by your ambition. This immorality has to go to your account.[21]

---

19 See: The Julia Creek fatality, *The Advertiser*, [Adelaide], 3 March 1914: 10.
20 Kaibel, letter to Reuther, 7 December 1905, quoted in Stevens (1994: 160).
21 Kaibel, letter to Reuther, 1906, in Stevens (1994: 160).

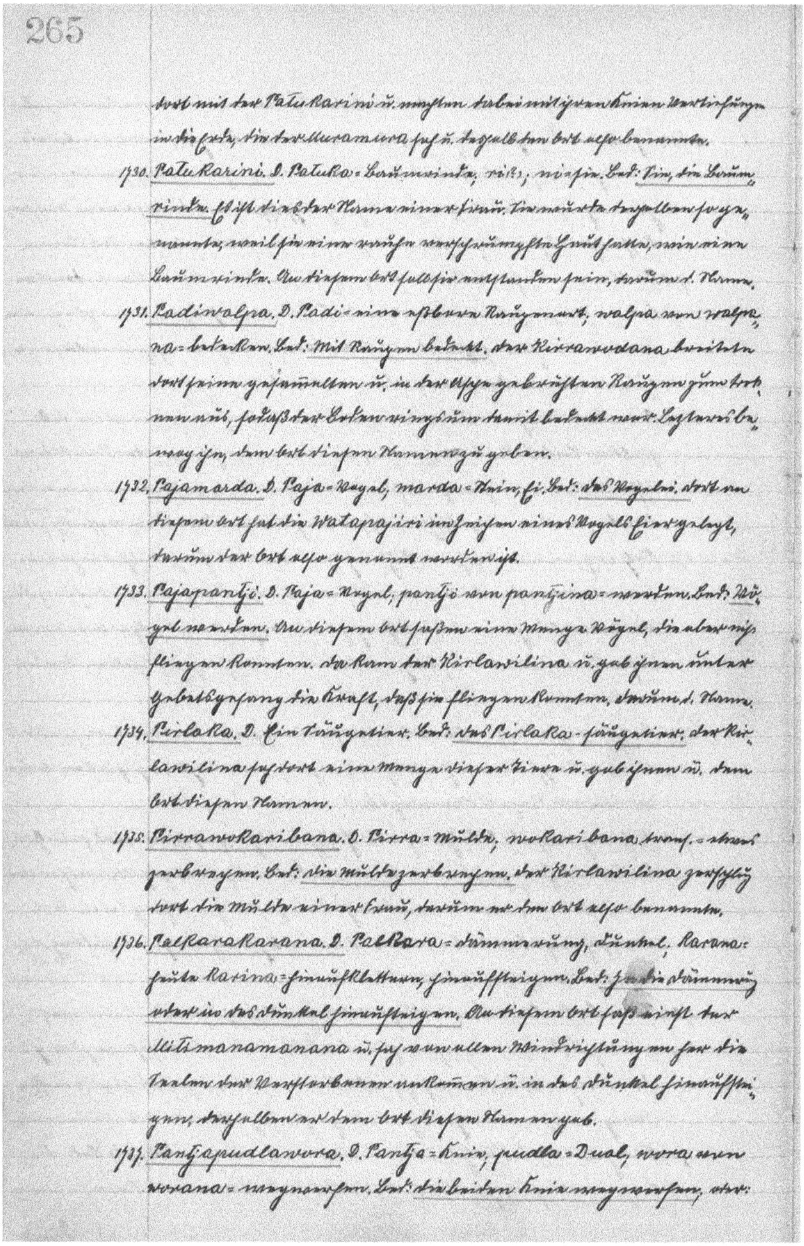

Plate 4.8 Page 265 of Reuther's manuscript of volume 7 titled 'Ortsnamen der Eingeborenen Australiens' ('Placenames of Aboriginal Australians'), 1905. It contains 2,468 placenames.

Source: South Australian Museum, Adelaide, AA-9-7, p. 265.

Here, Reuther's sheltering the all too human results of moral impropriety and his ethnographic collecting were conflated to condemn his anthropological work, and had precipitated his retreat from Killalpaninna to a Lutheran enclave on the edge of the Barossa Valley. Laura looked after Pauline Reuther until the latter's death in 1937. She is one of several Dieri descendants (women in particular) who were absorbed into Lutheran families and essentially 'lost' to the Dieri community today. Carl Oscar ('Os') Reuther sold Gumvale during World War II.

Pauline and J. G. Reuther are buried together in the cemetery alongside the former Lutheran church at Julia, South Australia, close to their Gumvale property.

Pulcaracuranie

Here we examine a process by which Reuther's collection of placenames (and their mapping by Henry Hillier)[22] has come to inform contemporary Dieri relations to country. We focus on a place, Pulcaracuranie, which marked an *axis mundi* in the Dieri cosmos, a place to which souls of the dead would travel, drink and ascend to the sky as Muramura had done in the beginning. This place had featured in white exploration of the region, and had been documented by pivotal anthropologists such as Elkin, yet its location had been lost to Dieri descendants. Reuther's detailed records (and a *toa* sculpture depicting the place), together with a triangulation of historical sources, allowed for its relocation and a renewed ascription of meaning.

The placename 'Palkarakarani' is shown on Hillier's map[23] in association with the edge of the flood-out of Cooper Creek on the western side of the 'Pulcaracuranie Flat' of current topographic maps. Goyder's map, which pre-dates the Hillier map by nearly two decades and appears to be its basis, identifies Pulcaracuranie Flat in the same location; Hillier's 'Palkarakarani' is written against this same feature (albeit to the left, presumably to avoid the other placenames along Cooper Creek), suggesting that he and/or Reuther concurred with this location.

---

22 Harry James Hillier arrived at Killalpaninna in June 1892 and stayed for 12 years, becoming especially devoted to J. G. Reuther (Scherer 1966a: 305). He was a gifted draftsman and illustrated Reuther's botanical and ethnographic collections, as well as transferring the placenames to a large linen map.
23 For a detailed account of the map, see Jones (2002).

Plate 4.9 A portion of Goyder's *Official Atlas of South Australia* … Sheet 5 (1885) overlaid with a portion of Hillier's map (c. 1904) of Reuther placenames (in red) showing a 'native well' at the northern end of Pulcaracuranie Flat.

Source: Compiled by Rod Lucas.

There are acknowledged difficulties in using the Hillier map of Reuther's names to identify places on the ground. In particular, it is often difficult to locate precisely what is being named on Hillier's map itself. As Hercus and Potezny (1991: 148) note:

> [S]ince there is no dot to show the precise point, we cannot know whether the place is to be found near the centre, near the beginning, or at the end of the written name.

This makes the precise location of placenames almost impossible to determine without extra information such as Reuther's accompanying descriptions, correlations with other maps, Aboriginal knowledge, field observations, archival references and so on (see Jones 2002: 194).

Neither Reuther nor Hillier is known to have travelled to this part of Cooper Creek and they are unlikely to have had any precise knowledge of the location of 'Palkarakarana' on the ground. Nor does Reuther record any specific physical or topographical features that might distinguish his 'Palkarakarana' or 'Palkarakarani'.

Plate 4.10 Pulcaracuranie, view north-west. The yellow sand dune at back left is likely the one climbed by the explorer John McKinlay in 1861 during his search for Burke and Wills.
Source: Rod Lucas, 2004.

On Wednesday, 27 November 1861, explorer John McKinlay wrote of travelling to:

> Pal-coor-a-ganny. At present this is the dry bed of a small lake with plenty of dry clover and grasses in the dry bed. On the north-east side of the lake is a well dug by the natives about ten to eleven feet deep with about one foot of water at present in it and good. I suppose a considerable quantity could be had if the hole were enlarged. Close by there was an encampment of blacks, in all about a dozen, not the same apparent well-fed fellows that frequent the lakes and main creeks. From inquiry it appears that during the dry season this is the sort of water they have to depend upon, and I think the wells are few and far between. A high sandhill was some little distance off and to it I went; from the top of which I had an extensive view. Could see nothing northward and westward but a jumble of lower sandhills looking very dreary without even a creek with its timber to break the monotony of the view.[24]

Field inspections confirm the accuracy of McKinlay's 1861 description of a small lake covered in dry clover and grasses; there is a conspicuous high sand dune to the north-west (reminiscent of the one McKinlay climbed and positioned to see the topographic features he described) and an Aboriginal camp to the north-east (evidenced today by a range of archaeological materials including stone artefacts, scarred trees, hearths and human burials).

Dieri people visited the Pulcaracuranie area within the Dieri #1 native title claim area for Work Area Clearance (WAC) surveys in November 2003 and again in November–December 2004. A further survey of this

---

24 *Diary of Mr. J. McKinlay*, South Australian Parliamentary Paper, No. 12, 1862, p. 10.

area was undertaken in August 2006 in respect of proposed petroleum wells on the edges of Pulcaracuranie Flat. In that context, the historical and anthropological records relating to the area became relevant to decision-making about the protection of Aboriginal heritage in the area. Reuther's mythological data, his placename record and the Hillier map became central to this assessment. Further Dieri WAC teams visited the area again in November and December 2006.

A distinctive form of vegetation on the north-eastern edge of the dry lake is indicative of a source of water where none is obvious—something that early pastoralists also seemingly took advantage of with the construction of a water 'whim' or 'race' on this same north-east corner. Dieri representatives identified sedges, a type of 'couch' grass and *Trichodesma zeylanicum* (water bush)—all found at this location—as growing only where there is water. Dieri have thus viewed this vegetation as suggesting the location of a former 'native well'.

Plates 4.11a–c Artefacts at the Pulcaracuranie campsite, including grinding stones and worked glass.

Source: Photographs by Deane Fergie, Andrew Nettlefold and Jan Scott, December 2006.

The associated campsite area is extensive, contains an array of artefacts (stone tools, grinding stones, hearths, skeletal remains) and extends from pre-settlement into settlement times (as evidenced by the presence of worked glass) (see Plates 4.11a–c).

Reuther's extensive manuscripts contain various references to Pulcaracuranie. Here we re-present just a few, which are also indicative of the cultural richness to be found throughout his corpus:

Reuther place name material[25]

No. 1736 Palkarakarana, D[ieri] Palkara = 'twilight, dawn, dusk; darkness'; karana—(nowadays karina) = 'to climb upwards; to ascend.' Meaning: 'to ascend in the twilight or darkness'

Once, as he was camped at this spot, Mit[j]imanamanana saw the souls of the departed arriving from all points of the compass, and ascending upwards in the darkness. He therefore gave the place this name.

Reuther dictionary entry[26]

1520. Mura (n, m) = 'the deity'

(16) … The soul ascends in Palkarakarani, where the souls ('heart of the deity') of the muramuras once ascended. At the grave the soul's ceremonial song is sung to it, so that it may accompany it [on its last journey].

1522. muramura (n, m & f) … The souls of the deceased muramuras rose heavenward at Palkarakarani, and [today] many of them shine resplendently in the vault of heaven as stars in the constellations. Even the sun and moon are the souls of one-time muramuras.

Other 'Dictionary' entries include:

1634. mungara (n, m) = 'the soul.'[27]

I. Murangara as heart of the deity. With this meaning the legend is in agreement. In the beginning there lived on earth only the muramuras, that is, the demi-gods, the progenitors, the primeval ancestors. These were mortal human beings, but were brought into existence by the Mura 'deity'.

---

25 Reuther's volume 7 (SAM AA266/09/7); Scherer's translation, volume VII.
26 Reuther's volume 3 (SAM AA266/09/3); Scherer's translation, volume IIIA.
27 Reuther's volume 3 (SAM AA266/09/3); Scherer's translation, volume III.

While Kakalbuna was [once] sitting at Palkarakarani—he was a muramura—he saw the souls of the muramuras who had just recently died winding their way upwards from this place; whereupon he remarked: '"Those are muramura-ngaras ("the hearts of the tribal ancestors").' From here the term mungara takes its origin.

Scherer Vol 2

813. mungara (n, m) = 'soul'

2) nauja mungara ngakani, nauja ngani mungara narini puntila nganai ja Palkarakarini palkarakarala nganai = he soul mine, he I soul in death go away will (leave) and in Palkarakara upwards ascend will, i.e. 'this is my soul; [when my soul departs in death] I will make my upward ascent in Palkarakarani'

Shortly prior to death the soul, since it cannot endure physical pain leaves the body and wanders southward. For this reason all 'native' people are buried with the head facing south. Without the soul, the body may still live on for some time, but [eventually] it must die.

Soon after the body is dead, it is buried. The soul turns around to watch its body being buried, and when it sees the latter being carried to the grave on the head [of two people], it says to itself: ngakani palkuni kawalka mapateriji = 'the crows are gathering around my body'.

The soul now turns towards Palkarakarani, where it ascends upward.

There are other references to Pulcaracuranie in Reuther's manuscripts. In Volume 11, for example, Reuther recorded the following in the context of discussing illness:

The fact is, it was here that the muramura Balungopina saw the souls of the various muramura winding their way, in spiral fashion, upward on something in the twilight. [Just] as the souls of the muramura wended their way upward here at Palkarakarani, so, it is believed, all the souls of men will go that way ...

Already while he is sick, the Aboriginal [man] frequently arranges for his ceremonial mura-songs to be sung to him. Thereby he consoles himself in his suffering. With the same ceremonial mura-songs [his] soul is accompanied to Palkarakarani.[28]

---

28   Reuther's volume 11 (SAM AA266/09/11); Scherer's translation, volume XI.

Finally, in his volume on *toa*s, Reuther notes that 'Palkarakarani' was a place of paramount importance to traditional Aboriginal people. The passage of souls between earth and sky was represented in a *toa* sculpture that depicts these two fundamental dimensions of the Dieri universe and their connection at the place called 'Palkarakarani' (*toa* number 145 in the catalogue by Jones and Sutton 1986: 99; Reuther #190):

> Toa 190 (630) Palkarakarani
>
> Meaning: 'to ascend in the dark.'
>
> With respect to the religion of the Aborigines, this is the most important place [of all], and so we must go into the matter a little more closely.
>
> Palkara signifies 'twilight, dusk;' ngalpura = 'dark' [or darkness], and paratji = 'light.' Palkara is the light of dusk [or the gloaming], and karani from karana means to climb up on something, e.g. on to a tree,—but not to fly up or lift oneself up without some [visible] means. The word therefore signifies: 'to climb up on to something in the twilight.' This much the Aborigine does know: that here the souls of the dead from all points of the compass wend their way ('climb') upwards.
>
> Here the muramura Milkimadlentji (meaning 'evil eye') and Mitjimanamana saw, in their mind's eye, the souls of the dead climbing upwards …
>
> The white [section] at the lower end of the toa indicates the earth, and the recessed [portion] the atmospheric region between earth and heaven. The upper white [section] denotes the heavens which surround us. The [white] vertical lines are the souls of the dead, as they climb upwards.
>
> The dots above the upper white [section] are the stars. Beyond the stars the local pagan knows of no [further] space. For him, the stars are the souls of the dead, the most pre-eminent of these being those of the muramuras, as he tries to explain this in [the case of] the constellations.
>
> The toa intends to say: 'We have gone to the place where the souls of the dead climb upwards [in the dark].'[29]

---

29   Reuther, The Diari, vol. XII, 1976–77: 100–1 [SAM AA266]; see also vol. XIII, 1976: 92.

Plate 4.12 Pulcaracuranie (Palkarakarani) *toa*.
Source: Jones and Sutton (1986: 99).

Reuther's material includes a number of placenames—Palkarakara, Palkaratarana, Palkarakarana, Palkarakarani—which could be said to confuse any issue of location. The last two forms, however, are the most common and Reuther himself accounts for their correlation on linguistic grounds. Similarly, there are a number of *muramura* associated with the mythology recorded by Reuther: Balungopina,[30] Mitjimanamanana,[31] Kakalbuna[32] and Milkimadlentji.[33] These multiple associations (or the relationship between these *muramura*) are uncommented on and unexplained by Reuther.

Verifying the location of Pulcaracuranie on the ground is, however, made easier by a number of other records, including McKinlay's diary and other ethnographic materials recorded by Otto Siebert.

In a collection of 'legends and customs' published in German in 1910, missionary Siebert[34] noted the following in respect of the three Dieri souls, *kutchi, mungara* and *jaola*:

> Of the mungara, the Dieri say that it may go after death southward, but there it continually wanders around in order to see how they bear the corpse to the grave. Jaola is the personal ghost. The jaola goes after death first of all to Palankarani, a place not far from Lake Hope where the ground is much cracked and full of holes; from that place, it goes to heaven, Pariwilpa, and is seen as a shooting star.
>
> 'Woe! Who has died?' they say if a shooting star is seen.

Siebert refers to 'Palankarani' as a place where the ground is cracked, broken up or full of holes. Reuther's material does not include such a topographical association. But this is an apt description of parts of the Pulcaracuranie Flat where the occasional floods have left deep 'crab-holes'. These are physically distinctive and quite unlike the 'crab-holes' of Bulpanie to the south, for example.

---

30   Reuther's volume 11 (SAM AA266/09/11); Scherer's translation, volume XI.
31   Reuther's volume 7 (SAM AA266/09/7) and volume 13 (SAM AA266/09/13); Scherer's translation, volume VIIB and volume 13.
32   Reuther's volume 3 (SAM AA266/09/3); Scherer's translation, volume IIIA, word #1634.
33   Reuther's volume 12 (SAM AA266/09/12); Scherer's translation, volume XII.
34   Siebert is acknowledged to have been dedicated to the collection of information from Aboriginal people associated with the mission—so much so that he was reprimanded by the Mission Committee for his ethnographic work in collaboration with Howitt. Siebert, Letter to Howitt, 27 February 1900, Howitt Papers, Box 3, Folder 1, State Library of Victoria, Melbourne.

Others have collected material about Pulcaracuranie, including A. P. Elkin, who conducted fieldwork throughout north-east South Australia in 1930. He later published an article summarising traditional beliefs and practices connected with death throughout South Australia, based on his own and others' work. This article refers to 'Bälkärakärinyi' or 'Palankarani' as a place associated with those beliefs. Referring to processes of inquest following a death among the tribes of north-eastern South Australia, Elkin wrote:

> [T]he corpse ... is placed across the men's heads. One of the old men then takes two lighted sticks, from fifteen inches to three feet in length, called the kunya, and amidst complete silence calls out the name of the place whither the dead person is going, apparently for the purpose of calling his attention to the inquest rite. The words as given me are: Gäla gala gala gala (wake him, or let him know), Bälkärakärinyi (the place), mili waruka (travelling in the air), napa (water), tapari (drink). This Bälkärakärinyi seems to be a spring out west where the spirit has its last drink on its way to the home of the dead. (Elkin 1937: 281)

Conclusions

A crossreferencing of various historical data on placenames, mythology and geography suggests that the Pulcaracuranie area was a particularly important place in Dieri religion. This importance was reflected in songs and stories relating to the *muramura*, the ancestral beings who created the landscape and shaped much of traditional Aboriginal social life. Correlating the sources on mythology with present-day topography suggests that the Pulcaracuranie area was seen as a passageway between the everyday world in which people lived on the land and a sky world where people's souls were believed to have lived for a time after death.

Triangulating Reuther's mythological materials, McKinlay's geographic description and field observations provides extremely strong evidence that the 'Pulcaracuranie' area—encompassing the Pulcaracuranie Well and Pulcaracuranie Flat of current topographic maps—was a place of paramount significance within Dieri traditions, it being an *axis mundi* connecting the realms of sky and earth; in effect, a central pillar or pathway of the Dieri cosmos via which human souls were believed to travel between distinct realms of existence. Through this work, some of the difficulties and uncertainties of locating mythology in a particular place can be reduced.

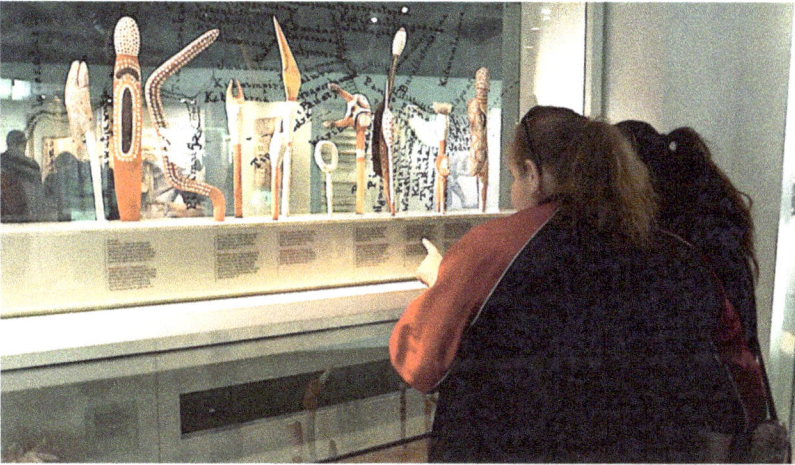

Plate 4.13 Dieri women Melanie Warren and her daughter Jaima Warren viewing *toas* in the South Australian Museum.
Source: Deane Fergie, 23 July 2014.

But, more importantly, using these materials has allowed contemporary Dieri people to protect important sites and to reconnect with country in ways they have not been able to for several generations. In the process, they are able to use all the materials available to them—from oral history to archival records—to reinscribe the country with meaning.

Plate 4.14 Carl Strehlow's farewell from Killalpaninna.
Source: Lutheran Archives.

Dieri representatives travelled to Canberra in October 2014 to view a range of material culture items and human skeletal remains from their country held in the National Museum of Australia. They talked with museum staff about repatriating the latter. Dieri man Willie Dawson said after viewing these holdings:

> We don't know the exact location [from which the human remains came], but I know a location where all the spirits go to at the end of the day— so long as they are back on country that is the best thing for them.[35]

There is talk of returning these human remains to Pulcaracuranie.

References

Austin, P. 1981. *A Grammar of Diyari, South Australia.* Cambridge: Cambridge University Press.

Austin, P. 1986. Diyari language postcards and Diyari literacy. *Aboriginal History* 10(2): 175–92.

Austin, P. 2015. And still they speak Diyari: The life history of an endangered language. *Ethnorema* 10: 1–17. Available from: www. academia.edu/10050989/And_still_they_speak_Diyari_the_life_ history_of_an_endangered_language, or: eprints.soas.ac.uk/20134/1/ 03%20Austin.pdf.

Elkin, A. P. 1937. Beliefs and practices connected with death in north-eastern and western South Australia. *Oceania* 7(3): 275–99. doi.org/ 10.1002/j.1834-4461.1937.tb00384.x.

Flierl, J. 1880. Christianieli Ngujangujara-Pepa Dieri Jaurani. Adelaide.

Hercus, L. and Potezny, V. 1991. Locating Aboriginal sites: A note on J. G. Reuther and the Hillier map of 1904. *Records of the South Australian Museum* 24(2): 139–51.

---

35   Willie Dawson, personal communication.

Jones, P. 2002. Naming the dead heart: Hillier's map and Reuther's gazetteer of 2,468 placenames in north-eastern South Australia. In *The Land is a Map: Placenames of Indigenous origin in Australia*, (eds) L. Hercus, F. Hodges and J. Simpson, pp. 187–200. Canberra: Pandanus Books.

Jones, P. and Sutton, P. 1986. *Art and Land: Aboriginal sculptures of the Lake Eyre region*. Adelaide: South Australian Museum in association with Wakefield Press.

Kenny, A. 2009. Carl Strehlow's mission. In *Migration and Cultural Contact: Germany and Australia*, (eds) A. Brandauer and M. Veber, pp. 91–112. Sydney: University of Sydney Press.

Kenny, A. 2017. *A preliminary assessment of J. G. Reuther's ethnographic work (1899–1908)*. LocuSAR report, Adelaide.

Koch, W. and Homann, E. 1870. Nujanujarajinkineixa–Dieri Jaura Jelaribala. Tanunda, SA: Lutheran Mission Committee.

Lucas, R. 1996. The failure of anthropology. *Journal of Australian Studies* 48: 40–51. doi.org/10.1080/14443059609387265.

McKinlay, J. 1962 [1862]. *McKinlay's Journal of Exploration in the Interior of Australia*. Melbourne: F. F. Bailliere. [Reprint of *Diary of Mr J. McKinlay, Leader of the Burke Relief Expedition, being Journal of Explorations in the Interior of Australia, together with Chart, South Australia*, Parliamentary Paper No. 12, 1862. Australiana Facsimile Editions No. 1. Adelaide: Public Library of South Australia.]

Peters, P. W. n.d. The fruits of Luther's mission-mindedness. Wisconsin Lutheran Seminary, Mequon, WI.

Proeve, H. F. W. 1976. Rechner, Gustav Julius (1830–1900). *Australian Dictionary of Biography*. Canberra: National Centre of Biography, The Australian National University. Available from: adb.anu.edu.au/biography/rechner-gustav-julius-4456/text7261. Published first in hardcopy 1976. Accessed online 10 June 2015.

Proeve, H. F. W. and Proeve, E. H. 1952. *A Work of Love and Sacrifice: The story of the mission among the Dieri tribe at Cooper's Creek*. Point Pass, SA: E. H. Proeve.

Rechner, J. G. 2008. *G. J. Rechner and His Descendants: Rechner, Fischer/ Fisher, Stolz and Reuther journeys.* Adelaide: Self-published.

Reuther, J. G. 1899–1908. Volumes 1–13. SAM AA266/09/1-13, South Australian Museum, Adelaide.

Reuther, J. G. 1970. Diary of J. G. Reuther 1888–1914. Translated by R. B. Reuther. Unpublished ms.

Reuther, J. G. 1981. *The Diari.* Translated by P. A. Scherer. Microfiche No. 2, Australian Institute of Aboriginal Studies, Canberra.

Reuther, J. G. and Strehlow, C. [translators]. 1897. *Testamenta Marra: Jesuni Christuni ngantjani jaura ninaia karitjimalkana wonti Dieri jaurani.* Tanunda, SA: G. Auricht.

Scherer, P. A. 1966a. Looking back on a hundred years of Bethesda mission. *Lutheran Herald*, 8 October: 291, 304–5.

Scherer, P. A. 1966b. Looking back on a hundred years of Bethesda mission. *Lutheran Herald*, 22 October: 314–15, 317.

Scherer, P. A. 1979. Donor of Aboriginal heritage. *The Lutheran* 13(12): 12–15.

Schoknecht, A. C. and Schoknecht, C. P. (compilers) 1997. *Missionary Carl Schoknecht, Killalpaninna Mission 1871–1873: Selected Correspondence.* Melbourne: Self-published.

Siebert, O. 1910. Sagen und Sitten der Dieri und Nachbarstamme in Zentral-Australien. *Globus* 97(4): 44–50; 53–9. [English translation held in the Archives of the South Australian Museum, Adelaide.]

Stevens, C. 1994. *White Man's Dreaming: Killalpaninna mission 1866– 1915.* Melbourne: Oxford University Press.

Strehlow, C. 1907–1920. *Die Aranda- und Loritja-Stämme in Zentral-Australien.* 7 vols. Frankfurt am Main: Joseph Baer & Co.

Valleskey, D. J. [1993]. Luther's impact on mission work. Wisconsin Lutheran Seminary, Mequon, WI. Available from: www.wlsessays.net/ bitstream/handle/123456789/1327/ValleskeyLuther.pdf?sequence= 1&isAllowed=y. Accessed 29 April 2015.

Veit, W. F. n.d. Labourers in the vineyard or the uneducated missionary: Aspects of the non-theological education of missionaries. Unpublished ms.

Warneck, G. 1897. *Evangelische Missionslehre*. 3 vols. Gotha: Friedrich Andreas Berthes.

Appendix 4.1: The titles of J. G. Reuther's 13 volumes

Reuther, J. G. 1904–06. Wörterbuch. Vols 1–4. SAM AA266/09/1–4. South Australian Museum, Adelaide.

Reuther, J. G. 1899–1904. Diari Gramatik, Wörterverzeichnis, Taufordnung etc., Wankaguru-Sprache, Wörterverzeichnis Wonkanguru, Iuyani Nganmeni, Tirari, Wunkarabana-Jaurawurka-Jendruwonta-Wonkaranta, Jandruwonta Sprache. Vol. 5. SAM AA266/09/5. South Australian Museum, Adelaide.

Reuther, J. G. n.d. Vol. 6. SAM AA266/09/6. South Australian Museum, Adelaide.

Reuther, J. G. 1905. Ortsnamen der Eingeborenen Australiens. Vol. 7. SAM AA266/09/7. South Australian Museum, Adelaide.

Reuther, J. G. n.d. Bedeutung und Herkunft von Namen der Eingeborenen Australiens. Vols 8 and 9. SAM AA266/09/8-9. South Australian Museum, Adelaide.

Reuther, J. G. n.d. Die Entstehung der Mardu. Vol. 10. SAM AA266/09/10. South Australian Museum, Adelaide.

Reuther, J. G. 1907–08. Von der Götter- und Geisterwelt der Eingeborenen Australiens, Bezeichnung der Toa. Vol. 11. SAM AA266/09/11. South Australian Museum, Adelaide.

Reuther, J. G. 1905. Museum und Toas. Vol. 12. SAM AA266/09/12. South Australian Museum, Adelaide.

Reuther, J. G. n.d. Bedeutung der Toa. Vol. 13. SAM AA266/09/13. South Australian Museum, Adelaide.

5

Looking at some details of Reuther's work

Luise Hercus

The surviving work of J. G. Reuther fills 13 volumes and is an easy target for comments about Germans' meticulous attention to detail (see Lucas and Deane, Chapter 4, this volume, for details). A single word in Reuther's 4,035-word Diyari dictionary may have well over 30, and in a few cases even over 60, illustrative sentences. These sentences are important not only for their anthropological content, but also linguistically: they contain special idioms and turns of phrase that are characteristic for a whole area. The richness of detail is characteristic of his massive work, compiled at the Lutheran mission at Killalpaninna.

I focus here mainly on matters of detail in Reuther's comparative wordlists[1] in volume V and in his volume VII on placenames, using individual entries to illustrate general points. There is a bit of 'devil' in the detail: there are many difficulties of interpretation. I will show how evidence gathered in the 1960s and 1970s from speakers of the nearby languages—particularly Arabana/Wangkangurru, Yaluyandi and Kuyani—may help to solve some of these difficulties.

---

1   Information on Diyari is largely from Austin (1981); on Yandruwandha from Breen (2004a, 2004b); and data on adjacent languages is from Hercus (1994) and from other publications and fieldwork by the author.

Background

The mission at Killalpaninna in Diyari country was a long way from any major centre of white population, and could only be reached via the Birdsville Track. Travelling there in the latter part of the nineteenth century and in the first decades of the twentieth century was still a major undertaking. Killalpaninna was a centre for Diyari people but also a refuge for people of many other groups. Despite its isolation, it was once a vibrant place with Aboriginal people coming and going. It had a school and a church and a supply of food; there were rations and the daily bread was baked there (Jones and Sutton 1986: 35).

The people from neighbouring groups who had come there were the ones involved with the wordlists of seven Aboriginal languages: Wonkarabana, Jauraworka to English, Wonkanguru, Kuyani to English, Ngameni, Tirari to English and Jendruwanta to English. In modern spelling, these language names are Arabana, Yawarrawarrka, Wangkangurru, Kuyani, Ngamini, Thirrari and Yandruwandha. These wordlists are single glosses and have no illustrative sentences. They figure as four lists in the English translation by P. A. Scherer from the original German.[2]

In addition, there was some information from groups of people from:

- Pilardapa (Reuther's Pillatapa) from the nearby Blanchwater area: their language was very close to Diyari (Austin 1981).
- Yaluyandi (Reuther's Jeluyanti) from the Diamantina to the north of the Ngamini.
- Wangkamadla (Reuther's Wongamarla) from west of Bedourie in far western Queensland.
- Karangura adjacent to Yaluyandi: this was always a small group and just a couple of people from there are known to have gone to Killalpaninna.

So, including Diyari and the seven groups who contributed to the comparative dictionaries, there were therefore 12 different groups of people speaking separate languages who had been resident at one time or another at Killalpaninna. We must be grateful to Reuther for continuing

---

2   Scherer's English translation of much of Reuther's work, including the wordlists, was made available on microfiche by the Australian Institute of Aboriginal Studies (Reuther 1981).

to work undaunted, and contributing to the knowledge of all of them. What is perhaps the most impressive part is that Reuther must have used the Diyari language in eliciting the information in all of his many volumes.

After the mission effectively closed in 1915, the place went into decline. By 1969, there was only one building left standing and now there is nothing except one European gravesite. There are no Diyari or any other Aboriginal people living permanently anywhere in the vicinity.

In its heyday, Killalpaninna—despite the harsh climate and spartan conditions—was an ideal place for language studies because of the diversity of speakers. Reuther was there for 18 years, so it is not surprising that the sheer quantity of his work is overwhelming, his 13 volumes covering every imaginable aspect of traditional life, as well as general topics that one might not expect, such as the *toa*s and lists of personal names. The placenames volume has 2,449 entries.

Reuther's huge work is unique, but it cannot be considered in isolation: Regina Ganter[3] has recently discovered at Neuendettelsau a notebook from Reuther's predecessor, Flierl, which contains brief vocabularies and some grammatical features from four languages—Diyari, Ngamini, Wangkangurru and Arabana. One can tell it is an early work because the writer is just coming to grips with the sound system of these languages and has missed hearing the initial *ng*, writing *ura* for *ngura* ('camp'), and *Aumini* for *Ngamini*.

There are too many similarities between Flierl's four-language vocabulary and Reuther's seven-language vocabulary for this to be coincidental— for instance, the word for 'valley' is translated in both sets of vocabularies by the Arabana and Wangkangurru speakers as *jikara*, which means 'swamp', and the words for 'alive' are given as translations for 'life'. Both Flierl's list and Reuther's original manuscripts have glosses in German. Flierl's vocabulary and grammatical lists must have given an initial incentive and served as a model for Reuther's work, confirming his adherence to the German missionary linguistic tradition.

---

3   Personal communication.

Reuther's achievement

It is difficult to comprehend how Reuther achieved this work. He had no typewriter, as they were only just coming into usage; no filing cards, just sheets of paper; no encouragement apart from the work of Flierl and the collaboration with his co-worker Carl Strehlow; and there was hostility from the synod to contend with.

Reuther was describing Diyari and the neighbouring languages as living and evolving, and he followed the German missionary model in paying attention to the intricacies and details. His situation differed from that of Strehlow, who was later with Arrernte and Luritja people as the population at Killalpaninna contained not only local Diyari, but also displaced people from other parts of the Lake Eyre Basin.

The initial concept of Reuther's work seems to have been that the Diyari dictionary was going to include comparative material from all those neighbouring languages. Even he found this huge vision impracticable and there are hardly any parallel sentences from these languages after the first volume of the Diyari dictionary. But Reuther did not abandon the wider view; he followed the unwritten German missionary rule of 'never give up', so he produced dictionaries with German glosses, with 1,744 entries for each of the seven languages listed above as well as Arabana, Yawarrawarrka, Wangkangurru, Kuyani, Ngamini, Thirrari and Yandruwandha, except that the first 127 entries of the Ngamini–Thirrari vocabulary have gone missing, and Yandruwandha has only 857 words.[4]

---

4   A combined electronic version of these lists with the call number 0379 was prepared by Peter Austin and Pia Herbert, and consolidated by David Nash. However, during the decommissioning and transfer of this database from the Aboriginal Studies Electronic Data Archive (ASEDA) (see aseda. aiatsis.gov.au/) to the Australian Institute of Aboriginal and Torres Strait Islander Studies (AIATSIS), it went missing. ASEDA can now be found under the Australian Indigenous Languages Collection (AILC) at the AIATSIS.

Reuther's volume V, the comparative vocabularies: Problems

The only way to proceed when one has only sheets of paper is to keep on collecting and simply adding new material even if there is some duplication or contradiction. With the profusion of information that Reuther encountered, there can be a few problems. Here is just one example to show how data from Wangkangurru can clarify contradictions.

There is a Wangkangurru fixed locution *milyki warru withirnda* ('his eyes turn white'; literally, 'eye white becomes he'), which is used on a number of occasions in mythological texts to describe an impressionable young man watching a ceremony when girls are dancing. It is roughly equivalent to the expression 'his eyes lit up'. Reuther's lists use this expression to translate 'fornicator among relation' (no. 670), when it really means 'just looking' and has nothing to do with kinship. However, further on at word number 1,022, 'fornicator' is translated into the appropriate 'swearwords' in the Aboriginal languages, except for Kuyani, which still has the innocent expression *mini ngarla* ('eyes big').

This example shows the effects of Reuther simply adding on to existing vocabulary, rather than crosschecking or correcting. The contradictions show the probity of his work and seem to confirm that Reuther never tampered with his information.

With the constant inflow of new information and probably little opportunity for looking back, all kinds of other mistranslations can slip through. There are a number of entries in the comparative vocabularies where some knowledge of Wangkangurru and the other languages tells us that the speakers have marginally misunderstood Reuther. He had the horrendous task of having to operate via Diyari rather than his native German, while at the same time keeping track of seven other Aboriginal languages. Examples are:

- Number 70, 'to brood': All the speakers gave him the word for 'to sunbathe', and three have even included the word for 'sun', which is listed just before, at number 69.
- Number 44, 'oppress': The words given by the speakers simply mean 'to put something down on the ground'.

- Numbers 528 and 639, 'to graze', 'to eat' (of animals): Reuther appears not to have been told by his advisers that the widespread verb *marka* used by them means 'to crawl' and that this is an extended meaning of the verb 'to crawl' in all the languages of the area—that is, 'to crawl along, eating'.

- Number 212: The gloss 'friend' is wrong; the words given by the speakers mean 'one's own', referring to a close relative rather than a classificatory one.

- There is also confusion introduced by the translator (Scherer) over word number 1,518, 'otter': All seven Aboriginal languages answer with the word for 'poisonous snake', and it seems that the German word 'otter' simply has not been translated, and we are dealing not with the English word 'otter', but with a German word for 'poisonous snake', as in the once much feared '*Kreuzotter*'.

The glosses often ignore lively metaphors, as in number 87, 'obey, be obedient', when the Aboriginal terms say 'ears awake'. Numbers 263 and 274 refer to 'moderate with food' and 'sober', respectively; however, all speakers say 'strong liver' for both items, except the Kuyani speaker, who says 'sorry, sad', probably conveying the thought that being stingy about food is miserable.

It can happen that some of the speakers have interpreted the question differently from the others, as in the case of number 71, 'thorn, sting': one has given the word for 'sting', two have given the word for 'sharp thorn' and two have given the word for 'sandhill cane-grass'. These are just a few examples of problems taken from near the beginning of the wordlists; there are many more of the same kind.

There are also interesting and unexpected items that are listed without adequate explanations, such as number 217, 'thoroughly healthy food'. The answers are equally unexpected: the overwhelming reply is 'raw'; two speakers even say 'live meat'. What the speakers are telling us is that they are missing fresh meat. There is a special expression for this elsewhere in Reuther's data and in Wangkangurru data: 'my mouth is getting hard from eating only vegetable food'. In Wangkangurru stories, old women are the ones who say this, complaining that their male relatives are not bringing them any meat.

There are three entries with the gloss 'once, formerly' (nos 1,434–6) without any distinction made between them. The united evidence of the different languages makes it clear that the three entries are all distinct. Thus, number 1,434 is the base form in all three and it means 'once upon a time, long ago'; the second entry is a reduplicated emphatic form of this; and the third is an elative 'coming from', and it means 'from ancient times, of old', so, in the case of Wangkangurru, it is *waru*, *waruwaru* and *warungana* (*waru-nganha*).

This is not an isolated case: it shows that Reuther did not analyse these forms at the point of entry, nor did he ask what was the difference between these words, but simply assigned one and the same meaning to all of them.

A slippage is evident in the glosses of line numbers 330–3 and there are also some gaps in the glosses. All of these could be easily filled with some knowledge of the languages involved, particularly Wangkangurru. Because of the circumstances in which Reuther had to write, there is still a lot of work to be done to elucidate his massive work.

Reuther noted new words in the comparative dictionaries for concepts that did not previously exist; some of these are quite practical, such as number 51, 'sourdough leaven' ('eyes [holes] shut in food'), and these would be lively examples for use in modern language revival:

- Wangkangurru: *milki-wapili-workana*: eyes (holes)-shut in-food/bread.
- Arabana: *miltji-wapili-workana*: eyes (holes)-shut in-food/bread.
- Kuyani: *maji-pamara-nku-ni*: food-rise-CAUS-emphatic.
- Yawarrawarrka: *duldruwindribuka*: holes(?) gone-in food.
- Yandruwandha: *tjilawari*: meaning unknown.

The words for 'sourdough bread' died out with the closure of the mission.

None of the Christian-oriented vocabularies included in the comparative wordlists appears to have survived. Six Wangkangurru speakers who lived until the 1960s had spent some time at the mission. They included one man, Ben Murray, who had kept in touch with the last of the missionaries. None used any of those religious terms. The word *purrka*, which meant 'sad, sorry', was used by Reuther to mean 'conscience'. It formed the base of different compounds to express the notions of 'rueful, to humiliate, to repent, to be compassionate, to be dejected'. These have not survived.

The idea of 'fasting' never really caught on, nor did the religious meanings of words connected with this. Reuther himself explains this in the Diyari dictionary: 'By "fasting", of course, one must not understand something voluntary, but compulsory. The speaker has probably already eaten to excess, or has no appetite for some reason or another' (Reuther 1981: Vol. III, p. 1155.4).

There was also no sign of survival of the new words used in Bible translations connected with finance, such as 'debtor' and 'tax collector'. The Diyari, Arabana and Wangkangurru words for 'stone' are still used today for 'money', even by younger people—but Reuther's lists do not mention money! They do, however, represent a valiant effort to adapt seven different languages to European concepts.

Reuther's volume VII, the placenames: Methodology

Reuther's method of elicitation involved the use of the Diyari language, the local Aboriginal language at Killalpaninna. The alternative would have been English, which was not familiar to him nor to the Aboriginal population. So, when it came to getting information about other languages, he had to use one Aboriginal language, Diyari, to elicit another. This method can break down when the ways of expressing complex concepts differ between Aboriginal languages. This is what happened in the case of the Diyari words *Mura* and *muramura*.

Reuther in his Diyari dictionary made valiant attempts to clarify what was meant by the Diyari word *Mura*. His trouble was that he could not bestow any worthy definition on 'paganism'. Reuther defined the term *Mura* (entry 1.36) as 'supernatural ancestor' and he illustrated this by quoting sentences where it means 'a person's main totemic ancestor'. He cautiously added, after some sentences showing a man's devotion to his own *Mura*, 'I would not knowingly like to attach more meaning to a pagan point of view than actually applies' (Reuther 1981: Vol. I, p. 36, no. 29).

The translator, Scherer, here adds a footnote defining *Mura* as *Obergott*—that is, 'supreme God'. There are various instances where Reuther used the word *Mura* in the sense of something that represents one's *Mura*—that is, *churinga*, 'in the corner of the string-bag lies my *mura* "sacred stone"' (or '*churinga*') (Reuther 1981: Vol. I, p. 40, no. 42).

He also mentioned the very special notion of 'one's own *Mura* song'. When a man was dying, his *Mura* song was sung to him (Reuther 1981: 1200).

Reuther clarified this personal connection with the *Mura* when quoting the phrase *mura kamaneli* = 'one's own totemic ceremony' {\fn1} (Reuther 1981: entry 1295).

Furthermore, Reuther went through the difficult task of explaining the word *Mura* versus *muramura*:

> mura dikana = 'to teach or relate the stories [tales or legends] of the muramuras.'

> Note by Reuther: The expression is mura dikana (and not muramura dikana), because the mura is respected on account of or through the muramura. (Reuther 1981: entry 1109)

Later, in volume III of the Diyari dictionary, he addresses this problem directly:

> Let us now pass on to the word Mura, and observe in what relationship it stands to the reduplicated word, muramura. This form of reduplication is an [idiomatic] peculiarity of the local language, for it is to be found in all word-forms with the exception of the pronoun.

> The word Mura stands in relation to muramura as genus does to species. There is one Mura, whilst there are many muramuras. Mura is a personal name, whereas muramura is a generic term, for there are many of the latter who also bear a personal name. \fn1. Reuther: 'Stammvater.' P.A.S.[5] (Reuther 1981: Vol. III, p. 24, no. 1520)

Reuther was unaware that reduplication in nouns involved a diminutive and sometimes even a pejorative rather than a pluraliser, and that *muramura* basically meant 'lesser *Mura*'. He did, however, as in the quotation above, analyse it as a subdivision of the *Mura*. Reuther was clear when discussing *Mura* and *muramura*, stating that this was an idiomatic 'peculiarity of the local language'. Arabana and Wangkangurru people did not distinguish between a notion of *Mura* and *muramura*. For them, there was a creation time, or History Time, and that was called *Ularaka*. This term also covered the notion of 'ancestor belonging to the History Time', but was always accompanied by the name of that ancestor, whether important or not

---

5   This is a note from the translator, P. A. Scherer.

so important. This meant that a person would say *'antha Yaltya Ularaka'* ('I [belong to] Frog History') in the same way as one belonging to the important long *Kurrawara Ularaka* (the 'Cloud', i.e. the 'Rain History') would say *'antha Kurrawara Ularaka'* ('I Rain History'), and it would mean 'I identify with this history'. Although Reuther learnt about many myths from 'the Saltwater Blacks', I cannot find any reference to the word *Ularaka* in his works. He used only the Diyari terminology.

A search through the wordlists in volume V reveals that Reuther has, under item 723, a Yandruwandha entry, *jelkura*, and a gloss ('spirit, creator'— both crossed out), so he was having trouble with this gloss, presumably for religious reasons. There was no such trouble with the Arabana–Yawarrawarrka entries, where Yawarrawarrka has the same *jelkura* and Arabana has *muramura*, with the gloss 'ancestral being'. *Yelkura* is the word that is rendered by *'muda yalkurra'* in Breen's Yandruwandha dictionary, with the gloss 'God' (Breen 2004b).[6] Reuther's Wangkangurru–Kuyani comparative vocabulary has *muramura* throughout, with the same gloss of 'ancestral being'.

Both Ngamini and Thirrari are close to Diyari and one might have expected them to have the term *Muramura*, but the Kuyani entry *muramura* is surprising. One might be surprised, too, at the Arabana and Wangkangurru *muramura* because, in all the recorded material from their elders in the 1960s and 1970s, they used only their term *Ularaka*. Spencer's 1903 notebook from the Peake in Arabana country confirms this.[7]

There is, however, a word, *muramura*, in Wangkangurru. It refers to mythical beings, the 'little fellows' who were said to be living in stony cliffs and rises. We cannot know whether Reuther's speakers of Wangkangurru were thinking of the 'little fellows' when they must have agreed with *muramura* in answer to Reuther's question, or whether they simply went along with his word *muramura*. I would like to guess the latter, as this would account also for the Arabana and Kuyani entries. For Kuyani,[8] I have recorded only *Mura* ('ancestor, traditional story'), never *muramura* or anything like it. Adnyamathanha, closely related to Kuyani, also has only the one term, *Mura* ('history').

6 Breen writes 'd' for the tapped 'r'.
7 Spencer (1903: 1) has an entry *'ularra aka, ularaka–alcheringa'*.
8 The fluent Kuyani speaker who recorded her language, Alice Oldfield, was a traditional person and a rainmaker in her own right.

It seems, therefore, that only the Diyari and possibly their nearest neighbours, Ngamini and Thirrari people, made a distinction between *Mura* and *muramura*, while, for everyone else in the southern Lake Eyre Basin, such a distinction did not exist, and there was only one term. The difficulties involved in the definition of *Mura* and *muramura* are a clear example of the fact that one cannot always explain one Aboriginal language in terms of another, particularly where deeper differences in concepts are concerned.

Reuther was a careful observer, but, by always using the Diyari language, he was beginning to see the world through Diyari eyes.

Reuther's vision

Reuther's work on the dictionaries had him in constant contact with senior Aboriginal men, especially Diyari, and so, as indicated above, he came to have an understanding of how they viewed their world. He could see how they viewed the landscape, he could hear from them how all the natural features came to be and how this was part of a vast network of stories of creation. So he began to compile a list of placenames, which was, like his dictionaries, unique in size and detail. It forms volume VII of his work, and spans most of the southern part of the Lake Eyre Basin. It comprises the homelands not only of the Diyari, but also of those other people who participated in the work on the comparative dictionaries, as listed in section two above, as well as the Yaluyandi, north beyond the Ngamini. Karangura country was covered only indirectly by evidence from neighbouring people (see Hercus 1992); there had been only very few Karangura people at Killalpaninna. The sites of the Pilardapa to the south-east were classified under Diyari.

Reuther was a practical man and his vision went beyond the compilation of this huge listing; placenames had to have a map. He got the collaboration of the Killalpaninna schoolteacher, H. J. Hillier, who drew up an enormous map, based on the pastoral map. This map displayed inspirational foresight: it was intended to show the Aboriginal view of the landscape with all but the most prominent European names ignored. Clearly defined conspicuous features such as high hills and large lakes can be located easily with this map. It was ahead of its time and ahead of the infrastructure of its time. This had disadvantages in that many of the placenames, particularly those of the Wangkangurru in the Simpson Desert, were in unchartered territory. Most others were in poorly surveyed areas. In Hercus and Potezny (1990), we put the names (other than those of conspicuous features) into four categories:

1. Places within reasonable reach of Killalpaninna, along the old Kalamurina track and the southern portion of the Birdsville Track, which Reuther and/or Hillier are likely to have been able to visit personally.

2. Places with Aboriginal names that were shown on the pastoral map; these are mainly the prominent features mentioned above, such as hills and lakes, as well as some very conspicuous waterholes—as, for instance, Kantritya, Goyder Lagoon waterhole.

3. Places for which Aboriginal people were able to supply series of names in lines of travel or following watercourses in areas where European geographical knowledge was adequate for reasonably accurate positioning on maps.

4. Places for which Aboriginal people were able to supply a series of names in a sequence, but where European knowledge was so inadequate that the names simply appear as lists or are just put in a general location.

This means that the locating of sites from the Hillier map is very difficult in places of category three and almost impossible in category four.

Here are examples of this: in June 2003, John McEntee, Philip Jones, Vlad Potezny, Kim McCaul and I tried to locate some sites marked on the Hillier map along Strzelecki Creek. We were unsuccessful. Here is an extract from the record compiled by me (Hercus MS 1):

> Ngapamankamankani and Ngapamunari are two placenames on the Hillier map just south of Montecollina Bore (Mantukalina, Reuther X 138, but not listed in the placenames volume, VII), probably in the same small branch of the Strzelecki Creek. We assumed that we were looking for a soakage but did not find signs of one, but there was evidence of occupation all along the creek. Artefacts and remains of a hearth were identified as well as human skeletal material. As we had no additional information about the possible nature of these sites, neither could be positively identified.

Reuther has the following explanations for these names:

1376 Ngapamankamankani: ngapa = 'water', mankamankani = 'to find'

Leaving the creek behind, Mitikujana went overland, where he found water: he therefore named the place accordingly.

This implies that this particular site is not in the creek—but must be near it and we did not find any likely place.

1323 Ngapamunari: ngapa = 'water' munari = 'a steep bank' meaning: 'water near a steep bank'.

Here, at [the foot of] a steep bank, Marumaruna found water in the creek, he therefore gave the place the above name.

No particularly steep bank was found. (Reuther 1981)

These searches and subsequent attempts to find particular Swan sites around Lake Gregory confirmed the difficulty of locating sites using the Hillier map.

Nature of the entries

Reuther did not have the special personal intimacy with important sites that is displayed by T. G. H. Strehlow for *Akár' Intjôta* in lower southern Aranda country (Strehlow 1970: 134). Reuther's connection to country was mainly at second hand. As the items in volume VII show, he had developed a systematic set of questions for his advisors: 1) what was the meaning of a placename? If it is not a Diyari name, what would be the Diyari equivalent? 2) Why was it so called? 3) Who named it? In other words, he was asking for both the etymology and the etiology (the story of the bestowal of a name; see Koch 2009).

This does not leave any scope for the emotions displayed so frequently by people when talking about their country:

- 'I want to get back to my country, my country with the red sandhills': Murtee Johnny (Yandruwandha) talking about places off the Strzelecki Track.
- 'Makes me feel sorry to talk about this country': Linda Crombie (Wangkangurru/Yaluyandi) talking about sites on the Diamantina.

There is little doubt that Reuther's advisers must have felt the same.

As a result of the systematic nature of Reuther's methods, the entries for placenames in volume VII follow a distinctive pattern: Reuther's number comes first, then the name of the site, then the language, then the name of the ancestor who named the site. This means that important extra information can be left out simply because it does not fit into those exact slots. The names are often descriptive of the site, especially the vegetation of the site—for example: '2187, Wariwaringura, Tirari, Jikaura, Meaning: The Wariwari plant or creeper Jikaura always found this *species of grass here*, hence the name.' (Reuther does not tell us that *jikaura* is the name of the native cat, nor does he tell us that this creeper was the one used for making carrying pads. These would be vital pieces of information.)

Most, but not all entries adhere rigidly to the pattern of Reuther's three questions. The following is one of the cases where the *muramura* ancestor who named the site is himself not named: '2143 Wirramudla, Kujani, Wirra = D patara gumtree Meaning, The end of the *gum trees.*'

Here the gum trees along the creek finish up. The *muramura* therefore named the place accordingly.

As is often the case, the physical characteristics of the site are the source of the name. These may be anything but spectacular:

2334 Wirkaripudla, Wongkanguru, Kurkarli,

Wirkari=D wirka crack, crevice in the ground

Pudla the Dual form

Meaning Two cracks in the ground

Here Kurkarli came across two cracks in the ground and on that account gave the place this name. [Reuther does not tell us that *kurkarli* is the mulga snake.]

380 Karkumarra, Diari, Warliwuluna

Karku = red ochre; marra = with

Warliwulana found evidence here of red ochre ground, meaning 'the ground here is impregnated with red ochre'.

1153. Manakarlakarla, Wongkanguru

mana (as in Diari) = mouth, opening, inlet

karla = the fork of a tree

karlakarla = numerous forks

Meaning: Here where the creek runs into a main level expanse of water Kuruljuruna came across a tree which had many forks. He therefore gave the place the above name. (Reuther 1981)

Reuther does not tell us that the ancestor Kuruljuruna is in fact the diamond dove. Moreover, he always implies that reduplication of nouns means a plural (Reuther 1981: Vol. II, p. 1), whereas it implies 'little' in all the languages of the area, so the name actually meant 'it had little branches'.

These descriptions refer to ancestral times and may, of course, not be true of the present.

How easily things can change is shown by the following example.

Reuther has a site called Nganarawirli.[9] This is the large and permanent Andrewilla waterhole, and there is no difficulty locating it:

1475 Nganarawirli, Ngameni,

nganara as in D = munari 'bank'

wirli in D = jelpi = 'border, edge; end'

Meaning a steep bank on the edge (of the creek)

(Here) along the edge of the Cooper, Kimilina (found) a steep bank. He therefore named the place accordingly. (Reuther 1981)

This was a descriptive name, and remained descriptive of the site until 1974 when floods swept the bank away.

What strikes one immediately is that there is nothing important or dramatic in these entries, and that is true of the majority of the placenames: they may refer to a minor event—an ancestor may see a particular bird or animal in a place, or something unexpected may happen. Thus, we find entries such as:

843. Jelujanti. At Karatji waterhole Wutjukana discovered that his men 'were infested with a host of lice he therefore gave the place this name'.

1039. Wonkanguru. Madlabulu: 'Godagodana named this place after his dog'

madla in D = Kindala 'dog', la = he, bulu as in D = white. (Reuther 1981)

---

9   Although Reuther's text talks of it being on the Cooper, the Hillier map has it on the Diamantina in the right position, which shows that Hillier personally obtained independent information.

Madla is the Wangkangurru word for 'dog', as Reuther himself states, and cannot be split into *mad-la*. There is no word 'la' = he, and he does not tell us who Godagodana is.

What links these places to the main network of mythology is the ancestor who named the site; it means that the ancestor has been there and it is part of his/her journey. In the traditional Aboriginal view of the people in the area, the 'ancestral beings' were the ones who named most of the features of the countryside; modern humans had no part in this. This view was often expressed by senior Wangkangurru people and is also clear from Reuther's evidence. Reuther's huge list of placenames confines what is actually a great vision to precise slots. It also appears to contain trivia, but that is all part of his merit: he recorded simply what he was told, and fitted it into a system of data management. He never maximised or dramatised the importance of particular sites or even expressed particular views about them; in that sense he was a truly impartial observer and collector.

The names of the *muramura*, the ancestors

One likes to think of Reuther as perhaps being a little more easygoing than other missionaries, and he was well known, having been at Killalpaninna for such a long time. Above all, he had evidently built up lasting lines of communication with the senior men—his old advisers, whom he never names (see Jones and Sutton 1986: 52).

This might explain the way in which the ancestors were named in his works. In traditional times, the creation stories were told over campfires to an audience which already knew the gist of them—and so did Reuther. There was no need to name the main protagonists, though they might be referred to occasionally by nicknames—insider terms that were understood by this audience. They were not secret terms, just familiar. It seems that Reuther's mythological stories in volume X were based on an open version of the myths, as were the discussions in volume XI. The names used in the placenames volume, VII, however, were based on insider versions of the stories, and some of these insider names recur in the *toa* volumes.

Philip Jones (2002: 196) drew attention to this situation, stating: 'It appears that Reuther may not have understood that the same Ancestor could be referred to in several ways, and by various cryptic terms.' These insider or cryptic terms are numerous; they are basically nicknames.

From the way they are used in volume VII, one cannot deduce any coherent story from them, as each entry refers to a particular place, but, at the same time, each entry helps to plot the route of the ancestor.

A striking case of the use of nicknames is that of the ancestral turkey, who is associated with initiation over a large area south and west of Diyari country. The ordinary word for 'turkey' is never used as the name of a *muramura* throughout Reuther's data, be it in the 'open' myths of volume X or among the placenames and the *toa*s. The ancestral turkey is always called *Papapa* ('maternal grandfather') (in Kuyani) because he is associated with one particular story. In this story, grandfather (i.e. turkey) repeatedly warns his grandson not to touch his bag of ceremonial objects, but the young boy escapes with a bullroarer and races from hill to hill all over the landscape. He swings it standing on top of the hills, with the furious grandfather struggling along after him until ultimately grandfather cuts him off on a narrow peninsula and kills him. In this case, the identity of the 'grandfather' is obvious.

The aim of the following pages is to solve some of the more cryptic terms with the help of information learnt from Wangkangurru people. The insider terms are often hard to analyse because volume X with the open names tells only some of the stories and volume VII has only fragmentary references spread out among the placenames. A *muramura* called 'Godagodana' appears over and over again as the main ancestor for particular placenames, somehow connected with eagles and with rain. There is no mention that he is in fact a bird. But when one has learnt from Arabana and Wangkangurru people the story of the origin of the *Wilyaru* higher initiation rite and the associated myth of the eagles and the rain (as in Spencer and Gillen 1912: 24; and Hercus MS 3), one would realise that he is Kuta-kuta, the spotted nightjar. He pretends to be a piece of bark in this story, and, in fact, that is what he looks like. His actions ultimately bring the rain, so he is part of a major line of mythology.

Naming from what the *muramura* said

Some *muramura* ancestors are named for their favourite sayings. One can work this out only if one has heard the story from another source—in the following case, from the descendants of the 'Saltwater Blacks', the Wangkangurru people who told Reuther the story in the first place.

The ancestor Namparlinamparli figures prominently in Reuther's volume VII on placenames. This esoteric nickname refers to Wurru, the heron. In an Arabana–Wangkangurru story and song cycle (recited in the 1960s by the Wangkangurru elder Mick McLean; Hercus 2007), Wurru leads the waterbirds purposely into the desert 'to perish them' while he himself knows where to find water. He fakes sunstroke, calling out over and over again with a pathetic voice in an archaic form of Arabana: '*Nhampali nhampali nganha!*' (Cover me over, cover me over [with cool sand]), which was the traditional treatment for sunstroke.

Reuther tells the story of Marikilla in volume X (1981: entries 114–23). Marikilla is the Diyari name for the mulga snake; Wangkangurru, Ngamini and Yaluyandi people called it Kurkari. Most of Kurkari's later exploits are in Ngamini country. In volume VII, Reuther calls him Kurkarli, and also Ngaltimpara, which is the Ngamini word for 'bachelor'. This is because in the story he repeatedly called out loudly, speaking in Ngamini: 'I am a bachelor, looking for girls.' Linda Crombie was the last person who could still recall his utterances in Ngamini ('*Ngaltimpara nganyi mankara kapukapu!*'), and she could show the place north of Mount Gason where 'the Bachelor' abducted two Goanna girls, and the Milkiparda swamp where he ended up.

Naming from what the *muramura* did

The story of the Two Boys is one of the most important in the Lake Eyre Basin. Wangkangurru people called them Thutirla-pula ('Two Boys'); their eastern neighbours called them Kanku-wulu ('Two Boys'). They are mentioned under their ordinary name in volume VII: entry 1,443 speaks of 'the Province of the Kankuwulunas', because the area along the lower Eyre Creek and Mithaka country to the east was the centre of the Two Boys Cult. They usually appear under their main insider name, which is Kunjarlikunjarli ('One by One'), because they sometimes acted in unison, and sometimes separately. It is never stated in Reuther's works that this is another name for the Two Boys. He uses at least two further esoteric names for them further north, mostly in Wangkamadla country. We can explain these from Mick McLean's version of the story: *Kadlaburu Kadla-purru* ('carrying a bag') and *Kadlatjuwari Kadla-tyuwiri* ('[with] a bag that is long and narrow'), because they carried a bag full of brightly coloured feathers for a major ceremony, the Warrthampa ceremony, and they thereby introduced the use of feather decorations to people to the east of the Simpson Desert.

The Two Men of Initiation are the most widely known and most celebrated of the ancestors. They come from the Simpson Desert and travel all around to teach people about the use of knives in circumcision. Reuther has written about them as 'Malku-malkuwulu' (1981: Vol. X, entries 108–13), a name interpreted by Wangkangurru speakers as 'the two with the bilby-tail small headdress'. Reuther does not give an interpretation. Siebert has written about them as the Yuri-ulu (Howitt 1904: 783). They are listed in Reuther's placenames work as having named a number of sites. They also appear in the same volume under the pseudonym of Wutyuka, who is spoken of as a single entity. This name is based on the Wangkangurru word connected with initiation. And, as in the case of the Two Boys, it is never stated by Reuther in volume VII or elsewhere that Malku-malkuwulu and Wutyuka are alternative names for the same pair of ancestors.

The many different names that are given to the *muramura* ancestors are not readily comprehensible, but some are explained by more recent information—mainly from Wangkangurru speakers of the 1960s and 1970s. The world of the *muramura* and their link to the landscape become clearer when, with the additional information, we can begin to see who is who in that ancestral world and by what routes and with what motivations they travelled.

Concluding remark

The work of Reuther is still the main source of information, not just for Diyari, but also for the whole of the southern Lake Eyre Basin. Without Reuther, and without the Aboriginal elders who put in many hundreds of hours working with him, much of that wide landscape would be meaningless. Reuther went on getting data without going back to correct, to change or to interpret, so he has left a unique unaltered written record of what those elders told him over his many years at Killalpaninna. There is, however, much editorial work that still needs to be done to deal with the inevitable inconsistencies and to learn more about the identity of the ancestors.

References

Austin, P. 1981. *A Grammar of Diyari, South Australia.* Cambridge: Cambridge University Press.

Breen, G. 2004a. *Innamincka talk: A grammar of the Innamincka dialect of Yandruwandha with notes on other dialects.* Pacific Linguistics 558, The Australian National University, Canberra.

Breen, G. 2004b. *Innamincka words: Yandruwandha dictionary and stories.* Pacific Linguistics 559, The Australian National University, Canberra.

Hercus, L. A. MS 2 [n.d.]. Arabana–Wangkangurru dictionary. Available from PARADISEC: www.paradisec.org.au.

Hercus, L. A. 1992. Glimpses of the Karangura. *Records of the South Australian Museum* 25(2)(1991): 139–59.

Hercus, L. A. 1994. *Grammar of the Arabana–Wangkangurru language, Lake Eyre Basin, South Australia.* Pacific Linguistics Series C128, The Australian National University, Canberra.

Hercus, L. A. MS 1 [2003]. Report on fieldwork in the lakes area of South Australia, with input from J. McEntee, P. Jones, V. Potezny and K. McCaul.

Hercus, L. A. 2007. The story of Wurru the crane. [Electronic version with sound-files 2008.] Privately distributed and at Australian Institute of Aboriginal and Torres Strait Islander Studies and National Library of Australia, Canberra.

Hercus, L. A. MS 3 [in progress]. The rain from the Peake. Arabana/ Wangkangurru text with verses and illustations.

Hercus, L. A. and Potezny, V. 1990. Locating Aboriginal sites: A note on J. G. Reuther and the Hillier map of 1904. *Records of the South Australian Museum* 24(2): 139–51.

Howitt, A. W. 1904. *The Native Tribes of South-East Australia.* London: Macmillan.

Jones, P. 2002. Naming the dead heart: Hillier's map and Reuther's gazeteer of 2468 placenames in north-eastern South Australia. In *The Land is a Map: Placenames of Indigenous origin in Australia*, (eds) L. Hercus, F. Hodges and J. Simpson, pp. 187–200. Canberra: Pandanus Books.

Jones, P. and Sutton, P. 1986. *Art and Land: Aboriginal sculptures of the Lake Eyre region*. Adelaide: South Australian Museum in association with Wakefield Press.

Koch, H. 2009. The methodology of reconstructing Indigenous placenames: Australian Capital Territory and south-eastern New South Wales. In *Aboriginal Placenames: Naming and re-naming the Australian landscape*, (eds) H. Koch and L. Hercus. Aboriginal History Monograph 19, pp. 115–71. Canberra: Aboriginal History Inc. and ANU E Press.

Reuther, J. G. 1981. *The Diari*. Translated by P. A. Scherer. Microfiche No. 2, Australian Institute of Aboriginal Studies, Canberra.

Schürmann, C. W. 1844. *A Vocabulary of the Parnkalla Language. Spoken by the natives inhabiting the western shores of Spencer's Gulf, to which is prefixed a collection of grammatical rules, hitherto ascertained*. Adelaide: George Dehane.

Spencer, B. 1903. Urabunna Old Peake Station. Ms. Museum Victoria, Melbourne.

Spencer, B. and Gillen, F. J. 1912. *Across Australia*. London: Macmillan & Co.

Strehlow, T. G. H. 1970. Geography and the totemic landscape in Central Australia. In *Australian Aboriginal Anthropology*, (ed.) R. M. Berndt, pp. 92–140. Perth: University of Western Australia Press.

6

German Moravian missionaries on western Cape York Peninsula and their perception of the local Aboriginal people and languages[1]

Corinna Erckenbrecht

From 2004 to 2007, I conducted in-depth research about the German physical anthropologist and collector Hermann Klaatsch (1863–1916), who travelled around Australia from 1904 to 1907. This research examined newly available personal and scientific documents (Erckenbrecht 2010).[2] Klaatsch was a medical doctor, comparative anatomist and Darwinist, who firmly believed in the origin of species by natural selection as outlined in Darwin's famous book in 1859. By the end of the nineteenth century, more scientists believed that similar selection processes must have caused the human species to evolve; however, no one could say then where the development of humankind had taken place in prehistoric times. Thus, Klaatsch and many of his fellow anthropologists around the turn of the nineteenth century felt that more world-changing evidence for the new theory would soon be found. Eugéne Dubois, for instance, went to Indonesia specifically to look for archaeological sites and human fossils, because the tropics were seen as a likely place for these kinds of discoveries.[3]

---

1   I would like to thank Geoff Wharton for his comments on an earlier draft of this chapter.
2   The documents are kept by the Klaatsch family in the United States.
3   Africa, however, was not on anyone's list yet and it was hardly mentioned in the literature of that time.

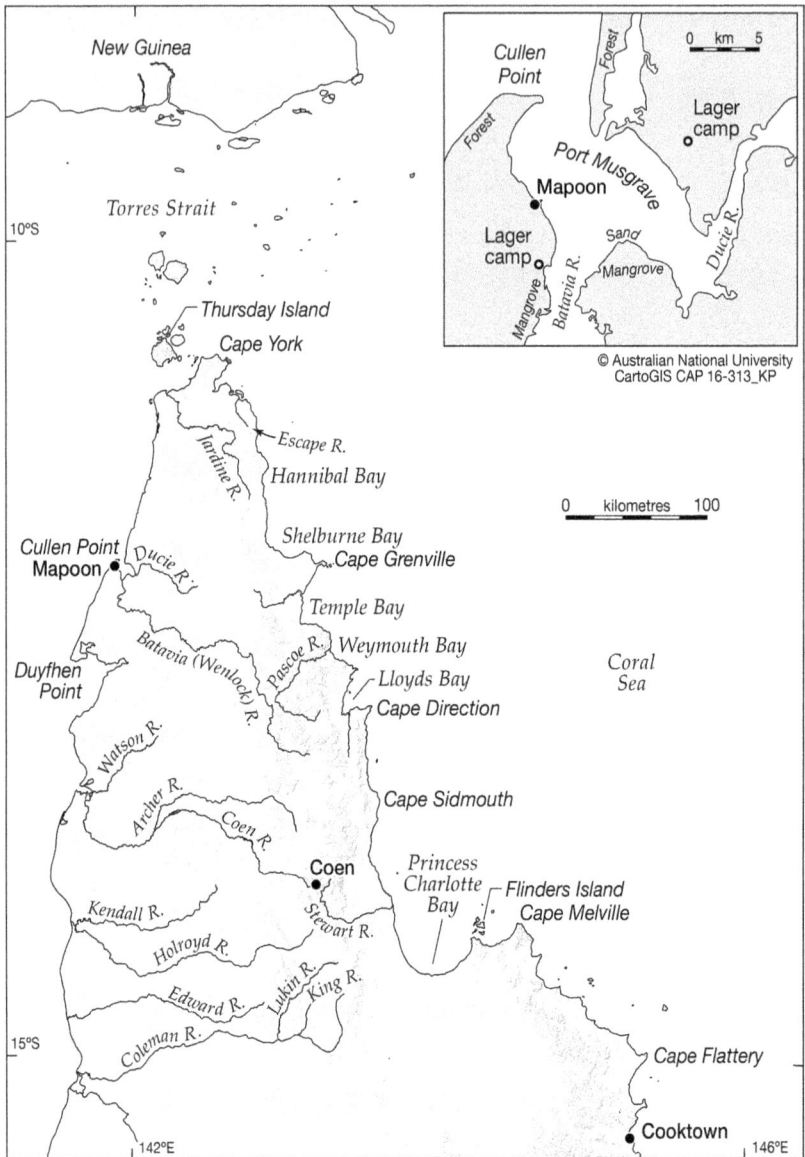

Map 6.1 Location of Mapoon Mission on Cape York Peninsula, 1892.

Source: CartoGIS, The Australian National University, based on a historical map drawn by the missionaries in 1892 and first published in the *Periodical Accounts Relating to the Foreign Missions of the Church of the United Brethren* (1894: Vol. 2, No. 17, p. 263).

Klaatsch's friend and colleague Otto Schoetensack (1850–1912) was convinced that the anthropogenesis had in fact taken place in Australia in prehistoric times (Schoetensack 1901, 1902, 1904), thus following some indications that British naturalist Thomas Huxley had mentioned in his book (Huxley 1863). Schoetensack's poor health prevented him from going on long overseas journeys. His younger friend Klaatsch, however, was prepared to go as soon as the opportunity arose. In August 1903, Klaatsch met a wealthy German representative of a north Queensland mining company, Francis E. Clotten, who planned a journey to Australia to inspect his mine and invited Klaatsch to accompany him. They left Europe in February 1904 and in March arrived in Brisbane, where Klaatsch remained for a few months. He was introduced to Walter E. Roth, the north Queensland protector of Aborigines at that time, and the two scientists became good friends. In his capacity as protector, Roth paid regular visits to various settlements, mission stations and Aboriginal camps in north Queensland using the government sailboat *Melbidir*. When Roth was asked to go to Western Australia in 1904 for an investigation into the mistreatment of Aboriginal people, he allowed Klaatsch to use the *Melbidir* on his behalf. Thus, Klaatsch went on a four-month journey to the Gulf of Carpentaria and visited, among other places, the Presbyterian mission station at Mapoon on western Cape York Peninsula at the end of July and the beginning of August 1904. Mapoon was established for the Presbyterian Church by Moravian missionaries James Ward and Nicolaus Hey in 1891 (see below).

When Klaatsch arrived at Mapoon, preparations were under way for the founding of another station at the Archer River, later called Aurukun. The new German missionary, Arthur Richter, was to establish the station. Klaatsch, being a guest at Mapoon, was invited to go along to the Archer River as well. There, Klaatsch was an eyewitness to the landing at the shore and the carrying of all provisions to the spot where the mission station was going to be established and where the first house was to be built. He took photographs of these scenes and also described it vividly in his notebooks and diaries (see Erckenbrecht 2010: 69ff).

Plate 6.1 Missionaries and their helpers at the landing place on their first day at the Archer River in August 1904.

In his notes, Klaatsch described many of the people in this photo, including an Indigenous 'Mamoos'. The same photo exists in the Moravian Church Archives, thus proving the contacts between Klaatsch and the Moravians.

Source: Hermann Klaatsch, 4 August 1904. Scan of historical photograph, Klaatsch family archive, USA.

These connections between a German scientist and traveller and the German Moravian missionaries in north Queensland brought me in touch with the Moravian Church Archives in Herrnhut, Saxony. I discovered their extensive and unique records, and especially their collection of historical photographs from north Queensland. The Herrnhut Museum of Ethnology also keeps an ethnographic collection by the German missionaries from north Queensland (as well as from Victoria, where the Moravians ran mission stations for several decades until 1908).

Following this first visit to Herrnhut, I planned to conduct research at the museum and archives, and, after having secured funding from the German Research Foundation (DFG) for a two-year research project, I started working at Herrnhut in November 2013, also moving to the Upper Lusatia region in Saxony for this project. Living in the very place where the missionaries had lived and where they had attended the Moravian Mission College in the nearby town of Niesky gave me additional inspiration for my research.

My research project: Method and focus

My research focuses on the 'Early missionary and colonial perspectives on the Indigenous cultures and languages of western Cape York Peninsula, Australia, and the documentation of the cultural changes in this region based on written documents, ethnographic artefacts and historical photographs'.[4] Originally, I intended to cover the whole period of the Moravian-run mission stations in north Queensland, from 1891 to 1919,[5] for all three stations (Mapoon, Weipa and Aurukun). But the Moravian Church Archives resources proved to be too numerous for just two years of research (including publishing the results in a book). Given this background, I decided to focus on the first five years of culture contact between the missionaries and the local Aboriginal people, from 1890 to 1895. This was the time of the initial contact of the German and British missionaries with the local Indigenous population at Cullen Point, later called Mapoon. The written records of this time—that is, the letters and reports that the missionaries wrote home to their mission board, their former mission college and friends and to the editorial boards of the Moravian journals—provide a fascinating insight into this first contact situation and the brethren's feelings, perceptions and efforts, and also doubts.

Moreover, the head of the mission station, James Ward, died in 1895, possibly from typhoid fever. The rest of the staff, also sick and demoralised by this experience, left the station temporarily to recover in a cooler climate in southern Australia. For all of them, it was a time to look back and review what had happened. This break was also the time for me to stop my research at 1895 and look back. I decided that the best time span for my research would be these early days of the mission. This was the period of various comparable written sources, when both Ward and Hey wrote their letters home. Their varying first impressions and thoughts to

---

4   This is the English title of my research proposal.
5   In 1919, the Moravians left north Queensland for various reasons and the Presbyterian Church took over with its own staff.

different addressees, their various perceptions and documentations, trials and errors, their feelings of desperation, but also of joy, and critiques were contained in these first years.

Almost all of these sources are written in German, most of them in old German script. They are not well known in Australia. So, my idea was to provide a unique contribution to north Queensland anthropology and mission history, and to 'excavate' and transcribe these early German sources to make them accessible for research and study—and, of course, for the personal use of the local Aboriginal people today as well.

But the written sources are just one part of the material, as mentioned above. The two other parts are the collection of historical photographs at the Moravian Church Archives and the collection of ethnographic artefacts at the Museum of Ethnology. Accordingly, I am interested in the triangulation of all three sources, studying them together at the same time. Further sources from the United Kingdom and, of course, Australia are included. I am especially interested in finding overlapping information to understand the meaning, intention and background of them all. This includes the question, for instance, of why certain photographs were taken in the first place. What are the photos about? What do they depict? How, by whom and in which context were they later used? Which captions were given by the missionaries themselves, by their wives or, later, by the brethren in Herrnhut? All these questions and their answers provide new and fascinating insights.

While conducting this research I am, of course, also interested in what can be said about the local Aboriginal society at that time. However, all sources are by the missionaries only and what they saw in the Aborigines or thought worthwhile to write home about them. There are hardly any relevant firsthand quotes by Aboriginal people themselves in those documents. So one has to be very careful in examining and evaluating the content of the text (or photos). The sources carry a palimpsest—something that shines through, but cannot be read easily or straight away. Rather, it has to be carefully identified, extracted, interpreted and assessed. Therefore, I would like to make it very clear in the theoretical, methodological and also practical approach of my research that I can produce results only about the Moravian perception of the Indigenous world in north Queensland: what they had on their mind when they came to Australia and whether or not they were able to understand what they saw and heard. It's about their perception on the basis of their specific background.

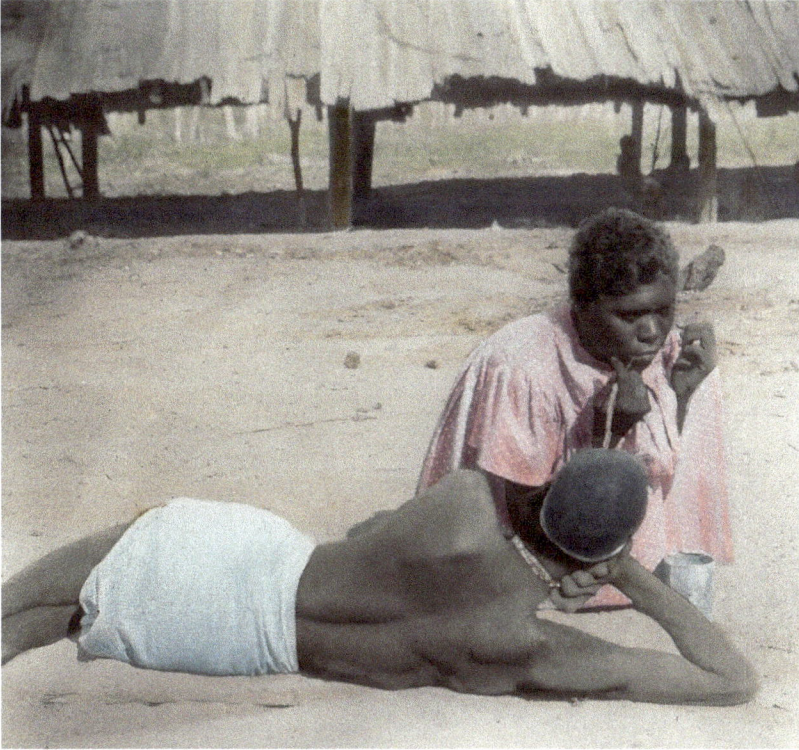

Plate 6.2 An example of a historical photograph in the Moravian Church Archives with an unclear motive.

Further research revealed that it can be compared with scenes published by Roth (1903: 38, pl. 40) showing the use of 'sucking strings', thus depicting a healing ceremony or medical treatment. This kind of treatment was described in the missionaries' letters.

Source: Collection, Moravian Church Archives, Herrnhut, Germany, LBS 02843_C_2-R_56-No_24.

Moravia and Moravian Church history

Moravia is a large geographic region in the eastern part of what is now the Czech Republic. The largest city is Brno. The region takes its name from the main river running through it, the Morave. Moravia is just a region and was never a nation-state. Thus, people from Moravia—Moravians in general—such as the well-known Sigmund Freud (Austrian), Oskar Schindler (German) and Ivan Lendl (Czech), belong(ed) to different states, nationalities and/or empires in the past. Together with Bohemia, Moravia forms the core region of the Czech Republic.

The Moravian Church originated in this region (as well as in neighbouring Bohemia). It is a pre-Reformation Protestant denomination dating back to the fifteenth century. Its members are followers of Jan Hus (1370–1415), a very influential Czech reformer. Jan Hus (English: John Huss) was a professor of theology and head of the university in Prague. He expressed ideas similar to those of Martin Luther, who came 100 years after him, including translating and teaching the Bible in the native tongue, criticising the sins and low morals of the monks and the clergy, opposing the sale of indulgences, emphasising the importance of the holy script only ('*sola scriptura*') and accepting laypeople to receive communion. Therefore, the chalice used in Holy Communion is one of their symbols.

Jan Hus was burnt at the stake for his beliefs 600 years ago (on 6 July 1415) at the council in Constance. This had far-reaching consequences. War broke out in the following years (the Hussite wars) and his followers were persecuted. They split into several groups with different aims, beliefs and politics, which are beyond the scope of this chapter to explain. One group re-formed officially in 1475, 50 years after Hus's death, and it was called the Unity of the Brethren or the Bohemian Brethren. This was the beginning of the new and independently organised Moravian Church.

In 1720, Count Nicolaus Ludwig Zinzendorf (1700–60) bought an estate at Berthelsdorf in the Upper Lusatia region in Saxony where he offered sanctuary to the Bohemian and Moravian Brethren in 1772, after their continuing persecution. Following their arrival, they cleared the woods and built a new village called Herrnhut ('under the hat of the Lord' or 'Lord's watch'). There was a renewal and reunification and, in 1732, after some quarrels in 1727, they decided to start their mission work again.

Moravian missionary activity and mission ethics

The Moravians first worked with African slaves in the West Indies (St Thomas), because Count Zinzendorf had heard sad stories of the lot of these slaves through a personal acquaintance with a black servant from St Thomas at the court of the Danish king in Copenhagen. Zinzendorf, himself an active member of the religious community and later bishop of the United Brethren, brought this slave with him from Copenhagen to Herrnhut in 1731. This sparked the enthusiasm for mission work, and, in 1732, the first brethren went to St Thomas. Later, the missionaries went to many other and quite different countries, such as Suriname, Labrador, Nicaragua and Tibet, to name just a few. They did not follow the paths of German—or British—colonial rule, but acted on the needs or requests they felt necessary to address. Altogether, they were active in 32 countries worldwide.

In their mission work, they were quite specific about which ethnic or cultural group they would like to address. In Labrador, for instance, they were only interested in the Inuit—not in the local tribes of Native Americans who also lived there. In Suriname in South America, they were interested in some coastal tribes, but also escaped slaves in the interior, called Marrons. In Nicaragua, they worked with several tribes on the remote Atlantic coast. Thus, they paid attention to remote ethnic and cultural groups at a time and in places when nobody else was interested in them. This is one of the reasons the Moravian Church Archives are so extremely valuable today and why they are consulted by visitors and researchers from all over the world.

Moravian mission ethics included to work with the poorest of the poor, to go where no one else wants to go, to live with people with whom no one else wants to live and to really love the mission work and really love the people. This caused great concern for the Moravian missionaries at Mapoon and also their wives, because they felt unsure as to whether they really loved Aboriginal people with all their heart. They remarked on their feelings and doubts in this regard in their letters. For them, it was a prerequisite for their mission work, no matter where they went.

At Niesky, another Moravian settlement near Herrnhut, there was a mission school at which Moravian teachers trained future missionaries. Nicolaus Hey went to school there for two years before he was called to the mission field in Australia. The school had a wide variety of subjects being taught, but it focused mainly on instructing its pupils in practical skills such as gardening and farming, but also, for instance, photography, especially since the head of the school in Hey's time, Hermann Kluge, took a special interest in it.

Formative influences for Moravian thought and identity

The Moravian Church and its missionaries were heavily influenced by their history and experiences, which I have tried to outline above and which I would like to summarise briefly as follows. They were a persecuted religious minority in exile, having successfully survived in a foreign and hostile environment through brotherly love and unity, which provided spirit, strength and endurance. This was based on the Protestant work ethic and a belief in education and lifelong learning. They also applied a surprisingly progressive working scheme: unmarried brothers and sisters could live on their own in separate houses and work independently in a communal way. Thus, progress and modest prosperity were achievable through a rural yet industrious lifestyle. And, last but not least, they had a centuries-long history of successful missionary work.

Moravians in Australia: Moravians in north Queensland

There had been Moravian missionaries in Australia since 1849. Charles La Trobe (1801–75), Superintendent of the Port Phillip district of New South Wales and then Lieutenant-Governor of Victoria, had invited Moravian missionaries to Australia. The La Trobe family belonged to the British branch of the Moravian Church. The Moravian missionaries tried to set up mission stations at several places in Australia. The first attempts were made in Victoria (at Lake Boga in 1851, Ebenezer in 1859 and Ramahyuck in 1864) and in northern South Australia, at Kopperamana and Killalpaninna (1866–68), following the ill-fated Bourke and Wills expedition. But these stations were given up after only a few months or years.[6] The mission station with the longest duration was Ramahyuck and the main missionary there was Friedrich August Hagenauer (1829–1909), who ran the station for many decades, until 1908.

---

6   See the *Missionary Atlas* published by the Mission Board (Missionsdirektion 1895, 1907), and missionary Gottlieb Meißel's fascinating report (1898)—and also his drawings—of his time in northern South Australia. His subsequent travels around the world to Jamaica, where he was going to team up with other Moravian missionaries, are also fascinating. Felicity Jensz (see e.g. 2007, 2012) undertook extensive research about the Moravians in Victoria.

In 1885, Hagenauer was asked to travel to north Queensland to assess the prospects of future mission work there. He wrote a report about this trip in 1886 called 'Notes of a missionary journey to north Queensland 1885' (Hagenauer 1886). However, Hagenauer came only as far as the Bloomfield River (Vilele plantation) on the east coast of Queensland and was never at the western Cape York Peninsula or Mapoon.

The British colony of Queensland was separated from New South Wales in 1859. By the 1880s, the Cape York Peninsula experienced the extension of goldmining and pastoralism. Conflicts broke out between the local Aboriginal people and pastoralists over the various uses of land, food, cattle and water. Many problems arose and many atrocities were committed against the Aboriginal people, which have been documented by Australian historians such as Rosalind Kidd (1997). Frequent calls by trepang, pearl and bêche-de-mer boats looking for new crew also added to a major upheaval in the living conditions of coastal Aborigines through long absences, the introduction of diseases and high death rates from tuberculosis onboard crowded sailing luggers. However, north Queensland and especially the Cape York Peninsula were still seen as quite well populated by Aboriginal people (in contrast with Victoria, where Hagenauer was constantly facing the closure of the mission station due to a steady decrease in the number of people living there). Therefore, the Presbyterian Church of Australia eventually decided to establish an Aboriginal mission in north Queensland and asked the Moravian Brethren in Herrnhut for suitable brothers to be sent over. The decision was first made in 1886 and, in 1890, the Moravians were contacted in Germany.

The Moravian Mission Board accepted this request and chose two brethren, according to the Australian Presbyterian Church wishes: one should be a good farmer, the other should be English or at least able to communicate fluently in English so as to easily handle all negotiations and correspondence in Australia. Accordingly, one British and one German brother were chosen (see below).

John Douglas (1828–1904), government resident at Thursday Island and a former premier of Queensland, was a crucial supporter of the establishment of an Aboriginal mission station in north Queensland. Two delegates of the Presbyterian Church, Reverends Hardie and Robinson from Melbourne, travelled to north Queensland, and, together with John Douglas, in July 1891, they went on a prospecting tour along the west coast to select the site for the future mission station.

At that time, the Moravian missionaries had already arrived in Melbourne. They still believed, as they had been told, that they were going to be sent somewhere on the east coast of north Queensland next to white settlements (as Hagenauer had suggested) and were very surprised when Douglas and the Presbyterian delegates decided on the west coast at short notice.

Douglas remained a very influential political and practical supporter of the Moravian Brethren until his death in 1904. Without him, the missionaries would not have survived. Therefore, it is easy to understand why there is a photograph of John Douglas in the Moravian Church Archives photograph collection from north Queensland.

The first missionaries in north Queensland and their background

The first missionaries at Mapoon were James G. Ward (1857–95), a Jamaican-born son of a British Moravian missionary, and his Irish wife, Mathilda Ward, née Barnes. Ward came to Europe at the age of eight and visited the Moravian schools in England and Germany before settling in Northern Ireland (at Ballinderry near Belfast). Nicolaus Hey (1862–1951) was from a small village called Dörrenbach near Bergzabern, Palatinate, and his wife was Mary-Anne (Minnie) Hey, née Barnes, the sister of Mathilda.[7]

Neither couple knew anything about Australia, the Aboriginal people or the place where they were going to start the mission. They had heard only rumours or clichés. On their arrival in Melbourne, they were met by Friedrich Hagenauer and, a few weeks later, they were taken to his mission station, Ramahyuck, for a visit. Nicolaus Hey reported when he saw Aboriginal people and a Moravian mission station in Australia for the first time: 'I am not able to express my feelings that overwhelmed me at the first sight of the mission station.'[8]

---

7 Before departing for Australia, Hey spent several months with the Wards in Ballinderry to learn English. Here, he met his future wife, the sister of Mathilda Ward, who played the organ at the local church. The Moravian missionary at the second station, Weipa (established in 1898), was Edwin Brown from England, and the Moravian missionary at the third station, Aurukun (1904), was Arthur Richter.

8 'Ich bin nicht im stande meine gefühle auszudrücken, die ich beim ersten Anblick der Station empfand', Letter No. 6(2) from Hey to the Mission Board from Melbourne, 21 August 1891, p. 3, Moravian Church Archives, Herrnhut, Saxony (translation by Anna Kenny).

Plate 6.3 The two missionary couples at Mapoon.

Standing at the back: James Ward (1857–94); Mary-Anne Hey, née Barnes (1869–1970). Sitting in front: Mathilda Ward, née Barnes (1861–1953); Nicolaus Hey (1862–1951). This well-known photo has—as a paper print—handwritten colouring instructions on the back, but no year. It must have been taken in 1893 or 1894.

Source: Collection, Moravian Church Archives, Herrnhut, Germany, LBS_00455_C_1-R_52-No_68.

In addition to taking part in all kinds of practical work at the station and attending the church services, Hey and Ward were shown such things as boomerang throwing by the Aborigines. Later, in north Queensland, Ward was very surprised that the Aboriginal people had no boomerangs at all, which made him wonder whether perhaps the Cape York Aborigines were a complete 'swindle'. He used this particular word and it was also used later in the Moravian journals as a headline for the latest news from north Queensland:

> No Boomerangs. The Menti. In one respect the blacks about here are a swindle. We always heard so much about the boomerang at home. We saw the Victorian blacks use it, but these blacks have no such thing. Nor have they a shield. Their only weapons are light or heavy spears, and the 'menti', an instrument for giving greater force to the spear when thrown. This serves for warding off the spears of their enemies in the fight as well.[9]

---

9   *Moravian Missionary Reporter and Illustrated Missionary News*, III(8)(NS)(August 1893), p. 59.

Their unpublished records: Letters, photographs and artefacts

The two Moravian Brethren wrote regular letters to the Mission Board in Herrnhut, and Nicolaus Hey also wrote long letters to his teacher at the mission college at Niesky. He included photographs and sketch maps he had drawn. Both missionaries also wrote letters to the editorial boards of the Moravian journals such as the *Periodical Accounts Relating to the Foreign Missions of the Church of the United Brethren*,[10] the *Moravian Missionary Reporter and Illustrated Missionary News*, the *Moravian Messenger* and the German *Missions-Blatt der Brüdergemeine*. Sometimes, personal letters to friends, including those written by the missionaries' wives, were published in these journals.[11]

Ward and Hey wrote about their daily life, their work and experiences, their establishment of a school and an orphanage[12] and the building of the first church, as well as many other things, including their problems with the Queensland authorities. Of course, descriptions of their attempts to put the Christian message across formed a major part of their correspondence. They also talked about their difficulties in learning the local Indigenous language(s). In addition, they were also asked by the Mission Board to answer specific questions, such as how many and which

---

10   Printed for the Brethren's Society for the Furtherance of the Gospel among the Heathen in London.

11   All these published letters, however, were slightly altered by the editors without pointing this out. The quotation marks placed by the editors indicating the beginning and ending of quotes create the impression that these paragraphs are direct citations, but they are not. So, these secondary sources have very limited value, in contrast with the original letters.

12   The missionaries established an orphanage in the early stages of the mission settlement. It began when John Douglas, government resident at Thursday Island, brought three orphans to Mapoon in October 1892. He thought this was a good idea because they had no home and no one to look after them. The missionaries, on the other hand, were willing to start an orphanage on the spot (the brethren in Germany were surprised by this development). They built a grass house on a sand hill for the orphanage, which was completed on 30 October 1892. The missionaries then formed a family from the orphans: a teenage girl and two young boys, still children. The missionaries married the teenage girl to an Aboriginal man at Mapoon, and the two young boys were given to them as if they were their children. The young Aboriginal couple was also supposed to act as the wardens or heads of the orphanage and of all the children who would enter the orphanage in the future. The orphanage was an unstable institution at first and the young couple later split. Nevertheless, the idea and intentions were genuine, and it was officially mentioned as being the orphanage. The sources for the whole story can be found in several letters by Hey and Ward, one of the more relevant of which is No. 58 by Ward to the Mission Board, written in October 1892 from Cullen Point (ref. no. R.15.V.II.B.3.a.2, Moravian Church Archives).

tribes lived around the station, their names and their languages. As Ward's and Hey's knowledge of these issues was quite poor in the beginning, their answers were not extensive or reliable in the first years.

The two brethren had quite different styles of writing. Hey often used his diary as the basis for his reports about events over long periods between letters; he was more systematic, albeit somewhat unsure and apparently ill at ease about writing, for instance, to the honourable elders of the church. After all, he was just a farmer. Ward, who had already worked as an ordained minister in Ireland, wrote more spontaneously and emotionally, but in a scholarly fashion, about events that had just happened. He also expressed more self-assurance and an ability to deal with conflicts— in many cases, expressing independent opinions.

Plate 6.4 One of the very first photographs taken at Mapoon, showing an Aboriginal camp at the seashore. It was taken by a visiting boat captain, Mr Smith, in the second half of May 1892.
Source: Collection, Moravian Church Archives, Herrnhut, Germany, LBS_00184_B.

Most of the Moravian missionaries took photos (and, prior to the availability of photography, they did drawings and paintings), documenting one way or the other their mission stations and the local Indigenous people. As mentioned above, Hey and Ward in particular were asked by the head of the mission school to take photos. There was also a Moravian Juvenile Missionary Association in London that equipped Hey and Ward with a camera while they stayed in London for a few days before their departure for Australia. The first photos were to be sent to these supporters. There were, however, practical problems with the glass plates and the paper. Thus, the first photographs at Mapoon were taken by a visiting boat captain who happened to call at the mission station in May 1892. He was a photography enthusiast and had all the necessary equipment on board his ship. It was part of my research project to try to identify these first photos. The Moravian Brethren did eventually begin to take photos, but not for long, as they lacked time for the cumbersome preparations necessary for the activity. Instead, their wives took over and, later, photographs of official visitations were added. Thus, the collection of historical photographs from north Queensland has a diverse and unique history.

The missionaries also collected cultural artefacts, but not on a large scale. The artefacts were sent home to Herrnhut for the local Museum of Ethnology, but were also sold to other museums and to raise money for the mission. These were mostly practical objects such as weapons, tools, baskets and ornaments, with a few exceptional ones such as message sticks, initiation girdles or bracelets made of shark vertebrae. In some but not all cases, these are accompanied by documentation or a list of artefacts. There are collections in Berlin, Dresden and, of course, in Herrnhut, which holds the majority of all collections in one museum.[13]

Their perception of the local Aboriginal people and languages and their approach to interaction

From the start, the Moravian missionaries in Australia were overwhelmingly confronted with unfavourable judgements of and prejudices about Aboriginal people. Some common views of Aboriginal people at that time were that they were wild and shy, treacherous and could not be trusted, and that they were cannibals. Some white Australians also believed Aborigines were not humans and had no souls, and that contact with Aborigines was dangerous so one should always carry a rifle.

---

13 Duplicates were also given to the museums in Frankfurt and Genk, Belgium, according to the inventory books at the Berlin Museum.

The missionaries believed many of these stories at first; however, they had a different approach. They went to the camps unarmed trying to settle conflicts whenever they occurred. Nevertheless, they also took or used photographs to show how wild Aboriginal people had been before and how peaceful and happy they were after contact with the missionaries.

In general, however, the Moravian perception of Aboriginal people arose from a different angle than that usually applied in the wider Australian society. First, they saw Aboriginal people as human beings who had an eternal soul. (However, no one had yet prayed for their souls, which was a great concern for the missionaries.) Furthermore, they were heathens and lived in darkness. They lived a sinful life in filthy camps. They had an Old Testament kind of law: 'An eye for an eye; a tooth for a tooth.' Both Ward and Hey mention this phrase, and it is not hard to believe that they could relate to this legal system quite well. However, spiritually, the Aboriginal people lived in darkness and in fear of numerous evil spirits and devils: 'It is a religion gone mad', Hey (1912) remarked later, although he emphasised that it was still a religion.

In Hey's point of view, there was a lot of 'darkness'.[14] This may sound absurd to us today considering the bright tropical conditions on Cape York Peninsula; however, it also illuminates Hey's perception of the Aboriginal way of life. It was necessary to bring some light into this darkness, which was one of the explanations for the opening of a second and third station. To light up a wide hall, one candle was not sufficient; only several would do.

First interactions

While erecting the mission house in the very first days in November 1891, Hey went to the nearby Aboriginal camp daily, establishing regular contact with the local Aboriginal people. He fed and nursed the sick and commented on his reasons for doing so. In turn, the Aboriginal people acknowledged his attention and also took care of him. He described to the Mission Board the contact situation at the Cape York mission station and wrote from Mapoon on 1 March 1892:

---

14   This is a recurrent phrase in his letters to the Mission Board, describing the various difficulties and failures in their attempts to Christianise Aboriginal people and to influence their beliefs.

When I realized that my strength was fading daily, I strived to spend as much time as I could with the Blacks, as I had to tell myself that I am here because of the Blacks and the Blacks are not here because of me. I went to the camp of the Blacks every day. Initially all women and children ran away when they saw me approaching, but with small presents I soon won the children over. I also took care of the sick. An old man had a dangerous wound on his foot and I feared the worst. I cleaned and bandaged it every day as well as using an ointment I had brought with me—and after four weeks his foot was completely healed. Another man had been prevented from hunting and gathering his food by a light illness, but had been nevertheless severely weakened by it and was unable to walk. Every day I took some of our food to him and he soon recovered. These small services of love made a big difference and changed their perception, they realized that I only had the best intentions for their wellbeing in mind. I was often surprised by their tenderness when they brushed an ant or some other small animal off me or when I had to carry something, they wanted to do it for me, though there are also exceptions, which require a lot of patience.[15]

This letter ends with the sentence: 'Please don't forget us in far away Australia.'[16]

Learning the local Aboriginal language(s)

From the start, the missionaries were keen to learn the local language(s); however, it was difficult for them to get words and they were also perplexed by the multitude of languages.[17] The very first word the missionaries wanted

---

15   *Da ich jeden Tag immer mehr merkte wie meine Kräfte dahinsanken, suchte ich so viel als möglich mit den Schwarzen in Berührung zu kommen, da ich mir sagen mußte, ich bin hier um der Schwarzen willen und die Schwarzen nicht um meinetwillen. Ich ging jeden Tag in das Lager der Schwarzen in der ersten Zeit so bald ich sichtbar wurde liefen alle Frauen und Kinder davon doch durch kleine Geschenke hatte ich bald die Kinder auf meiner Seite. Auch nahm ich mich der Kranken an ein Mann hatte eine gefährliche Wunde am Fuße ich fürchtete das Schlimste, ich unternahm jeden Tag die Reinigung der Wunde und verband es + machte gebrauch von einer Salbe welche ich bei mir hatte in 4 Wochen war der Fuß vollständig geheilt. Ein anderer Mann war durch leichtes Unwohlsein verhindert worden seiner Nahrung nach zu gehen und dadurch war er so herunter gekommen, daß er nicht mehr gehen konnte, ich brachte ihm jeden Tag von unserm Essen und auch er war bald wieder hergestellt. Solche kleinen Liebesdienste // brachten eine große Veränderung hervor, sie merkten bald daß ich nur ihr gutes im Auge habe und ich bin oft ganz erstaunt über ihre zärtlichkeit wenn eine Ameise oder sonst ein Thierchen sich an mir befindet wie sie es wegnehmen oder wenn ich etwas zu tragen habe wollen sie es für mich thun, doch giebt es auch Ausnahmen welche oft viel Geduld erfordern.* Translation by Anna Kenny.
16   Letter No. 10 by Hey to the Mission Board, from Mapoon, 1 March 1892, ref. no. R.15.V.II.b.3.a.2, pp. 10 and 11, Moravian Church Archives.
17   The language spoken by the people on the Mapoon peninsula was Tjungundji. During the first 10 years of the mission, people from other language groups, such as the Thaynakwith, Mpakwithi and Yupungathi, came to live at the mission. For a discussion of Mapoon area languages, see Crowley (1981).

to know was the word for 'heart'. In Christian belief, and especially in the Moravian belief, the heart is the organ where love and emotion—the core elements of Christianity—reside. Love and charity 'come from the heart' in Western, Christian and Moravian beliefs. Therefore, to teach Aboriginal people the Christian message, they wanted to tell them about the heart. And not only about the physical heart as such, but also about the 'good heart' and the 'bad heart'. This insistence on hearts went so far as to show pictures of a good heart and a bad heart to schoolchildren—until they were moved to tears, according to the Moravian Brethren's observations.[18] One wonders whether these tears were really caused by enlightenment and wonderment, or whether the children were simply scared. Later, the missionaries changed from the 'bad heart–good heart' dichotomy to the 'bad fellow–good fellow' dichotomy—an indication that they changed from their special Moravian way of thinking and talking to the lingua franca of the area more comprehensible for the Aboriginal people.

Before Ward died in January 1895, Hey reported that Ward had given a last sermon to the Aborigines in their own language.[19] Whether this is true or not we have no way of evaluating. However, Hey also mentioned that Ward had already translated the Christmas tale into the local language. Hey also points out in July 1892—only eight months after the start of the mission station—that they were already giving all their talks and sermons in the Aboriginal language, which was a lot of work (and which was admittedly still mixed with a lot of English words).[20] However, it shows their strong determination to communicate fluently in the local language.[21]

In 1903, Hey published his well-known 'An elementary grammar of the Nggerikudi language' as one of Roth's *North Queensland Ethnography Bulletins*. Hey admitted in his foreword that he still did not fully understand the language. In my opinion, Hey was considerably influenced by Walter E. Roth, an academic and medical doctor with considerable contemporary expertise in ethnographical studies. Hey saw himself

18 How these good or bad hearts were in fact depicted in the pictures, with what kind of abilities, qualities or outward appearances, we cannot know. A guess is that missionary brochures or Moravian children's books may have been used.
19 Letter No. 22 from Hey to the Mission Board, 18 January 1895, from Thursday Island, p. 8, Moravian Church Archives.
20 Letter No. 7 from Hey to Kluge, 30 July 1892, from Cullen Point, p. 7, Moravian Church Archives.
21 There is also evidence that both Ward and Hey compiled vocabularies of Tjungundji and Yupungathi during the 1890s (see Mathew 1899).

primarily as a farmer and not as a studied man, and his attitude towards science remained reserved. Christianity was the way to understand and to interpret the world, man and nature—not science. In his later years, he stated very clearly: 'Science is knowledge, Christianity is revelation' (Hey 1912).

Understanding photographs: (Hidden) messages of missionary photographs

Snapshots were not possible in early photography, so almost all photographs in colonial and missionary times were carefully composed. These compositions were meant to consciously or unconsciously transmit messages. One important message certainly was the sheer number of people: look how many we are; a mission station at this place is worthwhile. That was an important point in arguments with politicians, local enemies of the mission or competitive missionary congregations or denominations: to document the usefulness and the popularity of a mission station at a certain locality.

Another point was the evidence that Indigenous people were willing to stand still in a row for at least some time, according to the missionaries' instructions. As mentioned above, snapshots were impossible, so people had to stand still for at least a few minutes. So, apparently, the people did what the missionaries told them to do and this was proof of the cooperation the missionaries had gained.

Another important message was the successful pacification of the area. Aboriginal people were imagined as wild, unreliable and treacherous, as discussed earlier. The missionaries had been told many times to 'never let them get behind you' or they would invariably be killed. Thus, if a missionary stood unarmed in front of Aboriginal people, with his back turned to them, he was, first, very courageous and, second, had pacified the situation successfully.

Plate 6.5 A photo often used in Moravian journals with the intention of showing European readers how Aboriginal people looked before contact with the missionaries.

Source: Collection, Moravian Church Archives, Herrnhut, Germany, LBS_00548_C_2-R_58-No_59.

Plate 6.6 One of the first photos taken at Mapoon with a whole group of Aborigines and the missionaries standing among or in front of them.

These kinds of photos carry important and complex messages for European readers and fellow missionaries in regard to worthwhile, successful and pacificatory mission work in an imagined hostile and/or void environment.

Source: Collection, Moravian Church Archives, Herrnhut, Germany, LBS_00181_C_1-R_53-No_13.

Concerning Aboriginal ceremonial life and religion there was another message to be shown in missionary photography, or, rather, in a caption that was applied later: the missionaries' perception that Aboriginal culture and religion were childish. Plate 6.7 shows dancers dressed for the crocodile dance. The brethren at Herrnhut, however, added the caption '*Heidnisches Krokodilspiel*', which can be translated as 'a game of crocodiles by the heathens'. Thus, for them, this traditional ceremony was just a game. The missionaries wanted Aboriginal people to drop these 'plays' and were also opposed to traditional dance ceremonies (corroborees) of any kind, though this attitude changed later. To eliminate these 'heathenly' games, they tried to introduce other plays and (children's) games.

Plate 6.7 Dancers and their masks for the crocodile dance.

Such dances were often perceived by the missionaries as mere games of the heathens, not as serious choreographies with religious meanings.

Source: Collection, Moravian Church Archives, Herrnhut, Germany, LBS_01349_C_2-R_56-No_20.

Understanding artefacts

The message stick in Plate 6.9 belongs to the Australian collection at the Museum of Ethnology in Herrnhut, and is displayed in the permanent exhibition. There are no records or explanations accompanying it. However, in an article in one of the Moravian journals, I discovered the story of Aboriginal people arriving too early for Christmas at Aurukun in 1911. Christmas was very popular with Aboriginal people, as they were invited in great numbers, were given presents and received big meals for several days, so they were always eager to arrive in time. As they had no calendar to tell them when it was 24 December, they arrived at a time they hoped would be right. At Aurukun in December 1911, they arrived too early. Nothing was happening. So they left again. Arthur Richter sent them a messenger with a message stick, saying: 'Come back in seven days—then it's Christmas time.' As authorisation, he also attached a white man's envelope to the message stick, indicating that he had sent it. Aboriginal people knew that white people used paper and envelopes for messages, and the only white person in the neighbourhood was the white missionary. Thus, they could be assured that the missionary had sent this message.

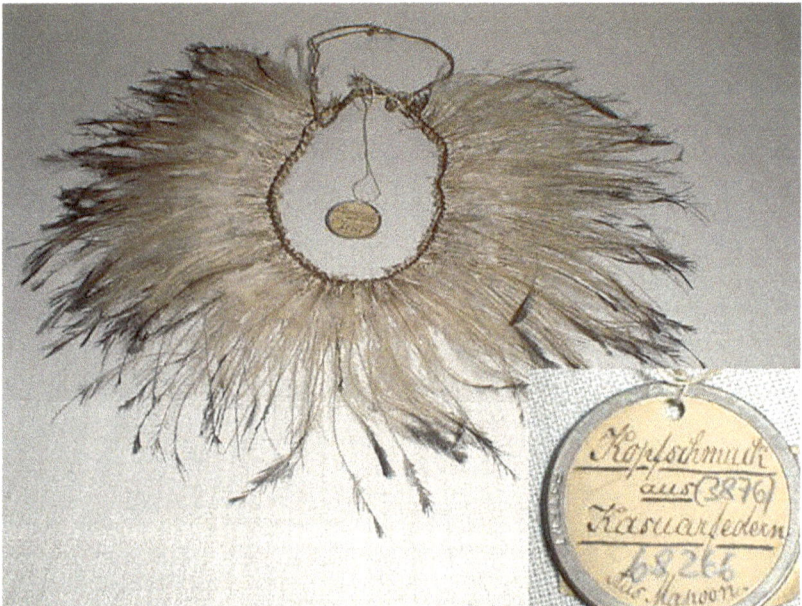

Plate 6.8 A head ornament made of cassowary feathers, from Mapoon.
Source: Inv.-No. 68266, Archives, Museum of Ethnology Herrnhut, State Art Collections, Dresden, Germany.

Plate 6.9 A message stick from Aurukun, probably used as a calendar to indicate the days until Christmas in 1911.

Source: Inv.-No. 68322, Archives, Museum of Ethnology Herrnhut, State Art Collections, Dresden, Germany.

Understanding religion by (tin plate) names

All Aboriginal children at the mission station had a tin plate for their food. Their names were marked at the side. However, as the missionaries explained in one of their letters, they did not have ordinary names, but the names of all kinds of animals, trees, stones and many other things. In other words, these were their totem names. The *Beiblatt zur Allgemeinen Missions-Zeitschrift* (Bechler 1913: 94) reported:

> The boys and girls can read now, that is why there are names on the rims of their plates. But what strange/fantastical names! Dalamany, Yampa, Gaddy and others! And even more curious are the meanings of these words! Kangaroo, dog, snake, tree, stone and many other things are the meanings of these names. Not unlike the savage's view that he can gain all attributes of a person when he eats a person's body, these people believe that they are descended from the animals, stones, trees whose names they

carry. The stronger the animal, the more powerful the tree, from which they descend, the more powerful they believe they are. This is how they perceive their beautiful names and are proud of them, similar to the ones of us, who descend from the heroes of ancient times.[22]

The missionaries described and understood the system of totemic ancestors well and the pride that Aboriginal people took in it, but summarised it as a question of names. Accordingly, Hey (1903), in his 'An elementary grammar of the Ngerrikudi language', explained the totem names and the totemic system as just a question of 'names'—not a question of religion.

Moravian contribution to Australian anthropology: Summary and conclusion

The Moravian archival records and museum collections are a rich source for western Cape York Peninsula anthropology. I have detailed only a few examples. The records are not accessed easily by any researcher from Germany or Australia, or by people of that region. They are written mostly in old German script and are not labelled or described adequately as ethnography as such. Neither are they translated into English or assembled in a publication under adequate titles and headings. To the contrary, the records have to be searched for among many different sources, extracted, transcribed and analysed very carefully. A sound knowledge of the Moravians' background, of the old German handwritten script and of Aboriginal people and their material culture is necessary to identify the key information that opens the door to rich anthropological data. Moreover, one has to be prepared to search in unlikely places, or under different labels, and to work through numerous archival records written in old German. The results, however, are very rewarding and can be used for very fruitful research and study in the future.

---

22 *Jetzt können Buben und Mädchen lesen, darum stehen jetzt Namen auf dem Tellerrand. Aber was für wunderliche Namen! Dalamany, Yampa, Gaddy und andere! Und noch viel wunderlicher die Bedeutung dieser Worte! Das Känguruh, Hund, Schlange, Baum, Stein und mancherlei andere Dinge, das ist die Bedeutung der verschiedenen Namen. Wie das Menschenfressen darin seinen Grund hat, daß der Wilde der Meinung ist, er könnte mit dem Leibe auch die Seele seines Opfers mit all ihren Tugenden und Vorzügen in sich aufnehmen, glauben diese Leute den Tieren, Steinen, Bäumen, deren Namen sie durchs Leben tragen, abzustammen. Je stärker das Tier, je mächtiger der Baum ist, von der er seine Herkunft ableiten kann, um so kraftvoller dünkt sich der Mensch. So sehen sie auf ihre schönen Namen und fühlen sich stolz in deren Besitz, ähnlich wie bei uns alle die, welchen ihren Stammbaum von Helden grauer Vorzeit herleiten.* Translation by Anna Kenny.

References

Bechler, T. 1913. Kulturarbeit der Brüdergemeine in Nordaustralien. Ein Kabinettstück neuerer Missionsgeschichte. *Beiblatt zur Allgemeinen Missions-Zeitschrift* 40(Jhg., 11)(Heft No. 6)(November).

Crowley, T. 1981. The Mpakwithi dialect of Anguthimri. In *Handbook of Australian Languages. Volume 2*, (eds) R. M. W. Dixon and B. J. Blake, pp. 146–94. Canberra: Australian National University Press. doi.org/10.1075/z.hal2.07cro.

Darwin, C. 1859. *On the Origin of Species by Means of Natural Selection, or the Preservation of Favoured Races in the Struggle for Life.* London: John Murray.

Erckenbrecht, C. 2010. Auf der Suche nach den Ursprüngen. Die Australienreise des Anthropologen und Sammlers Hermann Klaatsch 1904–1907. *Ethnologica N.F.* 27.

Hagenauer, F. A. 1886. Notes of a missionary journey to north Queensland. Special print.

Hey, N. 1903. An elementary grammar of the Nggerikudi language. In *North Queensland Ethnography Bulletin*, No. 6, (ed.) W. Roth. Brisbane: Department of Public Lands.

Hey, N. 1912. Substance of an address delivered by missionary N. Hey on 'Foreign mission night' during the sitting of the Presbyterian General Assembly of Queensland, May 14th 1912. Typed manuscript in Hey's personal file, ref. no. MD 925, Moravian Church Archives, Herrnhut, Saxony.

Huxley, T. H. 1863. *Man's Place in Nature.* Ann Arbor: University of Michigan Press.

Jensz, F. 2007. Collecting cultures for God: German Moravian missionaries and the British colony of Victoria, Australia, 1848–1908. PhD thesis. School of Historical Studies, Faculty of Arts, University of Melbourne, Melbourne.

Jensz, F. 2012. Collecting cultures: Institutional motivations for nineteenth-century ethnographical collections formed by Moravian missionaries. *Journal of the History of Collections* 24(1): 63–76. doi.org/10.1093/jhc/fhq043.

Kidd, R. 1997. *The Way We Civilise: Aboriginal affairs—The untold story.* Brisbane: University of Queensland Press.

Mathew, J. 1899. *Eaglehawk and Crow: A study of the Australian Aborigines, including an inquiry into their origin and a survey of Australian languages.* London: D. Nutt.

Meißel, G. 1898. Lebenslauf des verheirateten Bruders Gottlieb Meißel, heimgegangen in Niesky am 27. Juni 1897. *Mitteilungen aus der Brüder-Gemeine zur Förderung christlicher Gemeinschaft* (2)(S): 59–98.

Missionsdirektion (eds). 1895. *Missions-Atlas der Brüdergemeine.* Herrnhut: Mission Board.

Missionsdirektion (eds). 1907. *Missions-Atlas der Brüdergemeine.* Herrnhut: Mission Board.

Moravian Church Archives. n.d. Letters Nos 1–16 from Hey to Kluge, ref. no. NKH 9, Moravian Church Archives, Herrnhut, Saxony.

Moravian Church Archives. n.d. Letters Nos 5–22 from Hey to the Mission Board, ref. no. R.15.V.II.b.3.a.2, Moravian Church Archives, Herrnhut, Saxony.

Moravian Church Archives. n.d. Letters Nos 46–70 from Ward to the Mission Board, ref. no. R.15.V.II.b.3.a.2, Moravian Church Archives, Herrnhut, Saxony.

Moravian Missionary Reporter and Illustrated Missionary News. 1893. [London.] Vol. III(8)(NS)(August): 59.

Roth, W. E. 1903. Superstition, magic, and medicine. *North Queensland Ethnography Bulletin*, No. 5. Brisbane: Government Printer.

Schoetensack, O. 1901. Die Bedeutung Australiens für die Heranbildung des Menschen aus der niederen Form. (Vorgelegt in der Sitzung der Berliner Anthropologischen Gesellschaft vom 27. Juli 1901.) *Zeitschrift für Ethnologie* 33(S): 127–54.

Schoetensack, O. 1902. Erläuternde Bemerkungen zu meiner Abhandlung 'Über die Bedeutung Australiens für die Heranbildung des Menschen aus einer niederen Form'. *Verhandlungen der Berliner Anthropologischen Gesellschaft*, 34(S): 105.

Schoetensack, O. 1904. Die Bedeutung Australiens für die Heranbildung des Menschen aus einer niederen Form. *Verhandlungen des naturhistorisch-medizinischen Vereins zu Heidelberg* 7(S): 105–30.

Part II: Impact of the Aranda

7

Early ethnographic work at the Hermannsburg Mission in Central Australia, 1877–1910

Anna Kenny[1]

The early ethnographic work by the German Lutheran missionaries A. H. Kempe (1844–1928), L. G. Schulze (1851–1924) and Carl Strehlow (1871–1922) at the Hermannsburg Mission among the Aranda in Central Australia is not well known. Kempe and Schulze, for instance, are better known for their reporting of killings of Aboriginal people, their efforts to stop frontier violence and for their epic journey from Bethany in South Australia to the unforgiving centre of Australia that lasted nearly 18 months. Their journey has been immortalised in a booklet called *Venture of Faith* (Scherer 1963), which describes the missionaries' route of 900 kilometres through waterless desert stretches with an entourage of 37 horses, 20 cattle and nearly 2,000 sheep in the 1870s (Kenny 2013: 15). Immediately after their arrival at Hermannsburg, while they were still building houses for themselves and pens for their livestock, they began their study of Aranda, which Carl Strehlow would continue into the early 1920s.

---

1   A postdoctoral fellowship at The Australian National University that is part of an Australian Research Council Linkage grant (LP110200803) has made it possible to write this chapter.

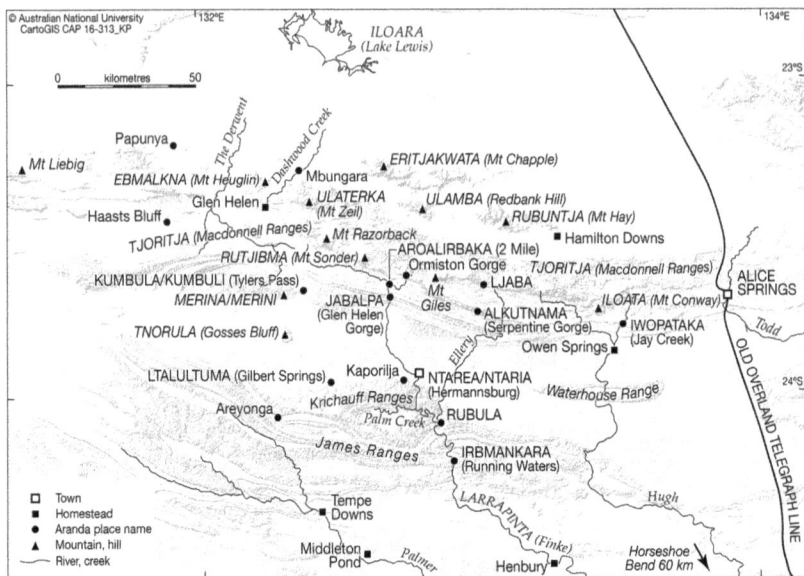

Map 7.1 Aranda names with their European equivalents for the area west of Alice Springs.

Source: CartoGIS, The Australian National University.

Plate 7.1 Hermannsburg, 1895.

Source: SRC 05846, Strehlow Research Centre, Alice Springs.

The training they received assumed that they would learn the language of the people whom they were sent to serve. It was a crucial part of Luther's reformation that the word of God was to be taught in the vernacular and translated into a people's mother tongue (Moore 2015: 39; Wendt 2001: 8). At the mission seminary in Hermannsburg, Germany, for example, they even used the Bible in Plattdeutsch (the German vernacular of that region). As a consequence, it was characteristic of nineteenth-century German Protestant mission theology and practice to pay special attention to a people's language and its implications for idiom and other dimensions of culture (Schild 2004: 54).

The site on the upper Finke River the missionaries chose for the mission is known as Ntaria and is associated with the *ratapa* ('twin') dreaming.[2] They named the mission Hermannsburg after the seminary in which they had trained and tentatively called the Aboriginal people 'Aldolinga', meaning 'from the west'.

Today, the local people call themselves Western Aranda or Tjoritjarinja, meaning 'belonging to the Western MacDonnell Ranges' (Kenny 2013: 17). These Arandic people used to be hunters and gatherers; now they live in scattered small remote communities. They still speak their own language, hold their own beliefs glossed in English with the terms 'The Dreaming' or 'The Law' and perceive their surroundings as a 'totemic landscape'. Their society is structured by a classificatory kinship system and their landownership system is essentially traditional with some adaptations resulting from settlement. At the same time, there is a strong Lutheran imprint on their society (Austin-Broos 2010).

According to Schulze (1891), Central Australia was very sparsely populated when they set up the mission, and during their residence they could see that the local people were 'considerably' reduced due to internal feuding, low birth rates, shootings by Europeans and smallpox, which seems to have arrived in the area just before Europeans. Progress in spreading the Gospel was slow and life on the frontier incredibly harsh. By 1891, the mission was abandoned and the missionaries had succumbed to the hardship and challenges of the desert. However, three years later, Carl Strehlow arrived to re-establish the mission, in 1894.

---

2   See Carl Strehlow (1907–20: Vol. I, pp. 80–1; Vol. II, p. 72, fn. 3; Vol. III, part 2, pp. 122–4) and T. G. H. Strehlow (1971: 758).

Plate 7.2 Carl Strehlow in his garden, 1901.
Source: SRC 07760, Strehlow Research Centre, Alice Springs.

In the course of learning Aranda, these missionaries collected and published not only linguistic, but also ethnographic data. Thus, the documentation of Aranda culture began at first contact in 1877.

Early Arandic ethnography

By 1880, the missionaries' language work had progressed well and they had produced a school primer and a book of Bible stories, psalms, hymns and prayers in the local language. Also, their studies of the local customs and practices had made some headway.

In 1882, Kempe published a paper on the plants of the Finke River in Central Australia in which he describes some of their local uses. One year later, in 1883, he published the first, very short ethnographic account about the people they had met at Ntaria called 'Zur Sittenkunde der Centralaustralischen Schwarzen' ('About customs of Central Australian blacks') (Kempe 1883). Although it is only five pages long, marred with common stereotypes of the time and first impressions (Kempe 1883: 52), it contains data that were of interest to anthropological investigation at the time. It covers in a very preliminary manner gesture language, sections, totems and *altjira*. Other than this short piece, he published only texts for mission purposes and 'A grammar and vocabulary of the language spoken by the Aborigines of the MacDonnell Ranges' (Kempe 1891a). His vocabulary is noteworthy because it contains nearly 2,000 words; many Australian languages have survived in samples of only 17–100 words in works such as Curr's compilation (1886–87). Kempe's strength was clearly linguistics and not ethnography.[3]

In 1886, based on data collated by Kempe and Schulze, F. E. H. Krichauff published a short paper called 'Customs, religious ceremonies, etc., of the "Aldolinga" or "Mbenderinga" tribe of Aborigines of the Krichauff Ranges, South Australia'. He extracted data from papers and letters Kempe and Schulze had sent to their superintendent, G. A. Heidenreich. Krichauff mentioned 'religion', 'festivals' in which emus and other species were worshiped, ceremonies, myths relating to the ancestral being Malbanca and how ancestors originated from primordial beings, beliefs about celestial bodies, *erinja* ('evil spirits'), mortuary rites and '*Altegiva*' (a misspelling of *Altjira*) (Krichauff 1886: 35–6). Krichauff's paper has to be treated with great care because he conflated and confused concepts and mythical narratives of the original findings of the missionaries.

---

3   Kempe's language work and his interest in flora and fauna—an acacia, *Acacia kempeana*, was named after him—were what made a lasting contribution to the knowledge of Australia's centre.

During the 1880s, both Kempe and Schulze corresponded with A. W. Howitt on aspects of Aboriginal culture. Schulze's letters included data about 'marriage rules' and, in particular, the 'eight-class' system,[4] which was a 'new discovery'. At the end of a letter written on 16 November 1887, he let Howitt casually know: 'P.S. Our tribe divides in more than 4 classes, as soon as possible I shall write it.'[5] While Howitt did not use Schulze's materials in his classic *The Native Tribes of South-East Australia*, he used information obtained from Kempe about the gesture language of the 'Aldolinga' (Howitt 1904: 727–35).

Schulze wrote in 1891 the first substantial ethnographic piece on the Aranda, called 'The Aborigines of the upper and middle Finke River: Their habits and customs' (Schulze 1891). His work shows that he was an apt ethnographer and had a flair for social observations. Although he makes some derogatory remarks about Aboriginal people (Schulze 1891: 219, 221), he does not descend to evolutionary sequencing. After describing the harsh nature of the Aranda's country—which he thought was 'at some places most striking and picturesque' (Schulze 1891: 211)—he briefly described the flora and fauna (pp. 214–17) and listed animals that were of particular importance to the Indigenous population. He collected, for example, Aboriginal names of nine different lizards, 22 different snakes and nine different fish. Among other topics, he discussed social organisation—in particular, the subsection system (Schulze 1891: 223–7)—mother's place (pp. 238–9), *altjira*, customs relating to death, *ltana* ('ghost'), *guruna* ('soul'), art forms, bush medicines, shelter, ceremonies and increase rites; he even recorded a *tjurunga* song (pp. 243–4).

Both Schulze and Kempe witnessed ceremonies (Schulze 1891: 221, 242–4). They were present at 'festivals or dances' called by the Aranda *tjurunga* and *ildada*, which:

> are ordered and arranged by the old people. Each one of these has one or more of these *tjurunga* as his special privilege or monopoly. This right does not pass to his sons as an inheritance. (Schulze 1891: 242)

These ceremonies—such as 'the *ilia tjurunga*, or emu festival', 'the *jarimba tjurunga*, or fish *tjurunga*, &c' (Schulze 1891: 242)—related to the earthbound mythical beings and became one of the central interests

4   Five letters by Reverend L. Schulze to A. W. Howitt, 1887–89, *Howitt Papers*, MF 459, Box 1051/Icc, State Library of Victoria, Melbourne.
5   L. Schulze to A. W. Howitt, 16 November 1887, *Howitt Papers*.

of Australian ethnographers (Spencer and Gillen 1899, 1904; Strehlow 1907–20: Vol. III, part 1, Vol. IV, part 1; Strehlow 1947, 1971). Schulze observed that they were not 'mere pleasure-bouts', but had 'a religious significance', and he wrote:

> If one attempts to deprecate the *tjurunga* of the old, it may happen one day that the traducer is killed for this offence, a case of the kind having occurred in the MacDonnell Ranges only a few years ago.

> These festivals serve as reminders, and extol the past, conjoined with prayers that these animals &c., may again appear in the same numbers, of similar size, &c.

> When everything is ready, the festival commences towards the evening. Women and children hurry towards the spot, and sit down together in a mass at one end of the arena, the men sitting in front of them. The chief old man and the festive dancers sit apart at a little distance. The singing, conducted by the onlookers, begins. One or two dancers then step forward and execute a dance consisting in keeping time to the singing by vigorous stamping with the feet, endeavouring at the same time to imitate the peculiarities of the particular animals that lends its name to the festival. After a while a pause is made, succeeded by the performance of another, and thus it goes on throughout the whole night, and for three or four nights in succession, while they rest and sleep by day. (Schulze 1891: 243)

> Most of the words of these songs are partly obsolete, and partly taken from other dialects. This explains why they are not understood by every one. One knows one song, another a different one, all being connected with the particular *tjurunga*, and derived from their ancestors. Their festivals of circumcision have not been seen by us. What I know of it is only by hear-say, hence I merely mention it. Their youths are circumcised at puberty. (p. 244)

Baldwin Spencer's, Frank Gillen's and Carl Strehlow's data about ceremonies suggest that the events Kempe and Schulze had witnessed were certainly not just entertainment, but were rites that were commonly performed at important places in Central Australia and also at public sessions of male initiation. Carl Strehlow (1907–20) made extensive records of both *tjurunga* and *ltata* (Schulze's *ildada*) ceremonies that can be stand-alone ceremonies or part of the initiation process, which, according to Strehlow, had seven stages at the turn of the twentieth century. The last stage was the *inkura* (Spencer and Gillen's *engwura*) ceremony; it was the largest and most prestigious ceremonial gathering and drew people together from far-flung places to witness the conclusion of the rites that brought young men into adulthood. All types of ceremonies and performances had either the purpose of *intitjiuma* (Luritja equivalent: *tintinpungañi*), meaning 'to initiate into something, to show how something is done', or the purpose of *mbatjalkatiuma* (Luritja equivalent: *kutintjingañi*), meaning 'to bring about, make fertile, improve the conditions of' (Strehlow 1907–20: Vol. III, part 1, pp. 1–2), and had public aspects that were witnessed by women, children and the uninitiated. At many stages of initiation women played a role, performing, for instance, dances called *ntaperama* (Strehlow 1907–20: Vol. IV, part 1, p. 19) and smoking ceremonies called *ulbuntakalama* (p. 36). The general public was usually never far from the privileged procedures, offering practical, ceremonial and emotional support.

Following in the footsteps of his predecessors, Carl Strehlow started his linguistic as well as his ethnographic investigations on arrival in Hermannsburg in 1894, drawing on Kempe's and Schulze's work. His previous experience at Bethesda (Killalpaninna) with the Dieri (Diyari)[6] people and his knowledge of their language and their joint work on the Bible translation are likely to have helped him quickly grasp the intellectual concepts of the Aranda and Luritja at Ntaria.

Carl Strehlow had been educated at the Neuendettelsau seminary in southern Germany, which trained its graduates rigorously. The classical orientation of the Neuendettelsau curriculum gave its students a solid basis from which to recognise structures of foreign languages, and assisted the writing of grammars and dictionaries—essential for the translation of the Scripture, mission preaching and schooling. In addition to classical languages, correct German style and essay and speech writing were taught, along with English. Other subjects that were prominent were music, which is deeply embedded in Lutheran tradition, and, under the director Johannes Deinzer, ethics. Neuendettelsau was less conservative and pietistic than other mission training institutions, such as Hermannsburg in northern Germany or the Basler Mission in Switzerland.

Strehlow arrived with an open mind and respect for the cultures of others. He combined all the interests of his predecessors in his work, which took on a cosmographic character covering most aspects of Aboriginal life and resulted in his classic ethnography, *Die Aranda- und Loritja-Stämme in Zentral-Australien* (*The Aranda and Loritja Tribes in Central Australia*) (Strehlow 1907–20), published in German, and a large comparative

---

6 The spelling Dieri is still commonly used by Dieri people today, while Diyari is a modern rendering.

dictionary with about 7,600 Aranda, German, Luritja and Dieri entries. Unlike the work of Kempe and Schulze, Strehlow's was influenced by views that would shape modern anthropology and were taken forward by his son, T. G. H. Strehlow (see Morton, Chapter 8, Austin-Broos, Chapter 9, and Gibson, Chapter 10, this volume).

Plate 7.3 Aranda Lutheran people and a group of visiting Luritja people at the Hermannsburg Mission, 1910s.
Source: SRC 06192, Strehlow Research Centre, Alice Springs.

In the following, I discuss briefly three topics—the subsection system, the *altjira* concept and mother's place—and show how the data of Kempe, Schulze and Strehlow senior not only contributed to the archival record of Central Australian anthropology, but also remain highly relevant today in land and native title claims.

Sections and subsections

Section systems among Aboriginal Australians had been known since 1855 from Reverend William Ridley's journey through the inland of south-east Queensland (Ridley 1861). Thus, Kempe (1883: 52), reporting on the section system among people at the Hermannsburg Mission in 1883—presumably based on information obtained from Southern Aranda people who still had not fully embraced the subsection system (Kenny 2013: 177)—was nothing unusual or new. However, Schulze's first observations about the 'eight-class' or subsection system that is found only in northern and Central Australia, were new (Kenny 2013: 169; Koch forthcoming). He mentions the subsection system in letters (1887–89) to A. W. Howitt that show that he was having a hard time understanding how it worked and in obtaining reliable data from his Aranda informants, whom he had to interrogate over and over again[7] and still could not quite make sense of what they were telling him. On 20 November 1889, for example, he wrote, confused and irritated, to Howitt:

> So for example, a Beltara is also Bungata; a Gomara also Mbitjana; a Bunanka also Gnuria; a Burula also Ngala, just with the difference, that one would like to be more Beltara than Bungata, the other would like to be more Bungata than Beltara.[8]

He spent many hours trying to elicit from them how this eight-class system worked, concluding that there used to be eight classes, but, due to demographic loss, only four classes remained.[9] On 10 December 1889, after further attempts to get to the bottom of the eight-class system, Schulze wrote:

> I have queried the natives several times for hours, but have not been able to discover anything too astonishing, which supports my view that a long time ago, they [the Aranda] certainly had 8 classes, in which only two particular classes could marry each other. For example, a Beltara-man may only marry a Gomara woman, a Bungata man may only marry an Mbitjana woman, and so forth. As the population diminished there were for example not enough Gomara women left, so they dropped the older regulation, and permitted Beltara men to also marry Mbitjana women and Bungata men could also marry Gomara women; and vice versa Gomara men may not only marry Beltara but also Bungata women, and Mbitjana men can not only marry Bungata but also Beltara women. Likewise with the other two class pairs. A Bunanka man who usually may only marry Burula, may now also marry a Ngala, if he cannot get a Burula.[10]

In his 1891 paper, Schulze maintained that the only way he had been able to understand this system was to collect as many examples as possible and then discuss them with informants. He remarked that when his

---

7 L. Schulze to A. W. Howitt, 8 May 1888, *Howitt Papers*.
8 L. Schulze to A. W. Howitt, 20 November 1889, *Howitt Papers*.
9 ibid.
10 L. Schulze to A. W. Howitt, 10 December 1889, *Howitt Papers*.

informants were asked to explain their social and religious customs, their final reply was always '*Wara*', meaning 'Our habit; nothing else' (Schulze 1891: 219). This reasoning added substantially to:

> the difficulty of discovering their motives, and caused the investigation of their social regulation in respect of their Eight-class system to be so troublesome. Information can only be obtained by accumulating many examples from their actual life, and then directing their attention to them. (Schulze 1891: 219)

Although Schulze had spent considerable time trying to solve the eight-class puzzle, he got muddled. He had not realised he was in an area where the section and subsection systems converged. The systems were straining to interlock, which was still the case in the 1930s (Strehlow 1947: 72), and he may have had among his informants some Luritja people who claim subsection affiliation through their mother if their parents' marriage had been irregular, in contrast with Aranda, who are always patrilineal in this regard. Finally, it might have been the case that the eight-class system had gone into temporary disuse as broader social networks waxed and waned in Central Australia.

Males.		Females.		Children.
Beltara	...	Gomara	...	Bunanka
Pungata	...	Mbutjana	...	Knuraia
Gomara	...	Beltara	...	Purula
Mbutjana	...	Pungata	...	Ngala
Bunanka	...	Purula	...	Beltara
Knuraia	...	Ngala	...	Pungata
Purula	...	Bunanka	...	Gomara
Ngala	...	Knuraia	...	Mbutjana

Plate 7.4 Schulze's version of the eight-class or subsection system.
Source: Schulze (1891: 224).

However, Schulze did get some aspects right, which was an achievement considering his circumstances. He first concluded correctly that, regarding marriage, it is ideally between 'a prescribed pair, thus forming four pairs of classes by prescription, although eight by name' (Schulze 1891: 223), but he did not get all pairs properly matched. Second, he also correctly asserted that 'paternal descent' was always the rule regardless of whether a man had married into the right Arandic subsection group.

According to Koch, Schulze's claim that, regardless of the subsection of the mother, the child's subsection is always determined by that of its father is inconsistent with his own data. Schulze contradicted his claim by placing the children of a male Bunanka in the Beltara subsection and those of a Knuraia in Pungata, which would be accurate if the subsection of the child had been determined by that of the mother or if, in Schulze's time, the joining of the original four terms and their filiations with the new set of terms was applied—that is, Penangke–Petharre (Schulze's Bunanka–Beltara) continued as a patrifilial pair rather than switching it to Penangke–Pengarte (Schulze's Bunanka–Pungata) beside Kngwarraye–Peltharre (Schulze's Knuraia–Beltara) (Koch forthcoming).[11]

Contemporary Indigenous views of the system as well as data from Spencer and Gillen (1899, 1927) and Carl Strehlow recorded only some years later, by contrast, match the subsections as Kamara–Purula, Ngala–Mbitjana, Paltara–Knuraia and Bangata–Pananka, and have Aranda marriage rules prescribing that Kamara marries Paltara, Purula marries Pananka, Ngala marries Knuraia and Mbitjana marries Bangata. Carl Strehlow (1907–20: Vol. IV, part 1, p. 63) showed the Aranda marriage rules of the eight-class or subsection system (Plate 7.4); A and B are parents and C their children.

Third, Schulze (1891: 224) observed correctly that 'those who stand on the same line marry first, but under certain circumstances marriages in a diagonal line are permitted to take place', which is correct in terms of the section system. He explained second-choice marriage to have come about because the Aranda:

> became much reduced in number, one class may have contained only a few men, and the other a few women, they then resorted to the relaxation of the rule to avoid extinction. (Schulze 1891: 224)

---

11   Koch uses the modern spelling of Central and Eastern Arrernte, a system that is called the IAD or common system.

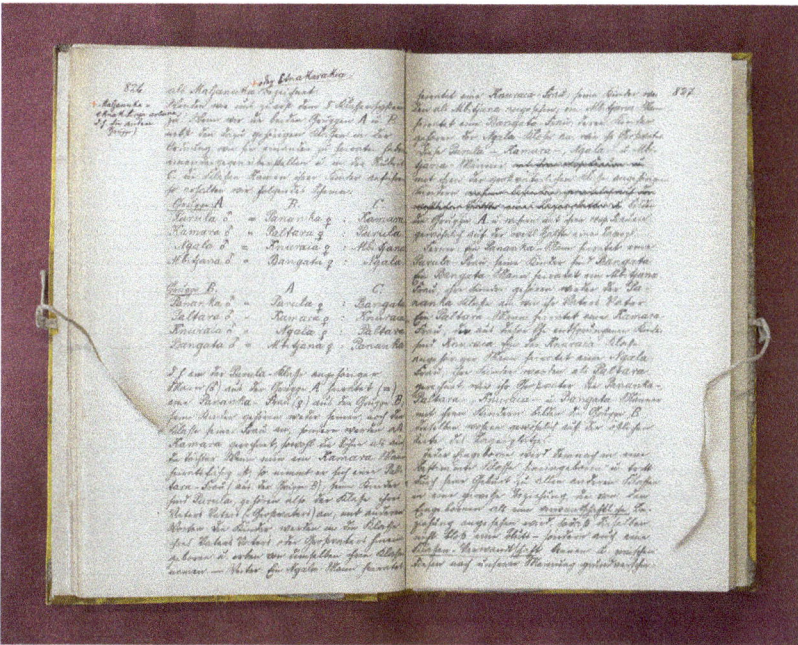

Plate 7.5 Pages 826–7 of Carl Strehlow's manuscript *Leben*. On page 826, centre, he illustrates how the subsection system of the Aranda works.
Source: Image courtesy of Strehlow Research Centre, Alice Springs.

To illustrate this point, he added that the numbers of the local population had been significantly reduced and marriages could not take place within the prescribed limits, especially as many white people attached 'to themselves native women' (Schulze 1891: 224).

Subsequent researchers amended his views and findings. Carl Strehlow (1907–20: Vol. IV, part 1) elaborated substantially on both the four-class and the eight-class systems, clarifying how they worked and other aspects of Aranda and Luritja social organisation and life. Through Spencer and Gillen (1899, 1927), the Aranda's social classification scheme became a seminal case—in particular, the eight-class system, called the 'subsection system' by Radcliffe-Brown, who named the system's related kinship classification system 'Arandic'.

Spencer and Gillen maintained that the subsection system had only been introduced into the Arandic world of Central Australia in the 1880s. However, Schulze's observations made at Ntaria at precisely that time on Western Aranda territory suggest otherwise, which is supported by Carl Strehlow's reports in the first decade of the twentieth century that, in mythology, the subsections were already well in place and their introduction did not seem that recent (Kenny 2013: 176). He wrote: 'This division of the people into different marriage-classes is regarded as being of very ancient origin and is already hinted at in the legends concerning the people of primordial times' (Strehlow 1907–20: Vol. IV, part 1, p. 62).

Strehlow's data on the mythical ancestors called Mangarkunjerkunja and Katukankara might also suggest that the subsection system had fallen into disuse as interactions and social networks had been disrupted, possibly due to events in the 1870s and 1880s, such as the building of the overland telegraph line, diseases such as smallpox, the Barrow Creek massacres or simply due to the unpredictable arid environment in which droughts and demographic losses occurred. He wrote:

> He [Mangarkunjerkunja] also gave them a marriage system, which regulated marriage between the classes. According to his instruction the two groups, which had been differentiated and separated at the beginning of time, should marry each other in the following manner:
>
> I. Land dwellers II. Water dwellers
>
> *Purula* should marry *Pananka*
>
> *Kamara* should marry *Paltara*
>
> *Ngala* should marry *Knuraia*
>
> *Mbitjana* should marry *Bangata*
>
> and vice versa. Then *Mangarkunjerkunja* divided the large territory, which the Aranda inhabit today, among the classes. (Strehlow 1907–20: Vol. 1, p. 6)
>
> The marriage system that *Mangarkunjerkunja* had taught also disintegrated. (p. 8)
>
> The moral decline spread further and further north, until a *tnunka* [kangaroo rat] man by the name of *Katukankara* [the immortal father] left *Anjatjiringi* in the north and once more re-enforced the marriage laws amongst the Aranda that *Mangarkunjerkunja* had given to them. (p. 8)

According to recent research by Koch on subsections and their spread, the subsection system would have arrived among Kaytetye and Anmatyerr(e) (northern neighbours of the Aranda) at the latest in the first half of the nineteenth century, which would be one generation before the Aranda (Arrernte) had the subsection system (Koch forthcoming). Based on

Schulze's letters to Howitt in the late 1880s, Carl Strehlow's data collected between 1894 and 1910 and estimates based on phonological change and the principles of adaptation of loan words (Koch forthcoming), it is likely that the subsection system had certainly arrived by the 1870s among the Western Aranda, if not decades earlier.

'Altjira'

A concept that becomes well discussed in Arandic ethnography as we pass through the twentieth century is *altjira* and its significance in Central Australian totemic beliefs and ceremonial life. According to Austin-Broos (2010: 16), *altyerre* (*altjira*) and *altyerrenge* are 'possibly the most contested words in modern Australian ethnography'.

It appears that the first written remark on the concept of *altjira*, and relating, among other things, to a 'high being', was made by Kempe over 130 years ago, in 1883. Kempe (1883: 53) recorded that '[c]hildren are a gift of Altjira (God)',[12] but did not make any other comment about what this might mean, and, interestingly, did not include it among the 2,000 words of his published wordlist. In his mission publications, he used the word *altjira* to denote the Christian God.

Schulze added to Kempe's scrap of information that *altjira* means 'not made'[13] and was connected to mother's place called *tmara altjira*. He wrote:

> They pretend that the *tjurunga arknanoa* ['festival plates'] were altjira— that is, were not made—but I suspect, as they occasionally give some to white people, that the old men and sorcerers make them themselves. (Schulze 1891: 242)

Carl Strehlow confirmed that the place called *tmara altjira* was associated with mother's totem and he added many more details to the written record about a 'supreme being' called *altjira*, unwittingly antagonising Sir Baldwin Spencer and triggering a debate about a high god among the Aranda and the meaning of this word that continues into the twenty-first century (see, for instance, Strehlow 1907–20: Vol. I; Vol. II; Vol. III,

---

12   Original: *Die Kinder, sagen sie, schenkt Altjira* (*Gott*).
13   Carl Strehlow to Moritz von Leonhardi, 13 December 1906, SH-SP-7-1. Held at the Strehlow Research Centre, Alice Springs.

part 1; Spencer and Gillen 1927; Strehlow 1971; Swain 1985; Kolig 1992; Hiatt 1996; Hill 2002; Strehlow 2004; Austin-Broos 2010; Green 2012; Kenny 2013; Moore 2015).

Carl Strehlow found that the term *altjira* was polysemic and covered an enormous amount of ground depending on the context in which it was used. He provided several meanings of this term and elaborated on them (see Kenny 2013). He maintained explicitly that the word *altjira* related to the spiritual and physical world of the totemic earthbound beings, but an *altjira* was also a 'sky being' called 'Tukura' in Luritja and could be interpreted as a 'high god', as it was the specific being of one of the myths he had recorded. Among its many references, *altjira* meant 'mother's totem' and had a providing and protecting role, 'like a mother feeds and protects her children during the early years of their lives', and appears in dreams to warn them of danger but also to tell friends about a person's wellbeing (Strehlow 1907–20: Vol. II, p. 57). The particular *tjurunga* associated with a man's mother, he regarded 'as the body of his altjira (mother's totem ancestor), who would accompany him on his lonely journeys' (Strehlow 1907–20: Vol. IV, part 1, p. 25).

While Strehlow's understanding of the term is evident, it is difficult to judge, based on Kempe's and Schulze's brief remarks on the concept of *altjira*, what they had understood about it. It appears though that they felt ambivalent about their use of *altjira*. Kempe, for instance, wrote to Spencer in 1910, 20 years after he had abandoned the mission:

> As regards the word '*Altjira*' in the language of the natives of Central Australia, I beg to tell you that, so far as I know the language, it is not 'God' in that sense in which we use the word—namely, as a personal being—but it has the meaning of old, very old, something that has no origin, mysterious, something that has always been so, also, always. Were *Altjira* an active being, they would have answered '*Altjirala*': the syllable 'la' is always added when a person exercises a will (force) which influences another being or thing. We have adopted the word 'God' because we could find no better and because it comes nearest to the idea of 'eternal'. The people through the usage of a word often use it as a name for a person. This, according to my conviction, is the true meaning of the word *Altjira*. (Spencer and Gillen 1927: 596)

It appears that Carl Strehlow also felt some ambivalence or even unease about its use in the Christian context, after he started corresponding with his editor, Moritz von Leonhardi, who wrote to him in 1905 that it rather surprised him to see that he still used *altjira* for 'Christian God'.

With their initial limited knowledge about Aboriginal cosmology and ontology, Kempe and Schulze, too, soon adopted the word *altjira* to denote the Christian God in their efforts to convey their Lutheran beliefs to the Aranda. Besides *altjira*, they had been told about *laia*, a kind of paradise, where the souls of people go to after death and where eternal joy lies (Kempe 1883: 56). Beliefs surrounding death were emphasised in Kempe's and Schulze's writing, because what happened to the soul (*guruna*) after death was, of course, of great interest to them.

While the information about *laia*, a type of paradise, and *altjira*, a being of some kind of higher order, appears to be accurate, how the missionaries interpreted the term was another matter. What they had heard about *altjira* and *laia* seemed familiar and, since they were trying to find contact points between themselves and the Aranda, what they had elicited from their Indigenous informants seemed to be related to their own concepts of their God and they decided to use it for their own purposes. Although Carl Strehlow kept on using the term *altjira* in the mission context, he was well aware of the term's large semantic field, discussing it for years with his editor (between 1901 and 1910). By the time he had realised the word's meaning, it was probably too late to replace the word *altjira* with another for the Christian God. It is noteworthy that at Killalpaninna the missionaries used the loan word *Godaia* for their own god (Moore 2015), rather than the word *mura*, which referenced a higher being among the Dieri people of the Lake Eyre region.

Despite their differences in quality and quantity, these early materials on *altjira* suggest that sky beings of some kind of 'higher order' are likely to have existed at the time of contact in 1877 alongside equally important totemic earthbound beings called dreamings today. It is clear now that *altjira* covers a very complex domain and that its semantic field and syntactic range were vast. Another example described by Carl Strehlow is the word *tjurunga*. He found that it had many very complex meanings depending on its context. *Tjurunga* could mean songs, stories, dances, paraphernalia or sacred objects—for instance, associated with the ancestral beings.[14] In his unpublished dictionary, *heilig* ('sacred') is part of its meaning as well as 'change into wood or stone' at the end of creative activities (Strehlow 1907–20: Vol. II, p. 77). *Tjurunga* today usually means 'sacred object' and is not often spoken about (Breen 2000: 60).

Other than providing evidence of a complex belief system, the materials of these early ethnographers make it possible to study language change and trace the semantic shifts of key words such as *altjira, tnankara, inkata* or even *tjurunga* back to the first contact period. The examination of *altjira*'s meaning, for instance, indicates that it has undergone some major semantic changes during the past century. Carl Strehlow, as well as Kempe, had observed a wide semantic field for the term *altjira* and Strehlow had discovered a synonym of the word: *tnankara*. Géza Róheim (1971: 211), shortly after Strehlow, also noted that this synonym for *altjira, tnankara*, 'is not often used', and, in his time, T. G. H. Strehlow (1971: 614) found that *altjira* was rarely used. Today, the Western Aranda use the term *altjira* to denote the Christian God and *tnankara* for concepts relating to Indigenous spiritual beliefs (Kenny 2013). Green (2012: 171) has observed a similar development for the Anmatyerr words *altyerr* and *anengkerr*, which used to be synonyms.

Mother's place (*tmara altjira*)

At the time of these early writers, the subject of territorial organisation was barely on the horizon in Australia. Indigenous landownership and rights became major subjects of research only in the second half of the twentieth century. Kempe and Schulze did not investigate territorial organisation as such when they arrived in Central Australia, though it seems that it was clear to them that the land they had come to was owned by the Indigenous population. Kempe remarked in 1883 that every group named themselves after a particular place, such as a water source or a waterway, or after the region from which they came (Kempe 1883: 52), while Schulze argued that they followed paternal descent and authority was held by the 'aged men and medicine-men' (the *knirabata* and *ngankara*), but that their rule was usually ineffective, as they did not form a 'nation, nationality, tribe, or tribelets', but the main unit was the family (Schulze 1891: 240–2).

---

14   See Carl Strehlow (1907, 1908, 1910); T. G. H. Strehlow (1947: 84–6; 1971: 770–1); and Carl Strehlow's letters to Moritz von Leonhardi (1906–09) held at the Strehlow Research Centre in Alice Springs.

Most importantly, though, Schulze (1891: 238–9) made the first remark on matrifiliation in Aranda country. He recorded the term *tmara altjira*, meaning 'the place where the mother of a dead person was born'. The deceased were oriented to face towards their mother's place, *tmara altjira*, to which their *ltana* ('ghost') hurried after death. Also T. G. H. Strehlow wrote in 1964:

> when a man died, he was buried (generally in a sitting position) in such a way that his face was turned towards the conception site of his mother: for that was his pmara altjira, his 'eternal home'. (Strehlow 1978: 39)

In this respect, Schulze had recorded that in 'an after-life, the natives say that the souls of all go to *laia*', but they were not able to explain to him how to reconcile this view with the information about *tmara altjira* (Schulze 1891: 244), where the soul is supposed to go after death as well.

About 15 years later, Carl Strehlow recorded further details surrounding the *tmara altjira*, meaning 'maternal totem place' (Strehlow 1907–20: Vol. IV, part 2, p. 16). He was able to explain why Schulze found his informants' view surrounding this place inconsistent. He was told that after a boy has carried his knocked-out tooth with him for several weeks, he tossed it in the direction of his *tmara altjira* (Strehlow 1907–20: Vol. I, p. 9) and that, after his death and the completion of his second burial ceremony, he would go to his *tmara altjira* to collect his tooth, which would show him the way to the Island of the Dead (*Laia*) (Strehlow 1907–20: Vol. III, part 2, p. 9, fn. 4).

Strehlow, too, mentioned connections to mother's conception dreaming, called in Aranda *altjira*, which is associated with a totem such as *ara* ('kangaroo'), *ilia* ('emu'), *jerramba* ('honey ant'), and so on. He described the relationship of an individual to the mother's dreaming, also called *garra altjira* or *deba altjira*, and to mother's conception site, called 'tmara altjira or more precisely, tmara altjirealtja, i.e. the place of the totem associated with me' (Strehlow 1907–20: Vol. II, p. 57; Vol. III, part 1, p. 2). He mentioned the right question to ascertain the totem place of a person's mother—namely, 'tmara altjira (or altjirealtja) unkwanga ntana?' ('Where is the place of the totem associated with you?') (Strehlow 1907–20: Vol. II, p. 58).

In 1927, Spencer wrote in a postscript that he and Gillen[15] had also encountered the *tmara altjira* in the 1890s. Spencer wrote:

> Gillen and myself describe the grave as having a depression facing the Alcheringa camp (the Tmara alchera) of the deceased. The difference between Schulze and us is that the former describes the Tmara as being that of the mother, whilst we describe it as that of the dead person. The important point, however, is the evident significance of the word Altjira, used by Schulze, as implying something associated with past times, and not as the name of any person or individual. He defines the Tmara altjira as the place where the mother was born; Gillen and myself as the place where the 'spirit' lived and entered the mother when she became pregnant, and Strehlow, who in this says that Tmara altjira as meaning 'mother's totem'. (Spencer and Gillen 1927: 591)

The important point here is that all three parties found the *tmara altjira* to be somehow associated with 'mother', which references matrifilial connections to place and country in the contact era. Together, these early remarks on matrifiliation to country indicate what the land tenure system might have been like. In the second half of the twentieth century, research for claims under the *Aboriginal Land Rights (Northern Territory) Act 1976* (Cth) and the *Native Title Act 1993* (Cth) provoked considerable academic debate around land tenure issues. This is where the material of Kempe, Schulze, the Strehlows as well as Spencer and Gillen, Róheim or Olive Pink becomes particularly interesting.

In addition, Carl Strehlow observed that sets of siblings with the same mother shared a dreaming and the site associated with it. He had found that one of the larger ceremonial objects was associated with *altjira* ('totem') and could be inherited from mothers.[16] This seems to be the first indication in the written record of Central Australia that mother's dreaming and place were collectively held, as all children of one mother had the same *altjira*, implying rights in the mother's place, and that, possibly at different times, different 'totem' affiliations were more or less important or emphasised. Unfortunately, these thoughts were not

---

15   Spencer references this section to their *Native Tribes of Central Australia* (Spencer and Gillen 1899: 497). The relevant passage reads: 'It [the body] is placed in a sitting position with the knees doubled up against the chin, and is thus interred in a round hole in the ground, the earth being piled directly on the body so as to make a low mound with a depression on one side. This is always made on the side which faces the direction of the dead man or woman's camping ground in the Alcheringa, that is the spot which he or she inhabited whilst in spirit form.'

16   Moritz von Leonhardi to Carl Strehlow, 2 June 1907.

developed any further. Nevertheless, they show that the right questions and concepts were emerging. A passage written on 6 April 1907 by Carl Strehlow to von Leonhardi indicates this clearly:

> As the tjurunga ['sacred property or object'] is the symbol of the personal totem, some blacks have told me, that the wonninga ['a ceremonial object'] can be seen as the symbol of the maternal totem or altjira. However, I am not yet certain about this, and will make further inquiries. While the tjurunga of individuals are different (each individual has his own totem ancestor), the wonninga as the symbol of altjira would tie the members of a family together, because they all have the same altjira, but all have different ratapa ancestors. It is hard to tell which of the two totems is older, the personal or the one inherited from one's mother.[17]

Although Kempe, Schulze and Strehlow did not connect the issues of social classification, knowledge and land in an understanding of territorial (local) organisation or land tenure, they recorded data on the different ways in which individual people could be connected with place. These data suggest that traditional ownership was dynamic and involved in change that intensified with the impact of settlement.

Conclusion

Despite their limitations, Kempe and Schulze laid the linguistic and ethnographic groundwork for the study and, more importantly, to some degree the continued vitality of Aranda language. Carl Strehlow's language work and, in particular, his ethnography *Die Aranda- und Loritja-Stämme in Zentral-Australien* secured the basis for ongoing value being placed on Western Aranda culture. Their Lutheran language tradition, which was fundamentally based on the Herderian view that language contained the spirit of a people, contributed significantly to the cultural survival of the Western Aranda by explicitly emphasising the importance of language.

While Kempe's and Schulze's work is still part of nineteenth-century ethnography, Carl Strehlow's work in its relation to modern anthropology has a transitional status, as it was influenced by anthropological thought developing in Germany and provided the blueprint for his son's seminal work. Although limited by the available tools (as were his predecessors),

---

17   Carl Strehlow to Moritz von Leonhardi, n.d. [possibly 6 April 1907], SH-SP-11-1. Held at the Strehlow Research Centre, Alice Springs.

his approach allowed him to collect material for the emerging discipline of anthropology; the ingredients that are essential for a modern comparative study of societies and their cultures are present in his ethnographic work.

In the second half of the twentieth century, it became possible for Aboriginal people in Australia to claim their traditional lands and native title rights under the Commonwealth's *Aboriginal Land Rights (Northern Territory) Act 1976* and *Native Title Act 1993*. The missionaries' ethnographic work showed the Aranda's cultural continuity and that the Aranda were, without a shadow of a doubt, among the original inhabitants of Central Australia. In this context, Schulze's paper is of particular value, because it is based on observations made during the first contact period and treats a particular people rather than seeking to explain 'origin' or trying to systematise social phenomena. His data on *tjurunga* ceremonies, *altjira, tmara altjira* and the subsection system are the earliest evidence for the continuity of these features of Arandic culture. In the context of land rights, native title, mining and royalty agreements, their ethnography is still playing an important role in contemporary Australia.

References

Altmann, M. 1980. *The Silver Miner's Son: The history of Louis Gustav Schulze missionary*. Hahndorf, SA: Fox Publishing.

Austin-Broos, D. 2010. Translating Christianity. *The Australian Journal of Anthropology* 21(1): 14–32. doi.org/10.1111/j.1757-6547.2010.00065.x.a.

Breen, G. 2000. *Introductory Dictionary of Western Arrernte*. Alice Springs, NT: IAD Press.

Curr, E. M. 1886–87. *The Australian Race*. 4 vols. Melbourne: J. Ferres.

Green, J. 2012. The Altyerre story: 'Suffering Badly by Translation'. *TAJA* 23(2): 158–78. doi.org/10.1111/j.1757-6547.2012.00179.x.

Hiatt, L. R. 1996. *Arguments about Aborigines: Australia and the evolution of social anthropology*. Cambridge: Cambridge University Press.

Hill, B. 2002. *Broken Song: T. G. H. Strehlow and Aboriginal possession*. Sydney: Knopf/Random House Australia.

Howitt, A. W. 1904. *The Native Tribes of South-East Australia*. London: Macmillan & Co.

Kempe, H. 1882. Plants indigenous about the River Finke, Central Australia. *Transactions and Proceedings and Report of the Royal Society of South Australia* 5: 19–24.

Kempe, H. 1883. Zur Sittenkunde der Centralaustralischen Schwarzen [About customs of Central Australian blacks]. *Mitteilungen des Vereins für Erdkunde zu Halle* [*Journal of the Halle Geographical Society*]: 52–6.

Kempe, H. 1891a. A grammar and vocabulary of the language spoken by the Aborigines of the MacDonnell Ranges. *Transactions of the Royal Society of South Australia* 14(1): 1–54.

Kempe, H. 1891b. *Galtjintana-Pepa Kristianirberaka Mbontala*. Hermannsburg in Hannover: Missionshandlung.

Kenny, A. 2013. *The Aranda's Pepa: An introduction to Carl Strehlow's masterpiece Die Aranda- und Loritja-Stämme in Zentral-Australien (1907–1920)*. Canberra: ANU E Press.

Koch, H. forthcoming. The development of Arandic subsection names in time and space. In *Skin, Kin and Clan: The dynamics of social categories in Indigenous Australia*, (eds) P. McConvell, P. Kelly and S. Lacrampe. Canberra: ANU Press.

Kolig, E. 1992. Religious power and the all-father in the sky: Monotheism in Australian Aboriginal culture reconsidered. *Anthropos* 87: 9–31.

Krichauff, F. E. H. 1886. Customs, religious ceremonies, etc., of the 'Aldolinga' or 'Mbenderinga' tribe of Aborigines of the Krichauff Ranges, South Australia. *Proceedings of the Royal Society of Australia, SA* (1886–87): 32–7, 77–80.

Moore, D. 2015. The Reformation, Lutheran tradition and missionary linguistics. *Lutheran Theological Journal* 49: 36–48.

Pink, O. 1936. The landowners in the northern division of the Aranda Tribe, Central Australia. *Oceania* 6(3): 275–305.

Ridley, W. 1861. Journal of a missionary tour among the Aborigines of the western interior of Queensland, in the year 1855. In *Queensland, Australia*, (ed.) J. D. Lang, Appendix I. London: Stanford.

Róheim, G. 1971 [1945]. *The Eternal Ones of the Dream: A psychoanalytic interpretation of Australian myth and ritual*. New York: International Universities Press.

Scherer, P. A. 1963. *Venture of Faith: An epic in Australian missionary history*. Tanunda, SA: Auricht's Printing Office.

Scherer, P. A. 2004. Kempe, Friedrich Adolf Hermann (1844–1928). *Australian Dictionary of Evangelical Biography*. Sydney: Evangelical History Association of Australia. Available at: webjournals.ac.edu.au/ojs/index.php/ADEB/article/view/1064/1061. Accessed 29 July 2015.

Schild, M. 2004. *Heading for Hermannsburg: Notes on Carl Strehlow's early career path*. Occasional Paper No. 3, (ed.) W. Veit, pp. 51–58. Strehlow Research Centre, Alice Springs, NT.

Schulze, L. 1891. The Aborigines of the upper and middle Finke River: Their habits and customs. *Transactions and Proceedings of the Royal Society of South Australia* 14(2): 210–46.

Spencer, W. B. and Gillen, F. J. 1899. *The Native Tribes of Central Australia*. London: Macmillan.

Spencer, W. B. and Gillen, F. J. 1904. *The Northern Tribes of Central Australia*. London: Macmillan.

Spencer, W. B. and Gillen, F. J. 1927. *The Arunta*. 2 vols. London: Macmillan & Co.

Strehlow, C. 1907–1920. *Die Aranda- und Loritja-Stämme in Zentral-Australien*. 7 vols. Frankfurt am Main: Joseph Baer & Co.

Strehlow, J. 2004. *Reappraising Carl Strehlow: Through the Spencer–Strehlow debate*. Occasional Paper No. 3, (ed.) W. Veit, pp. 59–91. Strehlow Research Centre, Alice Springs, NT.

Strehlow, T. G. H. 1947. *Aranda Traditions*. Melbourne: Melbourne University Press.

Strehlow, T. G. H. 1971. *Songs of Central Australia*. Sydney: Angus & Robertson.

Strehlow, T. G. H. 1978 [1964]. *Central Australian Religion: Monototemism in a polytotemic community*. Adelaide: Australian Association for the Study of Religion.

Swain, T. 1985. *Interpreting Aboriginal Religion: An historical account*. Adelaide: Australian Association for the Study of Religion.

Wendt, R. 2001. Einleitung: Missionare als Reporter und Wissenschaftler in Übersee. In *Sammeln, Vernetzen, Auswerten. Missionare und ihr Beitrag zum Wandel europäischer Weltsicht*, (Hrsg.) R. Wendt, pp. 7–22. Tübingen: Gunter Narr Verlag.

8

Sigmund Freud, Géza Róheim and the Strehlows: Oedipal tales from Central Australian anthropology

John Morton[1]

As almost every parody of Sigmund Freud reminds us, his native tongue was German. Although 'the German anthropological tradition' is hardly synonymous with his name, there is no doubting his more than occasional impact on the discipline of anthropology, in Australia as elsewhere. Psychoanalysis is occasionally known as the 'Jewish science' (Frosh 2005)—a term first conferred by its Nazi detractors—but it also has deep roots in German romanticism, principally through Freud himself, who claimed that he launched his career after hearing a public reading of Goethe's 'dithyrambic essay' depicting 'Nature as a beautiful and bountiful mother who allows her favourite children the privilege of exploring her secrets' (Jones 1964: 55).

Of all of Freud's works, *Totem and Taboo*, published in German as *Totem und Tabu* in 1913, is the most explicitly anthropological (Wallace 1983). It is also the work he claimed to be his best (Bakan 2004: 295) and which placed the Oedipus complex at the very heart of culture, with some illustrations drawn from Aboriginalist ethnography. In the first part

---

1   I thank Anna Kenny for her invaluable assistance in sourcing images for me at the Strehlow Research Centre, Alice Springs.

of this chapter, I look further into the Germanic roots of Freud's work and its relation to his 'armchair' encounter with Australian Aborigines, particularly those he wrote of—following Spencer and Gillen (1899) and Frazer (1910)—as the 'Arunta' of Central Australia. I do this in part to arrive at a view about Freud's impact on the later ethnography of Géza Róheim and T. G. H. Strehlow, both of whom also dealt with 'Arunta' (Aranda, Arrernte) people.

It was 15 years after the publication of *Totem and Taboo* that psychoanalysis produced its first field ethnographer: Géza Róheim. Róheim was Hungarian by birth and upbringing, but Hungary was at that time politically united with Austria, so he was fluent in German, the language in which a number of his early publications were issued. Fascinated by folklore from an early age, his higher education took him to Leipzig and Berlin to study geography (ethnology being unavailable under that name at the time), but, by then, he was already well acquainted with psychoanalysis, as well as writers such as Boas, Crawley, Frazer, Frobenius, Tylor and van Gennep. However, he did not formally encounter and 'convert' to psychoanalysis until 1915, when he began an analysis with Sándor Ferenczi (Muensterberger and Nichols 1974: xii–xiii). In 1928, Róheim, along with his wife, Ilona, embarked on a journey to Africa, North America and Oceania, with his most significant fieldwork done in 1929 in Central Australia, where his informants were both Arrernte and Western Desert people (Morton 1988: viii–ix). As I illustrate in the second part of this chapter, although Róheim generally remained faithful to Freud and to ideas put forward in *Totem and Taboo*, he both grounded his own ideas in more detailed, firsthand ethnography and extended Freud's ideas in novel directions. Although his influence on Aboriginalist anthropology as a whole was relatively slight during his lifetime, his work was significant and prescient in certain respects.

Róheim arrived in Central Australia just three years before T. G. H. Strehlow returned there in 1932 to embark on an ethnographic career that would see him elevated to the region's most authoritative and influential ethnographer. Strehlow was an enthusiastic, yet guarded, reader of both Freud and Róheim (see Gibson, Chapter 10, this volume), although, as I show in the third part of this chapter, it appears that Freud, largely through *Totem and Taboo*, probably had the greater bearing on Strehlow's work. This influence seems to have been as much personal as theoretical, having a lot to do with Strehlow's subjective orientation to his German missionary father, Carl, who also produced outstanding ethnographic work in Central Australia in the early part of the twentieth century. Carl Strehlow was radically empiricist in method (Kenny 2013: 116–24) and so was his son (see Gibson, Chapter 10, this volume); but there were times when the latter's writing seems to have been strongly over-determined by his encounter with Freud's *Totem and Taboo*. As I demonstrate below, this intimate orientation to *Totem and Taboo* mirrors only to some extent Freud's own or Róheim's reaction to it before and after his fieldwork in 1929.

Sigmund Freud

Although Freud once fantasised about migrating to Australia (Kaplan 2010: 208), he lived almost his entire life in German-speaking areas of Europe, principally Vienna. He wrote overwhelmingly in German and was by all accounts a consummately precise artist in his native tongue, modelling his style on the German classics—particularly Herder's sometime companion and kindred spirit, Goethe. He won praise from the likes of Thomas Mann and Hermann Hesse for his prose (Bettelheim 1985: 8–9), and won the City of Frankfurt's prestigious Goethe Prize for science and literature in 1930 (Jones 1964: 598–9). Although Freud's career began in medicine, he forged psychoanalysis by deepening his interests in literature and philosophy. Hence, as Bruno Bettelheim (1985) has spelt out in his book *Freud and Man's Soul*, Freud's approach to psychology became fundamentally humanistic, hermeneutic and idiographic—in a word, *geisteswissenschaftlich*—a matter that is often difficult to appreciate in the poor-quality English translations of the *Standard Edition*. The translation problem is especially acute where Freud's German phrasing *die Seele* ('the soul') is rendered simply as 'the mind' (Bettelheim 1985: 70–8) or where his terms of human subjectivity—*das Es* ('the it'), *das Ich* ('the I') and *das Über-Ich* ('the upper-I')—are medicalised as 'id', 'ego' and 'super-ego' (Bettelheim 1985: 53–60).

Along with his particular crafting of the German language, Freud also constructed psychoanalysis on the model of *Bildung* (Winter 1999: 40–53)—that is, as an educational method of self-discovery, self-cultivation and self-fulfilment that is at once personal, cultural, emotional and intellectual. This notion of *Bildung* can be traced back to Goethe and Herder's contemporary, Wilhelm von Humboldt (Dumont 1994: 82–144; Sorkin 1983), the linguist and educationalist perhaps better known in anthropology for his idea of *Weltansicht* or 'world view'—a forerunner of the now better known *Weltanschauung* (Underhill 2009). But it was Goethe himself who is sometimes said to have written the archetypal *Bildungsroman, Wilhelm Meisters Lehrjahre* (*Wilhelm Meister's Apprenticeship*) (Curran 2002: 2; Dumont 1994: 145–95), the novel genre that portrays *Bildung* as 'coming of age' or self-realisation through change and moral or cultural development. Matters connected to *Bildung* and the relationship between the individual and culture would eventually find their way into American anthropology after Boas, classically in Ruth Benedict's *Patterns of Culture* (1934), but in Freud's hands the associated life-narrative function was transferred to the methodological injunction 'know thyself', the most famous of the maxims inscribed on the Temple of Apollo at Delphi, where, in Greek mythology, both Laius and Oedipus consulted the oracle to be warned about parricide and incest (Graves 1960: 9–15). The story of Oedipus would, of course, become the basic narrative on which the entire edifice of psychoanalysis was built, not only as a therapeutic method, but also as a cultural phenomenon with wide effects and applications—including in relation to understanding Freud's own life.

Freud arrived at the idea of the Oedipus complex largely by introspection and intersubjectivity. That is to say, Freud came to the idea over a number of years, prompted initially by the death of his father, Jakob, in 1896, which brought about a sustained period of self-analysis (Jones 1964: 276–83) and a quickening of his vocational desire (pp. 293–8). In turn, the self-analysis fed into his dialogues with patients (Barron 1993: xix–xx; Sulloway 1980: 209–10). In line with the idea of *Bildung*, Freud began to understand both of these in terms of what he called *Kulturarbeit*—literally, 'culture work' or the work that is necessary to achieve culture (Bettelheim 1985: 63)—a term that is found, for example, in Freud's most famous statement: '*Wo Es war, soll Ich werden. Es ist Kulturarbeit etwa wie die Trockenlegung der Zuydersee*' ('Where It was, I should come into being. It is the work of culture, like the draining of the Zuider Zee'). Although it has not been established with certainty, it appears that the second sentence in this statement is probably an allusion to Goethe's *Faust*, where Faust reclaims his erstwhile restless soul from Mephistopheles and finally embodies his salvation in productive work—in fact, in the disciplined and fulfilling action of reclaiming land from the sea for cultivation (Bettelheim 1985: 64).

Hence, *Kulturarbeit* is fundamentally the unfolding of ethical projects defined as contributions to civilised society. For Freud, there was no fundamental distinction in kind between the 'culture work' he did for himself after his father's demise (his self-analysis) and the 'culture work' he did for or with others, be they patients, colleagues or general readers. In psychoanalysis, the social and psychological fields are inextricably linked as effects of 'sublimation'—the art of finding grace as equilibrium between inclination and obligation. This idea is yet another that Freud seems to have appropriated and reworked from Goethe, as well as from Schiller, Schopenhauer and Nietzsche (Goebel 2012: 1–155), but the idea that the Oedipus complex was the most suitable way of grasping sublimation came from elsewhere—from the symbolism implicit in Sophocles's famous play, *Oedipus the King* (Bettelheim 1985: 20–30), whose tragic appeal suggested to Freud that the complex was both universal and innate.

Totem and Taboo alludes to Goethe's *Faust* with its final quotation: 'in the beginning was the deed' (Freud 2001a: 161). In Goethe, this line inaugurates Faust's encounter with Mephistopheles and so signals the transgression—the vital 'deal with the Devil'—from which Faust must eventually be extricated and win redemption (Redner 1982: 41–62). As is well known, Freud's 'deed' was oedipal, involving the slaying of the father of the 'primal horde' due to envy of his sexual privileges, but it also led to the sons' remorseful response to their actions that resulted in the prohibition of incest and the institution of religion, law and morality. Hence, in both *Faust* and *Totem and Taboo*, we are treated to transgression as the first aspect of a rite of passage—a structure that Freud thought was echoed in contemporary rituals in Central Australia and elsewhere. Furthermore, he believed this structure to be at the heart of inheritance and tradition—again, taking his cue from *Faust*: '*Was du ererbt von deinen Vätern hast, Erwirb es, um es zu besitzen*' ('What thou hast inherited from thy fathers, acquire it to make it thine') (Freud 2001a: 158).

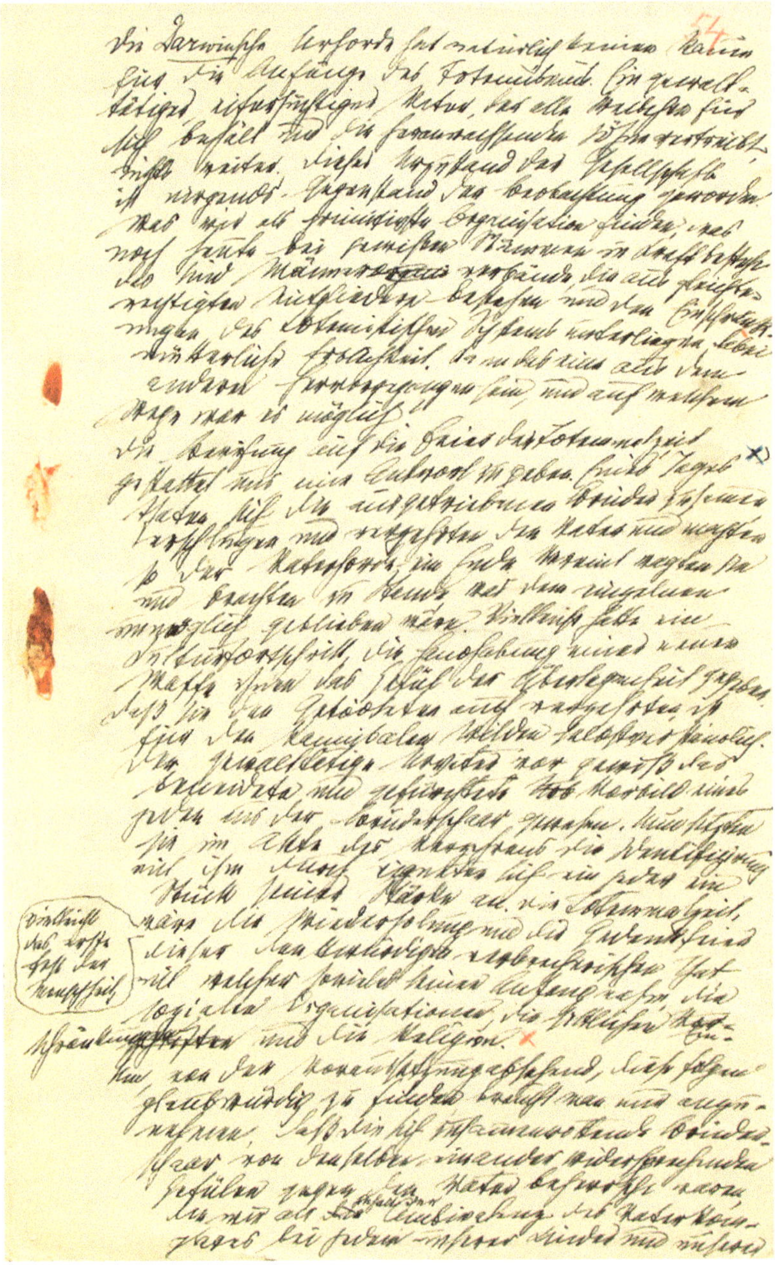

Plate 8.1 Extract from Freud's handwritten German manuscript for *Totem and Taboo*.

The extract contains Freud's famous description of the primal crime and its consequences, indicated between the blue and red crosses. It reads: *'Eines Tages taten sich die ausgetriebenen Brüder zusammen, erschlugen und verzehrten den Vater und machten so der Vaterhorde ein Ende. Vereint wagten sie und brachten zustande, was dem einzelnen unmöglich geblieben wäre. (Vielleicht hatte ein Kulturfortschritt, die Handhabung einer neuen Waffe, ihnen das Gefühl der Überlegenheit gegeben.) Daß sie den Getöteten auch verzehrten, ist für den kannibalen Wilden selbstverständlich. Der gewalttätige Urvater war gewiß das beneidete und gefürchtete Vorbild eines jeden aus der Brüderschar gewesen. Nun setzten sie im Akte des Verzehrens die Identifizierung mit ihm durch, eigneten sich ein jeder ein Stück seiner Stärke an. Die Totemmahlzeit, vielleicht das erste Fest der Menschheit, wäre die Wiederholung und die Gedenkfeier dieser denkwürdigen, verbrecherischen Tat, mit welcher so vieles seinen Anfang nahm, die sozialen Organisationen, die sittlichen Einschränkungen und die Religion.'* See pages 141–2 of the *Standard Edition* (Freud 2001a) for the English translation.

Source: Image courtesy of the Library of Congress, Washington, DC. *Sigmund Freud Papers*, MSS39990, Box OV 4, Reel 2, 1912–1913, IV, Folder 2, p. 54.

It is often said that, alongside the work of Frazer and Durkheim, *Totem and Taboo* was significantly influenced by early Central Australian ethnography, particularly the work of Spencer and Gillen (e.g. Kuklick 2005: 19; Morton 2005: 3489; Petch 2013: 804), but this needs to be qualified. Spencer and Gillen receive just three brief mentions in *Totem and Taboo* (Freud 2001a: 7, 114, 121) and there are relatively few references to Australian Aborigines at all, with most coming second-hand through Frazer—including one fairly short passage referring to the 'Arunta' (pp. 114–18). It may be true that Freud 'systematically read all the available ethnography' (Paul 1976: 333) pertinent to *Totem and Taboo*, but there is little evidence that the Central Australian material was especially important to his thinking in any direct way.

While few anthropologists have taken Freud's historical speculations about the primal horde too seriously, there have been some stout and reasonably convincing defences of his anthropological program (Fox 1967; Paul 1976, 2010). When thinking about the significance of *Totem and Taboo* for Aboriginalist anthropology, it is important to be clear about Freud's intentions in positing his version of 'original sin', which is closely wedded to his idea of 'culture work'. One way to look at those intentions is to say that, much in the spirit of Durkheim (whom he occasionally cites in *Totem and Taboo*) or Lévi-Strauss, Freud was looking for 'elementary structures'—not in 'collective representations' or 'the mind', but in the human organism. His speculations in *Totem and Taboo* were in part a response to what he regarded as the wrongheaded direction being taken by Jung (1956) in relation to (what Jung later came to call) the 'collective unconscious' (Freud 2001a: xiii), but they were also part of his own version of a pan-human 'archaic heritage' (Smadja 2015: 133–5), an emotional-cum-intellectual structure inherited and inescapably ingrained in the psyche, yet requiring effort for proper realisation.

The 'scientific myth of the father of the primal horde', as Freud (2001a: 135) later called *Totem and Taboo*, was indeed a myth: a story about human origins acting as a shorthand account of human evolution over the longue durée. But it was also a story about the emergence of *Kulturarbeit*, about how obligations to culture, law and morality came to be inscribed as part of humanity's organic constitution. The primal horde story illustrated what Freud evidently considered to be the most dramatic fraction of this inscription: inherent conflict between fathers and sons, together with its implications for the dynamics of succession (as in the myth of Oedipus). Yet there was much else to consider, because humanity's 'archaic heritage' also involved matters such as infantile sexuality, the formation of gendered identity and the reproduction of the family, not to mention the facility for language and symbolism. In regard to these other matters, the ethnography of Central Australia made no real impact on Freud's writing, but it did loom large in their reworking by Freud's ethnographer disciple, Géza Róheim.

Géza Róheim

Róheim began publishing, mostly in Hungarian, but also in German and English, in 1911. At the International Psycho-Analytical Congress in 1920, he gave what Ernest Jones (1964: 497) called 'an astonishing extempore address in English on Australian totemism', for which (together with another piece of writing) he would later be awarded a prize by Freud (La Barre 1966: 273–4; Muensterberger and Nichols 1974: xiii–xiv). By 1925, he had completed the book *Australian Totemism* in English—almost 500 rambling pages of densely argued elaboration of Freud's primal horde scenario in relation to an encyclopedic coverage of Aboriginal (and some other) ethnography, including that of Spencer and Gillen and Carl Strehlow. It also exhibited an idiosyncratic commitment to historical methods otherwise associated with the diffusionist schools of Fritz Graebner and Wilhelm Schmidt—although Schmidt himself would later become a bitter critic of *Totem and Taboo* (Wallace 1983: 141–2).

Robinson (1972: 76–80; also see Hiatt 1973: 242) provides a summary of *Australian Totemism*, emphasising how Róheim posited a 'Primeval Australian Horde' that spawned the varieties of totemism found across the continent. Different forms of moiety antagonism—what we are now likely to call 'complementary oppositions'—were summarily reduced to universal projections of the conflict between fathers and sons, the history of which was carried in mythology—for example, in the struggle between Eaglehawk and Crow. Increase rituals were said to re-enact the homoerotic bonds of the 'band of brothers', while initiation rites were said to have their origins in self-punishment and the mourning of the deceased father. One significant departure from Freud was Róheim's suggestion that the 'totemic meal' was the consumption not simply of the murdered father, but also of the incestuously claimed mother. While the book was welcomed in psychoanalytic circles, it is not the work through which Róheim made his mark in anthropology, heavily tainted as the tome was with the stain of speculative history, which Clark Wissler (1927: 520) in a review politely referred to as 'deduction'. But Baldwin Spencer (1925), who shared Róheim's evolutionist assumptions, reviewed it comprehensively, critically and sympathetically as soon as it was published. Much later, on the occasion of the book's reprinting in 1971, L. R. Hiatt (1973: 241) called it 'doctrinaire, though not unimaginative'.

Róheim's psychoanalytic understanding seemed to change dramatically after his fieldwork, although differences from Freud's approach in *Totem and Taboo* were already in place from as early as 1923 (Muensterberger and Nichols 1974: xiv–xvii). According to Jones (1964: 587), there was 'great excitement' in psychoanalytic circles about Róheim's impending journey in 1928, which in no small measure was prompted by Malinowski's controversial modification of Freudian theory in *Sex and Repression in Savage Society*, published in 1927 (parts of it having been previously published in 1924). Unsurprisingly, Róheim remained, post-fieldwork, a staunch defender of the idea that the Oedipus complex was universal, but his direct experience of Aboriginal people and other groups also made him rather less easy to ignore in anthropological circles; his work was, for example, taken up by Margaret Mead (La Barre 1966: 275). At the same time, his appreciation of the 'archaic heritage' that Freud had tried to capture through the story of the primal horde also changed, so that it is commonly stated that, by the 1930s, he had given up on *Totem and Taboo* and put in its place 'the ontogenetic theory of culture' (Morton 1988: x–xi; Paul 1976: 312; Robinson 1972: 80; Wallace 1983: 159–60). However, as I indicate below (and see Muensterberger and Nichols 1974: xviii–xxvi), this was not so much a full rejection of *Totem and Taboo* as a reorientation towards aspects of humanity's 'archaic heritage' that were either unannounced or underappreciated in Freud's book.

Magyar Tudós vezeti az első pszichoanalitikai expediciót AUSZTRÁLIA vad népei közé.

Mire e sorok megjelennek, egy lelkes magyar tudós van útban a Csendes-óceánon Ausztrália felé, egy kisebb, háromezer tonnás gőzösön. Róheim Géza, a kitünő magyar pszihoanalitikus és etnológus expediciót tervezett, amelynek célja tudományos alapon tanulmányozni Afrika és Ausztrália bennszülött lakosainak lelki életét.

Szinte magam előtt látom trópikus egyenruhájában ezt a lelkes magyar tudóst, amint feleségével és néhány bennszülött szolgával magára hagyva baktat mérföldeken keresztül a végtelen ausztráliai homoksivatagon. Fegyver nincs nála, elutazása előtt azt mondta, hogy utazásai közben sohasem visel fegyvert. Ha harcra kerül a sor — mondolta, — akkor úgyis reménytelen ez a küzdelem. Néhány ember harca egész törzsekkel, ismeretlen, embertől elhagyott vidéken. Mindössze egy kis gyöngyháznyelű, ezüstcsövű pisztolyt visz magával, ez is inkább emlék, mint fegyver.

— Furcsa érzés az, elindulni, úgyszólván egyedül, ismeretlen vidéken, ismeretlen, rosszindulatú bennszülöttek közé. Ez az érzés különösen akkor lepi meg az embert, amikor az expedició elhagyja az utolsó emberlakta helyet. Néha napokig, sőt hetekig valami reszkető, bizonytalan érzés tartja hatalmában az embert. Nem a reális veszedelmektől való félelem ez, hanem az isme-

retlen ellenségtől való veszedelem tudata. A pusztában való vándorlásnak minden bizonytalansága jól ismert előttem, hiszen nem ez az első utam ismeretlen országban, ismeretlen emberek között.

Ma ott tartok, hogy megvalósíthatom céljaimat és amikor útra indulok, vissza kell emlékeznem arra a mérhetetlen

Róheim Géza és felesége

munkára, amit addig kellett végezni, amíg az expedíciót megszerveztük. Évekig tartó levelezés, szervezkedés folyt, számtalan ajánlatot kaptam filmvállalatoktól, külföldi tudósoktól, akik felajánlották, hogy szívesen megfizetik az expedició részvételi díját, csak vigyem őket magammal. Kénytelen voltam minden ajánlatot visszautasítani, mert egyedül akarok dolgozni. A feleségemen kívül, aki a legkitünőbb munkatársam, csak egy német operatört viszek magammal, aki résztvett már a legkalandosabb vállalkozásokban is és azonkívül, hogy egyike a legkitünőbb szakembereknek, hideg, nyugodt és elszánt ember, akinek helyén van az esze és a szíve. Remélem, hogy az expedició útján nemcsak mint szakembernek, hanem mint bátor útitársnak is hasznát fogom venni.

Visszagondolok a gyerekkoromra, amikor hallatlanul lelkesítettek az ilyen kalandos vállalkozások. Akkoriban persze egy ilyen expedícióban csak a kalandlehetőségeket láttam, nem is gondoltam arra, hogy az ilyen vállalkozásokban rendszerint komoly tudósok vesznek részt. A pszihoanalizis természetesen rendkívül érdekel. Azt hiszem, életem fő munkája lesz az a könyv, amit a vad népek lelkiéletéről fogok írni, ha hazajövök Ausztráliából.

Amíg az expedició olyan stádiumba juthatott, hogy útrakészen állottunk, öt-

30

Plate 8.2 Extract from Hungarian magazine *Tolnai Világlapja* announcing the Róheims' departure for fieldwork.

The headline reads: 'Hungarian scientists lead the first psychoanalytic expedition among Australian savages.' The caption for the photograph reads: 'Géza Róheim and his wife.' Róheim's wife, Ilona, whom he married in 1918, accompanied and assisted him during his entire journey between late 1928 and early 1931. The journey took in not only Central Australia, but also parts of the Horn of Africa, Melanesia and North America. Originally published in *Tolnai Világlapja*, 26 December 1928, vol. 30, no. 52, p. 30.

Source: Image courtesy of Arcanum Database Ltd, Budapest.

Before coming to Australia, Róheim had begun to familiarise himself with Melanie Klein's psychoanalytic work with children, particularly in relation to pre-oedipal stages of development. Taken with her methods, he resolved to work with children as part of his broad study of Aboriginal life (Róheim 1932: 23). After his first field report, written in English and containing a groundbreaking section on psychoanalytic fieldwork technique (Róheim 1932: 6–22), he set about writing a sustained revision of Freud's idea of 'archaic heritage' by partially shifting the focus away from adult relationships between fathers and sons, and on to infancy and the mother–child bond—a matter that would preoccupy him for all of his career. The result was the 1934 publication *Das Rätsel der Sphinx, oder Die Menschwerdung*, which was quickly translated into English as *The Riddle of the Sphinx, or Human Origins*, a book that put together ideas about neoteny (prolonged infancy or delayed maturation) and the ontogenesis of religion in nightmarish fantasies of monsters of the kind that Klein had shown to be associated with the 'paranoid-schizoid position', and which took specific shape in Central Australia as terrible images of sorcery and demonic visitation (Róheim 1934: 23–41, 57–81). These demons, as he earlier pointed out in his field report (Róheim 1932: 14), partook of 'a deep-reaching unity' with 'ancestral spirits'—the totemic gods of *Totem and Taboo*.

In *The Riddle of the Sphinx*, Róheim argued that demons had their origins in the 'primal scene', the forerunner of oedipal dynamics—dynamics that were successfully dealt with by projection and the subsequent latency period retention of idealised images of self and kin as non-sexual beings. For Central Australian men at least, this 'complex' had to be re-engaged at adolescence and took the form of initiation, and later the begetting of a family and a ritual career—all of which meant the transformation of fear of foreclosed demons into respect for introjected gods (Róheim 1934: 83–157; and see Morton 2011: 17–27; 2014). The remainder of *The Riddle of the Sphinx* was written to support an 'ontogenetic interpretation of culture', but there is no real abandonment of *Totem and Taboo*, only a sustained attempt to integrate it with an ontogenetic outlook that Róheim (1943) would later try to systematise into a more general theory of 'the origin and function of culture'. He did not engage with *Totem and Taboo* when outlining that theory, and he would later say that Freud's 'Primal Horde theory' was untenably 'ultra-Lamarckian' (Róheim 1950: 424), but when he published *The Eternal Ones of the Dream* in 1945, basically as an update to *Australian Totemism*, he brought the primal horde back into view, referring to it as 'our old friend' (Róheim 1945: 16). Among the sporadic references to his 'old friend' in *The Eternal Ones of the Dream* was the claim that his interpretation of Arrernte primal horde mythology had been accepted by T. G. H. Strehlow (Róheim 1945: 17)—a matter on which I comment further below.

Róheim's near abandonment of the myth of the primal horde was less a desertion of Freud and more the outcome of his founding of a particular version of culture and personality theory. He never gave up on what he said in his first field report, echoing both Freud and Goethe—namely, that 'as every analysis shews, the stand we can make against reality is based on the stand we could make against the father' (Róheim 1932: 73). But the dramatic encounter between ageing fathers and their up-and-coming sons had to be merged into a more integrated appreciation of evolutionary dynamics that resulted in a distinctively human type of infant care, latency, adolescence, maturity, ageing and death. What is often not appreciated, largely because of his generally reckless and uneconomical approach to writing—what La Barre (1966: 281) calls his 'defects of structure and style'—is that Róheim systematically mapped this comprehensive scheme on to Central Australian Aboriginal culture, hardly an aspect of which remained unexplored before his death in 1953, even though some of his most important ethnographic observations were published only posthumously (Róheim 1974, 1988). Some of this corpus was novel not only in its psychoanalytical approach, but also in its focus—for example, on the life and character of Aboriginal women (Róheim 1933) and children (Róheim 1932: 23–37; 1974: 65–121). The comprehensiveness of Róheim's purview was, one might say, implicit in his post-fieldwork concern with the riddle of the sphinx, which alludes to emergence and decline in the life cycle:

> 'What being, with only one voice, has sometimes two feet, sometimes three, sometimes four, and is weakest when it has the most?'—'Man' answered Oedipus, 'because he crawls on all fours as an infant, stands firmly on his feet in his youth, and leans upon a staff in his old age.' (Graves 1960: 10)

It is symptomatic of Ronald and Catherine Berndt's relative proximity to continental anthropological traditions (see Peterson, Chapter 18, this volume) that they were among the few Australian anthropologists who read Róheim extensively and engaged his views. For example, the Berndts published a 12-page review dealing with *The Eternal Ones of the Dream*, which began with the statement: 'This is a valuable and extremely stimulating volume, even should one not subscribe completely to certain theoretical aspects—which however do not detract from the main thesis' (Berndt and Berndt 1946: 67). They also wrote of 'the convincing force of Dr. Róheim's line of thought and discussion', even though they could 'not feel entirely convinced' (Berndt and Berndt 1946: 67). Ronald Berndt (1952) would later sympathetically review Róheim's *Psychoanalysis and Anthropology* and, with Catherine Berndt, contribute to Róheim's *Festschrift*, their paper addressing 'the concept of abnormality' in Gunwinggu society (Berndt and Berndt 1951)—although this paper was typically descriptive and did not engage psychoanalytic theory. But it was another Australian anthropologist atypically close to continental traditions, T. G. H. Strehlow, on whom Róheim, as well as Freud, arguably had the greatest impact in the mid-twentieth century.

(Carl and) T. G. H. Strehlow

T. G. H. Strehlow's view of Róheim was laid out in a paragraph in *Songs of Central Australia* (1971: xvi–xvii), where Strehlow refers to his 'admiration for [Róheim's] amazing knowledge of Australian anthropological literature' and his belief 'that the Freudian school has some excellent suggestions to offer in regard to the elucidation of the aboriginal sacred myths and songs'. But he also takes Róheim to task for undisciplined partiality and the fact that 'many half-truths mar his writings'. Róheim, he suggested, put theory before facts, whereas Strehlow (1971: xvii) preferred 'to ensure absolute accuracy in whatever documents we are accumulating now for future research'. This empiricist stance not only was shared with his father, Carl Strehlow, but also was characteristically Boasian, and could be read as a methodological injunction to return psychoanalysis to its more idiographic roots in Freud, and ultimately Goethe (although that was hardly Strehlow junior's intention). For it was Boas himself who cited Goethe to this effect:

> It seems to me that every phenomenon, every fact, itself is the really interesting object. Whoever explains it, or connects it with other events, usually only amuses himself or makes sport of us, as, for instance, the naturalist or historian. But a single action or event is interesting, not because it is explainable, but because it is true. (Goethe, cited in Boas 1996: 13)

T. G. H. Strehlow's anthropological journey is inseparable from his father's. Carl Strehlow graduated from a German seminary in 1891 and soon after migrated to South Australia, where he worked at the Bethesda Mission at Killalpaninna, South Australia, before leaving to take over Hermannsburg Mission in 1894 (for further details, see Kenny, Chapter 7, this volume; 2013: 23–35). An accomplished linguist and translator of Christian texts into Diyari, Arrernte and Loritja (Kenny 2013: 28–9), Carl Strehlow published *Die Aranda- und Loritja-Stämme in Zentral-Australien* between 1907 and 1920—work that gave him fame in continental Europe, if not so much in Anglophone circles (Kenny 2013: 101). As a fluent German speaker, Róheim read Carl Strehlow's work keenly and used it freely, both pre- and post-fieldwork, although he suggested that it was somewhat 'introvert' due to Strehlow's dependence on native exegesis and refusal to witness un-Christian ceremonies (Róheim 1932: 20). Nevertheless, Carl Strehlow's missionary training provided him with 'a classical, humanistic orientation' (Kenny 2013) and his work is informed by ideas about vernacular usage and translation generally associated with both Luther and Herder (Benner 2013: 42); although the likes of Goethe and Schiller appear to have been suppressed in his education (Strehlow 2011: 217).

Plate 8.3 Carl Strehlow, Frieda Strehlow and their six children, Germany, 1911.

T. G. H. Strehlow, the youngest sibling, is at bottom left, with Frieda. His brother Hermann is at bottom right, with Carl. The other siblings, from left to right, are Rudolf, Friedrich, Martha and Karl. The photograph was probably taken in Berlin, or perhaps Angermünde, during the family's single visit to Germany in 1910–11. Of the six children, only T. G. H. returned to Australia with his parents. Frieda returned to Germany in 1931. T. G. H. returned to Germany to visit his mother just once, in 1950–51.

Source: Image courtesy of John Strehlow.

Carl Strehlow's life was a joint mission to convert Aboriginal people to Christianity and do justice, through ethnography, to their 'genius' as a 'folk'. To the extent that each was to be achieved through language and translation, the two aspects of his *Bildung*, his 'mission in life', were obviously closely related, exemplifying the more generally profound historical relationship between vocational anthropology and mission activity (Morton 2013: 238–41). One thing we know about this career is that it was the long-term outcome of longings and aspirations that were to a considerable degree thwarted by Carl Strehlow's father, Carl senior, who mistrusted, and tried to interfere with, his son's desire for higher learning on the grounds that it would lead to enfeeblement of mind and character, and perhaps atheism (Strehlow 2011: 221–4). Strehlow family tradition has it that Carl senior simply 'did not want his son to be better than him' (Strehlow 2011: 195) and the prevention of Carl junior's higher education led directly to his exile in Australia (p. 224). Hence, Carl senior's efforts to hobble his son read like a direct analogue of the relationship between Laius and Oedipus, who also lived in exile thanks to his father's fears of being overtaken, the Delphic oracle having told him that 'any child born to [his wife] Iocaste would become his murderer' (Graves 1960: 9). But there is no obvious sign of this tension in Carl Strehlow's ethnographic output beyond the fact of its learned character being a triumph of the will—a kind of victory. While Freud, for his part, seems to have been hardly aware of Carl Strehlow's ethnography (Gutjahr 2009: 32), Strehlow himself probably knew less about the atheistic Freud than he knew about Goethe and Schiller, so likely would not have reflected on or refracted his struggle with his father in psychoanalytic terms; rather, the exile in Australia was to be the making of him, intended as 'God's plan' (Strehlow 2011: 224). But it was to be a very different story with Carl junior's son, Theodor ('Theo' or 'Ted'): T. G. H. Strehlow.

Although we do not know for sure, it is possible that T. G. H. Strehlow read Herder (Gibson, Chapter 10, this volume), perhaps during his university training in English literature and classics, since he did once conclude a discourse on Arrernte myth by opining that 'the soul of a race is enshrined in its legends' (Strehlow 1947: 46). What is more certain is that he studied works such as Freud's *Totem and Taboo* and Róheim's *Australian Totemism* and 'Psycho-analysis of primitive cultural types' in detail and that, as a result, he found the idea of a pan-human collective unconscious to be of some interest (Gibson, Chapter 10, this volume). When in 1932 he arrived back in Central Australia, 10 years after his father's death (about which I say more below), T. G. H. apparently had a copy of *Totem and Taboo* 'in his saddlebag' (Hill 2002: 147). His first publication, in *Oceania* in 1933, concerned a myth and song powerfully and evocatively profiling murder, cannibalism, sexual jealousy and castration—a situation that Strehlow likened to 'the primitive horde as pictured by psychoanalysis' (Strehlow 1933: 199), which was enough to convince Róheim that Strehlow junior had 'accepted' his views (see above). Hill (2002: 210–14) calls the 1933 paper T. G. H. Strehlow's 'brilliant debut' on the academic stage. While this 'debut' contained a brief statement on how his method and understanding were superior to those of Spencer and Gillen (Strehlow 1933: 199), there was symptomatically no mention of the fact that Carl Strehlow (1907–20: Vol. I, pp. 92–3) had also recorded and published (without the song) a version of the same myth.

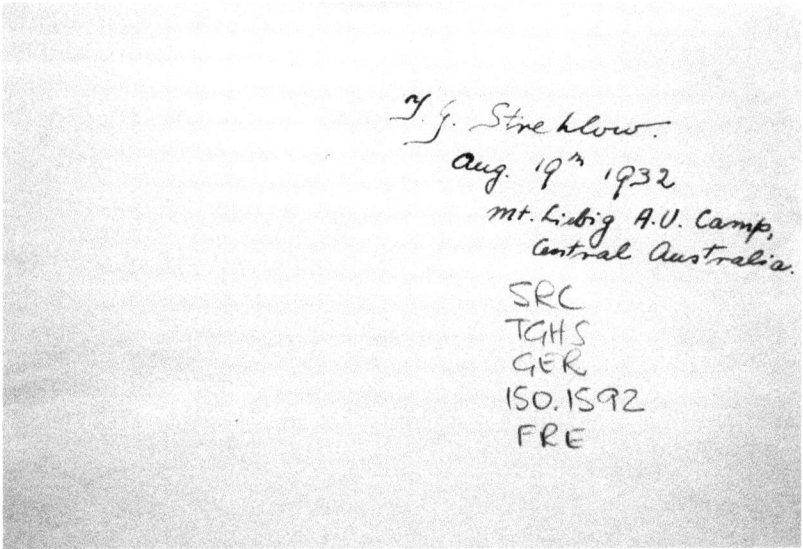

Plate 8.4 T. G. H. Strehlow's inscription in his copy of *Totem und Tabu*.

T. G. H. Strehlow read *Totem and Taboo* in its original German, his copy being the third edition published in 1922 by Internationaler Psychoanalytischer Verlag. This copy is now housed in the Strehlow Research Centre Library in Alice Springs. Hill (2002: 147) states that Strehlow 'did not write a word about the book in his diary', but the inscription suggests he received his copy at Mount Liebig in August 1932 while assisting an Adelaide University Board of Anthropological Research expedition. During the previous month at Mount Liebig, Strehlow witnessed his first secret-sacred ritual and found its symbolic violence most confronting. Hill (2002: 178) says Strehlow responded by writing in his diary: 'Gods everywhere at all times have been honoured and appeased by gifts of blood.' It is tempting to think that his confrontation with the ceremony prompted a request for delivery of *Totem und Tabu* to Mount Liebig.

Source: Image courtesy of the Strehlow Research Centre, Alice Springs.

This lack of recognition of Carl Strehlow's work by his son became something of a pattern, as has been noted or hinted at by others (Hill 2002: 224–5; Kenny 2013: 1; Strehlow 2011: 46–7). Exaggerated (if politely expressed) animus towards Spencer and Gillen (Strehlow 1963: 6–13; 1971: xx–xxxiii), who unfairly criticised his father (Strehlow 2004), seems to have been the other side of this pattern, although it also contained a reasoned critique of Spencer and Gillen's ethnography. In *Aranda Traditions*, which T. G. H. Strehlow (1947: 7–14) penned in 1934, but did not publish until 1947, he gave examples of 'Great Father' myths that contained bloody conflicts with sons, leaving, as Barry Hill (2002: 221–2) notes, his most dramatic account until last. His narrative concludes with a distorted echo of Sophocles's play:

Namatjirea is left behind deprived of sight; a pitiful half-wit, whose strength has been broken for ever: his eldest son, after breaking through the earth-mound, had chanted magic spells and destroyed the sight of his father, *because the latter had not taken him to his side as his equal*, so that father and son could both have sat at the foot of the tnatantja ['ceremonial pole']. (Strehlow 1947: 14; original emphasis)

Although T. G. H. Strehlow had a gift for dramatic free translation, these oedipal stories were obviously not entirely figments of his imagination. They were heavily worked ethnographic reports intended to expand readers' appreciation of the vividness of Aboriginal mythopoeia, although his translations in general tended to 'domesticate' the originals by assimilating them to a European classical (sometimes Biblical) heritage (Hill 2002: 434–57; Jorgensen 2010)—the same heritage that also informed Freud's and Róheim's appreciation of Oedipus. But Sophocles and Oedipus are only ever implicit in T. G. H. Strehlow's descriptions. He was happy to say that 'Aranda traditions' contained records of a 'lower and earlier stage of human society' and expressed, with 'veils torn aside', 'wishes and desires' that Aboriginal people are 'unable to realize' in their ordered society (Strehlow 1947: 45–6), but the oedipal drama of *Totem and Taboo* is never named as such.

He did, however, vividly describe how Arrernte men completed their long-term initiation by seizing and violently destroying the material emblems of power with which the senior generation oppressed its juniors during earlier ritual ordeals. The ceremonial pole, he says, 'is violently uprooted' by the 'excited' young men, who 'dance savagely' and 'weary it and exhaust its strength'. They 'rudely strip the pole of its decorations' and throw it 'into a deep gutter'. They form a 'single file' and proceed to 'cleave a deep breach' in the 'sacred earth mound'. 'The great tjuruŋa ['sacred object'] had been shattered; its spell has been broken; its power is no more' (Strehlow 1947: 111). As Barry Hill (2002: 223) says, 'Freud himself could not have dreamed a text more thematically expressive of his grand thesis'—except that Strehlow's account nowhere engages with Freud's insistence that the sons felt remorse for the murder of their father. The parricidal account is entirely Dionysian in tone. Hence it was left to Róheim (1945: 130–54) alone to emphasise the reciprocal relationship between 'destruction and restitution' and the nature of post-initiation rituals ('increase rites') as 'dramatized reparation' (p. 149).

It is a great irony that T. G. H. Strehlow could be far more persuasive about the importance of Oedipus and *Totem and Taboo* in making sense of Aboriginal life than Freud or Róheim—Freud not sharing Strehlow's command of ethnography and Róheim not sharing Strehlow's command of imaginative language and style. But Strehlow was not a fully committed Freudian. While he revisited Freudian ideas from time to time, he never did this thoroughly, or with the zest characteristic of *Aranda Traditions*—because, as Barry Hill (2002: 224) has rightly divined, the making of that book was Strehlow's own dramatic moment of displacement, of assuming power and becoming a man. And he followed in his father's footsteps very closely indeed, leading the same hermeneutic double life as ethnographer and God's messenger, except that the emphasis was inverted. Carl Strehlow's career was as a missionary, with ethnography an absorbing sideline; T. G. H. Strehlow's first string was his documentation of Arrernte culture, but he also spent much time with the translation of scriptures, where he would improve earlier renditions by his father at the same time as he was refining his father's appreciation of Arrernte people's 'world of the mind' (Strehlow 1969: 5). This is what Barry Hill (2002: 412–546) refers to as T. G. H. Strehlow's 'day work for Caliban' and 'night work for Luther'.

It is one thing to assume the father's place, to succeed him and even exceed his achievements; it is another to strike a balance between continuing a tradition and obliterating the past, or to prepare oneself for succession by becoming the dying father and no longer the rising son. This moment of reckoning came to T. G. H. Strehlow during the 1960s and his response was to write his most sustained oedipal tale, *Journey to Horseshoe Bend* (1969). However, this book is not genuinely ethnographic, even though it contains a significant amount of historical and cultural material. Rather, it is intended as a historical novel addressing the shocking death of Carl Strehlow in 1922 en route to Adelaide, where he hoped to find treatment for a life-threatening medical condition. It is also about the circumstances of the arduous overland journey, including T. G. H. Strehlow's involvement as part of the travelling party. While the book is a novel, it is also key to understanding the partiality of T. G. H. Strehlow's approach to Freud and Róheim.

Plate 8.5 T. G. H. Strehlow at his father's grave at Horseshoe Bend, 1936.

Strehlow briefly visited Horseshoe Bend in 1936 as part of a long, exhausting camel trek taken with his first wife, Bertha, whom he had just married, and three Aboriginal assistants. The journey took them south to Macumba, in South Australia, and back to Central Australia via Ayers Rock (Uluru), lasting the best part of five months. This was not Strehlow's first return to the site of his father's death, as he had previously conducted work at Horseshoe Bend during an intensive period of field research between 1932 and 1935. This research was the basis for his book *Aranda Traditions* and for a large part of his magnum opus, *Songs of Central Australia*.

Source: Image courtesy of the Strehlow Research Centre, Alice Springs.

Much has already been said about this award-winning book (Carter 1996: 21–2, 26–7, 39, 48, 59, 83, 107–14; Hill 2002: 642–60; Jones 2015; Morton 1995: 59–64; 2004). My own view, stated very briefly, is that it is more a myth—a literary vision or 'dream'—than a historical novel. Moreover, it is less about Carl Strehlow's death and more about the imagined forestalling of T. G. H. Strehlow's own. For readers unfamiliar with the plot, it describes Carl Strehlow's pain-wracked journey, with his wife and 14-year-old son, along the Finke River towards death at Horseshoe Bend. At the end, the son, who is always referred to in the third person as 'Theo', in response to the disaster that has befallen his family, lies alone in the bed of the Finke River and feels reassured about his future, somehow knowing that he will one day return to Central Australia to fulfil his destiny in an Aboriginal homeland. Hence, Carl dies and 'Theo' comes of age, recapitulating the whole saga of T. G. H. Strehlow's uptake of his father's authority a generation before. 'Theo' and Carl never speak to or set eyes on each other in the book and only occupy the same space after Carl dies. Nor is there any great sorrow expressed by 'Theo' or any reflection on the meaning of his father's passing. As opposed to Sophocles and Freud, here there is no genuine sense of tragedy in the story. All blame for Carl's death is sheeted home to darkly portrayed authorities in the Lutheran Church, and both father and son remain without flaws.

There is no mystery about why T. G. H. Strehlow turned the clock back at this particular moment in time, since we know well that, after severe illness and a brush with death, he was dogged by an acute midlife crisis—partly a crisis of Christian faith—that caused him to desert and disown his wife and children for the favours of a much younger woman. The other thing we know well is that, far from actually revitalising him and his career in the long run, those events presaged an ongoing threat to the security of his ethnographic collection of objects and manuscripts, which, long after his death in 1978, eventually had to be forcibly rescued and placed in public hands (Morton 1993). T. G. H. Strehlow's life after *Journey to Horseshoe Bend* was in fact plagued by alienation, misery and paranoia (McNally 1981: 144–201), its narrative being empty of 'reparation'—a sort of *Bildungsroman* in reverse, or a *Faust* without terra firma reclaimed from a tempestuous sea.

While this situation in itself invites psychoanalytic interpretation, I gesture towards *Journey to Horseshoe Bend* here only to underline the extent to which T. G. H. Strehlow remained untouched by Freud and Róheim. There is no doubt that *Aranda Traditions* was in no small way inspired by *Totem and Taboo*, but *Journey to Horseshoe Bend* indicates the limit of

T. G. H. Strehlow's understanding of psychoanalysis, both as a whole and in relation to *Totem and Taboo* alone, which he did not really 'get'. It also indicates, albeit more obliquely, how he was not fully interested in Freudian theory so much as the selective dramatic effect that the myth of the primal horde could lend to his constructions of Arrernte 'legends'. But when Strehlow came to write his own legend—to enshrine his own soul—Freud, like T. G. H.'s father, was nowhere to be seen.

Conclusion

The currents that link Freud, Róheim and the Strehlows are many and varied. They shared not only a Middle European, mostly Germanic, background, but also a commitment to humanistic research. They also shared vitalist views of cultures: all believed in something called 'the soul', even though they had different visions of its nature and development. All, for reasons connected with their continental background, were marginal to Australian anthropology. Psychoanalysis was largely not credible in the British traditions of anthropology that dominated Australia; Carl Strehlow wrote and published his major work entirely in German, so few in Australia managed to read him; and T. G. H. Strehlow, although well known and often courted for his work, had difficult relationships with Anglo colleagues, due largely to differences of outlook in how to approach anthropology. Symptomatically, Ronald Berndt remained his closest ally to the end—and it was Berndt who wrote T. G. H. Strehlow's glowing obituary in *Oceania* in 1979.

As far as Oedipus and *Totem and Taboo* are concerned, they clearly operated at a number of different levels in relation to Central Australian ethnography. If one is interested in how those stories might illuminate the genius of Aboriginal life there, one has to turn first to Freud and Róheim, and only then to the Strehlows; but if one wants to see how they might illuminate the genius of anthropology in that location—how its ideas are generated and regenerated across its cohorts of scholars— one might do no better than turn first to the relationship between Carl and T. G. H. Strehlow as ethnographers, each with a mission, the one succeeding the other. When Róheim (1932: 16–18) came back from the field, he underscored the importance of recognising transference and countertransference in anthropological work. Another way of putting this would be to say that, ethically, both the genius of the people and the genius of anthropology entail *Kulturarbeit*, the fundamental precept of which is 'know thyself'.

References

Bakan, D. 2004. *Sigmund Freud and the Jewish Mystical Tradition.* Mineola, NY: Dover.

Barron, J. 1993. Introduction. In *Self-Analysis: Critical inquiries, personal visions*, (ed.) J. Barron, pp. xix–xxii. Hillsdale, NJ: Analytic Press.

Benedict, R. 1934. *Patterns of Culture.* Boston: Houghton Mifflin.

Benner, E. 2013. Nationalism: Intellectual origins. In *The Oxford Handbook of the History of Nationalism*, (ed.) J. Breuilly, pp. 36–55. Oxford: Oxford University Press. doi.org/10.1093/oxfordhb/9780199209194.013.0003.

Berndt, R. 1952. Review of Géza Róheim's 'Psychoanalysis and Anthropology: Culture personality and the unconscious'. *Oceania* 22(3): 242–3. doi.org/10.1002/j.1834-4461.1952.tb00563.x.

Berndt, R. 1979. T. G. H. Strehlow, 1908–1978. *Oceania* 49(3): 230–3. doi.org/10.1002/j.1834-4461.1979.tb01392.x.

Berndt, R. and Berndt, C. 1946. The Eternal Ones of the Dream. [Review.] *Oceania* 17(1): 67–78. doi.org/10.1002/j.1834-4461.1946.tb00143.x.

Berndt, R. and Berndt, C. 1951. The concept of abnormality in an Australian Aboriginal society. In *Psychoanalysis and Culture: Essays in honor of Géza Róheim*, (eds) G. Wilbur and W. Muensterberger, pp. 75–89. New York: International Universities Press.

Bettelheim, B. 1985. *Freud and Man's Soul.* London: Fontana.

Boas, F. 1996 [1887]. The study of geography. In *Volksgeist as Method and Ethic: Essays on Boasian ethnography and the German anthropological tradition*, (ed.) G. Stocking, pp. 9–16. Madison: University of Wisconsin Press.

Carter, P. 1996. *The Lie of the Land.* London: Faber & Faber.

Curran, J. 2002. *Goethe's Wilhelm Meister's Apprenticeship: A reader's commentary.* Rochester, NY: Camden House.

Dumont, L. 1994. *German Ideology: From France to Germany and back.* Chicago: University of Chicago Press.

Fox, R. 1967. Totem and Taboo reconsidered. In *The Structural Study of Myth and Totemism,* (ed.) E. Leach, pp. 161–78. London: Tavistock.

Frazer, J. 1910. *Totemism and Exogamy: A treatise on certain early forms of superstition and society.* 4 vols. London: Macmillan.

Freud, S. 2001a [1913]. Totem and taboo: Some points of agreement between the mental lives of savages and neurotics. In *The Standard Edition of the Complete Psychological Works of Sigmund Freud. Volume 13,* pp. vii–162. London: Vintage.

Freud, S. 2001b [1921]. Group psychology and the analysis of the ego. In *The Standard Edition of the Complete Psychological Works of Sigmund Freud. Volume 18,* pp. 65–143. London: Vintage.

Frosh, S. 2005. *Hate and the 'Jewish Science': Anti-Semitism, Nazism and psychoanalysis.* London: Palgrave Macmillan. doi.org/10.1057/9780230510074.

Goebel, E. 2012. *Beyond Discontent: 'Sublimation' from Goethe to Lacan.* New York: Continuum.

Graves, R. 1960. *The Greek Myths 2.* Rev. edn. Harmondsworth, UK: Penguin.

Gutjahr, O. 2009. Missionary scholarship and cultural theory: Carl Strehlow's Aboriginal studies in the context of European knowledge discourses on Taboo and Totemism. In *Migration and Cultural Contact: Germany and Australia,* (eds) A. Bandhauer and M. Weber, pp. 15–44. Sydney: University of Sydney Press.

Hiatt, L. R. 1973. Review of Géza Róheim's 'Australian Totemism'. *Oceania* 43(3): 241–2. doi.org/10.1002/j.1834-4461.1973.tb01215.x.

Hill, B. 2002. *Broken Song: T. G. H. Strehlow and Aboriginal possession.* Sydney: Knopf.

Jones, E. 1964. *The Life and Works of Sigmund Freud.* Abridged edn. Harmondsworth, UK: Penguin.

Jones, P. 2015. Afterword. In *Journey to Horseshoe Bend*, T. G. H. Strehlow, pp. 292–310. Sydney: Giramondo. doi.org/10.1515/9781400870653-011.

Jorgensen, D. 2010. Simulating the sacred in Theodore Strehlow's 'Songs of Central Australia'. *The Bible and Critical Theory* 6(2): 22.1–22.10.

Jung, C. G. 1956 [1912]. *Symbols of Transformation: An analysis of the prelude to a case of schizophrenia*. London: Routledge & Kegan Paul.

Kaplan, R. 2010. Freud's excellent adventure down under: The only publication in Australia by the founder of psychoanalysis. *Australasian Psychiatry* 18(3): 205–9. doi.org/10.3109/10398561003682952.

Kenny, A. 2013. *The Aranda's Pepa: An introduction to Carl Strehlow's masterpiece Die Aranda- und Loritja-Stämme in Zentral-Australien (1907–1920)*. Canberra: ANU E Press.

Kuklick, H. 2005. Interpreting Aboriginal religion: From nineteenth-century evolutionism to Durkheimian sociology. *Humanities Research* 7(1): 567–72.

La Barre, W. 1966. Géza Róheim, 1891–1953: Psychoanalysis and anthropology. In *Psychoanalytic Pioneers*, (eds) F. Alexander, S. Eisenstein and M. Grotjahn, pp. 272–81. New York: Basic Books.

McNally, W. 1981. *Aborigines, Artefacts and Anguish*. Adelaide: Chi Rho.

Malinowski, B. 1927. *Sex and Repression in Savage Society*. London: Routledge & Kegan Paul.

Morton, J. 1988. Introduction: Géza Róheim's contribution to Australian ethnography. In *Children of the Desert II: Myths and dreams of the Aborigines of Central Australia*, G. Róheim, pp. vii–xxx. Sydney: Oceania Publications. doi.org/10.1017/cbo9780511624483.002.

Morton, J. 1993. Romancing the stones. *Arena Magazine* 4: 39–40.

Morton, J. 1995. 'Secrets of the Aranda': T. G. H. Strehlow and the course of revelation. In *Politics of the Secret*, (ed.) C. Anderson, pp. 51–66. Sydney: University of Sydney Press.

Morton, J. 2004. Krippendorf's lesson in the centre: The shaping of the Arrernte through T. G. H. Strehlow's 'Family Romance'. In *Traditions in the Midst of Change: Communities, cultures and the Strehlow legacy in Central Australia*, (ed.) M. Cawthorn, pp. 42–7. Alice Springs, NT: Strehlow Research Centre.

Morton, J. 2005. Gillen, Francis James, and Baldwin Spencer. In *Encyclopedia of Religion*, (ed.) L. Jones, 2nd edn, pp. 3489–91. Detroit: Macmillan.

Morton, J. 2011. 'Less was hidden among these children': Géza Róheim, anthropology and the politics of Aboriginal childhood. In *Growing Up in Central Australia: New anthropological studies of Aboriginal childhood and adolescence*, (ed.) U. Eickelkamp, pp. 15–48. New York: Berghahn Books.

Morton, J. 2013. Durkheim, Freud and I in Aboriginal Australia. *Australian Journal of Anthropology* 24(3): 235–49. doi.org/10.1111/taja.12049.

Morton, J. 2014. A murder of monsters: Terror and morality in an Aboriginal religion. In *Monster Anthropology in Australasia and Beyond*, (eds) Y. Musharbash and G. H. Presterudstuen, pp. 75–92. New York: Palgrave Macmillan. doi.org/10.1057/9781137448651_5.

Muensterberger, W. and Nichols, C. 1974. Introduction: Róheim and the beginnings of psychoanalytic anthropology. In *The Riddle of the Sphinx or, Human Origins*, G. Róheim, pp. ix–xxvi. New York: Harper & Row.

Paul, R. 1976. Did the primal crime take place? *Ethos* 4(3): 311–52. doi.org/10.1525/eth.1976.4.3.02a00030.

Paul, R. 2010. Yes, the primal crime did take place: A further defense of Freud's 'Totem and Taboo'. *Ethos* 38(2): 230–49. doi.org/10.1111/j.1548-1352.2010.01137.x.

Petch, A. 2013. Spencer, Walter Baldwin, and Francis James Gillen. In *Theory in Social and Cultural Anthropology: An encyclopedia*, (eds) R. J. Magee and R. Warms, pp. 802–5. Los Angeles: Sage.

Redner, H. 1982. *In the Beginning was the Deed: Reflections on the passage of Faust*. Berkeley: University of California Press.

Robinson, P. 1972. *The Sexual Radicals: Reich, Róheim, Marcuse*. London: Paladin.

Róheim, G. 1925. *Australian Totemism: A psycho-analytic study in anthropology*. London: George Allen & Unwin.

Róheim, G. 1932. Psycho-analysis of primitive cultural types. *International Journal of Psycho-Analysis* 13(1–2): 1–224.

Róheim, G. 1933. Women and their life in Central Australia. *Journal of the Royal Anthropological Institute of Great Britain and Ireland* 63: 207–65. doi.org/10.2307/2843917.

Róheim, G. 1934. *The Riddle of the Sphinx, or Human Origins*. London: Hogarth Press.

Róheim, G. 1943. *The Origin and Function of Culture*. New York: Nervous & Mental Disease Monographs.

Róheim, G. 1945. *The Eternal Ones of the Dream: A psychoanalytic interpretation of Australian myth and ritual*. New York: International Universities Press.

Róheim, G. 1950. *Psychoanalysis and Anthropology: Culture, personality and the unconscious*. New York: International Universities Press.

Róheim, G. 1974. *Children of the Desert: The western tribes of Central Australia*. New York: Basic Books.

Róheim, G. 1988. *Children of the Desert II: Myths and dreams of the Aborigines of Central Australia*. Sydney: Oceania Ethnographies.

Smadja, E. 2015. *Freud and Culture*. London: Karnac.

Sorkin, D. 1983. Wilhelm von Humboldt: The theory and practice of self-formation (Bildung), 1791–1810. *Journal of the History of Ideas* 44(1): 55–73. doi.org/10.2307/2709304.

Spencer, B. 1925. Review of Géza Róheim's 'Australian Totemism'. *The Argus*, [Melbourne], 22 August: 10.

Spencer, B. and Gillen, F. J. 1899. *The Native Tribes of Central Australia*. London: Macmillan.

Strehlow, C. 1907–1920. *Die Aranda- und Loritja-Stämme in Zentral-Australien.* 7 vols. Frankfurt am Main: Joseph Baer & Co.

Strehlow, J. 2004. Reappraising Carl Strehlow: Through the Spencer–Strehlow debate. In *The Struggle for Souls and Science: Constructing the fifth continent—German missionaries and scientists in Australia,* (ed.) W. Veit, pp. 59–91. Alice Springs, NT: Strehlow Research Centre.

Strehlow, J. 2011. *The Tale of Frieda Keysser: Frieda Keysser and Carl Strehlow—An historical biography.* London: Wild Cat Press.

Strehlow, T. G. H. 1933. Ankotarinja: An Aranda myth. *Oceania* 4(2): 187–200. doi.org/10.1002/j.1834-4461.1933.tb00100.x.

Strehlow, T. G. H. 1947. *Aranda Traditions.* Melbourne: Melbourne University Press.

Strehlow, T. G. H. 1963. *Anthropology and the Study of Languages.* Adelaide: Hassell Press.

Strehlow, T. G. H. 1969. *Journey to Horseshoe Bend.* Sydney: Angus & Robertson.

Strehlow, T. G. H. 1971. *Songs of Central Australia.* Sydney: Angus & Robertson.

Sulloway, F. 1980. *Freud, Biologist of the Mind: Beyond the psychoanalytic legend.* London: Fontana.

Underhill, J. 2009. *Humboldt, Worldview and Language.* Edinburgh: Edinburgh University Press. doi.org/10.3366/edinburgh/97807486 38420.001.0001.

Wallace, E. 1983. *Freud and Anthropology: A history and reappraisal.* New York: International Universities Press.

Winter, S. 1999. *Freud and the Institution of Psychoanalytic Knowledge.* Stanford, CA: Stanford University Press.

Wissler, C. 1927. Review of Géza Róheim's 'Australian Totemism'. *Social Forces* 5(3): 519–20. doi.org/10.2307/3004519.

9

Of kinships and other things: T. G. H. Strehlow in Central Australia

Diane Austin-Broos

Theodor George Henry (T. G. H.) Strehlow, son of German-born missionary Carl Strehlow and his wife, Friedericke, was born at Hermannsburg, Northern Territory, on 6 June 1908. Following the death of Carl in 1922, T. G. H. Strehlow's mother took her son to reside in Adelaide, where he attended the Lutheran Immanuel College and subsequently completed degrees in classics and English literature at the University of Adelaide. Strehlow was an outstanding student. Thereafter he returned to Central Australia and pursued studies of Arrernte language, society and, in particular, the poetry and performance in ritual song cycles of the Arrernte and other peoples of Central Australia. The notable publications from this early research included an Arrernte (Aranda) grammar in 1944 and a study of cosmology, ritual and related social organisation entitled *Aranda Traditions*, in 1947. Late in 1946, T. G. H. became a patrol officer in Central Australia—'the first full-time Commonwealth public servant dedicated to Aboriginal affairs' (Jones 2002). Along with Pastor Friedrich Albrecht at the Hermannsburg Mission, Strehlow was a strong advocate for the Indigenous residents of Central Australia. A sense of alienation from the larger society was fuelled by prejudiced views both of his commitment to Indigenous affairs and of his German heritage. Notwithstanding this, Strehlow regarded himself as an Australian. T. G. H. was called up for domestic military service in 1942 and, at the war's end, he returned to academic work, first in Adelaide, and then, in 1949, at The Australian National University in Canberra. He continued his Central Australian research.

In 1947, Strehlow chaired the anthropological section of a conference in Perth convened by the Australian and New Zealand Association for the Advancement of Science. In the course of the conference, he rued the limited expertise in linguistics among Australianist anthropologists. Subsequently, Professor A. P. Elkin of the University of Sydney proposed that T. G. H., in turn, extend his knowledge of anthropology—a discipline he had not studied formally. Strehlow went to the London School of Economics (LSE) in the middle of 1950 and remained there until early 1952. New Zealander Raymond Firth, an eminent ethnographer in Oceania, was head of the anthropology department. Strehlow sought Firth's support in the hope that the LSE might confer on him a doctorate for his already published work. Firth, like Elkin, remained unimpressed with Strehlow's anthropology, much to Strehlow's disappointment (Hill 2002: 472–3). He returned to Australia and, in 1954, became a reader in Australian linguistics at the University of Adelaide.

Subsequently, his relations with Australian academic anthropology and its supporting research institutions became strained. Strehlow remained an outsider and tailored neither his major interests nor his analyses to the normal science of British social anthropology. He published three further major works in the postwar period: an Arrernte translation of the New Testament (in 1956); a partly autobiographical narrative pertaining to his father's death in Central Australia, *Journey to Horseshoe Bend* (1969); and, finally, his extraordinary *Songs of Central Australia* (1971), a record and analysis of Central Australian ritual songs studded with allusions to classical (Greek and Roman) myth (Jones 2002; Hill 2002). In his later years, Strehlow's view of his custodianship of Indigenous artefacts and knowledge—tantamount to that of an Indigenous ritual leader—made him a controversial figure. Notwithstanding Strehlow's seminal publications, Australianist anthropologists were often critical of his stance. He died in 1978.

Strehlow on kinship, marriage and 'social control'

To consider Strehlow's contribution to those areas of anthropology generally described as 'kinship and social organisation', as opposed to 'myth and ritual', is also to address his status as a relative outsider. While Strehlow's research was focused on ritual dimensions of Indigenous life, kinship was central to an academic anthropology influenced most by British practice. To throw light on Strehlow's contribution therefore throws some light as well on the specificity of Australianist anthropology. A short story sets the scene.

On my return from Hermannsburg in 1990, I had a conversation with anthropologist Les Hiatt about my ongoing research. Previously, he had made me a gift of *Journey to Horseshoe Bend*, a book he admired, though not the missionary links of the author. In the course of our discussion, he remarked that T. G. H. Strehlow would have felt more at ease with the Australianist anthropology of the 1980s than with its counterpart in the 1950s. Hiatt was referring, I think, to the impact of the *Aboriginal Land Rights (Northern Territory) Act 1976* and its tendency to foster a concern with song, ceremony and authority regarding sites—as well as a gaze concentrated on descent. Strehlow's work would act as a resource for documenting some claims under the Act. Moreover, at a time when ritual life had declined in many areas where he worked, Strehlow's records of songs and genealogical connections, as well as his detailed maps of sites, provided a useful sense of traditional relations to the land. Hiatt's contrast was between this type of 'landed' focus and an earlier one on corporate structures, kinship terminologies and marriage practices—matters addressed in Hiatt's own early work (1962, 1965, 1966; cf. 1975, 2002). More generally, his reference to the 1950s concerned a period in which anthropologists saw Indigenous social life as structured first and foremost through kinship and marriage relations—a predictable conclusion perhaps when fairly sedentary settlement life for many Aboriginal peoples in Central and northern Australia was bringing the attenuation both of hunting and gathering and of ritual (see Barnes 1963). Hiatt was proposing that notwithstanding the extensive genealogical records that T. G. H. compiled, building on his father's work, Strehlow was not first and foremost a student of kinship or social organisation. His forte, like his father's, was definitely myth, and ritual as well.

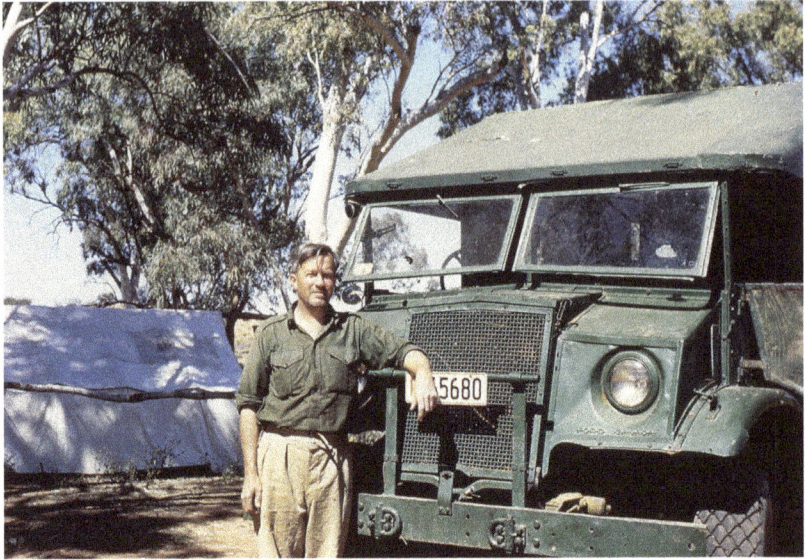

Plate 9.1 T. G. H. Strehlow with a Ford Blitz at Hermannsburg, 1960.
Source: SRC 01885, Strehlow Research Centre, Alice Springs.

Features of the Strehlow genealogies, and his essays on kinship, support this view and yet his research in this area should not be simply dismissed. Let me address the essays first and then the genealogies to put his work in context. Most of Strehlow's direct remarks on kinship and social organisation are contained in articles published in 1964 (republished 1978), 1965 and 1970, the last two in Australianist collections. Two further essays, published posthumously in 1997 and 1999, were in fact written much earlier. One, on 'social control', was composed in 1950 when Strehlow was in London at the LSE. The other, on 'regular and irregular' marriage, was undated but written soon thereafter. The 1950 paper is perhaps the most informative for Strehlow's views on units of social organisation in Central Australia. He discussed just two: the 'family', by which he meant a hearth group of parents and children; and the intergenerational patri-pairings, which he most commonly called *'njinaŋa' (–nhenge)* sections.[1] His treatment of the family was, if anything, Malinowskian (1913). He focused on various functions, among them

---

1   The Arrernte term has the sense of a 'relational' status and is used more commonly as a suffix for terms that describe dyadic kin relations both within and between generations. But, for this particular word, throughout this chapter, I have employed a more contemporary orthography. Strehlow's spelling of this particular term will be the more familiar to some readers. For my comment on the use of Arrernte orthographies as scholarly tools, see Austin-Broos (2009: 273).

nurturance, education (childrearing) and marriage customs, including love magic and the chastising of reluctant brides. The kin composition of this domestic group was assumed to be more or less nuclear. Despite the fact that in the 1950s Strehlow used the term 'clan' and once remarked that his *njinaŋa* section was the equivalent of Radcliffe-Brown's 'patrilineal horde', his approach to the patri-pairings was circumspect (Strehlow 1999: 40; Radcliffe-Brown 1930–31). He underlined that they were 'small' social units and designated these father–child relations in terms of subsection names used in Western Arrernte marriage classification— that is, as one among *pengarte/penangke, peltharre/kngwarreye, pwerrerle/kemarre* and *ngale/mpetyane*. His emphasis was more on a dyad than on lineal relations, although he may have tried to present his material, with its reference to Radcliffe-Brown, in terms of known sociological categories— for a London audience perhaps. Whether or not he distinguished between a corporate group and a residential one is unclear.[2] Consistent with his focus on dyadic relations though, he rightly repudiated Mathews's view that the intergenerational links between women in a subsection system constitute a matriline (Strehlow 1999: 41; Mathews 1907).

The 1950 paper is interesting in a further respect. In his narrative concerning one man's ritual path, Strehlow gave an account that is the closest I have noticed in his work to an ego-centred field of kin. He described relatives that fell under various subsections from the point of view of Nathanael Rauwiraka, an Ellery Creek *pengarte* man. To offer a sample of his remarks:

> Rauwiraka … regards all people who live in other *pengarte-penangke* … areas as people related to him patrilineally and … as people having the same status as himself … Since Rauwiraka's mother was a *pwerrerle* woman, he calls all males living in a *pwerrerle/kemarre* area … mother's brothers and refers to the whole district as 'land of my [MoBrs].' Again, Rauwiraka's own wife had to be an *mpetyane* woman. Hence any district [so settled] was to him a district settled by potential wives, brothers-in-law, and fathers-in-law. (Strehlow 1997: 11–12)

Strehlow goes on to remark that while *pwerrerle/kemarre* and *ngale/mpetyane* were to him *melyenweke*, people who supplied wives, *pengarte/penangke* and *peltharre/kngwarreye*, were *ilakekeye*, 'us two' or 'our own mob'.

---

2   Scheffler (1978: 522–3) tries to get around this issue by terming these units 'patrifilial kinship groups'.

Plate 9.2 Nathanael Rauwiraka, c. 1910s.
Source: SRC 05806, Strehlow Research Centre, Alice Springs.

In his article on marriage, Strehlow expanded. He offered a putative history of the use of subsection names to sort kin into marriage-relevant classes. He also described the way in which this system could have been embedded in 'geography'. As part of this putative history—always a precarious enterprise, from Lewis Henry Morgan through W. H. R. Rivers to the present—he indicated how this system might involve class 'shifting' with, on occasion, the re-rendering of a section as a subsection name; or an arbitrary allocation in the case of a person from the south-west where such names were not used. He remarked that the latter type of designation was done 'on the basis of physical characteristics'. 'Such men were regarded as *pwerrerle* if they had large heads and bushy beards; as *kemarre* if they had broad faces' and so on (Strehlow 1999: 21). Of these section and subsection names, which Strehlow called 'class' names, he noted that they postdated the actual classifications of a kinship and marriage system. Probably, he suggested, these summary names facilitated marriage and other forms of cooperation between different 'tribes' and 'tribal subgroups'. They acted to standardise 'social behaviour over the whole of Central Australia' (Strehlow 1999: 21).

Laurent Dousset (1999) points out that, in fact, Strehlow's treatment of so-called irregular marriages, which involved bringing new people into the system and turning to lesser preferences, not least when wives were scarce, constituted a 'new approach' to kinship and marriage. In this approach, 'contextual strategies are not seen as a deviation' from a normative kinship model. Regular variations in practice do not necessarily contradict an ideal statement of a marriage rule. Dousset (1999: 46) notes that this treatment preceded Hiatt's, which came in the form of a study of 'disputes' around bestowal caused by wife scarcity. Both preceded David Schneider's (1968: 4–8) view that situational practice need not undermine a 'cultural' unit of kinship. Strehlow was clear throughout his discussions that the Western Arrernte subsections were a system of classification and that the moieties they defined were simply named categories of people, not social groups and definitely not corporate ones. They were not a 'tribal structure'. Moreover, in these two early papers, Strehlow emphasised that this social system was sustained between multiple quite small groups stretched across a region. One might add that the patrifilial relatives involved (not the only members of these residential groups) shared alternating subsection names with the estate or country they called their 'own' place. As Morton has shown, all these classifications can 'shift' through time (see Morton 1997).

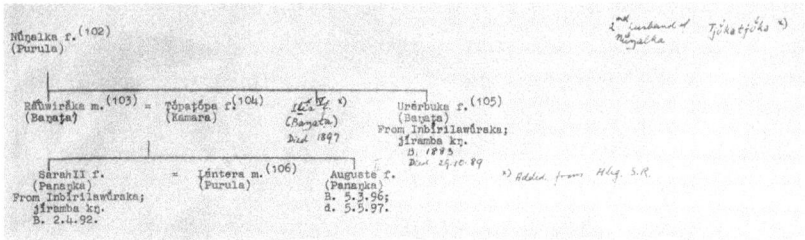

Plate 9.3 Excerpt of Nathanael Rauwiraka's genealogy.
Source: SRC FT I, 8, p. 13, Strehlow Research Centre, Alice Springs.

In the essays published before and after Strehlow's death, two things stand out. First, his discomfort with a specifically kinship account of the Western Arrernte's regional system. The songs in Rauwiraka's knowledge portfolio were by no means all acquired through kinship links; they were sometimes acquired at sites beyond the section/subsection regions. In the 1950 paper, and under the eye of Raymond Firth at the LSE, Strehlow made the following somewhat testy remark:

> Throughout this account it may seem to a *social anthropologist* that an altogether unbalanced emphasis has been laid on the importance of religion and ritual in native society. It is, however, an emphasis made by the natives themselves. (1997: 37; emphasis added)

This was his general conclusion from a more specific argument that 'the complete dependence upon one another of the various totemic clans both in their marriage arrangements and in their ceremonies' was the product of an environment where people lived 'in small groups scattered over a vast land' (Strehlow 1997: 36, 37). In a 1970 version of this point, Strehlow wrote that 'social control' and 'law and order' were ensured by notions of 'totemic landscape' anchored in a 'geographic environment'. Therefore, he suggested:

> [I]t is ... all the more surprising that ... so little attention has been given ... to the plotting of accurate maps ... and [to] listing the Aboriginal place-names, accompanied by detailed notes [of the latter's] totemic significance. (Strehlow 1970: 92)

The Strehlow genealogies

The curious documents that are the Strehlow genealogies—inherited by T. G. H. from his father, Carl,[3] and to which he added—became the repository for these data pertaining to a regional system. As anyone familiar with these documents would know, a majority of entries done or redone by T. G. H. involve the name of a person, a section or subsection name, the name of a conception site and the relevant conception or personal totem. In prolific footnotes to each genealogy, written in Arrernte, English or German, and sometimes scribbled or pasted on to parts of a genealogy itself, additional information is given. It may bear on the exact location of a conception site, on connections across genealogies, marriage details, conversations had or precis of police reports. Some entries also contain the colour shade or so-called caste of a person.

Further to the point that Strehlow resisted understanding a Western Arrernte system first and foremost in kinship terms, these records diverge markedly from the genealogies of British structuralism. The latter could serve two types of role. One was to show the contours of a kinship terminology and practice, the point being that *kinship as such is a system of social relationships* that renders or interprets biology. As Fortes (1970: 43–4, 46, 60) puts it, these renderings or 'recognitions' must be 'bodied forth' in 'objects and places' and in 'words, acts, ideas, attitudes, rules and sanctions'. Hence, the revelation of 'classificatory' kinship systems in which, for example, siblings of the same sex in a parental generation share terms translated as 'mother' and 'father' while siblings of the opposite sex are differentiated. The children of these siblings are classified accordingly. Parallel cousins are classified as siblings while cross-cousins are differentiated. Parallel cousins call both a mother and her sisters by the term translated as 'mother'; similarly, a father and his brothers are all called 'father'. This particular system is known as 'bifurcate merging', and, of course, there are a number of such classificatory systems known to anthropologists.[4] Strehlow knew about such things and the Arrernte kinship terms (which involve bifurcate merging) are recorded in his

---

3   The original genealogies are included in Strehlow (1999).
4   Lewis Henry Morgan is credited with an early appreciation of this phenomenon (see Fortes 1970). An excellent, very short introduction to the significance of kinship terminologies is Buchler and Selby (1968: 1–8).

dictionary. *But they were not his concern in these genealogies*, which were gathered mainly secondhand from senior Arrernte men. They have no 'ego' reference point.

The genealogies *are* named—often with reference to a deceased socially significant person. Sometimes this will be an apical ancestor, but not always. Nonetheless, all genealogies are anchored with reference to an apical ancestor or a small set of ancestral siblings. Carl Strehlow called them 'family trees'—a term that remains on the documents today. Moreover, introducing his essay on 'social control', T. G. H. remarked that all societies are interested in 'land and property'. Accordingly, these charts present as shallow family trees of five or fewer generations, informed by European notions of descent and relying on a naturalised, biological grid (see Morgan 1877; Maine 1861).[5] One might conclude that they were meant to demonstrate a jural structure such as lineage segmentation—the formation, over time and across a domain, of related corporate groups with inherited rights and reciprocal roles. Strehlow's remarks on the interdependence of 'clans' seem to suggest this.

Yet, the genealogies no more address corporate groups than they address kinship as such. They do not record the patrifilial inheritance of ritual status but rather the more variable conception sites and 'personal' totems that, as Strehlow (1947: 139) notes in *Aranda Traditions*, were employed to distinguish between patrifilial relatives. The genealogies are notable for spread, not depth, and for their cognatic nature. Moreover, at least in the larger genealogies, they seem to aim for inclusiveness. Elsewhere, T. G. H. remarked that the conception totem of a person was remembered as long as the person was remembered—like a nickname (Strehlow 1955). Therefore, if one aimed to record as many sites as possible, to demonstrate their density perhaps, and their implications for personal identity, one might privilege conception totems over patrifilial ones. Such an approach would also make the most of recall among a small group of ageing informants. Although my impression is that the children of male affines are more commonly recorded on another genealogy, suggesting something of a patrifilial bias, the air of cognatic inclusiveness remains.

---

5   In a fascinating note, Fortes (1970: 294–5, fn. 21) makes a distinction between Morgan, who suggested that material property confers status, and Maine, whose view was that status makes property significant and a matter of inheritance rather than (mere) acquisition. On the naturalisation of descent, see Schneider (1984).

Nor do the charts reflect the way in which Western Arrernte 'talk' filiation today. In a land claim context, the common refrain is that 'father's side is stronger'. In daily conversation, though, the more usual starting point is two or more consociates for whom a person wishes to demonstrate the relevant kin connection that makes them 'same family': same Mo, MoFa, FaSi or whatever. The lines of filiation described need not exhaust a memory and reach only to the relevant nexus. The modern term '*rame rame*' (meaning 'one family') can be described in terms of multiple such filiations (Austin-Broos 2009: 133–7). These daily references are more parsimonious than either the Strehlow genealogies or Sutton's (1998) 'families of polity'. They are not intended to specify a whole. Nor do they require an opt-in/opt-out clause.

Some of these matters bear on the 'West versus the rest' debate, even back to the 'African bias'. The relevance of unilineal descent and of consequent clearly bounded groups to Aboriginal social formations has been debated over many decades (Myers 1986; Sutton 1999; Barnes 1962; cf. Strehlow 1965). But that is not my reference here. Rather, my point is that T. G. H. used these genealogies for a very particular purpose: far from an interest in renderings of biology, property or corporate groups, he was focused on a socially saturated landscape made by marriages across a region and 'bodied forth' in networks of ritual. As Fortes (1970: 101–21) would have it, reviewing Aboriginal social organisation, jural concepts such as they were revolved around marriage and 'metaphysics'. Strehlow's claims for the family trees were as a spreadsheet of desert sociality understood in these terms.

Neither of Strehlow's two extended works, *Aranda Traditions* (1947) nor *Songs of Central Australia* (1971), leads with kinship as the pre-eminent framework. The contrast with Warner's (1958), Meggitt's (1962) and Hiatt's (1965) ethnographies is marked. Each approaches kinship in a different way. Warner, mindful of Radcliffe-Brown, remarks:

> The kinship system is the fundamental form into which the rest of the social organization has been integrated … The [Murngin's behaviour] can be understood only in terms of his behaviour as a kinsman. (Warner 1958: 7)

He saw a homology between the socially defined person and an integrated kinship structure. Meggitt, more mindful perhaps of the newly minted contrast between jural and domestic aspects of kinship, struggled nonetheless with Radcliffe-Brown's 'patrilineal horde', made his major unit a 'community' and discussed 'the family' separately and in detailed situational terms. Hiatt focused on social dramas around bestowal and was influenced not only by Meggitt's situational ethnography, but also by John Barnes's emerging network method (Barnes 1960, 1963: 204–6). Strehlow's work fell outside this normal science of British structuralism and influenced Firth's view of him. At the LSE, Firth remarked that, from an anthropologist's point of view, language mastery did not obviate the need for 'social' (meaning 'kinship') context. In describing ceremony, Strehlow 'should have said how the various actors were related' (Hill 2002: 472–3, 478–9). Firth sidestepped Strehlow's bid for a doctorate.

The second thing that stands out in Strehlow's essays is the crossness and also the stiffness with which he addressed social organisation. In the face of a Warner (1958: 15)—who described Murngin 'institutions' in terms of patrilineal clans, moieties, phratries, tribes and economic groups— Strehlow would insist on only three such units: the tribe (a language and territorial grouping), the patri-pair based *njinaŋa* section, and the family. He railed against the idea that moieties were Arrernte corporate groups in the style reported by Warner (1958: 32) for the Murngin or by Elkin (1979: 120). In the face of Meggitt's (1962: 248, 250–1) comment on the Walbiri that 'the community had … no formal hierarchy of government', Strehlow (1970, 1997) was almost apoplectic in his repeated attempts not to confirm that hierarchy, but rather to explain the way in which the ritual authority of Arrernte men seeped into mundane life. Possibly, this emphasis on ritual led him to reify *njinaŋa* sections in terms of bounded estates, with a main inherited site from which its patri-related custodians seldom moved, except to arrange either marriage or ceremony—so invested were they in their ritual 'property' (Strehlow 1965). John Morton (1997) has provided a cogent critique of this model, which sits awkwardly with the genealogies and rules out foraging and visits on account of kinship amity, as female aspects of a regional system. Except as brides, women barely figure in Strehlow's scheme (cf. Hamilton 1987).

Yet he did see something: a very particular social milieu linked with climate and geography. One way to approach Strehlow's view would be to observe that, in a period prior to the advent of 'alliance' theory as an alternative to 'descent', his interest in particular personnel contracting marriages that reproduced kin and ritual links distributed across a region was at odds with kinship accounts in terms of descent (also see Maddock 1972: 69–71). But this view as such does not capture Strehlow's reiterated point that marriage and its affinal links were integral to a 'totemic geography'. Meggitt comes closer to the point when he rereads Walbiri social organisation in terms of 'intersecting patri- and matri-lines' given spread by the marriages involved in an alternating generation subsection system (cf. Meggitt 1962, 1987). Not only did this apparatus organise life crises, it also assimilated groups and individuals to places in the landscape. All three had subsection names. How to account for this? Meggitt's (1987: 118–20) revelation was that one should come to kinship via 'Walbiri cosmogony and cosmology'. One can only read Indigenous kinship through an understanding of how people see the world and its initial genesis. Meggitt's essay was subtitled 'Kinship systems or cultural categories?'. He also cited Peterson (1969) on female (secular) and male (ritual) principles as defining themes in Walbiri life. Not so different, one might note, from Strehlow's focus on marriage and ceremonial practice in, and interpretation of, a landscape. What Strehlow saw went beyond the terminology and the sociology of kinship, into cosmology and the very beginnings of ancestral beings, species and geography.

Some other considerations

It seems appropriate before a conclusion to mention some other implications of Strehlow's work distinct from the more analytical ones. There are few ethnographic records for an Australian Indigenous language group that can reward careful study as much as his Arrernte corpus does. Crucially, this involves considering his published work in conjunction with the genealogies and his mapping of significant sites across the Arrerntic region of Central Australia. The map included in *Songs of Central Australia* is impressive enough but becomes even more so when consulted in conjunction with relevant notebooks held at the Strehlow Research Centre in Alice Springs in the Northern Territory. Especially for routes along major rivers travelled mostly north and south, and sometimes east and west, the dense lists of placenames make one realise that the published map marks only a modest selection of actual named sites in an Arrernte geography. In addition, one needs to consult a family group who can guide an interested observer, also able to access the texts, in an understanding of their 'own place' and the travels back and forth to other places for betrothal, marriage, other kinship events, secular ceremony, sacred rite and hunting and foraging. It was not just that Strehlow found the kinship and structural analysis of his time unamenable. Owing to his focus on 'religion', he was also looking at something else: the embedded, landed nature of this social system, which the sociology within anthropology at the time could not quite grasp. At least some of the passion in his writing, it seems, came from his unusual knowledge and the difficulty he may have had in communicating it to others. The references to classical myth, the appeal to a distant gravitas in attempts to capture one geographically close but conceptually distant to all but a few professional colleagues, also may have stemmed from this difficulty. Keen (1988) presents a most able overview of Australian Aboriginal kinship studies that surveys their many, often abstract, complexities—reaching sometimes to the esoteric. With good reason, Strehlow receives just one citation. And yet his legacy has been much more.

Another contribution was to the mission at Hermannsburg. Strehlow's dictionary and translations of the Bible and liturgical works are well known. Less known is a working everyday compilation made by the mission and entitled 'The birthday book'—a document in typescript form updated from time to time. The book contains 37 'family' lists with at least five lists that involve two surnames used by relatives located at two or more different and distant places in the region.[6] The birthday book is not a paired down version of the Strehlow genealogies, although significant amounts of data were clearly drawn from the genealogies begun by Strehlow's missionary father. This record is a more contemporary one, employed mostly through the mid to late twentieth century by the mission and then by non-Indigenous Lutheran personnel residing at Hermannsburg. It lists family members of the same surname most commonly across one to four generations along with their spouses. Each person's subsection is listed along with a birth date and a place of birth. Year of death is also recorded. An index of every relative, with the 'baptismal' (or first) name cited first, allows the user to crossreference a spouse's natal family. The book is an example of a mission's effort to remake an Indigenous people in terms of their own notions of naming, kinship, genealogical connection and domestic life. The provision of a first-name index also seems to imply that those using the book may likely only know an Indigenous person's first name—'Rosie', 'Jim' or the like. This is a reflection of the asymmetrical relations in settlement life between Indigenous and non-Indigenous people. Rowse (1998: 80–91, 147–83) has written on these not so subtle forms of domination pertaining to the Arrernte at Hermannsburg.

---

6   This could happen when some among a group of relatives adopted an Indigenous name as a surname while others in the larger group adopted a settler name as their surname.

The birthday book smacks of surveillance and, perhaps, of a Lutheran mission's love of lists. Nonetheless, the birthday book also records subsections and birthplaces. In a fieldwork that engaged non-Indigenous Lutherans as well as Indigenous ones, I noted that this book allowed non-Indigenous personnel to establish links and also formal distances between particular Western Arrernte—to learn a little of the Indigenous etiquette integral to everyday sociality. I, too, used the book when it was offered to me and, when I was trying to establish regional connections, consulted it in the company of Arrernte. As a European artefact, the book bears both negative and positive aspects.

So far as kinship practice is concerned, Strehlow was no ethnographer. The styles of in situ observational studies, evident in Meggitt's and Hiatt's work, were not Strehlow's interest. I have sought to underline that Strehlow's gaze was fixed on ritual and song and a regional system. Kinship analysis as practised in a mid-twentieth-century social anthropology was of interest only to the extent that it illuminated, mainly through marriage practices, this larger system. The intimacy of kin relatedness and the personae so defined through a sociality infused with kinship were not his empirical or conceptual interest. Although much transformed, it is this dimension of Indigenous life in Central Australia and elsewhere that has persisted to the present. Dramatic statements of grief and immense sorrow regarding the collapse of a magisterial system mark many of Strehlow's publications. One wonders whether or not this grief might have been mitigated had he been more engaged with, and comforted by, the minutiae of Arrernte kinship practice. Such an engagement also may have constrained his claims not only to the status of extraordinary scholar, but also to the status of an Arrernte ritual 'chief'.

Conclusion

One could interpret the Strehlow genealogies—with the songs and the extensive mapping and the ideas that inform their presentation both in charts and in texts—as an immense venture into particularism, prompted by the empirical facts. I suspect that, in part, T. G. H. saw it this way. But, of course, he was also immersed in religion—in *Geist* or, as Kroeber would have it, 'superstructure'. In our conversation, Hiatt noted Strehlow's orientation—not fashionable in Australia in his time, but worthy of respect nonetheless. Meyer Fortes once traced two 'lines of descent' in social anthropology's 'intellectual heritage'. One pursued 'structural concepts and theories'; the other, 'the facts of custom and culture'. Regarding the latter, Fortes (1970: 14) listed 'Kroeber, Malinowski and Frazer, to Tylor' and then 'to some extent Boas'; Boas only to some extent because, even more than Malinowski, he was a historical particularist interested in symbol and song but, in addition, in the ethos of a people, 'primitive' or 'civilised'. These two aspects of the 'German tradition'—historical particularism and romanticism—equally inform Strehlow's work.

References

Austin-Broos, D. 2009. *Arrernte Present, Arrernte Past: Invasion, violence and imagination in Indigenous Central Australia*. Chicago: University of Chicago Press.

Barnes, J. 1960. Marriage and residential continuity. *American Anthropologist* 62: 850–66. doi.org/10.1525/aa.1960.62.5.02a00060.

Barnes, J. 1962. African models in the New Guinea Highlands. *Man* 62(2): 5–9. doi.org/10.2307/2795819.

Barnes, J. 1963. Social organization: Limits of contemporary studies. In *Australian Aboriginal Studies*, (ed.) W. E. H. Stanner, pp. 197–210. Melbourne: Oxford University Press.

Buchler, I. and Selby, H. 1968. *Kinship and Social Organization: An introduction to theory and method*. New York: Macmillan.

Dousset, L. 1999. *On reading T. G. H. Strehlow's 'Aranda Regular and Irregular Marriages'*. Occasional Papers No. 2, December, pp. 45–59. Strehlow Research Centre, Alice Springs, NT.

Elkin, A. P. 1979 [1938]. *The Australian Aborigines*. Sydney: Angus & Robertson.

Fortes, M. 1970. *Kinship and the Social Order: The legacy of Lewis Henry Morgan*. London: Routledge & Kegan Paul.

Hamilton, A. 1987 [1980]. Dual social system. In *Traditional Aboriginal Society*, (ed.) W. H. Edwards, pp. 34–52. Melbourne: Macmillan.

Hiatt, L. 1962. Local organization among the Australian Aborigines. *Oceania* 32: 267–86. doi.org/10.1002/j.1834-4461.1962.tb01782.x.

Hiatt, L. 1965. *Kinship and Conflict: A study of an Aboriginal community in northern Arnhem Land*. Canberra: The Australian National University.

Hiatt, L. 1966. The lost horde. *Oceania* 37: 124–8. doi.org/10.1002/j.1834-4461.1966.tb01789.x.

Hiatt, L. 1975. Swallowing and regurgitation in Australian myth and rite. In *Australian Aboriginal Mythology: Essays in honour of W. E. H. Stanner*, (ed.) L. Hiatt, pp. 143–62. Canberra: AIAS.

Hiatt, L. 2002. *People of the Rivermouth: The Joborr texts of Frank Gurrmanaman*. Canberra: National Museum of Australia.

Hill, B. 2002. *Broken Song: T. G. H. Strehlow and Aboriginal possession*. Sydney: Knopf/Random House Australia.

Jones, P. 2002. Strehlow, Theodor George Henry (Ted) (1908–1978). In *Australian Dictionary of Biography*. Canberra: National Centre of Biography, The Australian National University. Available from: adb.anu.edu.au/biography/strehlow-theodor-gearge-henry-ted-11792/text21095. Published first in hardcopy 2002. Accessed online 2 August 2015.

Keen, I. 1988. Kinship. In *Social Anthropology and Australian Aboriginal Studies: A contemporary overview*, (eds) R. Berndt and R. Tonkinson, pp. 79–123. Canberra: Aboriginal Studies Press.

Maddock, K. 1972. *The Australian Aborigines: A portrait of their society*. Harmondsworth, UK: Penguin Press.

Maine, H. 1861. *Ancient Law*. London: Murray.

Malinowski, B. 1913. *The Family among the Australian Aborigines: A sociological study*. London: University of London Press.

Mathews, R. H. 1907. Notes on some Aboriginal tribes. *Journal and Proceedings of New South Wales Royal Society* 1: 67–87.

Meggitt, M. 1962. *A Desert People: A study of the Walbiri Aborigines of Central Australia*. Sydney: Angus & Robertson.

Meggitt, M. 1987 [1972]. Understanding Australian Aboriginal society: Kinship systems or cultural categories? In *Traditional Aboriginal Society*, (ed.) W. H. Edwards, pp. 113–37. Melbourne: Macmillan.

Morgan, L. H. 1877. *Ancient Society*. New York: Henry Holt.

Morton, J. 1997. *Arrernte (Aranda) land tenure: An evaluation of the Strehlow model*. Occasional Papers No. 1, October, pp. 107–26. Strehlow Research Centre, Alice Springs, NT.

Myers, F. 1986. *Pintupi Country, Pintupi Self*. Washington, DC, and Canberra: Smithsonian Institution Press and AIAS.

Peterson, N. 1969. Secular and ritual links: Two basic and opposed principles of Australian social organisation as illustrated by Warlpiri ethnography. *Mankind* 7(1): 27–35. doi.org/10.1111/j.1835-9310.1969.tb00383.x.

Radcliffe-Brown, A. R. 1930–31. The social organisation of the Australian tribes. *Oceania* 1: 34–63, 322–41, 426–56. doi.org/10.1002/j.1834-4461.1930.tb00003.x.

Rowse, T. 1998. *White Flour, White Power: From rations to citizenship in Central Australia*. Cambridge: Cambridge University Press. doi.org/10.1017/CBO9780511518287.

Scheffler, H. W. 1978. *Australian Kin Classification*. Cambridge: Cambridge University Press. doi.org/10.1017/CBO9780511557590.

Schneider, D. 1968. *American Kinship: A cultural account*. Englewood Cliffs, NJ: Prentice-Hall.

Schneider, D. 1984. *A Critique of the Study of Kinship*. Ann Arbor: University of Michigan Press. doi.org/10.3998/mpub.7203.

Strehlow, C. 1991 [1913]. The Aranda and Loritja tribes of Central Australia. Part IV, 1: The social life of the Aranda and Loritja. Translated by H. Oberscheidt. Unpublished ms.

Strehlow, T. G. H. 1947. *Aranda Traditions*. Melbourne: Melbourne University Press.

Strehlow, T. G. H. 1955. Collection of statistical evidence on the social organisation of a Central Australian tribe (the Aranda). Draft submission for grant of funds from the Social Science Research Council of Australia. Typescript.

Strehlow, T. G. H. 1956. *Testamenta Ljatinja. Anjkatja Arandauna Knjatiwumala*. Adelaide: Council of the British and Foreign Bible Society in Australia.

Strehlow, T. G. H. 1965. Culture, social structure, and environment. In *Aboriginal Man in Australia*, (eds) R. M. Berndt and C. H. Berndt, pp. 122–45. Sydney: Angus & Robertson.

Strehlow, T. G. H. 1969. *Journey to Horseshoe Bend*. Adelaide: Rigby.

Strehlow, T. G. H. 1970. Geography and the totemic landscape in Central Australia: A functional study. In *Australian Aboriginal Anthropology: Modern studies in the social anthropology of the Australian Aborigines*, (ed.) R. Berndt, pp. 92–140. Perth: University of Western Australia Press.

Strehlow, T. G. H. 1971. *Songs of Central Australia*. Sydney: Angus & Robertson.

Strehlow, T. G. H. 1978 [1964]. *Central Australian Religion: Personal monototemism in a polytotemic community*. Special Studies in Religion 2. Adelaide: Australian Association for the Study of Religion.

Strehlow, T. G. H. 1997 [1950]. *Agencies of social control in Central Australian Aboriginal society*. Occasional Papers No. 1, October, pp. 1–50. Strehlow Research Centre, Alice Springs, NT.

Strehlow, T. G. H. 1999. *Aranda regular and irregular marriages*. Occasional Papers No. 2, December, pp. 1–44. Strehlow Research Centre, Alice Springs, NT.

Sutton, P. 1998. Families of polity: Post-classical Aboriginal society and native title. In *Native Title and the Descent of Rights*, P. Sutton. Perth: National Native Title Tribunal.

Sutton, P. 1999. The system as it was straining to become. In *Connections in native title: Genealogies, kinship and groups*, (eds) J. Finlayson, B. Rigsby and H. Bek, CAEPR Research Monograph No. 13, pp. 13–58. Centre for Aboriginal Economic Policy Research, Canberra.

Warner, W. L. 1958 [1937]. *A Black Civilization: A social study of an Australian tribe*. New York: Harper & Brothers.

10

'Only the best is good enough for eternity': Revisiting the ethnography of T. G. H. Strehlow

Jason Gibson[1]

In September 2006, I sat with one of the few men still alive who had performed, in 1965, for the films of Theodor George Henry (T. G. H.) Strehlow (1908–78). We watched an hour-long silent colour film that depicted more than 27 different Anmatyerr ceremonies and included the participation of up to 10 individuals. The film had never been publicly screened before and had certainly never been viewed by Aboriginal people in the four decades since its making. I became fascinated with the manner in which films like this had been made and curious as to the intellectual style, theoretical agenda and methodological processes that drove this ethnographic project.

Though plentiful analyses of Strehlow's moral character and his intriguing life abound (Hill 2002; Morton 1993; McNally 1981), there have been very few attempts to interrogate the theoretical influences and motivations that shaped his ethnographic practice. One exception is Philip Jones's

---

1   Harold Payne Mpetyan, Ken Tilmouth Penangk, Max Stuart Kngwarraye (deceased), Paddy Willis Kemarr, Archie Mpetyan, Ronnie Penangke McNamara, Malcolm Heffernan Pengart and Huckitta Lynch Penangk were particularly generous in their memories of 'Strehlow-time'. I am grateful to the Monash Indigenous Centre and the Strehlow Research Centre for making the fieldwork and archival research for this chapter possible.

(2004) discussion of the young Strehlow's 'mentors', although this analysis is deliberately contained to the earliest stages of his career. Others have touched on his theoretical framework (Rowse 1992) and some of his contributions to Australian anthropology (Morton 1997; Austin-Broos 1997; Dousset 1999; Kenny 2004), but in-depth examinations of Strehlow's methods and achievements as an ethnographer are not particularly well developed. This chapter attempts to combine an overview of Strehlow's theoretical and methodical influences with an assessment of the contemporary usefulness of his singular approach.

First, I begin by examining the absolute commitment to empirical data-gathering that characterised Strehlow's ethnographic career over four decades, and which has been described as approaching 'perfection' in its technical execution (Morton 1995: 55). Strehlow operated according to his own program and often deliberately worked to set himself apart (Jones 2004: 36), so zeroing in on his inspiration is not easy. This chapter sketches his general intellectual style and points to some of his influences in Australia, the United Kingdom and Europe. Second, I outline the less widely appreciated regional scope of his inquiries and draw attention to his significant work among the Anmatyerr (a distinctive language and cultural group to the north of the Arrernte).[2] Third, in the course of discussing this material, I sketch out some of the changes that occurred in Strehlow's theoretical thinking and fieldwork methods over the course of his career and associations with particular intellectual disciplines. And last, I assess the utility of Strehlow's work via the commentaries of the handful of Anmatyerr men still alive who remember working with Strehlow. This reinterpretation of Strehlow's data (the audio and film recordings and field diaries) also demonstrates a tension between particularism and generalisation in his work.

'Preserving' information

T. G. H. Strehlow's approach to ethnographic record-taking was very much like that of his father, Carl, in that it was humanistic and emphasised mythology, song and language (cf. Kenny 2013). The 44 field

---

2   The orthography favoured in this chapter is the one currently dominant in most Arandic language communities, including the Anmatyerr communities. It was developed through the work of the Institute of Aboriginal Development (see Dobson and Henderson 1994; Green 2010). Strehlow's original spelling has been included in parentheses following the current spelling.

diaries produced during his four-decade-long career are replete with some of the most meticulously detailed descriptions of content of this type ever produced. When rereading the original field diaries, listening to the song recording or viewing the films produced by Strehlow over his career, one is struck by the tremendous commitment to documenting not only the particularities of Central Australian languages, mythologies and songs, but also their interrelationships and sophistications.

Strehlow's emphasis on empirical documentation has, thankfully, made his work amenable to reinterpretation and reanalysis by interested researchers and has provided further avenues for re-engagement with the material (Gibson 2015; Kenny 2004; Morton 1997). There are, however, stumbling blocks. The majority of the film and song recordings made by Strehlow contain ceremonial content of a secret-sacred nature, and thus access is nominally reserved for those who can demonstrate significant cultural rights to the material. These restrictions, coupled with the fact that detailed cataloguing of the film and song recordings has been completed only in recent times, have meant that the extensive audio and filmic collection has been largely inaccessible to researchers and Central Australian Aboriginal people. As a consequence, analysis of both the *contents* of these recordings and the *context* of their production has been incredibly limited.

The personal biography of T. G. H. Strehlow, complete with analyses of his personality and upbringing (Morton 1995, 2004; Hill 2002) and the later controversies surrounding the handling and ownership of his collection (Kaiser 2002; Smith 2009), has largely overshadowed discussions regarding his legacy and influence in anthropology. Barry Hill's (2002) dense and compelling narrative of Strehlow's life, for example, never seriously engages with Strehlow as an ethnographer and therefore glosses over the incredibly significant changes that occurred in not only his methods, but also his engagement with anthropological theory. This focus on the personality of Strehlow has obscured not only the dialogical properties of the ethnography and its relevance to contemporary Arandic[3] lifeworlds, but also, as Michael Jackson (2003: 88–9) has pointed out, its wider social and historical influences.

---

3   Arandic languages are a subgroup of Australian languages consisting of two dialect clusters, Arrernte and Kaytetye (Koch 2006). Anmatyerr is a part of the Arrernte dialect cluster.

Strehlow's intellectual style

An appreciation of Strehlow, and the fiction of who he thought he was in the field, is, of course, important to understanding this collection. Strehlow (1950: 129) described himself as being 'trained by natives' and not by 'armchair anthropologists', and his very personal, long-term and deep attachment with his region of study was uncommon in Australia at the time (Hinkson and Beckett 2008: 7). Strehlow approached his research in a way that may have resonated with his contemporary, the American sociologist C. Wright Mills. Mills (2000: 215) wrote that 'the individual social scientist' working in the 'classic tradition' sees their effort as the 'practice of a craft'. They are 'made impatient and weary by elaborate discussions of method-and-theory-in-general', as it 'interrupts' their 'proper studies' (Mills 2000: 215). Working from a similar premise, Strehlow's ethnography was undoubtedly a serious personal obligation. This intense focus led to a proprietorial attitude that ultimately intimidated many other researchers interested in conducting either linguistic or anthropological studies within the Arandic region (Green 2001: 33–4; Hill 2002: 336; Marcus 2001: 111).

Having grown up with knowledge of his father's work and later trained in English literature and the classics, Strehlow gradually became committed to the idea of ensuring that Central Australian oral literature was regarded as an equal to the poetry and literature of Europe's past. He studied Latin and Greek in his undergraduate years and emerged from Adelaide University with first-class honours in English. Under the tutelage of Professor Archibald Strong, the author of an acclaimed translation of the Anglo-Saxon poem *Beowulf*, Strehlow's keen interest in the literature and mythologies of Europe matured. Thus, with his feet firmly planted in the traditions of the Old World, Strehlow turned his mind to postgraduate studies and, under the careful guidance of professor of classics John Aloysius FitzHerbert (1892–1970), he devised a master's research proposal that went on to shape the remainder of his academic career.

In hindsight, Strehlow's MA thesis proposal looks like an early sketch of the themes that came to dominate his most significant work, *Songs of Central Australia*, published more than 40 years later. The proposal outlined an examination of the 'Primitive elements in Old Icelandic mythology and in Old English heroic verse, in the light of Aranda myths

and legends' (Hill 2002: 121).[4] Given that Strehlow was only in his 20s
at the time, and had not been to Central Australia since he was 13, we
can only assume that his knowledge of these 'Arrernte myths and legends'
came primarily from his father's work, *Die Aranda- und Loritja-Stämme
in Zentral-Australien.*[5] In these formative stages of his fieldwork career,
T. G. H. also found guidance from a number of individuals associated
with the University of Adelaide's Board for Anthropological Research,
including Professor John Burton Cleland, Dr Thomas Draper Campbell,
Henry Kenneth Fry and Norman B. Tindale (Jones 1995; Strehlow
1932: 203). As explained below, his first episode of fieldwork research
in the Anmatyerr region was interrupted by his brief role in locating and
encouraging Pintupi people to attend the Board for Anthropological
Research expedition team at Mt Liebig (see Batty 2013).

Strehlow's intellectual engagement with anthropology was undoubtedly
secondary to his training in literature and languages (Jones 2004: 37;
Ronald Berndt, in McNally 1981), and, despite a number of publications
firmly within the discipline, he found himself largely on the peripheries
of mainstream Australian anthropology (Austin-Broos 1997: 51).
What social anthropologist John Barnes described as Strehlow's 'odd
frame of reference' left those in mainstream Australian anthropology
perplexed (Barnes, in Gray 2007: 224). Raymond Firth, too, struggled
to comprehend Strehlow's approach and, despite publicly acknowledging
T. G. H. as the son of a 'famous father' (Strehlow 1950: 165) and thus
part of an Australian anthropological lineage, he paid scant attention to
his early manuscripts for *Songs of Central Australia.*

Strehlow strove for a detailed record of the linguistic, mythological and
symbolic repertoires of Central Australians, and fitting this material into
the conceptual apparatus of social anthropology was mostly a secondary
concern. Ethnographic fieldwork, he argued, was at the heart of all
worthwhile research and led to the gathering of 'stubborn and intractable'
'facts' that would 'outlive and outlast all theories' (Strehlow 1969: Vol. 15,
no. 2, p. 1). 'Isn't it the field workers that matter', Strehlow (1968: 80)

---

4   This thesis never came to fruition. Instead, he submitted a thesis in linguistics that was later
published as 'Aranda phonetics' (Strehlow 1942).
5   The focus on heroic verse in old European and Arrernte traditions had obvious resonances with
Frazer's comparative analysis of world mythologies; however, it was not until 1949 that mythologist
Joseph Campbell published his influential *The Hero with a Thousand Faces.*

asked rhetorically during one of his later trips in the Anmatyerr region.[6] This commitment to 'facts', rather than being interpreted as a complete rejection of theory, should rather be seen as positing that all theory 'must hover close to and emerge from data' (Hedican 2009: 424). Of course, the notion that 'facts' can be discovered via 'dutiful empiricism' (Geertz 1961) has been heavily criticised in anthropology. Strehlow's 'facts' were, of course, assembled within a conceptual framework characterised by a nostalgic longing for an Arandic past, and a blinkered commitment to the documentation of ritual and song.

Continental connections

Despite some speculation that Strehlow—either via his father or independently—found inspiration from a distinctively German-speaking tradition in anthropology (Austin-Broos 1997: 54), there is no direct link in Strehlow's corpus to either the German romantic tradition of the nineteenth century or the Boasian school. While Strehlow may have read Johann Gottfried Herder at some stage in his life, as Hill (2002: 23) suggests, there is little to indicate that this had any significant influence on him.[7] Nor is there evidence of influence via American anthropology, although things may have been different had Strehlow, as was suggested by Raymond Firth in 1932, travelled to Yale to receive training from Edward Sapir (Jones 2004: 37).

Strehlow's methods do nevertheless share some of the key accents typically attributed to German-speaking approaches, such as an emphasis on the detailed observation and documentation of local languages, myths and beliefs. He also committed to learning from one's informants and letting the findings emerge from extended periods of fieldwork. Observing the methods of German Lutheran missionaries (such as his father) translating and working in local vernaculars also affected his orthography for the Arrernte language, his method of genealogical record-keeping and his translation of myth and song. Both T. G. H. and Carl Strehlow in fact relied on a similar approach to linguistics that was influenced by Wilhelm

---

6   He had already been busy mapping sites along the Stuart Highway in South Australia. Before this, he had been obtaining mapping information and songs from Wangkangurru and Lower Arrernte speaker Mick McLean in Port Augusta.

7   There is no mention made of Herder in either Strehlow's published works or his diary. There are no copies of any Herder text in his personal book collection held at the Strehlow Research Centre in Alice Springs.

von Humboldt and the classicist Georg Curtius (Moore 2008, and cf. 2003). These methods were generalist, fieldwork-friendly and had been embraced by the Neuendettelsau Mission Society, where Carl Strehlow was trained.

There were other German-speaking ideas, however, that came to occupy an important place in Strehlow's thinking. The allure of psychoanalysis, with its links to studies in comparative mythology, is particularly recognisable in Strehlow's published and unpublished works. As a young master's student, he read a German edition of Freud's *Totem and Taboo* (1922) and avidly worked through Géza Róheim's *Australian Totemism* (1925). Róheim's contributions to the *International Journal of Psychoanalysis* (1932) were also heavily annotated by Strehlow.[8] References to Carl Jung in the introduction of Strehlow's first book publication, *Aranda Traditions* (1947: xv), and his stated interest in the possible 'parallels' between Central Australian traditions and those of past European societies reveal a sincere interest in prospects of psychoanalytic theory.

His song data, too, he later claimed, demonstrated not only the possibility of a commonality of human emotions, but also 'uninhibited subconscious drives' (Strehlow 1971: xvi). Although careful not to make definitive statements in support of psychoanalytic theory, he did, however, conclude that, from the type of comparative analysis offered in *Songs of Central Australia*, 'new light may eventually be thrown on the real reasons for the existence of the parallels', and 'even on the process of human thinking itself' (Strehlow 1971: xl). Unlike his father, who was advised against delving into parallels with European traditions (Kenny 2013: 121), T. G. H. felt freer to entertain comparative and theoretical investigations.[9]

Strehlow maintained his links with German-speaking ideas and academics throughout his career. As early as 1936, he was contacted by representatives from the Frobenius Institute who were already familiar with the work of Carl Strehlow about the possibility of assisting with their planned expedition to Australia (Beinssen-Hesse 2004). Though the Frobenius Expedition (1938–39) ended up travelling to the Kimberley

---

8   See Strehlow's personal library collection at the Strehlow Research Centre in Alice Springs. The inside cover of the *International Journal of Psychoanalysis* (vol. XIII, 1932) reads: 'T. G. Strehlow June 25th 1933, Alice Springs.'
9   Others influenced by comparative mythology, psychoanalysis and cultural diffusion, such as the American mythologist Joseph Campbell, also received some support from Strehlow (Campbell 1974: xii, 185).

region of Western Australia, contact with what Gingrich (2005: 108) has described as the 'late-Romantic', 'speculative' and yet 'fieldwork-oriented' school of cultural morphology continued. Most notably, Strehlow contributed to the *Festschrift* of Adolf Ellegard Jensen (Schuster et al. 1964) and received encouragement from Helmut Petri, whom he met with in London and Frankfurt in 1950 (Strehlow 1950: 130).[10]

A collection of regional scope

Perhaps one of the biggest misconceptions about Strehlow's ethnographic collection is that its contents pertain almost exclusively to the Arrernte. This emphasis on Arrernte and, more specifically, Western Arrernte material has almost certainly emanated from the largely biographical approach to Strehlow's corpus with his ties to the Hermannsburg Mission and the status of his father, Carl. Most analyses of Strehlow's anthropological material have accordingly focused on this Western Arrernte content (Morton 1997; Austin-Broos 2004, 2009) and overlooked material from other language or cultural groups. For example, when I first came to specifically explore the extent of the Anmatyerr collections at the Strehlow Research Centre close to 10 years ago, I discovered that the genealogies of over 370 Anmatyerr individuals were absent from the listings used by Aboriginal clients and other researchers visiting the centre.[11] The presence of Anmatyerr-related ceremonial objects, films, song recordings or documents was also incorrectly denied.[12]

A purely quantitative analysis of the Strehlow collection reveals the limitations of these past analyses. Although there is undoubtedly a very significant amount of Western Arrernte material in Strehlow's collection, the Eastern Arrernte content slightly outweighs it and the Southern, Central and Northern Arrernte material is also extensive. Crucially, Strehlow also made extremely significant recordings of both Anmatyerr and Luritja songs and ceremonies as well as far smaller collections of Alyawarr and Wangkangurru material. In the Anmatyerr area alone, more than 55 individuals (mostly men) acted as informants, guides or

---

10   Strehlow also wrote a favourable review of Andreas Lommel's 'humanitarian' and 'emotional' *Fortschritt Ins Nichts* (see Strehlow 1970a).

11   Anna Kenny has, however, in recent times included the Anmatyerr genealogies in her research (2013: 219).

12   I first began looking into the possibility that Strehlow had collected Anmatyerr sacred objects at the behest of the late Don Campbell in March 2006.

performers over four decades of research. Many hours of recordings were made of Anmatyerr songs and well over 150 song texts were transcribed.[13] Close to 50 different ceremonial 'acts' from across the length and breadth of the Anmatyerr region (approximately 4,000 square kilometres of the Northern Territory) were filmed and photographed in colour (Strehlow 1971: xiv, xx) and Strehlow's field diaries contain detailed maps of the 'totemic geography' for the region. In addition to this anthropological material, the diaries also contain important social histories of early Anmatyerr interactions with Europeans and thus undoubtedly comprise the most voluminous and important ethnography of the Anmatyerr prior to the land rights era (beginning in about 1975).

Though undoubtedly Arandic in linguistic terms, the Anmatyerr have a distinctive social and cultural history that differs from their neighbours to the south, the Arrernte. While the Arrernte region has been, at least in part, shaped by a history of two competing missions (Catholic in the east and Lutheran in the west) and an expanding township (Alice Springs) at its centre, the Anmatyerr region has never hosted a sizeable township, mission or government settlement and has instead been characterised by a long-term engagement with pastoralism.[14] Anmatyerr familial and cultural links with the Warlpiri to their west, as well as their strong links with the Alyawarr and Kaytetye, suggest that Strehlow's work in this region be considered in its own right and not subsumed within an analysis of his Arrernte work.

The following sections explore the nature of Strehlow's work with Anmatyerr people over four decades. By drawing out this history of ethnographic exchange and encounter, I hope to reveal more about Strehlow's changing methods and influences.

Fieldwork transformed

T. G. H. Strehlow's fieldwork career began with a journey north from Alice Springs into Anmatyerr country in the winter of 1932.[15] He was 24 years of age at the time and, armed with his humanistic and philological

---

13   Catherine Ellis used many of these Anmatyerr song recordings in her groundbreaking dissertation on Central Australian songs.
14   The ration depot at Bullocky Soak, near Central Mount Stuart, was very small and short-lived (between 1945 and 1947).
15   Strehlow first wrote 'Unmatjera' and revised his spelling to 'Anmatjera' in 1968.

outlook, he set out to ascertain the boundaries of what would later be defined as the Arandic 'language-dialect complex' (Hale 1962), which included the different kinds of Arrernte, Kaytetye, Pertame, Alyawarr and Anmatyerr. By leveraging his personal association with the Western Arrernte and enlisting the critical assistance of the skilled Northern Arrernte interpreter and go-between Tom Ljonga, Strehlow found Anmatyerr people were eager participants in his recording and documentation work. It was with these various Anmatyerr and Arrernte informants that his eyes were first opened to the storied landscape and the ritual cosmology of Central Australian people.

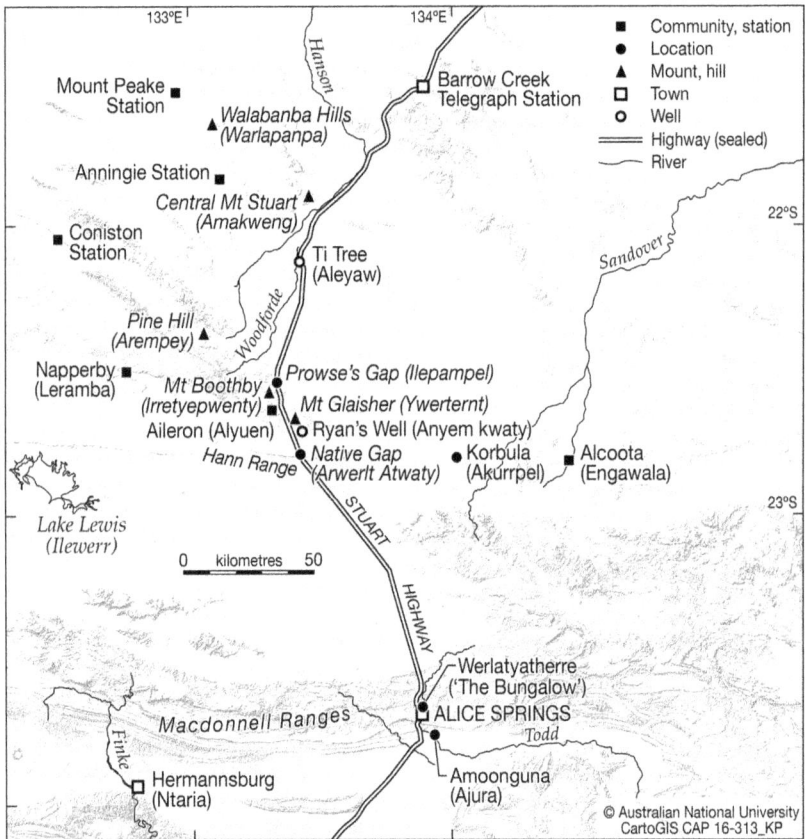

Map 10.1 The area north of Alice Springs where Strehlow worked.
Source: CartoGIS, The Australian National University.

This fieldwork expedition—what he called the 'Northern Trip'—took him to the far north-western corner of the Anmatyerr territory and along its northern and eastern boundaries. It was here he recorded his very first song verses, collected his first *tywerrenge* (*tjurunga*: 'sacred') objects and encountered men with whom he was utterly unfamiliar, but who were nevertheless willing to trade their ceremonial material (see Strehlow 1932). Following a brief diversion from his own research to assist with the University of Adelaide's expedition to Mt Liebig (see Batty 2013), Strehlow immediately returned to Anmatyerr territory, eager to resume his own studies. What he later called the 'Round Trip' began at Napperby Station and followed the perimeter of the Anmatyerr region from west to east (Strehlow 1932: 88). Wordlists, mythologies, song texts and translations were accrued along the way. These two month-long expeditions in Anmatyerr lands, coupled with his time in Arrernte, Luritja and Pintubi territories in 1932, were absolutely critical to Strehlow's understanding of the inherent connection between mythologies, people, landscape and ancestral beings across linguistic or cultural divides.

It wasn't until 1953, over 20 years later, however, that any significant Anmatyerr-related material was again documented. This was the beginning of a new period in Strehlow's research, following two years studying social anthropology at the London School of Economics (LSE) and a brief and yet very successful tour of Europe. Despite his aversion to British social anthropology, Strehlow's research during and after this period in London began to incorporate social anthropological ideas and he became increasingly interested in cultural geography (Strehlow 1952: 1).[16] While Morton (1997: 107) may be correct in surmising that Strehlow felt pressured to adopt some of the language and conceptual apparatus of the functionalists, he nevertheless did adopt this language on numerous occasions (see, for example, Strehlow 1956, 1970b, 1997). As exemplified by his numerous visits to the Assyrian, Egyptian and Greek collections at the British Museum, Strehlow's interest in the classics, however, continued to be his primary source of intellectual stimulation. His audio and film recordings of song and ceremony also remained central to his project even though they were less than enthusiastically received by those at the LSE (Strehlow 1952: 71a–5). In Austria, Belgium, Switzerland, France and Germany, however, his films were given the respect they deserved (Hill 2002: 484).

16 Morton (1997: 107) suggests that he may have been 'pressured' into using these social anthropological theories.

Admitting that he was 'set in his ways' and that he detested 'both the sort of linguistics and the sort of social anthropology' 'of the functional type' being taught in London, Strehlow (1950: 121, 154) desperately wished to return to his fieldwork and continue his recordings. Returning to Australia in the early 1950s, Strehlow changed his research methods somewhat and began to adopt what were then revolutionary audio and visual technologies such as colour film, colour slide photography and wire audio recording. As 'new ways of preserving this material had been perfected', he later commented, 'it was now possible to take good colour movies of the ceremonial "acts" (performances) and wire recordings of the songs and myths' (Strehlow 1964a: 110). This period of fieldwork (between 1953 and 1962) was also characterised by the staging of ambitious ceremonial 'festivals' in proximity to the Aboriginal settlements in Alice Springs. While Arrernte traditions remained the central focus of the festivals, interlinked Anmatyerr, Luritja, Alyawarr and Pintubi ceremonies and songs were increasingly introduced.[17]

As each ceremony was performed, Strehlow gave it a number, filmed it, photographed it, wrote up a description of the ritual paraphernalia and, in many cases, produced detailed 'film scripts' of the ceremonies. His methods of documentation were being carefully perfected so as to be as thorough as possible.

Revisiting the fieldwork

The filmic, photographic and audio recordings made during these festivals have in recent years been digitised and are now regularly accessed by Aboriginal men with personal connections to the material. Foreshadowing the uses of this material, anthropologist John Morton noted some time ago that the collection suited 'a new generation of researchers' wishing to 'breathe life' into the 'once dormant' collection via its 'collaborative opening up'. This collaborative rereading of the collection, Morton (2004: 46) suggested, would be most fruitful when it combined 'Aboriginal and anthropological investigations'. As indicated at the beginning of this chapter, it is exactly this experience that sparked my initial interest in the Strehlow materials. The memories and perspectives of Aboriginal people implicated in this wideranging regional ethnography

---

17 Particularly in 1955 when Bob Rubuntja planned the staging of honey-ant performances linking the Pintubi and Alyawarr populations.

not only make an important contribution to our understanding of their role in the production of this corpus, but also reveal new perspectives on Strehlow's methods.

A number of Anmatyerr men now aged in their 70s and 80s to whom I have presented some of this material remember witnessing Strehlow's 'festivals' in Alice Springs. One man, Paddy Kemarre Willis, who was in his 20s at the time, remembers Anmatyerr people—from as far afield as Coniston Station (to the north-west) and the Sandover River areas (to the east)—performing for Strehlow's cameras in 1955. These 'high school'[18] festivals, he remembered, had been organised and choreographed by senior Arrernte men but many of the participants had been sourced from the general itinerant Aboriginal population in Alice Springs. These people often resided on Aboriginal settlements, either at 'The Bungalow' (between 1953 and 1955) or at the Amoonguna settlement (in 1960 and 1962).

Willis and other Anmatyerr men with whom I have discussed Strehlow's films have noted the opportunistic nature of Strehlow's documentation during these Alice Springs festivals. One of the principal Anmatyerr performers in Strehlow's recordings, a man simply identified as Kwetyaney (Kutjania) by Strehlow, is well remembered by many in the contemporary Anmatyerr community.[19] Local histories tell us (and are confirmed in Strehlow's notes) that Kwetyaney belonged to the Warlapanpa estate (over 300 kilometres to the north-west of Alice Springs) and was resident at The Bungalow in 1953. Furthermore, Kwetyaney would have been in his early 50s at the time of the recordings and, contrary to the conventional narrative, he and other Anmatyerr participants were not driven by the need to see their traditions preserved. They had not, as is often assumed, chosen Strehlow as a 'guardian' of their ritual material (see Jorgensen 2010). Instead, these men had found themselves caught up in an ethnographic project largely outside their immediate concerns. Kwetyaney, and many of the other Anmatyerr men who feature in Strehlow's films at this time, were roving labourers or stockmen and their involvement in Strehlow's project was often unanticipated and opportunistic.[20]

18 The term 'high school' has been adopted by some Central Australian Aboriginal people to refer to the educational aspects of traditional ceremonial practices where knowledge of 'Dreamings', songs and other aspects of religious life were taught to young men during religious festivals.
19 Strehlow writes this name as 'Kutjania' and the estate name as 'Walabanba'. Kwetyaney was widely recognised and remembered as a man of the Ngal subsection who had, in later life, lived at Anningie Station and the Warrabri settlement.
20 Audio File: Paddy Don 10092013 (10 September 2013).

Anmatyerr descriptions of Strehlow's participation in these 'festivals' also complicate the otherwise tidy narrative of Strehlow as an *ingkarte* (*ingkata*)—a boss or leader of Arrernte ceremonies.[21] On the whole, Strehlow is remembered by those with whom he worked or who encountered him as a privileged documenter of men's ceremonial life in the region and commonly referred to as an '*urrempele*-man', meaning someone connected with a series of travelling ceremonies that move across Central Australia. Bob Rubuntja, one of Strehlow's most significant informants in the 1950s, also pointedly referred to Strehlow as *akiw-arenye*, meaning someone belonging to or inhabiting the ceremonial ground (Strehlow 1953: 50), not someone leading or controlling it. These are important semantic differences seemingly deployed to denote a common category of inclusion or membership in ceremonial activity, but they equally emphasise Strehlow's role as a documenter. The *urrempele*-man appellation, too, given its reference to regional peregrinations, highlights an awareness of Strehlow's aim to detail the connections between dreaming stories, estates, people and sites. Indeed, it was this attentiveness to the interconnectivity in the storied landscape that continued to drive his research outside the Arrernte area and into the Anmatyerr (Luritja, Warlpiri, Alyawarr, Kaytetye, and so on), particularly in the later half of the 1950s and until the early 1970s.

Recollections of the final years

The systematic methods of documentation that were developed during the 1950s were continued in Strehlow's final fieldwork period (1964–74); however, the staging of large-scale ceremonial festivals was abandoned. In its place came the fuller documentation of traditions that were linked to particular estates, as well as concerted efforts to map totemic sites and *anyenhenge* section areas across much of Central Australia. It was also during this time that Strehlow returned to the Anmatyerr region, at the request of Mick Werlaty (Wolatja), an Anmatyerr elder in his 70s. Werlaty had initially approached Strehlow for help in protecting the site of Akurrpele (Korbula) from the construction of a road (Strehlow 1964b: 49–50). Despite being 'sympathetic' to Werlaty's pleas, Strehlow admitted

---

21 *Ngkart* appears to be a distinctively Western Arrernte term that has now been adopted into Anmatyerr, although is used almost exclusively to refer to Christian missionaries. The term was never recorded by Spencer and Gillen, who alternatively use what is most likely the Eastern Arrernte variant, *Alartetye* (*Alatunja*), which carries a similar meaning (see Wilkins' glossary to Gillen et al. 2001).

that he felt powerless to act; however, the following year he returned with a proposition to protect the site in the only way he knew how: by filming its ceremonies and recording its songs.

Plate 10.1 Ken Tilmouth Penangk, photographed by Strehlow at Alcoota in 1965.
Source: SRC 03707, Strehlow Research Centre, Alice Springs.

The films that were produced during an intensive five-week period document over 28 separate performances from what Strehlow described as an 'inner cycle'. The Akurrpele films, along with 225 recorded verses, the hundreds of pages of fieldnotes, 140 photographs and the 32 ceremonial objects collected, constitute what is possibly the most complete document of a single estate ever produced in Australia.[22] Ever striving for the most comprehensive and best-quality recordings possible, Strehlow wanted to create a collection that would endure. 'Only the best is good enough for eternity', he declared when working with the same group again three years later (Strehlow 1968: 58). Werlaty's son, Ken Tilmouth, was in his late 20s at the time of these recordings and remembers performing in front of Strehlow's cameras. In recent years, Tilmouth has spent considerable time with staff at the Strehlow Research Centre effectively completing some of Strehlow's work. Using the extensive descriptions provided by

---

22 See Strehlow catalogue listing spreadsheet at the Strehlow Research Centre, Alice Springs.

Strehlow in his field diaries and Tilmouth's own first-rate knowledge of the Akurrpele ceremonies, individual song recordings have now been matched to the specific segments of silent colour film footage.[23]

The hubris that came to dominate Strehlow's later career not only blinkered his interpretation of these exchanges, but also limited his appreciation of the prospects for collaborative research of this kind. Instead, he arrogantly claimed to be the sole heir and possessor, not only of the ritual objects presented to him by the men at Alcoota, but also of the ceremonial designs, songs and stories (Strehlow 1965: 8–10, 48). Tilmouth recalls the exchange differently. While his father had presented the ceremonial cycle for Strehlow's documentation purposes, it had been simultaneously and unambiguously shown for the edification of all the men present.[24] Strehlow's presence, Tilmouth posits, while being a catalyst to stage the ceremonies, was in no way a prerequisite for its occurrence or persistence. The older men had not, as Strehlow imagined, shared this material with him simply because they were sceptical of their sons' abilities to safeguard these customs, but had recognised a new and changing context in which this symbolic labour could be organised and legitimated. Similar Aboriginal responses to the 'new all-inquiring, all-encompassing world' of intercultural relations have been noted elsewhere in Central and Western Australia (Anderson 1995).

The ongoing centrality of *tywerrenge* ownership and ceremonial life within a changing social, political and cultural context is something that Strehlow chose to either ignore or give only cursory attention to. The changed political context of the 1960s did nevertheless affect Strehlow's practice. The social and political upheaval of the late 1960s and early 1970s produced a period of estrangement between anthropologists and Aboriginal people in Australia (and in most other colonial societies) and led to a new unwillingness among Aboriginal people to play the passive object of study any longer (see Starn 2011: 183–4; Gray 2007: 226–7). An instance of this changed attitude is observable in Strehlow's interactions with these Anmatyerr men at Alcoota in 1968.

---

23   Interview with Ken Tilmouth at Alcoota, NT, 4 June 2014.
24   Alcoota notes, 15 August 2013. The Arrernte man was Sandy White Penangke, who married into the Anmatyerr/Kaytetye region.

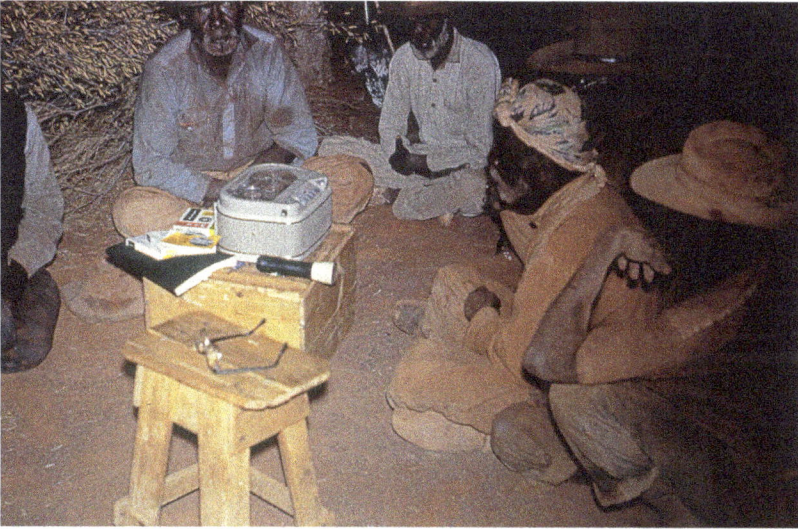

Plate 10.2 Singers gathered around T. G. H. Strehlow's tape recorder at Alcoota in 1965. The man immediately behind the recorder is Mick Werlaty Pengart.
Source: SRC 0370, Strehlow Research Centre, Alice Springs.

Strehlow had arrived at the 'native camp' at Alcoota Station just as a truckload of Anmatyerr men from Napperby Station were on their way to begin staging a circumcision (*apwelhe*) ceremony. Werlaty quickly reminded Strehlow that as soon as the 'singing began' for these ceremonies, he and his cohort would be obliged to devote all of their attention to the initiation rituals, regardless of Strehlow's desires (Strehlow 1968: 101, 111–14). Recently instituted improved wages for Aboriginal cattle station labour had at this time (1968) led to increased ownership of vehicles and increased mobility, and across the region there was greater intercommunity attendance for initiation ceremonies (see Peterson 2000; Curran 2011). The initiate and a large group of Anmatyerr men from Napperby arrived in their so-called red truck,[25] and other Anmatyerr people from the north were also making their way in a mixture of station and privately owned vehicles.

---

25   It is not clear whether this truck was in fact red in colour or whether the name indicated its dangerous cargo—that is, men on restricted ceremonial business.

Plate 10.3 T. G. H. Strehlow at Wolatjatara camp, 6 October 1953.
Source: SRC 00812, Strehlow Research Centre, Alice Springs.

Rather than noting the affects of a changing economic and social context on ceremonial life, Strehlow instead fumed that he had for the first time 'been disowned as *ingkata* [*ingkarte*] by a section of the Aranda-speaking population' (Strehlow 1968: 114–15). Strehlow's diaries remain silent on the significant social, economic and political changes and their influence on ceremonial practices. Indifferent and perhaps theoretically inept, he failed to grasp social change. The European bourgeois notions of spirituality and sacredness that produced an 'etherealised and aestheticised' conceptualisation of Aboriginal culture (Jackson 2003) failed to grasp the conditions of mundane social existence. It was the 'choice of classical forms', Darren Jorgensen (2010) has argued, that ultimately condemned Strehlow's work to the 'vagaries of the arts in Western culture' that eulogise the past.

These failings do not, however, dominate Anmatyerr memories of Strehlow. Instead, he is discussed as an ethnographer of exceptional skill, particularly when documenting song.

Remembering his methods

Reviewing the song and filmic material produced during this final period has also led to a better appreciation of Strehlow's methods. Harold Payne Mpetyan, for example, recalls Strehlow's excellent memory skills and his talents as a singer of Arrernte verse:

> He could talk Arrernte language and he could sing, too. Ken and me bin hear him that one. He was singing. We all bin there. Three blokes. He would sing, too [with us], *ya* proper really one that bloke! [He sang] That *apmwa ikwelengk* ['king brown snake'] song now.[26]

Harold went on to note that on at least two occasions Strehlow stopped the two men to correct them. Strehlow's diary remains silent on this exchange, but Harold distinctly remembers Strehlow writing down the verse lines and listening carefully to the version being recorded. As Ken and Harold sang the song, they had apparently missed a line. Strehlow stopped them:

> He said 'You two fellas just missed a line'. We started to sing another song. And when we started another one, then he called out, 'hey!'. And he was looking down at his paper. [Strehlow said,] 'You missed that one [line] hey?' 'You missed that one,' he said. 'Hey you bin ... why you bin miss that one?' he bin tell me. 'Oh we missed that one,' we bin tell him[27].

Harold laughed about the irony of the exchange. 'Was Strehlow right?' I asked. 'Had you in fact missed a line?' Shaking his head, Harold replied, '*Yewe yewe* [yes, yes]. He was right. He's a singing bloke that one!'[28]

Having spent the first phase of his career largely dependent on written transcriptions of song and only beginning to make audio recordings of songs in the late 1940s, Strehlow's ear had been finely attuned. Paul Albrecht, a Lutheran pastor who, like Strehlow, is fluent in Western Arrernte and has made recordings of Anmatyerr song, has similarly testified to having seen Strehlow take down a song verse as he heard it for the first time.[29] Strehlow's method in obtaining these recordings has never been closely analysed, however, it appears that he would listen to

---

26 See recordings SOU 00218: Tape No. 1, 1971, and Tape No. 2, 1971 (SOU 00219), at the Strehlow Research Centre, Alice Springs.
27 ibid.
28 ibid.
29 Paul Albrecht, personal communication to Jason Gibson, Adelaide, 3 July 2013.

the songs before recording them and, as this audition was taking place, he would write down the verses as he heard them. Following this, the songs would be committed to tape. Tape was expensive at the time so presumably he thought it best to save tape space and simply document the song, without explanatory discussions. At the end of each verse it was common for Strehlow to either remind himself or check the contents of the next verse about to be sung. Describing his role in this process as a 'prompter' (Strehlow 1965: 60), he would give a cue to begin recording particular verses.

The utility of the method

A range of Central Australian Aboriginal people now commonly access the Strehlow collection. Many are looking for anthropological evidence to validate their associations with parcels of land within the Australian legal framework (Wilmot and Morgan 2010). Others, as Berndt (1979: 88) predicted, have turned to the Strehlow collection simply to 'find personal and social meaning and emotional stability in contemporary society'. Strehlow's immersion in the mainly Arandic languages, songs and ceremonies has produced a collection of great utility and value to researchers and Aboriginal people alike. This is not to suggest, as I hope some of the examples cited above have clearly demonstrated, that his body of work is without flaws, contradictions or omissions. On the contrary, the sheer volume and longevity of Strehlow's focused documentation have allowed ample opportunity for these limitations to come to the fore.

John Morton (1997) has also shown how Strehlow's model of land tenure, which stresses the autonomy of the *anyenhenge* (*njinanga*) section areas or estates, can be effectively challenged using some of Strehlow's own contradictory fieldwork data. Strehlow's work on 'regular and irregular marriages' also demonstrates the failures of conceptualising human activity with a social 'system' and inadvertently challenges some of Strehlow's own functionalist tendencies (Dousset 1999). Strehlow's genealogical records, too, were set down in a manner that allows for new readings. For example, when working in the western Anmatyerr communities in 1968, Strehlow encountered information that suggested that Anmatyerr practices of land and mythological inheritance were, in his view, anomalous—where children inherited their father's totemic centres and did not appear to have their own private conception totems. Although this practice sounded 'rather doubtful' to Strehlow, he decided to record exactly what he had been told:

> [I]t is best to jot down what one is told instead of trying to 'tidy' up one's material. Genealogies are, after all the property of the heirs that figure in them; and what they know—or believe to know—must take precedence over the doubts and theories of the person who collects F.T.s [family trees].' (Strehlow 1968: 66)

Revealing his aversion for theoretical anthropology and his preference for a rather simplistic conception of pure ethnographic evidence, he writes that, 'in a hundred years' time future research scholars will be much more interested in knowing what' the Aboriginal informants 'had to say about their own traditions and institutions than in any explanatory theories advanced by Freud, Malinowski, Frazer, Róheim and the rest' (Strehlow 1971: xxxix). '[W]here local traditions are paramount and where myths, songs and ceremonies have always been regarded as private property', he argued, it was imperative that the anthropologist 'indicate clearly the names of his informants and the area for which that information is true' (Strehlow 1971: xxxii). The collection of detailed provenance data was therefore vital to understanding the interconnected webs of song verses, myths, ancestors, places and people that characterise Central Australian lifeworlds. It is this punctilious recording that facilitates current research into the Strehlow materials.

Conclusion

It was Strehlow's distinctive style of ethnography that led to his considerable achievements in anthropology, and the humanities more generally. Certainly, it was the intensive and particularistic documentation, as Ronald Berndt (1979: 88) notes, that offers so much to professional scholars and coming generations of Central Australians. Coming to his ethnographic practice from a perspective that privileged language and narrative led to an adoption of 'native concepts' and 'classifications' that were exceptional at the time. Moreover, this attention to song, religious belief and ritual led to an appreciation of the beauty and mystery of Central Australian lifeworlds, albeit often framed within Eurocentric comparisons and an undeniable primitivism. Strehlow's intellectual foundations ultimately led him towards a nostalgic search for rootedness (in geographically determined language regions) in opposition to abstracted theorisation or analysis.

It is this tension between classicism and social anthropology in Strehlow's work that gives it its singular character. In this sense, Strehlow's ethnography was an extremely significant forerunner to 'modernist Australianist ethnography' (Rumsey 2001: 20) that bridged artistic and anthropological perspectives. Anthropology, Strehlow (1966: 75) argued in the later stages of his career, ought to 'regain above all other things' its 'human view' where 'man' is put back into the 'Science of Man'. It is this descriptive approach to ethnography that makes both T. G. H. and Carl Strehlow's collections such valuable resources for researchers and Central Aboriginal people today.

What makes Strehlow's fieldwork data particularly interesting and useful to those now coming to this material is his particularistic approach to ethnographic documentation, his admission of contradictory data and the wideranging regional scope that reveals interconnections involving people, song and ritual repertoires across the landscape. What we might describe as the sociological or anthropological aspects of his work that elaborated 'models' or 'structures' of kinship, land tenure or social organisation were equally crucial in describing Arandic ontology. Much of this work, however, arose from Strehlow's methodological commitment to explicating the 'full details … of every informant responsible for each piece of mythological and sociological information' (Strehlow 1971: xviii). This was imperative to interpreting the data from within a specifically Central Australian context.

Strehlow's diaries do not compartmentalise his experiences into different domains. His fieldwork experiences run seamlessly into personal reflection, mundane travel logistics, personal dalliances and, of course, thick ethnographic description. We might now wonder whether Strehlow respected phenomenology's critique of the division between social scientific inquiry and everyday experiences. I imagine he would have agreed with the intentions of the phenomenologists to seek direct understanding and in-depth description (Jackson 1996: 2–7). Where Strehlow fails in this realm though is in his inability to acknowledge not only the dialogical origin of his data, but also the intercultural aspects of his work where Aboriginal men from varied backgrounds and experiences acted as co-producers in this collection. As a result, his ethnography is wilfully blind to the evidence of cultural continuity and ill equipped to theorise these issues.

The often backwards-looking frame of his romantic classicism prohibited any serious engagement with such notions. Strehlow's work, although interspersed with his personal musings, is almost devoid of any reflexive agonising about his ethnographic practice. The punctilious detail of his field collection, when coupled with the perspectives of Central Australian Aboriginal men, does, however, gives us scope to introduce these analyses. Strehlow's field diaries reveal someone deeply familiar with their anthropological subject but falling short of using these experiences to reflect critically on one's own assumptions or position. Collaborative rereadings of this archive with Anmatyerr and Arrernte people, while recognising the inescapable centrality of Strehlow 'the man' to the collection's production, give priority to the material itself. How and where this information—be it genealogies, song or film recordings—sits in its historical and cultural contexts is emphasised over and above the particular role of ethnographer or informant.

References

Anderson, C. (ed.). 1995. Politics of the secret. In *Politics of the Secret*, Oceania Monographs No. 45, pp. 1–14. Sydney: Oceania Publications.

Austin-Broos, D. J. 1997. *On reading Theodor Strehlow's 'Agencies of Social Control in Central Australian Aboriginal Societies'*. Occasional Paper No. 1, pp. 51–6. Strehlow Research Centre, Alice Springs, NT.

Austin-Broos, D. J. 2004. Western Arrernte endogenous change and the impact of settlement. In *Traditions in the Midst of Change: Communities, cultures and the Strehlow legacy in Central Australia— Proceedings of the Strehlow Conference, Alice Springs, 18–20 September 2002*, (ed.) M. Cawthorn, pp. 60–5. Alice Springs, NT: Strehlow Research Centre.

Austin-Broos, D. J. 2009. *Arrernte Present, Arrernte Past: Invasion, violence, and imagination in Indigenous Central Australia*. Chicago: University of Chicago Press.

Batty, P. 2013. 'Primitive Blacks Face White Man's Laws': The 1932 anthropological expedition to Mt Liebig, Central Australia'. In *Recreating First Contact: Expeditions, anthropology, and popular culture*, (eds) J. Bell, A. Brown and R. Gordon, pp. 197–239. Washington, DC: Smithsonian Institution Scholarly Press.

Beinssen-Hesse, S. 2004. Correspondence of Leo Frobenius and colleagues with Ekkehard Beinssen concerning proposed activities of the Frankfurt Institute for the Morphology of Culture in Australia. In *The struggle for souls and science: Constructing the fifth continent— German aries and scientists in Australia*, Occasional Paper No. 3, (ed.) W. F. Veit, pp. 152–82. Strehlow Research Centre, Alice Springs, NT.

Berndt, R. M. 1979. T. G. H. Strehlow 1908–1978. *Aboriginal History* 3: 84–8.

Campbell, J. 1949. *The Hero with a Thousand Faces*. Princeton, NJ: Bollingen Foundation/Pantheon Press.

Campbell, J. 1974. *The Mythic Image*. Princeton, NJ: Princeton University Press.

Curran, G. 2011. The 'expanding domain' of Warlpiri initiation rituals. In *Ethnography and the Production of Anthropological Knowledge: Essays in honour of Nicolas Peterson*, (eds) Y. Musharbash and M. Barber, pp. 39–50. Canberra: ANU E Press.

Dobson, V. and Henderson, J. 1994. *Eastern and Central Arrernte to English Dictionary*. Alice Springs, NT: IAD Press.

Dousset, L. 1999. *On reading Theodor Strehlow's 'Aranda Regular and Irregular Marriages'*, Occasional Paper No. 2, pp. 45–59. Strehlow Research Centre, Alice Springs, NT.

Fabian, J. 1983. *Time and the Other: How anthropology makes its object*. New York: Columbia University Press.

Freud, S. 1922. *Totem und Tabu: Einige Übereinstimmungen im Seelenleben der Wilden und der Neurotiker*. Leipzig: Internationaler Psychoanalytischer Verlag.

Geertz, C. 1961. Studies in peasant life: Community and society. *Biennial Review of Anthropology* 2: 1–41.

Gibson, J. 2015. Central Australian songs: A history and reinterpretation of their distribution through the earliest recordings. *Oceania* 85(2): 165–82. doi.org/10.1002/ocea.5084.

Gillen, F. J., Mulvaney, D. J., Morphy, H. and Petch, A. 2001. *'My Dear Spencer': The letters of F. J. Gillen to Baldwin Spencer*. Melbourne: Hyland House Publishing.

Gingrich, A. 2005. The German-speaking countries: Ruptures, schools and nontraditions—Reassessing the history of sociocultural anthropology in Germany. In *One Discipline, Four Ways: British, German, French, and American anthropology*, (eds) R. Parkin, S. Silverman and A. Gingrich with F. Barth, pp. 76–153. Chicago: University of Chicago Press.

Gray, G. G. 2007. *A Cautious Silence: The politics of Australian anthropology*. Canberra: Aboriginal Studies Press.

Green, J. 2010. *Central and Eastern Anmatyerr to English Dictionary*. Alice Springs, NT: IAD Press.

Green, J. A. 2001. 'Both sides of the bitumen': Ken Hale remembering 1959. In *Forty Years On: Ken Hale and Australian languages*, (eds) J. Simpson, D. Nash, M. Laughren, P. Austin and B. Alpher, pp. 29–43. Canberra: Pacific Linguistics.

Hale, K. 1962. Internal relationships in Arandic of Central Australia. In *Some Linguistic Types in Australia. Part 2*, (ed.) A. Capell, pp. 171–83. Oceania Linguistic Monographs. Sydney: University of Sydney.

Hedican, E. 2009. Ways of knowing in anthropology: Alexandre Chayanov and the perils of 'dutiful empiricism'. *History and Anthropology* 20(4): 419–33. doi.org/10.1080/02757200903219621.

Hill, B. 2002. *Broken Song: T. G. H. Strehlow and Aboriginal possession*. Sydney: Random House.

Hinkson, M. and Beckett, J. 2008. *An Appreciation of Difference: W. E. H. Stanner and Aboriginal Australia*. Canberra: Aboriginal Studies Press.

Jackson, M. 1996. Introduction: Phenomenology, radical empiricism, and anthropological critique. In *Things As They Are: New directions in phenomenological anthropology*, (ed.) M. Jackson, pp. 1–50. Bloomington: Indiana University Press. doi.org/10.1007/978-1-349-13729-9_1.

Jackson, M. 2003. Broken Song: T. G. H. Strehlow and Aboriginal possession. [Book review.] *Australian Aboriginal Studies* (1): 88–9.

Jones, P. 1995. Norman B. Tindale: An obituary. *Records of the South Australian Museum* 28(2): 159–76.

Jones, P. 2004. A maverick and his mentors. In *Traditions in the Midst of Change: Communities, cultures and the Strehlow legacy in Central Australia—Proceedings of the Strehlow Conference, Alice Springs, 18–20 September 2002*, (ed.) M. Cawthorn, pp. 36–41. Alice Springs, NT: Strehlow Research Centre.

Jorgensen, D. 2010. Simulating the sacred in Theodore Strehlow's 'Songs of Central Australia'. *The Bible and Critical Theory* 6(2): 22.2–22.10.

Kaiser, S. 2002. The Stern case. In *Traditions in the Midst of Change: Communities, cultures and the Strehlow legacy in Central Australia—Proceedings of the Strehlow Conference, Alice Springs, 18–20 September 2002*, (ed.) M. Cawthorn, p. 205. Alice Springs, NT: Strehlow Research Centre.

Kenny, A. 2004. Western Arrernte Pmere Kwetethe spirits. *Oceania* 74(4): 276–89. doi.org/10.1002/j.1834-4461.2004.tb02855.x.

Kenny, A. 2013. *The Aranda's Pepa: An introduction to Carl Strehlow's masterpiece Die Aranda- und Loritja-Stämme in Zentral-Australien (1907–1920)*. Canberra: ANU E Press.

Koch, H. 2006. The Arandic subgroup of Australian languages. In *Australian Languages: Classification and the comparative method*, (eds) C. Bowren and H. Koch, pp. 127–50. Amsterdam: John Benjamins Publishing Company.

McNally, W. 1981. *Aborigines, Artefacts, and Anguish*. Adelaide: Lutheran Publishing House.

Marcus, J. 2001. *The Indomitable Miss Pink: A life in anthropology*. Sydney: UNSW Press.

Mills, C. W. 2000. *The Sociological Imagination*. New York: Oxford University Press.

Moore, D. 2003. T. G. H. Strehlow and the linguistic landscape of Australia 1930–60. Honours thesis, University of New England, Armidale, NSW.

Moore, D. 2008. T. G. H. Strehlow and the linguistic landscape of Australia 1930–1960. In *Encountering Aboriginal Languages: Studies in the history of Australian linguistics*, (ed.) W. McGregor, pp. 273–300. Canberra: Pacific Linguistics.

Morton, J. 1993. Romancing the stones. *Arena Magazine* (April–May) (4): 39–40.

Morton, J. 1995. 'Secrets of the Arandas': T. G. H. Strehlow and the course of revelation. In *Politics of the Secret*, Oceania Monograph No. 45, (ed.) C. Anderson, pp. 51–66. Sydney: Oceania Publications.

Morton, J. 1997. *Arrernte (Aranda) land tenure: An evaluation of the Strehlow model*. Occasional Paper No. 1, pp. 107–26. Strehlow Research Centre, Alice Springs, NT.

Morton, J. 2004. Krippendorf's lesson in the centre: The shaping of the Arrernte through T. G. H. Strehlow's 'Family romance'. In *Traditions in the Midst of Change: Communities, cultures and the Strehlow legacy in Central Australia—Proceedings of the Strehlow Conference, Alice Springs, 18–20 September 2002*, (ed.) M. Cawthorn, pp. 42–7. Alice Springs, NT: Strehlow Research Centre.

Peterson, N. 2000. An expanding Aboriginal domain: Mobility and the initiation journey. *Oceania* 70(3): 205–18. doi.org/10.1002/j.1834-4461.2000.tb03019.x.

Róheim, G. 1925. *Australian Totemism: A psycho-analytic study in anthropology*. London: George Allen & Unwin.

Róheim, G. 1932. Psychoanalysis of primitive cultural types. *International Journal of Psycho-Analysis* 13: 1–224.

Rowse, T. 1992. Strehlow's strap: Functionalism and historicism in a colonial ethnography. *Journal of Australian Studies* 16(35): 88–103. doi.org/10.1080/14443059209387120.

Rumsey, A. 2001. Tracks, traces and links to land in Aboriginal Australia, New Guinea, and beyond. In *Emplaced Myth: Space, narrative, and knowledge in Aboriginal Australia and Papua New Guinea*, (eds) A. Rumsey and J. Weiner, pp. 19–42. Honolulu: University of Hawai'i Press.

Schuster, M., Haberland, E., Straube, H. and Jensen, A. E. 1964. *Festschrift fur Ad. E. Jensen/herausgegeben von Eike Haberland, Meinhard Schuster und Helmut Straube.* Munich: Klaus Renner Verlag.

Smith, R. 2009. 'Stuff at the core of land rights claims': The Strehlow collection. *Journal of Northern Territory History* 20: 75–93.

Starn, O. 2011. Here come the anthros (again): The strange marriage of anthropology and native America. *Cultural Anthropology* 26(2): 179–204. doi.org/10.1111/j.1548-1360.2011.01094.x.

Strehlow, T. G. H. 1932. Book I: Field diary (1)1932, Strehlow Research Centre, Alice Springs, NT.

Strehlow, T. G. H. 1942. Aranda phonetics. *Oceania* 12(3): 255–302. doi.org/10.1002/j.1834-4461.1942.tb00360.x.

Strehlow, T. G. H. 1947. *Aranda Traditions.* 2nd edn. New York: Johnson Reprint.

Strehlow, T. G. H. 1950. London diary 1(b), Strehlow Research Centre, Alice Springs, NT.

Strehlow, T. G. H. 1952. London diary 3(1951–52), Strehow Research Centre, Alice Springs, NT.

Strehlow, T. G. H. 1953. Book XVIII: Field diary and myths 18(1953), Strehow Research Centre, Alice Springs, NT.

Strehlow, T. G. H. 1956. *Friendship with South-East Asia: A cultural approach.* Melbourne: Riall Bros.

Strehlow, T. G. H. 1964a. Book XXXII: Field diary (32)1964, Strehlow Research Centre, Alice Springs, NT.

Strehlow, T. G. H. 1964b. Book XXXIII: Field diary (33)1964, Strehlow Research Centre, Alice Springs, NT.

Strehlow, T. G. H. 1965. Book XXXVI: Field diary (36)1965, Strehlow Research Centre, Alice Springs, NT.

Strehlow, T. G. H. 1966. Relative Relatives. [Review.] *Australian Book Review* 5(4): 74–5.

Strehlow, T. G. H. 1968. Book XXVIII: Field dairy (38)1968, Strehlow Research Centre, Alice Springs, NT.

Strehlow, T. G. H. 1969. Ayers Rock and Winbaraku by C. P. Mountford: A critical examination. *The Strehlow Research Foundation* 11–15(2).

Strehlow, T. G. H. 1970a. Fortschritt Ins Nichts. [Review.] *Journal of the Australasian Universities Modern Languages Association* (3): 365–6.

Strehlow, T. G. H. 1970b. Geography and the totemic landscape in Central Australia: A functional study. In *Australian Aboriginal Anthropology: Modern studies in the social anthropology of the Australian Aborigines*, (ed.) R. M. Berndt, pp. 93–140. Perth: University of Western Australia Press.

Strehlow, T. G. H. 1971. *Songs of Central Australia*. Sydney: Angus & Robertson.

Strehlow, T. G. H. 1997 [1950]. *Agencies of social control in Central Australian Aboriginal societies*. Occasional Paper No. 1, pp. 1–51. Strehlow Research Centre, Alice Springs, NT.

Sutton, P. 2003. *Native Title in Australia: An ethnographic perspective*. Melbourne: Cambridge University Press. doi.org/10.1017/CBO9780511481635.

Wilmot, H. and Morgan, R. 2010. Written proof: The appropriation of genealogical records in contemporary Arrernte society. *Land, Rights, Laws: Issues of Native Title* 4(5).

Part III: Widening the interest

11

The Australianist work of Erhard Eylmann in comparative perspective

Francesca Merlan[1]

Paul Erhard Andreas Eylmann is still little known to most Australianists because his significant major work, *Die Eingeborenen der Kolonie Südaustralien* (1908), remains largely untranslated.[2] This chapter provides perspective on Eylmann and his work, partly by comparison with that of Spencer and Gillen, who are much better known. Their research took place around the same time, in some of the same places. Eylmann made personal contact with Gillen in Central Australia, and continued to correspond with him from Germany, where he wrote his 1908 book. I contend that Eylmann, in combining in a single work both an effort at documentation and his subjectively framed experiences of travel and fieldwork, achieved a quality of writing that is in many ways more in tune with our sensibilities today than is the work of his major contemporaries, including Spencer and Gillen.

---

1   Thanks to Anna Kenny for sending me the Monteath paper, and to Jesse Rumsey-Merlan and Alan Rumsey for comments on a draft.
2   The Australian Institute of Aboriginal and Torres Strait Islander Studies (AIATSIS) library refers to partial translations into English of Eylmann's major work as follows: by Kevin Sherlock, of chapters XIV, XIX and XX (Call no.: SF 57.5/1), held in the same library; selected chapters compiled by Robin Hodgson, translated by Renate Hubel, 1994, MS 3369. Further, Courto's (1990) thesis gives an account of Eylmann's life and studies, and includes a two-page translation of Eylmann's introductory remarks to his 1908 work.

To what extent are significant differences in their work relatable to Eylmann's belonging to a hypothetical 'German' anthropological tradition (Gingrich 2005)? In brief anticipation of my conclusion, there is some connection between what we may consider German work of the period and Eylmann's orientation. But the difference between him and them is multifactorial. This chapter attempts to specify some of the relevant differences and what they indicate about the writing of ethnography, the overall Australianist ethnographic tradition, German contributions to it and German developments of the period.

Biography and orientation

Eylmann (1860–1926), scion of a well-off farming family from near Hamburg, was professionally trained in natural sciences and medicine (Schröder 2002). After practising as a doctor in Cairo for three years (1891–94), the tragedy of his wife's death there was the impetus for him turning to research in Australia. He studied further in numerous relevant fields in Germany to prepare himself for this. During this time, Eylmann came into contact with Adolf Bastian, who had by then been director at the Museum für Völkerkunde in Berlin for nearly two decades, and was also a mentor of Franz Boas.

Eylmann made his first solo expedition of over two years' duration, 1896 to 1899, crossing Australia south to north from Adelaide to Darwin, with a shorter side-trip to Lake Albert and the Grampians; another trip, in 1900, to Point Macleay, Kopperamana and other nearby destinations; and a third and final expedition, in 1912–13. Between the second and third trips, back in Germany, he completed his major work of 1908. Eylmann hoped to visit other parts of Australia, but, in the end, his research concentrated on the north–south swathe between Adelaide and Darwin—his principal contacts with Indigenous peoples (so far as these can be reduced to known tribal identities) having been with Ngarrindjeri, Diyari, Luritja, Arrernte, Warumungu, Kaititja, Wagaj, Tjingili and Waray. His work was wideranging and never concentrated in just one region, as was the initial work of Spencer and Gillen in Central Australia. Eylmann did, however, spend periods of months in a number of locations. He also visited towns on his route, considering them scenes of interest. He inquired of all Aborigines he met where they came from, often finding people in towns and at other points of settlement to be well outside their country of origin. He roughed out a social and linguistic mapping of groups. His work thus provides clues to earlier distributions of named sociolinguistic groupings in a number of places where these have changed quite significantly over the decades since Eylmann's publication.

Plate 11.1 Erhard Eylmann and Frieda, the daughter of one of the missionaries.
Source: SRC 06342, Strehlow Research Centre, Alice Springs.

Eylmann never held a university post. He was a research 'loner', for the most part: he travelled alone, but stopped and visited or made acquaintances at many places. He found temporary companions on the way, made acquaintance with pastoralists on whose properties he camped and also took advantage of German-speaking contacts in Adelaide and at mission stations such as Bethesda in South Australia and Hermannsburg in Central Australia, to assist him in making further acquaintance and advancing his research.

Eylmann was a relatively liberal-minded, non-evolutionary empiricist; he believed in the value of field investigation and observation. With his background in the medical and natural sciences, he displayed a strong interest in human physicality but also human social qualities of a generally comparatist and non-racist sort. He also developed a keen interest in and practice of collecting and museology. There was no touch of diffusionist or *Kulturkreislehre* ('culture circle theory') thinking about him such as was gathering steam in Germany at the time. He was acquainted with the various schools of physical anthropology of his day but was comparatively liberal in tendency. He closely observed the nature of interactions between Indigenous and non-Indigenous Australians, but harboured no evident negative thoughts concerning race mixture or what some (Fischer 1913)[3] called 'bastardisation', as had a subset of German natural scientists from the eighteenth century onwards, and as did also many Australians and anthropologists informed by Anglo intellectual developments.

Australianist field research and formal and informal writing

Certain understandings configured Anglo-linked ethnographic research and related writing in the early phases of Australianist work in the late nineteenth and early twentieth centuries. The period's scholarly interests—shaped largely in major intellectual centres of Europe and North America—focused on comparative institutions and an evolutionary framing of societies. In the resulting scholarly economy, highest value was attributed to the description of recently contacted, colonised people and

---

3   Fischer was director of the Kaiser Wilhelm Institute of Anthropology, Human Heredity and Eugenics between 1927 and 1942. He was appointed rector of the Frederick William University of Berlin by Adolf Hitler in 1933 and later joined the Nazi Party.

cultures as they were before Western intervention, with special reference to topics including (group) marriage, totemism and rite. This complex was later superseded intellectually by Radcliffe-Brown's structural functionalism and its particular synchronic orientation.

The period was marked by a gradual shift away from study of comparative institutions largely intellectually grounded in the ancient Western world, towards study of colonised peoples. An approximate division of labour developed in Australia and elsewhere between what counted as scholarship, on the one hand, and fieldwork, on the other, defined by the necessity to get information on certain topics from immersion 'in the field', but to shape it, descriptively and interpretatively, in terms of the prevailing scholarly interests.

Individuals and (often) pairs of workers bridged this division between scholarship and fieldwork in a variety of ways. In the United States, Lewis Henry Morgan—lawyer, would-be Iroquois Indian, founder and participant in numerous investigative, activist and scientific associations, fieldworker among Indian tribes, businessman, public servant, supporter of causes and traveller—was both scholar and fieldworker, but was crucially informed and assisted by his Iroquois protégé and colleague Ely Parker.

Lorimer Fison and Alfred Howitt formed an Australianist scholar–fieldworker pair (publishing *Kamilaroi and Kurnai* in 1880).

The division was famously bridged in the work of Émile Durkheim through his reliance on Spencer and Gillen as the empirical basis for his own intellectual grappling with questions of religion, the sacred and profane and morality. Spencer and Gillen, in turn, formed a pair roughly personally matched to, and bridging, the difference between scholarship and fieldwork. Spencer, a professor of biology, was acknowledged between them as the intellectual leader of their joint research, and Gillen, employed in postal and telegraph work in Alice Springs, was the indispensable person with extensive knowhow, local knowledge and contacts with Indigenous and non-Indigenous people, especially in Central Australia.

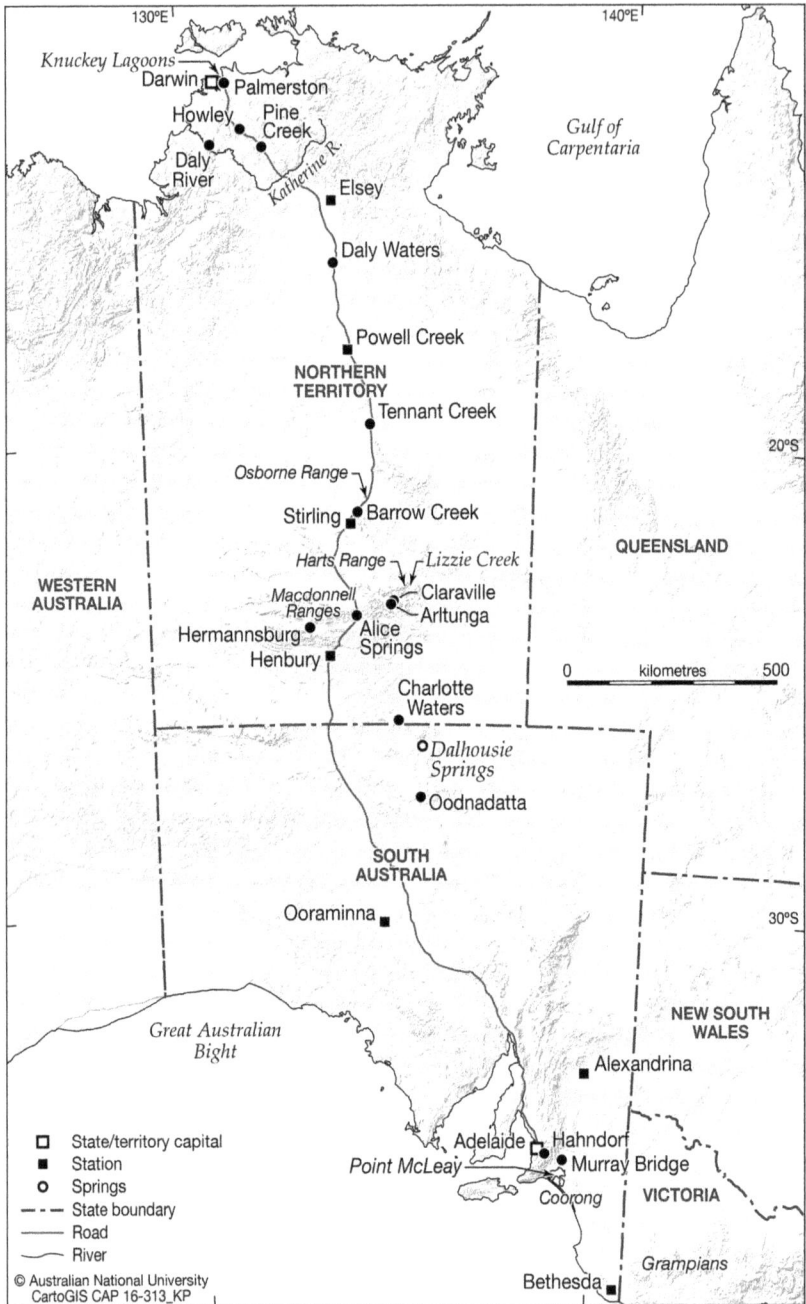

Map 11.1 Places visited by Eylmann on his travels.
Source: CartoGIS, The Australian National University.

The difference between intellectual framing and scholarship, on the one hand, and fieldwork, on the other, was largely realised in a related polarity between formal, objectifying ethnographic representation and the more subjectively framed experience of travel and fieldwork. Most researchers of the time published on these two aspects of the research work separately, even where—as in the comprehensive works of Spencer and Gillen, individually and jointly—we clearly see connections between the scholarly and travel works, and references to the same anecdotes and events in both kinds of writing. Formal writing counted as professional publication, capital and authoritative representation. The informal work of Spencer was intended for a wider, general, if not exactly popular, audience.

Spencer and Gillen published together *The Native Tribes of Central Australia* (1899) and *The Northern Tribes of Central Australia* (1904) as scholarly works under both their names. Later, Spencer published the large two-volume *Wanderings in Wild Australia* (1928), which covered in diarist and travel-writing mode his comprehensive experiences as researcher, scholar and administrator in Central and northern Australia. Gillen, on the other hand, produced a diary that has been issued by the Libraries Board of South Australia with the subtitle *The camp jottings of F. J. Gillen on the Spencer and Gillen expedition across Australia 1901–1902* (Gillen 1968). This diary, his son noted on its issue, was written in four exercise books to give Gillen's wife—who he had to leave for a year to travel with Spencer—an idea of his day-to-day activities. Consistent with his own sense of his contribution to the research project, the writing of the diary was in some large part an act of devotion to his wife and family rather than something he intended for wider publication.

Characteristic of the formal writing of the period is the elevation of description over narrative and certainly over reports of conversations or interactions, producing a sense of generalisation and normativity from close description of particular events. The formal is also characterised by effacement of the speaking and experiencing subject to a significant extent (see Pratt 1986), particularly the authorial subject, how he may have been part of the scene and how he experienced events and people. The focus is decidedly on the 'object', the 'other', not on self or relationship.

Characteristic of the informal or travel writing is a diarist's organisation—a chronological account of things done, undertaken, places and people visited and events—and a narrative style much more fully involving the authorial personality. Their travel works contain many incidents of Spencer and Gillen's being together with Aborigines, often providing some background concerning how particular ceremonial events or other encounters were organised or came about, and a dimension of humour or implicit comment that the writers do not allow themselves in the formal works.

Eylmann's major work on the Northern Territory melds the two dimensions—personal writing and scientific account—to a much greater extent than do Spencer and Gillen. The divide exists in some ways in his work, but in a less distinct form, and many parts of his text are permeated by descriptions and expositions in which he appears as experiencer and recorder, as well as by descriptive, 'scientific', interpretative and analytical passages. Eylmann does not seem to imagine himself losing what was later called 'ethnographic authority' (Clifford 1983) through his own inclusion, even in the recounting of episodes that many of his contemporaries, probably including Spencer and Gillen, would have deemed unacceptably low-life, even off-colour. In fact, his work breaches the convention of the division in many ways; overall, the weighting of personal narrative and scientific description and analysis is very different than in Spencer and Gillen.

As he travelled, Eylmann kept field journals and notebooks, which served him as sources for his published work. There was never any question of his intending to publish those field materials as such. They are, in the main, descriptive, not reflective or analytic, and daily entries often consist of remarks on a number of diverse topics, while the 1908 work is organised much more thematically.

Eylmann's book begins with a short preface outlining his travels. The reader has a sense of him as traveller all the way through the book as he contextualises the Aborigines and others whom he meets. One encounters them in large part in their relation to him, and not as if they were entirely separate from him and other colonials. While this may not adequately represent those parts of their lives that were lived in greater separateness from whites, locating them in colonial context often seems fully justified in that many were living near or on stations, at missions or around towns, where they were sometimes deliberately placing themselves in contact with whites, Chinese and other Aborigines. The overall effect is quite the opposite of a portrait of Indigenous society as if it were entirely separate from the colonial one.

Eylmann met Francis James Gillen, Spencer's collaborator on *The Native Tribes of Central Australia* (Spencer and Gillen 1899) and the postmaster of the Alice Springs Telegraph Station, on his first trip north, in 1896, on the recommendation of Amandus Zietz of the Adelaide Zoo.[4] Gillen gave Eylmann the benefit of his great practical knowledge of the region, helping him to make contacts with Aborigines and Europeans alike (see Monteath 2013: 4). Eylmann and Gillen had common interests in geology and other natural sciences, and Eylmann shared with Gillen his Berlin-period exposure to the work of the German natural and cultural scientists including Bastian, Häckel, Virchow and Graebner. According to Schröder's account, Baldwin Spencer, who first met Gillen in 1894, harboured some concern that Eylmann might get in his way or be interested in some of the same subjects as himself (Schröder 2002: 193; see also Monteath 2013: 4). Again, according to Schröder, Gillen was at some pains to convince Spencer that Eylmann's interests were quite different from his own and that they were not anthropological—seemingly a distinct prevarication of Gillen's understanding of the situation. Eylmann never met Spencer himself.[5]

Organisation of the 1908 work: Margins and middle

The organisation of Eylmann's book overall does reveal a manifest and even encyclopaedic plan to portray Australian Indigenous people, society and especially material culture in traditional terms (as Eylmann would have absorbed from Bastian, and also from other field manuals available at the time; see footnote 5). Besides chapters that are fairly standard in

---

4   Monteath (2013: 4) mentions the significant number of Germans hired into scientific and organisational posts in Adelaide by the time of Eylmann's first visit.

5   Monteath (2013) argues that Eylmann and Spencer and Gillen operated with a view of their research as entirely within a scientific paradigm devoted to observation and factuality. Though this may have been the contemporary normative ideal, I think this is a serious underestimation of the Eylmann text's subjective dimensions, which Monteath does not make much of. Monteath (2013: 3) mentions that Eylmann probably would have read the *Anleitung zu wissenschaftlichen Beobachtungen auf Reisen* (*Guide to Scientific Observations on Travels*), brought together by Georg Balthasar von Neumayer (1875) and available as a compendious field guide (of 1,600 pages!), with the needs of the German Navy to collect data particularly in mind. Von Neumayer had considerable field experience in land survey in Victoria. This volume is now available online. It certainly has a scientific caste but in no way forms *the* model for Eylmann's main work, although undoubtedly he was possessed of some of the same drive for detail and exhaustiveness as von Neumayer. *Anleitung zu wissenschaftlichen Beobachtungen auf Reisen* includes sections on such subjects as photography as an aid in land survey, botanical geography, collecting and pressing plants, magnetic observations, marine animals and a host of other topics.

encyclopaedic ethnographic works of the period (e.g. on religion, burial and material culture), Eylmann also features chapters on 'Bodily and spiritual character', as well as 'Illness and treatment of the sick', reflecting his medical and wider interests. Two final two chapters, entitled 'Relations between Indigenes, Europeans and Asians' and 'Missions', would never have appeared in Spencer and Gillen, given their conception of their work; a scan of the table of contents of their *Native Tribes of Central Australia* (1899) suffices to demonstrate this. Spencer's disparagement of Aborigines encountered at Oodnadatta as 'well clothed as we were and too civilised to be really interesting' is also indicative (Spencer 1928: Vol. I, p. 16).

Spencer's attitude is not surprising for the time, but highlights two important differences that Eylmann represents in this period. First, despite the obvious architecture of his work, bookended by travelogue at the beginning and Indigenous relations with outsiders at the end, the book is permeated by a sensibility for the nature of Aborigines' changing relations with outsiders and, relatedly, among themselves. To convey this sense, the work is punctuated throughout by comments from Indigenous people, which Eylmann reproduces fairly directly about all of the subjects he attempted to investigate. He regularly depicts himself as the traveller, the asker, the experiencer and a person approached by Aborigines as well as attempting to find ways to spend time and talk with them. This contextualises and renders the particularity and often the expression of the Indigenous people he was meeting. He identifies by name some, though not all, of the Aborigines from whom he gained detailed information. He also regularly wrote into his journals information and hearsay he gathered from settlers and officials who claimed knowledge of Aboriginal practices: Mr Bogner at Hermannsburg, Mr Cowle at Illamurta, Frank Gillen at Alice Springs, Pater Marschner at Daly River, and so on. He cites his interactions with Aborigines, in particular, and with others, evidently without anxiety concerning whether his relaying of many events and experiences in ways that reveal his personal involvement casts any shadow on their documentary value. For him, that documentary value was evidently not neatly or completely identified with scientism or rigorous 'factuality' conceived purely observationally, apart from the human relations in which the Aborigines, and he himself, were entangled.

This points to a second aspect of Eylmann: he occupied a dual position as fieldworker and researcher, interested both in traditional society and in contemporary social relations. On the one hand, he was interested, like others of the period, in documenting traditional Indigenous society as it was before colonisation; but, on the other hand, he was not an ideological evolutionist. That is, he did not come fully immersed in that logic by which Aboriginal society was revelatory of earlier human history and social arrangements, and by which its primary interest lay in what research through that lens could reveal. Like Spencer and Gillen and many others, he did see, and to some extent lament, that Indigenous society was changing rapidly, and, like them, he believed and observed that it was changing for the worse—largely through their interaction with Europeans. But he also recognised in his observations ways in which Aborigines were making new terms for themselves in the various structures and conditions of colonial settlement, and he was clearly very interested in how they were doing so. In these terms, his ethnographic interest focused on the relations of Aborigines and himself in interaction with Europeans of the outback— his portrayal of them, in drink and other ways given to excesses, often not very flattering—and with Chinese, with whom Aborigines of Pine Creek and Darwin had a great deal to do, mostly by way of material and sexual trafficking.

In looking at these relations, Eylmann's observations often come to rest on what seemed to him confronting and perhaps confounding, such as the fact that Aborigines newly arrived into Knuckeys Lagoon around Darwin—the 'uncivilised Aborigines'—manifested extreme jealously concerning their wives and women, and sent them out of sight to keep them away from strangers, but rapidly took to offering them, and under-aged girls, to anybody who had a little bit of tobacco in his possession, as well as to Chinese to obtain opium. At the same time, he notes:

> Any time an indigenous married couple made its way to my camp, and sat down with me without having been asked, I knew that, after a long talk about quite indifferent things, I would be asked if I wanted a woman. (Eylmann 1908: 459)

He was, of course—like Spencer and Gillen—fully aware of the extent to which the offer of women among Indigenous men was a regular aspect of social relations. With respect to the puzzle set up by these different behaviours, he tended to explanation simply as a difference between the 'uncivilised' and more acculturated Indigenes, and never arrived at any deeper insight concerning gendered relations in the Indigenous–non-Indigenous context, save one: that to an extent, the women themselves had some personal investment in sexual self-valuation, and rapidly took to demeaning him as a cheapskate when he refused such offers. In any event, his interest in such frictions of intercultural contact keeps his text from becoming generalising in many places. Instead, it remains more often narrative, with some focus on specific interactions and conversations. And in these ways, too, the overall portrayal is not of Aborigines as untouched by history nor as survivor-victims of European imperialism (which he even tends to downplay in places), but as human beings whom he could approach in their present condition, and himself as someone who was regularly approached by them for their own purposes.

Medical man

As medical man, Eylmann displayed great interest in the bodily character of Australian Aborigines and their skeletal remains, as well as in their notions of sickness, health and curing, and their everyday practices relating to bodily condition in their own terms. He begins his volume, in fact, within the chapter on 'Bodily and spiritual nature', with a long (Eylmann 1908: 1–33) disquisition on the physical characteristics of Aborigines, justifying this on the basis that these are overall among the people most strongly differentiated from other peoples in the world, but also noting that there are significant regional differences among them. His discussion moves from physical properties of every part of the body to hair types, skin colouration, the physiology of ageing, bones, teeth, bodily strength, bodily capacities of sight, hearing and movement to sleep, tolerance of cold, damp and pain, and food preferences and tastes. He also comments extensively on evidence of introduced disease, such as syphilis. He remarks on what he found to be a lively aesthetic, visual and musical sensibility. This discussion grades into what his chapter title labels the 'mental[6] nature' of Aborigines, to which I return below.

Given his frequent comments on sexual practices and relations, especially between Aborigines and non-Aborigines, it is again worth mentioning that he speaks of *Mischlinge* ('half-castes') without apparent disparagement, generalising that they are physically larger than the mother and her kin, and that the offspring seem generally healthy, of pleasing appearance and somewhat more intelligent than 'full-bloods' (Eylmann 1908: 65).

---

6   Perhaps the best translation of German *geistig* is 'mental' in this context, contrasting with *körperlich* ('bodily') in the chapter title. But *Geist* is clearly broader than simply mentation, and can encompass the 'psychological' and 'moral'.

In other places, he refers to specific part-caste children as 'pretty'—one like a German farm girl in her blooming appearance (Eylmann 1908: 65)—also reporting from what he knew that the girls become sexually involved with whites and Aborigines from an early age. He noted that the number of part-castes was disproportionately small given the rather considerable sexual traffic between Aboriginal women and non-Aboriginal men, attributing this both to low fertility on the part of the women and to his understanding that many mothers killed such infants. (Spencer and Gillen similarly comment on the paucity of children; 1904: 327.) Eylmann also seems, whenever possible, to have asked after intimate sexual practices, reporting a finding that women apparently regularly expel the sperm following coitus—another explanation, he thought, for the small number of children, including part-caste ones.

Spiritual characteristics

Spencer and Gillen, like Eylmann, had some interest in the spiritual and moral character of Aborigines. Spencer reserved his most detailed commentary for *Wanderings in Wild Australia* (1928: Vol. I, pp. 197–204), consistent with what he seems to think is the more interpretative and tenuous nature of this compared with the more observationally grounded formal ethnography. The issues that people commented on back then seem to have been fairly standard: the gratitude or ingratitude of Aborigines; their capacity for cruelty or sympathy; men's treatment of women; cannibalism; and treatment of the elderly and sick. Comments on these matters by Spencer tend to be limited to what were contemporary commonplaces, such as that Aborigines do not express gratitude but simply treat whites as they would a fellow tribesman (1928: Vol. I, p. 199); that they are completely childlike, with no thought for the morrow (p. 203) and generally lighthearted; and that it is unsafe and unwise to judge the actions of a native 'from the standpoint of view of the motives and feelings that govern our own' (p. 202).

Eylmann goes much further in the fullness of his characterological discussion. He does so partly by considering certain commonplaces— 'what is often said'—but also by developing discussion from concepts that allow for elaboration and comparative comment, and of a range of phenomena that reveal new perspectives. He also regularly considers certain characteristics as he sees them among Aborigines, and between Aborigines and settlers.

In his discussion of the 'psychic nature' of Aborigines, he flatly rejects the settler commonplace that Aborigines have no feelings of love and compassion for each other, declaring this to be completely baseless; the result of a superficial knowledge of and lack of contact with Aborigines in daily life. In refutation, he describes moving scenes he has witnessed among Indigenous people.

He attempts to specify a range of feelings for and in relation to others, framing this to some extent under the rubric of *allgemeine Menschenliebe*— whether Aborigines display a generalised love of humanity. A certain inclination towards those with whom he regularly lives is present, he notes, but he says relations to distant people are characterised by lack of respect and even hostility. He wonders about Aborigines' relations to whites: do they ever really come to respect and like them? Certainly, he observes, kinds of dependencies develop on white suppliers of food and livelihood. He notes in several places Aborigines' purposeful avoidance of whites and apparent dislike of them (Eylmann 1996: 218, 256). These reflections are exemplified from his experiences (e.g. Eylmann 1908: 35).

His work provides insight into the kind of relations he cultivated with people and camps on his longer stays, not only with Aborigines (for example, at Knuckeys Lagoon in Darwin), but also with Europeans living at Sterling Station, whom he saw as among the roughest types he had encountered anywhere, with no kindly feelings for Aborigines (Eylmann 1908: 10).

In his survey of the kinds of emotions and feelings that Aborigines express, he notes their love for their dogs, which they value greatly, but also the regularity with which children torment and torture animals as a form of play. Exemplifying this, he records that the young children dealt with the proliferation of cats on Sterling Station by spearing them in the anus, and that even his threats to shoot the children had little effect. He compares them with young children back home in Germany who delight in blowing frogs up until they explode (see below on Eylmann's penchant for such comparison).

Eylmann discusses and offers examples of Aborigines being very self-preserving, such that in times of drought they will unhesitatingly leave the sick, weak and elderly behind, not harming but also not helping, and go off to seek a living elsewhere. He comments on the desire to obtain goods and the readiness of women to prostitute themselves, as he sees it, for any advantage of this kind.

He considers the topic of what we would now call 'demand sharing' (Peterson 1993)—that is, social demand on Aboriginal people who have food or other goods to share with their closest associates. With regard to this topic in Indigenous–non-Indigenous relations, he comments that Aborigines sometimes seem to have regard for whites only when they can fulfil their demands—and treat them with much less regard when they cannot. But, he observes, such behaviour is no rarity in 'our own country' (Eylmann 1908: 39).

Eylmann (1908) offers extensive commentary on the differences in behaviour and presentation that he observed between men and women, the former often presenting an outwardly composed and controlled mien (p. 38), the women exhibiting much less control under many circumstances. He also counters the commonplace that women are seen merely as slaves (Eylmann 1908: 51), though he does suggest there is a need for them to be urged to work by their men (p. 52) to combat their tendency, he thought, to take things easy. In a number of places, he compares what he sees as a certain limited set of mental foci on the part of women (matters to do with daily food supply, sex) with the greater breadth of men's interests, also commenting, typically, that women here resemble women at home in these ways (Eylmann 1908: 59; cf. Courto, in Eylmann 1996)!

Eylmann discusses jealousy, dislike and competitiveness, but also what he sees as admirable characteristics often encountered among Aborigines: physical courage (in which, he says, the Aborigines outstrip whites by and large) and uncomplaining behaviour even under extreme conditions of hunger, thirst and wounding. He sees men as not given to braggadocio (Eylmann 1908: 44), and their demeanour overall as generally somewhat withholding, though he does not discount the effects of white settlement on them (p. 45).

Eylmann suggests that Aborigines are not particularly given to high valuation of peaceableness for its own sake, nor do they particularly seek out fights; he credits women with being more *streitsüchtig*—readily looking for fights.

There is readiness to lie, but, he suggests, it is not so great as among ourselves (who he designates *Kulturmenschen* in this context). But he finds them to often give the answer that seems to be anticipated—what has been called elsewhere the 'pleasing answer'—noting that this presents special difficulties for the discovery of facts of matters.

Eylmann sees *Stehlsucht*, or a tendency to steal, as very limited, commenting that Aborigines in remote places he passed through, at least, regularly left things around their camps without fear of theft, and that he himself had things apparently stolen, or at least taken, from his camp only in a few limited instances.

He also writes extensively on the common attribution to Aborigines of laziness and lack of foresight or care for the future (*Sorglosigkeit, Unstetigkeit, Mangel an Voraussicht*; Eylmann 1908: 50). He has clearly closely observed the work of hunting, caring for and preparing weapons by men, and finds little justice in such attributions, especially under the environmental conditions he came to understand. While he found lack of cleanliness to be an objective fact, in terms of both lack of bodily washing and food preparation, he sharply condemned devaluation of Aborigines on account of their inattention to it, finding it consonant with often limited water supply and of no disadvantage to them.

He comes to a view on what we might translate as evaluative rationality (*Urteilsvermögen*): that whites tend to be superior in this regard, and that Aborigines find it difficult to overcome superstition (Eylmann 1908: 58) and are more suggestible. But he makes comparative comments favourable to Aborigines of his experience with respect to their ability to master foreign languages (Eylmann 1908: 58), a superlative awareness (*Wahrnehmungsvermögen*), an unmatched ability in spatial orientation (*Orientierungssinn*), memory and observational acuity (*Beobachtungsgabe*) and in no way inferiority in imagination and capacity to concentrate compared with the people of a north Hannoverian town!

And, with respect to children, after observing their performance at the mission school at Killalpaninna, for instance, he found them in every way equal to their German or English counterparts (Eylmann 1908: 60).

At the end of all these considerations, which make up the main 'mental' aspect of the chapter's attention to 'bodily and mental nature', Eylmann comes to a consideration that considerably alters his occasional use of the contrast between *Natur-* and *Kulturmenschen*, or 'uncivilised' and 'civilised', as we might best translate it. He says, in the end, that there are no thoroughgoing *Naturmenschen*, or uncivilised (French *sauvage*), peoples, but perhaps only 'half-civilised' ones (*Halbkulturvölker*). This is because all the characteristics that Aborigines display, and that he has tried to describe, come about because those people have lived for immeasurably long periods in the terms of their own societies, and have developed those characteristics that are necessary in their relations with their own kind (Eylmann 1908: 60). Thus, he reasons, there are no real *Naturmenschen*— in the primary sense of uncivilised 'children of nature'. They are children of society.

It is also worth noting that, although we may translate his *geistige Beschaffenheit* as 'mental nature', in contrast with the physical, he was interested in both, and generally considered practices and events as revelatory of character; he was not interested in romantic notions of spirit and soul. It has already become clear, I hope, that he did not posit any brute connection between physical characteristics and intellectual capacity. In general, he leans towards a view of general similarity of human capacity, which he occasionally pronounces to be slightly superior in the long run in the scheme of European human social development. He presents a view of Aborigines as highly active, capable and intelligent—with a certain caveat regarding the women, but all women, not just Aboriginal ones! Although Eylmann displays a certain elitism with regard to his German lower-class compatriots, in general terms, he inclines to a view of the largely shared nature of human capacities that are developed differently under different societal conditions.

Eylmann often adopts a comparative mode of making a point, as illustrated in several places above. His comparisons are made largely in relation to Europeans with whom he feels familiar, and generally to counter various negative commonplaces that he experienced north Australian settlers to express in relation to Aborigines. For example, he judged Aborigines as no more *arbeitsscheu* ('work shy') than Germans or other 'civilised' people— provided they may do the work they know and are not forced into 'narrow, dull spaces' for work that is unfamiliar to them and that has for them no apparent purpose (Eylmann 1908: 50). On lack of cleanliness, he compares Aborigines with the lower, and even upper, classes of north Hannover, and finds the latter to also not be assiduous about bathing (Eylmann 1908: 53).

Commenting on the fact that Aborigines often have limited English and that number systems are undeveloped in their languages, Eylmann (1908: 58) observes that Aboriginal boys and men, possessed of excellent memory and awareness, can usually tell much more quickly than white bushmen whether an animal is missing from their herd, and can describe exactly what the missing one looks like. He also attributes to them much more acute species recognition than to north German farmers, comparing them favourably in terms of imagination and concentration (Eylmann 1908: 59).

Against the constancy of such comparison, its relative scarcity in Spencer and Gillen's work is noticeable. A rare example is in *Wanderings in Wild Australia* (Spencer 1928: Vol. I, p. 200), in which Spencer, arguing that Indigenous women are not treated with excessive harshness, says: 'The life and treatment of the black lubra are far preferable to those of hundreds and thousands of women in British slums.'

To cite so many examples of comparison might make it seem that Eylmann tries too hard to prove the worth of Aborigines against opposing commonplaces. But, distributed as these examples are over the book, they do not seem strained, but rather point to his conviction that Aborigines were people who had, in general terms, no lesser capacity in many ways than his countrymen, and some of whose capacities outstripped theirs in their present condition. What is striking, however, is his insistence on the commonality of the sisterhood, both Aboriginal and European, in being strife-prone and given to pettier thinking than men.

Strategy and agency

Eylmann was very sceptical of the missionary project, and he seems to have let that be known in the various mission stations in which he spent time: Hermannsburg, Killalpaninna and the Catholic mission at Daly River.

In his view, the relations between mission and Aborigines were of an unhealthy nature. Eylmann saw that, out of their desire to gain converts, the missionaries placed too much trust in Aborigines' apparent piety, which he saw as largely situational. The converts were also not held to a work regime and were, as a result, overfed and underactive, in his view. He gives a lengthy, tongue-in-cheek account of a church service, held by Pastor Carl Strehlow in Arunta. He reports that, in his view, the sermon made little impression on its audience, except that they later recounted with great amusement the language mistakes the pastor had made.[7] Eylmann placed little stock in the sincerity of conversion of the majority of Indigenous people at Hermannsburg, understanding them to be more fully absorbed in their own social events and corroborees.

---

7   See Monteath (2013: 8) on the lack of warmth—indeed, the animosity—between Strehlow and Eylmann.

He describes 'corroborees' he saw at Hermannsburg and elsewhere, reminiscent of some of the long and detailed accounts in Spencer and Gillen of similar events. One of Eylmann's points in recounting this was how much notionally converted Aborigines continued to value sacred objects.[8] He observes that some Western Aranda and Jingili told him that these 'fetishes' were 'blackfellow money', with which one could negotiate for women, weapons and instruments. He found this equation interesting, and notes the men had independently come to making this equivalence through their exposure to work for settlers, not through any questions of his.

Though he admired and regarded key practitioners (of sorcery and healing) as adepts, keen observers and knowers of people, and as highly disciplined—even hardened—he does not idealise or in any way romanticise Indigenous ceremonial practices. Instead, in places he refers to them as *Hokuspokus* (Eylmann 1908: 225), raising the question, as he does for many Indigenes' relations to Christianity, how seriously people may take them.

Eylmann, German anthropological tradition and Spencer and Gillen

Although Spencer and Gillen, each in his own way, differentiated their formal work from their travel and personal accounts, this by no means guaranteed a greater sense of coevalness (Fabian 1983) between themselves and their subjects in the latter than in the former. I suggest that the primitivist and evolutionary prism through which they engaged their Aboriginal subjects as scientists was largely the same one through which they engaged with and wrote about them as part of their travelogues.

---

8   With some apparent compunction, Eylmann (1908: 199) admits to having removed some fetishes, learning their location from revelations of caches to him by people he calls 'boys'. (In using this word, he is apparently voicing the local English-speakers.) Of what he did, he uses the word *Entwendung*, which can only be understood as 'theft'. His phrasing suggests compunction, but the reader never learns any more about this, or what became of the material. On Eylmann's death, a significant number of artefacts he had collected went to the Übersee Museum in Bremen (Monteath 2013: 9). In addition to these appropriations, as Courto (in Eylmann 1996) notes, Eylmann reports himself going uninvited into camps and opening and examining graves, only prevented from doing so, for example, by missionaries at Killalpaninna (Eylmann 1996: 263) in the case of graves of people whose relatives were living at the mission.

Eylmann, too, made use of some of the framing organisation and discursive tropes of primitivism (specifically, engaging the originally Herderian opposition between *Natur-* and *Kulturmenschen* in some places, but sparingly). However, through personal inclusion of himself in his relations to Aboriginal people, Eylmann distinguishes himself from Spencer and Gillen. He blended 'scientific', or documentary, and personal writing in ways that make his work more fully in tune in many places with current ethnographic sensibilities and writing. In places, he tends towards comparison—between 'them' and 'us', the 'us' of his discourse often explicitly the working classes of his home region—much more than do Spencer and Gillen. While Eylmann never fully identifies himself with those working classes, his forthright inclusion of himself in many episodes, his presentation of himself in interaction with Aborigines and others, gives his portrayal of those relations a coeval quality that traditional ethnographic writing has often been accused of lacking.

Many of the kinds of things Eylmann wrote about were outside the framework of Spencer and Gillen. Their view of their research task was more fully enclosed in an evolutionary view, from which perspective they mainly saw and foretold degeneration and degradation, concerned that it would make impossible their research task as they saw it. As Spencer and Gillen say (1899: 8):

> When the remnant of the tribe is gathered into some mission station, under conditions as far removed as they can well be from their natural ones, it is too late to learn anything of the customs which once governed tribal life.

There is little flexibility, in Spencer and Gillen's view, on the part of the Aborigine, who is characterised by rigid conservatism: 'As amongst all savage tribes the Australian native is bound hand and foot by custom. What his father did before him that he must do' (Spencer and Gillen 1899: 11, 13–14, 510–11).

While it was certainly true that knowledgeable old men were disappearing and young men's interests were turning to other things, the statement has a characteristic death-knell quality. These attitudes did not, of course, diminish but rather fuelled Spencer and Gillen's zeal to conduct fieldwork of a particular kind, and they came up with valuable detailed descriptions of ceremonies, for example, that can never be reproduced in the same way.

Although Eylmann certainly thought that Aborigines were being radically and negatively affected by European settlement, he did not take the view that they were characterised by rigid conservatism. His narrative, event-based and subjective approach to his writing meant that he was constantly revealing unexpected and particular responses to situations that were incompatible with a view of them as rigidly conservative. His emphasis is, rather, more often on Indigenous accommodation or even—as in the case of Hermannsburg—on what he thought was Aborigines being able to adapt to and make use of the kinds of positions and flexibilities that a particular European settlement regime offered. Rather than being exclusively focused on tradition and custom, Eylmann saw Aborigines' relations with Europeans and Asians as worthy of being included in the main body of his work, even if at the margins to some extent, but also interspersed throughout the body of his narrative.[9]

In his view of the native as 'mentally' merely a child, who acts, as a general rule, on the spur of the moment (Spencer 1928: Vol. I, p. 204), without the 'slightest thought of, or care for, what the morrow may bring forth' and living 'entirely in the present' (p. 203), Spencer does not come close to thinking of Aboriginal 'character' in the more diverse terms that Eylmann set out. And it is no part of Spencer and Gillen's discussion to set out so many ways in which they found Aborigines to be particularly gifted or to be endowed with specially developed capacities, and to compare them favourably with other peoples.

Was Eylmann's style, or aspects of it, born of German training and thinking? Certainly, not being captivated by an evolutionist view was possible for a German trained in the natural sciences, with a strong empirical bent and a determination to do fieldwork, and only a studious rather than committed relationship to the evolutionist bent of many of the arguments coming out of emergent British anthropology and the study of comparative institutions. His concern with recording language is also typical of German interests in folklore, philology and linguistics.

Gingrich (2005: 86) has commented on some principal tendencies of the first period of academic anthropology in imperial Germany, and of the two central actors at the time, Bastian for *Völkerkunde* and physical anthropologist Virchow:

---

9   He also wrote a shorter work on European Australian travelling bushmen whom he encountered, and their indigence (Eylmann 1922).

Both were political liberals, both had received their first academic training in medicine and the natural sciences, and both were committed to an empiricist positivism of a nonevolutionary kind that followed the model of the natural sciences. (see also Berghahn 1994: 170–85)

Gingrich (2005: 89) also describes *Völkerkunde*—the comparative study of (non-European or other) peoples—as classifying and generalising the results of a strictly descriptive ethnography. While his work certainly fell within some of these terms, and he pursued *Anthropologie* in Virchow's sense of it as physical anthropology, Eylmann also had a sensibility for social relations that went well beyond the limits of contemporary conventions of natural science inquiry. Certainly, his inclusion of Aborigines, Europeans and Asians within his frame of interest opened on to a field of interrelationships that others did not consider worthwhile at this time in Australia or central to their ethnographic observations. While Eylmann documented these relations with interest, his interpretations of them were not as developed or rich as his observations.

Eylmann had a strong desire to accomplish documentary work of a lasting kind, and to that end assiduously studied the physical and material aspects of Indigenous life, coming up with what would count as objective representations of many phenomena. But he also remained committed, without ever saying so in so many words, to representing the subjective nature of his field research, giving the particulars of people and events as part of his efforts to provide a sense, and interpretation and analysis, of Indigenous life at the time.

Of course, many writers in the early period of anthropology were concerned to differentiate their work from travel writing and other similar genres, and to establish themselves as authoritative and scientific. Spencer was very consciously part of a natural science tradition, and this bounded his imagination concerning possible ways of understanding the situation of Aborigines in the Northern Territory. In reading both his and Gillen's main volumes, one feels that there is a large amount of description of ritual, but little interpretation or linking of that material to any discussion of Indigenous lives, social relations and colonial impacts. Because Eylmann was outside these debates—he was also a relative outsider to academic debate in Germany—he had no hesitation in presenting both documentation and subjective experience as part of his overall work. What Mary Louise Pratt (1986), for example, describes as a hegemonic divide in anthropology, a contradiction between objective and subjective representations, was preceded by some diversity in which practitioners such as Eylmann could present and interweave these two aspects of field experience in their writing. He did so without any metacommentary, of course, oblivious of explicit debate that was to emerge in anthropology only 50 years later.

It seems of likely relevance that Eylmann had been a medical practitioner and was presumably experienced at listening to and working closely with his patients. One might note that Spencer was a different sort of biologist, an academic one, who may not have been called on to develop that degree of immediacy of attention and empathy.

Despite what I have called a certain elitism in his attitudes towards his fellow Hannoverians, Eylmann spent a great deal of time with Aboriginal people, interacting with and accessible to them, and encountering them on a certain common ground, compared with the thinking and related field practices of Spencer and Gillen. In his field research, he located himself with Aboriginal others in the same time and space. His writing attempts a blend between ethnographic representation and the subjective experience of fieldwork without loss of acuity and with a strong component of interpretative and comparative comment, together with a certain amount of fairly ungrounded speculation common to the period. Spencer, on the other hand, remains fundamentally an evolutionist even in his personal, 'informal' writing. His personal narrative does not treat the Aboriginal other as coeval with him; rather the other, in his view, remains ruled by custom, childlike temperamentally, on the way out and of little interest to the extent that he has changed. Indigenous people as willing and forced to accommodate, living in unequal entanglements with variably well and ill-disposed outsiders were some of the things that Eylmann was able to describe, while Spencer and Gillen ruled them out.

References

Berghahn, V. R. 1994. *Imperial Germany 1871–1914: Economy, society, culture, and politics*. Providence, RI: Berghahn Books.

Clifford, J. 1983. On ethnographic authority. *Representations* 1(2): 118–46. doi.org/10.2307/2928386.

Courto, V. 1990. The tragical history of Doctor Eylmann: The ethnographer Erhard Eylmann and an assessment of his work. Unpublished BA thesis. Department of Prehistory and Anthropology, The Australian National University, Canberra.

Eylmann, E. 1908. *Die Eingeborenen der Kolonie Südaustralien*. Berlin: Reimer.

Eylmann, E. 1922. Das Bettelwesen in dem Staate Südaustralien und dem Nordterritorium vor dem Weltkriege [Begging in the state of South Australia and in the Northern Territory before the world war]. *Mitteilungen der Geographischen Gesellschaft in Hamburg* 34: 57–98.

Eylmann, E. 1996. *The Australian journals of Erhard Eylmann 1896–1912*. Introduced and translated by V. Courto. Research report. Canberra: Institute of Aboriginal and Torres Strait Islander Studies.

Fabian, J. 1983. *Time and the Other: How anthropology makes its object*. New York: Columbia University Press.

Fischer, E. 1913. *Die Rehobother Bastards und das Bastardierungsproblem beim Menschen: Anthropologische und Studien am Rehobother Bastardvolk in Deutsch-Südwest-Afrika, ausgeführt mit Unterstützung der Kgl. Preuss. Akademie der Wissenschaften*. Jena, Germany: G. Fischer.

Fison, L. and Howitt, A. W. 1880. *Kamilaroi and Kurnai: Group-marriage and relationship, and marriage by elopement*. Melbourne: George Robertson.

Gillen, F. J. 1968. *Gillen's Diary: The camp jottings of F. J. Gillen on the Spencer and Gillen expedition across Australia 1901–1902*. Adelaide: Libraries Board of South Australia.

Gingrich, A. 2005. *One Discipline, Four Ways: British, German, French and American anthropology*. Chicago: University of Chicago Press.

Merlan, F. 2004. Ich reiste wie ein Buschmann. [Review.] *Australian Aboriginal Studies* 1: 115–19.

Monteath, P. 2013. Globalising German anthropology: Erhard Eylmann in Australia. *Itinerario* 37(1): 1–12. doi.org/10.1017/S0165115313000247.

Peterson, N. 1993. Demand sharing: Reciprocity and the pressure for generosity among foragers. *American Anthropologist* 95(4): 860–74. doi.org/10.1525/aa.1993.95.4.02a00050.

Pratt, M. L. 1986. Fieldwork in common places. In *Writing Culture: The poetics and politics of ethnography*, (eds) J. Clifford and G. E. Marcus, pp. 27–50. Berkeley: University of California Press.

Schröder, W. 2002. *Ich reiste wie ein Buschmann: Zum Leben und Wirken des Australienforschers Erhard Eylmann*. Bremen: Science Edition.

Spencer, B. 1928. *Wanderings in Wild Australia*. 2 vols. London: Macmillan & Co.

Spencer, B. and Gillen, F. J. 1899. *The Native Tribes of Central Australia*. London: Macmillan & Co.

Spencer, B. and Gillen, F. J. 1904. *The Northern Tribes of Central Australia*. London: Macmillan & Co.

von Neumayer, G. B. 1875. *Anleitung zu wissenschaftlichen Beobachtungen auf Reisen, mit besonderer Rücksicht auf die Bedürfnisse der kaiserlichen Marine [Guide to Scientific Observations on Travels, with Special Attention to the Needs of the Imperial Navy]*. Hanover: Dr Max Jänecke doi.org/10.5962/bhl.title.59330.

12

Herbert Basedow (1881–1933): Surgeon, geologist, naturalist and anthropologist[1]

David Kaus

Herbert Basedow, born in Adelaide to German parents, was to become one of Australia's leading scientists of the first three decades of the twentieth century. He had broad-ranging interests in geology, zoology and botany, but, arguably, is now best remembered for his contributions to Australian anthropology. In his native South Australia, in particular, Basedow was a significant public figure and, by the time of his death in 1933, he was well known as a commentator on a broad range of issues, as an explorer and as a Member of Parliament (MP).

Early life[2]

Basedow's parents independently emigrated to Australia in 1848. They married in 1868, the second marriage for each (both of their previous spouses had died). Martin Peter Friedrich Basedow was the first Basedow to arrive in Australia, as an 18-year-old, on 31 March 1848. He was destined to become a prominent figure in South Australia, as a teacher,

---

1   The second part of this title was derived from Stanner (1976: 131).
2   This section is largely derived from Basedow (1990), except where noted.

journalist, newspaper owner, editor and MP. Anna Clara Helena came from another important German-Australian family in South Australia, the Mueckes. Herbert was born on 27 October 1881, the last of 13 children.

Plate 12.1 Herbert Basedow, about 1925.
Source: Copy of a portrait held by the National Museum of Australia, Canberra.

The Basedow family lived at Kent Town, within walking distance of Adelaide's city centre. In fact, Herbert lived there most of his life, later buying and living in the house next door to the family home. He attended Prince Alfred College, proving himself as both a scholar and a sportsman, playing Australian football for the college's First XVIII. Later, he rowed for the University of Adelaide, including in an intervarsity competition in Sydney in 1900.

Herbert's Australian primary schooling was put in abeyance in 1890 when his parents took him and seven siblings to live in Germany. His father's obituary in South Australia's *Australische Zeitung* (*Australian Newspaper*) stated:

> In 1890 Mr. Basedow after an absence of 43 years travelled with his wife and 8 children to his fatherland for a period of 3 years' residence. Taking a flat in Hannover, he spent a large part of the three years travelling. He journeyed over most of Germany and visited respectively France, England, Denmark, Sweden, Austria-Hungary, Switzerland and Italy. (Translation, Basedow 1993: 9)

If Herbert accompanied his father on these travels this may have given him his appetite for travelling for, as we shall see, his work would take him to widely varied places, many of which would be seen by only a handful of non-Indigenous people of his generation.

Herbert completed his schooling at Prince Alfred College in 1897, the year he won the Cotton Medal for academic achievement in agricultural chemistry. The following year, he commenced a science degree at the University of Adelaide, graduating in 1902. As well as science and mathematics, he also took subjects such as surveying and mechanical drawing, which would hold him in good stead when he later published his maps of little explored areas such as western Central Australia, which he travelled through in 1903 and 1926, and the north, in 1905, 1916 and 1928 (Basedow 1915, 1916, 1918, 1929b; Mackay 1929).

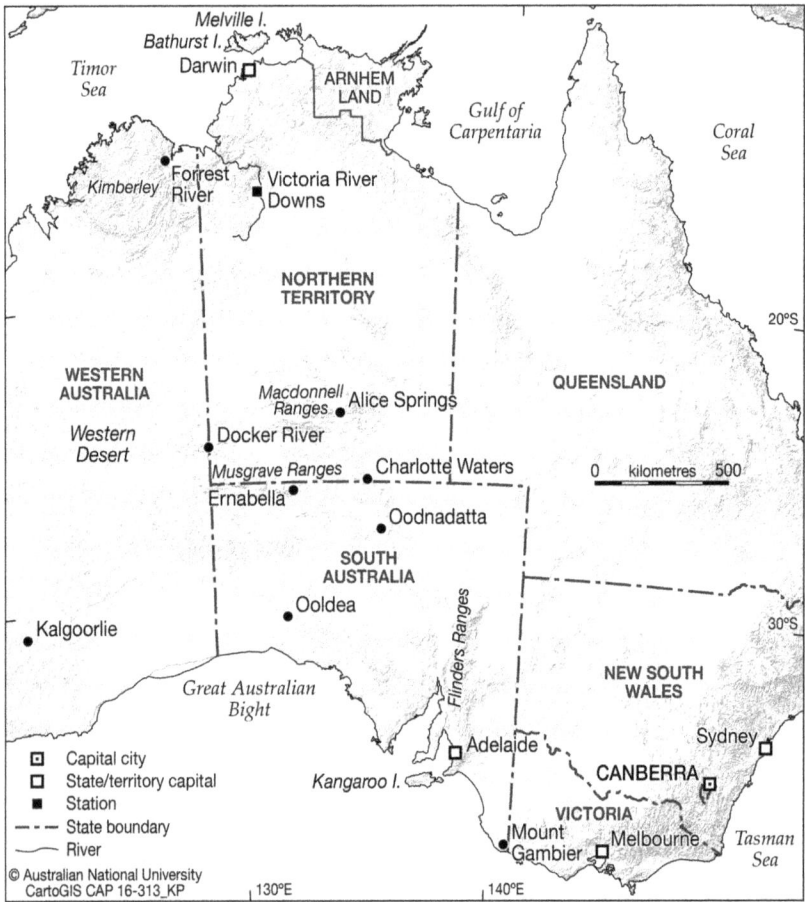

Map 12.1 Locations mentioned in the text.
Source: CartoGIS, The Australian National University.

Postgraduate study[3]

Basedow returned to Germany in 1907 to undertake postgraduate study in science and medicine. His first stint was at Breslau University, where he studied geology, physical geography, zoology and philosophy under the renowned scientist Hermann Klaatsch. Basedow and Klaatsch presumably

---

3   The first part of this section relies heavily on Zogbaum (2010: Ch. 3). She has looked at Basedow's German education more closely than anyone else. Furthermore, as a German speaker, Zogbaum was able to read Basedow's theses.

met in Adelaide in 1907 when the latter delivered a paper on Aborigines at the Science Congress. In his paper, Klaatsch singled out Basedow for high praise:

> Close association was secured with the Kunandja tribe, or Kunandra tribe,[4] as recorded by that gifted young scientist, Mr. Herbert Basedow, whose profound investigations had lightened his own task in that part of Australia.[5]

Klaatsch (1907: 584) made a similar comment in his published paper. He obviously recognised Basedow's potential, as had South Australia's government geologist H. Y. L. Brown earlier (see below), and no doubt encouraged him to go to Germany to study. At Breslau, the geologist professor Fritz Frech supervised Basedow's doctorate in geology and, after three semesters, Basedow obtained his degree. His thesis, a '43-page summary of his own observations and investigations', was on the geology of Australia (Zogbaum 2010: 29). The published version (Basedow 1909), though, has a wider coverage, as demonstrated through maps including localities not visited by Basedow.

In 1908, Basedow commenced medical studies. In preparation, he worked in anatomy establishments with Klaatsch and in Berlin, followed by three months' practice in Switzerland. Following this, he spent one semester at Heidelberg, before switching to the University of Gottingen later the following year. Here he was awarded another PhD, this time in medicine. His thesis was an analysis of craniometric measurements of 172 crania (36 of them Tasmanian), examined at the Hunterian Institute during his vacation in the middle of 1909. As Zogbaum (2010: 30) pointed out, the 36 Tasmanian crania did not suffice for a 'credible statistical average on which he could place weighty conclusions'; however, this was the sample that was available to him. Remarkably, Basedow was awarded two doctorates in a very short time, assisted, no doubt, through credit for work undertaken in Australia.

One idea in Basedow's second thesis, which he would continue to reiterate, was his promulgation of the outdated 'black Caucasian theory', which posited that Aboriginal people and Europeans shared a common

---

4   Klaatsch is talking about his visit to the Darwin–Daly River area, where Basedow undertook geological work as part of a government expedition in 1905. He later published his anthropological observations and, in his discussion of the 'tribes' of the area, does not mention a group whose name approaches Kunandja or Kunandra (Basedow 1907: 1–3).
5   *The Advertiser*, [Adelaide], 11 January 1907: 7–8.

ancestry. Klaatsch was an early proponent of this theory and Basedow was one of the next generation of scientists who continued with it. According to Zogbaum (2010: 1), Basedow 'was the first to supply scientific foundations' for this theory, in the form of 'detailed cranial measurements' presented in his doctorate. One of the unfortunate aspects of this theory as presented by Basedow was that it demonstrated that the intermixing of Aborigines and Europeans eventually 'breeds out the colour', without throwback or atavism, resulting in a complete loss of Aboriginal physical features because of their shared ancestry. Klaatsch had speculated that skin pigmentation was confined to the epidermis and, following death, the skin becomes lighter in colour. This theory was to provide a scientific basis for later government policy to solve the 'half-caste problem', with the removal of children from their families its most evil consequence. Basedow could not have foreseen this, but it would mean the complete extinction of the 'Aboriginal race', for those of unmixed descent were also disappearing, as a result of coming into contact with a 'superior race', as far as Basedow was concerned. This was a constant theme with Basedow—something that will be briefly considered below.

Apparently, the change in skin colour could work in reverse, if a newspaper report of one of Basedow's lectures is to be believed:

> When something unexpected happens some day to hurry along the development of Northern Australia, blondes need not apply. Those who are so unfortunate as to 'favour' their Nordic ancestors must be content to dwell in the South. Tropical Australia is safe only for people with dark complexions, dark eyes, and black hair. They may go in and possess the land, but, dreadful consequence, must pay for it in terms of skin pigment. In an 'age or two,' they will be black. Dr. Basedow is too merciful to say so directly. He adopts a euphemistic negative. Their whiteness, he says, will disappear. Anthropologically, they are more or less identical with the aborigine already; and the black-fellow who does not regard them as 'radically different from himself,' will have all the less reason to do so, one must suppose, when the difference becomes indistinguishable.[6]

In 1911, Basedow's medical qualifications were called into question during the so-called Glacial Controversy, originally a dispute between Basedow's geology professor, Ralph Tate, who died in 1901, and another geologist, Walter Howchin. Briefly, Howchin had discovered a site that he determined to be a Cambrian glacial site, while Tate—and, after his death,

6   *Register*, [Adelaide], 11 December 1926: 8.

Basedow—put forward an alternative theory for its creation. In a brief look at Howchin's career, Selby (1991: 569) noted that his theory was eventually 'completely vindicated'.

A large part of the Glacial Controversy was played out in the media and in this Howchin was joined by geologist Fritz Noetling. In 1911, Noetling inspected the location of the disputed site and, while Basedow was living for a brief stint in Darwin, said he was going to deliver a paper at one of the next meetings of the Royal Society of South Australia. While Noetling did not want to 'anticipate the contents of [his] paper', he was quite happy to professionally denigrate Basedow, saying his paper would 'show how futile and superficial Dr. Basedow's observations, and his theory based thereon, were'.[7] Basedow had published his theory in his German paper on Australian geology (Basedow 1909). Basedow returned to Adelaide soon after and was interviewed by the *Register* on 18 September. The last comment in the interview, published the following day, referred to his appointment as chief medical officer in Darwin. In a subsequent letter, Noetling finished by questioning Basedow about his medical qualification.[8] There is nothing to indicate why he asked this or what it had to do with the Glacial Controversy. Noetling even wrote to the University of Breslau to seek clarification on the nature of Basedow's medical degree. As far as he was concerned, he obtained evidence that Basedow had not obtained the correct qualifications that would entitle him to practice medicine in Germany and outlined the case in another letter to the *Register*.[9] Basedow received his share of support, with three South Australian medicos writing letters to the *Register* in support of him: Dr Alex Henry,[10] Dr F. Angas Johnson[11] and Dr J. R. Kelman.[12] It was not until the following January that Basedow himself responded, after also seeking written advice from the University of Breslau.[13] It would seem Basedow did not have a case to answer and the South Australian Government, having registered him as a medical practitioner, on 8 September 1910,[14] obviously accepted his credentials.

---

7 ibid., 4 September 1911: 9.
8 ibid., 2 October 1911: 10.
9 ibid., 27 October 1911: 5.
10 ibid., 28 October 1911: 5.
11 ibid., 30 October 1911: 9.
12 ibid., 11 November 1911: 15.
13 ibid., 18 January 1912: 5.
14 *South Australian Government Gazette*, 1 December 1910. Basedow's Christian name was given as Hubert; this was corrected in the following *Gazette*.

Noetling was not the only one who regarded Basedow in a bad light. As Mulvaney and Calaby (1985: 276) pointed out:

> [Baldwin] Spencer regarded Basedow's qualifications and self-promotion with contempt. So did F. Wood Jones, the South Australian anatomist, who described his credentials as an 'impudent parade of degrees, real or assumed; and knowledge, borrowed, stolen or feigned'.

As Mulvaney and Calaby (1985) suggested, perhaps it is time for a reassessment of Basedow. Even though he had his detractors, there is little doubt he achieved a lot over his career.

Basedow's career

By the time Basedow graduated from the University of Adelaide in 1902, he had delivered at least three papers, all on geological subjects, to the Royal Society of South Australia, two of which were later published, along with a summary of the third (Basedow 1901, 1902a, 1902b). The following year, he participated in the first of many major expeditions; between 1903 and 1928, he was to be involved in more than 15 expeditions in Central and northern Australia.[15] He also made shorter trips, mostly in South Australia, but also to other states. These included places such as Mount Gambier, Kangaroo Island, Kalgoorlie and north Queensland. None of these trips was for anthropological purposes, but all were opportunities to undertake anthropology.

The six-month-long 1903 expedition searched for mineral deposits in the far north-west of South Australia and adjoining country in south-western Northern Territory, then under South Australian control. Basedow's role was as prospector, engaged 'through the courtesy of the late Government Geologist (Mr. H. Y. L. Brown, F. G. S.)' (Basedow 1915: 60). According to one newspaper report,[16] Brown selected the expedition's four prospectors and originally Basedow's name was not among them. It was not until Arthur Warman pulled out that Basedow was added, as indicated by other newspaper reports. It would seem Brown, like Klaatsch later, recognised Basedow's abilities and, although he may not have been a first choice

---

15 See Kaus (2008) and the National Museum of Australia's website (www.nma.gov.au/exhibitions/expedition_photographs_h_basedow_1903_1928/central_australia) for overviews of Basedow's major expeditions apart from the vice-regal expedition of 1924. At the time the exhibition and accompanying book were being produced, insufficient detail was known about this expedition for it to be included.
16 *Register*, [Adelaide], 24 February 1903: 3.

for the 1903 expedition, evidently Basedow proved himself worthy of Brown's faith for he was to join him, along with Lionel Gee, on an even longer official geological exploration trip in the north of the Northern Territory two years later (see Brown et al. 1906). From 1906, Basedow began his association with the Flinders Ranges, returning periodically for geological purposes until around 1913. Two papers resulted, one on burials (Basedow 1913a) and a much longer one on rock engravings (Basedow 1914). While he probably did not discuss the former with local Aboriginal people, he may have tried to elicit information about the engravings:

> The living generation of blacks in the Flinders Ranges know nothing about the carved productions of art here discussed. They barely recognise in them the handicraft of a people who, in all probability, were their direct ancestors. (Basedow 1914: 198)

At least some of his visits to the Flinders Ranges were undertaken on behalf of the South Australian Government, and his 1910 trip may have been while he held the position of assistant government geologist. He had been appointed on 10 August that year,[17] at 'the expressed request of Mr. Brown'.[18]

The following year, Basedow left to take up a Commonwealth appointment in Darwin, advertised as Chief Protector of Aborigines.[19] He was to remain in the position for only six weeks, dissatisfied with his working conditions and unable to get on with the administrator. Basedow had had his title changed to Chief Medical Inspector and Chief Protector of Aborigines in the Northern Territory and, despite holding the position for just a short period, he would continue to refer to it as one of his credentials for many years to come. Before he left Darwin, Basedow made a trip to Melville and Bathurst islands, observing cultural practices and making a collection of artefacts. This also resulted in a published paper (Basedow 1913b).

Around the time of his return south, the positions of chief government geologist and assistant government geologist were advertised. Apparently, it was suggested to Basedow that he not apply, to save him the embarrassment of not being appointed. It seems Adelaide did not want a repeat of recent events in Darwin. Instead, Basedow served locum tenens with a medical practice in 1912, and, in 1913, went into private

---

17 *South Australian Government Gazette*, No. 38, 11 August 1910: 290.
18 *Public Service Review*, November 1910: 301.
19 *Commonwealth Gazette*, 1911: 774.

practice as a general practitioner and consulting geologist. His business card for the latter reads: 'Geological, Mining, and Petroleum Reports. Examinations undertaken in any part of Australia.'[20] After a time, Basedow again became acceptable to both the South Australian and the federal governments, for, in 1919–20, he was to undertake medical inspections of Aborigines at their behest. These expeditions, jointly funded with a number of wealthy pastoralists, medically inspected Aboriginal people in the settled districts in South Australia and the southern part of the Northern Territory. Basedow produced four substantial reports that gave accounts of the expeditions, notes on the Aboriginal groups encountered and information regarding their health (Basedow 1920, 1921a, 1921b, 1921c). These reports remain unpublished and it would not be until 1932 that he published his six-part paper on the health of Aboriginal people. Perhaps surprisingly, given his medical background, this would be his only publication on the subject.

In the interim, in 1916, on behalf of a syndicate of prominent Adelaide citizens, Basedow investigated a reported deposit of 'certain tungstate ores' in the western Kimberley. Again, he planned to undertake scientific investigations:

> Realising the rare opportunity for conducting scientific research in a tract of practically unknown country, I resolved that, after the work entrusted me by the Syndicate had been completed, I would on my own account continue the explorations farther afield. (Basedow 1918: 106)

Again, his 'scientific research' included anthropological work and he acknowledged a number of missionaries for 'facilitating [his] ethnological investigations among the local tribes' (Basedow 1918: 106–7).

Basedow was involved in several expeditions in the 1920s. The first was in 1922, a search for oil in the Victoria River area in the Northern Territory, and, in 1923 and 1924, he was a member of two vice-regal trips that travelled to Central Australia by car. There were no anthropological papers published after these trips and his anthropological observations made during these expeditions were incorporated into *The Australian Aboriginal* (1929a), his first book (see below). Finally, in 1926 and 1928, wealthy New South Wales grazier Donald Mackay engaged him and they explored the Western Desert area and Arnhem Land, respectively.

---

20   Card in State Library of South Australia, Adelaide, PRG 324, Item 3, p. 62 (between items dated 1922 and 1923).

This time, short papers followed, usually just a page or two, sometimes in newspapers, in anticipation of more extensive publications. A brief paper on the 1926 expedition concludes with a note that '[f]ull reports on the scientific results of the Expedition will be published in due course' (Basedow 1929b: 176). It would seem the same was true of the 1928 expedition if the statement saying the 'extensive' collections made would be 'submitted to specialists in due course for identification and description' is any indication (Basedow 1928). These did not eventuate, but there is a suggestion that when Basedow went to London at the end of 1931, he took with him the manuscript for a book to be published there. If this is true, it must be languishing in a publisher's basement or in an archive somewhere or is lost.

Basedow was never to hold a position in anthropology. The first chair of anthropology was created in Australia at the University of Sydney, and the appointment of A. R. Radcliffe-Brown led *The Bulletin*[21] to question filling professorships from overseas. *The Bulletin* continued: 'But neither case is quite so dreadful as the appointment of a young gentleman in S' Africa to the chair of Anthropology while the Australian Dr. Basedow was available.'

Soon after, Basedow turned to politics. He had first stood as a Liberal Party candidate in 1924, but was not elected. He stood again in 1927 and this time was successful. He missed out at the 1930 election, but was successful at the following election, in 1933. However, Basedow was not to serve his constituency for long, for he died later that year, on 4 June.

By this time, Basedow was a prominent citizen, was regarded as a more than capable scientist and explorer and was recognised at many levels. He was also adept at self-promotion, and newspapers, not just in South Australia, are full of stories about him, contributing to this widespread recognition. By 1920, they often sought him out for comment.

Basedow and Aboriginal people

Basedow engaged with Aboriginal people at a personal level, which is indicated by such things as his frequent recording of people's names when he photographed them and the fact that he gained access to secret

---

21   *The Bulletin*, 23 December 1926.

men's ceremonies when he did not have long-term relationships with people. He explained his approach, a little fancifully, as an anthropologist in *Knights of the Boomerang*:

> My work kept me constantly among the natives, who learned to regard me as one of themselves. I used to camp among them and accompany them on their hunting-excursions. An accurate shot from my rifle or occasional minor surgical feat helped to win me their confidence; and so I was able to study them intimately, without allowing my presence to disturb them in the slightest degree. (Basedow 1935: 16)

There are instances where observers have claimed that his interactions in the field could be abrupt and impersonal. Daisy Bates was one of these critics, and, after Basedow's expedition across the Nullarbor in 1920, she wrote to a newspaper implying that all Basedow did at Ooldea was to get Aboriginal people to 'strip and be photographed'.[22] Bates had an axe to grind, as she saw Basedow's success in securing the medical relief expeditions as preventing her from securing her desired position as protector of Aborigines (Salter 1972: 180).

Basedow also hosted Aboriginal people at his Adelaide home. One such visitor was Erlikilyika, or Jim Kite, known for his work with Spencer and Gillen and his art (Mulvaney 2001). While little is known about these casual visits, the presence of two young Aboriginal women in the Basedow household from 1920 presents a rather incongruous picture. Unndela, daughter of Charlie Apma, one of Basedow's Arrernte informants, and Tjikana (Aluridja)[23] were taken by Basedow and his wife, Nell, when they were in Central Australia to their home to work as servants.[24] Basedow claimed that he had the approval of the 'elders' to take the girls:

> When in the MacDonnell Ranges I was desirous of taking two aboriginal children away with me. The circumstance was mentioned to one of the influential old men, who thereupon called together the elders of the tribe; and my request was considered in all its aspects. After a lengthy meeting, during which it was apparent there were two or three dissentient voices, I was finally informed that the children could accompany me under certain conditions which I had to take upon myself to guarantee. This

---

22   *The Advertiser*, [Adelaide], 28 June 1920: 9.
23   This is not the place to consider the validity of this name. It was the term Basedow used for some Western Desert peoples with whom he was involved and was probably first encountered by him on the 1903 expedition, where he recorded the two female Aboriginal assistants as Aluridja speakers (Basedow 1915: 59). Five years later, he published an Arrernte and Aluridja vocabulary (Basedow 1908).
24   See, for example, *Register News–Pictorial*, [Adelaide], 8 January 1929: 10.

agreement arrived at, the children were given to understand that they were going by the direction of the old men, and I officially received the spokesman's word of honour that, firstly, the children would never desert us *en route,* and, secondly, no attempt would be made on the part of the tribe to interfere with us, or steal the children from the camp at night. Had one attempted this under any other conditions and against the will of the tribe, there would have been serious trouble. (Basedow 1929a: 226–7)

There is evidence that shows this 'transaction' was not as amicable as Basedow would have us believe.[25] There is also a certain irony here. Apparently, Basedow did not see any conflict in having Aboriginal servants while at the same time pushing for better treatment of Aboriginal people as a whole. He was outspoken on issues such as brutal treatment in the outback, supported relief efforts and was heavily engaged with organised groups such as the Aborigines' Protection League of South Australia; he was its foundation president in 1925. His efforts to obtain better conditions for Aborigines were widely reported in the press and attracted praise in letters to newspapers from time to time. For example, 'Eroosnal' wrote: 'All honour to Dr. Basedow and all other true Christians who are trying to get justice for the black men.'[26]

A disturbing aspect of Unndela and Tjikana's time in the Basedow household is revealed through Basedow's photographs. Twenty-six photographs of them in Adelaide are known and, of these, six show them topless. While this is revealing about the power relationship between 'employer' and 'staff', it possibly has more to do with Basedow's interest in physical anthropology than anything. It was by no means the only occasion he photographed people in this fashion. There are a few more obvious examples among his photographs where there are front and side views of the same people, either naked or where they have some of their clothing removed. Also see Plate 2 of *The Australian Aboriginal* (Basedow 1929a), which has side views of a white woman and an Aboriginal woman, both naked, presented for comparative purposes. The Aboriginal woman is not Unndela or Tjikana.

---

25 The author has been shown documentary evidence that Unndela and Tjikana did not want to leave the territory, that efforts were made by Charlie Apma to have Unndela returned to him and his wife, Yoolda, on at least three occasions and that the South Australian authorities were at first unaware of Basedow's 'arrangement', even though it had been made through the office of the Chief Protector of Aboriginals. This is a complex story and worthy of telling in full.
26 *Register,* [Adelaide], 13 November 1928: 8.

L. C. E. GEE. H. Y. L. BROWN. H. BASEDOW.

PEDRO. F. J. WILLIAMSON. PETER.
TOBATCHIE. BUBS. LOMAN.

Plate 12.2 Aboriginal people were often engaged to assist on expeditions. This photograph shows members of the 1905 expedition to the north-west of the Northern Territory.

Source: Brown et al. (1906: facing p. 45).

Basedow's anthropology

Basedow was one of those highly educated individuals who undertook anthropological work secondary to their main line of work. His anthropological activities included all those things modern anthropologists do. He observed and documented Aboriginal people and their activities and he lectured and published on the topic. He also held a relevant postgraduate qualification. The major difference was that Basedow did not have a paid position in the field. In the first decades of the twentieth century, jobs for anthropologists were rare, so this is not surprising. We have already considered his qualifications and some aspects of his work, so let us now look at how he undertook his anthropology.

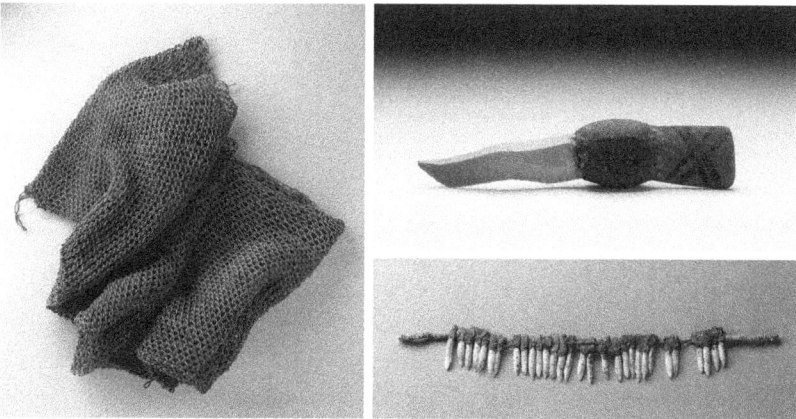

Plates 12.3a–c Aboriginal artefacts collected by Herbert Basedow.
Knife, northern Central Australia, probably collected 1920–24; fishing net from Arnhem Land, probably collected 1928; headband from the Northern Territory, possibly collected 1905.
Source: Photographs by Lannon Harley. National Museum of Australia, Canberra, nma. img-ci20082084-012-wm-vs1 and nma.img-ci20082084-029-wm-vs1.

Most of Basedow's fieldwork was a secondary activity of his many expeditions and shorter trips—that is, his anthropology was done on top of the duties, mainly to do with geology, he was expected to undertake. As he was continually on the move, it was unusual for him to spend more than one or two nights in any one place. This in large part accounts for the often superficial nature of his records. He could not observe extended activities, such as complete ceremonial activities, and much of his observation was serendipitous—that is, he was only able to witness what was happening at the time of his visits.

Basedow's first known venture into anthropology occurred on the 1903 expedition. Expedition leader, Larry Wells, 'kindly permitted [him] to make use of [his] spare time by studying the natural history of the region and collecting what specimens opportunity afforded' (Basedow 1915: 60).

Presumably, anthropology came under the heading 'natural history' and Basedow made extensive records about Aboriginal people. After his return to Adelaide, he presented papers based on his anthropological and geological observations to meetings of the Royal Society of South Australia and the University of Adelaide Scientific Society. He published these and one other article in the following five years and the illustrated ones used his photographs and drawings (Basedow 1904, 1905, 1906, 1908). The first of these was his 'Anthropological notes' and the last was a vocabulary of Aluridja and Arrernte, published in Germany while he was studying there. The other two papers were geological in nature and for one he was awarded the University of Adelaide's Tate Memorial Medal,[27] presented for original work in geology. There were only two candidates and Sir Edgeworth David, the examiner, recommended the medal go to Basedow for his 'Geological report on the country traversed by the South Australian Government north-west prospecting expedition, 1903' (Basedow 1905; see Kaus 2008: 19). On this expedition, Basedow made geological, zoological and botanical collections, and he probably collected Aboriginal artefacts as well. As yet, none of the many Central Australian artefacts in his collections can be associated with this expedition. The drawings of 10 artefacts illustrating his 'Anthropological notes' are of such detail that suggest they were drawn from 'life' after he returned to Adelaide (Basedow 1904: Plates III, IV).

Broadly speaking, this was a pattern that he was to follow on the several subsequent expeditions with which he was involved, until a trip to Arnhem Land in 1928. That is, on these trips he would make observations of Aboriginal people and natural history and collect artefacts and specimens as an aside to the chief purpose or purposes of the expedition. After returning home, he would publish on his findings (see below regarding the 1926 and 1928 expeditions) and he would give lectures to learned societies. Eventually, he would also give public lectures; these were well attended and it was not uncommon for prominent people such as the state governor to chair them.

27　See Basedow (1990: 108) for photographs of this medal.

Like many others, Basedow used photography as part of his record-making, and it was usual for him to use more than one camera. On the 1903 expedition, for example, he used two Kodak cameras, a No. 2 pocket folding and a No. 1 panorama (Basedow 1915: 240). Many of his published works include photographs and it was his preference to use his own images. While some publications include a handful of photographs by others, his 1907 'Anthropological notes' is an exception in that all of its 17 photographs were taken by others: Paul Foelsche, N. Holtze and W. Holtze (Basedow 1907: 59)—Nicholas and, presumably, Wladimir Holtze). The numerous drawings, however, are his. Basedow was a capable artist and, again, he provided the drawings reproduced in his publications.

By 1919, Basedow started using additional forms of recording equipment. The 1919 expedition is his first known use of a cinematograph, to take moving pictures. Shortly after, possibly in 1920 in the Alice Springs area, he began to record ritual songs using a wax cylinder recorder. Only a little is known about either. None of his moving footage has apparently survived and, for the cylinders, little beyond the 'tribe' (mostly Arrernte and Kaytetye) of the singers and the subject of the songs is known. Several of the songs are 'inside' or secret, and, until they have been played to the appropriate Traditional Owners, it will not be known if they are all restricted.

There is one other aspect to Basedow's work: the promotion of his work, and himself, through newspapers. This took different forms and seems to have begun by providing expedition photographs for reproduction, starting with the 1903 expedition and continuing until his 1928 Arnhem Land expedition. By the time of the 1905 expedition, Basedow was being interviewed both before and after expeditions. His appearance in the media was not restricted to expedition-related matters; there was also extensive coverage of other aspects of his life, including his education in Germany and his later political activity.

Today, material collected by Basedow is to be found in repositories mainly in Australia, but also in several overseas collections. The Australian collections comprise 1,300 Aboriginal artefacts as well as unknown numbers of geological, zoological and botanical specimens. The National Museum of Australia in Canberra houses the bulk of his anthropological material, almost 80 per cent of his Indigenous artefacts and most of his recordings and photographic negatives and slides. The state museums in Adelaide, Melbourne and Sydney hold smaller parts of his artefact collection, and other photographs (including albums and prints) and papers are in the Mitchell Library in Sydney, the South Australian Museum Archives and the State Library of South Australia. The full extent of Basedow's collections and the complexities surrounding their generally poor level of documentation and the reasons for their distribution are the subject of ongoing work, along with work on improving the collection's documentation.[28]

Plant specimens collected in 1919 link Basedow's anthropology and botany. Labels in his hand with some of the specimens record Aboriginal names for plants and sometimes their uses. This did not happen consistently, either on this expedition or in his later plant collecting, but, for those that do have labels, this is an important source of information.

It would seem one rationale for Basedow's collection of artefacts was tied in with his firm belief that Aboriginal people were doomed to become extinct. This is an often-repeated theme with Basedow and, in terms of artefacts, he stated: 'Bones, stone artefacts, and wooden implements will remain in our museums for ever, but the habits, laws, beliefs, and legends are doomed to rapid extinction' (Basedow 1929a: xiii).

Basedow continued to espouse this notion of extinction during his trip to England and Europe late in 1931 and into 1932. In fact, he even put a time limit on their extinction—within 12 years! Reports of this reached Australia and were published in the local media.[29] Both the *Argus* and *The Advertiser* ran responses from eminent anthropologists on the same day, by Professor Frederic Wood Jones and Norman B. Tindale, respectively. Jones was reported as being 'surprised' at Basedow's 'unduly pessimistic' prediction.

Thomas (2001: 15–16), in his discussion of Aboriginal health, pointed out how researchers claimed in the late nineteenth century and well into the twentieth century that Indigenous Australians 'might become extinct and their potential contribution to science lost'. He goes on to refer to Russell McGregor's statement that sometimes the same people also campaigned against frontier violence and the bad treatment of Aboriginal

---

28   For a discussion on work undertaken to date on the photographs, see Kaus (2008: 28–30). It should be noted that Basedow collected some Aboriginal remains in addition to the material discussed here.

29   For example, *The Argus*, [Melbourne], 23 December 1931; *The Advertiser*, [Adelaide], 23 December 1931.

people (McGregor 1977, cited in Thomas 2001: 16). As we have seen, Thomas could be talking about Basedow. That Basedow probably believed the extinction of Aboriginal people would be a loss to science is inferred in the following quote taken from the preface to *The Australian Aboriginal*: 'I could not allow this opportunity to pass without brief reference to the causes of the early extinction which is threatening this inoffensive, useful, and scientifically important people' (Basedow 1929a: xiv).

Later anthropologists have frequently referred to Basedow's observations. As they often noted, his observations were made at an early time and this makes them important, despite their often limited scope. The nature of the expeditions in which he took part meant he rarely spent much time at any one place, unlike later anthropologists, who tended to spend extended periods in one place. This is reflected in Yengoyan's summary of previous work with Pitjantjatjara people prior to his own fieldwork, in 1966–67, where he commented: 'Furthermore, the Pitjandjara are known to the Social Anthropology of the Australian Aboriginal through the early observations of Basedow and more definitive accounts of Elkin, Berndt, Tindale and Mountford' (Yengoyan 1970: 71).

Presenting information

Basedow had intended to 'write a progressive series of treatises on the Australian aboriginal, embodying observations as they were being made' (1929a: vii). In reality, he achieved this until 1914, since he published articles on anthropology following the two major expeditions in 1903 and 1905, a series of trips to the Flinders Ranges between 1905 and about 1913 and a relatively short trip to Melville and Bathurst islands in 1911 (Basedow 1904, 1905, 1908, 1913a, 1913b, 1914). Between 1914 and his next major trip, in 1916,[30] to the western Kimberley, he published his journal for the 1903 expedition (Basedow 1915); he also published his 1916 expedition journal (Basedow 1918). Both journals include anthropological material, but Basedow would not publish any further articles of an anthropological nature until 1925. There were geological papers and some newspaper articles, however, as well as the four reports following his 1919–20 medical relief expeditions.

---

30   There may have been an expedition to Central Australia about 1914, but nothing concrete has been found about this.

Perhaps Basedow decided that it would be better to embody his anthropological observations in a more substantial form. It is also likely that the six years following 1918 were busy ones for him, with expeditions every year except 1921. In 1924, he also stood for parliament, which would have been another call on his time. For at least part of this period, he would also write his first book, *The Australian Aboriginal*, a 405-page tome published in 1925 (reprinted in 1929). It is a scholarly work, encyclopedic in approach, which covers every aspect of the lives of Aboriginal people from birth to death, with chapters on topics including art, music, religious life, origins and several on physical anthropology. It embodies his own observations along with information from areas that he never visited. It reflects his wide knowledge but it lacks the referencing of the work of others. He wanted 'to make it of general interest' (Basedow 1929a: ix), at a time when an overview of Australian Aboriginal people and their cultures was not really available to the general public. It was still a scholarly book, although its lack of referencing is something to be deplored. He excused this approach in his preface:

> I have to offer an apology to any authors who may claim priority to some of the facts which I mention in this book. I have written this account of the Australian aboriginal without attempting to consult previous literature, for the simple reason that, had I started looking up all necessary references, the volume might never have been completed. (Basedow 1929a: xii)

Basedow continued with his justification, saying that his 'time at headquarters' had been 'so limited' during the previous 15 years that it was 'impossible for [him] to adopt any other method than to write up [his] observations at first-hand and run the risk of a certain amount of trespass' (Basedow 1929a: xii). In the final piece of this justification, he effectively lets himself off the hook, saying:

> Our knowledge of Australian ethnology is so meagre that every man who has had first-hand experience among the tribes should consider it his bounden duty to place on record any facts he possesses, however trivial they may be. Every year the number of people who have seen the unsophisticated savage is dwindling. (Basedow 1929a: xiii)

Mention should also be made of *Knights of the Boomerang*, Basedow's second book, published in 1935, two years after his death. This book was more of a narrative and is told from an 'Aboriginal perspective'. The Berndts (Berndt and Berndt 1981: 539) found it to be a popular affair and 'less careful with both "facts" and interpretation', while McCarthy

(1935: 22), in his review of the book, stated it to be 'reliable' and seemed pleased that it was 'at a price within the reach of everybody'. Nonetheless, it suffers from irregularities this author believes are not down to Basedow, particularly a number of incorrectly captioned photographs and what appears to be an abrupt ending, as if someone took the manuscript and decided not to publish the final chapters (see Kaus 1984).

The point was made above about Basedow being unable to spend much time at any one place and how this affected what he was able to observe and record. In *Knights of the Boomerang*, he dealt with this by amalgamating observations from different times:

> The observations which have been pieced together in this volume have been made at different times, in different localities, and under different conditions; but I have taken the liberty of bringing them into chapters in order to make them read in sequence. (Basedow 1935: 17–18)

This unusual approach needs to be considered when reading this book; however, it is particularly useful for those interested in Basedow's work, as its narrative form fills out some of the bare details that we would otherwise be left with. It would help to have a basic understanding of Basedow's travels to place what he says into cultural, geographical and chronological contexts.

Linguistic capabilities

Both English and German were spoken at home as Basedow was growing up. His two stints in Germany, in 1890–93 and 1907–10, no doubt contributed to his competency in his parents' native tongue. In a curriculum vitae in Basedow's hand, he stated (probably understated): 'I possess a fair knowledge of the German and French languages.'[31] It is unlikely his work as an anatomy assistant while in Germany could have been undertaken unless he was a competent German speaker. Basedow was also fluent, according to one newspaper, in Italian, Spanish and Danish and had a 'fair knowledge of the various Slavonic dialects'.[32] He also had capabilities in at least two Aboriginal languages, Arrernte and Aluridja. One can imagine Basedow, Unndela and Tjikana conversing in these languages at home.

---

31 Mitchell Library, Sydney, MSS Set 161/5 Box 3(11), Folder 5/4.
32 *Muswellbrook Chronicle*, 16 May 1933: 4.

His competency in speaking Aluridja would come in useful when the Mackay expedition of 1926 encountered Aboriginal people in the country between Charlotte Waters, Docker River and Oodnadatta. For example, the day after leaving Ernabella, in the Musgrave Ranges, heading towards Oodnadatta, the expedition came across some people camped at a waterhole. Basedow was able to find out that the older people remembered Immalangenna, an old man he had met on the 1903 expedition.[33]

Plate 12.4 On his expeditions, Basedow travelled by buggy, wagon, horse, car and camel. This is the 1926 expedition photographed at an unknown location between Charlotte Waters and the Petermann Ranges, Northern Territory.
Photograph: Herbert Basedow, National Museum of Australia, Canberra, 1985.60.3935.

An indication of Basedow's competency in Arrernte comes from T. G. H. Strehlow when discussing execution for sacrilegious acts.[34] Basedow related a song in connection with this with sufficient accuracy that Strehlow (1970: 137) was able to identify the place with which the ceremony Basedow witnessed was associated. Basedow did not provide this information.

---

33 Mitchell Library, MSS Set 161/5 Item 17, 29 July 1926.
34 Because this relates to secret totemic activity, this description is necessarily brief and general.

It is difficult to fathom Tindale's comment in relation to Basedow's linguistic ability in the 'Blunders' chapter of his *Aboriginal Tribes of Australia* (1974). Tindale said that Basedow was 'often far from the mark in transcriptions'. By way of example, Tindale (1974: 155) said that Basedow's 'most notable blunder probably was Herrinda for the well-known tribal term Aranda'. Given Basedow's linguistic background, one would expect him to have a reasonable if not high level of linguistic competency, but, for Aboriginal languages, this would require the expertise of a linguist to properly assess. Nevertheless, Tindale was wrong, as Basedow did not use 'Herrinda' in place of Aranda (Arrernte). He first used this term in his 1908 vocabularies publication where he actually stated 'Herrinda' to be a local group of Arrernte (Basedow 1908: 208).[35] This was the country of Arrerika (aka Punch), who had been an expedition assistant on at least two major expeditions with which Basedow had been involved, in 1903 and 1920. Most likely, Arrerika was Basedow's only informant for the Arrernte (Basedow = Arrunndta) part of his vocabulary of Aluridja and Arrernte (Basedow 1908). It is also likely that Arrerika enabled Basedow to witness a secret emu ceremony in the eastern MacDonnell Ranges, probably in 1920. In his account of this, Basedow (1935: 152) again used the term 'Herrinda', the name for the 'local groups of the Arrunndta' in the area where he was camped at the time.

Summary

Basedow's employment and related opportunities were generally not directly associated with anthropology. They were mainly geology-related and his recording of Aboriginal cultures was undertaken secondary to this. Even so, he was to make substantial records of Aboriginal cultures, resulting in several publications, numerous photographs depicting Aboriginal people in the first three decades of the twentieth century and a large collection of artefacts. He was a man of many talents, with a career in medicine and geology and with a deep interest in natural history. He published in these areas and he also made important collections of plant and geological specimens as well as some animal (both vertebrate and invertebrate) specimens. Overall, his contribution to anthropology, geology, botany and zoology was substantial but, as Ian Harmstorf (2015),

---

35 I would like to thank Anna Kelly for translating for me this part of Basedow's article, which is in German.

his *Australian Dictionary of Biography* biographer, stated: 'It was frequently said of him, after his early death, that he would have achieved greater eminence if he had not spread his remarkable talents so widely.'

References

Basedow, B. 1990. *The Basedow Story: A German South Australian heritage.* Adelaide: Self-published.

Basedow, H. 1901. On the occurrence of Miocene limestones at Edithburg, and their stratigraphical relationship to the eocene of Wool Bay, with description of a new species by Professor R. Tate. *Transactions of the Royal Society of South Australia* 25: 145–8.

Basedow, H. 1902a. Descriptions of new species of fossil mollusca from the Miocene limestone near Edithburg (including notes by the late Professor Ralph Tate). *Transactions of the Royal Society of South Australia* 26: 130–2.

Basedow, H. 1902b. A brief note on the occurrence of a raised beach on Hindmarsh Island, South Australia. *Transactions of the Royal Society of South Australia* 26: 324–5.

Basedow, H. 1904. Anthropological notes made on the South Australian Government north-west prospecting expedition, 1903. *Transactions of the Royal Society of South Australia* 28: 12–51.

Basedow, H. 1905. Geological report on the country traversed by the South Australian Government north-west prospecting expedition, 1903. *Transactions of the Royal Society of South Australia* 29: 57–102.

Basedow, H. 1906. Sources of Central Australian water supply. *Proceedings of the Adelaide University Scientific Society*: 3–11.

Basedow, H. 1907. Anthropological notes on the western coastal tribes of the Northern Territory of South Australia. *Transactions of the Royal Society of South Australia* 31: 1–62.

Basedow, H. 1908. Vergleichende Vokabularien der Aluridja-und Arrundta Dialekte Zentral-Australiens. *Zeitschrift fur Ethnologie* 40: 207–28.

Basedow, H. 1909. Beitrage Zur Kenntnis Der Geologie Australiens. *Zeitschrift der Deutschen Geologischen Gesellschaft* 2: 306–79.

Basedow, H. 1913a. Burial customs in the northern Flinders Ranges of South Australia. *Man* (13): 49–53. doi.org/10.2307/2788101.

Basedow, H. 1913b. Notes on the natives of Bathurst Island, north Australia. *Journal of the Royal Anthropological Institute* 43: 291–323. doi.org/10.2307/2843169.

Basedow, H. 1914. Aboriginal rock carvings of great antiquity in South Australia. *Journal of the Royal Anthropological Institute* 44: 195–211. doi.org/10.2307/2843536.

Basedow, H. 1915. Journal of the government north-west expedition. *Proceedings of the Royal Geographical Society of Australasia, South Australian Branch* 15: 57–242.

Basedow, H. 1916. Physical geography and geology of the western rivers' district, Northern Territory of Australia. *Proceedings of the Royal Geographical Society of Australasia, South Australian Branch* 16: 148–217.

Basedow, H. 1918. Narrative of an expedition of exploration in north-western Australia. *Proceedings of the Royal Geographical Society of Australasia, South Australian Branch* 18: 105–295.

Basedow, H. 1920. *Report upon the first medical relief expedition amongst the Aborigines of South Australia*. GRG 23/1 1920 144. State Library of South Australia, Adelaide.

Basedow, H. 1921a. *Medical report upon Aborigines of the lower Northern Territory of Australia*. CRS A3 Item 22/2805. National Archives of Australia, Canberra.

Basedow, H. 1921b. *Report upon the second medical relief expedition among the Aborigines of South Australia*. GRG 23/1 1921 87. State Library of South Australia, Adelaide.

Basedow, H. 1921c. *Report upon the third medical relief expedition among the Aborigines of South Australia*. GRG 23/1 1921 330. State Library of South Australia, Adelaide.

Basedow, H. 1928. Through unknown Arnhem Land: Mackay exploring expedition—Some nature studies. *Brisbane Courier*, 12 September 1928 [part 5 of 6].

Basedow, H. 1929a [1925]. *The Australian Aboriginal*. Reprint. Adelaide: F. W. Preece & Sons.

Basedow, H. 1929b. Notes to accompany the 'Map of the Mackay exploring expedition in Central Australia, 1926'. *Proceedings of the Royal Geographical Society of Australasia, South Australian Branch* 29: 171–6.

Basedow, H. 1932. Diseases of the Australian Aborigines. *Journal of Tropical Medicine and Hygiene* 35(12): 177–85; 35(13): 193–8; 35(14): 210–13; 1 August 1932: 229–33; 15 August 1932: 247–50; 35(18): 274–8. [Issued as consolidated reprint.]

Basedow, H. 1935. *Knights of the Boomerang*. Sydney: The Endeavour Press.

Basedow, M. K. (ed.). 1993. Basedow family newsletter, No. 2, 1913, 'Martin Peter Friedrich Basedow (1829–1902)' (copy of obituary from 'Australische Zeitung', March 1902). In *The Basedow Family History 1230–1943: English translation & Basedow family reunion—Launch of the 'The Basedow Story: A German South Australian heritage' by Bernard Basedow, 1990*, pp. 7–12. Sydney: Self-published.

Berndt, R. M. and Berndt, C. H. 1981. *The World of the First Australians*. Rev. edn. Sydney: Lansdowne Press.

Brown, H. Y. L., Basedow, H., Gee, L. C. E. and Etheridge, R. 1906. *Northern Territory of South Australia, North-Western District: Reports (geological and general) resulting from the explorations made by the government geologist and staff during 1905*. Adelaide: Government Printer.

Harmstorf, I. 2015. Basedow, Herbert (1881–1933). *Australian Dictionary of Biography*. Canberra: National Centre of Biography, The Australian National University. Available from: adb.anu.edu.au/biography/basedow-herbert-5151/text8633. Published first in hardcopy 1979, accessed online 7 September 2015.

Kaus, D. 1984. Manipulation of photographs: A case study. *COMA: Bulletin of the Conference of Museum Anthropologists* (14): 2–20.

Kaus, D. 2008. *A Different Time: The expedition photographs of Herbert Basedow 1903–1928*. Canberra: National Museum of Australia Press.

Klaatsch, H. 1907. Some notes on scientific travel amongst the black population of tropical Australia in 1904, 1905, 1906. *Reports of the Australian and New Zealand Association for the Advancement of Science* 11: 577–92.

McCarthy, F. D. 1935. Knights of the Boomerang. [Review.] *Mankind* 1(12): 21–2.

Mackay, D. 1929. An expedition in Arnhem Land in 1928. *Geographical Journal* 74: 568–71. doi.org/10.2307/1785164.

Mulvaney, D. J. and Calaby, H. 1985. *'So Much That is New': Baldwin Spencer 1860–1929—A biography*. Melbourne: Melbourne University Press.

Mulvaney, J. 2001. Erlikilyika: Arrernte ethnographer and artist. In *Histories of Old Ages: Essays in honour of Rhys Jones*, (eds) A. Anderson, I. Lilley and S. O'Connor, pp. 277–86. Canberra: Pandanus Books.

Salter, E. 1972. *Daisy Bates*. New York: Coward, McCann & Geoghegan.

Selby, J. 1991. Geo-giants of the past: Walter Howchin (1845–1937). *Terra Nova* 3(5): 568–9. doi.org/10.1111/j.1365-3121.1991.tb00196.x.

Stanner, W. E. H. 1976. After the Dreaming—Whither? *Mankind* 10(3): 131–41. doi.org/10.1111/j.1835-9310.1976.tb01144.x.

Strehlow, T. G. H. 1970. Geography and the totemic landscape in Central Australia: A functional study. In *Australian Aboriginal Anthropology: Modern studies in the social anthropology of the Australian Aborigines*, (ed.) R. M. Berndt, pp. 92–140. Perth: University of Western Australia Press.

Thomas, D. 2001. *The beginnings of Aboriginal health research in Australia*. Discussion Paper No. 3, September. VicHealth Koori Health Research & Community Development Unit, Melbourne.

Tindale, N. B. 1974. *Aboriginal Tribes of Australia: Their terrain, environmental controls, distribution, limits, and proper names.* Berkeley: University of California Press.

Yengoyan, A. A. 1970. Demographic factors in Pitjandjara social organization. In *Australian Aboriginal Anthropology: Modern studies in the social anthropology of the Australian Aborigines*, (ed.) R. M. Berndt, pp. 70–91. Perth: University of Western Australia Press.

Zogbaum, H. 2010. *Changing Skin Colour in Australia: Herbert Basedow and the black caucasian.* Melbourne: Australian Scholarly Publishing.

13

Father Worms's contribution to Australian Aboriginal anthropology

William B. McGregor

I have previously discussed in some detail the contribution of Fathers Hermann Nekes (Society of the Catholic Apostolate, SAC, or Pallottine Society) and Ernest Worms (SAC) to Australian Aboriginal linguistics (McGregor 2005, 2007; Nekes and Worms 2006: 1–40; see also McGregor 2008b), and edited their magnum opus, *Australian Languages*, distributed in microfilm form in 1953, but not published until 2006 (by Mouton de Gruyter). In this chapter, I provide an overview of the contribution of Ernest Worms to Australian Aboriginal anthropology, which centred on Aboriginal religion, although missiology was always an applied side to his research. I will attempt to situate Worms's anthropological thought in German anthropology of the late nineteenth century and the *Kulturkreislehre* ('culture circle theory') school of anthropology. Before getting down to business, I provide a brief biography of Father Worms (see further Nekes and Worms 2006; and Ganter, Chapter 14, this volume).

Personal and intellectual background

Ernest (Ernst) Ailred Worms was born in Bochum, Germany, on 27 August 1891. Little information is available on his early life until he entered the Pallottine Society in 1912. His studies were interrupted by

World War I, when he was called up for military service; he was awarded the Kaiser's Iron Cross. After the war, Worms returned to the SAC and was ordained in 1920.

Worms's first posting was in Eastern European Pallottine jurisdictions; ultimately, he served as director of studies in Rössel in East Prussia. Worms was appointed to the Pallottine mission in the Kimberley in Australia in 1930. He arrived in Broome, Western Australia, on 17 December of that year by ship, with Father Francis Hügel and three religious brothers. There he served for eight years as Broome parish priest. Soon after his arrival, he began research on the Indigenous languages and peoples, starting with Yawuru in early 1931. After his former teacher Father Nekes (1875–1948) joined him in 1935, Worms became more active in linguistic investigations, though he always maintained a greater interest in anthropological issues.

Plate 13.1 Father Worms working in Broome, probably in the 1930s.
Source: Courtesy of the Australian Pallottine Archives.

In 1938, Worms took up the post of rector of the Pallottine College in Kew, Melbourne, where he remained for a decade. During this time, he continued his collaboration with Father Nekes, who was also in Kew for part of this period. Worms returned to the Kimberley in 1948, where he renewed his research on Aboriginal languages and cultures. In 1957, he again returned east, to Sydney, where he took charge of the Pallottine College in Manly. While there, he played a role in establishing the New South Wales Anthropological Society, and participated in the National Conference on Aboriginal Studies, held in May 1961, where he presented a paper on Aboriginal religion, which was subsequently published in the proceedings of the conference (Worms 1963). Also in 1961, Worms was appointed a member of the linguistic panel of the interim council for the Australian Institute of Aboriginal Studies (now the Australian Institute of Aboriginal and Torres Strait Islander Studies, AIATSIS).

Father Worms died of cancer in Saint Vincent's Hospital, Sydney, on 13 August 1963, aged 72. Today, Worms appears more dynamic, more widely published and is probably better known among Australianists than his co-author, Nekes. In the mid-twentieth century, however, Elkin's evaluation was that Nekes was a trained academic (see Capell 1956: ii); Worms an amateur.

Unlike the typical missionary, Father Worms was based mostly in urban centres, from which he undertook fieldtrips to numerous locations. And, unlike the typical missionary—or missionary linguist or anthropologist— he did not work for decades with one group of people, focusing his intellectual attention on that particular group. As far as I can determine, he did not gain speaking control of any Aboriginal language. Instead, his research—both linguistic and anthropological—was largely comparative, using a broad base of languages and cultures, albeit with a particular focus on the Dampier Land region.

Worms was educated in the Limburg Seminary, where he attended lectures in linguistics and anthropology by Father Hermann Nekes, who became a lifelong friend and mentor and subsequently joined Worms in Australia in 1935. Unfortunately, I have found little information on what was taught in the seminary at the time (see, however, Ganter, Chapter 14, this volume). Nor have I been able to find much information on the theoretical framework underpinning Hermann Nekes's anthropology and linguistics, beyond the fact that he had been heavily influenced by his well-known contemporary Father Wilhelm Schmidt (1868–1954), and presumably worked within the *Kulturkrieslehre* paradigm (see, again, Ganter, Chapter 14, this volume). It is therefore reasonable to assume that Worms's linguistic and anthropological training fell within that framework.

Another potentially significant influence on Father Worms's anthropological thinking was Helmut Petri (1907–86), professor of anthropology at Cologne University. Petri led the Frobenius Expedition into the Kimberley in 1938–39, and met Father Worms at the beginning and end of this expedition, as well as on various subsequent occasions (for details, see Ganter, Chapter 14; and Redmond, Chapter 16, this volume). The extent of their personal interaction is uncertain, although Petri is referred to as Worms's 'friend and colleague in anthropology' (Worms and Petri 1998: xi). As a former student of Koppers, Petri would have been familiar with the culture circle paradigm and may have influenced Worms's diffusionist thinking. In any event, it seems that Petri may have alerted Worms to the significance of rock art to the unpicking of layers in cultural diffusion (see Ganter, Chapter 14, this volume).

Overview of Father Worms's anthropological research

As already mentioned, Worms's anthropological interests centred on religion, while his linguistic interests were primarily in the domain of anthropological linguistics—in particular, he was interested in the domain of language and thought, where he upheld a fairly extreme Whorfian stance (see further below). One encounters very little in his writings on social concerns, either sociolinguistic or social anthropology.

Fieldwork

Father Worms undertook linguistic and anthropological fieldwork in a variety of locations throughout the country, including:

- the Dampier Land region, mainly Broome and Beagle Bay
- west and east Kimberley locations, in annual field trips from 1933 to 1938
- western New South Wales and southern Queensland, during the same years
- Palm Island, in 1946, where he worked on a number of rainforest languages and peoples of northern Queensland, and also carried out anthropometric measurements
- Balgo, in 1948 and 1950, where he discovered rock engravings

- the Pilbara region and Port Hedland hinterland, in 1952, where he also investigated rock art
- Central Australia and the Northern Territory in 1960, when he undertook a nine-month-long fieldtrip investigating cave paintings funded by the Wenner-Gren Foundation.

Map 13.1 shows the traditional locations of the languages and groups on which Father Worms did fieldwork (cf. Nekes and Worms 1953: 15); the fieldwork was not always in the traditional regions indicated (e.g. the northern Queensland fieldwork was probably all conducted on Palm Island). Information on locations visited during the 1960 fieldtrip is incomplete. It should be noted that Worms did both anthropological and linguistic research in each fieldwork location. Nekes's fieldwork was focused exclusively on the Dampier Land region.

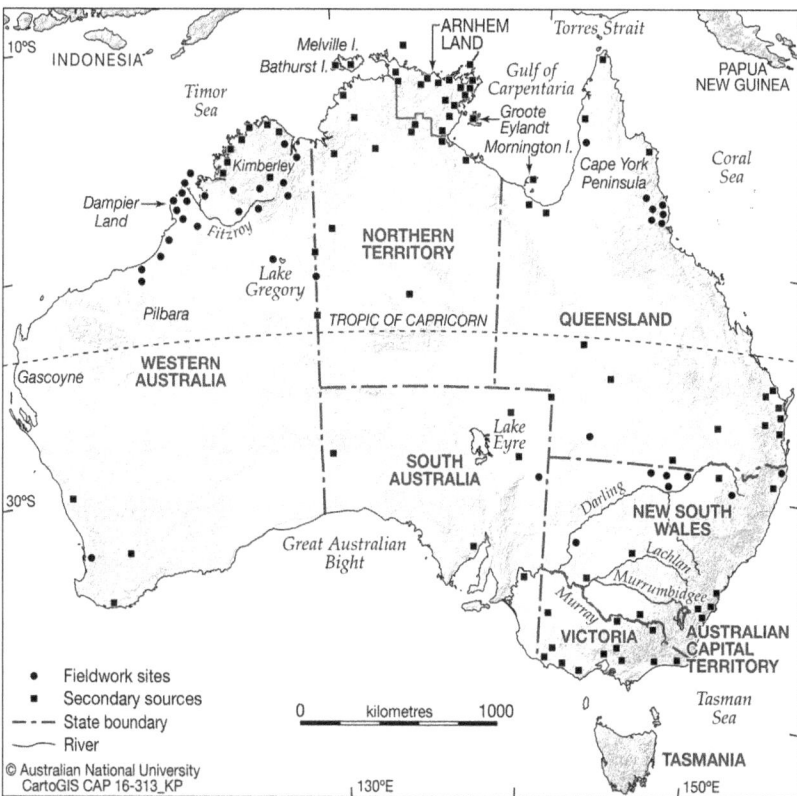

Map 13.1 Map showing the location of Worms's fieldwork languages and cultures.

Source: CartoGIS, The Australian National University.

Worms does not discuss his fieldwork methodology in detail anywhere in his published writings. I provide a brief description of what is known of his linguistic fieldwork methodology in Nekes and Worms (2006: 14–15). Even less is known of Worms's anthropological fieldwork methodology. One of the few descriptions of a fieldtrip comes from his colleague Father Francis Hügel:

> He learned also about the neighbouring tribes and was one day told about the hero GALALANG; the outstanding figure among the Njol-) Njol [sic], the residing tribe in Beagle Bay. So one day he came up to Beagle Bay, where I was appointed to and invited me to come with him to trace the last tracks of this hero. On mule back it took us almost a whole week to cross the Dampier peninsula, 65 km East to the King Sound, but what we found was rather disappointing: a clearing in the bush where [there] was gravel over the ground, on that ground a clearing in the shape of a human being: this was the place where Galalang rested and had gone back into the ground. For our guides, Abos and all the local tribe of the Nimanbur [sic] a sacred place. Fr. Worms travelled always with a good camera, a Leika, and so he took also a photo of Galalang. (Huegel 1981: 2–3)

Worms describes the figure as follows (Worms and Petri 1998: 116):

> In the country of the Bard, hidden in the mangrove thicket of King Sound, we found a large ground-figure of Galalang in sunk-relief which had been scratched into the gravelly ground.

Unfortunately, Worms and Petri (1998) contains no photographs; presumably, his photo of Galalang is somewhere in the uncatalogued collections in Kew, Rossmoyne or Limburg (see Ganter, Chapter 14, this volume). In fact, only a handful of photographs appear in publications, mainly in those concerning Aboriginal art (see below).

Worms gathered a range of texts in the languages he investigated, including mythological narratives and songs, some explanatory texts and a few narratives of personal experience. Most were taken down laboriously, verbatim, from native speakers, as they were produced. It appears that some form of shorthand may have been used in the online transcriptions, though no examples of these representations or information on this form of shorthand are provided (Worms 1953b: 967; Nekes and Worms 2006: 14–15). Just a few texts were recorded on wax cylinders, and these were all songs.[1] Fieldworkers at the time had to be very circumspect in their use of cylinders, which were quite bulky and inconvenient to use, and tended to record only music and song (see also McGregor 2008a).

Motivations

Worms's anthropological and linguistic research was motivated to a considerable extent by missionary concerns to develop more effective missionary practices, thus facilitating conversion. As Worms (1970: 374–5) himself put it:

> I believe the following to be important qualities for a missionary working among Aborigines.
>
> 1. He must have a good knowledge of classical and several modern languages, as well as history. The former will give him at least a linguistic feeling and adroitness for native languages; the latter, having made him conscious of the complexity and recentness of his own cultural background and of the problems which arose from the meeting of different cultures in the history of his own home country, will supply him with a sympathetic attitude for similar difficulties faced by his primitive natives, who find themselves in a similar, but far more intense, collision …
>
> 3. A fundamental anthropological knowledge is necessary, otherwise he would feel lost in strange surroundings and be blind to the exuberance of human life around him. This science will enable him to avoid a false impression that all he observes is unique and extraordinary, but will support him in his difficult task by adding to his experiences, that of other anthropologists and educated missionaries …
>
> 5. The missionary, too, must be a man of restraint and of untiring perseverance. Being an anthropologist and psychologist by his education and vocation, he clearly sees the impossibility of changing the style of living of a nomad within one generation—even the educational work of three generations will not bridge the immense distance between their culture stratum and that of the modern industrial age.

---

1   Their recorder—probably an Excelsior phonograph—was provided by the Berlin Phonogramm-Archiv and brought to Australia by Father Nekes in 1935. Father Worms cut a dozen wax cylinders in Beagle Bay in 1936 and duly forwarded them to the museum. The phonograph seems never to have been used again, probably because all of the cylinders were recorded in 1936. An offer of more cylinders was made by the director of the Phonogramm-Archiv, Dr Marius Schneider, in mid-1937; no action appears to have been taken on this, perhaps initially because of Father Worms's imminent move to Melbourne and, later, due to the war.

Father Worms's Kimberley fieldtrips of the late 1930s were also partly motivated by concerns to set up a new mission in the east Kimberley for the desert peoples, to replace Rockhole near Halls Creek, which had been encountering many difficulties. Thus, his favourable report on the area of Lake Gregory led ultimately to the establishment of the Balgo Mission.

However, Worms was also concerned about the loss of traditional languages and knowledge, and about their preservation:

> The compilation of this list of Aboriginal geographical names used by nine tribes of the Australian Kimberleys, together with etymological and mythological annotations, has a three fold purpose: first to prevent an irretrievable loss of verbal documents at a time when place names have already started to fade out of the memory of the younger natives, especially those living in the coastal regions ... Over a hundred names, hitherto unknown, are now rescued from falling into oblivion. (Worms 1944: 284)

Output and major themes

Table 13.1, which slightly revises Table 2 of Nekes and Worms (2006: 36), categorises the published and unpublished writings of Fathers Nekes and Worms according to their main topic. For the sake of completeness, both linguistic and anthropological writings are included. However, this division is somewhat misleading: Worms's anthropology was closely linked to his linguistics and (as we will see) most of his writings combined both fields. Note also that, in some instances, works are listed under more than one topic heading.

Table 13.1 Published and unpublished works by Fathers Hermann Nekes and Ernest Worms

Topic	Published	Unpublished
Grammar	Nekes (1938)	
Lexis and semantics	Worms (1938b, 1938c, 1942b, 1944, 1946, 1957b, 1960c)	Worms (1958b)
Texts (including translations)	Worms (1940, 1949, 1950a, 1950b, 1957c, 1959d)	
Historical	Worms (1941)	
General linguistics (grammar, lexis, texts)	Nekes and Worms (1953); Worms (1953b)	Nekes (1931–47)
Other linguistics	Worms (1958a, 1958c)	

Topic	Published	Unpublished
Religion and intellectual culture	Worms (1938a, 1942a, 1947, 1950a, 1952, 1953a, 1960a, 1963); Worms and Petri (1968); translations: Worms (1972, 1986); Worms and Petri (1998)	
Missiology	Worms (1959a, 1970)	
Art	Worms (1953c, 1954, 1955b, 1957a, 1957d, 1959b, 1959c)	
Material culture	Worms (1950b)	Worms (n.d.)
Mythology	Worms (1957b); see also under 'Texts'	
General anthropology	Worms (1955a, 1960b, 1961)	Worms (1974)

The remainder of this section provides brief discussion of the major themes in Worms's linguistic and anthropological thinking.

Lexis and semantics represented two of Worms's major concerns in linguistics and are dealt with in no fewer than seven published papers. In addition, they play a very prominent role in Nekes and Worms (1953); over half of this work is made up of an alphabetical listing of lexical items in a range of languages of the continent. As will become clear in the discussion below, Worms saw lexicon and semantics as windows into Aboriginal thought. He also believed they provided crucial evidence of diffusion of cultural traits and notions, as also discussed below. Aside from this, the lists of lexical items and the remarks on their meanings provide fascinating information on culturally relevant phenomena that are not dealt with in detail elsewhere in his works—for example, artefacts, such as *laŋgai* ('slowly burning tree, used as fire reservoir') (Nekes and Worms 1953: 644) and *nomolor* ('stern of boat, back of cart, big end of axe-head') (pp. 760, 765), and practices and/or beliefs, such as *djibeṛ* ('presentiment, foreboding of coming event on account of nervous jerks or palpitation of a vein') (p. 473; see further McGregor 2005: 12–13; 2007: 108–9).

About the same number of publications present texts in languages from various parts of the continent—again, with particular focus on the Dampier Land region. Mostly these texts are presented in the original language,[2] which is always identified (although not always correctly). In many instances, the narrator of the text is identified. The Aboriginal language transcriptions are accompanied by interlinear glosses

---

2   In a few instances (e.g. Worms and Petri 1998), just the English/German free translations— or summary translations—are provided.

(often somewhat lacking by modern standards) and free translations into English or German (usually separate from the original and interlinear representations); in many cases, they are replete with footnotes providing grammatical and lexical information that repeats information provided elsewhere in their work, as well as a limited amount of elaborating material. As already remarked, the majority of these texts were dictated—hence, their shortness and similarity to written texts and general lack of features characteristic of oral delivery—although, fortunately, a few characteristics of oral delivery are apparent in some texts.

It was the content of the texts (including songs) that most interested Worms, not their linguistic features.[3] Thus, in particular, Worms mined mythological texts for the insights they provide on religious beliefs; at times, he also used their content as evidence in support of his interpretation of Aboriginal prehistory. And sometimes he linked the myths to associated rituals and artefacts (e.g. *tjuringa*). This attention to texts is doubtless an inheritance from late nineteenth-century German ethnography, which held that the essence of a cultural group is inscribed in its mythology, folktales and songs.

Material culture figures but minimally in Worms's writings, although, as mentioned above, it does appear indirectly in wordlists and mythology (see also below on religion). Worms (1950b) presents a number of fire myths in Australian languages and provides discussion of fire-making tools and how they are used. As usual, he enters into fairly extensive discussion of terms for these artefacts. Worms (n.d.) is a 10-minute black-and-white 8 mm film illustrating pressure flaking of quartz spear tips.

Worms's research on rock art did not begin until some 20 years after his arrival in Australia, and may well have been stimulated by contact with Helmut Petri (see above). In 1953–54 and 1960, he undertook field trips to investigate rock art in the Pilbara, northern Kimberley and Northern Territory, funded by two grants from the Wenner-Gren Foundation. The findings of the first of these trips appeared in three articles published in *Anthropos* (Worms 1953c, 1954, 1955b). The second and third of these papers provide fairly detailed descriptions of the art and are illustrated by a number of photographs and drawings of a selection of artworks (see Plate 13.2 for an example). No publication resulted from the second Wenner-Gren grant, though the discussion of Aboriginal art in the first

---

3   That is, except their lexical choices, which he deployed in ways discussed above.

chapter of Worms and Petri (1968) draws on his findings. Evidently, Worms spoke to local Aborigines about the art and their interpretations of it (see e.g. Worms 1955b: 547). In the late 1950s, Worms also published two very brief, popularising pieces in magazines (Worms 1957a, 1957d) and two reviews of books on Australian Aboriginal art (Worms 1959b, 1959c).

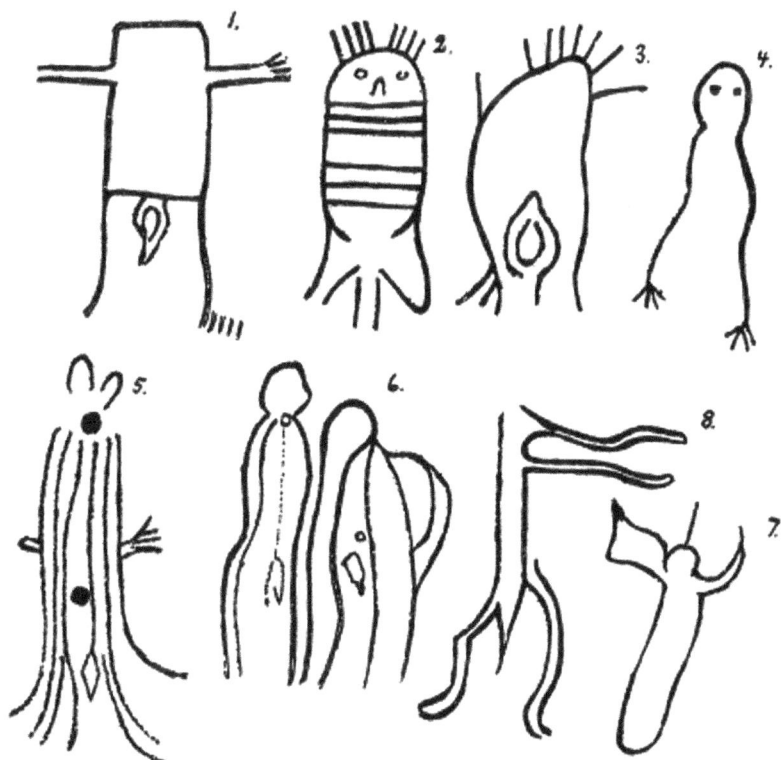

Plate 13.2 Figure D from Worms (1954: 1085).

The caption reads: 'Petroglyphs of Human Beings, Port Hedland, W. A. —2: 61 cm. long. — 3: 41 cm. × 17.5 cm. — 6: 56 cm. × 25.5 cm. — 8: 31 cm. × 24 cm.'

Source: Courtesy of Anthropos.

Religion, as already mentioned, was Worms's primary interest; the majority of his publications touch on religion in one way or another and it is the main topic of at least nine of them. Two are general works on religion in Aboriginal Australia. The first was an overview article (Worms 1963). The second was a much more substantial work—Worms's anthropological magnum opus, 'Australische Eingeborenen-Religionen', which was published in 1968 as volume 5.2 of the series *Die Religionen der Südsee und Australiens* (Worms and Petri 1968). A French translation of the volume was published in 1972; however, it was not until 1986 that an English translation of Worms's contribution appeared (Worms 1986). This was followed a decade later by a revised translation (Worms and Petri 1998). Worms died before he could complete work on 'Australische Eingeborenen-Religionen', and Helmut Petri completed the revision and editing of the manuscript.[4] He added a considerable amount of material to the text, which he distinguished by smaller font. In fact, his contribution was significant enough that the 1998 translation includes Petri as a joint author, at the request of Gisela Petri-Odermann, his widow. Having myself edited *Australian Languages* (Nekes and Worms 1953), I have no doubt that Petri had to do a considerable amount of editorial work to produce a publishable text.

'Australische Eingeborenen-Religionen' covers a range of themes concerning religion and religious thought, all of which are dealt with in previous publications, including mythology; sacred beings ('heroes') and their relation to the concept of god; sacred objects—the material culture of religion (the significance and use of these objects); music, song and dance (including musical instruments and song texts); art; symbolic representation (in sacred objects, art, etc.); the concept of the soul and beliefs about death; and initiation and other rituals (e.g. funerary rituals). Worms's treatment is, overall, quite descriptive and synchronic in orientation, and integrates evidence from his own fieldwork and from the contemporary literature, with which he appears to have been conversant. Nonetheless, the temporal dimension looms large, so that he continually returns to the topic of diffusion, which he attempts to substantiate through his interpretation of Australian Aboriginal linguistics, prehistory and physical anthropology.

'Australische Eingeborenen-Religionen' ranges over the entire continent, including Tasmania, which is dealt with in a separate chapter. Although mindful of the inadequacies of treatments of the religion of Tasmanian Aborigines, Worms felt there was sufficient evidence to conclude that the religious ideas of Tasmanians resembled those of mainlanders in key points, and that the similarities were indicative of an ancient cultural stratum.

---

4   It would be interesting to know how much interaction they engaged in during the preparation of the text before Worms's death, and the extent to which this shaped Worms's draft.

Worms's ideas on mission practice are overviewed in some detail in his last publication, also posthumous, Worms (1970), although his ideas on this theme are articulated elsewhere as well (e.g. Worms 1959a).

Some characteristics of Worms's anthropology

Virtually all of Father Worms's anthropological work was tied in one way or another with religion. It is impossible in the scope of this short chapter to provide a comprehensive account and evaluation of Worms's contribution to knowledge about Australian Aboriginal religion. Instead, I will identify and briefly discuss two recurrent themes and issues in Worms's contribution: 1) the role and place of language, which I will cover briefly, since it has already been discussed elsewhere; and 2) diffusion and *Kulturkreislehre*, on which I will provide more details, as this has been discussed less comprehensively in the literature.

The role and place of language

Language played a crucial role in the German anthropological tradition of the late nineteenth century (Kenny 2013: 5). There are two main aspects of this notion: first, from Herder came the idea that cognition is dependent on language; and second, it was considered that mythology, folktales and song constitute the essence of a cultural group. Both of these features, as was seen above, are characteristic of Worms's ethnography, just as they played a central role in the German-inspired Boasian tradition in the United States. Thus, Worms presumed a strong Whorfian stance, as I have observed elsewhere in discussing his linguistics (Nekes and Worms 2006: 18). Indeed, he imbued words with an almost mystical significance:

> Indeed, by an appropriate naming of places the Aboriginal depicts mentally a plastic map of his country and its geographical forms, shows parts of his economy by pointing to the prevalent kinds and regions of vegetation and animal life, reveals the practical mastery of his language and a faithful memory of an archaic vocabulary, and discloses involuntarily his carefully hidden mythology and actual religion by inter weaving natural features of the landscape with totems, heroes, and supernatural beings. (Worms 1944: 284)

Moreover, as already discussed, he recorded the mythology and songs of many of the groups with whom he worked—in many cases, in their traditional language. A number of articles reproduce them in the original language together with interlinear glosses and free translations, and with some explanation and/or discussion.

There is a third aspect of the significance of language to Worms's ethnography, which I have elsewhere referred to as *lexical syndromes* (Nekes and Worms 2006: 20), which I here refer to as *lemes*: a blend of *lexeme* and *meme*, since that is effectively what they are—the lexical correlate of memes. Whether or not this represents an original idea of Worms's or is something he borrowed from others remains to be seen.[5] I have discussed these in some detail in Nekes and Worms (2006: 20–24); however, since they play such a crucial role in Worms's anthropology, some general remarks are in order here.

Lemes are form-meaning correspondences that are recurrent across languages and that are indicative of underlying root forms that reveal, according to Father Worms, insights into the workings of the Aboriginal mind and, ultimately, Aboriginal beliefs and culture. For instance, Worms (1957b; see also Worms and Petri 1998: 8–10) identifies the leme *bag- ~ bug- ~ big-* ('the dead, ghost'), which is manifested, he avers, in a wide range of lexemes across the languages of the continent that concern the domain of ghostly activity (Worms's spellings; sources omitted):

* *baka* 'dead' Darling River, South Australia, New South Wales; *kuka-buk* 'dead' Streaky Bay, South Australia; and *buka-da* Kurnu (New South Wales)
* *biga* 'shade' Yawuru; *pega* Murray River 'ghost'
* *bag-wan* 'to hide' Brabralung (Victoria)
* *puka* 'ghost' Streaky Bay, South Australia
* *baga-djimbiri* 'two heroes' Karajarri
* *bagin* 'bad spirit' Wiradjuri
* *bagu-ṇan* 'ghost of the dead' Bardi, Jabirrjabirr, Nimanburru, Nyulnyul
* *bugan-di* 'walking without tracks' Mangala, Nyikina, Yawuru

5   Nowhere, as far as I am aware, does Worms actually discuss the concept or attribute it to any source. Schmidt (1919) does not employ any comparable notion, and Brandewie (1990) nowhere alludes to anything like the leme in Schmidt's thinking. Of course, the possibility that he employed it somewhere in his vast corpus of writings cannot be ruled out.

- *buga-di* 'hair dress' Kukatja; *puka-ti* Pitjantjatjara, *poko-ti* Ngalia
- *baka-li* 'power (in vocation) names' Yirrkala
- *buga-mani* 'spirits of deceased, burial ceremony with grave posts' Tiwi. Literally perhaps 'carvings of spirits'—cf. *mani* 'engraving, picture' Kukatja
- *mirrabooka* (*mira-buga*) 'group of stars, Southern Cross; The Primeval Old Man' (Perth)
- *lari-buga* 'initiation ceremony' Karajarri, Yawuru; *lari-big* Bardi, *lari-b* Nyulnyul
- *dil-bag* 'ritual snapping of fingers' Bardi, Jabirrjabirr, Nimanburru, Nyulnyul
- *gan-bag* 'music stick' Jabirrjabirr, Nyulnyul
- *bukwa nepi* 'spirit babies' Cape York
- *būgar-ri* 'dream, myth' Karajarri, Mangala, Nyikina; *būgar* Nimanburru, Nyulnyul; *būgir* Jabirrjabirr, *būar* Bardi, *bura* Jawi
- *ma-būgarin* 'to dream' Jabirrjabirr, Nyikina, Nimanburru, Nyulnyul, Yawuru; *būgari mana* Karajarri
- *ga-buguri* 'dreaming' Kukatja
- *bugaru* 'mythical time' Malyangapa (New South Wales), *pekere* 'dreamtime' Tangana [possibly Tanganekald, South Australia]
- *baguri-ji* 'I dream' Gumbaynggir; *baguri-nj* 'initiation ceremony' Gumbaynggir
- *būgari-gura* 'native law' Yawuru, Karajarri
- *bugerum* 'big bullroarer' Yakara (New South Wales).

There are many problems with Worms's implementation of the notion of the leme, which we need not go into in detail about here (for more detailed discussion, see Nekes and Worms 2006: 21–3). Suffice it to observe the following: Worms's implementation of the notion of leme is almost completely lacking in constraint, the only apparent constraint being that the lexemes must apparently come from Australian languages—otherwise, there would be no reason not to include, for instance, *bogey* (man) ('devil, ghost'; English, nineteenth century) and *bogle* ('phantom, goblin'; Scots English, sixteenth century) as instances of the leme. The fact that the lemes are—like *bag- ~ bug- ~ big-* ('the dead, ghost')—very short forms, often consonant–vowel–consonant, ensures that there is a high probability of false identifications. Furthermore, Worms frequently fails to systematically distinguish between segments that are phonemic in particular languages—which is especially the case for the apical tap/trill and apical glide rhotics, which are phonemic in most Aboriginal languages—adding to the probability of false identifications.

Worms employed lemes in his anthropology in a range of ways, including to argue (never very convincingly) for:

- directionality of borrowing/diffusion of words
- directionality of borrowing/diffusion of cultural items, material and cognitive
- directionality of movement of peoples
- fundamental cultural beliefs
- the significance of places and myths (including their 'heroes', etc.)
- the idea that there are just a few *demas* ('supreme beings') across the continent.

In fact, it is often unclear what the leme is imagined to motivate and/or precisely how it motivates a particular claim. Consider, for instance: 'But the etymology of Maŋulagura, the mythological name of Wamerana, gives us a satisfactory insight into the significance of the sacred place' (Worms 1954: 1079). The 'etymology' provided on the following page indicates that Maŋulagura means 'The Woman's' or 'The Place of the Woman', but no information is provided about the relation of the site to women, so the putative etymology falls far short of providing an insight into the significance of the place.

Diffusion and *Kulturkreislehre*

The second major influence on Worms's thought comes from the late nineteenth-century and early twentieth-century German–Austrian anthropological theory of *Kulturkreis* ('culture circles'). As we have already seen, his teachers and mentors were evidently strongly versed in and influenced by this theory, especially through Schmidt and Koppers. Culture circle theory and diffusion permeate Worms's linguistic and anthropological thinking, even though, as far as I am aware, Worms does not specifically mention the theory by name anywhere in his academic writings; nor, I think, does he ever use the word diffusion.[6] Other components of Father Schmidt's thinking about religion and culture circles are also evident in Father Worms's writings; again, these ideas are not always attributed to Schmidt.

Culture circle theory was developed by Leo Frobenius (1873–1938), and subsequently refined by Fritz Graebner (1877–1934) and Father Wilhelm Schmidt. The basic tenet is that cultural traits spread out from a centre of origin via diffusion of ideas and/or of cultural groups upholding those ideas. Schmidt developed the theory further, adding the notion of culture complex, an entity comprising various features embracing all cultural domains (material culture, economy, social life, religion, etc.) that form functionally interrelated sets of cultural traits. Culture complexes develop from a centre of origin and may diffuse over large areas of the world.

The former component, diffusion, is perhaps the more immediately obvious in Worms's writings, both linguistic and anthropological. However, culture complexes are more implicit, though discernible to some degree—in particular, Worms evidently presumes that sets of interconnected phenomena are what primarily spread as packages.

Crucial to the culture circle theory is the notion that ethnology is history: 'Ethnology is history or it is nothing', according to Schmidt (cited in Brandewie 1990: 99). This idea is strong in Worms's anthropology; the historical dimension is ever present in the synchronic facts, which are consistently interpreted diachronically. As usual, this is mirrored in his linguistics; as I have remarked elsewhere (Nekes and Worms 2006: 19), Nekes and Worms consistently confused synchronic and diachronic dimensions in their linguistics—and perhaps believed it artificial to separate them. And, although in many places in their writings they used temporal terms, apparently they did not always imbue them with temporal significance.

Diffusion is the primary historical mechanism that Worms alluded to, though it is often unclear whether he is talking about diffusion of ideas or movement of people; these are also often confused in his works. Where he apparently talks as though ideas have diffused, it is not always clear that this is not a consequence of movement of the people holding the

---

6   The only publication of Worms's that I am aware of (thanks to Ganter, Chapter 14, this volume) that mentions 'culture circles' explicitly is a newspaper report (Worms 1947).

ideas, and in places migration is explicitly mentioned as the vector for diffusion of ideas. Indeed, one gets little sense of internal developments within a culture (complex) or language (or language family). Thus, at times, he speaks of strata of Aboriginal languages or peoples as though some of the contemporary languages or societies have remained virtually unchanged—in both geography and their systems. This reading prevails in various places even though one finds a number of explicit statements to the contrary.

One such original stratum was the 'pygmoid' Tasmanian Negroid population, which, according to Worms, previously inhabited the entire continent. Contemporary remnants of this group are the Cairns rainforest people in Queensland (Worms and Petri 1998: 95). Mythological references to earlier 'races' of small stature in the western Kimberley, northern Central Australia and western Arnhem Land are taken as evidence supporting the original spread of these people. A later mainland Australoid population subsequently migrated into Australia, Worms maintained, taking over most geographical regions. The influence of Schmidt's notion that pygmies represent the ethnographically oldest people of the world (Brandewie 1990: 69), and were indeed the oldest group in Australia (p. 117), is obvious.

Another obvious influence from Schmidt concerns the earliest religion, which Schmidt argued in his 12-volume work on religions of the world was monotheistic—'primitive monotheism'—and that south-east Australians had a notion of a highest being. In Worms's writings of the 1940s (e.g. 1947) and 1950s (e.g. 1950a: 642), we find expression of this notion. By the time of 'Australische Eingeborenen-Religionen', however, Worms had moderated his views—or perhaps Petri moderated them for him. Thus, according to Worms and Petri (1998: 126), there is insufficient evidence for belief in a single highest god among mainland Aboriginal cultures. At best, there is evidence for belief in *demas*, or sublime beings. Belief in a single highest god may, Worms admits, have been present in Tasmania, but the evidence is insufficient to be certain.

If diffusion is so important, its direction immediately emerges as a concern—and Worms invariably identifies directionality. How does he motivate it? Sometimes it is simply stated and left unargued. In some instances, directionality follows from presumed prehistoric population movements—for instance, the migration of a 'powerful' group, the Aranda, who (it is claimed) moved down from Papua New Guinea to Central Australia and presumably represented a cultural complex.

In some instances, claims by Aboriginal people are used to motivate directionality. Evidently, Worms sometimes asked his consultants where particular phenomena came from—for example, fire-making artefacts (Worms 1950b). In some instances, mythological evidence was employed; this could be in the form of information contained in a myth or evidence of the spread of myths based on contemporary knowledge. Recent history in a few cases provided evidence, as in the case of diffusion of sections and section terms into Dampier Land, where both historical records and local knowledge of Aboriginal people indicate that these social categories and the terms for them are recent, and replace a former generation moiety system. Succession of styles in overlays in some rock art is interpreted as evidence for directionality of movement of styles and/or people, where some of the overlaying styles are limited in geographical distribution.

In some cases, Worms adduces linguistic evidence in support of directionality of diffusion. In no instance does this evidence make a convincing argument. Consistent with the idea that sets of cultural and linguistic phenomena diffuse together as a bundle, Worms presumes that the direction of borrowing of lexical items is consistently unidirectional, that lexical items are always borrowed in one direction and that this direction is also consistent with the direction of borrowing of corresponding cultural notions, artefacts, and so forth. Worms frequently uses these ideas in making his arguments, and in refuting counterclaims. Thus, he critiques Davidson (1947) on the directionality of diffusion of some fire-making artefacts on the grounds that this direction goes counter to the direction of borrowing of the terms for the artefacts.

Certainly, etymologies can be used to support diffusion of cultural phenomena, assuming that it can be shown that a term for a cultural notion or artefact was borrowed in a particular direction. But Worms never produces such evidence. His etymologies do not support directionality or, if they do, they are of items not directly relevant to the diffused phenomena, or the alleged 'etymologies' are in reality lemes, not etymologies.

As already mentioned, Worms showed little interest in social anthropology. The closest he comes to this theme is in his treatment of social divisions (moieties, sections and subsections) and, to a lesser extent, kinship. His treatment of these themes, however, largely concerns diffusion, and concerns of social organisation and interpersonal interaction are barely touched on. As mentioned above, Worms realised that sections were a relatively new introduction to the Dampier Land region and that they had begun to make inroads into the peninsula only in the early decades of the twentieth century, when they began replacing an earlier generation moiety system. The ongoing diffusion of the section system could hardly have escaped him and was obvious from statements from Aboriginal people themselves. In typical fashion, Worms put the centre of diffusion in Central Australia—in particular, the Arrernte people—and proposed that it emanated from there outwards to the southern Kimberley region and ultimately Dampier Land (Worms 1950b: 156–7).

Worms also discussed the diffusion of subsections and used lemes to support his story of their diffusion (Worms and Petri 1998: 180–1). In particular, he claimed that the 16 terms for the eight subsections (two terms, one male, one female, for each subsection) in Kukatja represented 12 words for 'human being'. Where the figure of 12 comes from is not explained and is inconsistent with the data he presents; nor does Worms say what the 12 words for 'human being' actually are or comment on their provenance. He correctly observed that terms for the males of subsections begin with the palatal stop while those for females begin with a nasal, and divided each of the 16 terms into two components, the first of which is a term meaning either 'man' or 'woman' (not 'human being'!). One infers that Worms sees the subsection terms as composites of pairs of lexical items meaning 'human being' and 'man'/'woman', and that these exemplify the leme 'human being'. Worms's excursus into this domain is a clear illustration of how badly one can be misled by lemes. There may be formal similarities between the components Worms identifies and terms for 'human being'. However, his proposed leme is not very convincing and has little explanatory adequacy; nor does Worms's discussion provide any insights into the diffusion of subsections or terms for them. More obvious and plausible correspondences are between initial syllables of the subsection terms in Kukatja (and a number of nearby languages) and gender prefixes in some languages of the Victoria River district, and the remainders with section terms from two different sets, as shown by Patrick McConvell (1985a, 1985b).

I wind up this discussion with an example of one of Worms's better arguments for directionality, albeit one that still falls short of being convincing. Worms (1950b: 152) uses the words of a Yawuru fire-making song to support the argument that the fire saw was borrowed from the south, and ultimately came from Central Australia and Papua New Guinea. Given the song words are from Aranda, the song may reasonably be presumed to originate there also, though whether or not it was contemporary with the development of the fire saw is impossible to say. If not, and the song developed much later than the implement itself—as would seem likely—it would be irrelevant to the direction of diffusion of the fire saw. And, surprisingly, Worms does not discuss the word for 'fire saw'; it seems more plausible to associate the direction of borrowing of the lexeme with that of the item than with the direction of borrowing of an associated song.

Conclusions

In this chapter, I have given an overview of Father Worms's contribution to Australian Aboriginal anthropology. There are many gaps in the story presented and further research is needed on a number of issues. I single out two of these as particularly important. First, what was the nature of the intellectual background of and influences on Father Worms? In particular, we need to know more details on what was taught at the Limburg Seminary, both by Father Nekes and by Worms's other teachers. Father Nekes still appears to me as a rather shadowy figure in the background (Nekes and Worms 2006: 11–12), and it would be useful to gain a clearer idea of his linguistic and anthropological thought and the influences on these from Schmidt, Koppers and others. Ganter (Chapter 14, this volume) provides some relevant information in this direction, though many details need to be filled in. In addition, we need to know more about Worms's interaction with Helmut Petri and his influence on Worms's thinking.

Second, what was the relationship of Worms's anthropology to mainstream Australian anthropology of the time, and Worms's relations with other Australianist anthropologists? Worms evidently read widely in the Australian anthropological literature and was familiar with relevant work, particularly in religion; however, the impact of his ideas on Australianist anthropology and of Australianist anthropology on his thinking remains somewhat uncertain. We know that personal relations with Professor A. P. Elkin were not always good and that Worms blamed Elkin—not entirely without justification, though in fact Elkin was right that the manuscript was really unpublishable—for problems in publishing *Australian Languages*. On the other hand, a number of his contemporaries were more favourably disposed to Worms. Norman B. Tindale (1974) dedicated his major work to Father Worms: 'To the memory of Father Ernest A. Worms whose active encouragement, beginning in the year 1952, led to the preparation of this work in its present form.' And W. E. H. Stanner had this to say in his 1967 address at the Australian Student Christian Movement conference in Canberra:

> [The Aboriginal religious mentality] is still only variably appreciated by Christian missionaries to the Aborigines—by some, not at all; by others, very sensitively understood. I can think of no one whose insight and empathy could compare with, let alone exceed, that of the late Fr. Worms. (Worms and Petri 1998: xi)

Regardless of Worms's difficult personal relations with Elkin, I think it is fair to say that the latter was not nearly as dismissive of Worms's anthropological work as R. M. W. Dixon was of his linguistic work, especially on Dyirbal (see Dixon 1972: 365–6; 1977: 510).

I conclude with my own evaluation of Worms's contribution to Australianist anthropology. To begin with, many of his diffusionist notions are interesting, though they lack clarity (e.g. movement of what exactly?) and have little evidential basis. Specifically, the linguistic evidence he cites to substantiate his proposals is completely unconvincing. The lemes he employs are almost completely lacking in constraint. Although some/many/all may have some viability, there is no compelling reason to believe they do, and there is no evidence that they show anything significant or unique about Aboriginal modes of thought. The person leme in subsection terms is a case in point.

The main value of Worms's anthropological research is probably descriptive and documentary. Some of the mythological materials he gathered, especially in Dampier Land and nearby areas, may be important, especially given the current state of the languages and (presumably) current knowledge of traditional mythology and culture. But, in many cases, the usefulness of this material is reduced by the lack of association with particular places. As remarked above, unlike the typical missionary, Worms's contact with Aboriginal groups was usually quite brief; thus, his descriptions and documentations of both religion and languages lack depth compared with those of missionaries such as Carl Strehlow. My own feeling is that Worms's and Nekes's contribution to Aboriginal linguistics is more significant than Worms's contribution to Aboriginal anthropology.

References

Brandewie, E. 1990. *When Giants Walked the Earth: The life and times of Wilhelm Schmidt SVD*. Fribourg: Fribourg University Press.

Capell, A. 1956. *A new approach to Australian linguistics*. Sydney: University of Sydney.

Davidson, D. S. 1947. Fire-making in Australia. *American Anthropologist* XLIX: 426–37. doi.org/10.1525/aa.1947.49.3.02a00040.

Dixon, R. M. W. 1972. *The Dyirbal Language of North Queensland*. Cambridge: Cambridge University Press. doi.org/10.1017/CBO978 1139084987.

Dixon, R. M. W. 1977. *A Grammar of Yidiny*. Cambridge: Cambridge University Press. doi.org/10.1017/CBO9781139085045.

Huegel, F. 1981. Memoirs about Fr Ernest Worms, missionary, pioneer and scientist. Unpublished ms, Beagle Bay Mission, WA.

Kenny, A. 2013. *The Aranda's Pepa: An introduction to Carl Strehlow's masterpiece Die Aranda- und Loritja-Stämme in Zentral-Australien (1907–1920)*. Canberra: ANU E Press.

McConvell, P. 1985a. The origin of subsections in northern Australia. *Oceania* 56: 1–33. doi.org/10.1002/j.1834-4461.1985.tb02105.x.

McConvell, P. 1985b. Time perspective in Aboriginal culture: Two approaches to the origin of the subsections. *Aboriginal History* 9(1): 53–80.

McGregor, W. B. 2005. Frs Herman Nekes and Ernest Worms' dictionary of Australian languages, Part III of *Australian Languages* (1953). In *Proceedings of the 2004 Conference of the Australian Linguistic Society*. Sydney: University of Sydney. Available from: ses.library.usyd.edu.au//bitstream/2123/108/1/ALS-20050630-BMc.pdf.

McGregor, W. B. 2007. Frs Hermann Nekes and Ernest Worms's 'Australian Languages'. *Anthropos* 102: 99–114.

McGregor, W. B. 2008a. History of fieldwork on Kimberley languages. In *Encountering Aboriginal Languages: Studies in the history of Australian linguistics*, (ed.) W. B. McGregor, pp. 403–35. Canberra: Pacific Linguistics. doi.org/10.1075/hl.35.1-2.07mcg.

McGregor, W. B. 2008b. Missionary linguistics in the Kimberley, Western Australia: A history of the first seventy years. *Historiographia Linguistica* 35(1–2): 121–62.

Nekes, H. 1931–47. Kimberleys language material: D'aro, N'ol N'ol, etc. Unpublished ms, 7 parts.

Nekes, H. 1938. The pronoun in Nyol-Nyol (Nyul-Nyul) and related dialects. In *Studies in Australian Linguistics*, (ed.) A. P. Elkin, pp. 139–63. Sydney: Australian National Research Council.

Nekes, H. and Worms, E. A. 1953. *Australian Languages*. Fribourg: Anthropos Institut.

Nekes, H. and Worms, E. A. 2006. *Australian Languages*. Berlin: Mouton de Gruyter.

Schmidt, W. 1919. *Die Gliederung der australischen Sprachen: geographische, bibliographische, linguistische Grundzüge der Erforschung der australischen Sprachen* [The classification of Australian languages: Geographical, bibliographical, fundamental aspects of research on Australian languages]. Vienna: Mechitharisten-Buchdrückerei.

Tindale, N. 1974. *Aboriginal Tribes of Australia: Their terrain, environmental controls, distribution, limits, and proper names*. Berkeley, CA, and Canberra: University of California Press and Australian National University Press.

Worms, E. A. n.d. *The Making of Stone Spear Points*. [8 mm film.]

Worms, E. A. 1938a. Die Initiationsfeiern einiger Küsten—und Binnenlandstämme in Nord-Westaustralien [The initiation rituals of some coastal and inland tribes of north-western Australia]. *Annali Lateranensi* 2: 147–74.

Worms, E. A. 1938b. Foreign words in some Kimberley tribes in north-western Australia. *Oceania* 8: 458–62. doi.org/10.1002/j.1834-4461.1938.tb00436.x.

Worms, E. A. 1938c. Onomatopoeia in some Kimberley tribes of north-western Australia. *Oceania* 8: 453–457. doi.org/10.1002/j.1834-4461.1938.tb00435.x.

Worms, E. A. 1940. Religiöse Vorstellungen und Kultur einiger nordwest-australische Stämme in fünfzig Legenden [Religious beliefs and culture in some tribes of north-west Australia in fifty legends]. *Annali Lateranensi* 4: 213–82.

Worms, E. A. 1941. Australian native languages disprove some theories of evolution. *The Advocate*, 13 March: 17.

Worms, E. A. 1942a. Die Gorangara-Feier im australischen Kimberley [The Gorangara ritual in the Australian Kimberley]. *Annali Lateranenses* 6: 207–35.

Worms, E. A. 1942b. Sense of smell of the Australian Aborigines: A psychological and linguistic study of the natives of the Kimberley division. *Oceania* 13(2): 107–30. doi.org/10.1002/j.1834-4461.1942.tb00373.x.

Worms, E. A. 1944. Aboriginal place names in Kimberley, Western Australia: An etymological and mythological study. *Oceania* 14(4): 284–310. doi.org/10.1002/j.1834-4461.1944.tb00405.x.

Worms, E. A. 1946. The Aboriginal mind at work: Semantic notes on Australian languages. *Mankind* 3(8): 231–2.

Worms, E. A. 1947. Primitives believed in one god not many. *The Advocate*, 5 March: 11–12.

Worms, E. A. 1949. An Australian migratory myth. *Primitive Man* 22(1–2): 33–8. doi.org/10.2307/3316209.

Worms, E. A. 1950a. *Djamar*, the creator, a myth of the Bād (west Kimberley, Australia). *Anthropos* 45: 641–58.

Worms, E. A. 1950b. Feuer und Feuerzeuge in Sage und Brauch der Nordwest-Australier [Fire and fire-making tools in myths and customs of the north-western Australians]. *Anthropos* 45: 145–64.

Worms, E. A. 1952. Djamar and his relation to other culture heroes. *Anthropos* 47: 539–60.

Worms, E. A. 1953a. Australian ghost drums, trumpets and poles. *Anthropos* 48: 278–81.

Worms, E. A. 1953b. H. Nekes' and E. A. Worms' 'Australian Languages'. *Anthropos* 48: 956–70.

Worms, E. A. 1953c. Petroglyphs at the headwaters of the Yule and Fortescue rivers. *Anthropos* 48: 630.

Worms, E. A. 1954. Prehistoric petroglyphs of the upper Yule River, north-western Australia. *Anthropos* 49: 1067–88.

Worms, E. A. 1955a. Bei den Australiern [Among the Australian Aborigines]. *Die Kath. Missionen* 5: 145–7.

Worms, E. A. 1955b. Contemporary and prehistoric rock paintings in central and northern Kimberley. *Anthropos* 50: 546–66.

Worms, E. A. 1957a. Art gallery found in the desert. *Catholic Weekly*, 13 June: 11.

Worms, E. A. 1957b. Australian mythological terms: Their etymology and dispersion. *Anthropos* 52: 732–68.

Worms, E. A. 1957c. The poetry of the Yaoro and Bad, north-western Australia. *Annali Lateranensi* 21: 213–29.

Worms, E. A. 1957d. Prehistoric rock carvings: Some fascinating discoveries in West Australia. *Air Travel*, March: 14–16.

Worms, E. A. 1958a. Capell's new approach to Australian linguistics. *Anthropos* 53: 270–1.

Worms, E. A. 1958b. Language of the Gogadja tribe (south and south-east of Gregory Salt Lake). Unpublished ms, Sydney.

Worms, E. A. 1958c. M. Fischer-Colbries linguistisch-ethnologische Untersuchung der Pankala [M. Fischer-Colbrie's linguistic-ethnological investigation of the Pankala]. *Anthropos* 53: 591–6.

Worms, E. A. 1959a. Der australische Seelenbegriff [The Australian concept of soul]. *Zeitschrift für Missionswissenschaft und Religionswissenschaft* 42: 296–308.

Worms, E. A. 1959b. Australian Aboriginal Rock Art, by F. D. McCarthy. [Review.] *Anthropos* 54: 640–1.

Worms, E. A. 1959c. The Tiwi: Their art, myth and ceremony, by C. P. Mountford. [Review.] *Anthropos* 54: 641–3.

Worms, E. A. 1959d. Verbannungslied eines australischen Wildbeuters: ein Beitrag zur Lyrik der Bad [Banishment song of an Australian poacher: A contribution on the lyrics of the Bad]. *Anthropos* 54: 154–68.

Worms, E. A. 1960a. The Aboriginal concept of the soul. *The Australasian Catholic Record* 37(2): 100–15.

Worms, E. A. 1960b. The changing ways of our Aborigines. *The Catholic Weekly*, 16 June: 1.

Worms, E. A. 1960c. Tasmanian mythological terms. *Anthropos* 55: 1–16.

Worms, Ernest A. 1961. Konferenz zum Studium der australischen Eingeborenen in Canberra, ACT, Australien [Conference on the Study of Australian Aborigines in Canberra, ACT, Australia]. *Anthropos* 56: 632.

Worms, E. A. 1963. Religion. In *Australian Aboriginal Studies: A symposium of papers presented at the 1961 research conference*, (ed.) H. Sheils, pp. 231–47. Melbourne: Oxford University Press.

Worms, E. A. 1970. Observations on the mission field of the Pallottine fathers in north-west Australia. In *Diprotodon to Detribalization: Studies of change among Australian Aborigines*, (eds) A. R. Pilling and R. A. Waterman, pp. 367–79. East Lansing: Michigan State University Press.

Worms, E. A. 1972. Les religions primitives d'Australie. In *Les religions du Pacifique et d'Australie*, (ed.) C. M. Schröder, pp. 153–391. Paris: Payot.

Worms, E. A. 1974. Cahiers de terrain, Kimberley, Australie du nord-ouest, 1937–1963 [Field notebooks, Kimberley, north-western Australia, 1937–1963]. Unpublished ms, Institut d'Ethnologie, Musee de l'Homme, Paris.

Worms, E. A. 1986. *Australian Aboriginal Religions*. Sydney: Nelen Yubu Missiological Unit.

Worms, E. A. and Petri, H. 1968. Australische Eingeborenen-Religionen [Australian Aboriginal religions]. In *Die Religionen der Südsee und Australiens* [*The Religions of the South Pacific and Australia*], Vol. 5, No. 2, (ed.) C. M. Schröder, pp. 125–329. Stuttgart: W. Kohlhammer Verlag.

Worms, E. A. and Petri, H. 1998. *Australian Aboriginal Religions*. Sydney: Nelen Yubu Missiological Unit.

14

Historicising culture: Father Ernst Worms and the German anthropological traditions

Regina Ganter

When the shy and unobtrusive, often trembling, Catholic Father Ernst Worms (SAC)[1] arrived in Broome at the end of 1930 and was asked 'and how do you like Broome, Father?', he responded with polite lies and presumably told his interlocutors what he thought they might like to hear. What he would have liked to tell them was that it was 'gross'.[2] He saw a society divided along the minute spatial geographies of race and class, and thoroughly exploitative. He sent his mentor in Limburg a West Australian pocket yearbook with the comment:

> [L]ook at the high wages in Broome, whereas the non-whites, i.e. blacks, half-castes, Chinese, Malays, and Japanese, are given dogs' wages [*werden mit einem Hundelohn abgespeist*]. Blacks are almost always given £1 a month! The government doesn't care.[3]

1   Worms later Anglicised his Christian name to Ernest. SAC stands for Society of the Catholic Apostolate, colloquially referred to as the Pallottines, named after their Italian founder, (Saint) Vincent Pallotti. The author acknowledges the assistance of the Australian Research Council Future Fellowship ARC FT100100364.
2   Kurt Benesch, *Mission Aktuell* 1/1975, in Worms, Ernst, P. (1891–1963), pp. 1–27, Zentralarchiv der Pallottinerprovinz [hereinafter ZAPP], Limburg.
3   Worms to Nekes, Broome, 22 March 1932, in Nekes, Australien B7d, l(2), ZAPP.

Worms's unpublished writing was often crafty, witty with a dry humour and gentle in his appraisal of the foibles of his brethren. He tried to live up to the expectations of his superiors as the pioneer of a new age of missions.

Father Worms (1891–1963) was the first of the Pallottine stormtroopers of the Prefect Apostolic in the Kimberley, Father Otto Raible (SAC), who had a grand vision for an expanded Pallottine presence in the Kimberley. In 1935, Raible became the first Pallottine bishop in Australia. The German Pallottines had been in the Kimberley since 1901, but it took until 1935 before they were awarded the ecclesiastic administration of the Kimberley vicariate. Raible defended their sphere of influence on two major fronts: against the competing Spanish Benedictines based at New Norcia, who had challenged the presumed Pallottine territory with their Drysdale River Mission, and against the increasing intervention of a secular state bureaucracy claiming absolute control over Aboriginal affairs in Western Australia. Raible's new age of mission involved the acquisition of a productive farm in the emerging southern wheatbelt (Tardun); the (short-lived) introduction of two experts in tropical medicine from the Würzburg institute for mission medicine, a Catholic college founded in 1922 (Leugers 2004: 112),[4] Dr Johann Betz and his wife, Ludwina Betz-Korte;[5] the introduction of a professor of linguistics from the Orientalist Seminar in Berlin, set up to train public servants in the German empire, Dr Hermann Nekes (SAC); and the establishment of a theological training college in Kew, Melbourne. The last initiative resulted in a generation of Australian-born Pallottines and stood the Society of the Catholic Apostolate (SAC) in good stead during and after World War II and eventually assisted the shift from remote Indigenous mission to urban youth work inspired by the German Pallottine *Schoenstatt* movement, which focused on the involvement of laity. The Pallottines in Melbourne became strongly involved with Catholic Action, an anti-communist movement associated with Bob Santamaria that caused the Labor Party split in 1956 (Nailon 2001: 161–3).

Worms, trained in the *Schoenstatt* tradition, had been associated with a similar youth initiative after his ordination in 1920, when he was stationed near Königsberg to minister to *Neudeutsche* ('new Germans') after the redrawing of national boundaries at the end of World War I (Ihle 1968: 405–27). Worms received two months of training in mission

---

4   For the Würzburg institute, see: www.medmissio.de/.
5   'Betz, Johann Dr and Ludwina Betz-Korte', in Ganter (2016).

medicine at the Würzburg college before he travelled to Australia in November 1930 on the German Lloyd ship *Trier*, which carried almost 100 German missionaries of different denominations to Singapore, destined for various parts of the Asia-Pacific.[6]

Worms's training in theology and philosophy at Limburg reflected the intellectual traditions of the German universities.[7] He commenced his Australian research very much within the vision explicated by Rudolf Virchow regarding the capacity of missionaries to inform, collect and research, which formed part of the German instructions for scientific travellers and collectors that left the theorising to the metropole and favoured the recording of observations in the field 'uncontaminated by theory'.[8] Worms began his work in the Kimberley with wideranging scientific observations. For at least the first three months in Broome, he meticulously recorded the weather, including temperature, cloud cover, wind direction, rainfall and any unusual phenomena. He inspected a petrified tree (at a place recorded as Ten Mile Mill) and followed up on reports of a figure of Christ appearing in the intertidal zone. He also visited the Port Hedland rock art galleries already described by Elkin and Basedow and subject to much discussion and speculation.

Worms spoke German, English, French and Latin and his theological training in Limburg had included linguistic training (1918–20) from Hermann Nekes (SAC), who was known for his work in Cameroon— the major field of Pallottine involvement—on tonology and foreign influences in the Bantu languages. During his first year in Broome, Worms began working on the Yawuru language under the guidance of Nekes in Limburg. Worms was very awake to the cultural influences and dramatic changes being wrought on the Kimberley communities by the lugger industries that brought many Asians to the northern ports and provided easy mobility for its Indigenous workers. Broome, in particular, had become a second home to many workers from Timor, Rote and other nearby islands (Yu 1999: 49–73). By May 1933, Worms urgently requested a Malay grammar. The core of his work became the attempt to decipher layers of cultural influences on the roadmap of the diffusionist

---

6   Josef Schüngel SAC to Bernd Worms, 2 August 1988, in Worms, Ernst, P. (1891–1963), pp. 1–27, ZAPP.
7   See, for example, descriptions of the training in Dresden and Neuendettelsau by Christine Lockwood (2014) and Anna Kenny (2013), respectively, and under the menu item 'More— Missionary training' in Ganter (2016).
8   Virchow (1888), discussed in Murray (2004: 130–42). See also Janice Lally (2008: 191–215).

and historicising German ethnographic tradition that survived until the 1950s and 1960s (Gingrich, Chapter 2, this volume), and it was this theoretical cage that prevented Worms from accepting the many voices arguing for extraneous influences on Aboriginal cultures and languages.

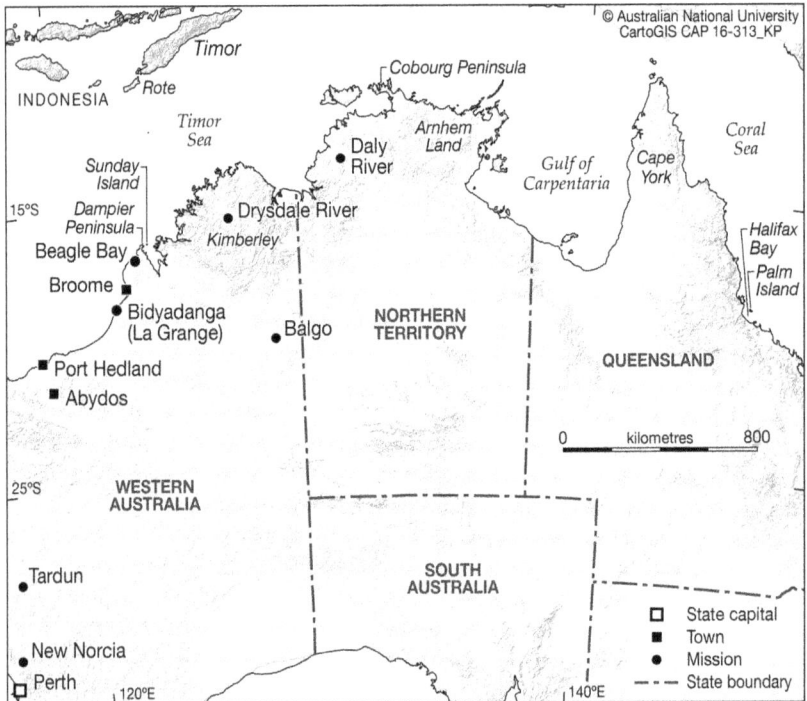

Map 14.1 Locations mentioned in the text.
Source: CartoGIS, The Australian National University.

Not a Malay grammar, but Nekes himself arrived in the Kimberley in 1935 with the newly appointed Bishop Raible. Nekes was very familiar with the work of Father Wilhelm Schmidt (SVD: Society of the Divine Word). Schmidt was founder and editor of the *Anthropos* journal, president of the International Congress of Anthropological and Ethnological Sciences and founder of the papal missionary ethnological museum in the Lateran Palace in Rome. Schmidt was known for his contribution to the study of the language families of the world, with the identification of the Mon-Khmer language as a link between Asian and Austronesian languages. Schmidt's eight-volume *Ursprung der Gottesidee* (*The Origin of the Idea of God*, 1955) asserted monotheism as the condition of primitive religions, and he subscribed to the idea of pygmy races as an *Urvolk* observable across the world—an idea that had emerged in Germany in the 1890s and was also adopted by Norman Tindale and Joseph Birdsell (1941).[9] Implicit in Schmidt's work was the deeply held assumption, shared with his German-speaking contemporaries, that language reflected the *Volksgeist*, so that language, culture and religion formed a cohesive cultural complex (Gingrich, Chapter 2, this volume; Kenny 2013).

These four ideas are mirrored in the work of Worms without being explicitly theorised: 1) an affirmation of a basic unity of Aboriginal languages, as distinct from the Tasmanian languages, which were ascribed to 2) a prior *Ur*-population, 3) traces of monotheism in these older cultural strata, and 4) the idea of the centrality of language in expressing and communicating culture. Worms did not see it as his task to develop new theories, only to map his findings on to the contemporary credible explanatory paradigms.

It was Schmidt's (1919) work on the structure of Australian languages that led Worms to think of his magnum opus on Australian religion along the fault lines of a significant distinction between 'Australian' and 'Tasmanian' religions as a working title for his book.[10] In 1962, Worms was 'just polishing' the manuscript, expecting an imminent publication; alas, the book did not appear until after his death, heavily edited and reconceptualised with the fault lines flagged in the title shifted for a more modern audience to 'Australian' and 'South Pacific' religions.[11] Worms had already realised in 1958, when he reviewed Arthur Capell's book on Australian languages, that Schmidt's structure of Australian languages was 'no longer tenable', but it was too late for him to rethink his book on religions and he could not give up the underpinning idea of migration and diffusion that had scaffolded all his work.[12]

---

9   Schmidt's urgent appeal in 1910 to study the pygmy races is discussed in Gusinde (1957).
10   Worms had as a working title 'Die Religion der australischen und tasmanischen Eingeborenen' (The religion of the Australian and Tasmanian Natives).
11   The work was published as Worms and Petri (1968).
12   In his book review, Worms conceded that the Victorian languages were not as archaic as Schmidt thought and that there was little evidence of a southward movement of the Victorians, nor could the Victorian languages be considered a block. Aranda, on the other hand, could not be considered an erratic appearance in the Australian languages as Schmidt had thought. A relationship between the Tasmanians and the northern Queensland pygmoids could not be established and it was likely that the languages that had developed in Victoria represented an autochthonous development that rendered Schmidt's theory of waves of migration untenable (Worms 1958).

Schmidt, in common with the weight of opinion among German ethnographers in the nineteenth century, was strongly anti-evolutionist, resisting the idea of a progression of humankind from primitive to cultured. One of Schmidt's disciples, Wilhelm Koppers, sent Worms a copy of a little-known 1959 German publication on 'the error of Darwinism' (Nachtwey 1959), which expressed the anti-evolutionist stance they all shared.[13] Worms felt that the German 'new ethnology' of Ratzel, Graebner, Frobenius and Schmidt 'harmonised with Catholic thought', because it resisted evolutionist thought and therefore made room for the Christian creation story, and because it affirmed the existence of monotheistic conceptions in primitive cultures rather than positing a unilinear development from atavistic to polytheist and finally monotheist religions. In one of his populist publications in 1947, Worms single-handedly dismissed the work of Frazer, Tylor, Spencer and Morgan as 'pre-modern ethnology' 'enslaved to evolutionism' and craftily asserted that only the English scholars ('except for Andrew Lang') still lagged behind 'new ethnology' (all of which was in German). He leaned on Max Müller's ideas about the 'heaven fathers' of ancient European societies to refute allegations by Australianists such as Howitt that the 'missionaries had invented the high God' in their interactions with Indigenous people (Worms 1947: 11).

Clearly, Worms's ethnography was driven by the desire to comprehend Aboriginal religion in terms that were decipherable to Christian thought. The basic, though largely implicit, tenet of Worms's work was that in the Kimberley an older stratum of beliefs included an all-father, who was public knowledge and could be freely referred to, and this was over-layered with more recent influences from the geographic centre (Worms 1955a). He observed about the Bardi that they practised monogamy and their initiation involved the knocking out of a tooth (Worms 1938a). He also discerned in the Bardi language a morphological connection between the word for sun and terms associated with initiation, and therefore supposed that the older culture may have had a sun-worshipping component (one of the 'lemes' identified by McGregor, in Chapter 13, this volume, as a linguistic technique used by Worms). All of these characteristics were taken as indicators of an older culture observable in the Kimberley in keeping with Schmidt. A shared and identifying element of the newer

---

13   This book, along with many others gifted to Worms by his German colleagues, even well after his retirement, remains in the library of the Pallottine house in Kew to which Worms retired.

ideas, stories, ceremonies and objects was that they were protected with restrictions and secrecy. Worms deciphered this diffusion through comparisons with the findings of Ronald and Catherine Berndt from Arnhem Land and of Carl Strehlow on the Aranda and Loritja/Gogadja. Worms gradually adjusted his orthography to that of these three authors, leaving behind his initial adherence to Schmidt's *Anthropos* alphabet, which was not favoured by English speakers, so *Bād* became *Bard*, *N'ol-N'ol* became *Njul-Njul*, *Jaueru* became *Yaoro* and *Gorañara* became *Guraɳara*, more akin to Berndt's *Kurangara*, a recent ritual complex to which Worms devoted much thought. Worms remained strongly devoted to the *Kulturkreislehre* ('culture circle theory') concept of Schmidt and Koppers, which he romanticised as a methodological tool:

> [We] must use historical culture-circle method, a very complicated and exacting technical procedure which could be compared to the work of a geologist in determining relationships and stratifications in the earth. (Worms 1947: 11)

Worms used every methodological instrument available to him—oral history, legends, observations of culture, language morphologies and, finally, rock art—to decipher diffusion, and attempted to place changes in a historical framework to match them with these German theoretical approaches.

A detailed description of the stages of initiation (published in German in 1938a) emphasised several *Kulturkreis* elements.[14] The quartz knives used had been brought from the mountainous inland and had the same name on the coast and in the desert. Several of the ceremonies required the collaboration of people other than one's own, and the ceremony of the Karajarri he witnessed was held on mission land much further north, outside their territory (Worms 1938a, 1938b). Elsewhere, Worms also noted that, among the Bardi, the four-week-long preparatory instructions taught the young men ceremonial words for everyday objects—often obsolete or foreign words (Worms 1950a). One of the Karajarri initiation songs could not be translated as the performers claimed not to understand the words. It was just the same with initiation songs of the Bardi, Dyaro and Nyulnyul, and Worms commented that he often encountered this with regard to texts that had been imported along the Fitzroy River.

---

14   Worms specified that he studied Karajarri (Garadyari at La Grange, Cape Bossute), Yawuru (Yaoro around Broome), Bardi (Baad at Lombadina), Nyulnyul (Beagle Bay), Jaru (Dyaro, south of Halls Creek) and also Walmajarri (Walmadyeri/Warmala, towards Gregory Salt Lake).

This comment served to support his suggestion of a cultural diffusion from the centre, but Worms omitted to mention that Strehlow had already described the same phenomenon—of a secret ritual language—among the Aranda.[15]

Worms managed to translate the Nyulnyul song and sent it, together with a wax cylinder, to Marius Schneider at the Völkerkundemuseum in Berlin. He realised early that the explanation that a text had come from elsewhere, and could therefore not be translated, might be a layer of protection. With regard to the curse incantations of the *Kurangara/Gorangara* complex, he wrote:

> This supposed untranslatability, and the endeavour to ascribe the origin of a curse song to another group of people, stems from the desire to protect a larger secret and leave to a distant tribe the odium of having created such a supposedly gruesomely effective saying. (Worms 1940: 221)[16]

Still, he lent much credibility to explanations of texts, objects and ideas as 'coming from the east'. Worms showed one *tjuringa* (he used the Aranda term with Strehlow's spelling) that was given to him (possibly his first) to several different people, all of whom gave somewhat different explanations of it. One said it had come from the Nykina (neighbours towards the east), one said it had come from the Ngarinyin (located in the north-east) and another said it had come from the Walmadjeri (located in the south-east) (Worms 1950a: 641–58). It is not clear whether the informants referred to the object itself, the meaning inscribed on it or the very idea of the *tjuringa*, as a cultural import. (Worms was well aware that *tjuringa* were also made locally.) Worms used this range of information on the same object to show the ubiquity of explanations of things 'coming from the east'. (In my opinion, a subject position on the west coast of a peninsula on the West Australian coast almost dictates that practically everything comes from the east—even if just a little further east, such as Galalang coming from Sunday Island.)

---

15 'Teil Das Soziale Leben der Aranda und Loritja, I. Abteilung' in (Strehlow 1907–20: Vol. IV, pp. 28–32) and 'II. Abteilung' (Vol. II, pp. 47–54).
16 *'Diese angebliche Unübersetzlichkeit und das Bestreben, die Herkunft der Fluchgesänge einem anderen Volke zuzuschreiben, entspringt dem Wunsche, ein grösseres Geheimnis zu schützen, und das Odium der Urheberschaft eines nach ihrer Ansicht so grausig wirksamen Spruches einem entfernt wohnenden Stamme zu überlassen.'*

Because of frequent references to influences coming from the east, and because of his theoretical mind map, Worms consistently discounted a cultural influence from the north. For example, in response to a study by Daniel Sutherland Davidson arguing that the fire saw had been imported 'from the direction of Timor' (Davidson 1947), Worms published an alternative explanation in the same year in which Griffith Taylor also reaffirmed a much older pygmoid migration from New Guinea or the Philippines (Winlow 2009). Worms agreed that the fire drill was the older technology, not subject to any restrictions, and that the fire saw was a more recent introduction and was used only by elder males. Worms had visited the so-called pygmy tribes of Halifax Bay and Palm Island and found that one of these groups did not have the fire saw. He also determined that the words for fire were similar between these north Queensland languages and those of Tasmania and the Kimberley (Worms 1950b). This observation is suggestive of the pygmy migration theory embraced by Schmidt, which imagined this older civilisation pushed to the margins of the continent. Worms agreed with Davidson that the older fire drill must have accompanied the 'earliest migration' from Cape York towards the west. But he discounted a South-East Asian origin for the fire saw—first, because it was also known to the eastern pygmoid people at Palm Island and Cape York; and second, because the Nyulnyul assured him that the fire saw had come to them from the east. On the basis of a comparison of 29 languages in the Kimberley, New South Wales and north Queensland, Worms assumed that the fire saw was imported from the southern suffixing languages, ultimately from Central Australia (Aranda), and had moved northwards across the Dampier Peninsula (Worms 1950b).

Worms's language morphologies were imaginative (see McGregor, Chapter 13, this volume), but, trapped by theory and a literal understanding of oral history, he never sought the same kinds of ('lemic') similarities between Australian and Malay languages. By Worms's own method, one might find the similarity between *garidja*, the mythical eagle ancestor that brought fire to the Bardi, according to Worms, and *garuda*, the Indonesian term for eagle deriving from Sanskrit, where it denotes a mythical bird-man, at least striking, and would begin looking for similar word/meaning pairs, perhaps at Cobourg Peninsula, where Father Confalonieri had already undertaken significant language work.

Similarly, although Worms recognised that circumcision and subincision (and the four-class marriage system) had been adopted in the Kimberley in the not too distant past, he ignored the potentially extraneous origin of some of the words given to him for the stages of male initiation. For example, at the second stage of initiation, a young man was called *nindi* or *orongganyano*. With recourse to a Malay grammar, Worms might have found the first part of the alternative term suggestive of the Indonesian word *orang* ('man'/'person'). The fifth level was described as *bungana*, not unlike the term *bunggawa* used in the trepang fishery for 'headman' and related to the term *abang* for 'elder brother'—an Indonesian respectful address (Macknight 1969, 1976). At Elcho Island, where a succession of elders have liberally revealed the Macassan connection, the secret-sacred language used in rituals was explained as a form of Malay (or at least containing many Malay words), the language that was also used to address the first Europeans in the Top End.[17]

Elders in the Kimberley have made no such disclosure and, at any rate, the theory underpinning the work of Worms did not countenance such an extraneous influence. The cultural and linguistic similarities between the Kimberley and the centre that Worms found reflected in the work of Carl Strehlow suggested a Central Desert origin for most phenomena that he identified in the Kimberley as more recent. He concluded that there were many signs of the imposition of a Central Australian culture on the more primitive north-west Australian culture (Worms 1950b). By more primitive, he meant an older culture that was less complex than the contemporary one, rather than undeveloped in the evolutionist sense.

Worms published 50 Kimberley legends in German (1940) to which he referred as migratory myths and plumped these for religious ideas. He attempted to arrange the various culture heroes in historical order of arrival in the Kimberley (Djanba – Djamar – Minau or Bamar – Galalang). This attempt at theorising (Worms 1952) is not very convincing,[18] perhaps because the project was upended by the regional 'nicknames' with which

---

17   Interview with Terichini Yumbulul, Galiwin'ku, Northern Territory, June 1995. He was the son of David Burrumarrra, a chief informant for the Berndts, Ian McIntosh, Peter Spillett and others regarding Macassan contact (McIntosh 1994; Ganter 2006: 42, and passim).

18   Djamar is judged to be extraneous although he was said to have come to Lombadina from (nearby) Sunday Island. Galalang, thought to represent the oldest and 'indigenous' stratum, was also described as having come from Sunday Island (like Djamar) when the informant was only a boy. Minau, also referred to as Bamar, were said to have introduced obscene dances as well as polygamy, circumcision and subincision (and therefore sound more like a composite of Djanba and Djamar). The Bardi informants (but not the Nyulnyul) thought Galalang's times were better, which suggests that Galalang's times had only recently receded, so that a two-tier cultural shift, rather than a four-tier one, seems a more credible interpretation of Worms's results. One Bardi man referred to the people at Cossack (pearling harbour) as cannibals, indicating that they had very different customs from the Bardi, and he himself preferred the 'olden time', related to Galalang (Worms 1952).

Luise Hercus also struggled in the Diyari legends.[19] Djanba, the most recent introduction, was associated with the '*Gorangara* cult', which Worms and Bishop Raible first encountered near Balgo in 1938. Worms described it as an immoral, dangerous cult of black magic that was spreading across the Kimberley, striking fear into people. Worms had no inkling that it was a contact cult directed against colonisation (Redmond, Chapter 16, this volume), just as the Jesuit missionaries on the Daly River had observed the *Tyaboi* in the 1890s without any idea that they themselves featured in its ritual enactments (Rose 1998).

Missing from Worms's historical line-up of culture heroes in 1952 was Djanggala, the supernatural being of the Kimberley, which Worms thought was a local version of Djanggawul, reported by Berndt in Arnhem Land. The Berndts were supplying ample evidence of a lively contact and traffic between Makassar and south-east Arnhem Land that had ended only in 1906, including the oft-cited story of Djalajari, who had spent many years in Makassar and had a family there (Ganter 2006: Ch. 2). But the Berndts rendered Macassan terms in unrecognisable spelling, often unsuspecting of a Malay origin of words they took to be Yolngu-matha. For example, the Berndts refer to a place in Arnhem Land as 'Libabandria' without realising that this is the Macassan name Lembana panrea (meaning Tradesmen's Bay) adopted into Yolngu-matha. Kampung Maluku, a district of Makassar, is rendered as Kambu'malagu, Captain Daeng Tompo appears as 'karei Deintumbo buga' (which includes both *karaeng*/'king' and *bunggawa*/'headman'). Captain Husein Daeng Rangka, also known as Jago ('fighting cock'), appears in Djalajari's story recorded by Berndt as Captain Jadjung, identifiable by his vessel, the *Patti Jawaya*, written as *Batadjowa*.[20] Similarly, among the 43 terms Mawulan gave to Berndt in 1947 for objects and parts of a lugger, there are also recognisably Indonesian words such as *gula* ('sugar') for syrup, rendered

---

19   Luise Hercus (Chapter 5, this volume) referred to some of the *mura-mura* recorded by Reverend Georg Reuther, which she was able to identify only through reference to the work of Spencer.

20   Other Macassan placenames in Arnhem Land were Lemba Moutiara (Pearl Shell Bay) and Lemba Bingangaja (Trepang Bay). The Yolngu also adopted the Macassan placename of Kodinggareng Island for Gunyanggarra (aka Ski Beach at Yirrkala), and Garra-mangalai in Caledon Bay (aka Grays Bay) derives from Karaeng Mangnellai (King Mangnellai, referring to the genealogy of the Macassan captain Mangellai Daeng Maro) (Ganter 2006: Ch. 2; Macknight 1969: 180–5; Berndt and Berndt 1954: 53).

as *gwula*.[21] What all this means is that the rendition of an unrecognised loan word must be read with some latitude (for example, Djalajari is also rendered as Charley Charley).

Worms's guiding theories prevented him from casting his inquiries towards such extraneous influences from the north, though he well knew that contact between different Aboriginal groups in the lugger industries had produced a bewildering array of new customs and ideas.[22] He assumed that the starting point of introduced terms and customs was somewhere in South Australia and the Central Desert, but he was, at this early stage of Australian linguistics, unable to draw on a consistent method to identify the changes to which word stems had been subjected. Much more recently, Nicholas Evans's study of Macassan loan words at Cobourg Peninsula, based to a large degree on the work of Father Angelo Confalonieri in the 1840s, found that the Iwaidjan languages are the 'linguistic equivalent of a well-stratified archaeological language site' (Evans 1997: 239). Evans uses a credible methodology for identifying linguistic adaptations, whereas, 50 years earlier, Worms was casting around, guided by the methods of Nekes and Schmidt (see McGregor, Chapter 13, this volume).

It was the Frobenius Expedition in 1938–39 that directed Worms's attention to rock art as a way of deciphering historical layers of culture. Before their arrival, Douglas C. Fox, the American journalist who accompanied the expedition and who had mounted an African and European rock art exhibition at the Museum of Modern Art in New York in 1937 with Leo Frobenius, sent the accompanying book to Bishop Raible.[23] Leo Frobenius had founded the Research Institute for the Morphology of Civilisations in 1923 (and the Deutsche Gesellschaft für Kulturmorphologie), a fringe school of thought hotly discussed in Germany but virtually

---

21 Not being familiar with Malay, Makassar or other regional languages, I am only able to identify Indonesian words. When I pointed out the *gula/gwula* similarity in a personal communication at the Berndt Museum in 2013, Sandy Toussaint's Indonesian-speaking assistant was able to identify further Indonesian words in the same document: Mawulan's drawing on butcher paper, June 1947, Berndt Collection, Nr. 7246, Berndt Museum of Anthropology, Perth.

22 Worms observed that much of this circulation of culture arose from the work on the pearling luggers and innovations were still within living memory. For example, the two-class skin system of the Kimberley had been replaced with the four-class system (of the Aranda, according to Worms) through contact with Ngamula people at Cossack since the 1870s (Worms 1952).

23 This book, with a dedication by Fox, is held in the Pallottine library in Kew (Frobenius and Fox 1937).

unknown elsewhere.[24] The idea of cultural morphology sat well with the historicising diffusionist empiricism also present in Schmidt, at least in methodological terms. The Pallottines welcomed this expedition to their northern missions and, in Worms's biographies, his role in the Frobenius Expedition is somewhat overstated, suggesting that Worms facilitated or hosted the expedition.[25] In fact, Frobenius was unable to accompany the expedition, and Helmut Petri's book arising from it makes little reference to Father Worms, other than a criticism of his 'Aranda origin' theory (Petri 1954). (Petri also omits to mention the Australian emerging scholar Arthur Capell, who accompanied them.) Worms met Petri on his arrival in the Kimberley (after which Worms and Raible set off to find an alternative site for the Rockhole mission in the desert area, later called Balgo) and again at the conclusion of Petri's northern fieldwork in January 1939. They also met many years later at the end of Worms's own Wenner-Gren Foundation–funded fieldwork in October 1960, when Worms met up with Petri and Gisela Petri-Odermann at La Grange mission to record Garadjeri (Karajarri) songs,[26] and presumably also during Worms's German lecture tour in 1947.

Petri and Lommel's exhibition of Aboriginal rock art in London in January 1947 received much attention (Worms 1953b) and spurred Worms into further work on northern Australian rock art, which was also receiving increasing attention in Australia (Basedow 1925; Elkin 1930). Unlike the visitors from overseas and the south, he was able to position himself as the resident expert, and based himself in Broome again for a Wenner-Gren Foundation research grant in 1953 and 1954 to decipher layers of cultural periods from petroglyphs and pictograms. He revisited the rock art galleries at Port Hedland and galleries in the Abydos/Woodstock area of the Pilbara, along the Gibb River and near Kalumburu. Worms became

24 Professor André Gingrich explained that the Frobenius school of cultural morphology might be characterised as a neo-Herderian German romanticism with an anthropomorphic frame that focused on cycles of emergence, maturity and decay of cultures. In a personal communication, he added that it was somewhat 'fringe'. See Gingrich (Chapter 2, this volume).
25 News reportage emphasised Worms's role in hosting the Frobenius Expedition. For example: 'Dr. Petri, of the Frankfort Ethnological Museum, who is the leader of the Frobenius expedition for the comparative study of primitive and prehistoric culture, will arrive to-day by the overland express. He made thorough researches of the cave paintings in the north of Western Australia. Dr. Petri will be the guest of Father Rector Worms, of the Pallottine Missionary College, Kew' (*The Argus*, [Melbourne], 10 January 1939: 6). See also 'Kimberley natives', *West Australian*, [Perth], 7 November 1938: 16.
26 Worms, E. P., *Cahiers du Terrain*, Musée National des Arts Africains et Océaniens, (fieldnotes, in German), Microfiche held by the Australian Institute of Aboriginal and Torres Strait Islander Studies (AIATSIS), Canberra.

the first to describe some sites near the government research station at Abydos/Woodstock, later called Father Worms Hills, and counted his work on rock art as his most significant contribution to science. Although Worms does not make this explicit, it is reasonable to assume that his ways of seeing rock art were by now guided by the work of Frobenius, Petri and Lommel. What he saw was 'a succession of aboriginal and ethnic migrations' (leaning now on ideas of migration rather than diffusion). At Gallery Hill, the depictions of sexual acts were confined to the upper stratum of the 'Woodstock figures'. The absence of traces of the masculinist *Gorangara* cult from the lower strata of rock images confirmed that it could not be autochthonous and was clearly introduced. Worms also observed that the *Gorangara* had not yet reached Port Hedland.

One of Worms's missionary predecessors, the Spanish Father Nicholas Emo, had already produced a sketchbook of the *giro-giro* (Bradshaw figures, aka Gwion Gwion) at the Drysdale River Mission in 1909.[27] These drawings had also been described in 1937 by C. P. Mountford, who felt that, along the northern coast, Aboriginal art had reached a higher state of development than elsewhere and presumed that this was through contact with Malay pearl and trepang fishers. Worms agreed that the style of the *giro-giro* figures was much more sophisticated than other rock art styles and most likely executed with a brush. But he did not accept a Malay influence, because the sheer number and ubiquity of these paintings 'render an esoteric isolation impossible'. Worms thought they were executed in a 'bushman-like' manner and favoured a comparison with various African and Spanish rock art styles. He reported that the local owners claimed that the authors of these paintings, which had no relevance to them, were a people called *giro-giro*. Returning to the pygmy tribe thesis, Worms suggested that they belonged to 'a pre-Australoid', a 'negrito-Tasmanoid settler period' (Worms 1955b: 565 ff.). Worms cited a number of legends from different areas about a now extinct people of short stature. For example, he cited Strehlow on the story of the Tuanjiraka, small men who once lived north of the MacDonnell Ranges—again, without suggesting any connection to *tua* ('old') or *tuan* (a polite address in Indonesian) (Worms 1955b). If not

---

27 'Emo, Nicholas Fr.', in Ganter (2016). Worms erroneously claimed that 'Emu' had drawn these in 1905; however, Emo was not at Drysdale that year, so perhaps Worms had this from hearsay and never saw the sketches. They ended up in the Museum of South Australia, where they are ascribed to the ornithologist Gerald Hill, who visited the Drysdale River Mission in 1910. Emo's diary at that time refers to his work of copying the rock art—mostly while lying on low ledges—and expresses the fear that Hill may claim the work as his own.

for the theoretical frame of reference supplied by Schmidt, the linguistic puzzle pieces of meaningful or accidental similarities could have formed a very different pattern for Worms. The once intriguing pygmy theory has certainly fallen into disfavour for lack of evidence, and, indeed, the idea of an older cultural stratum does not require a 'pygmoid' population. More recent work confirms a long period of desertion of the Kimberley between ice ages that may explain the traces of different cultural strata. Robert Bednarik now suspects a migration most probably from Timor or Rote about 60,000 years ago (Bednarik 2010). Julia Martínez and Adrian Vickers supply an overview of maritime mobility in eastern Indonesia in the historical past and speculate that 'the name *Jawi*' (neighbouring the Bardi on Dampier Land) 'may even come from reference to Indonesians' (Martínez and Vickers 2015: 49).

In 1953, Worms and Nekes's major work on Australian languages was finally being published (in microfilm), premised on the fundamental unity of Australian languages and religions. That year Worms also responded to Ronald Berndt's (1951) study of the Kunapipi complex in Arnhem Land, which included the suggestion that Kunapipi represented an Asiatic, pre-Islamic 'great mother' cult or a Macassan importation. Worms was aware that the dingo had come from South-East Asia 'in the mists of time' (Worms 1955a: 146), and he also observed that the bamboo trumpet described by Berndt was slowly progressing from the Northern Territory through the east Kimberley towards the west and the ceremonial pole had also made its appearance in the western Kimberley in two instances. However, Worms doubted that Kunapipi could be a Macassan importation, because the name Kunapipi was so strongly rooted in genuine Australian terms (Worms 1953a).

Worms's commitment to a basic homogeneity of mainland Aboriginal cultures that could be discovered through linguistic analysis prevented him from accepting the idea of foreign influences. He always returned to the idea that 'it must be endogenous' (Worms 1953a) in the sense that whatever it was that he was examining must have originated from somewhere on the Australian continent.

Worms's period of publications commenced in 1938 when he became the rector of the Pallottine College in Melbourne after a fall from his horse that exacerbated a wartime injury and confined him to a corset, which made fieldwork in the tropical north all the more uncomfortable. At Kew he sought publicity for the missionary work of the Pallottines, who were breaking out of their sphere of influence in the Kimberley into the south. Worms tried to resist cultural stereotypes about Aboriginal people and attempted to insert a humanist perspective, always emphasising their equal intelligence in the framework of Pastor Herder's model of the unity of mankind. In a radio interview with the *Südwestrundfunk* (SWR), he went so far as to perform a corroboree song on air. While practically under house arrest in Kew during World War II, Nekes (1875–1948) and Worms produced their oeuvre on the Kimberley languages.

Worms also published the results of an experiment on the sense of smell, which Nekes had replicated from C. S. Myers of the 1898 Cambridge anthropological expedition to Torres Strait. Nekes had intended it as a linguistic experiment, but Worms used it to demonstrate that, against many assertions about the 'uncanny' overdeveloped sense of smell among Aborigines, there was no evidence of any hyperacuity among Indigenous people. Their sense of smell showed the same ranges of perception and agreement as that of white people and, moreover, was overdetermined by recent experiences. The greatest gender difference was the smell of tar, which Worms suspected may stem from the identity-forming experiences of men on the luggers,[28] while women may associate luggers and tar with uncomfortable travel and sea-sickness. The greatest overall agreement was on the smell of incense, and Worms was quick to accede that this most likely stemmed from the use of incense in church (Worms 1942b).

Worms began his publication phase at the same time as Petri, with work in the Vatican's ethnological series *Annali Lateranensi* (1938a, 1940, 1942a and 1957b) and *Oceania* (1938b, 1942b), an Australian international journal established in 1931 and edited by the part-German Anglican rector Adolphus Elkin, who had a special interest in the Kimberley. However, in the early 1950s, one of Elkin's students, Mabel Wyllie, produced a scathing critique of Catholic mission policy.[29] From that time, Worms eschewed *Oceania* and began to publish in the ethnographic journal *Anthropos*, founded by Schmidt (two in 1950, 1952, three in 1953, 1954, 1955, 1957, two in 1958, 1959, 1960, 1961).[30] He produced two co-authored books, over 20 academic journal articles, several book chapters and many minor publications, including book reviews. Every publication required

---

28 On the sense of pride obtained through lugger work, see Ganter (1994).

29 Mabel Wyllie, 'A study of polygynous marriage with special reference to northern Australia … and the attitude thereto of administration and Christian missions' (1952), cited in Erckenbrecht (2003).

30 For a full list of Worms's publications, see 'Worms, Ernst Fr.', in Ganter (2016).

the prior approval of the Pallottine Provincial and was reviewed by two internal censors (Leugers 2004: 113). Nevermann commented that Nekes had brought photographic equipment from Germany in 1935, but Worms 'has hardly any photographs suitable for reproduction' (Worms and Petri 1968: 129). However, the Pallottine archives in Limburg and those in Rossmoyne (Perth) have many good-quality photographs, though unsorted and mostly without provenance. Worms curated the ethnographic exhibition housed until recently in the Pallottine mother house in Limburg, which included many of the objects he described in his publications, and several photographs in that exhibition (and presumably also many in the photo collection) were from Worms.

Worms gained an international reputation as a missionary anthropologist.[31] During a series of lectures in the United States in April 1960, he participated in a symposium at a Central States Anthropological Society meeting in Bloomington, Indiana, speaking about the cultural changes wrought in Indigenous society, alongside the grand and emerging figures of Australian anthropology, Adolphus Elkin, W. E. H. Stanner, Catherine and Ronald Berndt, Jane Goodale, Arnold Pilling, Peter Worsley, Jeremy Long and others (Worms 1970). The following year, W. E. H. Stanner invited Worms to present at the conference that inaugurated what is now the Australian Institute of Aboriginal and Torres Strait Islander Studies. At age 69, Worms obtained a second Wenner-Gren research grant for a nine-month-long expedition to Central, northern and Western Australia during which he visited Ayers Rock (Uluru), the Simpson Desert and rock art sites in Arnhem Land, and saw bark paintings for the first time. His fieldwork journal mentions Bathurst and Melville islands, the northern coast and Mangingrida, Daly River, Port Keats, Katherine, Borroloola, Amoonguna, Alice Springs, Yuendumu, Papunya, Santa Teresa, Balgo and La Grange (mostly mission stations). In the process, he was organising

---

31 Worms followed invitations to speak in Rome, Munich, Münster, Vienna and at the Frankfurt Frobenius Institute, as well as the Smithsonian Institute in Washington, DC, the Verley University in San Francisco and the Congress of Anthropological and Ethnological Science in Philadelphia. In his last year, Münster University obtained funds from the DFG (Deutsche Forschungsgemeinschaft, the German equivalent of the Australian Research Council) to invite him back for a semester of guest lectures in the theological faculty, but he became too ill to travel and had to decline this and invitations from Cologne and Nijmegen.

his ideas for his major oeuvre on Aboriginal religions. Religion was, after all, his area of expertise and the reason ethnography and linguistics were considered legitimate missionary tasks.[32]

Worms consistently discounted the impact of South-East Asian contact as a significant cultural factor and, rather, looked for the large-scale migration of ideas and people on the continent itself. Everywhere he found evidence of an intensive cultural and linguistic movement between the south-east and north-west of Australia, with 'relatively small and unimportant' traces of a foreign element from the East Indies (Worms 1957a: 762). Trying to make historical sense of the multitudinous cultural influences engulfing the Kimberley, Worms mapped his observations against contemporary theories. He was limited—as are we all—by his linguistic capacities, or else he might well have cast his net of imaginative language morphologies in very different directions and may have distanced himself from Schmidt's language structure much earlier.[33] The pygmy migration theory was not essential for his assertions of diffusion, but it guided him into a search for historical layers of culture and cultural shifts.

Worms was deeply imprinted by Christian and German intellectual traditions that led him to a humanitarian approach to Indigenous people and to attempt to historicise cultural influences with a range of methods. The greater parts of his publications were in German and, since evolutionary theory has now lost its supremacist edge, Christian creationism has lost its interest in scientific discovery and migration theory has been muted by fears over native title implications, Worms's work has been marginalised,[34] along with much of the work of German missionaries in Australia. For those interested in paradigm shifts, as well as for those interested in documenting attachment to place, there is still much to be discovered from the detailed empirical research left by Worms and other German missionaries, and my website on German missionaries in Australia attempts to render such work more easily accessible (Ganter 2016).

---

32   In his fieldwork diary, Worms noted pointers for inquiry ('religious indifference of the Australians?'), sources to which he wanted to refer and the major insights he wanted to demonstrate, such as 'the Australian indigenous expressions ("termini") are neither childish ways nor mere metaphors, but meaningful phrases—see Jungmann II', or 'the wanjina board and string figures (gamba) in Kew and Manly are ancestor figures' (Worms, *Cahiers de Terrain*, AIATSIS).

33   In his book review of Capell, Worms (1953b) admitted that the central planks of Schmidt's structure of Australian languages were no longer tenable.

34   McGregor (2005: 16; 2007) determined that the dictionary produced by Worms and Nekes 'presents particularly important information on cultural practices and phenomena that have to my knowledge long since been forgotten'.

References

Basedow, H. 1925. *The Australian Aboriginal*. Adelaide: F. W. Preece.

Bednarik, R. G. 2010. Australian rock art of the Pleistocene. *Rock Art Research* 27(1): 95–120.

Berndt, R. 1951. *Kunapipi: A study of an Australian Aboriginal religious cult*. Melbourne: Cheshire.

Berndt, R. and Berndt, C. 1954. *Arnhem Land: Its history and its people*. Melbourne: Cheshire.

Davidson, D. S. 1947. Fire-making in Australia. *American Anthropologist* XLIX: 426–37. doi.org/10.1525/aa.1947.49.3.02a00040.

Elkin, A. P. 1930. Rock-paintings of north-west Australia. *Oceania* 1(3): 257–79. doi.org/10.1002/j.1834-4461.1930.tb01649.x.

Erckenbrecht, C. 2003. Der Bischof mit seinen 150 Bräuten [The Bishop with the 150 wives]. *Leipzig: Jahrbuch des Museums für Völkerkunde* 41. pp. 303–322.

Evans, N. 1997. Macassan loans and linguistic stratification in western Arnhem Land. In *Aboriginal Australia in Global Perspective*, (eds) P. McConvell and N. Evans, pp. 237–60. Oxford: Oxford University Press.

Frobenius, L. and Fox, D. C. 1937. *Prehistoric Rock Pictures in Europe and Africa*. New York: Museum of Modern Art.

Ganter, R. 1994. *The Pearl-Shellers of Torres Strait: Resource use, development and decline, 1860s–1960s*. Melbourne: University of Melbourne.

Ganter, R. 2006. *Mixed Relations: Asian–Aboriginal contact in north Australia*. Perth: University of Western Australia Press.

Ganter, R. (ed.). 2016. *German Missionaries in Australia*. [Online.] Brisbane: Griffith University. Available at: missionaries.griffith.edu.au/biographies.

Gusinde, M. 1957. A pygmy group newly discovered in New Guinea: A preliminary report. *Anthropological Quarterly* 30(1): 18–26. doi.org/10.2307/3316681.

Ihle, R. 1968. 'Unter den Ureinwohnern Australiens': Biografie von Ernst Worms ['Among the Australian Aborigines': A biography of Ernst Worms]. In *Pioniere und Aussenseiter – 21 Biografien* [Pioneers and Dissidents – 21 Biographies]. Darmstadt: Turis Verlag.

Kenny, A. 2013. *The Aranda's Pepa: An introduction to Carl Strehlow's masterpiece Die Aranda- und Loritja-Stämme in Zentral-Australien (1907–1920)*. Canberra: ANU E Press.

Lally, J. 2008. The Australian Aboriginal collection and the Berlin Ethnological Museum. In *The Makers and Making of Indigenous Australian Museum Collections*, (eds) N. Peterson, L. Allen and L. Hamby, pp. 191–215. Melbourne: University of Melbourne Press.

Leugers, A. 2004. *Eine geistliche Unternehmensgeschichte – Die Limburger Pallottiner-Provinz 1892–1932* [A spiritual enterprise history – the Pallottine Province of Limburg 1892–1932]. St Ottilien: EOS Verlag.

Lockwood, C. 2014. The two kingdoms: Lutheran missionaries and the British civilizing mission in early South Australia. PhD thesis. University of Adelaide, Adelaide.

McGregor, W. B. 2005. Frs. Hermann Nekes and Ernest Worms's Dictionary of Australian Languages, Part III of 'Australian Languages' (1953). In *Proceedings of the 2004 Conference of the Australian Linguistics Society*, (ed.) I. Mushin. Sydney: University of Sydney. Available at: ses.library.usyd.edu.au/handle/2123/93.

McGregor, W. B. 2007. Frs. Hermann Nekes and Ernest Worms's 'Australian Languages'. *Anthropos* 102(1): 99–114.

McIntosh, I. 1994. *The Whale and the Cross: Conversations with David Burrumarra MBE*. Darwin: Historical Society of the Northern Territory.

Macknight, C. C. 1969. *The Farthest Coast*. Melbourne: Melbourne University Press.

Macknight, C. C. 1976. *A Voyage to Marege: Macassan trepangers in northern Australia*. Melbourne: Melbourne University Press.

Martínez, J. and Vickers, A. 2015. *The Pearl Frontier*. Honolulu: University of Hawai'i Press. doi.org/10.21313/hawaii/9780824840020.001.0001.

Murray, B. 2004. Georg Balthasar von Neumayer's directives for scientific research. In *The struggle for souls and science: Constructing the fifth continent—German missionaries and scientists in Australia*, Occasional Paper No. 3, (ed.) W. Veit, pp. 130–144. Strehlow Research Centre, Alice Springs, NT.

Nachtwey, R. 1959. *Der Irrweg des Darwinismus* [The error of Darwinism]. Berlin: Morus.

Nailon, B. 2001. *Nothing is Wasted in the Household of God: Vincent Pallotti's vision in Australia 1901–2001*. Melbourne: Spectrum.

Petri, H. 1954. *Sterbende Welt in Nordwest-Australien* [The dying world of north-west Australia]. Braunschweig, Germany: A. Limbach.

Rose, D. B. 1998. Signs of life on a barbarous frontier: Intercultural encounters in north Australia. *Humanities Research* 2: 17–36.

Schmidt, W. 1919. *Die Gliederung der Australischen Sprachen* [The structure of Australian languages]. Vienna: Mechitharisten-Buchdruckerei.

Schmidt, W. 1955 [1912–52]. *Der Ursprung der Gottesidee* [The origin of the idea of god]. 12 vols. Münster: Aschendorff.

Strehlow, C. 1907–1920. *Die Aranda- und Loritja-Stämme in Zentral-Australien*. 7 vols. Frankfurt am Main: Joseph Baer & Co.

Tindale, N. B. and Birdsell, J. B. 1941. Tasmanoid tribes in north Queensland. *Records of the South Australian Museum* 7(1): 1–9.

Virchow, R. 1888. Anthropologie und prahistorische Forschungen [Anthropology and prehistoric research]. In *Anleitung zu wissenschaftlichen Beobachtungen auf Reisen* [Instructions for scientific observations on journeys]. *Volume II*, (ed.) G. B. von Neumayer, pp. 295–326. Berlin: Verlag von Robert Oppenheim.

Winlow, H. 2009. Mapping the contours of race: Griffith Taylor's zones and strata theory. *Geographical Research* 47(4): 390–407. doi.org/10.1111/j.1745-5871.2009.00604.x.

Worms, E. A. 1938a. Die Inititiationsfeier in NW-Australien [The initiation ceremonies in North-West Australia]. *Annali Lateranensi* 2: 147–74.

Worms, E. 1938b. Foreign words in some Kimberley tribes in North-western Australia. In *Studies in Australian Linguistics*, Oceania Monographs No. 3, (ed.) A. P. Elkin, pp. 165–70. Sydney: Australian National Research Council.

Worms, E. A. 1940. Die Religiöse Vorstellungen und Kultur einiger Nord-westaustralischer Stämme in fünfzig Legenden [The religious beliefs and culture of some nort-western tribes in fifty legends]. *Annali Lateranensi* IV(4): 213–82.

Worms, E. A. 1942a. Die Goranara Feier im australischen Kimberley [The Goranara festivity in the Kimberley of Australia]. *Annali Lateranensi* VI: 207–35.

Worms, E. A. 1942b. Sense of smell of the Australian Aborigines: A psychological and linguistic study of the natives of the Kimberley division. *Oceania* 13(2). doi.org/10.1002/j.1834-4461.1942.tb00373.x.

Worms, E. A. 1947. Primitives believed in one god not many. *The Advocate*, 5 March: 11.

Worms, E. A. 1950a. Djamar, the creator. A myth of the Bad (west Kimberley, Australia). *Anthropos* 45: 641–58.

Worms, E. A. 1950b. Feuer und Feuerzeuge in Sage und Brauch der NW-Australier. *Anthropos* 45: 145–64.

Worms, E. A. 1952. Djamar and his relation to other culture heroes. *Anthropos* 47: 539–60.

Worms, E. A. 1953a. Australian ghost drums, trumpets and poles. *Anthropos* 48: 278–81.

Worms, E. A. 1953b. Die Unambal: Ein Stamm in Nordwest-Australien [The Unambal: A north-west Australian tribe]. *Man* 53: 163–4.

Worms, E. A. 1955a. Bei den Australiern [Among the Australians]. *Die Katholischen Missionen* 5: 146–148.

Worms, E. A. 1955b. Contemporary and prehistoric rock paintings in central and northern Kimberley. *Anthropos* 50: 546–66.

Worms, E. A. 1957a. Australian mythological terms: Their etyology and dispersion. *Anthropos* 52: 732–68.

Worms, E. A. 1957b. The poetry of the Yaoro and Bad. *Annali Lateranensi* 21: 213–29.

Worms, E. A. 1958. Capell's new approach to Australian linguistics. *Anthropos* 53(1–2): 270–1.

Worms, E. A. 1970. Observations on the mission field of the Pallottine fathers in north-west Australia. In *Diprotodon to Detribalization: Studies of change among Australian Aborigines*, (eds) A. Pilling and R. Waterman, pp. 367–80. East Lansing: Michigan State University Press.

Worms, E. A. and Petri, H. 1968. Australische Eingeborenen Religionen [Australian Aboriginal religions]. In *Die Religionen der Südsee und Australiens* [The Religions of the South Pacific and Australia], Vol. 5, No. 2, (ed.) C. M. Schroder, pp. 125–329. Stuttgart: W. Kohlhammer Verlag.

Yu, S. 1999. Broome Creole Aboriginal and Asian partnerships along the Kimberley coast. In *Asians in Australian History*, (ed.) R. Ganter, *Queensland Review* 6(2): 49–73.

Part IV: Academic anthropology

15

Doing research in the Kimberley and carrying ideological baggage: A personal journey

Erich Kolig

Is there a German tradition in anthropology?

In discussing the German anthropological tradition's involvement in Australian Aboriginal studies, my perspective in the first instance is that of 'participant observation'. That is, I am drawing on my personal acquaintance with some German anthropologists and on having used their work in my own research into Aboriginal socioculture. In this undertaking, I am instrumentalising my narrative to explore briefly and in some particular contexts what 'German tradition' means. On this level, I am purposely ignoring some poorly researched works that mistakenly refer to me as a German anthropologist (see Hill 2012). But by giving the preamble of the symposium from which this volume arises about the 'German anthropological tradition' in Australia a slightly wider scope and renaming it the 'German-language tradition of anthropology', it changes the perspective. By removing the nationalist innuendo and giving it a linguistic tinge, I become an exponent of this tradition, which I believe justifies my approaching this topic at least partly in terms of a personal journey. In my case, 'German anthropological tradition' thus needs to be understood in a larger context, which includes the Viennese school of anthropology.

In an intellectual sense, the close kinship—perhaps even identity—between German and Austrian anthropology is undisputed, although not so much in terms of homogeneity as in terms of incessant cross-fertilisation. To name only a few outstanding anthropologists who demonstrate by their career the closeness of German and Austrian anthropology: among the founding fathers of today's anthropology department at Vienna University, the Societas Verbi Divini (Society of the Divine Word: SVD) Patres Wilhelm Schmidt and Wilhelm Koppers, were German nationals by origin; Felix von Luschan, director of the Berlin Ethnological Museum for many years, was Austrian; and Helmut Petri, of whom I shall say more later, studied for a while at Vienna University under Schmidt, Koppers and Heine-Geldern,[1] before he became curator at the Viennese Ethnological Museum for a short period. In a much less fortunate sense, the closeness of the national branches of this discipline also manifested itself during the Nazi era prior to and during World War II, as in both countries the racist, politically instrumentalised agenda dominated (see Linimayr 1994).[2] Thankfully, globalisation processes have meanwhile already largely overcome nationally defined, even linguistically bounded, anthropologies and advanced the shaping of a largely global academic discipline that, despite its diversity, has created worldwide, transnational networks for the exchange of ideas, sharing of research and methodologies and, by and large, has developed a common foundation of ethical guidelines.

My investigation makes no claim to illuminate the essence of German anthropology—if there is one—or to strive for definitional objectivity; nor do I have normative ambitions to characterise the German input into Aboriginal anthropology. In this context, by interweaving the so-called German tradition rather egocentrically with my own work, I will examine only the 'German' sources that were relevant to my work. Moreover, the perspective of my contribution is located in the past (mainly the 1970s and 1980s). I cannot relate my experience to very recent developments in Aboriginal anthropology nor to the most recent evaluation or appreciation of the German-language contribution, as, for some time now, I have relocated my professional interests to other anthropological fields.

---

1   Lack of space prevents me from naming the dozens of similar careers.
2   The instrumentalisation of anthropology for colonialist purposes in the United Kingdom and France pales into insignificance in comparison with the misuse of anthropology by the so-called German Reich.

In the year before I joined the anthropology department in Perth (at the end of 1969), I had done fieldwork in the Hindu Kush mountains of Afghanistan. I then completed my PhD thesis at Vienna University and had a short stint at the Berlin Ethnological Museum, where I was selecting representative objects from the museum's large Australian Aboriginal collection for display in a new wing. By that time, I had accepted—with much optimism and a little trepidation—the challenge of doing fieldwork in Australia at the invitation of Ron Berndt, the then head of the West Australian anthropology department.[3] I was to undertake fieldwork in Fitzroy Crossing in the southern Kimberley; a place, as I learned later, where a couple of researchers had previously declined to work.[4]

Not long after my inauguration into Aboriginal research, I was invited to address the Anthropological Society of Western Australia on the topic of the Viennese school of anthropology. While I had fond memories of my years of study at the Viennese anthropology department, its fundamentally Catholic orientation had—for me, as an agnostically inclined Protestant[5]— been a source of alienation. (I felt I had been given to understand—in the nicest possible way, of course—that my professional future was not within the hallowed halls of this institution.) Another anthropological branch offered at the department, also historically oriented though less Catholic, was focused on Africa and worked in an ethno-historical mould. The Institut für Völkerkunde (Institute of Ethnology), as its proper name was at the time, was grounded in Catholicism because it had been dominated for a while by members of the Catholic order of the SVD. Most of them went on to become exponents of the *Kulturkreislehre* ('culture circle' theory) until its scientific demise shortly before my entry into the anthropological scene. But the institute's founding ethos lingered. Patres Wilhelm Schmidt, Wilhelm Koppers and others (Patres Gusinde and Schebesta) still had a shadowy presence (to some extent thankfully having survived the brief Nazi interlude). Among their legacy were the institute's totemism studies—mainly in terms of classification,

---

3   I owe Ron Berndt a debt of gratitude for having given me this chance and Catherine Berndt for her desperate attempts to mould my stubborn continental individualism into something more conventional in Australian anthropology.
4   A short personal résumé can be found in Burke (2011: 151–3). It would be churlish not to express my thanks to the many people—although I cannot name them here—in the field and in academia who helped with advice and deed: colleagues, missionaries, both Protestant and Catholic, welfare personnel, and many others.
5   Before the increasing secularisation of the bureaucratic apparatus wiped this practice out, all official personal documents (such as matriculation and enrolment papers) contained a reference to the person's religious affiliation.

definition and phenomenological description—which were, of course, of some interest to my new undertaking. But its hypothesis of the primeval *Hochgott* ('supreme god' or 'all-father') belief, vigorously propounded by Schmidt (1912–54) and Koppers (1949)—and, I believe, accepted by Carl Strehlow, but not by E. A. Worms[6]—was a different matter. It led me later to reject it in a small publication (Kolig 1992) in which I argued that where this belief could be found in Aboriginal Australia (e.g. the Baiame belief), it was of missionary provenance. In my view, it represented a cognitive shift in the traditional Aboriginal cosmology, but, at the same time, also revealed a clinging to a traditional conception of the workings and control of power. In my view, it was a first paradigmatic step in the transition from the somewhat static pre-contact mental universe towards a more fluid, innovative framing of political thought. This was quite different from the idea of the persistence of an ancient cosmological concept. However, at least the patres' firm argument about the primordial *Hochgott* cult turned the view of the *Naturvölker*'s primitiveness on its head by attributing respectable religious beliefs in a creator divinity—comparable with 'the best' of Christianity—to ethnicities that were widely regarded as the most 'ancient' and most 'primitive'. (In Lewis Henry Morgan's evolutionary diction, Aborigines represented primordial savagery par excellence.) It gave them at least a semblance of respect. I felt almost sorry that I could not agree with the monotheistic *Hochgott* theory.[7]

I am purposely referring to my background in some detail as an antidote to the mistaken belief that, as the label German tradition would insinuate, there is or was an intellectually cohesive, monolithic form of a coherent theoretical and philosophical orientation, perhaps even a school of thought, whether inspired by Herder or not. Viennese anthropology rested heavily on various brands of historical anthropology. However, I am doubtful that the Catholic manifestation of anthropology owed much to Herder's thought, despite its profound devotion to a historicist perspective. Equally, the purely ethno-historical school—an offshoot of the fundamentally diachronic approach of much of the German-language tradition, which was also represented at Vienna—had an exaggerated empiricist basis, probably as an antithesis to the speculative character

---

6   A short dalliance with this idea can be found in 'Djamar, the creator' (Worms 1950).

7   In the 1980s for a short while there seems to have been an attempt to create a centre for Aboriginal studies in the Viennese anthropology department. The initiative collapsed with the untimely death of the main agent. I believe it was meant to continue with the totemism studies that had been undertaken earlier. See Haekel (1950).

of other offshoots of the historical method. Lingering shades of the *Kulturkreislehre* and other cultural-historical perspectives were on offer, as well as extreme, empirically based diachronic serialisation, all of which provided a rather narrow theory range for aspiring adepts of anthropology. It meant that, by and large, I was without a spiritual home. Beyond that, the bewildering maze of what may be called the German-language tradition in anthropology invited me to construct, like a bricoleur, my own homespun anthropological nest. Internally totally incongruent and fragmented, not to say illogical, it was concocted from a mixture of holistic anthropology, relativism and phenomenology à la Husserl, Dilthey and Gadamer, with a shot of Bastian's *Elementargedanken* ('elementary thoughts'), ethno-science and Max Weber's melange of historical, idealist and materialist strands woven together. It then was rather wilfully and illogically pressed into G. F. Hegel's progressivist cosmology as presented in his *Phänomenologie des Geistes* ('phenomenology of the spirit') (see Kolig 1977). Cultural particularism and universalist leanings formed strange bedfellows in the composition of my anthropological world view. Looming in the background, though unacknowledged at the time, was probably also Herder's nationalist romantic legacy, which inclined me to turn my interest to 'culture' in the sense of world view, values, oral traditions, ethos and other intangibles and house all this within a relativist, mentalist framework, which, in turn, was cocooned in a universalist gossamer. With hindsight, it seems I embraced Herder's cultural relativism as a method of understanding, but not as an overarching cosmological structure where, in my mind, Kant and Hegel had the whip hand.[8]

Typical for my personal intellectual starting point was the recognition that the situation was far from presenting a monolithic German-language tradition in anthropology. The situation that confronted me was one of a bewildering multi-vocality, not to say a cacophony, of theoretical and philosophical positions. This heterogeneity was my spiritual home, leading to a fundamental confusion to which Herder had substantially contributed—a confusion that for a time I sought to mitigate with critical theory of the Frankfurt school kind, together with a good dose of Kantian

---

8   PhD students at Vienna University had to take courses in philosophy and pass exams as a precondition for gaining a philosophical doctorate. Most of the courses I chose were on Kant or in the neo-Kantian tradition—all, of course, in the broad tradition of German-language Enlightenment, which presupposes a kind of universalism adverse to relativism. I agree with Gingrich's (2005: 64) opinion when he rejects Norbert Elias's assessment that Enlightenment was carried mainly by French and Scottish philosophy and only in a minor and romantic-tainted way by German-language philosophy.

rationalism, before ruefully shifting back to Max Weber as the refuge for my theoretical inspiration. In all of this, overall, I regarded Herder as a distant figure, fairly much outside my magic henge of ancestor worship. I felt more fealty to Weber's brand of idealism through which he could argue that the rise of a religious belief—Protestantism of the Calvinistic kind—could bring about a socioeconomic revolution of a magnitude that would come to dominate the world today. It is possible, of course, that Weber's thinking was also guided by Herder's legacy, but I cannot recall that Weber explicitly acknowledges this. In any case, it was on a conscious level that Weber's capitalism argument led me into mentalist and ideological perspectives about Aboriginal socioculture. I augmented the potpourri with a precarious balancing act between Karl Popper's evolutionary philosophy of knowledge and my fascination with the Marxism-inspired sociology of knowledge represented by Karl Mannheim, Jürgen Habermas and others. Again, I linked my understanding of knowledge with Weber's idea of social and intellectual rationalisation and a slight modification of Popper's view by stressing a functional distinction between religious and scientific thought, whereby only the latter, on a rational-empiricist basis, is subject to evolutionary advance. This eclectic amalgam I brought to bear on my Aboriginal research.

Neighbourly relations with Helmut Petri and others

When I realised that my imminent career was to be centred on Aboriginal studies, and on the Kimberley in particular, the work and publications of Helmut Petri—who was based at Cologne University—became of great interest to me. (I knew Petri already from visiting seminars and lectures he had given at the Viennese department when I was a student.) Together with Andreas Lommel, Petri had undertaken fieldwork in the northern Kimberley (among Ngarinyin and to some extent Nyigena, while Unambal and Worora were more or less Lommel's domain) before World War II in the Frobenius Expedition. More recently, Petri was working in the Eighty Mile Beach area (in Anna Plains and especially on the Catholic mission station of La Grange, now called Bidyadanga) among mainly Nyangomada, but also desert people from the south and east (so-called Yulbaridja). Most of his publications were very ethnographically descriptively, empirically orientated with little theoretical underlay, although it can be argued that cryptically they contained the distant legacy of Herder and the concept of '*Kultur*' he had spawned. (The *Kulturmorphologie* Petri was trained in certainly took its cues from a humanist, culturist, relativist and historical perspective.) His publications and also those of his wife and research partner, Gisela Petri-Odermann, showed a fascination with the *geistige Kultur* ('mental culture'), the ethos and the political and religious culture of the people they studied. Their lively, descriptive ethnographic style made for interesting reading without making theoretical or philosophical demands. To my relief, there was nothing in their work of the boring kinship studies that seemed to dominate other ethnographies.

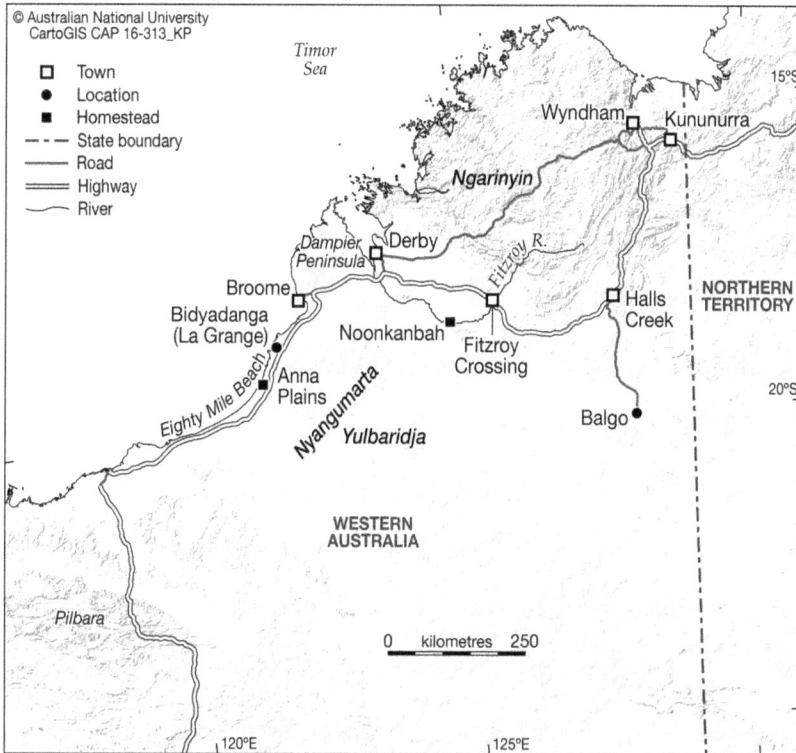

Map 15.1 Kimberley locations mentioned in the text.
Source: CartoGIS, The Australian National University.

The Petris' style of ethnography was often personalising and individualising their observations—in some cases, even mentioning the names of the people described or who were giving information. This closely descriptive style not only made for attractive reading, it also humanised Aborigines.[9] I am not sure if this style can be called proto-hermeneutic, but one of its strengths is that people are not subsumed under social functions, they do not become just anonymous agents exemplifying kinship systems or abstract cultural principles and as such are implied only in the narrative texture in sublimated form. They are identifiably individual actors with specific and quite different intentions and knowledge, day-to-day partisan political agendas and religious strategies—in short: possessing their own distinct personality.

The Petris' style of personalising and individualising their observations managed largely to avoid essentialisation, which today is so vehemently denigrated by positivist anthropologists. This descriptive, close-to-empirical-reality ethnography is absorbing to read but harbours a hidden difficulty. Referring to the personal views, thoughts and intentions of informants by name, even if it is done with the best and morally pure scientific intention and with the ideal of objectivity and emotional detachment in mind, may still invite protest, denial and even litigation by people so revealed, on grounds of defamation, false representation, insult or a number of other reasons. It can also have an unwanted side effect by creating internal conflict within the community. The German language protected the authors from such difficulties. The language barrier also allowed the Petris some liberties in another sense. It made it easier to set aside rules of religious secrecy and the gender barrier that applies in religious knowledge.

The linguistic discreteness of Petri's publications—from an Australian viewpoint—meant that preserving the secrecy of esoteric information to which he was privy was less of a problem, and other culturally based restrictions also could be circumvented with relative ease. That Petri-Odermann after Helmut's death was grappling with this is evidenced by an interview she gave (Beer 2007: 160) in which she muses over ethics concerning preserving the gender division in trying to publish her

---

9   In a review of Monteath (2011), Oliver Haag (2012: 134) remarks on the 'human twist in portraying Aboriginal people in German documents' referred to in this book. Haag notes that despite the inescapably racist perspective of these documents, they are inspired by the 'noble savage' trope rather than by the derogatory insinuations usual in English-language documents.

husband's religious material. On the other hand, she observes that much esoteric knowledge is lost to the younger generations and, if she does not publish it, it is in danger of being lost forever.[10]

As it turned out, in a substantive sense, culturally and religiously there was an important connection between Petri and Petri-Odermann's research area and mine.[11] This area was not only contiguous in a geographic sense with my research area in Fitzroy Crossing and the southern Kimberley in general, but also culturally closely related. Ron Berndt's strategic thinking was very much aware of these circumstances and placed me in the southern Kimberley to act as a kind of link or intermediary in a geographic and linguistic sense. (I seem to remember that in a conversation we had about my placement, Ron admitted as much. I believe the term 'spying' was also dropped in this context—though not by Ron or myself—which hinted at possibly another, deeper motivation.) Geographically, my position in the Fitzroy area was relevant in the sense that important cultural impulses moved from Central Australia across the southern Kimberley (especially Balgo, where the Berndts worked) to the Kimberley coast (where the Petris worked) via the cattle stations south of Fitzroy Crossing, and vice versa in the opposite direction.

Where Petri's work was of much value to me was the religious and cultural mobility among Aborigines of this region. The people the Petris were studying were culturally and linguistically closely related to the ones with whom I was dealing and these, in turn, shared cultural relations with the Balgo people. Myth, ritual and sacred objects were traded and handed on among desert and desert fringe groups in a sweeping movement spanning an enormous distance from the country's geographic centre to the Indian Ocean, where Petri and Petri-Odermann described them in tantalising glimpses.[12] In the process, of course, these religious elements underwent some change, which my research was able to highlight. Linguistically speaking, Petri's, and also Petri-Odermann's, publications were, with few exceptions, in the German language and therefore inaccessible to most Australian anthropologists at that time. In this sense, I presume I was meant to mediate between Petri's work and that of Australian anthropologists.

---

10 I recall that T. G. H. Strehlow made similar observations and claimed a similar defence.

11 See, for instance, Petri (1966, 1967), but also several other publications.

12 The phenomenon of *Wanderkulte* ('wandering or mobile cults') exerted some fascination at that time, harbouring shades of a modest form of diffusionism (see e.g. Kurangara described and analysed in several publications by various authors).

(Later, I translated one of Petri's key publications into English—Petri and Petri-Odermann (1988)—and, of course, in my publications I often referred to Petri's work.)[13]

Father Ernest A. Worms's work also provided valuable insights for me—especially his work on Kurangara (or Goranara, as he wrote) (Worms 1942; Worms and Petri 1968), which complemented Petri's and Lommel's work. But with Worms's work it was different insofar as most of it was centred on the Dampier Peninsula area (where he had several postings as a Pallottine missionary) and was not directly linked culturally with my fieldwork area, the southern Kimberley. Moreover, much of his oeuvre is published in the English language and is therefore better known to Australian anthropologists and less of an unknown cipher to the anthropological mainstream.

Herder's legacy and Carl von Brandenstein

Johann Gottfried Herder is widely acclaimed as the father of German—or better, German-language—anthropology by having set in motion an enduring tradition in perspective and focus. I believe he became the founding father more indirectly, in a very broad sense through his influence on scholars who came much later and paved the way for the formation of academic anthropology: from Wilhelm von Humboldt and Friedrich Schlegel to Wilhelm Wundt, Franz Boas and even Bronislaw Malinowski, to name only a few. The presumption sometimes seems to be that Herder's philosophy had a pervasive and lasting formative influence on German-language anthropology and that it can be expected that this influence made itself felt in the work of German-speaking researchers working in Aboriginal anthropology. This may be true only in a very generalised sense, as Herder's brushstroke was too sweeping and coarse to formulate a concise perspective on the human condition. His influence is more of a scattergun type, sparking major intellectual impulses in all directions.

His notion of *Volk* and his implicit idealist, romantic *über* value of the Germanic people foreshadowed, albeit in a much gentler way, later nationalist and even fascist ideological developments. This is so despite

---

13   One other paper appeared in English translation as 'Stability and change' (Petri and Petri-Odermann 1970). Petri's major work, *Sterbende Welt in Nordwest Australien* (1954), was translated only in 2011, as *The Dying World in Northwest Australia*.

the features in his work that clearly support the idea of democracy as the perfect political condition in which to unfold individuality and personal freedom, which he seemed to value highly. (This led him, for instance, to appreciate the French Revolution, which did not endear him to the aristocracy and the political elite of his time.) His emphasis on the concept of *Volk*—an entity characterised by a particular and unique configuration of language, religion, values, culture, ideals, oral traditions and so on—was counterbalanced and even contradicted by his emphasis on the unity of the human species, the assumption of a species-typical basis on which we can understand often seemingly radically different ethnic and cultural Otherness. (This seems to have had at least some influence on Husserl's phenomenology, on Bastian's *Elementargedanken* and on hermeneutics, but features of it can also be found in Jung's psychology, perhaps even in Freud's and other empathetically based theories and methods.) It is important to note that Herder's *Einheit in der Vielfalt* ('unity in diversity') prevented giving credit to the notion of 'race'—that is, to hold race responsible for the level of civilisation and for cultural achievement or 'failure'. Thus, blame for supremacist race theories that arose later in the German-speaking area—and not only there—cannot be put directly on his doorstep.

There is a basic irreconcilability between the traces of universalism in his work (though not in the Kantian sense) and his cultural relativism and ideas of a plurality of truths, the latter feeding into modern hermeneutics and postmodern thought. His hypothesis that language is not only important but also determines thought not only inspired Wittgenstein, but also eventually culminated in the Sapir–Whorf hypothesis—which, however, is far from being universally embraced. There are also traces of an incipient nature versus nurture debate in his work.

Like a Christmas sparkler, Herder's work not only shone brightly, it also spun off into many different directions, all carrying some of the original light. Herder's philological strand of thought, for instance, was carried forth into Aboriginal anthropology and linguistics by Carl Georg von Brandenstein.[14] His 'mercurial' work links language very much with culture, mentality, Aboriginal philosophy and world view, ritual and

---

14 Beyond professional help, I owe Carl and his wife, Carola, a considerable debt of gratitude for very personal 'moral' and practical support at a time my wife and I needed it very much when preparing for fieldwork in the Kimberley. All his material, published and unpublished, I had in my possession has been lodged in the Anthropos Institute in Sankt Augustin, Germany, where I presume it is publicly accessible.

myth. I am unable to judge what impact his linguistic work had overall on Aboriginal linguistics, but I am on safer ground with regard to his totemism studies, above all: von Brandenstein's articles on the Pilbara section system and its classificatory meaning (1972, 1974, 1977, 1978) and his book (1982) extending his notion into the subsection system. Some of his totemic work may be flawed in linguistic detail (as linguists are quick to point out), but the overall idea reflects Herder's anthropological humanism and its romantic legacy—apart from showing Lévi-Strauss's large footprint. Attributing to Aborigines a quality of philosophical thought comparable with that of classical Greece brushes both cultures with the same optimistic quality of genius. It is not to be mistaken as an argument in the vein of diffusionism, but as a signal of convergence through all humankind's cognitive tendency to order and systematise its comprehension of the world. Some cultures—such as Aboriginal cultures—come up with systematisations and an aesthetic sense of symmetry of a higher order and greater sophistication than others.

I built on this contention in a later small work in which I suggested that totemic systems and their inherent systemisation effort produced structures of power (Kolig 1988a). That is, I argued that the systematisation of world comprehension as espoused in the Aboriginal totemic systems represents the same idea of encapsulating and facilitating the empowerment of the cognoscenti as is the case with alchemy, for instance.[15] Perhaps unsurprisingly, this cognition-based interpretation of systematic totemism found no echo in Australian anthropology after decades of looking for explanations in another direction.

Von Brandenstein's linguistic diffusionist interests engaged in a major way with the hypothesis about an early Portuguese presence in Western Australia before Dutch, French and British mariners arrived on the scene. Apart from his earlier argument about the presence of traces of the Portuguese language in the Pilbara coastal area, in his last (unpublished) papers, he presented his views on a supposedly early Portuguese colonisation in the Fitzroy River Basin, my research area. Just to cite one example: the philological origin of the name of the well-known pastoral station Noonkanbah—or, as it is usually pronounced, 'Nukenbah'—is somewhat of a mystery. Aborigines call it a 'whitefella name', while 'whites' regard it as an Aboriginal word. Von Brandenstein traces it back to the Portuguese language and links it with navigation on the Fitzroy River. Unfortunately,

---

15   In this regard, I also owe a debt of gratitude to Lévi-Strauss, as did von Brandenstein.

for his argument, to date no supportive, hard, unambiguous archaeological evidence has been unearthed. The latest chapter in this saga is the discovery of an old Portuguese manuscript,[16] the text of which is adorned with a curious image of an animal with a short, slender, slightly pointed snout. Standing upright on its hind legs and clutching a leafy branch in its front paws, its posture suggests a herbivore. It has been argued that the image depicts a wallaby, while others pronounced it an aardvark or a deer. This, of course, is crucial: if the image depicts a wallaby, it would add some weight to the argument that early Portuguese explorers had visited Australia, while an aardvark could have been observed by them in South Africa, where the Portuguese presence at that time is well known and documented. But this is, of course, the subject of another debate.

As a sweeping generalisation on another level, it may be said that Herder's example of historical particularism led to an anthropological perception that acknowledged every culture as the heir of a distinct development. It needs to be carefully studied and should be entitled to intellectual respect—in contrast to another major inclination in anthropology that considers other cultures in terms of arrested developments along a pan-human sociocultural evolution. While the former viewpoint inclines to the notion that otherness possesses an inherent right to exist and to self-determination, the latter lends itself more readily to the subliminal notion of failure, which should be corrected by guided and goal-directed intervention motivated by varying degrees of benevolence. The discussions and conversations I had with Carl von Brandenstein over several years clearly showed his abiding respect—bordering on romantic admiration—for Aboriginal culture, although I do not know whether he had read Herder's works. In his linguistic work pointing to Portuguese influences, he seemed to emphasise the intelligent openness of Aboriginal culture to foreign influence and rejuvenation, even though in matters of technology and economy Aboriginal society remained staunchly conservative. In his book *Taruru*, he celebrated the epic eloquence and poetry of Pilbara Aborigines—in doing so, approaching T. G. H. Strehlow's classical study of Aranda traditions. Inspired by Lévi-Strauss's oeuvre, he also saw Aboriginal intellect as 'scientific', striving through classification and methodical ordering to a better understanding of the world couched in the mysterious paraphrases of totemism.

---

16 The manuscript held by the Les Enluminures gallery is dated between 1580 and 1620. For interpretations, see, for instance, Pridmore (2014).

Herder's influence worked itself out in unexpected major political orientations, even in very recent years—for instance, the Dutch multicultural policy of *Versuiling* and, much less commendably and paradoxically, in apartheid. Both pivot around the notion that exotic cultures need to be given the space to allow them to lead their distinctly separate existence. *Versuiling*, a species of multiculturalism, evinces the kind of respect for the cultural 'other' that concedes to it the right to unfold in a pluralist situation so as to maintain its essential integrity. Even in apartheid one can detect an ingredient of this kind, which shuns enforced assimilation, even though its reality had little of the intended benevolence of modern pluralism. I recall that erstwhile South African president Hendrik Verwoerd, one of the major architects of the policy of apartheid, once phrased it thus: whites and blacks should be living separately like the elephant and the lion. By this graphic reference, he rationalised his policy of 'separateness' as an ostensibly 'benevolent' approach to cultural incompatibility.[17] Modern pluralism seems to take important cues from Herder's legacy but arguably is more deeply grounded in up-to-date notions of human rights than any particular classical philosophy.

Diachronicity and its forward-looking implications

If there is a dominant topos in the 'German tradition of anthropology' then perhaps it is the conviction that a true understanding of cultural otherness comes through the study of world views, religion, beliefs, myths and oral traditions, values and ritual—things broadly called 'culture'. In contrast—at least in my subjective view—the mainstay of British-influenced Australian anthropology at the time appeared to be observable kinship and social structure and their workings as the key to understanding a society or an ethnicity. It seemed to me that in Australian anthropology at the time the legacy of Radcliffe-Browne and Malinowski reigned supreme, loyally carried forth by A. P. Elkin and others. What I call the 'culturist' approach seemed to be boutique anthropology, if not considered altogether eccentric. However, it had a strong supporter in Ron Berndt, who, by the way, is regarded by some as also standing in the 'German tradition'.[18] This is actually puzzling as he trained under

---

17   Gingrich (2005: 143) also refers to the role of anthropology in the formation of apartheid.
18   T. G. H. Strehlow sporadically also showed inclinations to move along similar lines.

A. P. Elkin in Sydney and, although of German ancestry, to my knowledge, he did not read German. If he read Herder and other salient German scholars in translation I do not know. That there was something in his Germanic background that inclined him to such a perspective may pander to a mystical viewpoint, but is certainly an 'unscientific' explanation.

There was also another distinction that seemed to separate Petri's and my approach (and also Lommel's) from the Australian mainstream. The synchronous, historically flattened perspective exercised a heavy dominance over diachronically intentioned studies. Diachronicity was used only for reconstructive purposes. It seemed to me that, in line with a cryptically underlying evolutionary predilection, the emphasis in Aboriginal anthropology lay heavily on reconstructing the pre-contact situation and bringing it into a framework of Eurocentric comprehension. Rather than analysing and comprehending current, contemporary processes and phenomena in the Aboriginal condition and projecting these forward into the future, the emphasis lay on reconstructing a supposedly unchanging past through the social detritus observable in the present. W. E. H. Stanner in *After the Dreaming* (1969: 14) also mentions that at that time there was little interest in 'actual life conditions' as 'living actuality', as he calls it, focused firmly on a reconstructive type of anthropology. Observations relating to sociocultural change and the fascinating phenomena it produced were subject to much neglect. This perspective was supported, it seemed to me, by a culture of pessimistic belief, unspoken but assuming the imminent demise of, given its fragility, traditional Aboriginal culture. The puzzle of how an Aboriginal form of sociocultural existence of such characteristic design unparalleled anywhere in the world could have emerged—and be preserved for such a long time before it was fatefully impacted and destroyed by colonialism—seemed to exercise paramount fascination for a majority of Australian anthropologists. The contemporary processes of change, their direction and their ideological and sociopolitical consequences seemed, by comparison, of minor interest, being regarded as a short flutter before extinction. In other words, it seemed to be largely a backward-looking anthropology burdened with a heavy reconstructive bias, rather than showing a contemporary and future-directed orientation based on a belief in the persisting robustness of Aboriginal cultural traditions; or, phrased differently, the imperative was overlooked to study how Aboriginal culture suspended between a lost past and a gleaming future was mustering its creativity to propel itself forward.

That this underlying pessimistic assumption was based on a misperception seemed plain to me. In my mind, it was obvious that Aboriginal culture and religion were not simply vanishing, incrementally disintegrating and crumbling under the onslaught of colonisation—which necessitated, of course, hurriedly collecting the few surviving sociocultural remains to facilitate an understanding of the past—but rather that the Aboriginal condition was actively and purposely changing and adapting. Not only that, in some cultural areas it put up an active, creative resistance rather than meekly succumbing (see Kolig 1981a, 1989a). Aboriginal communities constructively engaging with new realities seemed to me to be readily observable. The mythico-ritual field of Aboriginal culture, for instance, for decades already had shown attempts to bring modernity into its intellectual grasp, and perhaps harness it for tangible benefits, apart from making good use of modern organisational and technical opportunities to refresh and revitalise religious activity. This made it imperative to study and analyse what I could observe and witness with a view of how this fitted into the present, how it was influenced by the present and what it meant for the future. As an anthropologist with the West Australian Aboriginal Affairs Planning Authority (AAPA), I had the opportunity to point to a general cultural revivalism—a renaissance that at the time I called nativism (Kolig 1973–74a, 1973–74b, 1973–74c), a misnomer I owe to Ralph Linton (see also Akerman 1979).[19] I became aware of a strengthening of cultural Aboriginality with important political consequences—for example, the incipient, at the time emergent, land rights movement in the Kimberley, the formation of a pan-Aboriginal identity, the beginnings of politically effective organisation and active resistance to industrial interventionism (described by me, for instance, in *The Noonkanbah Story*, Kolig 1989b).

I believe at that time Petri was thinking in similar terms. He had changed his perspective since the Frobenius Expedition, when he had envisioned—just as Lommel had—the demise of Aboriginal culture in the Kimberley and Aboriginal culture as a whole. I believe that in his postwar studies he came to realise the dynamics of cultural change essentially were not to be interpreted as destructive, the last bizarre gasps of a dying culture, but that they signalled a victory over stagnation and heralded a cultural renaissance that represented continuity as well as a new beginning.

---

19 I pointed it out, for instance, to a royal commission into Aboriginal affairs in 1973 without stirring much interest.

He came to realise that syncretism and the *Heilserwartungsbewegungen* ('salvationist movements') he liked to study (Petri 1968) were not a dead end but a nascent future.

Like Petri, I was fascinated by the roots of this development in traditional myth and ritual and the adaptation of traditional thinking contained in them to contemporary opportunities and new formative conditions (e.g. Kolig 1973–74a, 1973–74b, 1974, 1990). Intertribalism (or the erosion of 'tribal' boundaries), the formation of heterogeneous local communities, the redefinition of traditional land rights (Kolig 1973), land entitlement and land inheritance, the gradual emergence of a more inclusive Aboriginal identity (Kolig 1972, 1977) at the expense of a language-based or 'tribally' based identity and the emergence of a more modern world awareness were all aspects of this development. I was also fascinated by what I believed were millenarian phenomena of the kind observed in other societies, which were rapidly changing under the impact of colonialism and Western cultural influence. While Petri in his writings seemed unconcerned about his intellectual borrowings, I used Weber's notion of increasing intellectual and social rationalisation to explain the processual, incremental shift from magical-mythical thinking to rationally based politics and organisation—a process I attempted to describe in *Dreamtime Politics* (Kolig 1989a).

Even seemingly traditional mythico-ritual cycles—such as *wandji*,[20] *woagaia* (see Kolig 1981b) and *ngamandji-mandji*—were used to construct wider intertribal identities commensurate with modern realities and superseding traditional forms of co-residence, reflecting the ever-widening intellectual and geographic horizon on which political aspirations could flourish. Identity changed from clannish and tribal to communal, societal and pluralistic. Exclusivist participation in myth and ritual changed to more open forms and from magical duty to identity generator. Within a very few years, a noticeable shift occurred from a plan to send sacred objects to 'Canberra' to stimulate the flow of goods (Kolig 1973) to engaging in political, rationally articulated dialogue. To me, this showed a rapid transition from a world view inspired by magical expectations and the need to appeal to and appease magical causalities to the domain of modern politics. Myth and ritual diminished as magical-

---

20 Described by Petri in great detail (1966, 1967).

religious instruments and were now meant to facilitate the construction of a collective identity commensurate with a modern reality, from which a modern political awareness could grow.

Of course, emphasising—or, as some would have it, overemphasising—change, be it creative, adjustive or disintegrative, as a logical consequence begs questions of cultural continuity, authenticity and the persistence of cultural identity. In fact, the relevance of this question of the sustainability of traditional cultural identity throughout—in many respects, profound—post-contact change was destined to become an important issue in native title claims, given the wording of the *Native Title Act 1993*. Native title legislation demanded the rigorous examination of whether claims were based on traditional legal and cultural criteria to determine validity. This meant—somewhat unrealistically—that this validity was either deemed extinct through profound change or presumed almost immutably preserved since pre-contact times. (This notion seems to have been based on the erroneous assumption that a culture left undisturbed would remain totally inert and unchanging.) But, admittedly, how else could one distinguish 'genuine' from 'fraudulent' claims in a Western court of law? This legal baseline leaves one question glaringly unanswered: how much of the cultural substance can change before it becomes innovation and invention and thus loses continuity with the past?[21] The requirements of the Act place this in the very centre of deliberation—yet without clarification.

The relevance of this question about the sustainability of traditional cultural identity throughout post-contact change had become apparent to me some time before the tidal wave of claims under the Act arose. A competently compiled summary of traditional Aboriginal culture in the Kimberley, written by a mining executive for 'industry–internal' use, forcefully brought that home to me.[22] It clearly advocated a mining industry agenda but was written in a spirit of firm belief in the truth of its assertions. It questioned the validity of traditional knowledge claimed by Aboriginal custodians of sacred sites in their strategy of achieving protection of such places and blocking mining. Referring mainly to Petri's and my publications, the report averred that the religious and cognitive background of Aborigines had shifted to the extent that the knowledge

---

21 I did not succeed in solving this conundrum in the Rubibi land claim. See Burke (2011) and Kolig (2003). I was also struggling with it in Kolig (2005).
22 I am withholding identification of this paper since it was not intended for public use.

relating to the sanctity of the land held out by them as traditional went far beyond embellishment and could at best be innovations accrued in post-contact time and, at worst, blatant, opportunistic misrepresentations for the sake of political and economic leverage.[23] After all, their relationship with the land had changed, traditional beliefs in the sacrosanctity of places had given way to more rationalist views, the original landowning groups had been replaced and supplanted with new 'immigrants' and—as Petri and I had written about the belief in Noah's Ark and the Christian eschatology associated with it—Aborigines had accepted Christianity. Cargo cults (*Wanderkulte*) and religious imports had replaced traditional beliefs and recognising this should now obviously engender acute scepticism in the mining industry vis-à-vis Aboriginal claims. That clearly was a consequence of Petri's and my writings that was totally unintended by me—and probably also by Petri, although I cannot be sure. As a guest at La Grange, he was somewhat constrained by the views of the Pallottine order's hierarchy, which was not entirely favourable to traditional Aboriginal relationships with the land.

There is another example of what seems to be the instrumentalisation of the German tradition in the fight over sacred sites and the beginning of the battle for land rights. At the height of the Noonkanbah controversy, a perceptive reviewer of the situation wondered why it was that three anthropologists with obviously Germanic names could admit what others steadfastly denied—namely, that the culture of Noonkanbah Aborigines had changed and thus their insistence that it had not was unmasked as just a ruse.[24] The three were Petri, myself and, characteristically so 'distinguished', Kim Akerman—probably because of his name as much as his publications.

The puzzle of nativism, millenarianism and Nazism

Early in my research among Aborigines and reading beyond the confines of Aboriginal anthropology, I had become fascinated by the topos of millenarianism (chiliasm, salvationism, revitalisation) as an expression of political thought and as the spectacular intellectual catharsis

---

23 This is not a verbatim quote, but is my inference of the clearly implied meaning.
24 I am relying on my memory here. Unfortunately, attempts to trace this newspaper column back about 30 years were unsuccessful.

of cataclysmic sociocultural change. Also, Weber's approach of paying careful attention to the role of charisma in fomenting ideological and social change intrigued me. (This interest led me a few years later to the New Hebrides—now Vanuatu—to study the Nagriamel movement on the island of Espiritu Santo and the Jon Frum movement on Tana.) As a student, I had avoided reading Wilhelm Mühlmann's famous study *Chiliasmus und Nativismus* (1964) because of his reputation as an opportunist ex-Nazi. I had few expectations that, as such, he would be able to treat this ideological-political subject matter with a modern, objective analytical viewpoint. But now I have to admit that I am consonant with his universalist argument about the 'normalcy' of millenarian movements in situations of sociocultural crisis and stress[25]—despite the suspicion that Mühlmann used this perspective to exonerate Nazism.[26] (Of course, causally contextualising the chiliastic phenomenon introduced a sizeable note of synchronicity into an approach that was otherwise heavily based on a diachronic foundation.)[27]

It is certainly true that there was a large body of literature at the time: Linton's and Mooney's nativism concept, Wallace's revitalisation and the many cargo cult studies from the Pacific area that were in vogue at that time—all dealing with the wide range of millenarian phenomena observed in the Third World, groaning under the impact of the colonising Euro-American culture.[28] Aboriginal Australia stuck out globally by the apparent absence of such ideological phenomena. Kenelm Burridge, in *Encountering Aborigines* (1973), tried to gloss over it with his assertion that Aborigines had skipped the magical-mystical phase of development and moved straight on to modern politics. I was not convinced and it seems neither was Petri.

---

25   My interest in the events around al Dawla al Islamiya fil Iraq wa'al Sham (Islamic State, IS, or Da'ish) may be related to this.

26   See also Gingrich (2005: 143–5). It is a sad reminder that it is all too easy to instrumentalise anthropology for partisan viewpoints (epitomised in recent years in the emergence of advocate anthropology in the age of postmodernism and the rising belief in the plurality of truth).

27   Max Weber's concept of *Realinteressen* also plays a role in this explanatory perspective, which combines idealism with materialism and diachronicity with synchronicity.

28   Vittorio Lanternari's *Religion of the Oppressed* (1963), Guglielmo Guariglia's *Prophetismus und Heilserwartungsbewegungen als völkerkundliches und religionsgeschichtliches Problem*, Peter Worsley's *The Trumpet Shall Sound*, Peter Lawrence's *Road Belong Cargo*, Norman Cohn's *The Pursuit of the Millennium* and Bryan Wilson's *Magic and the Millennium* were the 'classics' among the publications dealing with the efflorescence of cargo and millennial movements after World War II. Relative deprivation, cognitive dissonance, stress theory and so on supplied the theoretical instruments to try to understand the multi-causality of these phenomena. These theories have largely fallen into disuse in anthropology.

I was intrigued by the question of why Australian anthropology had apparently failed to notice anything ideologically millenarian in character, be it violently utopian, militaristic, apocalyptic, thaumaturgic or of a more dreamy, salvation-inspired nature, perhaps even derivatives of Christianity. Aboriginal Australia seemed remarkably devoid of charismatic, messianic or prophetic features—until I scanned Siebert's notes on the Diyari and read between the lines in Spencer and Gillen's voluminous tomes and, above all, Lommel's and Petri's works on the Kurangara. There was, of course, Ron Berndt's (1962) important study of the 'Adjustment' movement in Arnhem Land and Fredrik Rose's (1965) discovery of a 'cargo cult climate' in northern Australia. Petri's work led me to extend this into an investigation of Christian belief elements that had found their way into Aboriginal myth-ritual—for example, in the shape of the belief in Noah's Ark as an end-time vessel insinuating itself into Aboriginal political thought (Kolig 1980, see also 1988b), a mythico-political phenomenon Petri also noticed in the Eighty Mile Beach area. The myth of Captain Cook (Kolig 1979a) clearly was an attempt to fuse the European-dominated political reality with a more traditional comprehension of the world and its causalities. The earlier description of the Kurangara cult kindled my interest in the cult of Djuluru (Kolig 1979b), which I found drew in a very striking manner on modern images of war and, in so doing, utilised such names as 'Hitler' and 'German', while drawing on traditional concepts of empowerment through ritual and symbolism to bring these images into a useful ambience.

Petri's and Lommel's work—especially on the Kurangara mythico-ritual tradition (Lommel 1950, 1952; Petri 1950a, 1950b, 1950c, 1954) and its dynamic, which spread across the Kimberley—had laid a foundation on which Aboriginal contemporary ideology could be understood. Carl Strehlow's (1907–1910), E. A. Worms's (1930s–1960s) and Otto Siebert's (1910) works also made a contribution in this regard. Kurangara, Worgaia (Woagaia; Kolig 1981b), Molongo, Djuluru (Kolig 1979b), the Jinimin cult and so on were mythico-ritual traditions of pre-contact roots but with modern overtones that represented the shift from a pre-contact world awareness to contemporary cognitive comprehension, via redemptive aspirations, which eventually flowed into rational politics. Although Petri and Petri-Odermann (1988: 394) denied that the Kurangara he and Lommel had observed in the 1930s had any nativist or millenarian-prophetic undertones, the ceremony is open to being interpreted as an autochthonous tradition with soteriological expectations that had in various ways been adjusted to contemporary conditions. Rather than purely nostalgic, it was, in my mind, meant to be creative and effective in modern circumstances. Petri continued studying related traditions and their influence on cultural renewal, in the process changing his culturally pessimistic outlook—expressed in his original monograph *Sterbende Welt in Nordwest Australien* (1954; translated as *The Dying World in Northwest Australia*, 2011)—to a more positive, if implied, stance. Lommel, who did not renew his acquaintance with the Kimberley, extrapolated the opposite viewpoint from his original observations, clearly still under the impression of his earlier negative judgement. He saw by projection what he had witnessed as the cul-de-sac taken by an ultimately doomed culture. This led to his book with the telling title *Fortschritt ins Nichts* (Lommel 1969; translated literally meaning 'progress into nothingness'). From a brief exchange of communications, I infer that in later years he did not change his mind.

It should be mentioned that other anthropologists shared the view that incremental cultural change was worth studying, but few saw it in terms of its creative potential and perhaps not solely as a 'last gasp' phenomenon. Howitt, Siebert, Calley, Rose, Berndt and others included in their ethnographies the observation of new cultural phenomena.[29] Spencer and Gillen's hefty publications were an enormously important source of information, which, cryptically, also hinted at new developments. Some of their observations from earlier years afforded me a basis of understanding of several ritual and mythical traditions I was privileged to experience in and around Fitzroy Crossing. Petri must have felt the same way and indeed he implies that in his 'Nachwort' (1968). The cultural elements recorded by Spencer and Gillen derived from Central Australia, but, in renovated and revamped form, they crossed the southern Kimberley on their way to the western coast, representing new ideas and grasping at new opportunities. In this regard, the works of Petri, Lommel and the missionary Siebert, writing about his experience among the Diyari, turned out to be of great value to me.[30] They had all observed cultural change and attendant revivalist and even chiliastic, religious-political phenomena, by carefully screening religious and ritual features and analysing the underlying subtle shift in values and world perception.

---

29   For references, see Kolig (1987, 1988c).
30   There are several more ethnographers who had something to contribute—for example: Roth on the Molongo cult (see Kolig 1988c).

There was an interesting interpretation of this focus on cultural change and its ideological implications. In a review of my book *The Silent Revolution*, Kenneth Maddock (1984) mentioned what he saw as a similarity in approach and focus in the work of Petri, Lommel and myself.[31] For Maddock, there was a paradigmatic similitude between Petri's, Lommel's and my work, which was eloquent testimony to the national history of our respective countries. By our focus on cultural, religious and ideological change, and by our intense interest in the profound shift in *Weltanschauung* in Aboriginal culture, we showed that we were attuned to ideological volatility and attributed key significance to it. This sensitivity, he believed, had been engendered by the background of the political past in Germany and Austria where, from democratic roots, but under conditions of enormous social crisis and stress, a fascist fermentation with salvationist, millenarian overtones had rapidly grown and taken hold of society. The rapid transition from a relatively placid ideological situation devoid of flamboyant political utterances to the murderous antics of Nazism and its world-spanning dystopian aspirations had sensitised us to the significance of ideological transformation. It had created in us a heightened sensibility to, and curiosity in, the subtle nuances and subliminal currents of rapidly shifting perceptions, aspirations and myth-dreams—and the role charismatic leadership can play. Our relative proximity to a certain kind of collective political conscience, Maddock seemed to argue, had fostered our fascination with the intellectual and symbolic culture that is capable of leading to spectacular ideological eruptions, as our history had shown. Despite our generational and national differences, we lived in that no-man's land between guilt and victimhood, which had generated an awareness others did not have at that time.

References[32]

Akerman, K. 1979. The renascence of Aboriginal law in the Kimberleys. In *Aborigines of the West*, (eds) R. M. Berndt and C. Berndt, pp. 234–42. Perth: University of Western Australia Press.

Beer, B. 2007. *Frauen in der deutschsprachigen Ethnologie*. Vienna: Böhlau.

---

31 This was later confirmed and elaborated on in a personal communication.
32 The publications listed here under Kolig do not represent a complete list of my publications on Australian Aborigines. The same goes for Petri. A more extensive, although not complete, list of Petri's publications can be found in Craig (1968).

Berndt, R. 1962. *An Adjustment Movement in Arnhem Land.* Paris: Mouton.

Burke, P. 2011. *Law's Anthropology: From ethnography to expert testimony in native title.* Canberra: ANU E Press.

Burridge, K. 1973. *Encountering Aborigines.* New York: Pergamon.

Craig, B. 1968. *Kimberley Region: An annotated bibliography.* Canberra: Australian Institute of Aboriginal Studies.

Gingrich, A. 2005. The German-speaking countries. In *One Discipline, Four Ways: British, German, French, and American anthropology,* F. Barth, A. Gingrich, R. Parkin and S. Silverman, pp. 61–156. Chicago: University of Chicago Press.

Haag, O. 2012. Review of Peter Monteith (ed.), 'Germans, Travellers, Settlers and their Descendants in South Australia'. *Zeitschrift für Australienstudien* 26: 133–6.

Haekel, J. 1950. *Zum Individual- und Geschlechtstotemismus in Australien.* Vienna: Herold.

Hill, G. 2012. An honest look at flood mythology leaves Biblical literalists all at sea. 19 October. Available from: www.irefuteitthus.com/an-honest-look-at-flood-mythology-leaves-biblical-literalists-all-at-sea. html#axzz4pGII6ySw.

Kolig, E. 1972. Bi:n and Gadeja: An Australian Aboriginal model of the European society as a guide in social change. *Oceania* 43: 1–18. doi.org/10.1002/j.1834-4461.1972.tb01193.x.

Kolig, E. 1973. Aboriginal land rights, policies and anthropology: An anthropological dilemma. *Bulletin of the International Committee on Urgent Anthropological and Ethnolological Research* 15: 57–69.

Kolig, E. 1973–74a. Glaube als Rechtsmittel: Anatomie eines Landanspruchs moderner Schwarzaustralier. *Wiener Völkerkundliche Mitteilungen* 20–21(NS)(15): 69–93.

Kolig, E. 1973–74b. Progress and preservation: An Aboriginal perspective. *Anthropological Forum* 3: 264–79. doi.org/10.1080/00664677.1973.9 967279.

Kolig, E. 1973–74c. *Tradition and emancipation: An Australian Aboriginal version of nativism.* Supplement, Aboriginal Affairs Planning Authority, pp. 1–42. Perth: Government Printer.

Kolig, E. 1974. Der Kadjina: Mythos und Territorialismus moderner Schwarzaustralier. *Baessler-Archiv* 22: 283–304.

Kolig, E. 1977. From tribesman to citizen? In *Aborigines and Change: Australia in the '70s*, (ed.) R. Berndt, pp. 33–53. Canberra: AIAS Press.

Kolig, E. 1979a. Captain Cook in the western Kimberleys. In *Aborigines of the West: Their past and their present*, (eds) R. Berndt and C. Berndt, pp. 274–82. Perth: University of Western Australia Press.

Kolig, E. 1979b. Djuluru: ein synkretistischer Kult Nordwest-Australiens. *Baessler-Archiv* 27: 419–48.

Kolig, E. 1980. Noah's Ark revisited: On the myth–land connection in traditional Aboriginal thought. *Oceania* 51: 118–32. doi.org/10.1002/j.1834-4461.1980.tb01962.x.

Kolig, E. 1981a. *The Silent Revolution: The effects of modernization on Australian Aboriginal religion.* Philadelphia: ISHI.

Kolig, E. 1981b. Woagaia: Weltanschaulicher Wandel und neue Formen der Religiosität in Nordwest-Australien. *Baessler-Archiv* 29: 387–422.

Kolig, E. 1987. Post-contact religious movements in Australian Aboriginal society. *Anthropos* 82: 251–9.

Kolig, E. 1988a. Australian Aboriginal totemic systems: Structures of power. *Oceania* 58: 2112–230. doi.org/10.1002/j.1834-4461.1988.tb02273.x.

Kolig, E. 1988b. Mission not accomplished. In *Aboriginal Australians and Christian Missions*, (eds) T. Swain and D. Rose, pp. 376–90. Adelaide: Australian Association for the Study of Religions.

Kolig, E. 1988c. Religious movements. In *The Australian People: An encyclopedia of the nation, its people and their origins*, (ed.) J. Jupp, pp. 165–7. Sydney: Angus & Robertson.

Kolig, E. 1989a. *Dreamtime Politics: Religion, world view and utopian thought in Australian Aboriginal society.* Berlin: D. Reimer.

Kolig, E. 1989b [1987]. *The Noonkanbah Story: Portrait of an Aboriginal community in Western Australia*. Enlarged 3rd edn. Dunedin: University of Otago Press.

Kolig, E. 1990. Government policies and religious strategies: Fighting with myth at Noonkanbah. In *Going it Alone?*, (eds) R. Tonkinson and M. Howard, pp. 235–52. Canberra: Aboriginal Studies Press.

Kolig, E. 1992. Religious power and the all-father in the sky: Monotheism in Australian Aboriginal culture reconsidered. *Anthropos* 87: 9–31.

Kolig, E. 1994. Rationality, ideological transfer, cultural resistance and the Dreaming: The development of political thought in Australian Aboriginal society. *Anthropos* 89: 111–24.

Kolig, E. 2003. Legitimising belief: Identity politics, utility, strategies of concealment, and rationalisation in Australian Aboriginal religion. *The Australian Journal of Anthropology* 14(2): 209–28. doi.org/10.1111/j.1835-9310.2003.tb00231.x.

Kolig, E. 2005. The politics of indigenous—or ingenious—traditions: Some thoughts on the Australian and New Zealand situation. In *Tradition and Agency*, (eds) T. Otto and P. Pedersen, pp. 245–78. Aarhus: University of Aarhus Press.

Koppers, W. 1949. *Der Urmensch und sein Weltbild*. Vienna: Herold.

Lanternari, V. 1963. *The Religion of the Oppressed*. London: MacGibbon & Kee.

Linimayr, P. 1994. *Wiener Voelkerkunde im Nationalsozialismus*. Frankfurt: Peter Lang.

Lommel, A. 1950. Modern culture influences on the Aborigines. *Oceania* 21: 14–24. doi.org/10.1002/j.1834-4461.1950.tb00170.x.

Lommel, A. 1952. *Die Unambal, ein Stamm in Nordwest-Australien*. Hamburg: Museum fuer Voelkerkunde.

Lommel, A. 1969. *Fortschritt ins Nichts: die Modernisierung der Primitiven Australiens*. Zurich: Atlantis.

Maddock, K. 1984. Review of 'The Silent Revolution: The effects of modernization on Australian Aboriginal religion', Erich Kolig. *Oceania* 54(4): 340–1. doi.org/10.1002/j.1834-4461.1984.tb02070.x.

Monteath, P. (ed.). 2011. *Germans, Travellers, Settlers and their Descendants in South Australia*. Adelaide: Wakefield Press.

Mühlmann, W. E. 1964. *Chiliasmus und Nativismus*. Berlin: Reimer.

Petri, H. 1950a. Das Weltende im Glauben australischer Eingeborener. *Paideuma* 4: 349–62.

Petri, H. 1950b. Kurangara: Neue magische Kulte in Nordwest-Australien. *Zeitschift für Ethnologie* 75: 43–51.

Petri, H. 1950c. Wandlungen in der geistigen Kultur nordwetaustralischer Staemme. *Veröffentlichungen aus dem Museum für Natur-, Völker- und Handelskunde in Bremen* B(1).

Petri, H. 1953. Der australische Medizinmann. *Annali Lateranensi* 17: 157–225.

Petri, H. 1954. *Sterbende Welt in Nordwest Australien*. Braunschweig, Germany: Limbach. [Translated as *The Dying World in Northwest Australia*. Perth: Hesperian Press, 2011].

Petri, H. 1966. Badur (Parda Hills), ein Felsbilder- und Kultzentrum im Norden der westlichen Wüste Australiens. *Baessler-Archiv* 14: 331–70.

Petri, H. 1967. Wandji Kurang-gara, ein mythischer Traditionskomplex aus der westlichen Wüste Australiens. *Baessler-Archiv* 15: 1–34.

Petri, H. 1968. Nachwort. In *Die Religionen der Südsee und Australiens* [The Religions of the South Pacific and Australia], Vol. 5, No. 2, (ed.) C. M. Schroder, pp. 298–311. Stuttgart: W. Kohlhammer Verlag.

Petri, H. and Petri-Odermann, G. 1964. Nativismus und Millenarismus im gegenwärtigen Australien. In *Festschrift für A. E. Jensen*, (eds) E. Haberland, M. Schuster and H. Straube, pp. 461–6. Munich: Klaus Renner.

Petri, H. and Petri-Odermann, G. 1970. Stability and change: Present day historic aspects among Australian Aborigines. In *Australian Aboriginal Anthropology*, (ed.) R. Berndt, pp. 248–76. Perth: University of Western Australia Press.

Petri, H. and Petri-Odermann, G. 1988. A nativistic and millenarian movement in north west Australia. In *Aboriginal Australians and Christian Missions*, (eds) T. Swain and D. Bird Rose, Translated by E. Kolig, pp. 391–6. Adelaide: Australian Association for the Study of Religion.

Pridmore, P. 2014. That's no kangaroo on the manuscript—So what is it? *The Conversation*, [online], 17 January. Available from: theconversation. com/thats-no-kangaroo-on-the-manuscript-so-what-is-it-22115.

Rose, F. 1965. *The Wind of Change in Central Australia*. Berlin: Akademie Verlag.

Schmidt, W. 1912–54. *Der Ursprung der Gottesidee. Volume 1–12*. Münster: Aschendorff.

Siebert, O. 1910. Sagen und Sitten der Dieri und Nachbarstämme in Zentral-Austalien. *Globus* 97: 53–9.

Stanner, W. E. H. 1969. *After the Dreaming: The 1968 Boyer Lectures*. Sydney: Australian Broadcasting Commission.

von Brandenstein, C. 1970. The meaning of section and section names. *Oceania* 41: 39–49. doi.org/10.1002/j.1834-4461.1970.tb01114.x.

von Brandenstein, C. 1972. The phoenix totemism. *Anthropos* 67: 586–94.

von Brandenstein, C. 1974. Die Weltordnung der Frühzeit nach den vier Wesensarten. *Zeitschrift für Religions- und Geistesgeschichte* 26: 211–21. doi.org/10.1163/157007374X00781.

von Brandenstein, C. 1977. Aboriginal ecological order in the south-west of Australia. *Oceania* 47(3): 169–86. doi.org/10.1002/j.1834-4461. 1977.tb01286.x.

von Brandenstein, C. 1978. Identical principles behind Australian totemism and Empedoclean 'philosophy'. In *Australian Aboriginal Concepts*, (ed.) L. R. Hiatt, pp. 134–55. Canberra: AIAS.

von Brandenstein, C. 1982. *Names and Substance in the Australian Subsection System*. Chicago: University of Chicago Press.

Worms, E. A. 1942. Die Goranara-Feier im australischen Kimberley. *Annali Lateranensi* 6: 207–35.

Worms, E. A. 1950. Djamar, the creator: A myth of the Bad (west Kimberley, Australia). *Anthropos* 45: 641–58.

Worms, E. A. and Petri, H. 1968. Australische Eingeborenen-Religionen. In *Die Religionen der Südsee und Australiens* [The Religions of the South Pacific and Australia], Vol. 5, No. 2, (ed.) C. M. Schroder, pp. 125–329. Stuttgart: W. Kohlhammer Verlag.

16

Tracks and shadows: Some social effects of the 1938 Frobenius Expedition to the north-west Kimberley[1]

Anthony Redmond

In 1938, Andreas Lommel, newly graduated in anthropology and archaeology from the Frobenius Institute in Frankfurt, along with his colleagues Helmut Petri and Agnes Schulz and an Australian postgraduate student in psychology, Patrick Pentony, spent several months conducting fieldwork in and around Munja Government Station on Walcott Inlet in the north-west Kimberley region of Western Australia.

When I arrived in the Kimberley 56 years later, intent on studying *jurnba* (a Kimberley Aboriginal public song genre), together with its performers and composers, Lommel's German-language monograph *Die Unambal, ein Stamm in Nordwest-Australien* (1952) was an important source for approaching this subject. A newly published *Oceania* article compiled by Alan Rumsey as a collaboration between Lommel and senior Ngarinyin man David Mowaljarlai (Lommel and Mowaljarlai 1994), had already whetted my appetite for exploring the song texts composed by Alan Balbungu, which had been partially transcribed in Lommel's monograph.

---

1   This chapter is dedicated to the memory of Frank Zandvoort: adventurer, linguist, farmer and unforgettable friend.

Alan and Francesca Merlan had also recorded local people singing a number of these texts during their fieldwork in Ngarinyin country in 1993. These teachers and colleagues subsequently introduced me to Mowaljarlai during one of his visits to Sydney to work on their Ngarinyin-language texts, and a plan was put in place for me to begin fieldwork with Ngarinyin people in the following year.

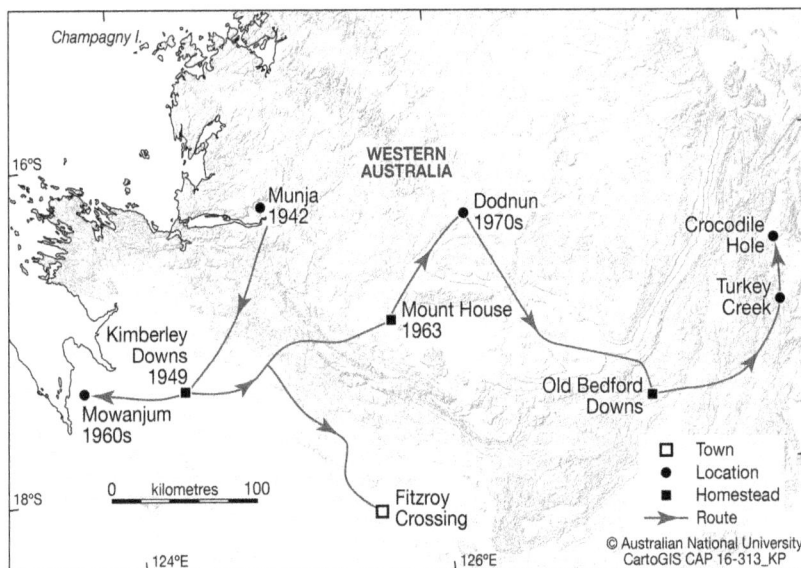

Map 16.1 The movement of the song cycle across the Kimberley.
Source: CartoGIS, The Australian National University.

One of my first points of call in July 1994 was to visit senior Ngarinyin man Laurie Gowanulli to talk about the Balbungu songs. While Mowaljarlai was a boy of just 10 in 1938, Gowanulli was already a young man of 20 or so when he first met Lommel during the Frobenius Institute group's visit to Munja.

Laurie was more than happy, as it turned out, to sit with me and my good friend, Frank Zaandvoort, who had recently completed a translation of Lommel's German-language monograph for me to work from. Laurie also agreed to sing and record more of the Balbungu song corpus with us and, in between those recordings, he reminisced at length about those pre–World War II times in Munja.

Plate 16.1 Laurie Gowanulli at Mowanjum, July 1994.
Source: Anthony Redmond personal collection.

By the time we had made our way through recording as many of the remaining Balbungu songs as Gowanulli (Gowan) could recall, I was very much under the spell of that charming gentleman's songs and stories and determined to follow up the possible implications of the songs themselves, the shamanic process involved in dreaming them and the ways in which they were used and distributed across that social world.

Gowanulli's reflections on Lommel's 1938 visit to Munja provide some interesting insights into what kind of sense Aboriginal people living in those settlements were making of the presence of these particular Europeans, who were so unusually interested in their sociocultural world, and how he and his countrymen contextualised this interest in them within the rapidly unfolding events that would soon draw the entire region on to a wartime footing.

In the first instance, Gowan described how he and his countrymen had generously taken care of Lommel and the other members of the Frobenius Expedition despite an uneasiness about the exact nature of these visitors' motivations for collecting examples of sacred ceremonial boards and making hand-drawn copies of the *wanjina* cave paintings to be subsequently shipped back to Europe:

Mark 'em [draw them] people.[2] I can't see how he drawing all the old people and all that, Wanjina too.

They [his countrymen] take 'em out, stockman boy took 'em up there in that cave place and deliver 'em there, one boy look after 'em, right, they all getting all that cave drawing and mark 'em all that exactly like that thing that was in the cave too, in that paper they bin put it. They all took 'em right back there but we never got answer from all that time. We don't know what they took 'em for. That Germany is a long way from Australia.

When I asked Gowan what he and his friends might have received in return for their investments of care, knowledge and time in their German visitors, he was emphatic that there had been little in the way of reciprocity (only lollies and tobacco), but he quickly located this in its particular historical context. In those days, he said, his people typically responded to requests from whitefella strangers much as they would to a request from an Aboriginal person coming from far afield and therefore in need of assistance and support because they were marooned in an unfamiliar social world. That was, he maintained, a very different situation to nowadays when Aboriginal people had become much more wary about requests for cultural, and especially ritual, knowledge and voiced their opinions and expectations much more stridently:

Nothing. No, we don't know what we give them for, we never had that thought, you know, we never thought about it. Not like now, everybody expecting, 'What for this, what for that, what you want this for?'

All that thing only coming out today. My time, when I bin grow, we only used do work, friend coming from there, long way we give what he ask for, he welcome, we give 'em anything, he can learn, something, well like the Germany mob they come there, we be good to them, give us everything what we needed like lolly and thing, and we give them thing and gone back home.

---

2   Agnes Schulz was by all accounts a very proficient portraitist and drew a number of portraits of people living at Munja, including Gowanulli's close friend, the late Paddy Wama.

To emphasise the cooperative and friendly approach his people had taken in those early days with white strangers, and Germans in particular, Gowan compared his countrymen's open-handed assistance to Lommel's party with the lifesaving kindness kinsmen from Drysdale River Mission had provided in finding two lost German airmen who had crash-landed their aircraft on the mudflats of the north-west coast in 1932:[3]

> Like that two bloke there, I don't know about two, when German travel back with the plane and when they crash somewhere in Wyndham, they crash there and Aboriginal people bin grab them, mind 'em—we see 'im in movie they make film all the time—the blackfellow look after them two German, they was still all right, fly 'em to Broome, nothing wrong with the people.

> But like this now what this one we give 'em [referring to Balbungu's songs], he welcome, good, old man was all right, old man he was the composer, he was the boss of the corroboree. We been pleased when anybody come up listen, recording, not this sort of one [pointing to my digital tape recorder], different one, long like that [early wax cylinder recording apparatus], like this he put that thing machine through from there and make him sing that he pick up like this cassette and he get a recording in there now. But that was old time, I never see that one now.

In these particular discussions, Gowan barely acknowledged the prevailing colonial context in which white managers infamously exerted an intermittent and often unpredictably violent control over the many Ngarinyin, Wunambal and Worrorra people who were by then living part of the year in and around Munja Government Station. In his view, although subjected to an onerous seasonal work regime in Munja's peanut oil plantations, the most senior Aboriginal men at least continued to exercise a high degree of personal autonomy and mobility. The implication was that the assistance offered to these European strangers was largely on his countrymen's own initiative and was derived from their traditional ethic of kin-based generosity rather than being coerced by mission managers:

---

3   Hans Bertram and Adolf Klausmann were flying the Junkers W33 seaplane *Atlantis* from Cologne, Germany, on a goodwill mission to Australia for the aircraft maker, Junkers, when they ran into a severe storm between Timor and Darwin. Flying during the night of 15 May 1932, they became lost in thick cloud. Eventually, at dawn, running short of fuel, they spotted the coast and landed in a sheltered bay. After a sleep and a think, they decided to use their remaining fuel to fly further down the coast, closer to where they believed the nearest town was located. In fact, they moved further away from civilisation, finally landing near Rocky Island, about 170 kilometres north-west of Wyndham. See: simplyaustralia.net/article-strangers2.html.

> Well, like the German mob, we just come friendly, well we know nothing. He give us what he give us, only give 'em lolly, he might get tobacco, he give 'em, not tea and sugar flour, no, only what he got it, he give them now lolly and that sort of thing, old people there, they give them whole lot and the old people go easy and give them.

Reflecting on that possibly naive and open-handed attitude to strangers, Gowanulli believed that, in recent times, his countrymen had developed a more knowing and self-protective diffidence in such dealings as they had become more conscious of the ways in which their cultural resources carried potential value in their negotiations with Europeans:

> You know if people come to ask to know everything, to understand, if people come they be surprised, what you, maybe you say, ask me, 'I want that.' 'What for?' 'Oh for so and so.' Might be you want me to get that thing. Well everybody find that very hard, difficult to know this time. Taking away country thing, you know … Yeah little bit changed this time. They want to come now well it little bit very hard for anyone coming here to ask what he want them for and all that. Everybody learn about this government business, 'What for he want, what he come for, what you gonna do with all that.'

> Like all this people now, this KLC[4] mob and all this, everybody all argue one another. I don't know nothing me because I'm don't interesting, you know.

After being in the field for some three months or so working with Gowanulli and his countrymen, Lommel and his companions, being mostly German nationals, had to make a hasty departure from Australia as the war threatened in Europe.

This 'second Germany war' remained rather remote for Kimberley Aboriginal people, whose knowledge of Anglo-Australian–German geopolitics was largely conditioned by their interactions with World War I veterans who had subsequently become stockmen, prospectors and missionaries in the Kimberley. These relationships ranged in emotional tone from the relatively respectful and friendly relationships established with returned Anglo-Scottish veterans, such as the supervisor of the Kunmunya Presbyterian Mission, 'Mr Love' (Reverend W. R. B. Love), and Dave Rust, the manager at Karunjie Station, to their interactions with

---

4   Gowan and some of his countrymen were, at the time of this interview, involved in a longstanding dispute with the regional Aboriginal political body, the Kimberley Land Council (KLC), in regard to the perceived infringement of Ngarinyin people's local autonomy in mounting litigation over land claims.

more violent, and sometimes positively deranged, veterans of the Light Horse Brigade, such as Scotty Saddler and Scotty Salmond (Redmond and Skyring 2010).

Plate 16.2 Gowanulli travelling in Garnlingarri country, 1996.
Source: Anthony Redmond personal collection.

Gowanulli suggested that the 'Germany war' may have been in some sense linked to the mystifying European interest in retracing *wanjina* images from the northern Kimberley cave galleries and the collection of ritual artefacts from ceremonial performances. He contrasted this link between the war and the German interest in collecting magico-material artefacts of Aboriginal ritual life with the much more pragmatic interests leading to the 'Japani war'. In his view, this latter war was driven simply by the Japanese appetite for mineral resources, particularly those located in his Worrorra countrymen's territory on Koolan and Cockatoo islands off the west Kimberley coast:

> Now we thought about this little way … Hey, German must be making war for this drawing business Australia, but it was Japanese mob start war second time, after Germany. German mob come here just to get 'em drawing and he took 'em back to Germany but it was Japanese was start the war—only for that goldmine, iron, there in Cockatoo [Island]. That wasn't long war, only short war and they finish.

Given Gowanulli's proposal that his countrymen's interactions with the visiting Frobenius Institute personnel were largely modelled on the ways in which they would have interacted with an Aboriginal relative stranger, at least part of the significance attributed to the German anthropologists' retracing of the *wanjina* cave art imagery might be illuminated by referring back to those local practices and beliefs.

Tracing the *wanjina*

Wanjina become incarnated in the living persons who identify with their *wanjina* by referring to it as 'I' or 'me' when narrating stories of events occurring in the *larlan* ('ancestral past'). Gowanulli, who belonged to the Brrejalngga clan, would narrate the story of how his *wanjina* was bitten on the upper arm by Bamali, a king brown snake in the *larlan*, by pointing to his own right arm and talking of the actual site where 'king brown bite 'em me'. One of Gowanulli's personal names, Nyajngo, derived from this biting action in the *larlan*. In a similar vein, another (now recently deceased) senior man, Neowarra, told me how:

> my father carried that Gayun.gu [Mt Barnett Range] on his shoulder right up to Manggurarri [near Doongan Station]. When he was carrying that ranges, that's *larlan di*, my grandfather found him there at Manggurarri— that's why my father got that name Manunggu, it's the same meaning as Gayunggu.

Here Neowarra was referring to his father as *wanjina*. The emphasis on the shoulders as the place on the body where country is carried reflects the fact that it is the father/son relationship that is figured in muscle twitchings at this bodily site, and also the place where child–spirit essences are often seen to 'sit'. Neowarra took his personal name from the black rocks (*nyawarra*) in the Munja area, where 'my father found my spirit when he was walking around that time'. Similarly, one of his classificatory sons takes his name from a female ancestral kangaroo, Nyenowarr, which gave birth to his actual father at Warr muj mulimuli in the Caroline Ranges. Thus, *wanjina* simultaneously carry the country and the clansmen who will care for it, carrying responsibility for that country across the generations. This concept of 'carrying' country and the burden of transmitting the law to the younger generations is a major concern of senior people.[5]

---

5   A similar image has been described by Myers (1980: 199) as focal among the Pintupi, for whom responsibilities of sacred knowledge are associated 'with phrases denoting some sort of physical object and indicating a weight burden, or responsibility for the "holder"'.

The maintenance of a fully vitalised natural and social world is something that senior Ngarinyin people say is achieved through their regular presence on country and conducting the appropriate ceremonial rites. The presence of the 'right people' for specific country is in itself believed to 'brighten' country and to release the inherent fecundity of its ancestral powers. This condition of abundant vitality is known as *yayiyurru* ('everything standing up in a bunch'). Senior people say the country recognises its own by *ngalug* ('odour') and the familiar sounds of such people's voices.

Conversely, the absence of the right people from country will cause diminished supplies of native fauna and flora, waterholes and rivers will become dry with the onset of a 'melancholy' or 'depression' in the country itself, in the same way that a person who is lonely or 'sorrowing' (*marari*) for a particular place might experience homesickness. Both the *wanjina* imagery and the country are said to become faint and lacklustre through the absence of this regular human contact. My Ngarinyin colleagues maintain that what were once extremely fertile breeding grounds for waterfowl at Munja, for instance, have become very depleted during a recent period of sporadic occupation.

One of the ways in which an ecological balance can be maintained is through the human attention given to maintaining the 'brightness' of the *wanjina* paintings in each clan country. People were said to have a ritual obligation to country where they have a strong connection deriving from one of a number of potential links. Mature persons other than clan members (but still belonging to the *wanjina* sociocultural domain) could be invited to repaint the *wanjina* images in another person's clan country. Those with a more direct responsibility for the sites would then give these painters gifts (*ngurli*) of kangaroo meat or sugarbag.

These *wanjina* images are not thought of as the artistic work of the ancestors of present-day people, but rather as the bodily imprint of autochthonous ancestors, whose images have merely been maintained—'kept bright'—by a ritual repainting. This repainting—'touch 'em meself' in Kriol—with its profound ecological and social consequences, is a self-generative action that humans should duplicate, augment and give an enhanced visibility to (Mowaljarlai and Malnic 1993; Mowaljarlai and Rumsey 1992; Rumsey and Mowaljarlai 1994; Crawford 1968; Blundell and Layton 1978; Blundell, Woolagoodja et al. 2005). Neowarra explained that the repainting process is initially activated by the emanations of wet season moisture from the rocky outcrops in which the paintings are located and that human agents then complete this revivification:

> In Winjin ['wet season'] time when that *wilmi* ['mist'] come out from the stone in early morning, *jurri* we call it, the 'smoke' goes into the paint and renews it and it's just like it paint up again so we can go always go back and renew it.

Lommel (1996: 17) found similar expressions among the Wunambal in 1938 and noted that people had told him how the *wanjina* at Merrinbini:

> still becomes ever stronger with each progressive completion of his image. When he painted himself in the Dreaming for the first time he shouted to his brothers and sisters exultantly;—look at me, how I paint myself, look here how my hands get stronger, how the picture takes shape.‖ He became stronger and stronger and there were tremendous rains. (Lommel 1996: 43)

The German anthropologists' persistent interest in the *wanjina* imagery was remarkable enough to local people that when Lommel returned in 1955 with his wife, Katerina, to conduct large-scale retracings of the *wanjina* images at the major sites of Wanalirri, Anggurrman and Ngalanggunda, local people living at nearby Gibb River Station named the well where the Lommels had established their base camp 'Lommel Yard'. High ritual status and associated ritual dangers attach to these particular ceremonial sites because it was from here that all of the region's *wanjina* had once gathered to wreak war and send world-destructive floods against humanity in revenge for humans' transgressive insults against them. During my fieldwork, many senior clanspeople for these sites refused to go anywhere near them for this reason:

> Yes. Yes, what's that—that crocodile been come from Box Hole, Wanalirri. And from there he been come from Lommel Yard. And that two crocodile meet now. But nobody won't go in that place—my place. I don't know how come. He doesn't—nobody won't go in that place, nothing. Can't do it. Yes. Everybody. All the Gibb River boys and Gibb girls, they don't go in—in that place, you know. Only just fishing, ride around. No, tourists wouldn't go in. I don't know. He don't go. Only in the Wanalirri they can go.

> Them two crocodile been—come from where he been drown them. I don't know … From there, he [*wanjina*] been come to—what that place? Box Hole [Wanalirri]. That drawing? And another one going to stop there, and these two [*wanjina*] they been walk away, go in that Lommel Yard. Two fella been stop there, find that cave, you know. Two fella been lay

down there. Wife and husband. From there, he been cross over, you know, go in that place there, low down to Wire Yard. I don't know what that place. I forget now. Diyan.gin. Yes. He been go right up there … and because he been find that cave, you know, he been stop there. One place he been stop. He never move anywhere no more. Three altogether they been go there. But I don't know what—when they feed them kangaroo, he go straight for that cave, but I won't go in that place. He's danger again. Big [rain]. He make big [flood] … everywhere. (Maudie White quoted in Federal Court of Australia 2001: 4883–4)

Close local attention, then, was being paid to Lommel and his party's intimate interactions with, and uncannily accurate retracing of, the *wanjina* images. Similarly close attention was being paid to the German anthropologists' collection and transportation of ceremonial artefacts just prior to the outbreak of the war.

Over the next three years, with the entry of Japan into World War II, the Kimberley region itself would become an intensively militarised zone. Airbases were established near Liveringa in the Fitzroy Valley and just outside the township of Derby. Australian and American military personnel were deployed across the region, including the servicemen involved in the construction of the US Navy's radar base at Champagny Island on the north-west coast, not far from the Presbyterian mission at Kunmunya. The town of Broome was bombed and strafed by Japanese fighter planes, killing scores of Dutch refugees from Java who had just landed in seaplanes on Broome's Roebuck Bay. The Benedictine mission at Kalumburu, on the far north coast, was bombed in 1943, killing five of the Aboriginal residents as well as the mission director.[6] A widespread fear of being shot by invading Japanese soldiers—something that then featured strongly in regional Aboriginal rumour mills—compelled many bush-dwelling Aborigines closer to European settlements, very much in accordance with wartime government policy (Crawford 2001: 245).

By 1942, at Munja Station, as throughout the rest of the northern Kimberley, the rumours of war had become a reality. For the majority of local people, this 'Japani war' would provide their first lived experience of the physical extent of modern military power as well as accelerating the integration of the more remote regions of northern Australia into the centralising bureaucracy of the modern war machine.

---

6   This was despite the precautions taken by the Benedictines in moving the mission further away from an airbase that had been established against their wishes in the vicinity of the original mission.

The West Australian state supply ship *Koolinda* and her 'classificatory sister ship', MV *Koolama*,[7] would both be memorialised in local Aboriginal song imagery following the sinking of the *Koolama* off the Kimberley coast by Japanese planes within two years of the Lommels' departure from the Kimberley.

The destructive drama of these sinking ships almost instantly provided the inspiration for a set of newly dreamt songs for Gowanulli's contemporaries. Gowanulli surmised that it must have been MV *Koolinda* that had, in fact, carried away the ceremonial paraphernalia collected by Lommel and Petri following their 1938 visit:

> They [his countrymen] took 'em [the anthropologists] with the camel. They go right round, pick 'em up with the camel and take 'em right round, show 'em everyway, they give them all this corroboree thing now, material, long long one [a reference to the secret-sacred Kurangara boards, photos of which were later featured in Lommel's monograph],[8] took 'em to right to Kalumburu, Wyndham, they get boat from there, ship steamer, might be *Koolinda*. Took them to England, from England then get another boat—might be another boat. German never come back again. That Dr Elkin mob (where he belong, Perth eh, round Sydney?). Same time he was round with that mob too. But his own, he running himself, this German mob self again. Dr Elkin mob was in Kunmunya and this mob Germans was in Munja.

---

7   'In 1941, the state ship *Koolinda* was travelling north when it encountered two lifeboats carrying 31 German sailors. The Germans were rescued at gunpoint and the few able to speak English explained that their German raider had sunk during a battle with an Allied cruiser which had also sunk. The cruiser was the Royal Australian Navy's *HMAS Sydney* which was lost with all 645 of its crew. The loss of the *Sydney* spurred significant mystery and controversy until the wreckage was found in 2008. In 1942, the state ship *Koolama* sunk alongside the Wyndham jetty after it was bombed by Japanese planes. The *Koolama* had been heading along the Kimberley coast from Darwin when long-range Japanese bombers scored two direct hits. Captain Jack Eggleston managed to beach the *Koolama* on the Kimberley coast where passengers were able to escape the ship and ultimately to be rescued with assistance from the Kalumburu Mission' (Collins and Smale 2014).

8   This was against the express wishes of Ngarinyin people who, with my assistance, had explicitly written to Lommel asking him to not include these photos of secret-sacred rituals in the English edition of his monograph.

Another travelling west Kimberley ceremony, Juluru, similarly employs scenes from the sinking of the SS *Koombana* during a cyclone in 1912.[9] Until its loss with all hands on board, the *Koombana*, like the other state supply ships, *Koolinda* and *Koolama*, had sailed between Fremantle and Derby servicing all the larger coastal towns en route. Juluru, by all accounts, had conflated historically separated events into a single time frame by condensing the much earlier sequence of events around the sinking of the state ship with those occurring during the World War II Japanese bombings of Broome, Wyndham and Kalumburu (Glowczewski 2002: 273). A number of other ceremonies had inducted the World War II imagery into traditional ritual forms, and in one of these the two main protagonists were named 'Hitler' and 'German' (Kolig 1989: 120–2; Widlock 1992; Glowczewski 1983).

I have recorded a number of songs deriving from composers' shamanic dreams of thematically related events. In one of these, the *dalabon jurnba* ('telephone *jurnba*'), the composer is a psychopomp who had received in dreams a series of urgent telegraph messages from the MV *Koolama* as it was being attacked and ultimately sunk midway between Kalumburu and Wyndham by Japanese planes. My narrator framed the composer's dream of telegraph transmissions within the local idiom of *lunggun*, the involuntary bodily 'signals' (sometimes explicitly glossed as 'telegraph') that are produced in a person's body by muscle twitchings, which act as presentiments of close kindred experiencing serious trouble:

Wey lejingara
Dalabon dalabon banga
Birrinye Kalumburu jila[10]

---

9   Launched in Glasgow in October 1908, the SS *Koombana* was operated by the Adelaide Steamship Company. It was the first ship built exclusively for passengers and cargo for service along the West Australian coast. Sailing from Fremantle, the ship made frequent visits to ports in the state's north-west from 1909 to 1912. Named after one of the pioneering Forrest family's properties near Bunbury, the word *koombana* is Noongar and reputed to mean calm and peaceful. Its last voyage from Port Hedland to Broome on 20 March 1912 was, however, disastrous. The ship, plus all crew and passengers, was lost in a tropical cyclone, never to be found, except for a small amount of wreckage found at sea near Bedout Island. The loss of the SS *Koombana* in 1912 caused much grief and anxiety in Western Australia, not least because of the loss of 150 lives. It has been said that the loss of the Koombana was a major impetus for the early development of the State Shipping Service, which was to dominate the north-west coastal shipping trade until the end of the twentieth century.

10   Anthony Redmond, fieldnotes, June 2007.

The man with whom I recorded this song is a Kija man who first heard it sung in Kija country at Bedford Downs Station in the eastern Kimberley (where an infamous massacre of his people had taken place in 1924). A recognisably similar version of this same song was recorded by R. M. Berndt in Halls Creek in 1962:

> *[D]alibun-dalibunba waiilidji barimrmbun, ngairabumana*
> At salt water wireless boat
>
> *galambaru djil agumanu*
> Kalumburu boat. By the salt water,
>
> (That) wireless boat at Kalumburu. (Berndt 1975: 134)

This man told me this *dalabon jurnba* evoked violent events in which 'lot of black people been killed at Kalumburu by *gardiya* [whites]'. Again, we are presented with a condensation of separate spatiotemporal events into a single song and time frame, taking one cue from the Japanese air raid on the Drysdale River Mission Station in 1943 but then enfolding the song into the traumatic reach of a set of songs that commemorate the massacre of Kija people at Bedford Downs some two decades previously.[11]

Throughout this range of performances, there is a recurrent thematic thread of Aborigines obtaining secret knowledge of (and sometimes ritual complicity in) the sinking of those ships—a knowledge denied to whites because they are seen to lack the capacity to hear the messages emanating directly from the realm of the dead.

It should not be forgotten here that the state ships memorialised in these songs were used to transport not just the materials of everyday European power, and subsequently the ceremonial boards collected by Lommel and Petri, but also the Kimberley Aboriginal prisoners to the state jails

---

11 'The men had been convicted by a local court of killing a bullock on Bedford Downs Station, and were sent back to the station with "tickets" hung around their necks as a sign to the station owner that they were guilty. Some of the men discarded these tickets before they got back, but others chose to keep them. On their return, those who still had their tickets were taken to a remote location and told to chop wood. After a morning's work, the men were given a meal and told to eat quickly—the food was heavily poisoned with strychnine and all those who ate it died painful deaths. Their bodies were then burned with the wood they had chopped that morning. Two men, however, had refused to eat and made their escape. These two, along with two women who had followed the party and also witnessed the killings, returned to tell the story to their people. Passed down through the generations both as oral narrative and in the form of a joonba, Timms relates the story of the Bedford Downs massacre, in visual form, to record this tragic event both for the Gija people and wider audiences. The joonba was recently staged as the performance "Fire Fire Burning Bright" at the Melbourne and Perth Festivals (Kjellgren 2004)' (Redmond, fieldnotes, June 2007).

of Fremantle and Rottnest Island in the south of Western Australia. These prisoners included the mixed-race children 'removed' to state institutions such as Moore River Settlement.[12]

In some of these songs, the sinking of the ships is attributed to the agency of local Aboriginal *barnman* (or 'wish-doctors') exacting vengeance in the context of localised feuds. The *dulugun jurnba* of the late Bruce Niltji, composed in the late 1970s, for instance, invokes the sinking of an 'old time one' ship off the west Kimberley coast during a massive storm whipped up by a 'doctor-man' who had invoked two destructive Wunggurr (Rainbow Serpent) snakes to sink the ship—purportedly to punish Aboriginal miscreants on board.

The strong association made by local people between European military technologies such as planes and the dangerous power of Wunggurr was further evident in a number of the dreams Patrick Pentony collected from people living at Munja during the Frobenius Expedition's 1938 visit:

> An aeroplane came out of the sky and landed on the ground. A mob of blacks came around and looked at the aeroplane. They were very frightened. I was very frightened. Then I awoke. *Comment*: This is a miriru dream. The aeroplane is Ungud. It is bad to dream of Ungud like that, for it means that he is going to kill someone. (Pentony 1938)

Pentony recorded a number of dreams in which a whitefella protagonist is either paired with or a mask for an Indigenous aggressor:

> I saw a rifle lying on the ground. Then I picked up the rifle and put it inside a house. A white man whom I did not know was talking to me. Then I went back to camp. I awoke. [Dreamer's] Comment: The policeman will come today. The rifle belongs to the white man. A blackfellow will come in too, because there was a white man in the dream. This blackfellow will be the tracker. (Pentony 1938)

In another dream, a man told Pentony that 'when one sees a strange blackfellow in a dream it means a white man will come according to Janba law' (Pentony 1938).

---

12 Tellingly, one of the passengers aboard the *Koombana* when it sank was the Derby police chief, 'Corporal Frank Buttle, who had been in charge of the Derby police for about three years. He had been returning from a holiday in Perth.'

An abiding local interest in harnessing, channelling and challenging the power of European technologies is also evident in the local Aboriginal incorporation of the dramatic power of cinema newsreels—the first harbinger of the local impacts of the looming military confrontations that would hit the region. The composer with whom Lommel worked in 1938, Alan Balbungu, had heard from various friends and countrymen working on the luggers sailing into Broome from Munja and Kunmunya for station and mission supplies about cinema's dream-like visual montages (Lommel 1996).

These films and newsreels were screened at Broome's Sun Pictures—the world's first 'picture garden'—built in 1916 by the Yamazaki pearling family, who had modernised a performance space where traditional Japanese Noh theatre had previously been staged.[13] Aboriginal people were permitted entry to a racially segregated area in the very front rows, and behind them were seated the Malay and Koepanger lugger crews. Overlooking those seated at the front was a set of cushioned cane chairs reserved for the Europeans in the centre of the floor,[14] and seated immediately behind them were the Japanese and then the Chinese.

The Sino–Japanese war had particularly strong local repercussions in Broome, which hosted very large Japanese and Chinese communities,[15] and Balbungu's integration of images of this war into his corroboree speaks to the composer's fascination with those cinematic images of military power and violent conflict.

---

13   'The Sun Pictures building in Broome's Chinatown was constructed at the turn of the century on a site owned by the Yamasaki family. Initially the spacious double-fronted tin structure served as an Asian emporium selling imported Asian foodstuffs, clothing and other household goods to Broome's polyglot community. The Yamasaki building was the most commodious store in Carnarvon Street, an area … [with] shops, bazaars, brothels, food stalls, in the Asian quarter known as Chinatown. The Yamasaki family's love affair with theatre however, saw them devote a portion of the building to a Japanese playhouse where traditional Noh theatre was performed.' See: broomemovies.com.au/history.html.

14   This situation resembles David Stout's ethnographic descriptions of racial divisions in colonial Panama, which Taussig (1993: 144) cites as evidence that 'the cultural politics of alterity should be seen as composed not simply of one-on-one, for instance Americans and Cunas, but as a hierarchy of alterities within a colonial mosaic of attractions and repulsions'.

15   Later, after the bombing of Pearl Harbor, Broome's Japanese residents were placed in internment camps or discretely left Australia.

Lommel described how Balbungu's *garlgudada* corroboree contained a number of verses evoking the *yalanganna jolja* ('soldiers from across the sea') in which a battle is being fought between members of the two north Kimberley patrimoieties, but employing imagery adopted from the newsreels showing scenes from the 1937 Sino–Japanese war:

> It shows two rows of spirits parading towards each other, as in battle and armed with rifles. The inspiration for this song has been taken by the poet (the Worrorra man, Balbungu) from a lively account of a friend who had seen a newsreel from the Chinese–Japanese War in the cinema in Broome. In the song it is described how during the battle, the spirits burst the mountains apart and blast the rocks to pieces—an idea of exploding grenades.

Paddy Neowarra described to me how one in another variant of this dance scene:

> Spotted Night Jar moiety spirit-people, Wodoy, came out in a vision of light as Jelarimirri continued to sing. A great light fell upon the ground. All the Wodoy ['spotted night jar'] people, were lit up as he sang. The composer was now singing only about this man connected with the devil-string—the 'death-cord' [human hair from deceased men plaited into a rope by widows and intimately associated with death ceremonies].
>
> That death-cord is laid out. Then that Brolga comes marching on in the afternoon time, dancing, pushing their beaks along the ground. Then one of them, she came to the death-cord laid across to divide Wodoy on one side from Jun.gun on the other. They were pulling on the cord from either end, pulling and pulling. A boughs screen of green was set up (so that the two different mobs were hanging on to the cord from either side and one end of the cord was attached to the singer). (Lommel 1996: 62)

It is said that this string—also used to construct *waranggi* ('string cross-dance emblems')—was originally made by *jilinya*, dangerous spirit-women who live an autonomous life in the paperbark swamps, feeding themselves by hunting game such as men and choosing their own lovers. In the performances of this *jurnba*, two older Ngarinyin men play this role, dressing as women, weaving the string over a campfire while dancing licentiously, supposedly to attract the attention of the white soldiers to seduce them. It is said white men were first attracted to Ngarinyin country by these beautiful women at least as much as by potential pastures for their cattle.[16]

---

16   There is an interesting parallel here in Sahlins's (1985) accounts of the role Hawaiians attributed to their women performing the *hula* and the subsequent resentment that was generated by whites possessing their women.

Gowanulli gave me an account of how a successful composer must visit Dulugun, the island of the dead, located off the west Kimberley coast very near to Champagny Island, where the US naval radar base had just been established. During this dream journey, the composer disappears into a trapdoor in the earth, which leads him to Dulugun, where the spirits of ancestral dead then showed him new songs over several days. When he finally awoke from his 'illness', the composer was in possession of the entire song corpus and its accompanying dances. The Ariadne's thread that the composer followed into Dulugun and back is represented in *jurnba* performance by a thin wire—now sometimes made of nylon fishing line—which both drags him to his destination and summons the spirits of the dead from behind their concealing bough screen. This thread, *buyu*, is often glossed as a 'radar' beam because of its invisible but irresistibly powerful pull.

Some of the most interesting aspects of Petri's (Petri and Petri-Odermann 1988) and Lommel's research from the Kimberley region were a product of the very close attention they had paid to the profoundly transformative historical processes unfolding before them, which were being locally articulated in new religious ceremonies, which they labelled 'travelling cults' and which were in full efflorescence during their visit.

The Kurangara cult, as Lommel saw it in 1938, was deeply saturated with symbols of European power. The principal figure, Tjanba, was said to live in a house made of corrugated iron, hunted game with a rifle rather than a spear and demanded tea, sugar and bread from his fellow ghosts. In this ceremony, the language used is Kimberley Kriol, proceedings are directed by a 'boss' and other ceremonial roles include the 'mailman', *pickyba* ('book-keeper') and 'police boys'. 'The symbols have changed. It is now no longer the Ungud snake but the Kurangara slab which incorporates life and death' (Lommel 1996: 28).

This figure was also associated with the spread of the then raging epidemics of leprosy and syphilis. Observing the trance states and creative shamanic illness of Balbungu, himself badly infected with leprosy, must have added considerably to Lommel's almost elegiac sense of an impending disaster looming over this particular lifeworld.

Lommel's informants had described the Tjanba cult to him as one in which

> the social order will be completely reversed: women will take the place of men; they will arrange the feasts and hand on the slabs, whereas the men will gather edible roots, without being allowed to participate in the feasts. (Lommel 1996: 29)

The travelling 'corroborees' that made their way across the Kimberley during these pre–World War II decades ranged across the secret-sacred spectrum, from highly dangerous types such as Juluru, Dingarri and Kurangara, to the more open, public performances known as *jurnba*. Each of these ceremonial genres has at various times been employed by Kimberley composers and performers to articulate grappling with a range of internal and exogenous conflicts engendered and/or enhanced by the impacts of colonisation. Aboriginal ritual efficacy can be seen here as struggling to reassert itself through investing doctor-men with an enhanced creative/destructive potential through an engagement with powerful European military technologies such as radars, telegraphs and aeroplanes.

The *jurnba* of Balbungu and his peers subsequently travelled through the Wurnan exchange network across a wide range of Kimberley settlements and across three or four generations to date. The songs themselves and their restless movement express local articulations of intercultural historical experience, which Lommel and his companions perceptively documented during their visits to Ngarinyin country. Patrick Pentony's contribution to the research by documenting the dreamt landscape of his Kimberley Aboriginal hosts added immeasurably to this portrait of a world not in its death throes, as Lommel and Petri suspected, but certainly beset by a massive realignment of both local and exogenous power relationships.

References

Berndt, R. M. 1975. Life and death: A Lungga (Gidja) mythic corollary. In *Explorations in the Anthropology of Religion*, W. E. A. van Beek and J. H. Scherer (eds), pp. 122–46. The Hague: Martinus Nijhoff.

Blundell, V. and Layton, R. 1978. Marriage, myth and models of exchange in the west Kimberleys. *Mankind* 11: 231–45. doi.org/10.1111/j.1835-9310.1978.tb00654.x.

Blundell, V., Woolagoodja, D. with Members of the Mowanjum Aboriginal Community. 2005. *Keeping the Wanjinas Fresh: Sam Woolagoodja and the enduring power of lalai.* Fremantle, WA: Fremantle Arts Centre Press.

Collins, B. and Smale, H. 2014. Remembering the state ship lifeline to the north west. *ABC Kimberley*, 19 February. Available from: abc.net.au/local/stories/2014/02/19/3948219.htm.

Crawford, I. M. 1968. *The Art of the Wandjina.* London: Oxford University Press.

Crawford, I. M. 2001. *We Won the Victory: Aborigines and outsiders on the north-west coast of the Kimberley.* Fremantle, WA: Fremantle Arts Centre Press.

Federal Court of Australia. 2001. Wanjina Wunggurr Wilinggin WAG6016/96 and WAG6015/99 [Transcript], pp. 4883–4.

Glowczewski, B. 1983. Manifestations symboliques d'une transition économique: le Juluru, culte intertribal du 'cargo' (Australie occidentale et centrale). *L'Homme* 23(2): 7–35. doi.org/10.3406/hom.1983.368369.

Glowczewski, B. 2002. Culture cult: The ritual circulation of inalienable objects and appropriation of cultural knowledge (north-west Australia). In *People and Things: Social mediation in Oceania*, (eds) M. J. Ballini and B. Juillerat, pp 265–88. Durham, NC: Carolina Academic Press.

Kjellgren, E. 2004. *Tradition Today: Indigenous art in Australia.* Sydney: Art Gallery of New South Wales.

Kolig, E. 1989. *Dreamtime Politics: Religion, world view and utopian thought in Australian Aboriginal society.* Berlin: Dietrich Reimer Verlag.

Lommel, A. 1952. *Die Unambal, ein Stamm in Nordwest-Australien.* Hamburg, Germany: Monographien zur Völkerkunde.

Lommel, A. 1996. The Unambal: A tribe in northwest Australia. Unpublished ms, Translated by F. Zanvoort. Missabotti, NSW.

Lommel, A. and Mowaljarlai, D. 1994. Shamanism in northwest Australia. *Oceania* 64(4): 277–87. doi.org/10.1002/j.1834-4461.1994. tb02472.x.

Love, J. R. B. 1917. Notes on the Wororra tribe of north-western Australia. *Transactions of the Royal Society of South Australia* 41: 21–38.

Mowaljarlai, D. and Malnic, J. 1993. *Yorro Yorro: The spirit of the Kimberleys*. Broome, WA: Magabala Books.

Mowaljarlai, D. and Rumsey, A. 1992. Ngarinyin customs and country. Unpublished booklet.

Myers F. 1980. The cultural basis of politics in Pintupi life. *Mankind* 12(3)(June). doi.org/10.1111/j.1835-9310.1980.tb01192.x.

Pentony, P. 1938. Collection of dream texts from Ngarinyin/Wunambal and Worrorra people. Unpublished MA thesis. University of Western Australia, Perth.

Petri, H. and Petri-Odermann, G. 1988. A nativistic and millenarian movement in north-west Australia. In *Aboriginal Australians and Christian Missions*, (eds) D. Rose and T. Swain, pp. 391–6. Adelaide: Australian Association for the Study of Religion.

Redmond, A. and Skyring, F. 2010. Exchange and appropriation: The Wurnan economy and Aboriginal land and labour at Karunjie Station, north-western Australia. In *Indigenous Participation in Australian Economies: Historical and anthropological perspectives*, (ed.) I. Keen, pp. 73–90. Canberra: ANU E Press.

Rumsey, A. and Mowaljarlai, D. 1994. *Report on Survey of Painting Sites in the Roe and Moran River Areas of Western Australia*. Canberra: Australian Institute of Aboriginal Studies.

Sahlins, M. 1981. *Historical Metaphors and Mythical Realities: Structure in the early history of the Sandwich Islands kingdom*. Ann Arbor: University of Michigan Press. doi.org/10.3998/mpub.6773.

Sahlins, M. 1985. *Islands of History*. Chicago: University of Chicago Press.

Sahlins, M. 2005. Structural work: How microhistories become macrohistories and vice versa. *Anthropological Theory* 5(1): 5–30. doi.org/10.1177/1463499605050866.

Taussig, M. I. 1993. *Mimesis and Alterity: A particular history of the senses.* New York: Routledge.

Widlock, T. 1992. Practice, politics and ideology of the 'travelling business' in Aboriginal religion. *Oceania* 63(2): 114–36. doi.org/10.1002/j.1834-4461.1992.tb02408.x.

17

Carl Georg von Brandenstein's legacy: The past in the present

Nick Thieberger[1]

Interned as a prisoner of war in Australia in the 1940s, the Hittite specialist Carl Georg von Brandenstein went on to work with speakers of a number of Australian languages in Western Australia. At a time when the dominant paradigms in linguistics were either Chomskyan reductionism or writing a grammar to the exclusion of textual material, Carl followed his own direction, producing substantial collections of texts and recordings in Ngarluma, Yindjibarndi, Nyiyaparli, Ngadju and Noongar, as well as information about a number of other Australian languages. Part of his motivation was to obtain examples to reconstruct what he considered to be the original human language that diffused to all corners of the world, so he put some effort into comparing Australian languages with the classical languages he had previously studied. He published on the nature of kinship and section systems, aligning characteristics similar to medieval European humours, and then extending that to the notion of active (nominative) and passive (ergative) verbal concepts. He interpreted symbolism in designs and in the categories and sounds of the languages he recorded. He was also convinced that Portuguese explorers had settled on the west coast of Australia and received public attention for his claims,

1   Thanks for reminiscences and other help to Reuben Brown, Pat Engberg, Erich Kolig, Jacqie Lambert, Merrin Mason, Anthony McCardell, Kirsty Murray, Ursula Oehme, Frank Rijavec, John Stanton, Dina and Henry Thieberger (for translations) and Anthony Thomas. Parts of this work have been supported by Australian Research Council grants DP0984419 and FT140100214.

which were partly based on comparisons of words from Pilbara languages with Portuguese. In Thieberger (2008), I showed that most of Carl's claims of Portuguese influence could not be substantiated, but, in this chapter, I will discuss the value of Carl's work despite the anachronous theoretical models that drove him. Since I wrote that earlier work, more details of Carl's life have emerged, which are included here.

Carl's studies and formation

Carl was educated in Berlin and Leipzig in the 1930s as a specialist in ancient Eastern studies and the history of religion (*Altorientalist mit Religionsgeschichte*) with two years of practical work at the Berlin Ethnological Museum. He began work on the Hurrian language, which was to be the topic of his habilitation, but the war intervened and he thought his material was lost in the war. He went to Persia with the German Army, was captured by the British in September 1941 and interned at Loveday and Tatura camps in Australia. His immigration documents list him as working for a pharmaceutical company and then, probably as a result, his profession is listed as 'pharmacist'—a fiction that was maintained in these documents until after the war—but his internee documents note that he was in counterintelligence and his own brief biographical notes make no mention of pharmaceuticals or pharmacy, but say he was in the Canaris Gruppe, an intelligence unit that was later involved in a failed attempt to assassinate Hitler.

An interview with Australian military authorities on 15 May 1946 resulted in the following 'character sketch':

> He admitted that earlier he had been very much impressed with Nazism which had brought economic order out of chaos. His enthusiasm however received a jolt when the pledge of 'No War' was not honored, but loyalty to his country stimulated a fervid hope for German success. Since the end of the war he has been disillusioned concerning the Nazi owing to the various facts revealed in the news, which he thinks cannot be all propaganda. He has been very much impressed with Australia and earnestly desires to remain here, is prepared to be naturalised and serve this country with the same fervor as he supported Nazism … He wishes to keep as far as possible from politics of all kinds, blames his extreme youth for earlier enthusiasm. A most desirable type, cultured and a serious thinker.[2]

2   E. A. T. Sgt Interpreter, Series A1838 1451/2/47, 15 May 1946, National Archives of Australia [NAA], Canberra.

Following internment, he refused paid repatriation to Germany in November 1947 and elected to remain in Australia, according to a memo to the Australian Military Mission, Berlin, from the internment camp authorities. This memo was in response to a request from Carl's wife (who, with their daughter, was left in Berlin when he was interned) asking why he could not be repatriated.

> He is alleged to have told his wife that much as he would like to return to her he cannot be repatriated, and he has not enough money to pay his own fare to Germany.[3]

At the time (September 1949), he had an address in west Melbourne.

He worked in the post office and also with Arthur Boyd in the 1950s, and then lived in New Zealand, where his second wife, Carola, worked at the German Embassy in Wellington, but there is not much more information about his life until he started working with Aboriginal people in Western Australia. According to a letter[4] by Dianne Barwick to Frank Gare, Commissioner for Native Welfare (dated 28 May 1964), 'Dr von Brandenstein did field studies of Aranda in 1959 and Western Desert languages in 1962 and 1963'. In his notes, Carl says he did a fieldtrip to Laverton at his own expense. I have been unable to find any records resulting from these earlier fieldtrips. During the 1960s, he received grants from the Australian Institute of Aboriginal Studies (AIAS; later renamed the Australian Institute of Aboriginal and Torres Strait Islander Studies: AIATSIS). These grant proposals were reviewed and received positive reports—for example, T. G. H. Strehlow noted that 'I am in favour of a renewal of his grant'.[5] Berndt observed that: 'Kept to his direct language survey, and actual recording, he does very well—but (as Capell will know) he is not structurally oriented and is philologically focused.'[6]

---

3   Series A1838, Memo 103, 1451/2/4/7, 20 March 1950, NAA.
4   In Registry files, Australian Institute of Aboriginal and Torres Strait Islander Studies [AIATSIS], Canberra.
5   Strehlow review to AIATSIS, 11 March 1965, AIATSIS.
6   Berndt letter to McCarthy, 22 February 1965, AIATSIS.

My connection to Carl

I met Carl on several occasions in the 1980s when I was working on a survey of West Australian Aboriginal languages (Thieberger 1993). He was very helpful in providing access to his work and we continued to correspond over the years. As I got more interested in the role of primary records of language performance in linguistic research, and the need to prepare and present the primary material together with the analysis, I found that Carl was one of the only linguists to provide such a connection, publishing a 45 rpm record with his texts of Ngarluma and Yindjibarndi (von Brandenstein 1970b). His interest in producing texts in Aboriginal languages, albeit written in his own orthography, meant that there are now sets of texts for Ngarluma, Yindjibarndi, Nyiyaparli and Ngatju (other languages included in his work are Mirning, Pitjantjatjara, Ngaanyatjara, Mardutjara, Manyjilyjara, Warnman, Dargudi, Nyiyapali, Nyamal, Inggarda, Jurruru, Warriyangka, Jiwarli/Thiin, Purduna, Payungu, Thalanyji, Pinikura, Martuthunira, Ngalawanga, Panyjima and Kurrama).

In 1999, AIATSIS asked me to visit Carl's house in Albany, Western Australia, to assess what was there and to suggest what should happen to it all. I was unable to find much of his primary research material and have been on the hunt for it ever since. I visited him in the local nursing home and had a conversation of sorts with him (he was already severely affected by dementia). I used his material in the linguistic reports for the single Noongar native title claim and for the Ngarluma/Yindjibarndi native title claim. A task for the linguist in these court processes is to show continuity of the language over time (since colonial 'sovereignty'). Carl's work was some of the most recent documentation of the languages, providing a basis for comparison with the earliest sources, and, in both cases, showing undeniable linguistic continuity over that period.

The themes in his work

The words used in reviews of Carl's work indicate the range of reactions it elicited—they include 'fanciful', 'unfashionable', 'rash', 'fantasy', 'cultural bric-a-brac', but also 'plausible'. We need to distinguish his earlier period, with fieldwork and writing up of results as a major focus, from his later writing, which became increasingly more speculative with time.

What did Carl's earlier work on Hittite iconography bring to his study of Australian languages? In part, he continued his interest. For example, in his article on 'The symbolism of north-western Australian zigzag design' (von Brandenstein 1972), in which he associated river directions with shield designs, he included images from fourth-millennium Egyptian design that also uses zigzags and made references to Mesopotamian art in which water is designed using curves, without sharp angles. This juxtaposition is not elaborated on in this article, which concludes: 'The identical zigzag line or band as a symbol of water was already known in ancient Egypt, from predynastic times on, whilst Mesopotamia had nothing like it to offer' (von Brandenstein 1972: 238). This might seem to imply that humanity's development of the zigzag pattern—'already known in ancient Egypt'—was somehow then diffused to all humans, but it is left more as a suggestion here than an overt statement. This interweaving of themes from the Old World with Indigenous Australia would be a continuing theme throughout his research in Australia.

I have asked specialists in Hurrian about Carl's work and had this response from Miroslav Salvini:

> I remember very well the works of Carl Georg von Brandenstein, especially the articles about the Hurrian language and the volume KUB XXVII [von Brandenstein 1934]. They were among the few Hurritological contributions at our disposal, when our Berlin Group began in the '60s the study of that language and the work at the Hurrian Corpus.[7]

> For us vBr belonged to the prehistory of Hurritology, a branch of Hittitology which we renewed. The most recent book in Hurritology still quotes 'Zum Churrischen Lexikon' by von Brandenstein. Undoubtedly he left a mark in Hurrian and Hittite (cf. e.g. Bildbeschreibungen) studies.[8]

Carl's work had a mixed reception among his professional peers. He was motivated to show diffusion, claiming that changes in language and culture are the result of contact from a single source spread through the world—in the particular case of Australia, by African slaves and Portuguese establishing colonies in north-western Australia. As I noted in Thieberger (2008), he regarded the languages of the world as having a pattern like a carpet, with the most worn areas of the carpet revealing the least about

---

7 Salvini, personal communication, 19 May 2015.
8 ibid., 22 May 2015.

the original pattern. In this view, the most traffic is in Europe, hence the need to study languages at the edges of the carpet, of which Australian languages, he posited, were an example.

A linguistic feature that was the focus of several of Carl's publications was what he called the 'active verbal concept' (AVC) and the 'passive verbal concept' (PVC). He thought the PVC (what is more commonly known as the ergative case, which marks the transitive subject only) was historically prior and the reflection of a 'language family' (von Brandenstein 1967: 5), the sole survivor of which in Europe was Basque. He suggested that the change to the AVC in some parts of Australia manifested 'as the result of a change to more individualistic thinking'. There is no evidence provided to link these, nor of what he means by 'individualistic thinking', but it is indicative of his view of the deterministic role of language in shaping culture. Yallop, in a review, noted:

> Not every reader will be willing to accept, for example, von Brandenstein's explanation of a linguistic change 'as the result of a change to more individualistic thinking' but we do well to ask ourselves whether von Brandenstein is wrong or merely unfashionable. (Yallop 1974: 86)

In the following passage, we see the linking of languages that are geographically widespread and quite unrelated but are regarded as part of a single family due to the presence of one grammatical feature, the PVC. The inclusion of Māori is quite peculiar, as we know that the Polynesian language family is relatively young, certainly in comparison with Australian languages:

> In the Caucasus ... Churrian and Biainian formed the oldest PVC group known ... Today the only PVC language of a similar type is the North-Caucasian Dagestan language Avaric with about 170,000 speakers, whilst Georgian, of the South-Caucasian group, stands more apart. If we look further east it is interesting to note in connection with the fate of the PVC allies of the conquerors of India, that a PVC substratum, apparently dormant until the 13th century (A. D.), has eventually reproduced PVC features in modern offspring like Hindi, Benghali, Nepali, etc. Going south-east we come across traces of PVC on Timor and—returning for a moment to Australia—we find PVC prevailing over a large part of the Suffixing Languages of the interior, perhaps the best known being the Western Desert group. Leaving aside an ambiguous brand of PVC in Indonesia and the Philippines we have, further east, the widespread Polynesian group, well illustrated by its eastern branch Maori. Finally we reach South America and close our list with Kechua in Peru and neighbouring states. (von Brandenstein 1967: 5)

The overall implication is that languages remain static unless influenced by some external force and, in the case of the north-west coast of Australia, this is the arrival of the Portuguese. Carl's field report in August 1965 is the first mention of the term '*tartaruga*' for turtle, with the note that it has been 'brought to the North Western shores between the De Grey and Nichol Bay by the Portuguese, less likely by the Late Romans' (von Brandenstein 1965: 2).

Baxter (1996: 300), in his work on Portuguese creoles in the region, points out that the crews of Portuguese ships were typically Asian and African slaves, thus it is unclear how much Portuguese would have been spoken. Nevertheless, even if it were Portuguese, the evidence provided by Carl may be restricted to the word '*tartaruga*'. He offers conjecture about the origin of this term, noting that:

> Although it seems absurd to consider, even as a last possibility, the origin of *tartaruga* and its spread to Europe during the Great Peoples' Migration by returning Roman, Greek or Teutonic seafarers, it should at least be mentioned. In this connection I have hesitantly to draw attention to a considerable number of genuine Australian word-stems which could be connected easily with Romance *resp.* Indo-European stems. (von Brandenstein 1967: 15)

Von Brandenstein (1970b) lists 60 'north-west' words that he claims derive from Portuguese. If we attempt to locate the same forms in other wordlists of Ngarluma (e.g. Hale 1982) or Yindjibarndi (e.g. Wordick 1982) (together denoted as NW—'north-west'—below), we can find, with a generous interpretation of similarity, only 23 of the 60 and, even then, there would need to be some explanation of semantic shifts that have taken place (e.g. Portuguese '*angle*' to NW '*elbow*'), or of why he considered there to be a relationship at all (e.g. Portuguese '*mortal*', NW '*marlba*'). Most importantly, there are terms included in this list that are widespread in Australia. They are unlikely to have originated in the north-west and can be regarded as only coincidentally similar (e.g. Portuguese '*mão*', NW '*mara*'). Beyond the borrowing of a word, he offers the following vision of a changed social organisation among the Ngarluma as a result of the alleged contact with the Portuguese. It is very unclear whether this is something he was told about or something he observed:

> The Ngarluma and, most likely also, the Karriera were exceptional and unaboriginal not only linguistically. Their spinifex seed harvest method is socially and technologically far advanced compared with the seed

gathering practices of other Aboriginal tribes. Under the supervision of specially appointed elders, the whole tribe, young and old, male or female, were equipped with specifically made cylindrical bark containers of equal height and diameter, to be filled by everyone with spinifex seeds (Triodia sp.). The full containers were delivered, checked and emptied at suitably situated caves, dry and cool and under constant guard; the contents were stored there until the time of need. The distribution was likewise strictly organised according to the principles of social justice, with age before youth. The Ngarluma never suffered from seasonal setbacks of grain supply. I suggest that this organisation was introduced by Portuguese elements of the Ngarluma population. (von Brandenstein 1989: 11–12)

The theory of Portuguese contact, settlement and ongoing cultural and linguistic influence was to drive Carl's later work, reaching its most peculiar in two manuscripts (von Brandenstein n.d., 1994), from the latter of which the following is part of the front matter:

> The chosen title *Early History of Australia* is, above all, clearly showing where the main interests and greatest chances of being successful must naturally lie: on a new and unique field of linguistics in North-Western and Northern Australia, involving Portuguese with Criolo and Creole, West-African Ful with nomadic Bororé-be'e cattlemen's 35-class-language, and the Bururú-biri's 3-, 4- and 5-class-languages in the Kimberley and related class-languages in Northern Australia (Arnhem Land); as well as Vulgar Latin, Old Indian, Iranian and Maghreb Arabian loan words in Aboriginal languages of Western Australia and Western Victoria. (von Brandenstein 1994: 5)

Note that the claims now also include Victorian languages, but with no indication of how the loan words travelled so far, what intervening steps there may have been and what traces they should have left. To be fair, at this stage of his life, Carl was soon to be committed to hospital care with dementia.

Among the themes he returned to in his work was the notion of sound symbolism or phonaesthesia. So, in his grammar of Ngadjumaja (south-east Western Australia), he discusses the 'static a and the dynamic u'; similarly, in the Ngarluma texts, he lists 'a' as static, 'u' as dynamic and 'i/e' as neutral (von Brandenstein 1970b: 301). Elsewhere, he talked of 'k' as the phonoseme of 'aggression', of 'm' as 'finite distance' and 'w' as 'infinite distance'. Again, it is unclear whether he is reporting on Indigenous ideas about these sounds or whether it is his own interpretation. He also wrote of the influence of environmental factors on the articulation of

Aboriginal languages, in which 'prevailing aridity would "dehydrate" the saliva-consuming sibilants and leave their functions to the dental palatal' (von Brandenstein 1980: 5). There are no sibilants (fricatives) in any southern language, but only a small number of these languages are spoken in arid zones; many are spoken in coastal or mountain regions. So the claim that aridity leads to a loss of sibilants would have to also suggest that the parent language was spoken in an arid region and that the descendant languages then inherited that characteristic. This is simply not tenable.

His theory of diffusion led him to look for similarities between widely separated (both geographically and genetically) languages, as in the following example in which he notes:

> the Finno-Ugrian essive—na is identical in form and function [to the Ngadumaja essive—N. T.]. The full range of functions of the Australian essive—na, ńa, -ni is met again in Churrian and Bianian, two ancient cognate languages from eastern Asia Minor. (von Brandenstein 1980: 21)

There is some merit in showing typological similarities between languages and in showing that features under examination in one language appear in other languages with the same or similar functions. However, the emphasis of Carl's work is on revealing origins of language, with examples of similarities implying common origins. The collocation of Finno-Ugrian and Australian examples, while never explicitly stated as being genetically related, implies relationships that Carl was keen to expose: 'I have hinted earlier … that Finno-Ugrian and Aboriginal Australian have more in common than just typological superficialities' (von Brandenstein 1970b: 298).

The distinction mentioned earlier between active and passive (or nominative/ergative) is one that Carl observed as having resonance more broadly: 'The whole world, preferably of animals and humans, is divided into the opposed temperaments "active" and "passive"' (von Brandenstein 1977: 171). This is aligned with two moieties in Noongar (south-west Western Australia), Corella and Raven. Carl then provides a four-page list of various plants and animals or 'totems' and their moieties, recorded with Charlie Dab of Esperance. He reports on characteristics of these and briefly extends the classification to section systems of kinship elsewhere in Australia. This was followed up in von Brandenstein (1970a), where he makes a plea for universal classification, appealing to the attempts at classification of 'human temperaments and somatic types' begun in the eighteenth century but failing to achieve its

GERMAN ETHNOGRAPHY IN AUSTRALIA

goals in the scientific twentieth century, while 'the great achievement of early mankind'—the recognition of essential temperaments associated with kinship categories—'still towers in the far distance of prehistory, unequalled and hardly known' (von Brandenstein 1970a: 49).

Carl elaborated this analysis in his 1982 book, *Names and Substance of the Australian Subsection System*, in which he suggests Karierra as the source for this kind of totemic affiliation:

> [I]f the substance of the Karierra section system is complex classification by opposed temperamental qualities, similar systems in other areas of Australia must likewise be based on the same contrast of temperaments … The rationale behind it must be expected to have remained of one cast and unchanged for ages. To think otherwise would mean to fail to gauge the substance of the eternal Aboriginal dream-time exactly, by applying again our old European yardstick, overworked as it is for measurement of 'change'. (von Brandenstein 1982: 5)

Yengoyan's review of this work notes:

> [W]hat is missing is any attempt to understand what are the linguistic and cultural processes in which the transformation and shift in terminology is accomplished from one society to another. (Yengoyan 1984: 346)

Heath's (1984: 466–7) review of the book says the overall argument is plausible and recommends the book to anyone interested in anthropological philology and structuralist theories of culture. Jorion's (1983: 794) review, on the other hand, says 'von Brandenstein's reconstructions of the ethnography are quite rash'.

While emphasising the importance of collecting primary records in Australian languages, Carl's analysis of this material was often significantly flawed. McConvell (1985: 61) details a number of errors made in the work on section names: 'Much of his linguistic evidence is coincidence, dressed up as historical connection.' He goes on:

> Von Brandenstein's approach contents itself with letting … crucial pieces of the puzzle go unsolved, while the collection of vaguely interesting cultural bric-a-brac, which neither proves nor disproves anything, is given priority. (McConvell 1985: 63)

The diffusionist nature of his argument can be seen in the following statement in his chapter on the 'Identical principles behind Australian totemism and Empedoclean "philosophy"' (von Brandenstein 1978):

> We have established as a fact the identity of the totemic classification system of the Australian Aborigines, in particular of the Karierra, with the elementary classification system handed down from primeval times in Greece by Empedocles …

> It should be kept in mind what an immense area of this planet had once been invaded and covered by the doctrine of the four basic qualities and been brought under the rule of the totemic order. Signs of it can be found in all continents. The author assumes that totemism has been the Weltanschauung of hunters and gatherers for thousands of years. The further the mode of living became removed from the original one of huntsmen in the course of strife and development, the more blurred or inflated with alien practices its fabric must have appeared.

> The fifth continent was spared historical upheavals most and therefore could preserve the social part of the totemic heritage the purest. The battered or shaken frontier between Asia and Europe, cutting right through the ancient Greek world, has been most successful in transforming totemism and passing on its essence to us Europeans. (von Brandenstein 1978: 143)

Morphy's review of the volume in which this chapter appeared says:

> Taken as a whole the volume is of uneven quality, varying from papers that make a genuine contribution to contemporary anthropological theory to ones that evoke not too happy memories of a bygone era … Von Brandenstein's paper on 'Identical principles behind Australian totemism and Empedoclean "philosophy"' is not credible, more rude than erudite. (Morphy 1979: 79)

Leaving his analysis of totemism and kinship, let us return to Carl's linguistic fieldwork. He spent a decade travelling through the Pilbara and recorded many audiotapes (AIATSIS has at least 39) with speakers of a range of Indigenous languages (listed later in this chapter). In his book of Tabi song and poetry, *Taruru* (von Brandenstein and Thomas 1974), he aims to show the lyrical nature of the allusions appealed to by the composers and performers. It is unclear how much poetic licence he applied to the interpretation of the lyrics, but it could be argued that he discussed the meaning with the performers to arrive at his translations.

In fact, as noted earlier, it is a common frustration with Carl's work that it is unclear how a certain result has been obtained and on what kind of evidence it is based. Elkin's (1975: 244) review of *Taruru* concludes:

> Dr. Brandenstein did Aboriginal Studies noteworthy service in recording the music and text of the tabi, and in providing the notes on each of the songs, including native text, word-for-word translation, and the comments on the singers and material … This is a welcome addition to the Australian Aborigine's own literature.

Nash (1982), in a review of the book *Ngadjumaja* (von Brandenstein 1980), praises the emphasis on texts, recognising the value of the work despite having some criticisms.

Interactions with colleagues

Despite his theories being so out of step with anyone else's work of the time, Carl nevertheless had financial support in the 1960s from the AIAS. This allowed him and Carola to drive from Perth to the Pilbara, spending around three months a year in the field. In the early to mid-1960s, he worked in the Gascoyne and Pilbara regions. Later, the couple was in the Goldfields and Esperance areas. Their base was an office in the anthropology department at the University of Western Australia, provided by Ronald Berndt, until 1970, when Berndt and von Brandenstein's relationship had broken down, with Carl feeling that he was not being treated with sufficient respect.

Professor R. M. W. Dixon's arrival as the chairman of the Linguistics Committee at the AIAS signalled a change in attitude to Carl's work (as I have written about in Thieberger 2008). So, for example: 'you build your etymological hypotheses into all of your transcriptions so that, in a nutshell, one cannot distinguish fact from fancy.'[9] However, as discussed earlier, all of Carl's work has been reused and can be interpreted and made useful to various kinds of language projects. The AIAS published the three-volume collection of texts in Ngarluma and Yindjibarndi (von Brandenstein 1970b), and Hale's (1971) review notes:

---

9   Dixon letter to von Brandenstein, 15 March 1973, AIATSIS.

The few reservations I have about these materials are not serious and do not detract from their value, in my opinion, I hope that the Australian Institute of Aboriginal Studies continues to publish material of this sort. (Hale 1971: 1369)

In fact, the institute subsequently refused to publish the sister volumes in Nyiyaparli. As Carl noted in correspondence:

I, as a Member of the Institute and colleague, expect you as the Linguistics Committee Chairman to speed up my unduly delayed publication of NNW II for which conditions and arrangements had been approved by the Institute prior to your commencement of office.[10]

The correspondence between Carl and the AIAS, on the one hand, and Ronald Berndt, on the other, became increasingly strongly worded over time. Carl felt he was not being accorded due respect. In response, Berndt had this to say:

Let me be quite frank, which I am sure you will appreciate, I personally think you are being very silly about this whole business: you are too ready to take offence, when none is intended. I have supported you for several years now, and—in my view—your rebuff is not in good taste. Don't 'stand on your high horse', especially where goodwill is to be found. And do be sensible and try to see my point of view and appreciate that I am helping you as best I can. And we expect you at the Christmas party on the 17th. All I can do is to assure you that no one is trying to get at you.[11]

The mystery of Carl's missing notes

When I visited Carl's house in Albany in 1999, I could not find much of the material that should have been there, including his notes, copies of publications and recordings. As early as 1974, Peter Sutton, in his role as an AIAS staff member, asked Carl about the diaries that 'do not include your data on the southern languages'.[12] The falling out with the AIAS (Thieberger 2008) seems to have resulted in Carl not depositing his field records there. In June 2015, I learned from Erich Kolig (at the conference at which this chapter was presented) that a woman who claimed to have been Carl's wife had been in touch with him for advice about where to

10 Von Brandenstein to Dixon, 15 April 1973, AIATSIS.
11 Berndt's lettter to Carl, 16 December 1970 (about Carl's claims he was not being offered proper office space), Berndt Museum.
12 AIATSIS Registry 64/4, letter from Peter Sutton to Carl, 12 February 1974, AIATSIS.

deposit Carl's material. I had spoken with her several times in the early 2000s when it seemed she had taken all of his material. Perhaps she saw me as an agent of AIATSIS and so was reluctant to reveal her possession of Carl's work. Happily, she followed the advice of Erich Kolig and deposited the papers at the Anthropos Bibliothek in Sankt Augustin, Germany. Thus, what had been the mystery of the location of these papers for some 40 years was now resolved.

Contribution

Having reached this point, you may well ask, why bother with this rather chaotic legacy? First, because there is great value to Carl's work that needs to be given its proper place in the history of Australian linguistics. Further, there is great public interest in possible early European contact with Australia (see, for example, Derriman 1990, 1992) and the evidence needs to be addressed and evaluated properly and not just dismissed.

But, most importantly, the valuable material in Carl's work can be separated from his personal theories, his spelling system can be deciphered and the texts, recordings and dictionaries he produced can be and have been reused, which is of huge value to the speakers he recorded and their descendants. His published narratives (von Brandenstein 1970b) in Ngarluma and Yindjibarndi from five speakers include topics ranging from practical knowledge ('Cutting up the kangaroo', 'How I prepare tobacco for chewing', 'Catching the dugong'), through the use of increase sites ('Smallpox talu', 'Snake talu', 'Paperbark blossom talu'), history ('Ambush at George River', 'Former war parties'), to origin stories ('Origin of Warmalana [Depuch Island]', 'A sea serpent made Millstream Pools') and a range of other themes.

The past in Carl's present was the diffusionism that was a constant theme, but also the rejection of what he perceived as being reductionist positivism, and what others saw as a lack of evidence for many, if not most, of his claims. He appears to have been an aristocrat with the time to pursue his theories unconstrained by the need for rigour or for the academic approval of others and used what could be termed statements from authority (*ipse dixit*) rather than testable arguments based on observable evidence. His later publications were not peer reviewed and were either self-published or produced as typescripts that he distributed to colleagues in an attempt to bring them over to what became his crusade.

There is much more to Carl's lifetime of recording and writing than can be presented here. Today, he could be a postmodern bricoleur, putting together odds and ends of cultural observations and daring the reader to believe it.

As I hope I have shown, Carl made a great contribution to our knowledge of Australian languages and created records for those languages that will be treasured into the future.

References

Baxter, A. N. 1996. Portuguese and Creole Portuguese in the Pacific and the western Pacific Rim. In *Atlas of Languages of Intercultural Communication in the Pacific, Asia and the Americas*, (eds) S. A. Wurm, P. Mühlhäusler and D. T. Tryon, pp. 299–338. Berlin: Mouton de Gruyter. doi.org/10.1515/9783110819724.2.299.

Derriman, P. 1990. Why Western Australia's Aborigines are speaking Portuguese. *Sydney Morning Herald*, 30 July: 3.

Derriman, P. 1992. Creole echoes from our past. *Sydney Morning Herald*, 9 May: 42.

Elkin, A. P. 1975. Review of 'Taruru'. *Oceania* 45(3): 244. doi.org/10.1002/j.1834-4461.1975.tb01861.x.

Hale, K. L. 1971. Review of C. G. von Brandenstein's (1970) 'Narratives from the North-West of Western Australia in the Ngarluma and Jindjiparndi Languages, Volumes 1–3'. *American Anthropologist* 73: 1368–9. doi.org/10.1525/aa.1971.73.6.02a00610.

Hale, K. L. 1982. Ngarluma dictionary and sentences. Unpublished ms.

Heath, J. 1984. Review of 'Names and Substance of the Australian Subsection System'. *Language* 66: 466–7.

Jorion, P. 1983. Review of 'Names and Substance of the Australian Subsection System'. *Man* 18(4): 793–4. doi.org/10.2307/2801915.

McConvell, P. 1985. Time perspective in Aboriginal Australian culture: Two approaches to the origin of subsections. *Aboriginal History* 9(1): 53–80.

Morphy, H. 1979. Review of L. R. Hiatt's (1978) 'Australian Aboriginal Concepts'. *Mankind* 12(1): 77.

Nash, D. G. 1982. Review of C. G. von Brandenstein's (1980) 'Ngadjumaja: An Aboriginal language of south-east Western Australia'. *Australian Journal of Linguistics* 2(2): 270–6.

Prichard, K. S. 1974. *Brumby Innes and Bid Me to Love*. Sydney: The Currency Press.

Thieberger, N. 1993. *Handbook of WA Aboriginal Languages South of the Kimberley Region*. Series C-124. Canberra: Pacific Linguistics.

Thieberger, N. 2008. Language is like a carpet: Carl-Georg von Brandenstein and Australian languages. In *Encountering Aboriginal Languages: Studies in the history of Australian linguistics*, (ed.) W. M. McGregor, pp. 321–35. Canberra: Pacific Linguistics.

von Brandenstein, C. G. 1934. *Kultische Texte in hethitischer und churrischer Sprache*. Berlin: Staatliche Museen zu Berlin, Vorderasiatische Abteilung.

von Brandenstein, C. G. 1965. *Interim report on fieldwork in north-west Western Australia, 15 July – 15 August 1965*. Report to Australian Institute of Aboriginal Studies, Canberra.

von Brandenstein, C. G. 1967. The language situation in the Pilbara: Past and present. *Papers in Australian Linguistics* (2)(A-11): 1–20.

von Brandenstein, C. G. 1968. Some new aspects of Australian Aboriginal language based on fieldwork in north-west Western Australia, 1964–67. Paper read at the General Meeting of the Australian Institute of Aboriginal Studies, Canberra. Typescript.

von Brandenstein, C. G. 1970a. The meaning of section and section names. *Oceania* 41(1): 39–49. doi.org/10.1002/j.1834-4461.1970.tb01114.x.

von Brandenstein, C. G. 1970b. *Narratives from the North-West of Western Australia in the Ngarluma and Jindjiparndi Languages. Volumes 1–3*. [Audio disc.] Canberra: Australian Institute of Aboriginal Studies.

von Brandenstein, C. G. 1972. The symbolism of the north-western Australian zigzag design. *Oceania* 42(3): 223–38. doi.org/10.1002/ j.1834-4461.1972.tb00315.x.

von Brandenstein, C. G. 1977. Aboriginal ecological order in the south-west of Australia: Meaning and examples. *Oceania* 47(3): 169–86. doi.org/10.1002/j.1834-4461.1977.tb01286.x.

von Brandenstein, C. G. 1978. Identical principles behind Australian totemism and Empedoclean 'philosophy'. In *Australian Aboriginal Concepts*, (ed.) L. R. Hiatt, pp. 134–45. Canberra: Australian Institute of Aboriginal Studies.

von Brandenstein, C. G. 1980. *Ngadjumaja: An Aboriginal language of south-east Western Australia*. Innsbruck, Austria: Institut für Sprachwissenshaft der Universität Innsbruck.

von Brandenstein, C. G. 1982. *Names and Substance of the Australian Subsection System*. Chicago: University of Chicago Press.

von Brandenstein, C. G. 1989. The first Europeans on Australia's west coast. Typescript.

von Brandenstein, C. G. 1994. Early history of Australia: The Portuguese colony in the Kimberley: Exploration – occupation – dissolution – vacation. Typescript.

von Brandenstein, C. G. n.d. [c. 1990?]. The Yawuji-bara and Yawuji-Baia: Two intermarrying groups of an Afro-Australian islander tribe. Typescript.

von Brandenstein, C. G. and Thomas, A. P. 1974. *Taruru: Aboriginal song poetry from the Pilbara*. Adelaide: Rigby.

Wordick, F. J. F. 1982. *The Yindjibarndi Language*. No. C-71. Canberra: Pacific Linguistics.

Yallop, C. 1974. Review of papers in 'Australian Linguistics' No. 2. by C. G. von Brandenstein, A. Capell and K. Hale. *Oceania* 45(1): 86. doi.org/10.1002/j.1834-4461.1974.tb01840.x.

Yengoyan, A. 1984. Review of 'Names and Substance of the Australian Subsection System'. *Anthropological Linguistics* 26(3): 345–9.

18

The end of an era: Ronald Berndt and the German ethnographic tradition

Nicolas Peterson[1]

In 1987, Ronald and Catherine Berndt (henceforth RMB and CHB) published a book titled *End of an Era: Aboriginal labour in the Northern Territory*. The core of the book was a report they had compiled of a survey of Aboriginal workers on pastoral stations in the Victoria River district of the Northern Territory in 1944–46. They chose the title not because there was any clear-cut break at that time but because it was evident in retrospect that the changes brought by the war, especially the experiences some Aboriginal people had working for the army in settlements along the Stuart Highway, foreshadowed the upsetting of the status quo (Berndt and Berndt 1987: xix). In fact, as far as the pastoral industry was concerned, it was another 20 years before there was a sharp break with the move to pay Aboriginal station workers full award wages, in 1965–68, bringing the regime of Aboriginal pastoral workers to an end. In the intervening period, the actions of the pastoralists had come under increasing surveillance.

---

1 This chapter has greatly benefited from detailed comments from John Stanton and a friendly if somewhat sceptical reading by Philip Jones, who, like Stanton, would place greater emphasis on the general ambience in which anthropology in Adelaide was carried out rather than on any specific German influence.

Ironically, and completely unintended by the Berndts, their use of the phrase 'end of an era' could have applied equally well, at the time of publication of this book, to a book about their life and work. Although 1987 did not mark any specific break—RMB died on 2 May 1990 and CHB on 12 May 1994—the late 1980s saw the ongoing decline in Aboriginal ceremonial life, the details and complexity of which RMB, in particular, had made the focus of his ethnographic work. Together, the Berndts published over 40 monographs and edited books and more than 200 articles and papers: 14 books were jointly written, seven individually authored by RMB, one ethnographic volume by CHB and four children's books, two jointly edited books and nine books edited by RMB, and then there are the numerous papers and chapters in books. RMB's seven single-authored books were monographs related to ritual and religion to which can be added a further seven more widely focused ethnographic publications authored jointly with CHB. This prodigious output is unlikely ever to be surpassed either in quantity or, more importantly, in its significance as ethnographic documentation of Aboriginal religion and classical Aboriginal societies and cultures more generally. It is a truly unique contribution.

In this chapter, I want to suggest that the uniqueness of this contribution to Australian anthropology owes something to RMB's German background and its influence, whether conscious or not, on his approach to ethnography and, one might say, in spite of his formal training in the discipline of anthropology. The significance of this suggestion is that it not only helps to identify the nature of RMB's lasting contribution, but also goes some way to explaining why his corpus has not had quite the influence it deserves but that it will surely gain in the future in respect of classical Aboriginal culture.

The Anglophone and Anglophile nature of Australian anthropology is not surprising despite the substantial number of German settlers, particularly in South Australia, or the number of German missionaries who worked with Aboriginal communities. As we have seen, much of the missionary work had a linguistic emphasis, because of the missionaries' background and training. However, it was the full-frontal attack by Sir Baldwin Spencer on the work of missionary Carl Strehlow (Kenny 2013: 105–9) that helped entrench the divide between two styles of anthropology. On the one hand, there was the positivistic social evolutionary tradition of British anthropology giving way to the structural functionalist tradition from World War I, with its particular interest in social organisation, and, on the other hand, a more humanistic German tradition with its greater acceptance of the idea of culture in the plural and its greater focus on religion, mythology and language, giving rise to an ethnographic emphasis and especially interlinear texts. As I hope to show, RMB straddled these two traditions, but it is from the influence of the German tradition that the uniqueness and importance of his contribution stem.

RMB's background and training

RMB was born in Adelaide in 1916. His father's parents were both German speakers, but RMB himself neither read nor spoke German and, while his mother's father was of German-Huguenot background, his mother's mother was of Irish-Scots descent (Tonkinson and Howard 1990: 18). The family broke with the Lutheran Church and sent RMB to an Anglican school, Pultney Grammar. RMB was clearly bookish and did not share his father's interest in soccer, but he did share his father's passion for the study of other cultures and, together, they regularly visited the State Library and the South Australian Museum. His father also had a collection of Aboriginal artefacts and was an avid reader of 'ethnological' works (Tonkinson and Howard 1990: 20–1). Unfortunately, it is not known what books these were.[2] By the age of 22, RMB was subscribing to *Oceania* and, in 1939, he became an honorary assistant ethnologist at the South Australian Museum, publishing his first paper in the same year. In August of that year, he joined the 12-day Board for Anthropological Research's expedition to Ooldea as the social anthropologist, along with J. B. Cleland, T. Harvey Johnston, E. C. Black, F. Fenner and A. Harvey, as an assistant. Cleland and Johnston, along with C. P. Mountford, were to be his patrons in this early period (Jones 1987: 88). With the exception of Mountford, all these men had medical or scientific backgrounds. With the encouragement of Cleland and Johnston, RMB enrolled for a Diploma in Anthropology at the University of Sydney in 1940 under Professor A. P. Elkin, which required coursework and a short thesis (Berndt 1982b: 50; Gray 2005: 80). There he met Catherine, who had come to Sydney from New Zealand with a BA in Latin and French and a one-year undergraduate unit in anthropology from Dunedin.

---

2   This reading did include James Frazer (presumably, *The Golden Bough*) and A. C. Haddon (see Gray 2007: 159).

In 1941, RMB published two papers, one with interlinear translation with Ted Vogelsang, the son of a missionary at Bethesda, who had an excellent command of Diyari (Berndt and Vogelsang 1941). By April 1941, RMB and CHB were married and on their way to Ooldea, funded by an Australian National Research Council grant for six months' research. In 1943, they both obtained their diplomas in anthropology; CHB graduated with an MA in anthropology in 1949 and RMB with a BA in 1950 and an MA in 1951, all from the University of Sydney. As is well known, Radcliffe-Brown, the father of structural functionalism, founded the Sydney department. From 1951 to 1953 (Berndt 1962a: xiv), the Berndts undertook pioneering fieldwork in the Eastern Highlands of New Guinea for which they both received their PhDs from the London School of Economics (LSE) in 1955.

Map 18.1 Locations mentioned in the text.

Source: CartoGIS, The Australian National University.

Thus, it can safely be said that the anthropological training that RMB and CHB received both in Sydney and at the LSE was firmly in the structural-functionalist tradition, although the teaching in Sydney was nothing like as narrow as it is often made out to be (see Berndt 1982b: 50–1). Raymond Firth, who had briefly held the chair at Sydney after Radcliffe-Brown's departure and was a core member of the structural-functionalist school, headed the department at the LSE (Kuper 1973: 156). Although Elkin's training in anthropology was in England, it was under G. Elliott-Smith and W. J. Perry, both of whom were diffusionists, with Elkin's own work focused particularly on social organisation in the structural-functionalist mode. However, RMB emphasises that once the Berndts had graduated:

> we were virtually on our own. There was little direction on Elkin's part. He appreciated independence and initiative. What he expected from us was two-fold: doing research and writing up the results, and taking an active part in furthering his humanitarian interests. (Berndt 1982b: 51)

Although almost all RMB's and CHB's fieldwork was carried out jointly, there is no doubt that RMB dominated the partnership, as is reflected in the fact that he was always the senior author of their joint ethnographically based publications and the sole author of the seven ethnographically focused books, as opposed to Catherine's one. However, the fact that all their fieldwork was carried out collaboratively raises the question of the nature of their collaboration. In several places (e.g. Berndt and Berndt 1945: 3; Berndt 1976a: xx; 1982b: 62), the gendered division of labour in their fieldwork is emphasised, but, at the same time, RMB acknowledges CHB's assistance in preparing various volumes that appear under his name alone (Berndt 1976a: xx). It would require a detailed investigation—with access to their field notebooks, which are under an embargo until 2024, and drafts of manuscripts—to adequately unravel the exact nature of the collaboration.

Early work

The Ooldea Report was RMB and CHB's first book-length publication, appearing initially as articles across a number of issues of *Oceania* from 1942 to 1945, and then reprinted as a monograph in 1945. It is a wonderfully rich ethnography based on only six months' fieldwork, covering most aspects of Aboriginal life, including a 31-page article on language. It is a tribute to the intensity and systematic nature of their work. At the time they were in Ooldea, the population of from 80 to about 500 people was mobile, with 13 moves of various camps that were to be found within 2.5 kilometres of the soak (Berndt and Berndt 1945: 6). They strategically placed their own camp—known through their presence as the 'place of currants'—on the main pathway to the soak, but within hearing distance of the main camp so that they could be present there in a short time, and their camp became a stop-off point for people throughout the day (Berndt and Berndt 1945: 7). The monograph is organised around the male life cycle running from conception through initiation, marriage to death and the religious life. There are several striking things about the monograph: on page eight, they name 27 of their informants in the body of the text and record their indebtedness to them; the second of the 12 papers is devoted to the discussion of acculturation and applied issues, including some policy recommendations (Berndt and Berndt 1945: 27–46); an impressive 48 pages are devoted to magic; and 49 pages are devoted to women's lives.

They spell out in some detail their field methodology, which included observing a strict sexual division of labour (Berndt and Berndt 1945: 3):

> All information was recorded in a series of notebooks. Direct observations were noted in a rough book in pencil at the time and written up at the earliest opportunity so that no detail should be omitted. When recording either directly from an informant, or indirectly through interpreters, details of the discussion were written almost verbatim. Native texts were recorded in phonetic script word for word as spoken by the narrator, there being no interruptions till the end. Then the document was read out by the investigator each work translated and the actual native word checked. A discussion would then follow on the particular subject matter of the text and other problems that might arise would be noted for further questioning. Each evening the text, translation and discussion of the day would when possible be entered in the field note-book and comments made. We would then discuss between ourselves the data obtained in the day's work and so, by the constant scrutiny of material, errors or omissions could be discovered, and on further enquiry corrected and rectified. (Berndt and Berndt 1945: 9)

They state explicitly that their aim was 'to make a complete study of the Ooldea aboriginal culture' (Berndt and Berndt 1945: 3) that was a holistic functionalist account, and, in a general sense, this is what they achieved. At the end of the introductory paper, they spell out their general intellectual orientation to the work, under the heading 'The mythological basis of the desert culture':

The myth is to these people a living reality believed to have once happened in the ancestral dream-times and to have brought about a social, moral and physical order. It dogmatizes on a 'way of life' … Within the mythology is found an explanation of desert cult totemism and its associate rites, ceremonies, mysteries and mediations. It lays down a sacred rule, embracing not only the religious and moral aspects of desert society, but also the secular. It is sacred as well as profane, and is the axis upon which the culture of these desert people revolves.

By the above it is not to be thought that the whole of Ooldea life is mythologically bound; far from it. (Berndt and Berndt 1945: 25)

Although they did write about social organisation, the whole tenor of their first field project was its emphasis on empirical observation and the collection of texts, especially on mythology, and language.

In 1950, CHB published her MA thesis, *Women's Changing Ceremonies in Northern Australia* (Berndt 1950), based on work she had done between 1944 and 1946 in the Victoria River district. This provides descriptions of three kinds of women's ceremonies in the area: *tjarada, jawalju (yawulyu)* and an example of an individual women's ceremony. The monograph is structured around the question of what effect contact has had on these ceremonies and her conclusion is that while it had given them some slight impetus, the overall effect was deleterious (Berndt 1950: 9). The monograph, introduced by Lévi-Strauss, is identical in approach to the couple's Ooldea work and RMB's later writings, including considerable detail, interlinear song texts and a strong emphasis on sexual themes. Over the course of her academic career, CHB was to return to the issue of women's relation to the secret life (C. Berndt 1965) and status (C. Berndt 1970), but she also directed considerable energy to educating younger Australians about Aboriginal societies and cultures (e.g. C. Berndt 1979).

The religious texts

RMB's and CHB's publishing careers divide quite clearly into two periods: pre- and post-1962. Prior to 1962, they published all but one of their major ethnographic works, reflecting quite closely the enormous amount of time they spent in the field—almost continuously from 1941 to 1950 in Australia (see Berndt 1982a: 51–2, 54) and in New Guinea from 1951 to 1953 (Berndt 1962a: xiv)—and the rapidity with which they published core aspects of their research. After 1963, the emphasis was on edited volumes and more general works once RMB had taken on the responsibility of building up and running the Department of Anthropology at the University of Western Australia.

After the initial fieldwork in the desert at Ooldea, the regional focus of their work shifted to Arnhem Land and led to the publication of four monographs covering eastern Arnhem Land, three on western Arnhem Land and two with broad coverage. The best known is RMB's work *An Adjustment Movement in Arnhem Land, Northern Territory of Australia* (Berndt 1962a), which dealt with a hitherto unreported kind of movement that involved the deliberate revealing of previously secret objects to the general population.

There is no doubt, however, that the two books *Kunapipi* (Berndt 1951b) and *Djanggawul* (Berndt 1952) are the most significant works.[3] These are extremely rich and highly specific accounts of two ceremonies held at that time in north-east Arnhem Land. While the Djanggawul ceremony relates to the *dhuwa ngarra* ceremony and was of long standing in the area, the Kunapipi ceremony was only just being introduced to the Yirrkala region at the time of the Berndts' fieldwork.

Kunapipi was RMB's first Arnhem Land ethnography. It benefited from his knowledge of the culture of the Victoria River district because it allowed him to see the wider regional connections of the ceremony—a point also emphasised in Elkin's introduction to the work. RMB sees the book as throwing new light on three aspects of Aboriginal religion (Berndt 1951b: xxvii): the concept of a fertility mother who is without totemic affiliation herself but who brought the totems into being; the relationship between the sacred and the profane, which he argues, contra Warner (1937), cannot be separated completely because each person has an 'individual germ' of the sacred or what he calls their 'own sacred aura'; and that women have a far greater part to play in sacred ceremonies than had been recognised before. Indeed, he argues, it is woman's unique ability to create life, together with man's power to inseminate, that has become a feature of Aboriginal religion in northern Australia (Berndt 1951b: xxviii).[4] As he was to later repeat in other works, he sees the fundamental doctrine of these kinds of ceremonies as based on the 'essential human and animal drives of food

---

3   His original spelling for Djanggawul was Djanggewul (see Berndt 1952: 28). Ron and Catherine wrote Chapters 2–8 of *Art in Arnhem Land* and Elkin wrote Chapters 1 and 9 (Elkin et al. 1950: xi).
4   Phyllis Kaberry, in her book *Aboriginal Women: Sacred and profane*, published in 1939, had first challenged Warner's typification of women as only profane.

and sex' (Berndt 1951b: 204, also p. 15). He states that the spread of cults such as the Kunapipi involved a certain amount of evangelisation by leaders interested in furthering the cult's activities (Berndt 1951b: xxix). In a rather obscure passage, he seems to suggest that the cults arise around individuals who become disguised as ancestral beings:

> This aspect of individual origins, in relation to specific Australian Aboriginal cults, is an important one. The contention, which may be substantiated by mythology and the traditional song-cycles, is that a powerful personality—such as the Great Mother, the acknowledged spiritual leader and inspiration of the Kunapipi cult—possessed of ability beyond the ordinary, can and does exert his or her influence on the society in which he is either temporarily or permanently living; and that influence, helped by favourable circumstances, is sufficient to establish a cult which attracts adherents, and becomes in its own right an important social function and institution. (Berndt 1951b: xxviii)

From this, it is clear that RMB's understanding of the origin of this cult is not in sociological terms but in contingent historical terms, even though the documentation of other religious festivals with their implied sociopolitical functions was already explicit in the works of Spencer and Gillen (1899) and T. G. H. Strehlow (1947).

At the core of the *Djanggawul* book are the 188 (Berndt 1952: xxi) songs detailing the travels and activities of two ancestral sisters and their brother as they populated eastern Arnhem Land. These songs are unique in Australia for the extended narrative style of the verses—most of them at least 10 lines long and some up to 25—and for being in everyday language, yet poetic and evocative. Peter Toner[5] has suggested that because the songs and their exegesis were recorded by writing, rather than by tape recorder, this method led to a more discursive style of transcription, which may in part account for the published features of this song cycle. However, John Stanton (2008) reports that the fieldnotes are word for word interlinear texts recorded by RMB and read back to the men for checking. The gloss on each section was, however, discursive text.

There is a high erotic content to the Djanggawul songs and mythology, as there is in the Kunapipi songs, leading RMB to feel it is necessary to counter the view that Aboriginal people are unduly concerned with the subject of sex 'and derive a morbid satisfaction from constant direct or symbolic reference to it' (Berndt 1952: 7). He goes on to say that

---

5   Personal communication.

Aboriginal people are frankly interested in the workings of the human body and in the satisfaction of its basic needs so that it is not unexpected to find manifestations of this interest in Aboriginal religious emblems and mythology, ritual and song. But he goes no further than this, basically eschewing any involvement with anthropological theory (e.g. Berndt 1952: xx, 10), and concentrates on presenting the field data.[6] From CHB, he learnt that women knew much information that is formally restricted to initiated men (Berndt 1952: 293).[7]

In addition to the above, RMB also collected three cycles of love songs at Yirrkala: the Goulburn Island cycle (*dhuwa*), the Rose River cycle (*yirritja*) and the Djarada. The first two cycles were in fact local creations but projected on to people elsewhere, and, by so doing, one might suggest, liberating their creative imagination (Berndt 1976a: xi, xviii). The third cycle was, however, definitely introduced. The book was not published until 1976, partly because RMB was 'not sure that its frankness and its erotic content would be appreciated by non-Aboriginal readers' (Berndt 1976a: xi). It is sobering to realise that by the 1960s these songs were no longer remembered (Berndt 1976a: xix). When it came to publication, two versions were produced: a long version aimed at academics and an abridged version for the general public (Berndt 1976b).

RMB draws attention to the difference in attitude to sex between eastern and western Arnhem Land:

> [W]estern Arnhem Landers who had seen the elaborate ritual which ordinarily accompanied traditional and public expressions of love in the north-eastern region, or those who had listened to one song after another and to the relatively indirect erotic references, wondered why it was necessary to spend so much time on extraneous matters when the sexual appetite could be assuaged much more easily and without such conventional preliminaries. Basically this is really a question of aesthetics. It could well be argued that if the sex object, and/or the whole erotic sequence for that matter, is to be attractive and desirable to those embarking upon such an experience, certain expectations must be fulfilled. (Berndt 1976a: xiv)

---

6   Sometimes one wonders about the empirical basis of these data, even when he acknowledges Catherine's help (Berndt 1952: xix), as when he comments that 'the clitorises of many Aboriginal women are fairly well developed' (p. 11).

7   From the Yirrkala area, Ron and Catherine moved west to Milingimbi, where they worked in 1946–47, recording a further 264 Djanggawul songs from which they prepared an unpublished volume called 'Daughters of the sun' (see Berndt 1952: xxi).

This kind of comparison of regional cultural styles is not what would be expected from a structural-functionalist approach and is much closer to the sort of comment that might be expected from an American-trained anthropologist.

There is a marked contrast between RMB's work and that of Lloyd Warner, who also worked with the Yolngu in north-eastern Arnhem Land. While Warner does include some listing of song content in his very detailed descriptive account of the organisation of the Kunapipi and Djunggawan ceremonies, along with an account of the myths, there is no evidence to suggest that the song and mythological material are based on the collection of interlinear texts. Warner (1937) is concerned with social analysis under the heading of 'Absolute logics', discussing the ceremonies in the two chapters headed 'Murngin totemism' and 'An interpretation of Murngin totemism and of its ritual logics'. RMB comments in his conclusion to Djanggawul that, in reading through the mythology and songs:

> it is possible for aliens such as ourselves to understand in some degree the fundamental issues involved in one Aboriginal religious cult. Moreover, it is only through the medium of such material, particularly in the form of interlinear translations, that we may attain more than a superficial understanding of Aboriginal thought and behaviour. These songs express what may be described as the spiritual quality of this particular Aboriginal society. (Berndt 1952: 292–3)

This emphasis is entirely consistent with the work carried out at Ooldea and not, as might be suggested, simply a reaction to the material published by Warner. RMB approached research with the Yolngu from a quite different angle, as becomes even more apparent in the light of the differences in approach to material culture, discussed in the next section.

The Berndts' work in western Arnhem Land continued with an emphasis on sexuality, leading to their monograph 'Sexual behaviour western Arnhem Land'. They write:

> When they first worked in these areas, the writers were interested more in a general approach to the local culture, but as work was intensified they observed that the sexual element was stressed above all else. That is, they did not enter field-work here with pre-conceived ideas on the subject nor with the avowed intention of investigating only the sexual aspect. (Berndt and Berndt 1951b: 29)

They comment in the introduction that the importance of sex has not been fully realised in Aboriginal anthropology and go on to say that it is 'only after the satisfaction of the bodily lusts of sex and eating that spiritual experience and growth can function smoothly and with some degree of expansion' (Berndt and Berndt 1951b: 15–16). They refer to Róheim's work but see this just in relation to mythology and ritual. In a footnote, they spell out their ideas a little further:

> That is, unless sexual desire can be successfully sublimated and diverted into other channels (cf. the voluntary celibacy of certain religious orders). However, this does not occur in Australian aboriginal society; and in present-day European society sexual maladjustment is a contributing factor to emotional and social instability and unrest. (Berndt and Berndt 1951b: 15)

This seems to be the most explicit statement that is provided anywhere of their underlying thinking about the place of sex in society. The actual statement of what they call their thesis is, in contrast, based simply on a distinction between what they see as social and what they see as individual, with an emphasis on the former:

> [T]he sexual act and the accompanying erotic play are incidental and personal, while the events leading up to, surrounding or resulting from this subject, and the institutions involved, are of general social importance to the community. (Berndt and Berndt 1951b: 17, 242)

The strength of this book is the highly specific detail deriving from texts of conversations, myths and songs of several kinds—much of it, to put it in today's terms, about desire. They conclude:

> The continual urge for sexual intercourse between men and women seems to be a primary consideration in Goulburn Island–Oenpelli–Liverpool society and receives far greater attention that the actual obtaining of and foraging for food. (Berndt and Berndt 1951b: 240)

Again, this does not read like a comment from the Sydney school. Typically, after 240 pages on the subject, they list some of the matter left out: the sexual life of widows and widowers, the ceremonies and restrictions that must precede remarriage and the sexual experience of people who have spent time in and near Darwin; no subject is ever exhausted.

Man, Land and Myth (Berndt and Berndt 1970), an ethnography of the Gunwinngu, is, by contrast, a much more holistic functionalist ethnography, written at a time of intellectual change in the discipline, which RMB saw as requiring the examination of ethnographic material in relation to specific problems (see below).[8] Unlike in the earlier ethnographies, here consideration is given to some of the other Australianist literature as it relates to land tenure, social organisation and religion (see Berndt and Berndt 1970: 210–36), but this is only at the end of the book following a quite generalised ethnography—for instance, the section on Kunapipi is only three pages of text and the engagement with the literature is really quite brief, being no more than a checklist.

The final ethnography for this region is a short book, *The Sacred Site: The western Arnhem Land example* (R. Berndt 1970a). In a way, this follows from RMB's important paper 'The Gove dispute: The question of Australian Aboriginal land and the preservation of sacred sites' (R. Berndt 1964), in that, like the paper, the book is an extensive piece of coastal mapping—in this case, of Croker Island and the adjacent mainland. Together, these two works foreshadowed what is now commonplace— mapping Aboriginal placenames—but which, surprisingly, was then a practice almost unknown among others working out of Sydney, but was the practice of Tindale and Mountford. Both were done at a distance and were greatly facilitated by being on the coast with its relatively easily identified features. Despite almost all of the sites being on the shore, or even in the sea, the analysis was entirely in respect of land, with nothing to say about sea estates. Nevertheless, these two studies were a major innovation, outside the published work done in either the German or the British tradition. *Man, Land and Myth* was the most mainstream of their ethnographies.

The revelation of the later years

The second book RMB published was titled *Art in Arnhem Land*, co-authored with Elkin and CHB (1950) and based on RMB's master's thesis. Although he later published three other books on the topic (Berndt 1964; Berndt and Phillips 1973; Berndt and Stanton 1980), as well as some important articles (see Berndt 1958), it was not widely understood until recently how strong RMB's interest in art was nor the magnificence of the collections he assembled. He made extensive collections not only

8   Although *A World that Was* appeared in 1993, up to Chapter 10 had been written in 1943–44, but was rewritten before publication (Berndt and Berndt 1993: 11). Even so, the nature of this ethnography is little different from their other writings from the pre-1963 period.

within Australia, but also privately of Asian art, the latter in conjunction with CHB, and the existence of which was concealed largely for insurance and security purposes (Brittlebank 2008). Although he published on aspects of his Australian collections from early on, the 'crown jewels', as RMB referred to them (Stanton 2013: 18), were not widely seen until 2013. These are the 365 truly wonderful crayon drawings on brown paper from Yirrkala collected between 2 December 1946 and 28 June 1947 (Stanton 2013: 18–19). Although a few of them had been displayed in a 1995 exhibition and some had been published in the books on Arnhem Land, where they were virtually all in black and white and reduced from their large size (mostly 115 x 74 cm), losing much of their visual impact, it was not until a large selection was displayed at the Art Gallery of New South Wales that they started to receive wide attention (see Pinchbeck 2013). There is yet another set of crayon drawings from the northern Tanami Desert of which only tantalising glimpses have been given and which is yet to be published in its full glory (Stanton 2008: 520–2, 534; Berndt and Berndt 1950).

Along with 219 bark paintings, the Berndts collected a wide range of three-dimensional items of material culture from Arnhem Land. In a conversation with Peter Lauer, director of the anthropology museum at the University of Queensland, RMB comments:

> Objects of all sorts abounded [in Arnhem Land]. They were part of the living culture, all of them in use. When I did commence to 'collect' there was nothing deliberate about it … the paintings and carvings themselves were vivid expressions of social relations on one hand, clusters of meaning on the other. They gave an additional, tangible dimension to understanding particular mythological situations that were not really explicable through oral communication alone. Through visual depiction … they created a multi dimensional … 'vision' of mythic events set within their situational contexts. (Quoted in Stanton 2008: 514)

Here the emphasis is entirely on meaning rather than the way material culture and painting relate to social organisation that a more Durkheimian approach would have emphasised. Indeed, RMB went on to say that his collections were made at a time when it was:

> popular among social anthropologists to denigrate the activities of museum ethnologists as not falling within the legitimate scope of what social anthropologists conceived to be their role on the field. (Quoted in C. Berndt 1979: 143)

Reflecting on what influenced him in making basic western and eastern Arnhem Land collections of bark paintings and sculptures, RMB comments: 'For myself, perhaps having been an ethnologist before becoming a social anthropologist had something to do with my making' the collections, although he also says he was 'not consciously oriented in museum terms' (C. Berndt 1979: 144). Association with the South Australian Museum was undoubtedly an explicit influence in some areas, as it was from Mountford that he got the idea of collecting crayon drawings (C. Berndt 1979: 145).

Conclusion

It is, perhaps, the focus on religion and mythology and the commitment to producing interlinear texts of the songs so central to Aboriginal religions that give a German inflexion to RMB's work. This emphasis may have come from Tindale, who was keen on this technique, but it was certainly not from Elkin, even though he did produce a few interlinear texts based on attending a *mardayn* ceremony in 1949 (Elkin 1972), possibly influenced by RMB. RMB indicates that he had sought some informal linguistic training from Professor J. A. FitzHerbert at the University of Adelaide and used Noel-Armfield's (1924) Cambridge University Press publication on phonetics as his practical guide for transcription before his first fieldwork, with Albert Karloan and Pinky Mack at Murray Bridge between November 1939 and February 1940 (Berndt and Berndt 1993: 3, 10). He had no other training at that time (Berndt and Berndt 1993: 3) and started out writing down texts in English, gradually moving to using Yaralde—commenting in his introduction to *A World that Was* that 'we place great value in the recording of interlinear texts, especially when a memory culture is concerned' (1993: 10). He also had the experience of collaborating with Ted Vogelsang in 1940 (Berndt and Vogelsang 1941) on the paper on Diyari medicine men in which they published interlinear texts.

In 1939, the only other ethnographers working in this mode were both from German backgrounds. Helmut Petri was here from Germany on the Frobenius Expedition in the Kimberley. He reports that a 'large part of my ethnographic fieldnotes fell victim to the bombing, in particular the original texts of the mythical traditions of the Ungarinyin with interlinear translation' (Petri 2011: 248).[9] It is also relevant that the Berndts visited these anthropologists and Pater Wilhelm Schmidt (see Tonkinson and Howard 1990: 30) and Humbolt and Leipzig universities during their trips to Europe and maintained correspondence with many German anthropologists over the years.[10]

Ted Strehlow was another person with anthropological training and a native competence in Aranda, as well as English and German, who would have been an influence on RMB, as they were close personal friends. But, although Strehlow maintained a lifelong interest in Arandic ethnography, his academic disciplines were linguistics and literature. Interestingly, he did receive some limited anthropological training at the LSE from Raymond Firth, but it seems to have had little influence on him, not least I suspect because of his isolation from the mainstream of the discipline here; as Diane Austin-Broos reports (Chapter 9, this volume), neither Firth nor Elkin was really impressed with Strehlow's anthropology.

The linguistic aspect of RMB's work pre-dated his time at Sydney and meeting CHB and, despite Malinowski's emphasis on the need for ethnographers to learn the local language, language was never central to British anthropology in the same way that it was in Germany. Further, even before the department of anthropology he founded at the University of Western Australia in 1956 separated from the psychology department that provided it an initial home, RMB had appointed an anthropological linguist, Susan Kaldor, to his staff in 1961 to teach anthropological linguistics as an essential prerequisite for any research (R. Berndt 1979: 509). While Dr Arthur Capell, a linguist, was employed in a research position in the anthropology department at the University of Sydney, there was no such emphasis on anthropological linguistics in teaching there.

So, this raises the question of what relevance this possible influence of the German humanistic tradition on RMB's work has for understanding why this enormously valuable corpus has not had quite as much impact as one might expect.

A factor that has contributed to the undervaluing of RMB's work is his writing style, which lacks a certain clarity and is full of qualifications and deferrals, as others have also commented (e.g. see Morphy 2009). I do not

9 Tindale (1937) also published some limited interlinear song text material from the Coorong area.
10 John Stanton, personal communication.

think, however, that this is an important reason. Much more significant, I think, is that RMB's explicit emphasis on placing ethnography before theory—indeed, largely ignoring theory (but see Berndt 1970b and 1974 especially)—makes for dense reading often attractive only to those with a specialised local interest. In RMB's first Arnhem Land monograph, *Kunapipi*, he states:

> The whole question of Australian Aboriginal religion needs far more consideration than has been accorded it to date; but before any reliable theoretical studies can be made, it is essential that anthropological field-workers should provide considerably more data than are at present available. (Berndt 1951b: xxvi)

In the following year when he published his foundational work on Arnhem Land Aboriginal religion, *Djanggawul*, he wrote:

> A considerable amount of thought has gone into the question of presenting the available data on the Djanggawul. It has finally been decided to present as much as possible of the 'raw' material without, apart from interpretation and partial analysis, engaging in theoretical discussion, for material of this type obviously lends itself to such treatment. It is our contention that the role of the anthropologist in the Australian Aboriginal field should be one of recording data, and of presenting these in an accessible form, so that the maximum amount of material may be available for the consideration of students interested primarily in theory. This is not to say that we disparage that particular branch of anthropological science, but that we ourselves are more intimately concerned with Australian Aboriginal problems ... we are acutely aware of the limitations of available anthropological data. (Berndt 1952: xx)

RMB never really moved from this position, although, by 1967, it is possible to detect a slightly defensive tone when making the same point.[11] In a paper presented at the 1966 general meeting of the Australian Institute of Aboriginal Studies (AIAS), as it then was, he comments:

> The strength of Australian Anthropology lay in the emphasis that has been placed on empirical material rather than on the pretentious generalizing on an insufficient basis of fact which sometimes passes for theorizing. It is my belief that much of the ethnographic reporting which has taken place on this Continent, and the subsequent analysis of that material,

11   In the foreword to the 1985 edition of *The World of the First Australians* (see Berndt and Berndt 1988: xi), they are saying the same thing: 'it is important, in fact, imperative, to have a reasonably good grasp of the "facts" of a situation before theorizing *about* that situation.'

will have currency in the future—which is more than can be said of a great deal of speculatory and fashionable 'theorizing for the sake of theorizing' produced elsewhere … The down-grading of ethnography, the use of this word as a term of disparagement, can do only harm to our discipline.

Nevertheless, our emphasis must shift, as it has to some extent already done, to looking at our material in relation to specific problems rather than simply recording the ethnographic material. (Berndt 1967: 42)

For this emphasis on ethnography over theorising, he will be thanked by future generations. A greater emphasis on analysis would have thinned the ethnography, although, in so doing, it would probably have made it easier for non-specialists to approach. It would be wrong, however, to give the impression that RMB did not have any analytical or theoretical contributions to make. While his theoretical orientation when exercised was undoubtedly functionalist, as one would expect, his study in the New Guinea Highlands—*Excess and Restraint: Social control among a New Guinea mountain people* (Berndt 1962b)—where he and Catherine were only the second anthropologists to work, makes it clear, as Raymond Firth (1990: 5) points out, that functionalists did not only study societies in equilibrium. Indeed, this was already clear from the section on acculturation in the Ooldea report and from the Berndts' book on social change in South Australia (Berndt and Berndt 1951a). Among the more influential papers are 'Ceremonial exchange in western Arnhem Land' (Berndt 1951a), the synthetic paper on 'Law and order in Aboriginal Australia' (R. Berndt 1965) and his classic paper on 'The concept of the "tribe" in the Western Desert of Australia' (Berndt 1959)—all papers in the structural-functionalist mode.

What makes RMB's work the end of an era are the changes that have and are taking place in both the Aboriginal and the anthropological worlds. The impact of the full incorporation of Aboriginal people in remote Australia into the cash economy from the 1970s has had both positive and negative consequences. The most negative have been the over-involvement with alcohol, which, along with an increasingly poor diet, has had a catastrophic impact on life expectancy and physical health, affecting the ratio of knowledgeable elders to the rest of the population, and which has seen a substantial decline in religious life and many areas being swamped with the holding of mortuary rites. The internet, television and media more generally have become a focus for the younger generations at the expense of Aboriginal religion, to be replaced in some areas with a wide range of Christian sects. In Yuendumu, in the Northern Territory, this has gone from one to five between the 1970s and today. On the other hand, anthropology has been dominated by an applied focus mainly around land claims and native title from 1978 to the present (see Austin-Broos 2011). Other factors are important, too, including an increasing emphasis on restricting outsiders' access to ceremonial life. Although there have been many excellent theses produced in the past 25 years, social change, health, women's lives and so on have taken the focus away from religion and mythology.

However, a new era of German-influenced ethnography began with the twenty-first century; this time, it is associated not so much with a topical focus as with a theoretical approach. With the arrival of a small but steady stream of students trained in the German tradition, phenomenology has come to feature alongside concerns with structure, agency and power, now taken up by some students trained in Australia, infusing the discipline with a new and rich seam of ethnography (e.g. see Musharbash 2008; Eickelkamp 2001; Heil 2003; Kenny 2013).

Work today in the areas that were of central interest to RMB is much more in the nature of salvage ethnography than anything he could have imagined. I leave RMB with the last word about his interests and the reader to reflect on the differences with today:

> 'It was in the sphere of religion, however, that I personally found greater satisfaction [than work in other areas] … particularly song-poetry' (1982: 55), going on to say that, 'Intellectually, the field of religion in its broadest sense offers perhaps the most rewarding area for continued investigation. This is because it is relevant to most of the features I have referred to [social organisation and social control], and because it concerns varying forms of aesthetic expression—myth and oral literature generally, song-poetry and music, ritual and dramatic performance, visual representations and art. (Berndt 1982b: 61)

References

Austin-Broos, D. 2011. *A Different Inequality: The politics of debate about remote Aboriginal Australia.* Sydney: Allen & Unwin.

Berndt, C. 1950. *Women's Changing Ceremonies in Northern Australia.* Cahiers D'Ethnologie, de geographie et de linguistique No. 1. Paris: Hermann.

Berndt, C. 1965. Women and the 'secret life'. In *Aboriginal Man in Australia: Essays in honour of Emeritus Professor A. P. Elkin*, (eds) R. Berndt and C. Berndt, pp. 238–82. Sydney: Angus & Robertson.

Berndt, C. 1970. Digging sticks and spears, or, the two-sex model. In *Woman's Role in Aboriginal Society*, (ed.) F. Gale, pp. 29–50. Canberra: Australian Institute of Aboriginal Studies.

Berndt, C. 1979. *Land of the Rainbow Snake*. Arranged and translated with illustrations by D. Yunupingu. Sydney: Collins.

Berndt, C. and Berndt, R. 1971. *The Barbarians: An anthropological view*. London: C. A. Watts.

Berndt, C. and Berndt, R. 1978. *Pioneers and Settlers: The Aboriginal Australians*. Melbourne: Pitman.

Berndt, R. 1948. A Wonguri-Mandjigai song cycle of the moon-bone. *Oceania* 19(1): 16–50. doi.org/10.1002/j.1834-4461.1948.tb00493.x.

Berndt, R. 1951a. Ceremonial exchange in western Arnhem Land. *Southwestern Journal of Anthropology* 7(2): 156–76. doi.org/10.1086/soutjanth.7.2.3628621.

Berndt, R. 1951b. *Kunapipi: A study of an Australian Aboriginal religious cult*. Melbourne: Cheshire.

Berndt, R. 1952. *Djanggawul: An Aboriginal religious cult of north-eastern Arnhem Land*. London: Routledge & Kegan Paul.

Berndt, R. 1955. 'Murngin' (Wulumba) social organization. *American Anthropologist* 57(1): 84–106. doi.org/10.1525/aa.1955.57.1.02a00100.

Berndt, R. 1957. In reply to Radcliffe-Brown on Australian local organization. *American Anthropologist* 59: 346–51. doi.org/10.1525/aa.1957.59.2.02a00180.

Berndt, R. 1958. Some methodological considerations in the study of Australian Aboriginal art. *Oceania* 29(1): 26–43. doi.org/10.1002/j.1834-4461.1958.tb02935.x.

Berndt, R. 1959. The concept of the 'tribe' in the Western Desert of Australia. *Oceania* 30(2): 81–107. doi.org/10.1002/j.1834-4461.1959.tb00213.x.

Berndt, R. 1962a. *An Adjustment Movement in Arnhem Land, Northern Territory of Australia.* Paris: Mouton.

Berndt, R. 1962b. *Excess and Restraint: Social control among a New Guinea mountain people.* Chicago: Chicago University Press.

Berndt, R. 1964. The Gove dispute: The question of Australian Aboriginal land and the preservation of sacred sites. *Anthropological Forum* 1(2): 258–95. doi.org/10.1080/00664677.1964.9967198.

Berndt, R. 1965. Law and order in Aboriginal Australia. In *Aboriginal Man in Australia: Essays in honour of Emeritus Professor A. P. Elkin*, (eds) R. Berndt and C. Berndt, pp. 167–206. Sydney: Angus & Robertson.

Berndt, R. 1967. The next phase of anthropological research in Australia. *Australian Institute of Aboriginal Studies Newsletter* 2(5): 42–52.

Berndt, R. (ed.). 1969. *Thinking about Australian Aboriginal Welfare with Particular Reference to Western Australia.* Perth: University of Western Australia Press.

Berndt, R. 1970a. *The Sacred Site: The western Arnhem Land example.* Canberra: Australian Institute of Aboriginal Studies.

Berndt, R. 1970b. Traditional morality as expressed through the medium of a Australian Aboriginal religion. In *Australian Aboriginal Anthropology*, (ed.) R. Berndt, pp. 216–47. Perth: University of Western Australia Press.

Berndt, R. 1974. *Australian Aboriginal Religion (in Four Fascicles).* Leiden: Brill for the Institute of Religious Iconography, State University of Groningen.

Berndt, R. 1976a. *Love Songs of Arnhem Land.* Melbourne: Nelson.

Berndt, R. 1976b. *Three Faces of Love: Traditional Aboriginal song-poetry.* Melbourne: Nelson.

Berndt, R. (ed.). 1977. *Aborigines and Change: Australia in the '70s.* Canberra: Australian Institute of Aboriginal Studies.

Berndt, R. 1979. Aboriginal studies within the Department of Anthropology, University of Western Australia. In *Aborigines of the West: Their past and their present*, (eds) R. M. Berndt and C. H. Berndt, pp. 509–16. Perth: University of Western Australia Press.

Berndt, R. (ed.). 1982a. *Aboriginal Sites, Rights and Resource Development*. Perth: University of Western Australia Press.

Berndt, R. 1982b. The changing face of Aboriginal studies: Some personal glimpses. In *Anthropology in Australia: Essays to honour 50 years of 'Mankind'*, (ed.) G. McCall, pp. 49–63. Sydney: Anthropological Society of New South Wales.

Berndt, R. and Berndt, C. 1945. *A Preliminary Report of Field Work in the Ooldea Region, Western South Australia*. Sydney: Oceania Publications.

Berndt, R. and Berndt, C. 1950. Aboriginal art in central-western Northern Territory. *Meanjin* 9(3): 183–8.

Berndt, R. and Berndt, C. 1951a. *From Black to White in South Australia*. Melbourne: Cheshire.

Berndt, R. and Berndt, C. 1951b. *Sexual Behaviour in Western Arnhem Land*. New York: The Viking Fund.

Berndt, R. and Berndt, C. 1954. *Arnhem Land: Its history and its people*. Melbourne: Cheshire.

Berndt, R. and Berndt, C. 1970. *Man, Land and Myth: The Gunwinggu people*. Sydney: Ure Smith.

Berndt, R. and Berndt, C. 1987. *End of an Era: Aboriginal labour in the Northern Territory*. Canberra: Australian Institute of Aboriginal Studies.

Berndt, R. and Berndt, C. 1988. *The World of the First Australians: Aboriginal traditional life past and present*. 4th rev. edn. Canberra: Aboriginal Studies Press.

Berndt, R. and Berndt, C. 1989. *The Speaking Land: Myth and story in Aboriginal Australia*. Melbourne: Penguin Books.

Berndt, R. and Berndt, C. 1990. A select bibliography. In *Going it Alone? Prospects for Aboriginal autonomy: Essays in honour of Ronald and Catherine Berndt*, (eds) R. Tonkinson and M. Howard, pp. 45–63. Canberra: Aboriginal Studies Press.

Berndt, R. and Berndt, C. 1993. *A World that Was: The Yaraldi of the Murray River and the lakes, South Australia*. Melbourne: Miegunyah Press.

Berndt, R. and Phillips, E. (eds). 1973. *The Australian Aboriginal Heritage*. Sydney: Ure Smith.

Berndt, R. and Stanton, J. 1980. *Australian Aboriginal Art*. Perth: University of Western Australia Press.

Berndt, R. and Vogelsang, T. 1941. The initiation of native-doctors, Dieri tribe, South Australia. *Records of the South Australian Museum* 6(4): 369–80.

Brittlebank, K. 2008. Two people, one life. *Australian Historical Studies* 39: 3–18. doi.org/10.1080/10314610701837201.

Eickelkamp, U. 2001. Pitjantjatjara women's art at Ernabella: Genesis and transformation. Unpublished PhD thesis. Heidelberg University, Heidelberg.

Elkin, A. 1972. *Two rituals in south and central Arnhem Land*. Oceania Monographs No. 19. University of Sydney, Sydney.

Elkin, A., Berndt, C. and Berndt, R. 1950. *Art in Arnhem Land*. Chicago: Chicago University Press.

Firth, R. 1990. The Berndts: An overview. In *Going it Alone? Prospects for Aboriginal autonomy: Essays in honour of Ronald and Catherine Berndt*, (eds) R. Tonkinson and M. Howard, pp. 3–9. Canberra: Aboriginal Studies Press.

Gale, F. 1972. *Urban Aborigines*. Canberra: ANU Press.

Gray, G. 2005. 'You are … my anthropological children': A. P. Elkin, Ronald Berndt and Catherine Berndt, 1940–1956. *Aboriginal History* 29: 77–106.

Gray, G. 2007. Cluttering up the department: Ronald Berndt and the distribution of the University of Sydney ethnographic collection. *Recollections: Journal of the National Museum of Australia* 2(2): 153–79.

Heil, D. 2003. Well-being and bodies in trouble: Situating health practices within Australian Aboriginal socialities. Unpublished PhD thesis. University of Sydney, Sydney.

Jones, P. 1987. South Australian anthropological history: The Board for Anthropological Research and its early expeditions. *Records of the South Australian Museum* 20: 71–92.

Kaberry, P. 1939. *Aboriginal Woman: Sacred and profane.* London: Routledge.

Kenny, A. 2013. *The Aranda's Pepa: An introduction to Carl Strehlow's masterpiece Die Aranda- und Loritja-stämme in Zentral-Australien (1907–1920).* Canberra: ANU E Press.

Kuper, A. 1973. *Anthropologists and Anthropology: The British school 1922–1972.* London: Penguin Books.

Morphy, H. 2009. Re-reading Ronald Berndt: Exploring the depths of his Yolngu ethnography. *Anthropological Forum* 19(1): 73–97. doi.org/10.1080/00664670802695624.

Musharbash, Y. 2008. *Yuendumu Everyday.* Canberra: Aboriginal Studies Press.

Noel-Armfield, G. 1924. *General Phonetics for Missionaries and Students of Languages,* 3rd edn. Cambridge: W. Heffer & Sons.

Petri, H. 2011 [1954]. *The Dying World in Northwest Australia.* English trans. Perth: Hesperian Press.

Pinchbeck, C. (ed.). 2013. *Yirrkala Drawings.* Sydney: Art Gallery of New South Wales in association with the University of Western Australia.

Radcliffe-Brown, A. R. 1956. On Australian local organization. *American Anthropologist* 58(2): 363–7. doi.org/10.1525/aa.1956.58.2.02a00140.

Róheim, G. 1945. *The Eternal Ones of the Dream: A psychoanalytic interpretation of Australian myth and ritual.* New York: International Universities Press.

Spencer, W. and Gillen, F. 1899. *The Native Tribes of Central Australia*. London: Macmillan.

Stanton. J. 2008. 'I did not set out to make a collection': The Ronald and Catherine Berndt collection at the Berndt Museum of Anthropology. In *The Makers and Making of Indigenous Australian Museum Collections*, (eds) N. Peterson, L. Allen and L. Hamby, pp. 511–36. Melbourne: Melbourne University Press.

Stanton, J. 2013. The crown jewels of our collection: The Yirrkala crayon drawings. In *Yirrkala Drawings*, (ed.) C. Pinchbeck, pp. 17–19. Sydney: Art Gallery of New South Wales in association with the University of Western Australia.

Strehlow, T. G. H. 1947. *Aranda Traditions*. Melbourne: Melbourne University Press.

Tindale, N. 1937. Native songs of the south-east of South Australia. *Transactions of the Royal Society of South Australia* 61: 107–20.

Tonkinson, R. and Howard, M. 1990. The Berndts: A biographical sketch. In *Going it Alone? Prospects for Aboriginal autonomy: Essays in honour of Ronald and Catherine Berndt*, (eds) R. Tonkinson and M. Howard, pp. 17–42. Canberra: Aboriginal Studies Press.

Warner, L. 1937. *A Black Civilization*. New York: Harper Brothers.

Index

'school' 43, 44, 383, 385, 386–7
see also University of Vienna
Virchow, Rudolf 18, 41, 42, 283,
    295–6, 359
von Brandenstein, Carl Georg 20,
    392–6, 435–49
    work on diffusionism 394, 439,
        443, 445, 448
von Chamisso, Adelbert 31
von Humboldt, Alexander 4, 31, 32,
    33, 34, 37, 42n.6
von Humboldt, Wilhelm 4, 31, 32,
    33, 34, 37, 42n.6, 197, 248–9,
    392
von Leonhardi, Baron Moritz 5, 10,
    185, 189
von Luschan, Felix 43, 46, 384
von Scherzer, Carl 33, 34

Walbiri 234, 235
Walsh, Grahame 5–6
wanjina 374n.32, 415, 416, 419,
    420–3
Ward, James 139, 141, 148–53, 155
Warlpiri 251, 156
Warneck, Gustav 8, 92, 93, 94
Warner, Lloyd 233, 234, 460, 463
Weipa 10, 141, 148n.7
Werlaty Pengart, Mick (Wolatja) 256,
    257, 259
West Africa 442
Western Desert 70, 196, 310,
    312n.23, 437, 440, 470
Willis Kemarre, Paddy 243n.1, 255
World War I 40, 43, 47, 330, 358
    impact on Aboriginal culture 418,
        419
    impact on Australian
        anthropology 46, 49, 454
    impact on ethnography 30, 46
    internment of Germans 46
    outbreak of 14, 46
World War II 45n.7, 99, 358, 388,
    418, 423, 431

destruction of ethnographic work
    12, 36, 436
impact on Aboriginal culture 20,
    402n.28, 403, 414, 418, 419,
    423, 425, 453
impact on ethnography 17,
    335n.1, 384
internment of Germans 17, 20,
    372, 435, 436
Worms, Ernest (Ernst) 329–50, 358,
    359, 362, 365, 366–72, 374, 392,
    403
    and A. P. Elkin 18, 331, 249, 350,
        372
    and 'culture circle' theory 17, 18,
        329, 341, 344, 363
    and Ronald Berndt 363, 367, 371
    in Arnhem Land 363, 367, 371,
        373
    in Kimberley 17, 330, 332, 336,
        358, 359, 362, 366, 367, 369,
        372
    influence of Helmut Petri 332,
        338, 349, 370
    influence of Hermann Nekes 331,
        349, 359, 368
    influence of Leo Frobenius 18,
        362, 370
    on diffusionism 17, 332, 337,
        340, 341, 344–9, 350,
        359–61, 363, 364, 369, 370,
        374
    role in Frobenius Institute
        Expedition 369
    work on songs 334–5, 338, 340,
        342, 348–9, 363, 364, 317,
        372
    work with Helmut Petri 334, 337,
        339, 340, 346, 369, 392
    work with Hermann Nekes
        17–18, 330, 331, 371, 372,
        374n.34

www.ingramcontent.com/pod-product-compliance
Lightning Source LLC
Chambersburg PA
CBHW051434270326
41935CB00019B/1823

* 9 7 8 1 7 6 0 4 6 1 3 1 7 *